An Introduction to Object-Oriented Design in C++

Jo Ellen Perry *and* Harold D. Levin

North Carolina State University

ADDISON-WESLEY PUBLISHING COMPANY

Reading, Massachusetts · Menlo Park, California · New York
Don Mills, Ontario · Wokingham, England · Amsterdam · Bonn
Sydney · Singapore · Tokyo · Madrid · San Juan · Milan · Paris

Lynne Doran Cote *Sponsoring Editor*
Helen M. Wythe *Production Supervisor*
Eileen Hoff *Cover Design Supervisor*
Roy Logan *Senior Manufacturing Manager*
Kenneth Wilson *Text Designer*
Alena Konecny *Art Coordinator*
Illustrations and Composition *Publishers' Design and Production Services, Inc.*

Library of Congress Cataloging-in-Publication Data
Perry, Jo Ellen
    An introduction to object-oriented design in C++ / Jo Ellen Perry
and Harold D. Levin.
        p.   cm.
    Includes index.
    ISBN 0-201-76564-0
    1. Object-oriented programming (Computer Science)   2. C++
(Computer program language)   I. Levin, Harold D.   II. Title.
III. Title: Object-oriented design in C++.
QA76.64.P527   1996
005.13'3—dc20   95-5965
                                                                    CIP

Reprinted with corrections January, 1996

The programs and applications presented in this book have been included for their instructional value. They have been tested with care but are not guaranteed for any particular purpose. The publisher does not offer any warranties or representations, nor does it accept any liabilities with respect to the programs or applications.

Many of the designations used by manufacturers and sellers to distinguish their products are claimed as trademarks. Where those designations appear in this book, and Addison-Wesley was aware of a trademark claim, the designations have been printed in initial caps or all caps.

3 4 5 6 7 8 9 10—MA—98 97 96

Preface

TWENTY years ago, there were no desktop PCs, most software was batch processed, and most program I/O was for unit records such as card images. Today most computers are desktop machines and we operate in an environment of networks, multimedia, and interactive graphical interfaces. This book is designed for use in introductory computer science courses that acknowledge these widespread and fundamental changes.

A couple of years ago, we heard people asking "Is object-oriented programming just a flash in the pan?" We don't hear this question anymore. Today, we are in the midst of a major paradigm shift affecting almost every aspect of computing—from commercial technology to fundamental theory. Elements of the diverse collection of topics lumped under the general heading "object-oriented" are at the center of the shift and provide the momentum that will determine the direction of the discipline into the next century.

What does all this mean with respect to teaching and learning about software development? Should students learn object-oriented techniques from the start? The answer is yes, even in the earliest portions of their training. Indeed, we think that it would be as counterproductive to teach standard techniques of structured programming early in the curriculum and then add in or switch to object-oriented methodologies in advanced courses as it would have been to first teach students to program in BASIC and later on to introduce structured programming as a portion of a specialized software engineering course. Two major ideas moved us toward the very early introduction of object-oriented concepts. One is that it is vital to take design seriously. The other is that concepts and technologies associated with software reuse are so important that they must be introduced at the earliest opportunity.

Where did we start?

We have both been teaching introductory computer science and computer programming to students for more than a decade. Until three years ago, all of our introductory teaching amounted to the same course that has been taught in Pascal since the beginning of structured programming. In the spring semester of 1992, partly because of the political pressure of other engineering departments and partly because of student demand, we taught an introductory course using C++. That first course was strictly experimental. We did not know if we could pull it off.

To make sure that students would not be shortchanged by programming in C++ rather than Pascal, we taught the experimental course as an exact mirror of the introductory course with Pascal. Pascal and C++ lectures were kept in lock-step. The day that Pascal CASE statements were discussed was the same day that C++ switch statements were discussed. The day that procedures were introduced in Pascal lectures, functions were introduced in C++ lectures. The students in Pascal and C++ wrote exactly the same lab assignments. Only the languages were different. No hint of object-oriented development was mentioned in the C++ course.

We came out of that experiment knowing that we had both succeeded and failed. We discovered that beginning students can learn C++ syntax as easily as they can learn Pascal syntax, and they can do traditional top-down design in C++ as easily as they can do it in Pascal. But that experimental course was still a C++ copy of a traditional introductory programming course. It was out of date before it started.

This book began as a result of that experience. We knew that we did not want another Pascal text in C++ clothing. At the same time, we knew that beginning students still have to learn concepts such as control structures and functions that are common to all general-purpose languages. While that knowledge is so ingrained in experienced programmers that many have trouble remembering when they did not know it, we recognize that students are not born knowing those concepts. Our first question was "How can we teach the new paradigms and still cover the fundamental concepts that every programmer knows?" Our answer is "Teach objects early along with the fundamental concepts." It is easy to teach fundamental concepts. What about objects?

Introducing object-oriented concepts

This book introduces objects at two levels: design and programming. At the design level, we began by *thinking* in terms of objects, comparing those objects and their interactions to animated cartoons. This is a comfortable context for most students. It is through this kind of object-think that students can apply their everyday intuition. Students know how to solve all sorts of difficult problems in ordinary life. They ought to be able to use that experience in solving programming problems.

At the programming level, objects can appear in various ways. In the beginning of this book, we use comments to bracket off the parts of programs corresponding to design objects. As we introduce new language features, we rely more on the code without the comments to describe the objects developed in our designs. With classes, we are able to capture in our code exactly what we had in our designs without relying strictly on comments to show us the way.

The focus from the beginning of the text is objects, not classes, and not C++ syntax for defining classes. Objects are concrete. Classes are the abstract mechanism for producing objects. We chose to leave classes until students could first become familiar with functions and control structures. C++ has built-in objects cin and cout that students can use from the start. Furthermore, students find it easy to use class libraries and class type objects quite early. When students can appreciate the need for producing many instances of new types of objects, they are ready to tackle the syntax and conceptual scheme for defining C++ classes.

Following through with major object-oriented concepts

Soon after we taught the first course using C++, we overheard some students saying that they knew all about object-oriented programming because they took a one-semester course in programming using C++. We knew they were wrong, but they did not find out until they tried to sell the skills they did not have. Soon, we began hearing from students asking where could they learn the important stuff— i.e., inheritance and polymorphism.

We think students need to see the whole picture in object-oriented program development. More importantly, students think they need to see the whole picture. And that picture includes first class types, inheritance, and polymorphism. Those topics are too important to be relegated to a footnote or a short appendix. Students—and people outside academia—do not think they should be ignored. And we do not think they should be ignored either.

As we remarked earlier, there has been a significant change not only in the economics and sociology of computation but also in what is at the leading edge and what is at the center of the discipline. If you think that the situation in computing today is not essentially different from the situation in the 1970s when Pascal and structured programming were new and important, then you may well be puzzled about why students should learn about objects, classes, inheritance, and polymorphism. However, neither teachers nor students can gain a full appreciation of object-oriented program development without inheritance and polymorphism.

A quick map of the book

Novice programmers who want to learn object-oriented program development in C++ from this book should start from the beginning and follow the sequence of chapters as we have laid them out. Experienced C programmers who are determined to read as little as possible can read Chapters 1, 3, and the beginning of Chapter 6 before going to Chapter 7, which gives the first full treatment on class definitions. Experienced Pascal programmers will also find it necessary to learn the syntax introduced in Chapters 2 through 6. Chapters 8 through 11 form the heart of the object-oriented features, syntax, and culture of C++. Chapter 12 introduces the reader to container classes and linked lists. Chapter 13 is a case study of the iterative process that we went through in developing a sophisticated class library.

This book is organized on two different themes. The first theme is design and analysis of programming problems; the second is the C++ tools that are useful in implementing solutions to these problems. Students who successfully complete a programming course should have practical programming skills when they leave the course. But to prevent creating a hacker mentality—going after an immediate solution in the quickest way possible—it is important to show students useful design methodologies from the start.

This book uses the familiar changemaker problem as a running example to illustrate iterations in design, enhancements, and implementation. The initial statement of the problem from Chapter 1 is very simple. As more programming tools become available, the changemaker is reanalyzed and redesigned to incorporate these new tools and to improve either the functionality of the program solution or to improve its organization.

For the teacher

This book contains material for a two-semester sequence in introductory design and programming. At North Carolina State University, the first course is organized into large lecture sections (175 students) with small closed labs. We have found that it is reasonable to cover Chapter 1 through the first half of Chapter 7 plus the Stream Appendices (D, E, and F) in a traditional three-semester hour introductory course. Students in four-semester hour courses could cover more material, or simply do the same material in more depth and with more examples.

The laboratory experience is important. Ideally, we would like all low-level syntax topics relegated to the lab. The lecture is a very inefficient way to cover that material. Through laboratories, especially those that have integrated support for software development, students can experiment with the language to see the practical results of the lectures.

We realize that the second course varies tremendously among different schools. The second course at North Carolina State University has traditionally focused more on software engineering concepts than data structures. The material in Chapter 7 through the remainder of the book is appropriate for such a second course.

Comprehensive exercises, varying from straightforward syntax exercises through programming projects are included at the end of every chapter. Answers to all of the exercises except the programming projects are available for instructors upon request from Addison-Wesley. For additional information, see the supplements section following. The programming projects are open-ended and can be modified to suit individual class needs.

We hope that this textbook will be useful not only for students but also for teachers who are just now starting to teach the introductory course using C++. That pedagogical task is not trivial. And it is especially not trivial to those who know C or Pascal and come to realize very late that C++ is not just a new version of C and not just Pascal with classes. Part of what we do in this book is addressed to helping our colleagues, who may be struggling just ahead of their students. We know about that struggle from our own experience.

Problem solving is difficult no matter what the language and what the tools. But be encouraged from our discoveries. The language switch—the syntax switch—is easy. Learning the culture, how good C++ programmers do things, is harder. But the most difficult thing is learning how to think in terms of object-oriented analysis and design as opposed to structured analysis and design.

For the student

You will begin learning by solving very simple problems and writing very short programs. Think about the programs that you use and like. If after three months, you still do not have a good idea of how to write such a program, all that indicates is that programming is a broad and deep subject. It will take considerable time and effort before you will realize the goal of having good object-oriented programming skills.

When you begin your work, you will discover ways to organize what you already know and ways to spell out things that you already know how to do. You will discover new ways of looking at problems and devising solutions to them. This book is full of advice on how to learn, what is important, when to exercise old skills, and when to learn new ones. We suggest that you read carefully. Read new material in the book before you go to class. Read it after you attend a lecture. Underline key points. And work problems. Programming is not for spectators.

Do not hesitate to experiment. If you are not sure how a piece of code works, try it out. All of us, even those of us who are professional teachers, are students too. And we learn what we know by falling into lots of holes and making lots of mistakes, just as you are almost certain to do. There is an extensive set of exercises at the end of each chapter. Answers to selected exercises are available via anonymous ftp to `ftp.aw.com`. For instructions to download these files, refer to the supplements section following.

Your compiler will not be perfect, and it may not support some features of C++ mentioned in this book. (For example, the type `bool` is not available on some compilers.) We have tried to warn you in the text where some of our compilers were deficient, and where you might run into the same problems. When possible, we have suggested simple work-arounds.

Technical standards

The code in the first seven chapters was tested on all of the following environments. All of the code was tested in at least one UNIX-based environment.

Borland Turbo C++ version 3.0 on DOS 5.0
Microsoft Visual C++ version 1.0 (Standard Edition) for Windows 3.1

Symantec C++ version 7.0 on Macintosh, system 7.0
AT&T version 3.0 on a SUN4 using SunOS 4.1
Gnu version 2.6.1 on a DECstation using Ultrix 4.2

The technical terms that we introduce in the text are not ours. Wherever possible, we have tried to conform our use of technical terms with the practice of the C++ community, its epicenter being at Bell Laboratories. We have also tried to conform with the language standards described in Margaret Ellis and Bjarne Stroustrup's *Annotated C++ Reference Manual* (the *ARM*),[1] which serves as the base document for the ANSI standardization of C++ currently in progress. In the few places where our code uses an operating system or other system-dependent headers or procedures, we isolated the nonportable features and indicated system dependence with comments.

We have entirely avoided the use of exceptions and exception handling for two reasons. First, exceptions are not as widely implemented in C++ compilers as are the other *ARM* language features, and standards for exceptions are more in flux than other parts of the language described in the *ARM*. Second, exception handling is an important addition to the control structures of the structured programming tradition but not an integral part of our central theme—object-oriented program development.

Supplements

The following supplements are available through the Addison Wesley ftp site:

- Source code
- Answers to selected exercises
- Instructor's solutions access information

To obtain any of the supplement files, ftp to `aw.com`. Log in with user name `anonymous` and use your internet address as the password. From there, type `cd sceng/authors/perry/oop.cs1`.

Acknowledgments

The authors gratefully acknowledge the help of many people in writing this book. Among our colleagues, Don Martin has been especially encouraging from the start. We doubt that we could have completed our work without the assistance of Susan Jones, who has worked tirelessly to check code, do problems, and suggest

[1] Ellis, Margaret A., and Bjarne Stroustrup. *The Annotated C++ Reference Manual*. Reading, Mass.: Addison-Wesley, 1990.

ways of formulating ideas. Both Susan and Don have been with us since the inception of this project, always giving constructive criticism and refraining from asking the question "Isn't it done yet?"

We appreciate the willingness of Don Martin, Susan Jones, Carol Miller, and Steve Worth to use a draft manuscript for their classroom text. We thank our students and colleagues alike for serving as guinea pigs in this project. All have provided valuable feedback.

The editorial staff at Addison-Wesley has been very helpful in preparing the final manuscript. Our editor Lynne Cote has offered valuable words of encouragement and has also provided us with a rich reference library from among the numerous excellent Addison-Wesley publications. We thank the authors of those books for pointing out to us and to their other readers the culture and use of object-oriented techniques and C++. In addition, our production supervisor Helen Wythe has been gracious and diligent in dealing with the endless problems of putting the book together.

We have taken advantage of extensive reviewer comments, incorporating many of the suggestions into the book. We thank especially James Adcock, Microsoft Corporation; Vicki H. Allan, Utah State University; Frank Cioch, Oakland University; H. E. Dunsmore, Purdue University; Thomas Hain, University of South Alabama; Dennis Heckman, Portland Community College; Robert Kline, Westchester University; Rayno Niemi, Rochester Institute of Technology; Christopher Skelley, Insight Resources; and Phil Sweany, Michigan Technological University. We also thank Pat Ryan of MicroSystems Integration for his early and consistent encouragement and helpful suggestions.

Finally, our families have lived with this project almost as much as we have. Lavon and Connie have demonstrated their love for us through their wonderful patience in our extended times away from home. They have had to put up with lost weekends and exhausted spouses for over two years, and they did it almost without complaint.

*for Lavon
and Dr. Myron J. Levin, M.D.*

Contents

Chapter 1

Object-Oriented Program Development

COMPUTERS are not smart; they just know how to follow instructions. Unlike dogs or cats or people, computers follow instructions very well, step-by-step. A computer **program** is a set of instructions to the computer. The purpose of this book is to teach you to write computer programs that will tell computers how to solve particular problems or do particular things.

This chapter begins with a look at how the entire process of creating a computer program originates. We will follow a special approach called **object-oriented**

1

program development, an approach that is somewhat new in the computing world but very old in the world of human experience. It involves creating models of real-world situations and building computer programs based on those models.

The best way to learn about object-oriented development of solutions to programming problems is through examples. There are no generic recipes that are going to work with all problems. Computer problem solving is a creative activity. It can be very simple or very complex, depending on the nature of the problem. And that's what makes it interesting. If solving problems were just a matter of following a simple list of instructions, then we wouldn't need programmers at all. We'd just write one program that would be able to write all other programs!

We'll examine two different problems to illustrate object-oriented development concepts, solving them step-by-step, from the beginning. First, we analyze the problems, then we design and draw out solutions on paper. We finish by writing the computer programs that are the actual problem solutions. The focus for this chapter is on analysis and design, because that constitutes the hard part of problem solving.

In this book we'll show you how to "object-think" when you are at the analysis or design levels of solving programming problems. We'll introduce specific details of how to code your solutions for the computer using the programming language C++. And we'll approach C++ programming tools gradually. Each program that you will encounter while studying this text uses the concepts of C++ that you already know or will soon learn. As you progress with your mastery of the features available in C++, you will see how some of the initial designs for problems can be changed to take advantage of increasingly sophisticated features of the language.

1.1 What is object-oriented program development?

A program is somewhat like the script of a play. A script describes the cast of characters, the environment in which they exist, and the things the characters do. The sets and the props of a play represent physical things, and the characters represent people that seem real (usually). The interactions among the characters represent situations and events. In many cases, computer programs contain computer-world representations of the things or objects that constitute the solutions of real-world problems. Executing a program such as this is like performing a play.

Object-oriented program development means constructing programs as models of real-world events. The entire programming process begins with construction of a model of the event. The end result of the process is a computer program that contains features representing some of the real-world objects that are part of the event. Execution of the program simulates the event.

Most of the things that you are asked to do in a beginning programming course are things that you know how to do without a computer. You know how to alphabetize a list of names, convert temperatures from Fahrenheit to Celsius, and determine the cost of a shopping cart full of groceries. But unless you've programmed before, you probably don't have the foggiest idea of how to make a computer solve these fairly simple problems. You probably don't even know where to begin.

As our first step in program construction, we'll look at an intuitive way to describe what is to be done. This description has nothing necessarily to do with computers. At this point, we will pay very careful attention to the objects involved in our intuitive solution and their behaviors. We will rely on our own real-world experiences and intuition for guidance.

Once we figure out what a program should do, we will be ready to create a model. Problem solving through model construction is not a new kind of intellectual activity. It's been going on since the beginning of civilization. Today we all use models constantly. Think about traveling by automobile from one city to another. Highway maps are models we use to solve the problem of getting from one geographical region to another. The objects that make up a highway map include representations of such things as cities, roads, and rivers. The relationships among these objects determine the routes that we can travel to go from one place to another.

What kinds of models can we create for computer programs? There are countless answers to this question. The basic requirement of any model is that it be useful. There can be many different models that will be useful in a given programming problem or task. Some models may even be radically different and still be useful. The modeling process itself is not rigid. For any one problem there is no unique answer to what model should be constructed and what objects must be involved.

Let's look at a list of problems that might be solved by computer programs. Think about each in terms of what situations the corresponding computer program can model. Imagine a cartoon for each situation. What are the objects in the cartoons? How do they interact? Some models are better than others. The best thing you can do is to pick out what you think is most useful. It takes experience and creativity to think up useful models.

- A video game software manufacturer wants to create a new video game that simulates a jet fighter.

- A physician needs software tailored to patients at her medical clinic. The patients have many varieties of illnesses and funding sources for their treatments.

- The Environmental Protection Agency needs a program that simulates acid rain deposition in the Appalachian Mountains under certain power plant location scenarios.

- An inventor is building a wheelchair that can climb stairs. The wheelchair must be simulated in software before the inventor is willing to pay for expensive tooling of the wheels, gears, and microprocessor that constitute the actual wheelchair.

You can't solve these problems now, but you can begin to think about the scenarios that they model. The video game will simulate interactions among fighter jets and is especially easy to imagine as a cartoon. The physician's software will take the place of the tedious bookkeeping and record keeping that used to be relegated strictly to hand calculations and notations. Acid rain deposition, which will take place as a story from the computer rather than as real rain in the Appalachian Mountains, will involve computer-world power plants and computer-world trees. The wheelchair simulator will be able to show how well a particular wheelchair design fits the specifications of the inventor.

The corresponding programs to solve these problems will differ immensely in length and complexity. Even the effort required to test the solutions to make sure they are correct will differ greatly among the programs. A program is **correct** if it does what it is supposed to do. The correctness of software may have an enormous impact on its users or it may be of relatively trivial significance. If the video game fails to keep correct scores for its players, the results may be of little consequence. But the failure of the wheelchair to climb a set of stairs properly could result in serious injury for the person in the wheelchair.

When you first start solving programming problems, your efforts will be very modest. You will not be able to solve the problems we just listed, and you will probably spend a considerable amount of time just figuring out how to write your solutions in C++.

C++ is a computer language specifically designed to support object-oriented program development. The new language tools that you will learn won't tell you how to solve the problem. But you will work within the confines of these new tools in order to create programs that will implement your solutions, programs that will actually solve the problems and perform the desired tasks.

What is an object?

In our discussions of problems and models, we will use the term **object** over and over again. The term object has the same meaning as a noun or noun phrase: It is a person, place, or thing. Examples of real-world objects are endless: person, table, vending machine, airline flight schedule, computer, dictionary, city, and the ozone layer to name a few.

All of the example problems in this chapter can be described in terms of real-world objects—from jets to ledgers to people to wheelchairs. When we look at a problem or situation to figure out what a program solution is supposed to do, we will do so in terms of the objects that make up the problem. We will identify those objects in terms of what they are, how they behave, and how they interact with each other.

Some objects—airplanes, people, and major cities—are very complicated, others are very simple. An object may include other objects. For example, a personal computer is an object. One of the objects that makes up the computer is the central processing unit (CPU). Another object is its main memory and another is the input/output (I/O) subsystem. The I/O subsystem also contains objects, including the keyboard, the mouse, and the display screen. A single key is an object that is part of the keyboard. Depending on just how fine a description is needed, the keyboard can be broken into even smaller objects—all the way down to molecules and atoms that form the plastic from which the keys are made.

Most objects in the real world have **attributes**, characteristics that can be described. For example, the attributes of a person include that person's age, name, gender, address, birthplace, parents' names, educational experience, physical condition, and so on.

Attributes can be of different types and different values. Consider a person as an object. One of the attributes is the person's name, which is a string of characters. Another is the person's weight, which is a number. Strings of characters and numbers are different types. The actual values of the names and weights differ from person to person. For example, for a particular person, the name attribute may have a value of "John Doe" and the weight attribute may have the value 158. For another person, those attributes may have the values "Jane Smith" and 134.

Objects have attributes and they have behaviors. **Behaviors** are things an object can do. Indeed, for some objects their importance lies in their behaviors rather than their attributes. Even inanimate objects such as computer keyboards can do things. We will be looking at objects as if they were intelligent beings. Objects *know* things and they *do* things. The things an object knows are its attributes. The things an object can do are its behaviors.

Most systems are made up of several different kinds of objects that interact with each other. For example, the keyboard may interact with the screen of the personal computer. In pressing a key, the image of a character appears on the screen. When we develop a model, we will look at objects individually to determine their attributes and behaviors. And we will look at them collectively to figure out how they interact with each other. In this chapter we will keep those interactions to a well-defined and highly controlled minimum.

Connections between computer-world objects and real-world objects

Real-world objects are almost always extremely complicated. In constructing a model, a programmer must create something very simple to represent a real-world system that is probably very complex. Models are usually simpler than the systems that they represent. Computer objects, which are created by the programmer as part of a model, are simpler than their corresponding real-world objects. Only the characteristics of the real-world system that are relevant to a problem are important for the corresponding model.

To construct a computer program using object-oriented program development techniques, a programmer must figure out what objects are important. For each object, the programmer determines what attributes are essential in solving the problem. For example, suppose the local library maintains information on its borrowers in order to keep track of its books. If a program is to maintain information on the library's borrowers in an accessible and ready-to-use form, then one useful model for constructing that program represents the borrowers as objects. Each borrower is a person.

People are extremely complicated things. However, with respect to the local library, the important attributes of each borrower may be limited to the following:

> Name
> Address
> Amount owed to the library for missing or overdue books
> List of books that the borrower currently has checked out of the library.

It is unlikely that the library needs to keep track of borrowers' weights, ages, genders, or physical conditions.

A model for a physician's office requires a different type of person object. What is important about a patient from the viewpoint of a physician? We could guess that a person's age, gender, weight, and physical condition are very important. However, the amount of money the person owes the local library is irrelevant.

In representing a real-world object as a computer object, always look for the important attributes that real-world object has with respect to the programming problem. Make it as simple as possible. Unnecessary details will only make your task harder to understand and to solve. Pick out only the relevant details and focus on them. For each object, describe its attributes (what it knows) and its behaviors (what it can do).

This process of picking out the essentials of an object is called **abstraction**. Real life is impossibly complicated. Models and objects, which are abstractions of their real counterparts, are simple.

Object-oriented analysis and object-oriented design

There are several important things that you must do as a programmer in order to go from the real world to the computer world. You must first figure out what specific task your program is to perform and the particular problem it is to solve. You must get an overall view of the problem. Even though the essential problem remains intact, details of the actual problem itself may change in scope or emphasis according to the wishes of your employer, client, or teacher.

A programming problem is usually described as a set of **specifications**, the details that constitute the actual problem. The specifications are part of what is called **object-oriented analysis (OOA)**, which answers the question *"What is to be done?"* During the analysis phase, you must think about the specifications in intuitive terms outside the realm of computers. The critical part of this activity is thinking up what kinds of real-world objects might be involved, then narrowing down the important attributes of these objects and determining their behaviors and interactions.

The answer to the question *"How* is it to be done?" describes another phase of the program development process: **object-oriented design** (**OOD**). During this phase, you will begin to create a computer model based on the analysis and make that model specific to the particular task at hand. At this time, you will think how the real-world objects may be represented as computer world objects. You must examine objects more carefully, specifying in detail what objects know and what they can do, and carefully describe their interactions. During the design phase, you may find additional useful attributes and behaviors for the objects that were not apparent in the analysis phase.

If the distinction between OOA and OOD seems unclear, don't worry. The OOA-OOD phases do not represent a strictly two-step process. Many times you will find yourself redoing some of the analysis in light of what you have learned in the design. You may find that the initial model that you selected is not appropriate, and that you need to go back and think the problem over again. You may discover additional specifications that you did not know about when you started your work. You may find that the attributes or behaviors of an object should be different from what you decided in the analysis state. It is a mistake to become so devoted to old decisions that you are unwilling to change them when the model that you have constructed is not useful.

Coming up with analyses and designs is not an obvious process and some people are better at it than others. The best way to learn how to do analysis and design is to look at good examples—and then to try to do some on your own. In fact, that may be the only way to learn. Many problems can be grouped into categories, where most of the ideas used to solve one problem can be used to solve a second and subsequent similar problems. This is very important. Be on the lookout to reuse good analyses and designs when they are appropriate for a new problem.

The design phase leads into the **implementation** phase of a design—translation of the design into actual code. During this phase, you look critically at objects with a view toward how they will be implemented in code. The coding phase of the object-oriented program development process is called **object-oriented programming** (**OOP**). After you understand your model, then you can translate that design model into code. That means you should stay off the keyboard for a while and take the time necessary to do reasonable analysis and design.

Just as the analysis and design phases interact with one another, the coding phase interacts with the analysis and design phases. (See Fig. 1.1.) Coding decisions may well change some of the aspects of the model, or they may actually refine some earlier decisions. Objects may change, or they may even be added to or taken away from other objects. Attributes and behaviors may be added or modified. Analysis, design, and coding do not compose a simple three-step process for solving a real-world problem. All steps interact with each other. However, some analysis must be done before any design, and some design must be done before any coding.

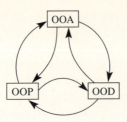

Figure 1.1 The object-oriented program development cycle.

Lessons for students

Students rarely get a glimpse of the world of programming that extends beyond their own academic environment. It is outside academia where the tangible benefits of object-oriented development techniques become apparent. In a nonacademic environment, programming problems typically start out ill-defined and open-ended. The problems are messy and difficult, and they don't have a clean set of specifications. A customer who needs a program may understand that there is a problem to solve but may not understand exactly what that problem is.

As a programmer is solving a problem, additional specifications and requirements may become evident. New information has a way of coming to the programmer incrementally rather than all at once from the beginning. As a result of this shifting platform, the problem is analyzed and reanalyzed. From the analysts' point of view, the hard part of object-oriented program development comes in the analysis.

Object-oriented program development of a solution organizes a model so that some of it can be completed before other parts are started. That same organization allows replacement of some of the model with more appropriate objects without having to redo the part of the model that remains valid. When part of a model is completed, it can be written in C++ code. So a partially working solution can be created before the overall problem is even analyzed. The discovery of new specifications can be accommodated after the programming process has already begun. It's not necessary to throw away the previous work and start again.

Object-oriented methodologies were invented to solve problems of the "software crisis" generated by large-scale programming projects. As software becomes increasingly important and also increasingly expensive to develop, test, and maintain object-oriented techniques will assume even greater importance.

The object-oriented techniques that we are going to introduce aren't necessary to solve small problems. In fact with small problems and adept programmers, little in the way of technique or methodology is necessary. But since we can illustrate the techniques with small problems, we will keep them small for a while so that you can focus a substantial part of your learning efforts on the techniques. Object-oriented methodologies for even simple problems scale up nicely to large projects.

There's no getting around the fact that for real-world projects (real-world in terms of size, reliability, or maintainability), much additional knowledge, experience, and a high level of programming ability are required. There is no magic bullet.

1.2 ▌ Sample problem: The convenience store

There is a large collection of programming problems that we will call the "special-purpose handheld calculator" problems. A model of a special-purpose calculator is useful for many of the problems that novice programmers typically are asked to solve when they first start programming.

We will examine in detail one special-purpose handheld calculator problem. You will be able to reuse the initial design for this problem over and over again, modifying it to fit new problems. It will not take you much time to realize that many of the problems that sound radically different are really variations on the same old theme. All of the final program solutions will look a little similar. Reuse of a model is one of the real benefits of object-oriented analysis and design.

Here is our first problem.

> Your uncle owns several convenience stores in New England and Canada. He originally prices all of the produce sold in his stores in terms of U.S. pennies per pound. In an effort to maintain uniform pricing of the produce for all of the stores, he must translate prices of produce in U.S. pennies per pound to Canadian dollars per kilogram. Your uncle assumes the exchange rate of U.S. dollars to Canadian dollars is US$ 1 = C$1.26. You have offered to solve this problem for him.

Analyzing and designing a solution

Imagine a physical scenario for this problem. Your uncle is holding a simple calculator in his hand, turning it on, entering numbers, and reading the results. Now let's analyze this situation. As a first step, we'll focus on the calculator in terms of its essential objects.

A calculator has a keypad on which the user can enter numbers. It is the part of the calculator that is used for input. The calculator also has a window that is used displaying answers or output, as well as showing input. The rest of the calculator is devoted to doing all of the hard work, the actual computing.

There are several objects in this scenario. The main object is the calculator itself, which consists of a human interface component and a computing component. The human interface component is the part of the calculator that interacts with the user (your uncle in this case). It is a collection of two objects, an input object (corresponding to the keypad) and an output object (corresponding to the display window) and it is responsible for communication between the user and the calculator. The computing component is a single object. It is the part of the calculator that figures out answers based on the numbers that have been entered.

> Many of the problems that you will encounter in your programming experience can be usefully analyzed into an object consisting of a human interface component and a computing component. This is classic, top-level analysis. You could reuse the analysis of the convenience store problem for many different problems just by changing the computing object or the human interface object.

We need to take a closer look at what each real-world object can do. Your uncle can interact with the calculator—he can turn it on. The input object can ask your uncle to enter a number. The computing object can compute an answer for a number. The output object can display the result of the computations.

We will stop our analysis here because we don't need anything else for now. It turns out for this problem that we don't need to be looking for the attributes of the individual objects during analysis. (The only object in our first model that will eventually have any attributes is the computing object.) We know that no more detail is necessary mainly because we've had enough experience to know so. Soon, you will be able to see when to stop the analysis. You will have enough experience to know what level of detail is sufficient.

Figure 1.2 is the model that we have described so far in the OOA phase of this problem solution. In this diagram, the objects are rectangles and the human interface object, which is made up of two different but related objects, is a rectangle with rounded corners. We know what the solution does, and now we must discover how it can do it. Our rough model needs to be translated and refined into a computer model.

The main object that we've decided upon is the calculator itself. With the hardware that we normally have to work with, this aspect of the model is difficult to design.

- Do we build an actual calculator, plastic and wires and all?

- Do we draw a picture of a calculator on the screen, complete with pictures of calculator keys that can be activated by a mouse?

- Do we just use the screen as a gigantic calculator display and the terminal keyboard as the calculator keyboard?

We'll go the easy route now by settling on the last option.

The input object will use the screen and the computer keyboard for its work.

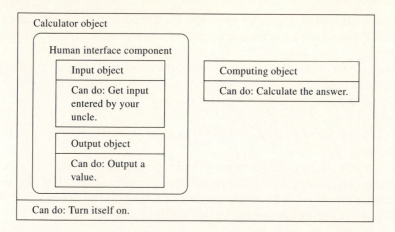

Figure 1.2 Analysis model of solution to the convenience store problem.

Your uncle pressing keys on his calculator's keypad will correspond to a user pressing keys on the computer keyboard. The input value to be entered by your uncle will represent the price in U.S. pennies per pound of an item. That value must be entered as one or more digits followed by a return, and it will be echoed on the screen as the keys are pressed.

The output object, which is the other half of the human interface component, is separate from the input object. But it will use the same display to show the results of the calculation. It will show a number (the answer) on the screen right below the number that was entered.

The computing object should do nothing except generate the answer. It should not try to read a value entered by the user; that's up to the input object to do. The computing object should not try to write the answer on the screen; that's up to the output object to do. This is an important concept to remember:

> Objects should not duplicate each other's tasks. If you find that your objects do duplicate tasks, that's a sign that those objects are too complicated and should be redesigned.

Although it is important that objects do not duplicate each other's tasks, that does not mean that the only object that is allowed to write something on the screen is the output object. The important point is that the output object is the only object that should be allowed to write *the answer* on the screen. Many times you will want to design an input object that can tell the user what kinds of values are supposed to be entered. This is known as **prompting the user**. The input object in that case would write a prompt message on the screen to tell the user what is expected. Prompts are especially important when more than one input value is to be entered.

How can the computing object compute the answer? That isn't too hard to figure out if you know the conversion factors, such as how many kilograms there are in a pound. Suppose we use the following terms:

`dollarsPerKg` is the price per kilogram in Canadian dollars of an item (the answer)
`penniesPerLb` is the price per pound in U.S. pennies of an item
`penniesPerDollar = 100` is the number of U.S. pennies in a U.S. dollar
`dollarsCanPerUS = 1.26` is the number of Canadian dollars in a U.S. dollar
`kgPerLb = .4536` is the number of kilograms in a pound

This formula provides the answer.

```
dollarsPerKg = penniesPerLb/kgPerLb *
                  dollarsCanPerUS/penniesPerDollar
```

One design based on this formula says that the computing object knows the three quantities `penniesPerDollar`, `dollarsCanPerUS`, and `kgPerLb`. These are the attributes of the computing object. The computing object can figure out the answer by taking the price in pennies per pound, dividing by the number of kilograms in a pound, multiplying by the number of Canadian dollars in a U.S. dollar, and dividing by the number of pennies in a U.S. dollar. This is the kind of behavior that most computer languages can describe easily.

Another design could use the fact that no matter what the value of `penniesPerLb`, the other numbers are the same. We could design the computing object to know a single value instead of three separate ones: `penniesPerDollar`, `dollarsCanPerUS`, and `kgPerLb`.

`toCanadian = .0278` is the quantity Canadian dollars per U.S. dollar /
(kilograms per pound * U.S. pennies per dollar)

The multiplication and division could be done once and for all instead of duplicating them each time the computing object needed to calculate the answer. The answer is computed as

```
dollarsPerKg = penniesPerLb * toCanadian
```

Which design is best? Probably the first. That's because the formula for computing the result is explicitly part of the first design. The multiplier, `toCanadian`, is not hidden as some mysterious number in the design (or in the actual code). In that sense, the first design is simpler, easier to understand, and easier to correct if it contains an error.

Unless the original problem statement itself mentions some kind of efficiency, go with the simpler design. The calculator should be reliable and correct. If you design the computing object to use the single multiplying factor rather than actually calculate the sequence of arithmetic operations, you're more likely to make a mistake. The code for that design will certainly be harder to read and understand than the code for the original design.

Now imagine what happens when the calculator object gets to work. The whole process begins when your uncle turns on the calculator. He punches in the number on the keypad and presses the enter key. Then the answer is displayed on the calculator's window.

In the real world, your uncle interacts with the calculator when he turns it on. In the computer world, we say objects interact by sending messages. A computer-world object responds to a message by performing one of its behaviors—the calculator responds to a message to turn itself on. After turning itself on, the calculator does three things: (1) It asks the input object to get a number; (2) after receiving the input number, the calculator object asks the computing object to figure out the answer based on the input number; and (3) the calculator object then asks the output object to display the answer.

Figure 1.3 illustrates the design we just developed. During the object-oriented design phase, we have greatly enhanced and clarified the model. Notice that in

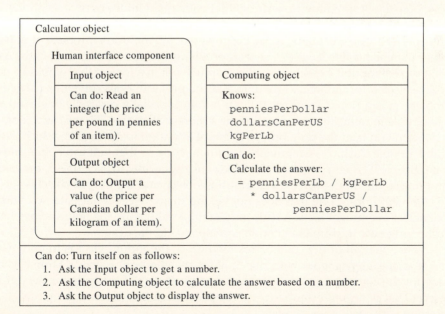

Figure 1.3 Design model of the solution to the convenience store problem.

this design, the input and output objects are not shown as having any attributes. Not all objects have attributes that are necessarily spelled out by each model that uses them. They can do things, but they may not know things that are tailored to the specific problem.

Implementing the solution

For most programming problems, the hard work should be done as soon as the design is finished. Implementation of the design—coding the design in a programming language—should be easy. We are showing you the implementation of our design so that you can get a feeling for how a C++ program looks. We do not expect you to understand how to construct code from design just by looking at this example. (Much of the second chapter of this book is devoted to detailed discussion of the exact meaning and significance of each line in the program.)

The analysis and design that we just finished can be used for a program written in any general purpose language. Our initial work does not require C++. And since C++ is full of features that promote object-oriented programming, our program could be implemented in a variety of ways. But we can also use C++ on an elementary level to capture the essence of our model.

The implementation that we show here is certainly not as simple as it could be. We could have settled for much less. But we really want to focus on design and not concentrate on the shortest code possible to solve a particular problem. Code constructed just from the "get it done the quickest way possible" standpoint tends to be limited. It's hard to reuse such code for similar problems. Such coding practices force the programmer to write similar code many times over.

Even though our implementation is not as simple as it could be, it is still far from perfect. The calculator must be powered up for every problem it solves, rather than being able to solve a several problems in a row. It does not tell the user what type of input it expects. And the output is not in a format that would be naturally selected for monetary amounts. But the program does solve this particular problem. It is a *correct* solution, though not an especially desirable one. And we will be able to refine it later to make it be a more realistic model of a calculator.

When you read the program, pay careful attention to comments, which begin with a double slash, //. Comments document code so that you can better understand the code when you read it. The code corresponding to each object, the calculator object, the input object, the computing object, and the output object is set off by comment lines. Code that does not belong to an object is not enclosed within that object's comment lines. At this time, comment lines are the only way we have of showing how the implementation corresponds to the design.

Notice that all of the code corresponding to the input object is in one place, and it is not intermingled with the code for the computing object. Similarly, the code for the computing object does not appear as part of the code for the output object. That is an important part of object-oriented programming: objects don't interfere with each other's code.

```
// Name: Convenience store owner
// Version: 1.0
// Purpose: Convert the price of an item in U.S. pennies per pound to
//    Canadian dollars per kilogram.

#include <iostream.h>

//----------------------- calculator object -----------------------------

void main()
{

    double theOutput;       // Answer displayed to the user
    double dollarsPerKg;    // Item's cost in Canadian dollars per kilogram
    int theInput;           // Input entered by the user
    int penniesPerLb;       // Price in U.S. pennies per pound of an item


    //------------------- input object ---------------------------------
    //  Get the input.
    cin >> theInput;
    //------------------- end of input object --------------------

    penniesPerLb = theInput;

    //------------------- computing object ---------------------------
    const double kgPerLb = .4536;          // Number of kilograms in a pound
    const double dollarsCanPerUS = 1.26;   // Number of Canadian dollars per
                                           //    U.S. dollar (exchange rate)
    const int penniesPerDollar = 100;      // Number of pennies per U.S. dollar

    dollarsPerKg = penniesPerLb/kgPerLb * dollarsCanPerUS/penniesPerDollar;
    //------------------- end of computing object ------------------------

    theOutput = dollarsPerKg;

    //------------------- output object --------------------------------
    // Display the answer.
    cout << theOutput << endl;
    //------------------- end of output object --------------------------

}
//-------------------- end of calculator object ------------------------
```

1.3 Sample problem: The changemaker

The next problem should be familiar to any of you who have ever gone into a coin laundry with only paper bills in your pocket. In that situation, you needed to exchange paper money for coins in order to operate a washer and dryer. We'll phrase a similar problem in this way.

> Write a computer program that can take an amount and compute the count of bills and coins of each denomination required to sum to the amount.

The problem statement is very brief. Is this U.S. currency? What are the sizes of the denominations? Is there an unlimited supply of each denomination so that the amount can be optimally divided? Let's begin with the assumption that there is an unlimited supply of U.S. currency as follows: $20 bills, $10 bills, $5 bills, $1 bills, quarters, dimes, nickels, and pennies.

Analysis and design

Here's another scenario for a model. A customer drives up to a bank window and gives the teller a check in exchange for cash. The teller then hands the customer an envelope that contains currency whose total value is the amount of that check.

Let's make a model for the changemaker problem as simple as possible. The main object in the model is a teller. The teller is like the calculator object in the convenience store problem. In fact, we could even look at this problem as another special-purpose handheld calculator problem. We could use the same input object and modify the output and computing objects to fit the new problem.

How must the output object and the computing object be modified for the new problem? The output object in the changemaker problem can't display simply a single number. It must display a sequence of numbers corresponding to the amounts of the different denominations. Rather than calculating a single number, the changemaker computing object must calculate a sequence of numbers. Figure 1.4 shows our analysis of this problem.

The teller waits for customers. This is similar to the process of turning on the calculator in the solution to our convenience store problem. What is the teller to look like? We face the same kinds of design issues we did in the last problem. (Only this time, the idea of creating a real, live teller is out of the question.) Once again, let's keep it simple. The teller will be the computer terminal. The input will be a single number. The output will be a sequence of numbers.

How is the input to be entered? The obvious choices are as a decimal number such as 23.41 or as an integer 2341. The first number represents an amount in terms of dollars; the second is the same amount in terms of pennies. For now, we'll choose to use the penny entry, just as we did in the convenience store problem.

The output object must be able to show a sequence of numbers. Suppose that sequence of numbers look like this:

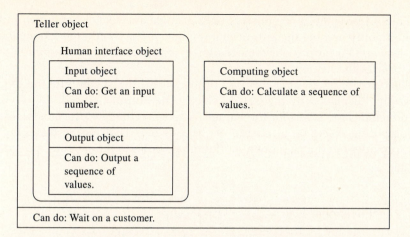

Figure 1.4 Analysis model of solution to the changemaker problem.

What could that sequence mean? One answer could be: 4 twenties, 0 tens, 0 fives, 4 ones, 3 quarters, 2 dimes, 0 nickels, and 2 pennies. Or it could just as easily mean: 4 pennies, 0 nickels, 0 dimes, 4 quarters, 3 ones, 2 fives, 0 tens, and 2 twenties. So that the user does not have to guess at what these numbers mean, why not indicate what each means in the output display? Let's change the output display design to be like this:

```
4 twenties
0 tens
0 fives
4 ones
3 quarters
2 dimes
0 nickels
2 pennies
```

Unless a program is to generate only a single answer for any given input, it should identify or label the output that it displays—it should tell the meaning of each answer. Our output object needs to be able to display a sequence of values and labels for the sequence.

The computing object is also part of the teller. It must compute the sequence that will be displayed by the output object. The output that will appear on the screen includes the labels for the values. Who is in charge of the labels? We'll let the computing object be in charge of the labeling. That means the computing object provides not only a sequence of numbers but also the appropriate sequence of labels.

Algorithms

Unlike our convenience store example, there isn't a mathematical formula that the computing object can use to figure out a sequence of values. The computing object needs an **algorithm**, which is a step-by-step finite process for solving a problem. You know this problem cannot be too difficult because people solve it all of the time. Think of how a real teller does it.

A real teller uses a helpful object to organize currency in order to make change, a cash drawer. A cash drawer is usually a shallow metal or plastic box partitioned into compartments. The compartments correspond to various denominations of currency: $20 bills, $10 bills, $5 bills, $1 bills, quarters, dimes, nickels, and pennies. (There may also be a compartment for larger bills, checks, or coupons.) The compartments are arranged in some sort of reasonable order.

How is the money given out? Assuming that the teller has an ample supply of all denominations, to give out $17.83, the teller would gather this from the cash drawer:

> a $10 bill
> a $5 bill
> two $1 bills
> three quarters
> one nickel
> three pennies

What conclusions can we draw from this example? The teller selects the money in order of denominations. All of the largest denomination is given out first, then the next largest denomination, then the next, and so on through the smallest denomination. The teller doesn't select a quarter, then a $10 bill, then another quarter, and so on. All bills or coins in a particular denomination are selected at the same.

Every teller can give out money in this fashion. The algorithm for giving out the money is most easily written to include exactly the same steps for each case, even though some of the steps may be superfluous for some cases. (In the $17.83 example, no $20 bills and no dimes were selected.) The following algorithm will thus work for all cases:

> select the correct number of $20's
> select the correct number of $10's
> select the correct number of $5's
> select the correct number of $1's
> select the correct number of quarters
> select the correct number of dimes
> select the correct number of nickels
> select the correct number of pennies

What is the correct number of $20 bills for our example of $17.83? The answer is none. How do we know that? If we select more than none, we would select a value that is more than the total amount that we are supposed to distribute in the first place. How about the correct number of $10 bills? We can select one $10 bill and not exceed the amount that we are to distribute. We cannot give out two of them.

At this point, after the $10 is selected, the additional amount of money needed to select from the cash drawer is $7.83. Continue to the next denomination, the $5 bills. The correct number must be the largest number of $5 bills whose value will not exceed the amount remaining, $7.83. There is one $5 bill to select.

The remaining amount is reduced to $2.83. The next denomination is $1 bills, and the largest number that make up that amount is two. So two $1 bills are selected, leaving the amount 83 cents. The next denomination is quarters. Three quarters can be selected without exceeding 83 cents, which leaves an amount remaining of 8 cents.

The correct number of dimes to select is none, still with 8 cents as the amount remaining. That leaves us with one nickel to select, and 3 cents left. The final amount to select is three pennies—with a final amount of $0.00 remaining to be distributed, which is what we want. There is no more money left to select.

That long explanation can be simplified:

> Beginning with the highest denomination not yet selected, find the largest number of that denomination (the count of that denomination) whose total value does not exceed the amount of money remaining to be distributed. Reduce the amount remaining by the value of that denomination times the count of that denomination. Continue this process through the remainder of the denominations.

How do we find the "count of a denomination"? Take a careful look at the computation for the number of quarters to be given back for $17.83. The amount left at the time the quarter denomination is determined was 83 cents. The value of a quarter is 25 cents. The number of quarters in 83 cents is 3, which is the quotient of dividing 83 by 25. The amount not yet divided among the smaller denominations becomes 8 cents, which is the remainder of dividing 83 by 25.

The algorithm relies on integer division with quotients and remainders to do the necessary arithmetic. Integer division is also something that most computer languages can perform very easily. In C++, the quotient of 83 divided by 25 is written as `83 / 25` and the remainder is written as `83 % 25`.

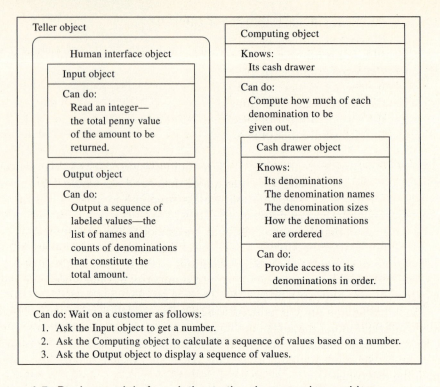

Figure 1.5 Design model of a solution to the changemaker problem.

Why did we start with the highest denomination and work our way to the smallest? Try going the other way. Try to construct an algorithm that starts with the smallest denomination and works its way to the largest. It can be done, but not nearly as easily.

The computing object knows its cash drawer. It utilizes the cash drawer object to figure out what currency to select. The cash drawer object has a life of its own. It knows its denominations and the size of each denomination, and how the denominations are ordered (largest to smallest). It knows the name or label of each denomination. What the cash drawer object can do is provide access to its denominations in order. (See Fig. 1.5 for the design model.)

It was not necessary to build a model that contained a cash drawer object. But the cash drawer was certainly helpful when we had to come up with an algorithm to distribute the change. Models and objects can be used in the most creative aspect of problem solving. Those objects may not show up in the analysis. For the design process, think of the cash drawer as an object that is actually part of the computing object. So the computing object contains another object, just as the teller object contains other objects. The fact that objects can contain other objects is an important design principle.

Implementation of the changemaker solution

This is our first implementation of the design of the changemaker problem. It is correct because it gives the right answers.

There are many standards for evaluating programs including correctness, efficiency, convenience of use, and organization of code. One aim of object-oriented program development is to offer guidelines for organizing code. The purpose of these organizational goals includes enhancing reliability, reduction of long-range costs, and developing software components that can be reused for a variety of tasks. With regard to the organizational goals of object-oriented program development, our first implementation of the changemaker is not very successful.

One element of the goodness of implementation code is how closely the pieces of the code correspond to the major portions of the design. The difficulties in this implementation are especially apparent in the computing and cash drawer objects. Using only elementary programming tools, it is impossible to separate the code of the output object from the code of the computing object or cash drawer object.

We are stuck with this solution until we see how to use C++ functions to organize code more effectively in Chapter 3. Even then, it won't be a perfect solution, but the solution will at least be a better organized one. As the text progresses, we will discuss more and more satisfactory ways to implement the design. Those successive implementations will use more advanced features of C++, such as aggregates and classes.

This program uses only elementary features of C++, but do not expect to understand what all of this code means until you finish reading the next chapter. Read the program for the purpose of understanding its organization as well as getting a feel for how C++ programs may look.[1]

```
// Name: The changemaker
// Version: 1.0
// Purpose: Determine the number of each denomination from twenty dollar bills
//    down through pennies that constitute a given monetary amount.

#include <iostream.h>

//----------------------- teller object ------------------------------------

void main()
{
```

---

[1] All compilers should find this program acceptable. However, some older C++ compilers may require you to put the word static in front of the names of the denominations. For example, the line

```
const char twentyName[] = "twenties";  // Label for $20 bills
```

must be changed to

```
static const char twentyName[] = "twenties";        // Label for $20 bills
```

```cpp
int countOfTwenties;        // Count of $20's to be returned
int countOfTens;            // Count of $10's to be returned
int countOfFives;           // Count of $5's to be returned
int countOfOnes;            // Count of $1's to be returned
int countOfQuarters;        // Count of quarters to be returned
int countOfDimes;           // Count of dimes to be returned
int countOfNickels;         // Count of nickels to be returned
int countOfPennies;         // Count of pennies to be returned

int theAmount;              // Amount to be changed

//------------------- input object -------------------------------------
// Get the amount from the user.
cin >> theAmount;
//---------------- end of input object ---------------------------------


//------------------- computing object ---------------------------------
//------------------- cash drawer object -------------------------------
const int twentyValue = 2000;    // Number of pennies in $20
const int tenValue = 1000;       // Number of pennies in $10
const int fiveValue = 500;       // Number of pennies in $5
const int oneValue = 100;        // Number of pennies in $1
const int quarterValue = 25;     // Number of pennies in a quarter
const int dimeValue = 10;        // Number of pennies in a dime
const int nickelValue = 5;       // Number of pennies in a nickel
const int pennyValue = 1;        // Number of pennies in a penny

const char twentyName[] = "twenties";    // Label for $20 bills
const char tenName[] = "tens";           // Label for $10 bills
const char fiveName[] = "fives";         // Label for $5 bills
const char oneName[] = "ones";           // Label for $1 bills
const char quarterName[] = "quarters";   // Label for quarter coins
const char dimeName[] = "dimes";         // Label for dime coins
const char nickelName[] = "nickels";     // Label for nickel coins
const char pennyName[] = "pennies";      // Label for penny coins
//---------------- end of cash drawer object ------------------------

// Determine the amount of each denomination to be returned.
countOfTwenties = theAmount / twentyValue;
theAmount = theAmount % twentyValue;
countOfTens = theAmount / tenValue;
theAmount = theAmount % tenValue;
countOfFives = theAmount / fiveValue;
theAmount = theAmount % fiveValue;
countOfOnes = theAmount / oneValue;
theAmount = theAmount % oneValue;
```

```
        countOfQuarters = theAmount / quarterValue;
        theAmount = theAmount % quarterValue;
        countOfDimes = theAmount / dimeValue;
        theAmount = theAmount % dimeValue;
        countOfNickels = theAmount / nickelValue;
        theAmount = theAmount % nickelValue;
        countOfPennies = theAmount / pennyValue;
        theAmount = theAmount % pennyValue;
        //---------------- end of computing object ---------------------------

        //-------------------- output object ---------------------------------
        // Display the results.
        cout << countOfTwenties << " " << twentyName << endl;
        cout << countOfTens << " " << tenName << endl;
        cout << countOfFives << " " << fiveName << endl;
        cout << countOfOnes << " " << oneName << endl;
        cout << countOfQuarters << " " << quarterName << endl;
        cout << countOfDimes << " " << dimeName << endl;
        cout << countOfNickels << " " << nickelName << endl;
        cout << countOfPennies << " " << pennyName << endl;
        //---------------- end of output object ------------------------------
}
//-------------------- end of teller object ------------------------------
```

If you want to see how this program executes, you'll have to create a file containing the program. This is done through a text editor. The next step is compiling, and after that, if you have made no mistakes, you can run the program.

1.4 Compilers and languages: Making the program run

You don't need to be an automobile mechanic to drive a car. You don't even need to know how an engine works. But you do need to have an idea of what cars, gasoline stations, and highways are all about. Since this text is about programming solutions and not simply designing models for real-world problems, you should understand a little of what it means to implement those models. The purpose of this section is to give you a rough idea of what programs, computer languages, and compilers are all about.

A computer program is a sequence of instructions to a computer to perform a particular task or collection of tasks. Computers have no intelligence on their own. They rely on instructions written by people. Each sequence of instructions—each computer program—is written in a particular language.

What kinds of languages can computers understand? Every computer has its own primitive language, which is called **machine language**. Machine languages vary among different computers. When people first began writing programs, they had to write them in machine language. This was very difficult and tedious. Machine languages don't even vaguely resemble natural languages such as English. One of the things that the earliest computer scientists did was to write other languages that contained symbols that resembled natural language words such as LOAD and STORE.

As computer science evolved as a discipline, increasingly sophisticated languages were created. These newer languages are called **high-level languages** because they look more like natural languages. Examples of high-level languages that were developed in the 1950s are LISP, FORTRAN, and COBOL.

C++ is the high-level language that this text uses for implementation of its designs. It is based on the popular high-level language C. C++ was created in the mid 1980s specifically for the purpose of supporting object-oriented programming. It has special features for implementing objects and models. Languages like C++, which are heavily used, undergo revisions and changes to increase their functionality and to make up for deficiencies.

Computers can understand their own machine languages—but how can they understand programs written in a high-level language such as C++? The answer is that computers rely on **compilers** to translate high-level language programs into machine language programs. A C++ compiler is a program that takes a C++ program as input and translates it into machine language. The input for the compiler (the C++ program to be compiled) is called **source code**. The output that the compiler produces is a machine language file called the **object code**.[2] The object code is used to create a file that can be executed—a file that consists of actual machine language instructions that the computer can follow. We sometimes call machine language files **binary files**.

For any given C++ program, the corresponding object code itself is not usually a complete set of machine language instructions that will perform the task that the original program set out to do. Most programs rely on other code to perform particular tasks such as input data from the keyboard and output information to the screen. Much of that code exists in libraries, which are supplied by the company that sells the compiler. A **library** is a collection of code that can be used to solve related tasks, and it is considered an essential part of the language itself.

What do libraries contain? Libraries that are always included in any C or C++ installation include functions for input and output, mathematics, some character-handling facilities, and system access (to the time and date, for example). Since the hallmark of C++ is code that can be reused in a variety of applications, programmers frequently create their own libraries. These libraries can be used the same way that the built-in libraries can be used.

After a C++ source code program is translated into machine language by the compiler, another program called a **linker** incorporates that library code into the object code produced by the compiler from the source code. The linker actually links in the necessary library code to create a file with all of the machine language

---

[2] The "object" in object code has nothing to do with the "object" in object-oriented program development.

instructions to perform the task at hand. The machine language file that is created in this entire process is an **executable file**. It can be run directly on the computer. When you compile a typical program, the compile command invokes the linker as well as the compiler.

It is not necessary for you to learn machine languages, to understand everything that the compiler and linker do, or to know how the inside of a computer is constructed. Most programmers do not have complete knowledge of any computer system. This overall view of source files, object files, compilers, and libraries should give you enough understanding of the programming process to do meaningful work. All systems are different. It is your task to figure out exactly how to use your system to create executable files.

1.5 Why is object-oriented program development so important?

Object-oriented program development is becoming very popular for software manufacturers as well as students and teachers. The traditional approach to programming has been limited to functional decomposition, a process that takes a problem and breaks it into series of steps and activities to be performed sequentially. The questions that you should ask are "Why the change? In what way is an object-oriented approach an improvement?"

One answer to these questions is illustrated by the computing industry itself. That industry produces two distinct products: hardware and software. If you compare making hardware with making software, you are going to find significant differences in the way two are produced.

To produce an actual computer, a manufacturer assembles a large number of components into a single product. There are many varieties of components used in many different computers. Manufacturers can share components and reuse them in different computers. They can redesign a couple of components and refit them into an old design to make a brand new computer. The benefits of being able to reuse components and designs are enormous. Hardware is cheap to produce, convenient to manufacture, and reliable.

Software is a different story. When a manufacturer produces brand new software to solve a new problem or perform a new task, the process often starts from the beginning. Old designs are not modified to suit new problems, and old code cannot be plugged into new programs. Each design-code-test process starts fresh, from the beginning. That's one of the reasons why new software is often expensive, unreliable, and not easily used by different computer systems.

While new software that solves new problems or performs new tasks is one issue for software manufacturers, old software is another. Most software is not created once and then left to be executed until something better comes along. Software is modified and enhanced many times over to meet new specifications and to correct defective features. Most of the time involved in software development is spent not on creating the original programs but on making these changes.

Changes can take lots of programmer time and effort—expensive time and effort. Much of the focus of object-oriented development is placed on reuse; of analyses, designs, and code. Old work that can be reused to create new products represents a savings in real money. So does new code that can be reused to enhance lots of different programs.

The hardware-software illustration can be extended to your local shopping mall. You can go into an electronics store and buy a design or a schematic for an AM radio receiver. You can even buy the components necessary to build the receiver. But you can't go into *any* store and find a schematic for a spreadsheet program. You certainly can't buy pieces of code that can be used to construct a program. You simply can't buy software designs and code in the same way that you can buy hardware designs and components.

One of the major goals of the object-oriented approach to programming is to make software production more like traditional design and manufacturing activities. Object-oriented programmers strive to make designs that can be used for a variety of different programming projects. The designs can be customized through small changes for particular purposes, and actual code can be reused. The entire software production process could thus become more efficient and the software itself more reliable.

1.6   Summary

In the object-oriented world of programming, a computer program is a model of the problem to be solved. The model consists of independent entities called objects, which are intelligent in the same sense that human beings are intelligent. They know things (their attributes) and they can do things (their behaviors). They can interact by sending each other messages.

Object-oriented program development describes a three-phase process for constructing a computer program: (1) object-oriented analysis, (2) object-oriented design, and (3) object-oriented programming. Analysis determines what is to be done in terms of real-world objects. During the analysis phase, the model and its objects are first sketched out. Design determines how it is to be done in terms of computer-world objects. During the design phase, the model is refined and the algorithms that describe the behaviors of objects are developed. The interactions among the objects are made clear. The programming phase finishes the actual solution to the problem. During the programming stage, the code that implements the design is written and tested.

Several computer languages have been developed just for object-oriented programming. The most popular languages are C++ and Smalltalk, although many others also exist. We say that those languages support object-oriented programming because they make it easy to write code that implements object-oriented designs.

Object-oriented program development does not require that the solution be implemented in C++ or Smalltalk or any other object-oriented language. It is possible to write object-oriented code in traditional languages such as Pascal and

FORTRAN. Indeed, any program you can write in C++ you can also write in machine language. But implementing object-oriented designs in machine language is so painful that it is rarely if ever done. The same can be said for implementing complicated object-oriented designs in traditional languages. C++ makes object-oriented programming easy.

Glossary

abstraction   The process of picking out the essential attributes and behaviors of an object.

algorithm   A finite, well-defined sequence of steps for solving a problem.

attribute   Something an object knows.

behavior   Something an object can do.

binary file   A file containing binary representation of data.

compiler   A program that translates high-level language source code into low-level language.

executable file   A file that can be run directly on the computer.

high-level language   A language such as C++, FORTRAN, or Pascal designed for writing computer programs.

implementation   The actual code that is the solution to a programming problem.

library   A collection of code designed for related tasks.

linker   A program that combines object code and library files to produce an executable program.

machine language   A computer's built-in native language.

object   An entity that has attributes and behaviors. Object-oriented models consist of objects.

object code   The result of compiling source code.

object-oriented analysis (OOA)   The initial stage of object-oriented program development that answers the question "What is to be done?" During the OOA phase, the model forming the solution of the problem is developed in terms of real-world objects.

object-oriented design (OOD)   The stage of object-oriented program development that answers the question "How is it to be done?" During the OOD phase, the model forming the solution of the problem continues to be developed in terms of computer-world objects. The objects and their interactions become better defined.

object-oriented program development   The process of constructing a solution to a programming problem as a model of the problem.

object-oriented programming (OOP)   The implementation of an object-oriented design into source code.

program   A set of instructions to a computer.

prompting the user   Displaying a message on the screen to tell the user what type or form of input is expected.

source code   A text file containing C++ (or other high-level language code).

specifications   A description of the problem to be solved.

1.7 ▌ Exercises

1. It can be helpful to think in terms of children's cartoons when trying to imagine that objects can have behaviors. Name some possible behaviors for each of the following objects—think cartoons.

   a. A broom

   b. An automobile

   c. A pencil

   d. An electric light

   e. A road map

2. Name some of the goals of object-oriented program development.

3. Check out your own computing system. What compiler will you be able to use to compile your C++ programs? What is its name and version number? Describe the sequence of steps that you would have to go through in order to compile the solution to the convenience store problem and execute it.

4. An algorithm for solving a problem is a sequence of well-defined steps that will solve the problem.

   a. Write the steps a robot wearing socks and shoes can follow in order to change into another pair of socks.

   b. Write the steps a robot can follow in order to swap two pictures on the wall of a dentist's office.

   c. Write the steps a robot can follow to find the number of the police department in the telephone directory.

5. a. Write the steps a person must follow in order to obtain a soft drink from a machine. Assume soft drinks cost 60 cents apiece and the person has quarters only.

   b. Write the steps the vending machine must follow in order to return a soft drink and appropriate change to the person.

6. Suppose you are given the task of going back in time to the nineteenth century. How will you describe the following ideas to a person living in that time? Which term will be the easiest to describe?

   a. Computer

   b. Model

   c. Input

   d. Output

   e. Program

   f. Software

   g. Hardware

The next three exercises are about object attributes and object behaviors.

7. A program is to be written to maintain information for the local public library. One of the objects in the program design is a borrower. Describe two attributes and two behaviors of the borrower that would be important to the library.

8. A software manufacturer is designing CAD (computer-aided design) software that can be used by architects to construct blueprints. One of the objects in the design is a pencil. Describe one attribute of the pencil that would be important to an architect. Describe one of the pencil's behaviors.

9. A program simulating acid rain deposition is based on a model in which one of the objects is a coal-burning power plant. Describe one attribute of the power plant that is important to the model. Describe one of the power plant's behaviors. Name another object which could be important in the model.

10. The following three problems can each be considered special-purpose handheld calculator problems. Design a solution for each one. Use as much of the original design of the convenience store solution as possible for each, changing the original design only when necessary to suit the new problem. Indicate what each object in each design knows and what it can do. (Do not try to implement a solution or to write code. Instead, draw a design diagram similar to the last diagram for the convenience store problem.)

    a. A laboratory needs to convert Fahrenheit temperature measurements to Celsius. Design a programming solution that will perform such a conversion.

    b. Assume that the average pulse rate for a person is 70 beats per minute. Design a computer program for which the input is the age of a person (in years) and the output is the number of heartbeats for that person from the time of birth up to the most recent birthday.

    c. Design a program that can compute the amount of money a customer must pay for a sale item. The sale price is 35 % off the original and the sales tax rate is 6.5%. The program user will input the original price of the item in order to get the answer.

11. Many programs begin execution with a banner or a message providing information on the program. You can easily include this feature as a specification of any of the special-purpose handheld calculator programs. Display of the banner is something that the calculator object itself does, prior to asking the input object to get a number.

    a. Redesign the model for exercise 10(a) by including the specification that the program display a message such as the following when it begins execution:

```
*******************************
Fahrenheit-to-Celsius Converter
*******************************
```

b. Another use of a banner is to tell users what kind or format of input data the program expects. Create a banner for the convenience store program that will tell users what the program does, what kind of input is expected (the meaning of the input), and the format in which the input should be entered.

12. These problems are similar to the changemaker problem. For each one, there is a single input value but there are multiple output values. A solution for each can be designed using features of both the changemaker model and the convenience store models. Use the output object from the changemaker model and modify the computing object of the convenience store model to design a solution for each one.

   a. Pieces of lumber have been measured in inches. Design a programming solution to the problem of converting the inch lengths into feet and leftover inches.

   b. A length of vinyl flooring has been measured in inches. Design a programming solution to the problem of converting the inch length into yards, feet, and inches.

   c. The total amount of time it took for an airplane to travel from New York to London was reported in seconds. Design a programming solution to the problem of converting the seconds to hours, minutes, and seconds.

13. These problems differ from the convenience store problem in that more than a single input value is required for each. Since there is a single output value for each problem, the output object of the convenience store design can be reused directly without modification. The input object, however, needs to be changed.

   If we merely redo the input object to read two integers instead of one, the new design will not work when three or more items must be read. This situation may be repeated and may end up constructing a new input object design every time the number of input values differs from previous problems. Let's take a different approach. We'll include a new object within the current input object, called an `inputAnInteger` object. The input object will need to know the order in which the values are to be read, and it can simply ask the `inputAnInteger` object to do the reading whenever reading is necessary.

   The process of getting multiple input values is complicated by the fact that the user needs to know which input value is being requested at which time. A crude program may leave the user guessing at which quantity is to be entered first. A better designed program will tell the user which quantity is currently being requested. This can be accomplished through user prompts, which can be very long and complicated or brief. The following are three examples of simple prompts informing users that a price of an item is to be entered:

```
Please enter the item price in dollars and cents $
Enter price -->
Price:
```

Design solutions for the following problems. For each design, let the input object know the prompts.

a. The exchange rate for U.S. and Canadian currency changes daily. Modify the design of the solution to the convenience store problem so that your uncle enters the exchange rate as well as price of an item in U.S. pennies per pound.

b. A manufacturer makes cylindrical tanks according to dimensions (radius and height) specified by customers. Each tank consists of a cylinder with a top and a bottom, all constructed of sheet metal. For each tank, the manufacturer needs to know the surface area of the tank in order to determine the cost of the sheet metal. Design a programming solution for this problem.

c. A building inspector has an instrument that can indicate the distance and the angle of elevation from the instrument to a building. By aiming the instrument at the top of the building, the inspector has enough information to determine the building's height. Design a program that reads the distance and angle of elevation and computes the height.

14. This problem is unusual in that there is no input. However, there are multiple output values.

The university gymnasium has a new indoor running track whose inside lane measures 510 feet. The head of the physical education department wants to post a table that tells joggers how many laps they must run in order to run distances of 1 mile through 10 miles (in 1 mile increments). Design a program that can produce such a table.

15. These problems require that you copy the code for either the convenience store problem or the changemaker problem on your computer. Be very careful with typing, since typing errors are usually disastrous when it comes to compiling code.

a. Copy the program for the convenience store operator onto your computer. Compile the program and then execute it. What modifications can you see that should be made to improve the behavior of the program? How would you change the output?

b. Modify the convenience store program so that the exchange rate is $1.29 Canadian = $1.00 U.S. Compile and execute the program to be sure that your modification is correct.

    c. Copy the program for the changemaker onto your computer. Compile and execute it.

    d. Modify the changemaker program to satisfy the following constraint. The cash drawer does not contain any quarters. It does contain 50 cent pieces instead. Compile and execute your program. Test it by entering the following data: 1783, 20467, and 15.

    e. Modify the original changemaker program to satisfy this constraint. The cash drawer contains 50 cent pieces in addition to all of the bills and all of the original coins. Compile and execute your program. Test it by entering the following data: 1783, 20467, and 15.

Chapter 2

C++ Tools: Anatomy of a Simple Program

Chapter Contents

THIS chapter is about programming in C++. Rather than looking at the analysis and design of programming problems, we will focus our attention on the essential coding tools that a C++ programmer must master in order to write simple programs. Later we will return to analysis and design, but at this point, we will simply look at some of the tools that are needed to implement designs.

Using tools means writing code in the programming language C++. Writing in a computer language is quite different from writing in a natural language like English. People often bend rules of grammar and composition when they use natural languages for speaking or writing. If someone speaks or writes using improper English grammar or syntax, we will probably be able to understand what they mean. The opposite is true of computer languages. If we use improper syntax when writing code in a computer language, the compiler will not be able to follow our instructions. People are much better than compilers at processing languages.

Programmers are confined to rigid rules of composition and syntax or grammar. This chapter will focus on some of the C++ rules to follow when writing your programs. You will see how to take advantage of some of the built-in features of C++.

The initial part of the chapter will explain the implementation of the convenience store solution in detail so that you can understand the purpose of each line of code. We will discuss some of the concepts illustrated by the convenience store program as well as tools that you will find useful for many other simple programs.

After reading this chapter, you should be able to write your own C++ programs to implement designs for simple programming problems.

2.1 The convenience store program, line-by-line

Most of the hard work in programming takes place in analyzing the problem in the first place and constructing the design model. It is in the design and analysis phases that the programmer decides on the essential structure and algorithms of the program. Good analyses and designs of programming problems usually lead to easy implementations of these designs into C++.

Coding of good designs is easy. But it can be tedious because it is such an exacting process. Just like all computer languages, C++ requires that programmers follow certain rigid rules of **syntax**, the rules for forming grammatically correct programs. The easiest way to learn C++ syntax is to read C++ code and to write your own programs. Let's look again at the convenience store program as an example of a simple program.

```
// Name: Convenience store owner
// Version: 1.0
// Purpose: Convert the price of an item in U.S. pennies per pound to
//   Canadian dollars per kilogram.

#include <iostream.h>
//----------------------- calculator object -------------------------------

void main()
{
    double theOutput;        // Answer displayed to the user
    double dollarsPerKg;     // Item's cost in Canadian dollars per kilogram
    int theInput;            // Input entered by the user
    int penniesPerLb;        // Price in U.S. pennies per pound of an item

    //------------------- input object -----------------------------------
    //  Get the input.
    cin >> theInput;
    //------------------ end of input object -----------------------------

    penniesPerLb = theInput;

    //------------------- computing object -------------------------------
    const double kgPerLb = .4536;          // Number of kilograms in a pound
    const double dollarsCanPerUS = 1.26;   // Number of Canadian dollars per
                                           //   U.S. dollar (exchange rate)
    const int penniesPerDollar = 100;      // Number of pennies per U.S. dollar

    dollarsPerKg = penniesPerLb/kgPerLb * dollarsCanPerUS/penniesPerDollar;
    //------------------- end of computing object ------------------------

    theOutput = dollarsPerKg;

    //------------------- output object ----------------------------------
    // Display the answer.
    cout << theOutput << endl;
    //------------------ end of output object ----------------------------

}
//------------------- end of calculator object -------------------------
```

This program contains three types of lines: (1) comments, (2) compiler directives, and (3) the lines that constitute main().

Comments

The first four lines in the program are called **comments**. A comment in C++ starts with the double slash, //, a symbol that is called a comment delimiter.[1] The comment continues to the end of the line in which the double slash appears. The compiler will not translate comments into machine code. Instead, the compiler ignores them, as if the double slash and the rest of the line were entirely absent from the program.

The comments placed at the beginning of a program are often called header comments. You can quickly get an idea of the problem that this program is attempting to solve just by reading its first four lines.

Programmers write comments in their programs to explain to other programmers (and to remind themselves) what their code is all about. Header comments indicate what the entire program is all about. Some comments will tell you what particular segments of code are supposed to do, others how certain names will be used. We have used comments and blank lines in the convenience store program as a way to organize our code for easier reading and to relate the program to its design.

Some comments, like this one, take up an entire line.

```
//------------------ end of calculator object --------------------------
```

Many lines of programs contain both working code and comments. The following line contains a comment that begins in the middle of the line.

```
int penniesPerLb; // Price in U.S. pennies per pound of an item
```

The code in the first part of the line, before the double slash, will be translated by the compiler, and the comment after the double slash will be ignored by the compiler.

In the end, there will be two readers of your source code, programmers and compilers. Even though compilers ignore comments, that does not mean comments are optional. They are the only reliable way you have to show programmers (including yourself) what the code in your program means. At this point, comments are the only way you have of tying the design to the code that implements the solution of the problem.

Include directives

The compiler ignores comments and blank lines. The first line in the convenience store program that it cannot ignore is the one containing a **compiler directive**, a special instruction to the compiler.

---

[1] C++ compilers accept the C-style comments as well as the // comment style. The delimiters for C-style comments are /* and */. A C-style comment which begins with /* does not end until the next */ appears. The advantage of C-style comments is that they can extend over several lines.

```
#include <iostream.h>
```

Programs may have many different kinds of compiler directives. They are easy to recognize because they start with the pound character, #. The convenience store owner program has only one compiler directive, and it is known as an **include directive**. An include directive instructs the compiler to treat a particular file as part of the program.

C++ has an extensive amount of built-in code to perform a variety of tasks. This is not unique with C++. Languages such as FORTRAN, C, and Pascal also have built-in code. Built-in code is kept in a collection of libraries that are available to the compiler. Libraries consist of header files, whose names end in .h, and object files. If you want to use the code in any of those C++ libraries, you should place an include directive with the appropriate library header file at the top of your program right under the program header comments. Be sure to enclose the name of the library header file in angle brackets, < and >.

The include directive in the convenience store program tells the compiler to treat the file named iostream.h as part of the program. iostream.h is the name of the header file of the built-in **iostream library**, which contains most of the code that the operating system uses for C++ input and output. The include directive is necessary because the program does input and output. When the program runs, the user (the person who runs the program) is expected to enter a number on the keyboard. The answer (the number generated by the program) then appears on the screen.

The main() function and its definitions

The code that follows the compiler directive consists of comments, blank lines, and the main() function. A **function** is a program building block. Every C++ program must contain a function named main. For most programs in this book, main() begins with the following line:[2]

```
void main()
```

Lines of code in main() that end with semicolons, ;, are called **statements**. When the program runs, those statements are said to be executed. You can think of the execution beginning with the first line of code in main(). Unless some error occurs during execution, you can think of the execution ending with the last line of code in main().

A program can have just one function—which must be main()—or it can have many functions. The body of every function, including main(), begins with

---

[2] You may see other forms of declaring main() including main(), int main(), void main(void), and int main(void), as well as more complicated forms. All of them contain the word main followed by parentheses.

a left curly brace, {, and ends with a matching right curly brace, }. Every segment of code that begins with a left brace and ends with the corresponding right brace is called a **block** or **compound statement**. Blocks always occur as function bodies or inside function bodies.

> A simple statement ends with a semicolon (;).
>
> A compound statement ends in a curly brace (}).

The first statements in the body of main() of the convenience store program are **definitions**. There are four of them at the beginning of main():

```
double theOutput;
double dollarsPerKg;
int theInput;
int penniesPerLb;
```

The remaining three definitions in main(), which appear in the code for the computing object, are:

```
const double kgPerLb = .4536;
const double dollarsCanPerUS = 1.26;
const int penniesPerDollar = 100;
```

The rest of the code in main() consists of comments, which you now recognize, and five statements. Each of those statements expresses an action to take place.

Let's back up for a moment to look at definitions in more detail. The computing object of the special-purpose handheld calculator must know three constants—items that remain the same for all computations: (1) the number of kilograms in a pound, .4536; (2) the number of Canadian dollars in a U.S. dollar, 1.26 (remember your uncle's naive assumption that the U.S. to Canadian dollar exchange rate would always be the same?); and (3) the number of pennies in a dollar. Those numbers must be stored somewhere so that the computing object will be able use them.

That's not all the storage that is necessary. The number that the user inputs during program execution as well as the final answer determined by the computing object must be stored somewhere at some time during program execution.

Data objects are places in computer memory where values that a C++ program uses or computes can be stored. A data object definition informs the compiler to create a data object by setting aside a location in memory to store a value of a specified type. It also tells the compiler the name of the data object.

This definition creates a data object whose name is `penniesPerLb`.

```
int penniesPerLb;
```

The type of data object tells how its value is to be interpreted. The type of `penniesPerLb` is `int`. So the information stored at the memory location of this data object is to be interpreted as an integer, a number with no fractional part. The definition of `penniesPerLb` does not specify any particular value to be stored at its memory location.

The following definition creates a data object whose name is `theOutput`.

```
double theOutput;
```

The type of `theOutput` is `double`. The value of a data object of type `double` is to be interpreted as a real number, which is a number with a possible fractional part rather than an integer. A more complete discussion of different numeric types is found later in this chapter.

Data objects whose values are allowed to change are called variable data objects, or **variables**. This program has four variables: `theOutput`, `dollarsPerKg`, `theInput`, and `penniesPerLb`. The values of these four data objects may vary from one execution of the program to another as well as during a single execution of the program.

Data objects whose values remain fixed during execution are called constant data objects, or **constants**. The following definition creates a constant whose name is `kgPerLb`:

```
const double kgPerLb = .4536;
```

A data object can be **initialized**, given a specific value when it is defined. The data object `kgPerLb` is initialized with the value .4536. The word `const` says that `kgPerLb` is a constant data object. The value of a constant data object cannot change.

> Constant data objects must be initialized when they are defined. That's the only way they can get a value.

Let's look at the next definition as it appears in the program.

```
const double dollarsCanPerUS = 1.26;      // Number of Canadian dollars per
                                          //    U.S. dollar (exchange rate)
```

This constant has the name `dollarsCanPerUS`, the type `double`, and the value 1.26. The meaning of the name is given in the two comments:

```
// Number of Canadian dollars per
//    U.S. dollar (exchange rate)
```

That second comment delimiter is necessary in order to continue the description of `dollarsCanPerUS` to the following line. Without that second `//`, the compiler would treat the following phrase as code to be translated into machine language rather than simply as text that it can ignore.

```
U.S. dollar (exchange rate)
```

The final constant, `penniesPerDollar`, has the type `int`. So the information stored at the memory location for `penniesPerDollar` is to be interpreted as an integer. The definition has the effect of setting aside a place in memory that has the name `penniesPerDollar` and in which the integer value 100 is stored.

> Attributes of objects in a design are often implemented in C++ programs as variable or constant data objects.

Input, output, and assignment statements

The definitions in `main()` create data objects, which thus reserves memory for storing certain types of values. The remainder of the body of `main()` contains statements that will actually do something when the program runs.

Let's examine the remaining code that is not comments. There are three more statements, beginning with this input statement:

```
cin >> theInput;
```

The effect of the execution of the input statement is as follows. When the program runs, it pauses until the user enters a sequence of characters (which should be digits for the convenience store program) and then presses return. That sequence of digits is interpreted as an integer and then stored in the memory location for the variable named `theInput`. So the value of `theInput` becomes the integer entered by the user.

The symbol `cin` (pronounced *C-in*) represents the **input stream**, the sequence of characters entered by the user while the program is executing. `cin` is defined and given many powerful features in the iostream library. That library lets you use `cin` without worrying about how the operating system and C++ interact to give the program access to the user's keystrokes.

The symbol `>>` is called the **input operator** or the **extraction operator**. You can read the code

```
cin >> theInput;
```

as this, "Extract the integer from the input stream `cin` and place it into the memory location for the data object named `theInput`." Most programmers would read that line of code as this, "Read `theInput`."

That entire line of code is called a statement. These lines are also statements.

```
penniesPerLb = theInput;
dollarsPerKg = penniesPerLb/kgPerLb * dollarsCanPerUS/penniesPerDollar;
theOutput = dollarsPerKg;
```

All three of these lines are **assignment statements** because the last operation each performs is to assign values to variables. The assignment operator is denoted by the symbol =. The effect of executing an assignment is that the variable data object on the left side of the assignment operator gets a new value. The left-hand operand of the assignment operator (what appears on the left-hand side of the =) is the name of a variable. The right-hand operand is an expression that will be evaluated.

Let's look at the middle assignment more carefully.

```
dollarsPerKg = penniesPerLb/kgPerLb * dollarsCanPerUS/penniesPerDollar;
```

Here is how the assignment statement is executed, starting with the value of `penniesPerLb`:

1. Divide that number by the value of `kgPerLb`.

2. Multiply the result of step 1 by the value of `dollarsCanPerUS`.

3. Divide the result of step 2 by the value of `penniesPerDollar`.

The value that results from performing this sequence of arithmetic operations is stored at the memory location for `dollarsPerKg`.

The final line of executable code in the convenience store program is an output statement. It is the last statement of the program:

```
cout << theOutput << endl;
```

When this code is executed, the value of `theOutput` will be displayed on the screen and the cursor will drop to the next line. The **output stream** `cout` (pronounced *C-out*) is also defined in the iostream library. It has many powerful features that you will begin to appreciate as you program more in C++.

The input stream `cin` represents the sequence of characters entered by the user. The output stream `cout` also represents a sequence of characters, which are placed into `cout` by the program when it executes and displayed on the screen. The operator << is called the **output operator** or the **insertion operator**. You can read the expression

```
cout << theOutput
```

as, "Insert the sequence of characters that represent the value of `theOutput` into the stream `cout`." Most programmers would read that line of code as this instead, "Write `theOutput`."

The entire output statement

```
cout << theOutput << endl;
```

is actually a compound expression containing two output operators that are processed from left-to-right. The first one inserts the value of `theOutput` into `cout` and the second one inserts a **newline** character into `cout`. This results in the value of `theOutput` followed by a newline character being displayed on the terminal screen. Displaying the newline character means that the screen cursor drops to the next line.

The output statement is the last statement in the program. The right brace, }, which is at the end of the source code file for the convenience store program marks the end of the block that is the body of `main()`.

2.2 ▌ Storing information

When a program executes, it uses the computer's memory to store data. It is the responsibility of the compiler to set aside memory to store that data. Let's take a quick look at main memory. In very primitive terms, a computer's main memory is organized into millions of tiny switches, each of which is either on or off. The on-or-off characteristic can be indicated by the numbers 1 and 0. These numbers are binary digits or bits. Each switch is represented by its corresponding bit. The bits (switches) are organized into groups of 8, called bytes.

Every place in memory is characterized by two things: its address (its actual location) and the sequence of bits that starts at that location. The value that is stored at a particular location depends on not only the pattern of bits that begins at that location but also on a way of interpreting that pattern. The type of a data object specifies the number of bits that make up the bit pattern and a way of interpreting that bit pattern as a value.

The exact size for each type varies among C++ compilers. Typical sizes of `int`s are 16 or 32 bits. Typical sizes for `float` and `double` are 32 and 64 bits or 64 and 128 bits. The type `char` requires 8 or 16 bits.

Data object definitions

C++ programmers define data objects in order to be able to store data during program execution. A data object is characterized by four things:

1. An **address**: the location in main memory where the data will be stored.

2. A **name**: a way the program can easily refer to the data object.

3. A **type**: a determination of how much memory is allocated to the data object (its size) and the way to interpret the bits at the memory location of the data object.

4. A **value**: the bits, interpreted according to the type, at the location of the data object.

Data objects are created in code through definitions, which set aside a fixed region in memory in which to store values of a particular type. The programmer must specify a name, a type, and possibly an initial value with each definition.

Data objects can be either variable or constant. When a new constant data object is defined, it must be initialized with a particular value. It is also possible to initialize a variable data object when you define it. The syntax for initializing a variable is identical to the syntax for initializing a constant.

While initializing a constant is a necessity, initializing a variable is optional but it can be a significant programming convenience. Initialization not only shortens the code by eliminating the need for a separate assignment statement but also helps document the code. The reader can see the initial value of a variable in the definition rather than having to scan for it later in the code.

Here are some sample definitions of variable and constant data objects.

```
int count = 0;                        // Count of test scores entered so far
const int maxGrade = 100;             // Largest possible test score
float x;                              // x-coordinate of endpoint
float y = 4.7;                        // y-coordinate of horizontal line
double rocketSpeed;                   // Speed of rocket at its peak height
const int daysInWeek = 7;             // Number of days in a week
char initial = 'A';                   // Initial of user's last name
const float speedOfLight = 1.863e5;   // Speed of light in miles per second
```

The data objects count, y, and initial are variables that are initialized to the values 0, 4.7, and 'A' respectively. The constant data object speedOfLight is initialized to the value 186,300.

There is an alternative syntax for defining and initializing data objects. The next two definitions are equivalent to the last two.[3]

```
char initial('A');                    // Initial of user's last name
const float speedOfLight(1.863e5);    // Speed of light in miles per second
```

Where in a program can data objects be defined? The answer is almost anywhere. Not all definitions need to come at the beginning of main(). Data objects can be defined right before they are needed. For example, the constants in the convenience store program could have been defined after the first input statement. We put their definitions at the beginning of main() just so they would be easy to

---

[3] Not all compilers will allow this form of initialization for built-in types.

find. That is not always the best choice, as you will understand when you start to write more complicated programs. The only hard and fast rule is that no object can be used before it is defined.

All of our definitions contain documentation to indicate the meaning of the data object in the solution to the problem. It is always a good programming practice to document definitions. It is often difficult to invent perfect names for data objects. Documentation helps explain the purpose of the data object, even if its name does not provide a complete picture.

Identifiers

Names that are devised by programmers are called **identifiers**. Most of the identifiers in the convenience store program are names of constant or variable data objects. Some identifiers, like `cout`, are defined in libraries that a program includes.

When you make up identifiers for your programs, try to select names that reflect the purpose or use of the identifier as it relates to the real-world problem that the program is trying to solve. Don't invent identifiers that are going to be mysterious to you a month after you write the code. Give data objects names that have some logical meaning.

You have many choices in making up identifiers. However, each name must follow two rules:

1. An identifier can be constructed of alphabetic characters (uppercase and lowercase), underscores, and digits.

2. Each identifier must begin with an alphabetic character or an underscore.

All of the characters in an identifier name are important. Uppercase alphabetic characters are distinct from lowercase alphabetic characters. The identifier `cat` is distinct from the identifiers `cAt`, `CAT`, and `_C_A_T`.

A popular C++ programming convention is to begin names of data objects and functions with lowercase letters. Identifiers that begin with underscores are traditionally used by special operating system facilities, so using them in ordinary contexts is uncommon. If an identifier is supposed to represent more than a single word, such as "price per kilogram," then those subsequent words are distinguished from the previous part of the identifier by beginning with a capital letter such as in `pricePerKg`. An alternative to this convention is to use underscores to separate the individual words, such as `price_per_kg`.

Here are some examples of legal C++ identifiers.

```
january      FLOAT      anExceedinglyLongButLegitimateIdentifierName
jane_doe     JaneDoe    anAmount     _a_problem
constant     month2     monthTwo     secondMonth
```

Here are some examples of illegal identifiers.

```
float      2months    money$    int
.period    no!!       123       stars*in*their*eyes
```

Certain words having special meaning in C++ cannot be used by programmers as ordinary identifiers. These words are called **keywords**. In the convenience store program the keywords are `double`, `int`, and `const`. A complete list of keywords is provided in Appendix B at the end of this book.

There are also some words that are not C++ keywords, but they are so commonly used for fixed purposes that programmers should not use them as ordinary identifiers. Examples of these words are `main`, `cin`, and `cout`. C++ compilers do not care what identifiers you use as long as they are legal. If you adopt a consistent programming style when selecting identifiers, your programs will be easier for you and for other programmers to read.

2.3 ▌ Expressions, statements, and numeric types

All computations in C++ are done by evaluating **expressions**. Many expressions are a combination of operands such as variables and literal numbers and operators such as = and +. The list below shows several C++ expressions. In those expressions, `count` is a data object of type `int`, `initial` is a data object of type `char`, and `x` and `speedOfLight` are data objects of type `float`.

```
count + 3
35
41 - 17.2
cin >> initial
x = 1 / speedOfLight
```

The first expression, `count + 3`, consists of the addition operator, +, and two operands, `count` and 3. If the value of `count` is 0, evaluation of `count + 3` results in the value 3. The use of blanks around the addition operator is optional. The compiler treats the expression `count+3` the same as `count + 3`. The evaluation of this expression does not change the actual value of `count`.

The second expression, 35, evaluates to 35. This is an example of a **literal value**, the simplest kind of expression—a single number 35 but no operator. The third expression, `41 - 17.2`, is almost as simple, but it requires a computation that uses the literal values 41 and 17.2.

The next example, `cin >> initial`, consists of a single operator, >>, and two operands, `cin` and `initial`. This expression has a **side effect**, a change in an object that results from evaluating an expression. This causes the value of `initial` to change. Frequently, expressions are placed in a C++ program for the sole purpose of creating side effects.

The final expression, `x = 1 / speedOfLight`, also has a side effect. The expression consists of two operators, `=` and `/`, and three operands, `x`, `1`, and `speedOfLight`. The evaluation is as follows. First, the subexpression `1 / speedOfLight` is evaluated then that value is assigned to `x`. Expressions such as `cin >> initial` and `x = 1 / speedOfLight` typically appear in a program just for their side effects. But those expressions do have values, just as the first three statements have values. The value of `cin >> initial` is the value of `cin`. The value of the expression `x = 1 / speedOfLight` is the value assigned to `x`.

Expressions such as the last two usually, but not always, appear in programs as **expression statements**, expressions terminated by semicolons. Most definitions are also statements (called definition statements). The body of `main()` in the convenience store program consists of a sequence of 12 statements—seven definition statements and five expression statements. When the program runs, those statements execute in the order in which they appear. The execution of each statement is completed before the execution of the next statement begins.

An expression that ends in a semicolon is a statement; an expression that does not end in a semicolon is not a statement. Here are some examples of expression statements. The last example contains a function call to the square root function `sqrt()`, which is part of the built-in math library.

```
cin >> initial;
x = 1 / speedOfLight;
dollarsPerKg = penniesPerLb / kgPerLb
              * dollarsCanPerUS / penniesPerDollar;
cout << sqrt(10 + x);
```

Statements can be extremely complicated or long. If you don't have enough room on a single line to write an entire statement, then you may continue the statement on the next line. The third statement above, which comes from the convenience store program, is an example of a statement that extends over two lines. Statements can also be extremely short. The shortest statement in C++ is the **null statement**. It consists of a single semicolon and nothing else.

```
;
```

Execution of the null statement results in no action taking place. Although you can put many statements on a single line (the C++ compiler looks for the semicolon at the end of a statement to tell where it ends) C++ programmers usually place no more than one statement on a single line of code. That makes their code easier to read, easier to modify, and easier to correct if errors are found.

Assignments

The assignment operator is used to store a value in a data object. We have already encountered three examples of assignment statements in the convenience store program.

```
penniesPerLb = theInput;
dollarsPerKg = penniesPerLb/kgPerLb * dollarsCanPerUS/penniesPerDollar;
theOutput = dollarsPerKg;
```

Let's look at some other simple examples. Suppose these are definitions for the variables x, y, and z.

```
int x = 3;      // x is initialized to 3
int y = 5;      // y is initialized to 5
int z;          // z is not initialized
```

The first two definitions are also initializations. Since z was not initialized when it was defined, the value stored at z is unpredictable until z is given an actual value during program execution. A picture of the memory allocated by execution of these three lines of code is as follows:

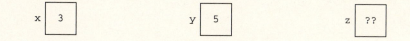

Consider this sequence of assignments.

```
z = y;   // z gets 5, which is the current value of y
y = x;   // y gets 3, which is the current value of x
x = y;   // x gets 3, which is the current value of y
```

In the first statement, the value of y is placed into the memory location for z. Other ways of stating this are "the value of y is stored in z" or simply "z gets the value of y" or even more succinctly "z gets y." In the second statement, the value of x is stored in y. In the third statement, the value of y is stored in x. The result of the execution of the three statements looks like this:

The assignment operator is not the same as "equals" in mathematics. In C++, the operands that appear on the left and right side of the = operator are not equivalent. The left-hand operand is always the name of a variable, and it refers to the memory location for that variable (the address of the variable). The right-hand operand is an expression that can be evaluated to something compatible with the type of the variable on the left-hand side.

In those last assignment statements involving x, y, and z, each left-hand operand is the name of a variable data object, but each right-hand side operand is also the name of a variable data object. There is a big difference between how those names are treated. When the name of a data object appears as a left-hand operand, it is considered to represent the address of the data object. When a data object appears as a right-hand operand, it is considered to represent the value of the data object.

C++ uses the terms **lvalue** and **rvalue** to distinguish the use of variable and constant names that appear on the left and right sides of assignment operators. If a use of the name of a data object refers to an address, then the name is an lvalue. If a use of the name of a data object refers to the value stored at an address, then the name is an rvalue. A name can be an lvalue or an rvalue, depending on where it appears in a particular expression. For example, in this statement

```
y = x;
```

x is an rvalue and y is an lvalue. In this statement

```
x = y + 34;
```

x is an lvalue.

> In any assignment, what appears on the left-hand side of the = must repre-sent a single address (lvalue). The right-hand side may involve values (rval-ues) of one or more data objects. When it is evaluated, the right-hand side produces a single value, which is stored at the address on the left-hand side.

Now let's look at some "assignments" that are not legal.

```
3 = x;          // illegal
x + y = 12;     // illegal
```

The first statement is not legal because 3 does not represent an address; it is just a value. The second assignment is not legal because x + y is not an address.

The following example of an assignment is legal, but it does not look like anything that you might write in a mathematics class.

```
x = x + 8;
```

The interpretation of that statement is as follows. Evaluate the right-hand operand by finding the sum of the literal number 8 and the value of x. Then store the result at the address of the left-hand operand. If the value of x is 3 immediately before the statement is executed, then the value of x is changed to 11 as a result of statement execution. This operation becomes more apparent if we use the modified assignment operator +=. The statement x = x + 8; is equivalent to this:

```
x += 8;
```

Read the statement x += 8; as "increment the value of x by the number 8." C++ has an entire collection of modified assignment operators that do arithmetic involving the value of the left-hand operand. The following statements illustrate some of the modified assignment operators.

```
x -= 34;        // Decrease x by 34
y *= x + 3;     // Multiply y by x + 3
y /= 3;         // Divide y by 3
x += x * 4;     // Increase x by its current value * 4
```

Integers and arithmetic operations

Recall that the type of a data object describes how the bits that reside at that data location are to be interpreted. You have seen definitions of objects of these types: int, double, and char. C++ supports two fundamental types of numeric data: integer and floating point. There are several variations of both integer and floating point types. Integers and floating point numbers are represented in main memory as binary (base 2) numbers rather than the ordinary decimal (base 10) numbers.

Everybody is familiar with decimal numbers. A nonnegative number can be expressed as a sum of products of the decimal digits 0 . . . 9 and powers of 10. For example, the decimal number 1092 can be written like this:

$$1 * 10^3 + 0 * 10^2 + 9 * 10^1 + 2 * 10^0$$

An nonnegative number can also be written as a sum of products of the binary digits 0 and 1 and powers of 2. The decimal number 1092 can be written like this:

$$1 * 2^{10} + 0 * 2^9 + 0 * 2^8 + 0 * 2^7 + 1 * 2^6 + 0 * 2^5 + 0 * 2^4 + 0 * 2^3 + 1 * 2^2 + 0 * 2^1 + 0 * 2^0$$

The binary representation of the decimal number 1092 is formed by taking the binary digits of the expression 10001000100. That sequence of 0's and 1's is used to construct the sequence of bits that represent the decimal number 1092 in computer memory.

We'll consider integer types first. An integer in mathematics is a number from the following double-ended infinite sequence:

$$\ldots, -4, -3, -2, -1, 0, 1, 2, 3, 4, 5, \ldots$$

Mathematical integers have no fractional parts. They are capable of representing many different kinds of real-world data such as test scores, seconds until liftoff, days in a week, penny value of a bank account, the number of periodical subscriptions for a public library, and elevation in feet above sea level. Literal integers, integers printed in the source code of a C++ program, are written as sequences of decimal digits that may or may not be preceded by + or − signs.

Programmers use type int when they need data objects that can hold integers. Data objects of type int usually require 16 or 32 bits of storage, depending on the particular computer or compiler. This means that the range of mathematical integers that can actually be represented by an int is limited. In the case of 16-bit integers, the range is −32,768 to +32,767. In the case of 32-bit integers, the range is −2,147,483,648 to +2,147,483,647.

Programmers occasionally need to represent integer data that may exceed those ranges or that may require a smaller or different range of values. For those instances, C++ provides a variety of short, long, and unsigned integer types. For example, five-digit zip codes cannot be represented by 16-bit ints. If the ints on your system are 16-bit ints, most implementations of C++ allow you to define a data object that is of type long int in order to represent a five-digit zip code.

If all of the data for a particular integer type are nonnegative, then you might choose the type unsigned int for a corresponding data object. There is one advantage of unsigned ints over int. The largest possible value that an unsigned int can represent is approximately twice the largest possible value that an int can represent. Here are sample definitions and assignments for both of those integer types:

```
long int fiveDigitZip;        // 5 digit zip code
unsigned int pinNumber;       // Bank customer id number
...
fiveDigitZip = 90617;
pinNumber = 61001;
```

Built into C++ are the ordinary arithmetic operators that one naturally expects to be able to use with integer data: addition, subtraction, multiplication, division, and negation. Let's look at some examples of their use. Assume the following variable definitions and initializations are given:

```
int x = 5;
int y = 17;
int z = -4;
```

Sample expressions based on these definitions and their evaluations are shown below.

Expression	Value
x - 4 + 12	13
y - (z * x)	37
x + y * 3	56
(x + y) * 3 - 4	62
-z	4
-z + 7	11

The only subtlety about those examples might be in the order in which the subexpressions are evaluated. **Operator precedence** determines the order of evaluation when there is more than one operator in an expression. The precedence of arithmetic operators in C++ should be familiar, since it is the same as that used in mathematics.

Addition and subtraction have the same precedence. Multiplication and division also have the same precedence, and it is higher than that of addition and subtraction. Negation (or unary - such as in -x) has the highest precedence of all arithmetic operators. The higher the precedence, the earlier the evaluation of the corresponding subexpression. Thus in the expression x + y * 3, multiplication will be performed before addition. In the expression x - 4 + 12, subtraction will be performed first and addition second. When two arithmetic operators have the same precedence, the evaluation proceeds from left to right.

Parentheses in numeric C++ expressions also follow the same rules used in mathematics. Parentheses allow you to control when operations are performed. The expression (x + y) * 3 is an example. Even though multiplication has a higher precedence than addition, the sum x + y is computed before multiplication by 3.

Many times programmers place extra parentheses in an expression just to clarify the order of evaluation to the reader. Whenever an expression is especially complicated or unusual, don't hesitate to use extra parentheses when they make your code easier to read.

None of the examples just given involve division. As a reminder of what integer division means, pretend that you are in grade school and the teacher writes the following division exercise on the board.

$$\begin{array}{r} 3 = \text{quotient} \\ 7\overline{)26} \qquad 5 = \text{remainder} \end{array}$$

Integer division yields two different answers, a quotient and a remainder. C++ has two different integer division operators: the **division operator** /, which yields the quotient, and the **modulus operator** %, which yields the remainder. The following are additional expressions that use the most recent definitions of x, y, and z and their evaluations. (The value of x is 5; y is 17, and z is -4.)

Expression	Value
x / 13	0
x % 13	5
13 / x	2
13 % x	3
34 / x / 2	3
34 / (x / 2)	17
x + y % 4 * 3	8

The arithmetic operations addition, multiplication, and subtraction can be performed on integers with predictable results. Division is not so straightforward. An error will occur if you attempt to evaluate the expressions a / b or a % b when b is 0. If a or b is negative, then the value of the expression a % b is unpredictable.

We used the division operator and modulus operator extensively in the change-maker program from Chapter 1. Look at the following pair of statements:

```
countOfTwenties = theAmount / twentyValue;
theAmount = theAmount % twentyValue;
```

The variable theAmount represents the total amount to be divided among the denominations. The variable countOfTwenties represents the number of $20 bills to be given from theAmount. The constant twentyValue represents the number of pennies equivalent to $20 (2000). Let's trace the execution of the two statements. Suppose that the value of theAmount is 67015, which represents $670.15.

theAmount	countOfTwenties	twentyValue	
67015	??	2000	Execution begins
67015	33	2000	After execution of first statement
1015	33	2000	After execution of second statement

The table shows how the values of the three data objects are affected by execution of the code. Notice that the value of `twentyValue` does not change. After all, `twentyValue` is a constant.

Tracing code, executing it by hand, is useful for understanding the effect of execution of that code. To trace code, list all of the data objects that appear in the code. Under each data object, write its value before execution of the code begins. Then execute the code by hand, line by line. After you execute each line, list the value of each data object underneath its value for the previous line.

Another integer type: `char`

Earlier in this chapter, we defined and initialized the variable `initial` this way:

```
char initial = 'A';    // Initial of user's last name
```

The possible values for `initial` are single characters such as `'A'`, `'x'`, `'8'`, or `' '` (the blank character). Most C++ literal characters are written as a single character enclosed in single quotes. Some characters are represented by two-character sequences called **escape sequences**. The first character in an escape sequence is the backslash character, `\`. The escape sequences are helpful for representing hard-to-express characters. For example, suppose `ch` is a variable of type `char`. The assignment

```
ch = '\'';
```

makes the value of `ch` the single-quote character. Without the backslash, the compiler cannot distinguish between the value that is the single-quote character and the final single quote that ends the character.

A listing of all of the C++ character escape sequences is provided in Appendix A at the end of this book. The more useful escape sequences include the newline character, `\n`, the horizontal tab, `\t`, the double quote, `\"`, and the backslash, `\\`.

C++ considers the type `char` to be a special type of integer. It may seem strange to you that `char` is an integer type, but C++ likes its primitive types to be numeric. This is part of the legacy that C brings to C++. But the question remains, "What is the connection between characters and integers?"

Computers use special encoding schemes that allow them to treat characters with the same ease that they treat numbers. Encoding schemes associate with each character a particular integer. Just as the integer 238 can be represented as a sequence of bits, the encoding scheme represents the character `'B'` as a sequence of bits. One of the most commonly used encoding schemes is the American Standard Code for Information Interchange (ASCII) character set.

It is not particularly helpful to memorize ASCII codes for all the characters. Most programmers remember a few of them. For example, the character `'A'` has ASCII code 65. The digit character `'0'` has ASCII code 48; the character `'a'` has ASCII code 97. The blank character, `' '`, has ASCII code 32. ASCII codes that are less than 32 are used for characters that cannot be printed or that appear as white-space, such as a tab. Appendix A contains a chart of ASCII codes.

Since the type `char` is actually an integer type, we can perform arithmetic on characters. This seems strange, but it can be useful. Let's look at the following example:

```
char ch;
ch = 'A';
ch = ch + 2;
```

The resulting value of `ch` is `'C'`.

Floating point types

Programmers use floating point types for numeric data that may have fractional parts or numbers that are too large to represent as integer types. There are several floating point types in C++, just as there are several integer types. The most commonly used floating point types are `float` and `double`. The amount of precision necessary for the floating point data determines which type is appropriate for a particular application.

Precision of a floating point type is indicated, of course, by the number of significant digits that can be represented by a data object of that type. The amount of precision for `float`s and `double`s depends on the particular hardware and compiler on which the program is to be implemented. A system which has 32-bit `float`s and 64-bit `double`s gives 7 significant digits for `float`s and 15 significant digits for `double`s. In such a system, the real number π is `3.141593` as a `float` and `3.1415926535898` as a `double`.

The range of numbers that can be represented in `double` or `float` types depends on the system also. The range of positive numbers that you can represent with a 64-bit `double` is larger than the range that you can represent with a 32-bit `float`. If your real-world problems depend on very small numbers such as 10^{-100} or very large numbers such as 10^{100}, then you may need to use the 64-bit representation just to be able to represent the magnitudes of such numbers.

The amount of precision for a floating point number depends on how much memory is allocated for its representation. The more bytes required by a floating point type, the higher the precision. The `sizeof` operator tells how many bytes are allocated for types, objects, and expressions. For example, `sizeof(double)` is the number of bytes are allocated for an object of type `double`. If x is an object, then `sizeof(x)` is the number of bytes that are allocated for x. The `sizeof` operator can be used with types, objects, and expressions.

Literal floating point numbers can be written as sequences of decimal digits that contain decimal points. C++ compilers consider floating point literal values to be of type `double`.

Frequently floating point data are very large or very small, so it is convenient to express the data in scientific notation. Such numbers can be written as an integer or a sequence of decimal digits that contains a decimal point and is followed by the letter e or E followed by an integer. The part of the number that appears before the letter constitutes the significant digits (or mantissa) of the number. The part of the number that appears after the letter is the exponent, which is the power to which 10 must be raised as a multiplier of the mantissa.

The following are examples of floating point literals:

```
23.134
.290            // It's not necessary put a digit before the decimal
-3456.78123
2.              // It's not necessary to put a digit after the decimal
2.0
3.45e4          // The same as 34500.0
3.45e-4         // The same as .000345
-9.8761E3       // The same as -9876.1
-9.8761E+3      // The same as -9876.1
3e4             // The same as 30000.0
```

The same primitive arithmetic operations that are built in for integer types—addition, subtraction, multiplication, and division—are available for floating point types. Unlike integer division, there is only one division operator for floating point data, the operator /. This makes sense in the mathematical world. There is no such thing as a remainder in real division. The remainder is included as part of the decimal expansion of the quotient.

C++ comes with a math library that contains many commonly used mathematics functions such as sin() (the sine function), log() (natural log function), exp() (the exponential function e^x), and fabs() (the absolute value function). Most of these functions are efficiently coded and not something that programmers ordinarily want to devise on their own. The following segment of code calculates the roots of a quadratic with coefficients a, b, and c.

```
float a, b, c;           // Coefficients of the quadratic ax^2 + bx + c

// . . .
// Assume a, b, and c have been assigned values and that a is not 0.

float firstRoot;         // One root of ax^2 + bx + c
float secondRoot;        // The other root of ax^2 + bx + c
float discriminant = b * b - 4 * a * c; // Discriminant of ax^2 + bx + c
if (discriminant >= 0) {
   firstRoot = (-b + sqrt(discriminant)) / (2 * a);
   secondRoot = (-b - sqrt(discriminant)) / (2 * a);
}
```

This code has several features that we haven't shown before. The three variables a, b, and c are defined on a single line in a single statement. Variables of the same type can be defined on a single line, although documentation of such declarations can be hard to read. Also, the definitions of `firstRoot`, `secondRoot`, and `discriminant` did not immediately follow the definitions of `a`, `b`, and `c`. Definitions may appear after other statements that are not definitions.

The code contains a selection statement, which causes some code to be executed under certain conditions. The selection statement starts with the keyword `if`. If the condition (`discriminant >= 0`) is true, then the two statements inside the braces will be executed. The left brace, the assignments to `firstRoot` and `secondRoot`, and right brace make a compound statement because they are two different statements grouped together by the braces. If the condition (`discriminant >= 0`) is false, the compound statement is skipped and the two assignment statements will not be executed.

The general form of an `if`-selection statement looks like this:

```
if (condition)
    statement-T
```

The execution is simple. The condition is evaluated. If it is true, then *statement-T* is executed; if it is false, *statement-T* is not executed. *Statement-T* can be either a simple statement or a compound statement. In our example of finding the roots of a quadratic equation, the curly braces indicate that *statement-T* is a compound statement.

Both statements in the body of the selection statement call the math library function `sqrt()`. The value of each function call is the square root of the value of `discriminant` which is the argument of the call. A function call consists of the name of the function followed by the argument written within parentheses, `sqrt(discriminant)`.

In order to use a math library, you must tell the C++ compiler about it. To do so, add the following include directive to the others in the program.[4]

```
#include <math.h>
```

There is an important characteristic that distinguishes between floating point and integer numeric types as follows. Any integer that is within the range of `int`s has an exact binary representation. If `int`s are 32 bits long, then any number within the range –2,147,483,648 to 2,147,483,647 can be written in binary (base 2) using no more than 32 binary digits. The same is not true for floating point numbers. That's pretty easy to see even in our own decimal system. It is impossible to represent the fraction 1/3 in base 10 as a finite number of decimal digits. An infinite decimal expansion is required: .333333.... The floating point number 1/3 cannot be represented in base 2 with any finite sequence of binary digits either, much less a sequence of only 64 binary digits. Even the decimal number 1/10 cannot be written in base 2 as a finite sequence of binary digits.

---

[4] For many systems and compilers, the include directive is not enough to use the math library. For them, you must also load the math library when the program is compiled.

If exact representation is required for all numeric data, use integer types rather than floating point types. Floating point numeric operations often yield **roundoff errors**, small errors that occur as a result of rounding off the least significant digit in a floating point number to represent it with the number of binary digits available for the floating point type.

If roundoff errors accumulate because of many operations on floating point data, then those errors can become unacceptably large. This is a tremendous problem for scientists and mathematicians who work with large quantities of data or who do large numbers of arithmetic operations on data. A major chore of numerical analysts, who are interested in calculations on numerical data, is controlling roundoff errors to acceptable levels.

Polymorphism and numeric conversions

Students in mathematics classes often perform calculations on integers and real numbers at the same time. You've done that whenever you have computed the circumference of a circle using the formula $C = 2\pi r$. In that formula, 2 is an integer, π is a real number that is not even rational, and r could be an integer, a rational number, or any nonnegative real number.

C++ is also able to deal with mixed arithmetic types. Consider this simple C++ expression:

```
1.2 + 5
```

There is something going on here that is actually quite complicated. You know that `int` type data and `double` type data have different representations in the hardware of the computer, but the operation + can be used for both of them. There must be thus at least two different ways the compiler implements +, one way for `int`s and another way for `double`s. The compiler can actually look at the two types of values to add and figure out which add operation the programmer intends to be used. The ability for such operations to be used in two different type contexts, *int + int* and *double + double*, is called **polymorphism**. For now, think of polymorphism as the ability of C++ to perform the same operation on different kinds of data. (Polymorphism is actually a little more complicated than that.) It so happens that polymorphism is pretty important to object-oriented programming. The numeric operations such as addition and subtraction have a special kind of polymorphism, which some programmers refer to as "ad hoc polymorphism."

Let's go back to that problem of evaluating `1.2 + 5`. Surely C++ can add two `int`s and C++ can add two `double`s, but how does it add an `int` and a `double`? Is there yet another addition operation that can add an `int` and a `double`? The answer is no. When integer and floating point numeric data are added together, C++ performs data conversion, temporarily changing integer values to floating point values to perform the computation. If an integer value is assigned to a floating point variable, then that value is converted to a floating point representation before it is assigned to the variable. One reason C++ does automatic conversions is so we can program in a language what we naturally do in mathematics.

For the expression 1.2 + 5, it is easy to believe that C++ can make a double out of an int. After all, in mathematics, every integer is also a real number. And it is always possible to add two real numbers. Just how do these conversions from int to float or int to double work?

Although an integer is also a real number in mathematics, in C++ that is not the case. An int is not a float or a double. You can see why if you look at some actual representations. Suppose a C++ compiler uses 16-bit ints and 32-bit floats. The number 5700 is represented as a 16-bit int as follows.

0001011001000100

The number 5700.0 represented as a 32-bit float is this:

01000101101100100010000000000000

The representations are different, but C++ can do conversions from int to float in the obvious manner if you think in terms of decimal notation instead of binary. We will illustrate integer type to floating type conversions with a few examples. Consider these definitions and initializations:

```
int x = 3;          // x is 3
int y = 5;          // y is 5
double r = 23.4;    // r is 23.4
float s = 5;        // 5 is converted to 5.0 before
                    // being used to initialize s
```

Now look at the following assignment statements:

```
r += x;             // r is now 26.4
s = x / y;          // s is now 0.0
s = 3.0 / y;        // s is now .6
```

In the first statement, the value of x, which is 3, is taken and converted to the double number 3.0. Then r is increased by that amount. (This all happens, by the way, without changing the actual value of x. The conversion does not change the data at a memory location for an object. The language can create a new value from the original one, which is a double rather than an int.)

In the second statement, the integer expression x / y is evaluated as 3 / 5, which is 0. The number 0 is then converted to 0.0, which is assigned to s. This is an example of a "gotcha." Even though the result is eventually converted to a float, the division operation is performed first on int data.

In the third statement, the mixed type expression 3.0 / y is evaluated by a conversion of the int value 5 to the float value 5.0. The division 3.0 / 5.0 evaluates to .6. So s is assigned the value .6.

What happens when we try to assign a floating point number to an integer variable? C++ does the best it can in that circumstance. If the floating point number is small enough (in the range of possible int values), it assigns only the integer part of the floating point number to the integer variable. The fractional part is thrown away, truncated.[5] Look at these assignment statements:

```
x = r;              // x is now 26
y = -23.4;          // y is now -23
```

C++ truncates .4 from 26.4 in order to assign the result to x and it truncates –.4 from –23.4 in order to assign –23 to y. (The truncation of negative floating point values to integer values depends on the hardware of the computer. Some machines truncate –23.4 to –23. Others truncate –23.4 to –24.)

The next assignment is more complicated:

```
x = sqrt(2) + 199 / 100;    // x is now 2
```

The expression sqrt(2) evaluates to a double value, which is approximately 1.14, and the expression 199/100 evaluates to the int value 1. To determine the sum, C++ converts the int value 1 to the double value 1.0 and then adds it to 1.14. The sum, 2.14, is then converted to the int value 2, which is assigned to x.

All of the examples we have discussed so far have been implicit type conversions, which means they are conversions that are automatically performed by the compiler. C++ also lets the programmer make explicit type conversions, which are conversions that are explicitly written in the code. Explicit conversion is done through **type casting**, which amounts to using type names the same as unary operators (operators with a single operand). If you want the value of x to be treated as a double and the value of r to be treated as an int, you can type cast them as follows.[6]

```
double(y)    // The value of the expression is -23.0 (assuming y is -23)
int(r)       // The value of the expression is 26 (assuming r is 26.4)
```

Here are some examples of statements involving type casting. (Assume that r is 26.4 at the beginning of execution of these statements.)

```
cout << int(r) << endl;    // Output: 26
s = (double(3)) / 2;       // Assigns 1.5 to s
s = double(3) / 2;         // Also assigns 1.5 to s
r = float (2/3);           // Assigns 0.0 to r. The integer division
                           //    takes place before the type cast to float.
```

---

5 Many compilers will give a warning when they convert a floating point value to an integer value.

6 In order to be compatible with C, C++ also allows you to write the type cast with the parentheses around the name of the type instead of around the value. For example: (float) x. Parentheses around the type are necessary when the name of the type is more than a single word description.

Since chars are numeric types, we can mix together chars, ints, floats, and doubles. Here are some additional definitions and assignments. (Assume that ASCII character codes are used.)

```
char ch;
ch = 65;                    // 65 is the ASCII code for 'A'; ch is now 'A'
ch = 66.8;                  // 66.8 is converted to 66; ch is now 'B'
x = ch;                     // x is now 66
r = ch;                     // r is now 66.0
cout << char(67) << endl;   // Output: 'C'
cout << "ASCII value of " << ch << " is " << int(ch) << endl;
```

The output generated by the code is shown below.

```
C
ASCII value of C is 67
```

That last statement illustrates how handy a tool type casting can be. It prints both the character value of ch and the ASCII value of ch.

```
cout << "ASCII value of " << ch << " is " << int(ch) << endl;
```

Type casting might be a handy tool, but it is also dangerous. If you try to assign to a char variable a number that is bigger than all ASCII codes, then the result may be unpredictable. That is why it is best not to do it. In general, when C++ converts data of one type to another type that requires less memory (fewer bits), important information may be lost in the conversion. Programmers rarely need to know the binary representation of a particular value, but they do need to keep in mind how those representations can vary among numeric types when evaluating expressions of mixed types.

2.4   C++ streams

The C++ iostream library defines the input stream cin and output stream cout so that programmers can read values into and print values from a program.[7] Simple input and output operations on these streams are very easy to perform. A program

---

[7] C++ does not insist that input come from the keyboard and output go to the screen. Input and output can be associated to other devices (such as printers) or disk files. The default for input and output, however, is that they are associated with the terminal.

that uses the iostream library must contain this include directive before it uses `cin` or `cout`.

```
#include <iostream.h>
```

Both the input stream `cin` and the output stream `cout` are objects. They are not mere data objects because they can do things. In object-oriented jargon, the way you get objects to do things is to send them messages. Messages to `cin` and `cout` have a variety of forms.

Input

The convenience store program and the changemaker program were two examples of the use of the input stream `cin`.

```
cin >> theInput;
```

For both programs, it was expected that the user would enter a sequence of digits by pressing several number keys in succession and then pressing the return key. Any tabs, blanks, or returns that the user might enter before pressing the first digit were ignored.

The input expression represents a message to `cin` requesting it to read an integer. When the expression is executed, `cin` determines what number is meant by the sequence of characters entered by the user. Then `cin` stores that value in `theInput`, which is the right-hand operand of the input operator, `>>`.

Input stream operations can be performed many times in the same statement. Suppose we use the following definitions:

```
int x;
float s;
int y;
```

Then execution of the statement

```
cin >> x >> s >> y;
```

requires the user to enter a sequence of characters that represent an integer followed by **whitespace**, characters such as blanks, tabs, and returns. This whitespace is then followed by a sequence representing a floating point value followed by more whitespace and then by another sequence representing an integer. For example, if the user types the characters

```
 21 13.4    -4
```

and then presses return, then `cin` stores 21 in x, 13.4 in s, and –4 in y.

That last run-on input statement is not a particularly good one, the reason being that it does not give the user any idea of how much data or what type of data is expected. Most good programs prompt the user when data is supposed to be entered to tell what kind or format of data is expected. (Our original versions of the convenience store and changemaker programs did not contain prompts. We should redesign our solutions so that they do.)

Later on in this text we will examine in detail what happens if the user enters unexpected input such as a sequence of alphabetic characters a b c rather than a sequence of numeric characters such as 123 45 67. Suffice it to say for now that the program does not crash, but that the values of x, s, and y do not change.

The input operator can be used with any of the built-in data types that you know about so far: int, char, float, and double. By default, the input operator causes cin to skip over whitespace characters. But not all input must be done through the input operator. Suppose ch is a char variable—a char type variable data object. Then the execution of this statement

```
cin.get(ch);
```

stores the value of the next input character into ch without skipping over whitespace characters. The expression cin.get(ch) represents a message to cin. The message is, "Get the next input character, whether it be whitespace or something else, and store it in ch."

Output

Just as the input can be thought of as a message to cin, output can be thought of as a message to cout. If x is any built-in type data object, the message cout << x can be translated as, "Figure out how to write the value of x and then put those characters at the end of the current output."

You don't have to think in terms of messages to objects to understand what happens with simple output statements. Here are some examples:

```
cout << "The answer to the first question is " << x << "." << endl;
cout << "Next is " << y;
cout << " and next is " << s << ".\n" << endl;
```

If the values of x, s, and y are 2, 29.7, and 5 respectively, then your screen could look like this after the statements are executed:

```
The answer to the first question is 2.
Next is 5 and next is 29.7.
```

Successive output statements can be combined into a single statement. Frequently such a statement extends over several lines of code. Here is the last output sequence written as a single statement:

```
cout << "The answer to the first question is " << x << "."  << endl
        << "Next is " << y << " and next is " << s << ".\n" << endl;
```

Of course, we could have done the opposite by combining the output statements into a single one and used a sequence of separate output statements instead:

```
cout << "The answer to the first question is ";
cout << x;
cout << ".";
cout << endl;
cout << "Next is ";
cout << y;
cout << " and next is ";
cout << s;
cout << ".\n";
cout << endl;
```

A sequence of characters enclosed in double quotes is called a **string literal**. The output above contains five string literals. One of them consists of a single period. Output of a string causes the characters of the string to appear on the screen. (The output of " . " , which is a string literal, looks the same as the output of ' . ', which is a literal character.)

A string can contain escape sequences (escape characters) as well as ordinary characters. The newline character, ' \n ', can be embedded in a string to terminate a line of output. That last code was one example. The following code is another. Its output is shown in the box below.

```
cout << "Daniel\nPaul" << endl;
```

```
Daniel
Paul
```

The difference between inserting endl and ' \n ' into the output stream is subtle. When endl is inserted into the output stream, the data in the output stream that has not yet been displayed are displayed. If ' \n ' is inserted instead of endl, the display may be delayed.

When output is generated, it is stored in a buffer, an area in memory. The output is displayed later when the buffer is flushed. Flushing occurs when the buffer becomes full, when the program terminates execution, or when `endl` is inserted into the output stream. Flushing does not automatically occur when `'\n'` is inserted.

Manipulators for output formatting

Programmers can control the appearance of the output generated by their programs by using **manipulators,** which are special data objects for changing streams. You already know about one manipulator, `endl`. The insertion of `endl` into `cout` does two things: It places the newline character into the output stream and it "flushes the output stream buffer." This means that all of the characters that have been inserted into `cout` that have not yet been displayed will now be displayed.

Manipulators are inserted into the output stream the same way that numbers are. They are used for formatting output rather than inserting new data. Most manipulators are defined in the C++ manipulator library. In order to use this library, a program must contain the following include directive:

```
#include <iomanip.h>
```

Four manipulators are very convenient: `setiosflags()`, `resetiosflags()`, `setprecision()`, and `setw()`. The first two can be used to alternate the display of floating point output between scientific notation and fixed decimal notation. The third controls the number of digits displayed, and the fourth adjusts the width of the display field for the next output value.

Let's look at scientific versus fixed notation. The number 1,341.215 in scientific notation is 1.341215e+03. In fixed decimal notation, it is 1341.215. Think for a moment about the circumstances in which you might want one format instead of the other. Suppose you were printing out the amount of a mortgage payment. A printout of $895.46 is much easier to read than $8.9546e02. On the other hand, if you are printing a table of galactic distances, you would probably use scientific notation.

You can set floating point output into one of these two forms. You can insert instructions to do so into the output stream the same way that you insert data or `endl` into the output stream.

To set floating point output to fixed decimal format, use `setiosflags()`.

```
cout << setiosflags(ios::fixed);
```

Once the fixed format is set, it remains set until you change it back. Do that by using `resetiosflags()`.

```
cout << resetiosflags(ios::fixed);
```

Think of the "reset" as an "unset." To set the output to scientific format, use `setiosflags()`, specifying scientific instead of fixed.

```
cout << setiosflags(ios::scientific);
```

And of course, to turn off the scientific formatting, use `resetiosflags()` again. This time, specify that it is the scientific format that is to be turned off.

```
cout << resetiosflags(ios::scientific);
```

If you are changing from fixed to scientific or vice versa, be sure to set the format *to which* you are changing and to reset the format *from which* you are changing. When both formats are set, the output format is not predictable.

The manipulator `setprecision()` establishes the precision of the floating point output. In C++, precision means the number of digits to the right of the decimal. In scientific format, precision is one less than the number of significant digits printed. The number 1,341.215 in scientific format and precision 2 is displayed as `1.34e+03`. With fixed decimal format and precision 2, it is displayed as `1341.22`. The final digit for each display is rounded up to the nearest integer. In either case, to set the precision to 2, use the following expression:

```
cout << setprecision(2)
```

The sample code below illustrates the use of `setiosflags()`, `resetiosflags()`, and `precision()`. The corresponding output is shown in the box.

```
double x = 32.1630, y = 67009.1223, z = 1000.84856;
// Print all three numbers in fixed notation with precision 1
cout << setiosflags(ios::fixed) << setprecision(1)
     << "Fixed notation, precision = 1\n"
     << "x = " << x << "\ny = " << y << "\nz = " << z << endl;

// Print all three numbers in scientific notation with precision 3
cout << resetiosflags(ios::fixed) << setiosflags(ios::scientific)
     << setprecision(3) << "\nScientific notation, precision = 3\n"
     << "x = " << x << "\ny = " << y << "\nz = " << z << endl;

// Print x fixed, y scientific, z fixed
cout << "\nPrecision = 3, x is fixed, y is scientific, z is fixed\n"
     << resetiosflags(ios::scientific) << setiosflags(ios::fixed)
     << "x = " << x
     << resetiosflags(ios::fixed) << setiosflags(ios::scientific)
     << "\ny = " << y
     << resetiosflags(ios::scientific) << setiosflags(ios::fixed)
     << "\nz = " << z << endl;
```

```
Fixed notation, precision = 1
x = 32.2
y = 67009.1
z = 1000.8

Scientific notation, precision = 3
x = 3.216e+01
y = 6.701e+04
z = 1.001e+03

Precision = 3, x is fixed, y is scientific, z is fixed
x = 32.163
y = 6.701e+04
z = 1000.849
```

The fourth manipulator, `setw()`, is used to right justify the next item to be output in a field of a particular width. Suppose this expression is evaluated

```
cout << setw(20)
```

Then the next item that is output will be displayed as 20 characters, with leading blanks if necessary to make up the total 20. If the next item requires display of more than 20 characters, then `setw()` is ignored and the item is displayed in the smallest space required.

Once the format and the precision are set, they remain that way until they are changed by subsequent invocations of `setiosflags()`, `resetiosflags()`, and `setprecision()`. However, `setw()` is effective only for the next item that is output. Without another `setw()`, the subsequent item will be displayed with the smallest possible number of characters.

The following code shows how `setw()` can be used to make a simple bill of sale for an item costing $127.10 and a tax rate of 6.5 percent. The corresponding output is shown in the box.

```
double price = 127.1;
double taxRate = .065;
cout << setiosflags(ios::fixed) << setprecision(2)
     << "Price    $" << setw(7) << price
     << "\nTax      $" << setw(7) << price * taxRate << " at "
     << setprecision(1) << taxRate * 100 << "%\n" << setprecision(2)
     << "Total    $" << setw(7) << price * (1 + taxRate) << endl;
```

```
Price      $ 127.10
Tax        $    8.31 at 6.5%
Total      $ 135.36
```

The manipulator `setw()` works for strings the same way that it works for numbers. In that case, the string is displayed right-justified in a field whose width is the argument to `setw()`. The following is some sample code and output:

```
cout << "12345678901234567890\n";
cout << setw(10) << "Hello" << endl;                          // Statement 1
cout << "Hello" << endl;                                       // Statement 2
cout << setw(1) << "Hello" << setw(10) << "Hello" << endl;     // Statement 3
```

```
12345678901234567890
        Hello
Hello
Hello       Hello
```

We could have written those last three output statements as a single statement. We coded the output in separate statements so that we could review them one at a time.

1. `cout << setw(10) << "Hello" << endl;`

    displays `"Hello"` right justified in a field of width 10. This means that the `'H'` is padded on the left by 5 blanks.

2. `cout << "Hello" << endl;`

    displays `"Hello"` with no padding. No field width is specified, so the minimum possible one is used.

3. `cout << setw(1) << "Hello" << setw(10) << "Hello" << endl;`

    `"Hello"` is not small enough to fit into a field of width 1, so it is displayed in the smallest possible field. The `setw(10)` forces the second `"Hello"` to be displayed in a field of width 10 (beginning after the first). The `endl` forces everything to be printed and drops the cursor to the next line.

The manipulators provide a convenient way to format output. It is also possible to format output through direct messages to the output stream, as follows:

```
cout.width(8);
```

The message is simple: "Set the field width of the next output to 8." The message statement does exactly the same thing as:

```
cout << setw(8);    // Equivalent to: cout.width(8);
```

The form you prefer to use is going to be largely a matter of personal preference. The iostream and manipulator libraries allow many more additional options as well. For example, the padding character for display in a field of a given width can be something besides a blank. The output items can be left justified instead of right justified. Appendixes D and E at the end of this book have more information on what is available.

2.5 ▌ Programming style: Does it matter?

Compilers are very picky about whether source code adheres to certain grammatical rules, but they don't care about how easy code is to read. Whether you name a variable x or `timeBeforeMidnight` is immaterial to the compiler. All names are equally acceptable as long as they obey the strict C++ rules about constructing identifiers.

C++ is a free format language, which means it has the following characteristics:

- Extra blanks or tabs before or after identifiers, literals, and operators are ignored.

- Blank lines are ignored just like comments.

- Code can be indented in any way.

- More than one statement can be on a line and the same statement can be continued over several lines.

If you were to take the entire convenience store program, remove the comments, and take out most of the extra whitespace, the compiler would still be able to compile it. But here is what you could end up with.

```
#include <iostream.h>
void main(){double theOutput,dollarsPerKg;int theInput,penniesPerLb;cin >>
theInput;penniesPerLb=theInput;const double kgPerLb=.4536;const double
dollarsCanPerUS=1.26;const int penniesPerDollar=100;dollarsPerKg=
penniesPerLb /kgPerLb*dollarsCanPerUS/penniesPerDollar;theOutput =
dollarsPerKg;
cout<<theOutput<<endl;}
```

How would you like to have to read programs that look like this? The compiler has certain requirements: that the identifiers are correctly spelled, that they aren't used before they are defined, that statements end in semicolons, and that there are no spaces between the two <'s in the operator << or between the two >'s in the operator >>. The programmer, as a result, is given many options in deciding how a program looks.

When you write a C++ program, you create a source code document that is to be compiled, executed, tested, and probably modified to eliminate errors or to incorporate new or different features. If you are a student, then your instructor will read that text document. If you are a professional programmer, then your coworkers may read your code. And in either situation, you will read your code, probably several times after it is written. A C++ source code file is created not just for the compiler but also for people.

Programming **style** refers to how your source code looks—how it is formatted, how indentation reflects the structure of the code, where blank lines and comments appear, how the identifiers are chosen, and how the program is documented with comments. You should write your programs in a style that makes them easy to read and easy to understand.

For the kind of code discussed so far, you can follow this brief list of style strategies.

1. Place each statement on a line by itself.

2. Unless there is a change in the structure of the code, indent each statement the same as the previous statement.

3. Use blank lines to separate different segments of code.

4. Use identifier names that have meaning in the corresponding real-world situation that your program models. If a data object is used only for internal object computations, make its name reflect its purpose.

5. Document each identifier with a comment telling what it means.

6. Document segments of code to tell the purpose of each. In particular, make sure your documentation relates the design to the code.

7. Document the beginning of the program with a header which, at a minimum, tells the purpose of the program. Other header documentation can include the name of the programmer, the date of completion or version number of the program, the kind and format of the expected input, the expected output, and any error checks that are made to guard against inappropriate input.

By the time you finish writing your program, you may have more lines of documentation and formatting than lines of statements. Novice programmers tend to write all of their code, then throw in the documentation at the end. That usually results in poor and inadequate documentation. In the situation where a programming project cannot be written over a single session with a text editor, it is essential that you document your code as you create it. For any subsequent programming sessions, that initial documentation can save you much time trying to figure out what the code written during the previous session means.

The bottom line on style is this. Your code is going to be read by people, including yourself. Make that reading task as easy as possible. Good programming style is not a luxury; it is a necessity.

2.6   Making sure that the analysis, design, and implementation are correct

No programmer would consider the implementation of a programming problem in C++ to be complete without going through the steps to verify that the program is indeed a solution to the corresponding real-world problem. The steps for evaluation, a key part of programming, are as follows:

1. Compile the program.

2. Execute the program with test data.

3. Fix any errors.

4. Repeat the steps until the program is correct.

Corrections may be simple to make, or they may require actual design or analysis modifications.

There are three kinds of errors that an implementation can generate: (1) syntax errors, (2) runtime errors, and (3) logic errors. The first two are detected as a result of the actions of the compiler and the operating system. The last one can be detected only by someone who sees that the program is misbehaving. All three programming errors are called **bugs** and the process of correcting them is called **debugging**.

Syntax errors

A **syntax error** is a grammatical error that breaks a rule in the language in which a program is written. As a consequence, the compiler will not be able to translate the program successfully, and it will not be able to create an object file or eventually an executable file.

Common syntax errors include the following:

- Using the name of a data object but forgetting to define it

- Misspelling an identifier

- Unintentionally substituting lowercase letters for uppercase letters or vice versa

- Forgetting to initialize a constant

- Using << instead of >> to read values; using >> instead of << to write them

- Forgetting to put a semicolon at the end of a statement

- Putting an extra semicolon after a right curly brace

- Missing a parenthesis or a brace

- Omitting a necessary include directive at the beginning of the program

This list is by no means all-inclusive. The more language features you learn, the more different kinds of syntax errors you will discover.

If your code has a syntax error, the compiler will give you an **error message**. The message that the compiler displays depends on the nature of the error and the actual compiler. Some messages are easy to understand

```
Line 48, E#742, y undefined
```

and some are not so easy to understand

```
Line 73, E#1499, pointer operand for <<
```

The compiler will indicate which lines in the code that it considers to contain errors. Sometimes an error is not detected in the line where it was actually made. Instead the compiler detects the error in a subsequent line. When you search for the source of an error, look at the line which the compiler flagged as erroneous as well as above that line.

Many times an error in one line of code will cause other lines of code to be considered incorrect also. That is, one error may cascade through many subsequent lines of code. You will obviously need to edit your source code file to correct errors. When you do correct them, begin your corrections with the first errors that were detected. That may eliminate the false error messages in those parts of the code resulting from early errors.

A compiler can display **warning messages** as well as error messages. An error prevents the program from being compiled. A warning does not prevent compilation, but it alerts the programmer that there may be an unintended logical error in the program such as forgetting to assign a value to a variable. Here is a typical compiler warning message for that situation:

```
Line 67, W#231, sum used but not set
```

It is up to you to decide whether or not to rewrite the code that causes the warnings since the compiler can create an executable file even if the code is not changed.[8] However, at a minimum you should carefully evaluate all warnings. Never ignore them. Failure to heed them can result in unpleasant and difficult to correct errors when the program executes.

Runtime errors

Suppose your code is free of syntax errors. Will it run? Is it correct? Executing a program with the intent of discovering errors is called **testing**, a process that will allow you to find errors before anybody else does. Errors that cause the program to terminate abnormally (to crash or abort) are called **runtime errors**. Runtime errors occur after the program has already compiled successfully. Examples of runtime errors are attempting to divide an integer by 0 or inadvertently referencing a part of memory not set aside for use by your program (that's not very common in simple programs such as the ones we have looked at so far). Another kind of runtime error is called an infinite loop, the unintentional endless execution of the same statement or group of statements over and over again.

When a program aborts, an error message may be displayed. Runtime error messages as well as syntax error messages can be difficult to understand. Runtime error messages usually do not indicate the line of code in which the error occurred, and they may fail to reveal the nature of the error. However, there are some program development environments that do provide the line of the source code in which the program actually crashed as part of the error message. If you do not have such an environment, you may resort to placing extra output statements in your program to find exactly where the crash occurred.

Frequently it is not the line that causes the actual crash that is defective but some code that was executed earlier. That previously executed code may propagate faulty data to the line in the program in which the crash occurred, a line that could not appropriately handle improper data. In that case, you must search for how that line ever received the improper data to begin with. This involves understanding how all of your code behaves.

Once you have removed the source of error from your program, you must test again. Elimination of one error does not necessarily mean that no errors remain. Sometimes elimination of one error causes another error to show up.

Logic errors

The last type of error we will look at is the **logic error**, which is an error that generates the wrong answers, or answers that may be wrong for just some of the input data. Errors in logic are the hardest errors to correct because they don't generate any error messages.

When it is time to check your program for any type of runtime or logic errors, you need data. It is important that for each test case, you know ahead of time what

---

8 A common industry convention is that all code must be free of warnings as well as errors. In that situation, programmers have no choice but to rewrite code that generates compiler warnings.

the results should be. It doesn't do you any good to see the results produced by
your program if you don't know what your program should do. If your program
fails a test case, it has an error and it will be your job to figure out why.

Finding the source of logic errors involves intensive examination and tracing
of your code to see how the error occurs. Some errors—such as having an incorrect
formula or improper value of a constant—can be easy to fix. That does not mean
they are easy to find. Usually the error is more subtle, and you need to hand trace
your code carefully to find out where you made a mistake.

Given the size of the programs that you have seen so far (they are very small)
and your inexperience, if your program does not contain syntax errors but
you still go through the execute-fix-compile process more than twice, you
should seriously consider completely discarding all of the implementation,
examining the design, and starting over again. There is something *seriously*
defective in your program solution. If the only way that you can tell what
your code will do is to compile and run it rather than checking it by hand,
then your code is surely defective. The only kinds of errors that you should
have are things like typing errors, slight errors in output format, and simple
logic errors.

You are in big trouble if you can't tell what your program will do without running it. You should be able to trace your own program by hand. If
your code is too convoluted to trace, don't be afraid to throw it away and
begin all over again. That is probably the best advice we can give.

If you think that you have corrected all of the logic errors in your program,
then run all of your test cases again. If the program passes all of them, you can
breathe a very short sigh of relief, then test all over again with different test cases.

It is unfortunate that there are no real testing schemes that are completely effective. A program that passes a huge battery of test cases may still contain errors.
Even with very sophisticated programs (written, of course, by fantastic programmers), it is often possible to discover logic errors. Everyone has seen commercial
programs that contain bugs. As a student programmer, your goal should be to find
and correct all of the logic errors that are likely to show up. You won't always find
all of them, but you can probably keep them to an acceptable minimum.

2.7 Summary

All of our discussions of object-oriented analysis and object-oriented design are to
no avail if the solutions are not implemented. The implementation of the solution
is the final product resulting from all of that analysis and design. If you don't

know how to code in C++ but you want to implement your solutions in C++, then you have a lot to learn. This chapter was about taking the necessary first steps.

The convenience store problem solution was used to illustrate simple features that almost every C++ program has: comments, compiler directives, functions, definitions, and input and output statements. Well-written programs contain comments to help programmers read them and understand what they do. Programs that rely on built-in C++ libraries such as the iostream library contain compiler include directives. All C++ programs contain major building blocks called functions, including a function called `main()`. Simple C++ programs consist of the following kinds of statements:

- Definitions

- Input and output statements

- Assignment statements

- Function calls

Information for simple C++ programs can be stored in data objects. Data objects have names, values, locations, and types. Numeric data types include integer and floating point types. Arithmetic operations are built into C++ to support numeric types. C++ will convert one type of numeric data to another when necessary to evaluate expressions.

Input and output in all good C++ programs is done through streams. While data objects cannot do anything on their own, the streams `cin` and `cout` can. We can look forward to a time when all of our design objects can be implemented as intelligent objects in our code.

Implementing the design of a solution to a programming problem is a two-phase process: (1) writing code and (2) testing code to determine if the solution is correct. Implementation is incomplete without the compiling, testing, and correcting of errors.

Glossary

address   The location of an object in memory.

assignment statement   A statement that uses the assignment operator, =, to specify a value for an object.

block   A segment of code enclosed in braces consisting of a sequence of zero or more statements. (Also a called a **compound statement**.)

comment   A segment of code to be ignored by the compiler. Comments start with // (the **comment delimiter**) and extend to the end of the line.

compiler directive   An instruction to the compiler beginning with the pound character, #.

compound statement   See block.

constant data object   A data object whose value cannot change during execution of a program. A constant data object must be initialized with a particular value when it is defined.

data object   A place in computer memory to store a value of a particular type. Data objects are usually characterized by name, value, type, and address.

debugging   The process of finding and correcting errors in a program.

definition (of an object)   A statement that creates a new object, specifying a name and a type.

division operator   The operator /. The value of a/b is the quotient of a divided by b.

error message   A message the compiler generates when it detects a syntax error in a source code file. The compiler will not be able to translate such source code into object code.

escape sequence   A two-character sequence in which the first character is a backslash. Escape characters are used in source code to stand for characters which are difficult (or impossible) to represent as single characters. Examples are '\n' (newline) and '\t' (tab).

expression   The primary unit of computation in C++. (An expression statement consists of an expression terminated by a semicolon.)

extraction operator   The input operator, >>.

function   The major building block of a C++ program whose body consists of a sequence of statements.

identifier   A name made up by the programmer. Identifiers begin with alphabetic characters or underscores and may contain alphabetic characters, underscores, and digit characters.

include directive   A compiler directive instructing the compiler to treat the named file as part of the source code.

initialization   Specifying a value for an object when it is created.

input operator   The operator >>, used for reading data into a program.

input stream   cin is the standard input stream, which is associated with the sequence of characters entered by the user from the keyboard.

insertion operator   The output operator, <<.

iostream library   The library containing code for doing input and output in C++.

keyword   One of a list of special words of significance to the C++ compiler. Keywords cannot be used for identifiers in a C++ source file. (See Appendix A.)

literal value   A number or character value in a C++ source code file.

logic error   An error in a program that may yield incorrect results when the program is executed.

lvalue   The name of an object when the name is used as an address.

manipulator   A tool used for controlling input and output stream formatting. C++ provides a manipulator library with the header file iomanip.h (See Appendixes D and E.)

modulus operator   The operator %, used with integer operands. The value of a%b is the remainder of a divided by b.

name   An identifier used to denote a particular object (or function).

newline The escape sequence '\n'. Inserting a newline into cout forces the cursor to drop to the next line.

operator precedence Rules to indicate the order in which subexpressions are to be evaluated according to the operators they contain. (See Appendix C.)

output operator The operator <<, used for writing data from a program.

output stream cout is the standard output stream, which is associated with the sequence of characters written by the program to the terminal.

polymorphism The ability to use an operator with different meanings.

roundoff error An error resulting from the inexact representation of floating point data.

runtime error An error that causes the program to halt execution abnormally.

rvalue The name of an object when it is used as a value.

side effect A change in an object due to the execution of code.

string literal A sequence of characters in a source code file enclosed in double quotes.

style The format, arrangement, and appearance of source code.

syntax error A violation of the syntax (rules of grammar) in a C++ source code file. A syntax error prevents the code from being compiled.

testing The process of executing a program with the intent of finding errors.

tracing Executing code by pencil and paper.

type A way of interpreting a sequence of bits to obtain a value.

type casting A method of explicitly converting one type of value to another type.

value The information stored at a data object interpreted according to its type.

variable data object A data object whose value can change during program execution.

warning message A message from the compiler about the source code. Warning messages do not prevent the compiler from generating object code.

whitespace Characters such as returns, blanks, and tabs that are invisible when printed.

2.8 ■ Exercises

1. Given the following C++ program.

```
// A simple program for computing gasoline cost for an automobile trip
#include <iostream.h>

void main()
{
   int gallons;                             // Number of gallons of gas used

   cout << "Enter the number of gallons used ";
   cin >> gallons;
```

```
const double pricePerGallon = 1.35;   // Price of a gallon of gas
float cost;                            // Total cost of gas for the trip

cost = gallons * pricePerGallon;
cout << "\nTotal cost of trip: $" << cost << endl;
}
```

    a. What are all of the program comments? (Write them down.)

    b. Does the program have a compiler directive? If so, what is it?

    c. What are the names of all data objects defined in the program?

    d. What are the types of the data objects from part (c)?

    e. What operators are used in the program?

    e. In the assignment to cost, which data object names are used as lvalues? Which names are used as rvalues?

    f. Write all of the output statements in the program.

2. List five C++ keywords. What happens if you use a keyword as the name of a data object that you define in your program?

3. Which of the following are valid C++ identifiers? For each one that is not valid, explain why it is not valid.

```
GeorgeWashington    byGeorge!    "George"    x-coordinate
billygoatgruff      A            'A'         _lying_low
dollar$andCents     double       a2          2a
my(dog)has(fleas)   SHORT        integer     C++
starry**night       FLOAT        float       U.S.A.
```

4. Write definitions for variable data objects to represent the following items. Select good names and appropriate types for the data objects. Comment each definition.

    a. Miles that a car can travel on a gallon of gasoline

    b. User's first initial

    c. Number of students in a programming class

    d. User's weight to the nearest half pound

    e. Speed of an express train at a given time traveling from Madrid to Seville

    f. Number of edges of a polygon

    g. Percentage of people in Canada who are under 21 years old

5. Write definitions for constant data objects to represent the following items. Select good names. Comment each definition.

    a. Number of inches in a mile

b. Number of seconds in an hour

c. Third letter in the alphabet (uppercase)

d. Speed of light

e. Number of sides of a hexagon

f. Normal human body temperature (Be sure to indicate if the measurement is in Fahrenheit or Celsius.)

g. Largest decimal digit

6. Correct the syntax errors in the following program:

```cpp
#include <iostream.h>
void main()
{
    int badInt = 2,367;
    cout >> "Hello world" >> endl
    cout >> "This is a test";    // it really is a test
        >> "\nEnter a number ";
    ////////////////////////////////////////////////////
    cin << x;
    int z;
    z + x = 10;
    cout >> "number +1 = " >> x + 1 > > endl;
}
```

7. Write a single line of code for each of the following tasks.

a. Allow the program to use `cin` and `cout`.

b. Allow the program to use the built-in function `sqrt()`.

c. Output the remainder of 245678 divided by 34567

d. Create a `char` type variable data object to represent the first character of the alphabet.

e. Create a `char` type constant data object to represent the first character of the alphabet.

f. Output the phrase `"Hello world"`.

8. Assume that x, y, and z are `double` data objects and i, j, and k are `int` data objects. Write a single expression to represent each of the following:

a. An expression using x and y that represents the mathematical expression $3x^2 + 4y - 7$.

b. An expression using x and y that represents the mathematical expression $x^3 + 4y + 5$.

c. The remainder of i divided by twice the value of j.

d. The average of x, y, and z.

e. The average of i, j, and k (be careful not to lose the fractional part).

f. The area of a right triangle with x for one leg and y for another. (Assume that both x and y are positive.)

g. The hypotenuse of a right triangle with x for one leg and y for another. (Assume that both x and y are positive.)

9. Find the values of the following expressions:

   a. `2 - 3 - 4 - 5`

   b. `2 - (3 - 4) - 5`

   c. `5 - 2 * 4 * 3`

   d. `12 / 5 * 5`

   e. `12 / 3 - 12 % 5`

   f. `0 / 5 - 21 % 6 * 5`

   g. `3.0/4 + 5`

   h. `3/4 + 5`

   i. `5 % 2 + 18 / 3`

   j. `(5 + 4) % 7 * 8`

   k. `int(3.5) + double(3)`

   l. `char(68)`

   m. `char('a' + 4)`

10. Assume that x, y, and z are variables of type `int`. Assume also that before execution of each code segment that x, y, and z have the values 10, 20, and 3 respectively. Find the values of the following expressions:

    a. `x + y + z / z`

    b. `x + (y + z) / z`

    c. `(x + y + z) / z`

    d. `x / y / z`

    e. `y % x - y / x`

11. Assume that x and y are a variables of type `int` and that the value of x is 2684. What is the value of y after each of the following assignment statements is executed?

    a. `y = x % 10;`

    b. `y = x / 10;`

    c. `y = x - x % 10;`

    d. `y = (x / 10) % 10;`

12. Write single statements for each of the following:

    a. Assume that x is a double variable data object. Assign to x the largest root of the quadratic $ax^2 + bx + c$.

b. Assume that `ch` is a `char`. Write a statement that outputs both `ch` and its ASCII code.

c. Suppose that `numStudents` is the number of students currently enrolled at the university and `numCStudents` is the number of currently enrolled students who are taking a computer science course. (Both `numStudents` and `numCStudents` are `int`s.) Write a statement that assigns to the `double` variable `percentCS` the percentage of university students who are taking computer science courses.

d. Suppose that `dozenCost` is a `double` representing the cost of a dozen hats in U.S. dollars and that `singleCost` is a `double`. Write a statement that assigns to `singleCost` the cost of a single hat (1/12 the cost of a dozen hats rounded to the nearest penny).

e. Use `singleCost` from part (d). Write an output statement that generates the cost of a hat in terms of dollars followed by cents. For example, if the cost of a hat is $17.83, then the output generated by your statement should be:

```
Cost is 17 dollars and 83 cents.
```

13. Assume that `x`, `y`, `z`, and `temp` are variables of type `int`. Assume also that before execution of each code segment that `x`, `y`, and `z` have the values `1`, `2`, and `3` respectively. Trace each code segment. For each trace, make a table of all four variables. Show the value of each one after the execution of each statement.

a.
```
x = y * z;
z += y + x / 4;
y = (x + 17) % (y + x);
```

b.
```
x = y;
y = z;
z = x;
```

c.
```
temp = x;
x = y;
y = z;
z = temp;
```

14. The modulus operator can be used to tell if one positive integer is divisible by another. Suppose that `x` is a positive `int`.

a. If `x` is an even number, what is the value of `x % 2`?

b. How can you tell if x is divisible by 10?

c. Suppose that y is an int with a value that is larger than x. What is the value of x % y?

15. Find out the values of the following expressions on your system. If you do not have access to an interactive development environment, you can write a simple program like this to test your answers.

```
#include <iostream.h>
void main()
{
    cout << " size of an integer is" << sizeof(int) << endl;
    // output any of the parts for a) through g)
}
```

a. sizeof(int)

b. sizeof(double)

c. sizeof(float)

d. sizeof(char)

e. sizeof("Hello")

f. sizeof("H")

g. sizeof('H')

Do the answers for (f) and (g) surprise you?

16. C++ does not have a "typeof" operator. What are the types as well as the values of the following expressions?

a. 'a'

b. 1 / 2 + 3 % 3

c. 1 / 2 + 3.0

d. 1 / 2 + int (3.0)

e. char(70)

f. char(70) + 70   // This one is tricky.

g. double (100/75)   // Be careful with this one, too.

h. int('A')

17. Suppose a, b, and c are char type variables.

a. Write a segment of code that will read the next three non-whitespace characters into a, b, and c.

b. Write a segment of code that will read the next three characters into a, b, and c, not skipping the whitespace characters.

18. Suppose that x is a variable of type int and that the value of x is 7. Show the output generated by each of the following statements:

    a. `cout << "x = " << x;`

    b. `cout << "x = 7" << x;`

    c. `cout << (x = 2) << x;`   `// This is a tricky part.`

19. Write a series of output statements that will do the following:

    a. Output the phrase `"Hello, Mom"` on one line.

    b. Output the phrase `"Hello, Mom"` on one line and `"I enjoy summer camp."` on the next line.

    c. Output the phrase `"Hello, Mom"` on one line and `"I enjoy summer camp."` on the next line. For this problem, combine `"Hello, Mom"` and `"I enjoy summer camp."` into single string to be inserted into `cout`.

    d. Make the cursor go two lines down the screen.

20. Suppose that x is an int and it has the value 123. What output is generated by execution of the following statement?

    `cout << "x" << ' ' << x << setw(6) << x << ' ' << x % 100 << endl;`

21. Suppose that x, y, and z are of type double and they have values 33.1670, –.000391, and 1.02e+8 respectively. Write a sequence of output statements whose execution will do the following:

    a. Display x, y, and z in fixed decimal format, each with two digits to the right of the decimal.

    b. Display x, y, and z in scientific format, each with three significant digits.

    c. Display x in fixed decimal format, then y in scientific format, then z in fixed format. Set all precision to 2.

    d. Display the phrase TABLE OF PRIMES with 20 leading blanks and 10 trailing blanks.

    Draw the displays that would be shown by executing the correct code for (a), (b), and (c).

22. Suppose x, y, and z are of type int and that their values are all positive but less than 100. Write a segment of code that will display the value, the square of the value, and the cube of each one in a labeled table. All the numbers should be right-aligned in their respective columns. For example, if their values are 8, 20, and 55 respectively, then the display should look like this.

```
Number         Square          Cube
-----------------------------------
   8            64             512
  20           400            8000
  86          7396          636056
```

What is the largest number that could appear in the table? Does your code display that largest number appropriately?

23. Suppose that x is a data object of type `double` and that its value is between 0 and 30,000. Suppose that `whole` is an `int` variable and that `fraction` is a `double` variable. Write a segment of code that assigns to `whole` the integer part of x and that assigns to `fraction` the fractional part of x. For example, if the value of x is 234.5678, the result of execution of the code should be that `whole` has a value of 234 and that `fraction` has a value of .5678.

If you have a C++ programming development environment that allows you to evaluate expressions directly, you can easily tell if the code that you wrote for this problem is correct. If not, you'll have to write a program just to test the code.

A program written just to test some code for correctness is called a **driver**, a minimal program into which the code to be tested is placed. It usually consists of the code to be tested, and input statements that allow testing on various datasets, and output statements that show the results of each test. All this is wrapped up into a source code file that can be compiled. Here's a driver program that you can use to test your answers to this question:

```
#include <iostream.h>
void main()
{
    int whole;
    double fraction;
    double x;
    cout << "Enter a floating point number between 0 and 30,000 --> ";
    cin >> x;

    // The code which you wrote to answer this question goes here.

    cout << "Integer part = " << whole << endl;
    cout << "Fraction part = " << fraction << endl;
}
```

24. You can figure out all of the digits in a nonnegative integer by performing a sequence of integer division and modulus operations. Suppose that the variables x, sum, onesDigit, tensDigit, hundredsDigit, and thousandsDigit are of type int and that x is between 0 and 9999 inclusive.

    a. Write a segment of code that assigns to:
       onesDigit the digit of x in the 1's position
       tensDigit the digit of x in the 10's position
       hundredsDigit the digit of x in the 100's position
       thousandsDigit the digit of x in the 1000's position

    b. Write a segment of code that finds the sum of the digits in x.

    c. Write a segment of code that finds the sum of the sum of the digits in x. (How many times do you have to repeat this process—finding the sum of the sum of the digits of the sum of the digits...—in order that the final sum is a single digit number?)

    d. Test your answers for (a), (b), and (c) to determine if they are correct. Write a driver program if necessary.

Programming projects

25. Write an implementation of the design for exercise 12 in Chapter 1. Make sure that the numeric output is formatted with two digits to the right of the decimal. Test your program with the following input values: $100.00, $99.99, $0.50, and $0.00.

26. Write an implementation of the design for exercise 16 in Chapter 1. Numeric output should be formatted with two digits to the right of the decimal.

27. Write an implementation of the design for exercise 17 in Chapter 1.

28. Write an implementation of the design for exercise 21 in Chapter 1. The output that execution of your program produces should look like a table, with two labeled columns (one for the distance and one for the number of laps) and easy-to-read numbers. When you execute the program, redirect the output in order to generate a text file for the table.

29. Every line in the real plane can be written in the following form, where A, B, and C are real numbers:

$$Ax + By + C = 0$$

    Design a program that takes as input the x- and y-coordinates of two different points in the plane and writes the equation of the line as output. Implement your design as a C++ program. Test your code using the following pairs of points as test cases:

(0,0) and (0,5)
(0,0) and (5,0)
(1,1) and (1,4)
(–7.5,7.5) and (1,–1)

The first line in this test dataset is a vertical line, so its slope is undefined. Your program may need a selection statement to trap vertical lines.

30. A furniture store has just lost the records of the wholesale prices it paid for certain items that it recently sold. However, it still has records of how much customers paid for those items. The ticket price of an item is always 40% above the wholesale price, and a 6.5% retail sales tax is levied on each item. Design and implement a solution to the problem of determining wholesale prices of items from the amounts of money customers paid to purchase the items.

Chapter 3

Implementing Object Behaviors with Functions

IN the world of object-oriented program development, programs contain models of the problems they address, and such models are made up of objects. All of the activity in a model takes place through the behaviors or methods of its objects. Objects interact by sending each other messages and receiving replies to those messages. With the exception of cin and cout, we have up to this point used only data object definitions to implement object attributes and simple statements to implement their behaviors. We have grouped the definitions and statements together by comments to show which code implemented which design object.

In this chapter, we will show you how to use C++ functions to implement the methods that objects use for carrying out their behaviors. We will show you how calls to these functions correspond to sending messages and how values returned from these functions correspond to the replies. We will be able to encapsulate some objects into single functions, wrapping all of the attributes and behaviors of an object into a single section of code.

You have already had experience with at least two functions in the previous chapter: a function named main, which is contained in every C++ program, and the function sqrt() from the math library. In this chapter, we will take advantage of functions as organizational tools for our own programs. We will show you how to use functions, and then we will illustrate their use by reimplementing the solutions to the convenience store and the changemaker problems. You will learn new ways to represent object behavior and how to write your own functions.

Near the end of this chapter, you will learn how to use code written by other programmers for your designs. C++ programmers typically implement their design objects through classes. Although we will focus for a while only on simple, nonclass implementations of design objects, the section in this chapter on using class libraries will give you a preview of what is to come later in this book.

From now on, we will see that objects always work through functions. The function feature of C++ allows you to write code that can work for a variety of different data and circumstances. Functions are the most primitive examples of reusable code that can be used for different programs.

3.1 C++ functions that return values

The word *function* is a term heard in mathematics classes. A mathematical function is like a black box. A number can be fed into the box, which in turn produces a single number as a result. The square root function is an example.

$$x \longrightarrow \boxed{\sqrt{}} \longrightarrow \sqrt{x}$$

If x is a nonnegative number, then $\sqrt{x}$ is the number which when multiplied by itself is x. The number x is called the *argument* to the function. Exactly how the square root is calculated is not part of the picture. That's what makes the box a black box. You cannot look into the box to see how the calculation is performed.

Built-in functions

C++ has functions, too. C++ functions have some features in common with mathematical functions. The C++ mathematics library contains a square root function, `sqrt()`. When we refer to a C++ function by name in this text, we will use the convention of writing the actual name followed by parentheses. The C++ square root function calculates numbers in the same sense that the black box above calculates them. That is, you can feed in a nonnegative number and it will return the square root of that number.

How can you "feed in a number" to the C++ square root function? How can you apply the function to a number? You do it by calling the function. The following expression is an example of a **call** or **invocation** of the function `sqrt()`:

```
sqrt(3.57)
```

The number 3.57 is the **actual argument** of the function call. The actual arguments provide the information in the function needs to do its calculation. The expression itself means the result obtained by applying the function to the actual argument. That result is the value that is computed and returned by the function.

In order to call the square root function, the programmer needs to know the following things:

1. The name of the square root function is `sqrt()`.

2. There is one actual argument to the function, and it must be a nonnegative number.

3. The result returned by the function is a number of type `double`, and it is the square root of the argument.

Exactly what the programmer must know is the **interface** of the function. The following C++ code specifies the interface of the square root function:

```
double sqrt(double x);
// Argument: x - a nonnegative number
// Returns: The square root of x
```

The specification of the interface of the function consists of a **declaration** of the function and function header comments, which describe the exact behavior of the function. The function declaration is a function header followed by a semicolon. A function header consists of the type of return value, the function name, and the list of **formal arguments** in parentheses.[1] Figure 3.1 illustrates how the declaration and header comments specify the interface of the function—they tell a programmer how the function can be used.

---

[1] In many texts, you will see the word *parameter* instead of the word *argument*. With respect to C++ and many other languages, the two words mean exactly the same thing. In this text, we will almost always use the word argument.

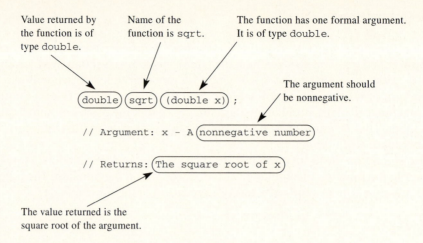

Value returned by the function is of type `double`.

Name of the function is `sqrt`.

The function has one formal argument. It is of type `double`.

The argument should be nonnegative.

```
(double) (sqrt) ((double x)) ;
```

```
// Argument: x - A (nonnegative number)
```

```
// Returns: (The square root of x)
```

The value returned is the square root of the argument.

Figure 3.1 Specification of the interface of `sqrt()`.

The implementation of the square root function is the **definition** of the function. The implementation is the code that shows exactly how the function works—and exactly what is inside the black box. Most C++ programmers do not have the slightest idea what the implementation code for the square root function looks like. They simply use the function, trusting that it behaves according to the specification of the interface.

The C++ mathematics library is a rich source of useful functions such as the square root function, the sine function, and the natural log function. But we are not limited only to these functions when a mathematical calculation is necessary. And more important, we do not need to restrict our use of functions simply to mathematical calculations.

User-defined functions

A well-known physics formula gives the power loss in an electrical cable as a function of the resistance and the current. The power loss (in watts) is the resistance (in ohms) multiplied by the square of the current (in amps). A black box diagram of the function is shown below.

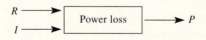

There is no function built into C++ for computing the power loss in an electrical cable. If we want such a function, we'll have to write our own. To begin our work, let's figure out the specification of the function's interface. Our function needs a return type, a name, and a list of formal arguments.

The type of value that our function will return should be a numeric type. Since power measured in watts is not always a whole number, the return value should be a floating point type. We will write our function so that it returns a `double`.

What about the name of the function? Since the name of any function is an identifier, the name of our function must conform to the valid identifier rules given in the previous chapter. That will satisfy a syntax requirement, but there is also a stylistic requirement. The name should describe what the function does. We can name our function `powerLoss()`.

The formal argument list shows what *types* of actual arguments are expected by the function and the *names* by which they will be known in the definition of the function. In order to compute the return value, `powerLoss()` needs two pieces of information: a resistance and a current, both of which are floating point numbers. An appropriate formal argument list is `(double resistance, double current)`.

We have enough information to make a function declaration, and we can supply header comments to describe what this function does.

```
double powerLoss(double resistance, double current);
// Arguments:
//    current - Current in the cable measured in amps
//    resistance - Resistance in the cable measured in ohms
// Returns: The power loss in watts over a cable with the given current
//    and resistance.
```

A programmer can tell from just the declaration that a call to `powerLoss()` consists of the name `powerLoss` and two `double` type expressions separated by a comma inside a pair of parentheses. The function declaration and header documentation tell how the function can be used. They constitute the specification to the interface to the function.

With the function interface specification, we know what the function should do. Now we must figure out how it will do it. We need to implement the function by writing its definition, which contains the code that indicates how the function computes its value.

The definition of a function consists of the function header and the function body. We have already constructed a header for `powerLoss()` in the declaration. The **body** of the function contains the code that will be executed whenever the function is called. If a function returns a value, there must be a **return statement** in the body of the function indicating the value that will be returned. Figure 3.2 illustrates an annotated definition for `powerLoss()`.

The first line of the definition is the function header. When it is used in the definition, the header does *not* end in a semicolon.

```
double powerLoss(double resistance, double current)
```

The body of `powerLoss()` is the remaining code. The body is a block, so it begins with a left curly brace and ends with a right curly brace.

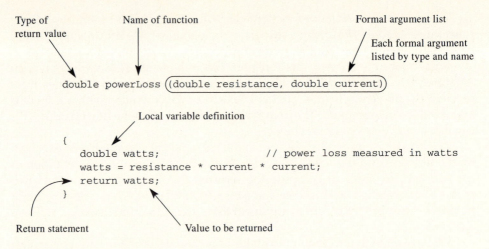

Figure 3.2 The definition of `powerLoss()`.

```
{
    double watts;
    watts = resistance * current * current;
    return watts;
}
```

The first statement in the body of this function is the definition of `watts`, a **local** data object, which can be used only in the body of a function. The last statement in the body of this function is a return statement which indicates what value the function will return to the calling code.

The definition of a function consists of the code that tells how the function computes its value. Notice that the function header, which is part of the function definition, actually contains all of the code necessary for a declaration. Indeed, since a function declaration tells how a function is to be used, then the definition for a function is one kind of function declaration.

Declaration vs. definition: What's the difference?

A **declaration** introduces an identifier into a program. A **definition** introduces an identifier and tells the meaning for that identifier.

- A function definition is a kind of declaration. It shows what code is to be executed when the function is called.

- It is possible to declare a function without defining it.

- A function can be declared many times, but it can be defined only once.

- An object can be defined only once.

- An object definition is also a declaration. Except for the example in the footnote below all of the examples of object declarations in this book are also definitions.[2]

There are two important rules about identifiers in C++:

1. Identifiers must be declared before they are used.

2. Functions and objects, whose names are identifiers, cannot be defined twice.

As long as a function is declared before it is called, its definition can be placed anywhere except inside another function. The following is a complete program using `powerLoss()`:

```
#include <iostream.h>

double powerLoss(double resistance, double current);    // Declaration
// Arguments:
//    current - Current in the cable measured in ohms.
//    resistance - Resistance in the cable measured in ohms.
// Returns: The power loss in watts over a cable with the given current
//    and resistance.


void main( )
{
    double aValue;
    aValue = powerLoss(3.5,7.26);                         // Call
    cout << aValue << endl;
}

double powerLoss(double resistance, double current)      // Definition
{
    double watts;                // Power loss measured in watts
    watts = resistance * current * current;
    return watts;
}
```

[2] An example of an object declaration which is not a definition is `extern int x;` the `extern` says that x is defined in another file.

The call to `powerLoss()` consists of the function name, parentheses, and the two `double` expressions that are the actual arguments. The call can be made inside `main()` because there is a declaration for `powerLoss()` before the call.

We could have put the definition of `powerLoss()` above `main()` and avoided its separate declaration. After all, a definition also serves as a declaration. But for most functions, we will make declarations that are separate from their definitions. We will follow conventional C++ programming practice and place the declarations above `main()` and put the definitions below `main()`. There is good reason for this. When C++ programmers put their function definitions below `main()` and all of their function declarations above `main()`, they remove any restrictions on where the functions can be invoked. Any function can call any other function (including itself) except `main()`.

A function declaration that is not a definition is called a **prototype**. C++ programmers put function prototypes above `main()` and function definitions below `main()`. The names of the formal arguments must be shown in the function definition. However, the same is not true for prototypes. In fact, the C++ compiler ignores the names of the formal arguments in a prototype but does not ignore the formal argument types.

All of the following are legitimate declarations for `powerLoss()`.

```
double powerLoss(double resistance, double current);
double powerLoss(double x, double y);
double powerLoss(double, double);                      // Signature form
```

All of these declarations could be made in the same program, for the same `powerLoss()` function. The last prototype, which shows only the return type, the function name, and the formal argument types, is called the function's **signature**. We usually prefer showing names for the formal arguments in the prototypes, since this usually helps us write good function header documentation. However, C++ programmers are not uniform in this practice. Select a style that you like, and stick to it.

Tracing function calls

What actually happens when `powerLoss()` is called? Suppose `main()` contains the following assignment statement:

```
aValue = powerLoss(3.5,7.26);
```

A trace of the execution of the assignment statement begins with the trace of the function call `powerLoss(3.5,7.26)`.

1. Two new data objects are created, `resistance` and `current`, to correspond to the formal arguments. They are initialized with the actual arguments 3.5 and 7.26.

```
double resistance = 3.5;
double current = 7.26;
```

2. The function body is executed

   a. The local variable data object `watts` is created via its definition in the body.

   ```
   double watts;
   ```

   b. A value is assigned to `watts`.

   ```
   watts = resistance * current * current;
   ```

   c. The value of `watts` is returned.

   ```
   return watts;
   ```

3. The function quits execution. The value that was returned is assigned to `aValue`.

You may find it helpful to draw a picture of what happens during the execution of a function call. Figure 3.3 shows a simple model of what happens to computer memory at the beginning of execution of the call `powerLoss(3.5,7.26)`. The objects on the right side are known by `powerLoss()`. The objects on the left side are known by `main()`.

You can also trace the function by hand by substituting the function call with code that is similar to the body of the function. The following illustrates how the function call might be shown in such a trace.

```
#include <iostream.h>

main()
{
  double aValue;
  aValue = { double resistance = 3.5;
             double current = 7.26;
             double watts;
             watts = resistance * current* current;
             return watts;
          }
  cout << aValue << endl;
}
```

This code is not a real program because it will not compile. (C++ does not accept underlined identifiers and it does not accept assignment statements for which the right-hand side is a block.) But our pseudo-program can be traced just

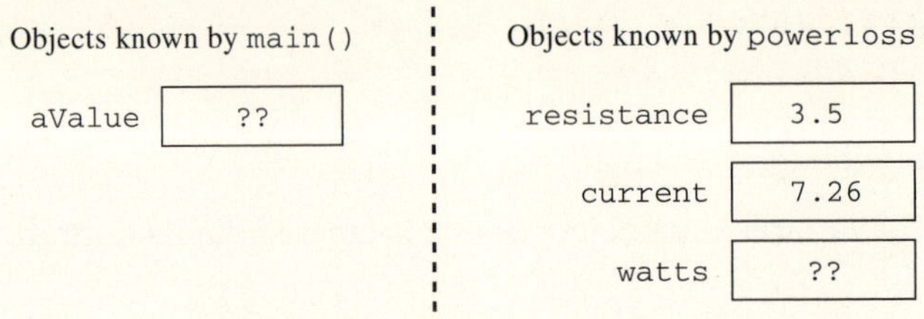

Objects known by `main()`   Objects known by `powerloss()`

aValue	??

resistance	3.5
current	7.26
watts	??

Figure 3.3 Memory model for the beginning of execution of `powerloss(3.5,7.26)`.

like real code. The identifiers <u>resistance</u>, <u>current</u>, and <u>watts</u> are underlined to show that they really belong to the function `powerLoss()` instead of `main()`. They are temporary data objects that go away as soon as the function quits executing.[3]

Formal and actual arguments

The term *formal arguments* refers to the list of arguments and their corresponding types in the function definition. The *actual arguments* are the arguments that appear in the function call. There is a rigid correspondence between formal and actual arguments.

The formal arguments are names of data objects for the duration of execution of the function. Actual arguments for all of our examples so far are expressions. When a function is called, the actual arguments are evaluated one at a time, and their values are used as the initial values of the formal arguments. The value of the first actual argument initializes the first formal argument, the value of the second actual argument initializes the second formal argument, and so on to the point where the value of the last actual argument initializes the last formal argument.

The correspondence between formal and actual arguments has nothing to do with the names of the variables that appear in the expressions of the arguments. Naming is completely irrelevant. (It is even possible for variables in `main()` to have the same names as the names of the formal arguments.) The position of an expression in the actual argument list determines which formal argument is to be initialized by its value.

To illustrate the formal-to-actual argument correspondence, suppose the following data object definition statements have been executed:

```
float x = 1.0;
float y = 2.0;
double z = 3.0;
double w = 40.5;
int a = 8;
int b = 9;
```

[3] A C++ compiler can actually substitute the text of a function body for the function call in a manner similar to this. When the programmer declares a function to be *inline*, that is exactly what may happen. Inline functions are usually reserved for functions that are *very* short and are called many times.

The following table shows some sample calls to `powerLoss()` along with the initializations of the formal arguments `resistance` and `current` and the values returned.

Function call	resistance	current	Value returned
powerLoss(x,y)	1.0	2.0	4.0
powerLoss(y,x)	2.0	1.0	2.0
powerLoss(x + 23,w)	24.0	40.5	39366.0
powerLoss(sqrt(a),b % 4)	2.828427	1.0	2.828427

What happens if we try to do something completely absurd such as make the call `powerLoss("Jane",2.3)`? The compiler objects. The string literal `"Jane"` is not considered to be a numeric type, and the compiler wants the arguments in any call to `powerLoss()` to be of type `double` or easily converted to `doubles`.

Additional examples of functions that return values

We will now look at several examples of function specifications and their implementations. These illustrations show some of the many ways that arguments, return types, and local data objects can appear in a function.

The first function is very simple. It has no arguments and it always returns the integer 0. When a function has an empty argument list as in this case, then the formal argument list is written as `()` or `(void)`, depending on the programmer's particular stylistic preference. We prefer to use `()`. The word `void` is a keyword.

```
int zeroFunction()
// Returns: The integer 0
{
    return 0;
}
```

If you prefer to use `void` to show that there are no arguments, here is the equivalent form of `zeroFunction()`.

```
int zeroFunction(void)
// Returns: The integer 0
{
    return 0;
}
```

A call to `zeroFunction()` should have no arguments. Regardless of whether or not you explicitly declare the formal argument list as `void`, a call to this function is written as the name of the function followed by an empty pair of parentheses—`zeroFunction()`.

The next function takes a digit character as an argument and returns its integer equivalent. For example, if the actual argument to the function is the character `'5'`, then the function will return the integer 5. Even though a similar function is built into a C++ library, it is easy to construct on your own. The formal argument type is `char` and the return type is `int`. (The implementation relies on the fact that `char` is actually an integer type. The result of subtracting an `int` from a `char` is an `int`.)

```cpp
int charToInt(char digitCharacter)
// Argument: digitCharacter - A character
//            (ASSUME: '0' <= digitCharacter <= '9')
// Returns: The integer equivalent of digitCharacter.
//   For example, if the argument is '0', the return value is 0; if the
//   argument is '9', the return value is 9.
{
   const int asciiZeroDigit = int('0');           // ASCII code for '0'
   return digitCharacter - asciiZeroDigit;
}
```

The documentation for the argument `digitCharacter` is important. It specifies the limitations on any actual argument used in a function call to `charToInt()`. That is a function **precondition**, an assumption that the function makes with respect to its actual arguments.

The function `averageFour()` computes the average of four integers. Notice that it divides the sum of the four integers by 4.0 rather than by 4 to avoid truncating the fractional part of the quotient.

```cpp
double averageFour(int firstNumber, int secondNumber,
                   int thirdNumber, int fourthNumber)
// Arguments: firstNumber, secondNumber, thirdNumber, and fourthNumber can be
//    any four integers.
// Returns: The average of four arguments.
{
   return (firstNumber + secondNumber + thirdNumber + fourthNumber) / 4.0;
}
```

The function `max()` returns the value of the larger of its two arguments. Its definition uses an `if/else` selection statement. In the next chapter we will look more carefully at `if` and `if/else` statements. But you should find them easy to understand right now. If the value of x is greater than the value of y, then the value of x is returned. Otherwise, the value of y is returned.

```
double max(double x, double y)
// Arguments: x and y are any floating point numbers
// Returns: The larger of the two values of x and y.
{
    if (x > y)
        return x;
    else
        return y;
}
```

The general form of an if/else-selection statement is as follows:

```
if (condition)
    statement-T
else
    statement-F
```

Execution is straightforward. The condition is evaluated. If the condition is true, *statement-T* is executed and *statement-F* is skipped. If the condition is false, *statement-T* is skipped and *statement-F* is executed. The statements can be either simple or compound. In the definition of max(), both statements are simple—both end with semicolons.

The last function, passFailLetter(), computes the final pass/fail letter grade for a student based on four test grades and a final exam grade. Tests are worth 60 percent of the average and the final exam is worth 40 percent. If the final average is 60 or better, the letter grade is P. Otherwise the letter grade is F.

```
char passFailLetter(int firstTest, int secondTest,
                    int thirdTest, int fourthTest, int exam)
// Arguments:
//    firstTest, secondTest, thirdTest, fourthTest - The four test grades
//    exam - Grade on the final exam.
// Returns: 'P' or 'F' based on scores of four tests and a final exam
//    Tests count 60% and the final exam counts 40%. 'P' is returned if the
//    weighted average is 60 or greater. 'F' is returned if the weighted
//    average is less than 60.
{
    const double testWeight = .6;    // Weight of test average in final grade
    const double examWeight = .4;    // Weight of exam in final grade
    float testAverage = averageFour(firstTest, secondTest,
                                    thirdTest, fourthTest);
```

```
   double finalAverage = testAverage * testWeight + exam * examWeight;

   if (finalAverage >= 60)
      return 'P';
   else
      return 'F';
}
```

The definition of `passFailLetter()` contains two return statements. Only one of them will be executed on any particular call. Which return statement is executed depends on the value of `finalAverage`. If `finalAverage` is at least 60, then the first return statement will be executed and the second one will not. If `finalAverage` is less than 60, then only the second return statement will be executed.

The following segment of code contains calls to the functions of this section. The statements may be placed in `main()` or in any other function that is defined below the function declarations. For each call, assume that `number` and `i` are `ints`, `myTestAverage` and `z` are `doubles`, and `myGrade` is a `char`.

```
number = zeroFunction();                          // number is 0
number = charToInt('5') * charToInt('7');         // number is 35
myTestAverage = averageFour(99,68,71,80);         // myTestAverage is 79.5
myGrade = passFailLetter(99,68,71,80,75);         // myGrade is 'P'
cout << "Grade is "
     << passFailLetter(99,68,71,80,75) << endl;   // Output: Grade is P
i = 20;
z = averageFour(i,i + 10,i * i,12);               // z is 115.5
cout << max(myTestAverage,z);                     // Output: 115.5
```

Execution of a function *ends as soon as a return statement in the function is executed*. A function definition can have several return statements. Both `max()` and `passFailLetter()` are examples of functions with two return statements. Once a return statement is executed, the function is exited—execution of that function call stops. Even if the body of the function contains additional code after that return statement, that additional code is not executed.

Since execution of a return statement terminates execution of the function call, we could have defined `max()` in the following way. The results are identical to the original definition.

```
// Alternative definition for max()
double max(double x, double y)
{
   if (x > y)
      return x;
   return y;
}
```

3.2 ▌ Procedures: Functions that do not return values

C++ has two kinds of functions: functions that return values and functions that do not. Functions that do not return values are sometimes called **void functions** or **procedures**. The function header for a procedure begins with the keyword `void` rather than the type of an object.

Since a procedure does not return a value, its definition does not contain a return statement that specifies a particular value to be returned. (We are not saying a procedure does not have any return statement.) A function that returns a value must have a return statement indicating the particular value to be returned. The only two differences between functions that return values and procedures can be summarized as follows:

1. The header for a procedure begins with the keyword `void`. The header for a function that returns a value begins with the type of value to be returned.

2. A procedure cannot have a return statement that returns a value. A function that returns a value must have a return statement that specifies a value to be returned.

Let's look at some simple procedures. The first example prints a number on the screen, right-justified in a particular field width. It has two formal arguments, one for the field width and the other for the number. In the header documentation for a procedure, we use the term "side effect" rather than the term "returns" to indicate what is supposed to happen as a consequence of function execution.

```
void printNumberInAField(int fieldwidth, int aNumber)
// Arguments:
//    fieldwidth - Exact number of characters to be printed
//         ASSUME: fieldwidth is large enough to print aNumber.
//    aNumber - The number to be printed
// Side effect: Prints aNumber right-justified in a field of the given
//    fieldwidth.
{
    cout << setw(fieldwidth) << aNumber << endl;
}
```

A function has a side effect if its execution changes any object besides its own local objects. The object `cout` is changed (data is inserted into `cout`) as a result of a call to `printNumberInAField()`.

Our second example is a procedure that displays 50 asterisks and then a newline. It does not have any arguments, but it does have a side effect.

```
void printARowOfStars()
// Side effect: Prints 50 asterisks followed by a newline
```

```
{
    cout << "*****************************************************" << endl;
}
```

Here are some example calls to these procedures. In each call to `printNumberInAField()` except the last one, all of the arguments are literal numbers. We could have used numeric variables, numeric constants, or any expressions that would evaluate to numbers. Of course, there are no arguments in any call to `printARowOfStars()`.

```
printARowOfStars();
printNumberInAField(6,13);
printARowOfStars();
printNumberInAField(13,6);
printARowOfStars();
printNumberInAField(6,zeroFunction());
```

The output generated via execution of these calls is shown in the box below.

```
****************************************************
       13
****************************************************
             6
****************************************************
       0
```

By using functions, a programmer can often avoid writing duplicate code. There is also the added benefit of simplifying the calling code so that a programmer can get an idea of what is happening just by reading the function calls.

The bodies of `printARowOfStars()` and `printNumberInAField()` do not contain return statements. Return statements inside bodies of procedures are optional as long as they do not specify a particular value to be returned. We could have had return statements at the ends of `printARowOfStars()` and `printNumberInAField()`. The body of `printARowOfStars()` could have looked like this:

```
{
    cout << "*****************************************************" << endl;
    return;
}
```

If a procedure contains a return statement, there is no expression written after the keyword `return`. The effect of placing the return statement at the bottom of the definition of `printARowOfStars()` is to emphasize that this is the last statement that will be executed in this invocation of `printARowOfStars()`. When a return statement is executed in any kind of function, whether it returns a value or not, that function does no additional work. Execution of the return statement terminates the function call.

Programmers sometimes place return statements in the body of a procedure simply to avoid the execution of the statements that follow them. If you want to be able to exit a function early (before the last statement), place a return statement at the point where you want the exit to occur. Just remember to return a value if the function is not void and not to return a value if the function is void—if it is a procedure.

Pass-by-value arguments

In all of the functions that we have discussed, the formal arguments were **pass-by-value arguments** or simply **value arguments**. When a call is made to a function with a pass-by-value argument, a new object is created for the formal argument and initialized with the value of the corresponding actual argument. The name of the new object is the name of the formal argument. The new object exists only for the duration of execution of the function.

Pass-by-value arguments have limitations on their usefulness. Look at the following void function, which does not really do what its name and documentation promise. This is an example of a function that has an incorrect implementation. The function's definition does not meet the function's specifications.

```
void swap(int x, int y)
// Arguments: x and y are variables
// Side effect: The values of the actual arguments are interchanged.
//    The new value of the first argument is the old value of second one
//    and vice-versa.
{
    int temp = x;       // Temporary buffer to hold the original value of x
    x = y;
    y = temp;
}
```

What happens when we call this incorrect version of `swap()`, as in the following situation?

```
int first = 12;
int second = 8;
// The value of first is 12, and the value of second is 8.
swap(first,second);
// The value of first is still 12, and the value of second is still 8.
```

Objects known by the function
invoking swap()

first	12

second	8

Objects known by swap()

x	12

y	8

temp	?

Figure 3.4 Memory model for the beginning of execution of
swap(first,second). This is a defective version of swap().

The call swap(first,second) has no effect on first or second. But from
the name of the function as well as its header documentation, we have a reasonable right to expect that swap(first,second) would exchange the values of the
two variables first and second. After the call, first should be 8 and second
should be 12.

Let's take a closer look at our simple function-tracing memory model to
understand exactly what happens during a call to this defective swap(). Figure
3.4 shows memory at the beginning of execution, right after the invocation
swap(first,second) is invoked.

Since swap() may be invoked by another function besides main(), the
objects first and second are shown as known by the function making the call.
Figure 3.5 shows memory immediately after the last assignment in swap(). Nothing in the execution of this defective version of swap() can possibly change
first and second.

If the actual argument corresponding to a formal pass-by-value argument is a
variable, then that variable will not be changed to a new value as a result of
changes in the formal argument. An actual argument corresponding to a formal
value argument provides one-way communication from the calling code to the
function. Value arguments protect against unwanted side effects to their actual

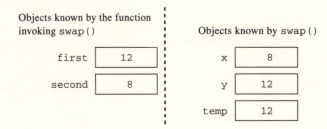

Objects known by the function
invoking swap()

first	12

second	8

Objects known by swap()

x	8

y	12

temp	12

Figure 3.5 Memory model for the end of execution of swap(first,second).
This is a defective version of swap().

arguments. In `swap()`, however, the last thing that we want is protection. We want a change in the actual arguments.

Pass-by-reference arguments

In order to get side effects when they are wanted, C++ offers another kind of formal argument known as a **pass-by-reference argument** or simply a **reference argument**. Programmers use reference arguments when they want the value of an actual argument to change as a result of executing the function. That means, of course, that the actual argument corresponding to a formal reference argument should be an object, not just an expression.

Let's rewrite `swap()` to use reference arguments. This is a correct implementation satisfying the function's specifications.

```
void swap(int& x, int& y)
// Arguments:
//   x - in - A variable
//       out - A variable whose value is the original value of y
//   y - in - A variable
//       out - A variable whose value is the original value of x
// Side effect: The values in the actual argument variables are interchanged.
{
    int temp = x;       // Temporary buffer to hold the original value of x
    x = y;
    y = temp;
}
```

The symbol `&` is called an ampersand. The ampersand after the `int` type tells the compiler that this is a reference argument. The ampersand can appear anywhere between the `int` and the name of the formal argument. The following declarations for `swap()` are equivalent:

```
void swap(int & x, int & y);
void swap(int& x, int& y);
void swap(int &x, int &y);
void swap(int&x,int&y);
```

Our documentation for a formal reference argument contains the word "in" if the value of the formal argument is important when the function begins execution. It contains the word "out" if the value of the formal argument is important when the function completes execution (when there is a side effect for the actual argument).

In the new, correct version of `swap()`, both of the formal arguments provide two-way communication between the calling code and the function. That is, their values coming into and coming out of the function are important. The documentation uses the labels "in" and "out" to describe this.

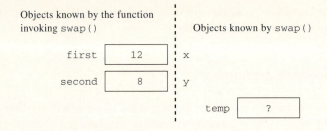

Figure 3.6 Memory model for the beginning of execution of swap(first,second). This is the *correct* version of swap().

What happens when the correct version of swap() is called? For a value argument, a new object for the formal argument is created and initialized with the value of the actual argument. For a reference argument, no new object is created. Instead, *the name of the formal argument becomes another name for the actual argument while the function is executing.* What does that mean with the correct version of swap()? Suppose the following statement executed:

swap(first,second);

During the execution of swap(), x becomes another name for the data object known in main() as first and y becomes another name for the data object known in main() as second. The data object named temp is known only in swap(). Figure 3.6 illustrates the memory model for the invocation of the new, correct version of swap().

In the memory model of the call to the correct version of swap(), x appears beside the box for the object whose name in main() is first. We use this drawing scheme to illustrate that x is a new name for an object that already exists when the function is invoked. Similarly, since y is a formal reference argument, y becomes a new name for an object that already exists.

Figure 3.7 shows the memory model at the end of execution of swap(first,second). Notice how the values of the actual arguments first and second have changed.

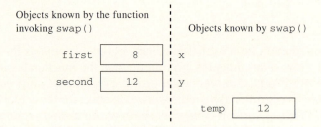

Figure 3.7 Memory model for the end of execution of swap(first, second). This is the *correct* version of swap().

Using reference arguments to establish values for variable objects

The function swap() is used to exchange the contents of two variables. It updates its two actual arguments, a process that is a typical use of reference arguments. Another common use of reference arguments is to establish values for variables. In this case, the formal reference argument provides one-way communication from the function to the calling code. The only purpose of readInteger() is to establish a value for its actual argument.

```
void readInteger(int& aNumber)
// Argument:  aNumber - out - Integer entered by the user
// Side effect: Reads aNumber from cin.
{
    cin >> aNumber;
}
```

Here is how readInteger() can be invoked:

```
int amount;
readInteger(amount);
```

The behavior of this function is very crude for the person who is actually entering a number. Most good programs would prompt the user to enter data rather than just showing a cursor on the screen and hoping for the best. Let's write a new function inputInt() with slightly different specifications. It will tell the user exactly what input is expected. So inputInt() will have two formal arguments: the number to be read and the prompt.

```
void inputInt(int& aNumber, const char prompt[])
// Arguments:
//   aNumber - out - The integer entered by the user
//   prompt - Prompt message to be displayed
// Side effect: Prompts for and reads aNumber.
{
    cout << prompt;
    cin >> aNumber;
}
```

The first formal argument type, int&, is a reference to an integer type. The second formal argument type, const char[], is a string type. Chapter 6 will focus on exactly what is meant by a string type. For now, think of an actual argument the same as a string literal like "Enter a number: ".

Any call to inputInt() must have two actual arguments: an int variable and a prompting message. Here's an example:

```
inputInt(amount,"Enter a number: ");
```

You can think of the code that is being executed at this point like this:

```
cout << "Enter a number ";
cin >> amount;
```

Of course, this code is not part of the actual program. The formal argument `prompt` means the actual argument `"Enter a number: "`, and the formal argument `aNumber` means the actual argument `amount`. At least that is the correspondence for this particular function call.

As another illustration of how to use the new `inputInt()`, suppose `width`, `depth`, and `height` are `int` type variables that represent the dimensions of a box. The following three calls to `inputInt()` get values for them.

```
inputInt(width, "Enter width of box in inches: ");
inputInt(depth, "Enter depth of box in inches: ");
inputInt(height, "Enter height of box in inches: ");
```

For each of these function calls, `aNumber` and `prompt` correspond to different things altogether. And that is part of the beauty of functions. We do not have to write four different pairs of statements to write a prompt and read a number. We can get by with only one pair.

The input objects of the convenience store and the changemaker problems were designed to read numbers. If we redesign them to prompt the user and then read, we could use `inputInt()` or something very much like it to implement the behavior of those input objects.

Functions can have reference arguments as well as value arguments in the same formal argument list. The only syntactic difference between the two kinds of arguments is that a formal reference argument has an ampersand, `&`, to modify its type name. The following function `writeCheck()` has both kinds of arguments. It could be used as a method for a checking account object.

```
void writeCheck (float debit, float& balance, float& overdraft)
// Arguments:
//     debit - Amount of money to be debited from the account
//         (ASSUME: debit >= 0)
//     balance - in  - Amount of money in the account
//             - out - Amount of money after recording the debit
//     overdraft - out - 0.0 if the balance was large enough to cover the
//         debit. Otherwise, the amount that the debit exceeds the balance.
// Side effect: Decrease the balance to reflect a withdrawal of the debit
//     If the balance becomes negative, set the overdraft to show the deficit.
{
    balance -= debit;
    if (balance < 0.0)
        overdraft = -balance;
    else
        overdraft = .0;
}
```

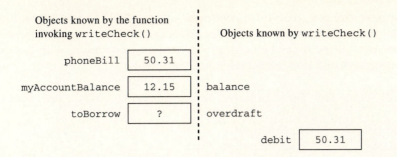
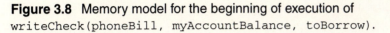

Figure 3.8 Memory model for the beginning of execution of
writeCheck(phoneBill, myAccountBalance, toBorrow).

Let's now look at some code to call writeCheck(). Suppose myAccountBalance is a float representing the balance of a checking account, phoneBill is a float representing a check that was written off that account, and toBorrow is a float representing the amount of money to borrow from the bank in order to keep myAccountBalance out of the red (with a negative balance). The following invocation of writeCheck() will change the balance according to the amount of the check and indicate how much should be borrowed from the bank to cover the overdraft created by paying the phone bill.

```
writeCheck(phoneBill,myAccountBalance,toBorrow);
```

Assume phoneBill has a value of 50.31 and myAccountBalance has a value of 12.15. Figure 3.8 shows the memory model at the beginning of the invocation of writeCheck().

Figure 3.9 shows the memory model at the end of execution of the call. Notice that the values of both myAccountBalance and toBorrow change as a result of the call while the value of phoneBill remains the same.

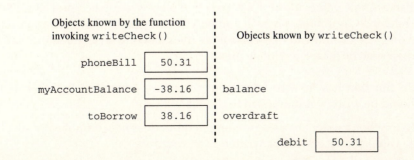

Figure 3.9 Memory model for the end of execution of
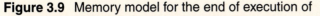
writeCheck(phoneBill, myAccountBalance, toBorrow).

Our next example, `divMod()`, performs integer division in a single function call. Integer division results in a divisor and a remainder, so `divMod()` needs to compute two values. It can be naturally written as a procedure with two formal value arguments and two formal reference arguments.

```
void divMod(int numerator, int denominator, int& quotient, int& remainder)
// Arguments:
//    numerator, denominator - two integers
//       (ASSUME: numerator >= 0; denominator > 0)
//    quotient - out - The quotient of numerator/denominator
//    remainder - out - The remainder of numerator/denominator
// Side effect: Finds the result of integer division of numerator/denominator.
{
    quotient = numerator / denominator;
    remainder = numerator % denominator;
}
```

The calls to `divMod()` should have numeric expressions for the first two actual arguments and `int` variables for the last two. In addition, the first actual argument should be nonnegative and the second actual argument should be strictly positive. Here are some sample calls:

```
int x;
int y;
divMod(47,8,x,y);          // x is 5, y is 7
divMod(x,2,x,y);           // x is 2, y is 1
divMod(26,4 * y,y,x);      // x is 2, y is 6
```

Whether you write a function to return a value or a procedure depends somewhat on your individual programming style. Most programmers would write a function that has no side effects but that returns a single result as a function that returns a value. That is part of the culture of C++ programming.

If the purpose of a function is to carry out a command such as "display the result," then it is usually written as a procedure. If a function needs to compute more than a single value, most programmers would write it as a procedure with formal reference arguments for each value to be computed. There are also exceptions to this. We recommend that you follow the following style guidelines unless you have a specific reason to violate them.

- If a function has no side effects but computes a single value, then it should be written as a function that returns a value.

- If a function carries out a single command but does not compute any single value, then it should be written as a procedure.

- If a function has more than one side effect, then it should usually be written as procedure with a reference argument for each side effect. (A popular exception to this is a function that may be unable to perform its intended operation. In that case, the function may return a value that indicates the success or failure of its operation.)

3.3 █ Scopes and lifetimes

In all of the previous examples we have not had to worry about confusions over names. All of the names in each program were unique. But that will not always be the case. Some names, like x and y, are so popular that you will be tempted to use them in a variety of different functions. And in situations where many programmers are writing code for the same program, it would be a terrible inconvenience if they had to tell each other which names they were using to avoid duplicating those names in different functions.

In this section, we will see how the compiler deals with apparent name conflicts and we will find out what is legal and what is not. We will also trace our examples using memory models to help explain what is happening.

Names are created through declarations. Since a definition is a kind of declaration, names are created through definitions also. A declaration associates a name (an identifier) with an object or a function. Each declaration has exactly one name, but the same name can be used in different declarations. The **scope of a declaration** is the set of lines in the program where the name introduced by that declaration refers to the object or function being declared. When there is only one declaration of a name, it is common to talk about the **scope** of that name, meaning the scope of that sole declaration of the name.

A **global declaration** is a declaration that is made outside any block. Since every function body is a block, a global declaration cannot occur in the body of a function. The scope of the identifier for a global declaration extends from the point of its declaration to the end of the file in which it is declared. Such declarations are said to have **file scope**.

Objects that are declared inside the body of a function are called **local** to the function. They have **block scope**. The name of a local identifier can be used from the point of its declaration to the end of the block in which it is declared.

Formal function arguments are considered to have block scope, even though they are not actually declared inside any block. Their names can be used anywhere in the blocks that are the bodies of their corresponding functions. The scope of a formal argument name includes the body of its function.

Figure 3.10 illustrates our first example of scoping: a program in which all of the identifier names are unique. The boxes around the code show scoping of identifiers and declarations. (This program does not do anything. It is just used as an illustration.)

The variable y is global. Its scope extends to the end of the file. The scope of z extends from its definition to the end of main(). The scope of a extends from its definition through the inner block of main() in which it is declared. The scope of s and t is the body of f(). The scope of r extends to the end of the body of f().

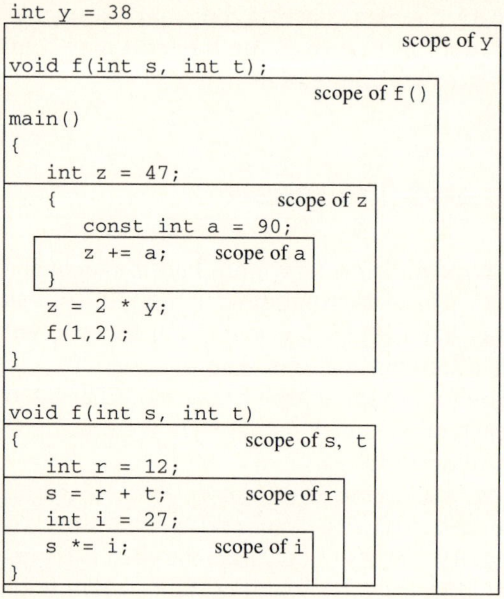

```
int y = 38
                                                     scope of y
void f(int s,  int t);
                                            scope of f()
main()
{
    int z = 47;
    {                                 scope of z
         const int a = 90;
             z += a;        scope of a
    }
    z = 2 * y;
    f(1,2);
}

void f(int s,  int t)
{                                    scope of s,  t
    int r = 12;
    s = r + t;              scope of r
    int i = 27;
    s *= i;            scope of i
}
```

Figure 3.10 An illustration of identifier scope.

The scope of i, which is defined after r, does not include any code in the body of f() that appears above its definition.

It is possible to have a local object with the same name as a global object. If the scope of the global declaration includes the scope of the local declaration, we say the local declaration **hides** the global one in its scope or that the global declaration is not **visible**. The use of the name in the local scope refers to the local declaration and not to the global declaration.

It is also possible to have two objects with the same name that are declared in the same function. The only way for the scope of the first one to include the scope of the second one is if the second one is declared in a block that is nested inside the block of the first. Again we say that the second declaration hides the first in its scope. The use of the name in the inner scope refers to the inner local declaration, not to the outer local declaration. The lifetime of the inner object extends from the time its definition is executed to the time the block in which it is defined quits execution.[4] C++ uses the following rule to determine which identifier matches which declaration.

> An identifier matches the declaration that precedes and is closest to its use and lies within the same scope.

---

[4] Programmers can create blocks to limit scopes of declarations (thus avoiding name conflicts) and to limit lifetimes of objects (for program efficiency).

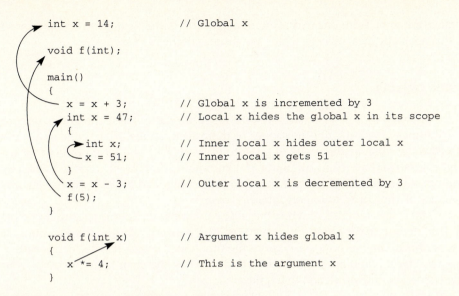

```
int x = 14;              // Global x

void f(int);

main()
{
    x = x + 3;           // Global x is incremented by 3
    int x = 47;          // Local x hides the global x in its scope
    {
        int x;           // Inner local x hides outer local x
        x = 51;          // Inner local x gets 51
    }
    x = x - 3;           // Outer local x is decremented by 3
    f(5);
}

void f(int x)            // Argument x hides global x
{
    x *= 4;              // This is the argument x
}
```

Figure 3.11 Hiding identifiers in their scopes.

It is easy to read the C++ matching and scoping rule and still not quite understand what is going on. The purpose of the program shown in Fig. 3.11 is to illustrate scopes of declarations of objects with the same names. All of the objects and arguments are named x. Rather than enclose all of the scopes in boxes, we illustrate which use of x matches which declaration of x. (The separate declaration for f() uses the function signature.)

No sane programmer would write code such as this. But this program is legal, and it is not too difficult to figure out what each occurrence of x means.

The **lifetime** of an object is the time during program execution when memory is allocated to the object. When the sample program is executed, the data object named y is created and exists for the entire execution of the program. The memory originally allocated to y remains allocated to y throughout program execution. The lifetime of y is the entire time the program is executing. When main() is executed, z comes into existence. It also remains in existence until the end of program execution. When the call to f() is made from main(), data objects named s and t are created. Their lifetimes extend to the end of execution of the function call. The lifetime of r is from the time of execution of its definition inside f() until the end execution of the call to f().

The lifetime of a formal value argument is the same as the time of execution of the function. The lifetime of a local object is similar. A local object is created when its definition is executed in the body of the function, and it dies when the function quits execution.

When the lifetime of an object is over, you cannot refer to that object. You cannot resurrect it. If the function is called again, then the definition will be executed again, creating a brand new object. Do not expect the values of local objects to remain the same from one execution of a function to the next. (The one exception to this are static local objects, which we discuss in the next section.)

Static objects

There are two kinds of local objects: **static** and **automatic**. These categories refer to the lifetimes of objects, not the scopes of their declarations. (The scope of a static object is the same as the scope of an automatic object.) The local objects that we have seen so far have been automatic. An automatic local object is created when its definition is executed. When the function containing its definition finishes execution, the lifetime of an automatic object is over.

A static object is created when the code containing its definition is first executed. The definition for a static object is executed only once during the execution of a program, no matter how many times the function in which it is defined is called. A static object is initialized only once and it exists and maintains its value from one execution of the function to the next.

A static object does not die after a function is executed only to be recreated when the function is called again. The lifetime of a static object begins with the execution of the first call to the function in which it is defined. A static object dies at the end of program execution.

A local object that is static must have the keyword static at the beginning of its definition. That is the only thing distinguishing it from a local object that is not static.

Consider the following function definition.

```
int f(int x)
{
    static int y = 3;        // Definition and initialization of y
    y += x;
    return y;
}
```

What happens when this initial call to f() is made?

```
cout << f(1) << endl;    // Output is 4
```

The local variable y is defined and initialized to 3. When the function quits execution, the value of y is 4.

Now consider this subsequent call:

```
cout << f(1) << endl;    // Output is 5
```

When the function begins execution, the definition of y is *not* executed. However, the data object y does exist having the value 4. When the function quits execution, the value of y is 5.

Finally, let's continue with the following call.

```
cout << f(2) << endl;    // Output is 7
```

When the function begins execution, y has the value 5. When it quits execution, the value of y is 7.

Function arguments

We turn now to the problem of scoping with respect to argument names and function calls. Confusion is most likely to occur over which name goes with which data object.

Identifier scope and lifetime make arguments very important. Arguments provide the major communication links between functions. If one function must know the value or location of an object belonging to another function, then one way that information can be communicated is through arguments or a return value. The only other way that two different functions can use the same object is if it has a global declaration.

The following is the definition for a new function f(). We will trace calls to f() with different arguments.

```
void f(int x, int& y)
{
    int w = 22;
    x += y;
    y = w + x;
}
```

The first call is straightforward.

```
{
...
    int x = 13;
    int y = 14;
    int w = 37;
    f(x,y);
    // x is 13, y is 49, w is 37
...
}
```

Let's use the memory model technique for tracing execution of the code. Observe that there are two different uses of the identifier w and two different data objects with the same name. One is local to the function f() and the other is local to the block containing the call to f(). Similarly, the formal arguments named x and y are not the same as the data objects named x and y, which are local to the calling

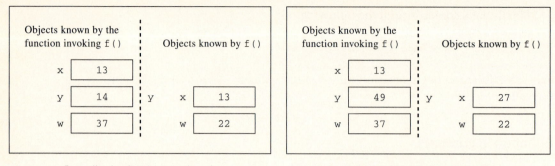

Immediately after the execution of
int w = 22; inside f()

At the end of execution of f(x,y)

Figure 3.12 Memory models for execution of f(x,y). The model on the left is near the beginning of execution of f(); the model on the right is immediately after the end of execution of the last statement of f().

code. But none of that should be a problem as long as we realize that while f() is executing, the names in the body of f() refer to the identifiers known to f(). In Fig. 3.12, those identifiers known to f() are on the right sides of the dotted lines.

Changes in the objects x and w that are local to f() (located to the right of the dotted line) did not effect the values of the objects x and w that are local to the calling code (located to the left of the dotted line).

We made the next call f() deliberately confusing. We switched the actual arguments x and y, making the call f(y,x). The first actual argument is y, so it corresponds to the formal argument x. The second actual argument x corresponds to the formal argument y.

```
{
...
    int x = 13;
    int y = 14;
    int w = 37;
    f(y,x);
    // x is 49, y is 14, w is 37
...
}
```

Figure 3.13 shows the memory model for the call f(y,x).

Our final example shows how a single argument can be used more than once. We'll use w as both the first and the second actual arguments for the call to f().

```
{...
    int x = 13;
    int y = 14;
```

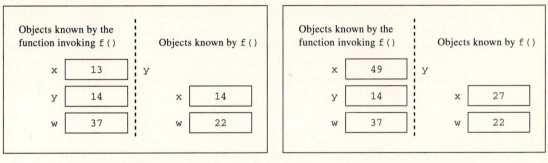

Immediately after the execution of
int w = 22; inside f()

At the end of execution of f(y,x)

Figure 3.13 Memory models for execution of f(x,y).

```
int w = 37;
f(w,w);
// x is 13,  y is 14, w is 96
...
}
```

Figure 3.14 illustrates the call f(w,w).

Although we have sometimes resorted to using global data objects in the first few chapters of this book, we do not like them for several reasons. They make any function that uses them less general and the code in that function is bound to a particular data object and will not be able to work on a variety of data. Furthermore, the information that only a single design object should know can be accessed by other objects. In object-oriented program development, however, data that is owned by a single object should not be accessible to another except by

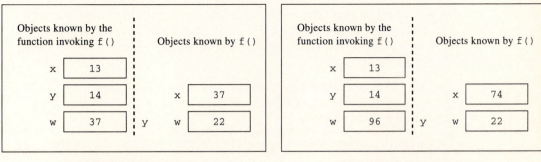

Immediately after the execution of
int w = 22; inside f()

At the end of execution of f(w,w)

Figure 3.14 Memory models for execution of f(w,w).

explicit permission of the owner through a function call with the data as an actual argument.

You will see an example of global constants in our next version of the change-maker program. Later in this text, when we discuss how to encapsulate all of the data and functions that make up an object into a single class, we will be able to get rid of these globals.

3.4 Programming errors and functions

If all the tools that programmers used were very simple tools, perhaps all of their mistakes would be simple mistakes—and all of their programs would be simple programs. New tools lead to more programming power and more opportunities to make errors. Novice programmers typically encounter several different kinds of errors when they first start writing functions. This should not discourage them from using functions, because the payoff for using them is so impressive.

The most common programming errors for novice (and occasionally for experienced) programmers fall into two categories: (1) syntax errors and (2) usage errors. The following are syntax errors to which we all fall victim:

- Failing to place a prototype for the function before `main()`.

- Having a different function header in the definition from that in its prototype.

- Placing a semicolon after the function header and before its body in the definition. The compiler treats the header and semicolon as a separate declaration that is independent of the block following it. The compiler interprets the block as "free floating" and not part of any function, which is an error.

- Mismatching formal and actual arguments. When a function is called, the call should have the same number of actual arguments as there are formal arguments. The actual argument types must be compatible with the formal argument types. This does not mean that the types must match exactly. (The C++ compiler will make conversions when it can to force a match.)

- Using a call to a procedure as an operand in an assignment expression or in an input or output expression. A procedure is a void function; a procedure call has no value.

- Failing to put parentheses in a call to a function with no arguments.

- Using an identifier in one function that is local to a different function.

Usage errors are not syntax errors. They frequently create unanticipated and unwanted results. Sometimes the results will lead to runtime errors and sometimes to corruption or loss of data. The following are errors in usage that programmers often commit:

- Using pass-by-value arguments when the intent is to change the corresponding actual argument. If one of the intents of the function is to change an object, then the corresponding formal argument should be pass-by-reference.

- Using a reference argument when no side effects on the actual argument are intended.

- Not using a variable as an actual argument for a reference argument. Many compilers treat this as a syntax error. Some compilers allow a programmer to use something like a literal, an arithmetic expression, or a constant as an actual argument for a formal reference argument. (The actual argument will not change in that situation since C++ creates a temporary object to take the place of the actual argument.)

- Returning from a function too early. Remember that a function quits execution as soon as a return statement is executed. If there are several return statements, there is a possibility that the function will be exited before all of the statements in the function are executed.

Other errors fall into the category of poor programming decision errors, some of which are propagated from the analysis and design phases to the programming phase. There are no obvious admonitions to give at this point, but here are some things that should alert you to poor design or poor implementation:

- Creating global data objects simply to avoid argument passing. This gives all objects access to common data. The programming principle that object-oriented designers and programmers enforce perhaps most vigorously is called **information hiding**—the rule that an object should know its own attributes, that access to those attributes must be limited to the object, and that an object's attributes should be changed only by the object's methods. It is a principle that you will appreciate as you become more experienced.

- Writing a function that is "too long." Programmers usually have several rules of thumb about when a function is too long. For example, a function that runs over a page in length is probably too long and is trying to do too many things. In terms of object-oriented programming, functions that are too long are evidence of objects that are too complicated. Objects and their behaviors or methods should be simple.

- Writing `main()` so that it is too long. (Remember that `main()` is actually a function.)

- Writing a function whose argument lists are too long. That may indicate that a message to the corresponding object is too complicated, which means that the object itself is too complicated.

- Failing to document a function so that a programmer who uses the function cannot tell by looking at the interface (prototype and documentation) what the function is supposed to do and what will be its side effects.

3.5 Refining object-oriented designs

Objects have attributes and behaviors. The behaviors of objects are called their **methods**. In C++, methods can be implemented as functions. In Chapter 1, the two designs we created for two problems were made with the idea that the only programming tools that were available were those found in Chapter 2, which covered only the bare essentials for C++ programming. Our initial strategy was simple: come up with the simplest design and simplest implementation possible in the context of these primitive tools.

We drew pictures for our designs and learned that objects in models interact with each other. In object-oriented lingo, they communicate with each other by sending **messages** and receiving replies. In our old design diagrams, we did not show how the objects communicated. We realized at the time we created these designs that we did not really know enough to separate code for one object from the rest of the code in the implementation. All we could rely on were comments.

Now we know about C++ functions and can refine the old designs to take advantage of functions. We will be able to encapsulate or represent some objects completely within single functions, including what the objects know and what they can do. For other objects, we will be able to implement their behaviors in functions. Our new representation still will not be perfect, but it will be better than what we had before.

We are going to change the old designs in light of this new programming tool. The programs that will implement these new designs will execute much the same as our old programs but with a couple of minor improvements in the user interfaces. The new designs and their corresponding programs will be easier to modify to suit changing specifications.

The messages and replies that constitute object communications will show up in the actual implementation code as function calls, arguments, and return values. The specification for each message will show up in the function's header documentation, and the communication of information will show up in the new design diagrams as arrows.

Redesigning the solution to the convenience store problem

Using our new language features, let's go back and redesign the solutions to old problems, beginning with the convenience store problem. We'll update the specification for the solution so that the user will be prompted to enter an amount in pennies. That will allow someone besides your uncle, who already knows how to work the calculator, to run the program and have an idea of what kind of data is to be entered. We can improve the specifications even more if the display shows the user not only the answer but also what that answer means. That should eliminate confusion on the part of the user with respect to pennies per pound and dollars per kilogram.

New specifications do not automatically determine how to make new design decisions. Where does the prompt belong? Who owns it? Where does the explanation of the answer belong? One could argue that the prompt belongs to the input object and that the explanation belongs to the output object. But that would mean those objects were very special-purpose indeed. Instead, we will place ownership of those two items with the calculator itself. This makes the input and output objects usable in other designs and other programs. The calculator remains special-purpose, but it has some generic pieces.

We can reuse our old design to assign ownership of all of the constant items (pennies per dollar, Canadian dollars per U.S. dollars, and kilograms per pound) to the computing object. But who should own the information that varies from one execution of the program to the next regarding the pennies per pound (the user's input) and the answer (the program output—Canadian dollars per kilogram)? That's not a very hard question to answer at this point. Clearly, the information that varies should not belong to the input or output objects. Those objects do not care what they read and what they display. They just transmit information between the calculator and the user. We'll place the information that varies with the calculator itself.

How does the calculator get the values to be entered by your uncle and how does it get the answer? It can ask the input object to get the pennies per pound and it can ask the computing object to calculate the answer. The calculator asks the input object to get the pennies per pound by sending it a message. In order for the input object to prompt the user, the message that the calculator object sends to the input object must include that prompt. The input object will reply to the calculator object with an integer value.

The calculator will ask the computing object for the answer. Since the computing object needs to know the price of the item in pennies per pound, the calculator will send along this information when it makes its request. In other words, the message that the calculator object sends the computing object includes the pennies per pound as part of the message. The computing object will reply to the calculator object with the answer.

The output object is the only object that can show the user what that answer is. The calculator object can send a message to the output object to display the answer along with an explanation of the answer. Again, the information that the calculator must send to the output object the display is the answer itself and the explanation.

The directions of the lines and arrows in Fig. 3.15 show how information is communicated among the objects.

It is now time to implement the new design with a program. The computing object, the input object, and the output object will be encapsulated into separate functions. The behavior of the calculator object will be in `main()`. Messages from one object to another will be function calls.

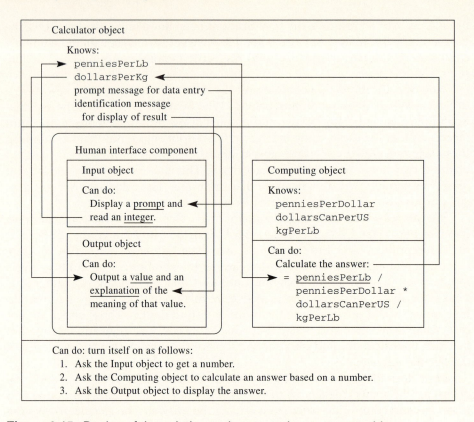

Figure 3.15 Design of the solution to the convenience store problem.

Reimplementing the solution to the convenience store problem

It will be easy to implement the new design in C++, and we can even use some of our old code and certainly the old variable and constant definitions.

It is not usually possible to encapsulate an entire object within a single function. But the objects in the convenience store problem are exceptions. All of the objects in the solution to the problem can be implemented as single functions.

Let's start with the computing object. Using the old constant identifiers, the computing object's attributes are kgPerLb, dollarsCanPerUS, and penniesPerDollar. These can be local data objects for a function that implements the computing object.

In order for the computing object to compute, it must be sent a message. According to the design diagram, part of the message is the price of an item in U.S. pennies per pound. A message is a function call. The actual argument in the call is an integer representing that U.S. price. When the computing object is sent such a message, it replies with the answer, the price per kilogram of an item in Canadian dollars. The reply is the function's return value.

A good name for the function that encapsulates the computing object is priceCanadian. Its type can be double. The specification of its interface consists of the function declaration and the header documentation.

```
double priceCanadian(int priceUS);
// Argument: priceUS - Price per pound of an item in US pennies.
// Returns: Price in Canadian dollars per kilogram for the item.
```

The implementation of the computing object is its definition.

```
double priceCanadian(int priceUS)
{
    const double kgPerLb = .45;              // Number of kilograms in a pound
    const double dollarsCanPerUS = 1.26;     // Number of Canadian dollars per
                                             //  U.S. dollar (exchange rate)
    const double penniesPerDollar = 100;     // Number of U.S. pennies in a
                                             //  U.S. dollar
    return priceUS/kgPerLb * dollarsCanPerUS/penniesPerDollar;
}
```

Like the computing object, the output object has only one behavior. We will implement it as a single function with two arguments. Sending the output object a message to print the answer means calling its function with the answer to be printed and the label indicating what that answer means. We'll call the function that represents the output object outputDouble(), a name that sounds like the task it has to do. Its interface specification is as follows:

```
void outputDouble(double aNumber, const char label[]);
// Arguments:
//  aNumber - The number to be displayed
//  label - An explanation of the number which is displayed
// Side effect: Displays aNumber on the screen followed by a newline.
```

The second formal argument is a label for the number that will be displayed. The implementation of the output object method is a four-liner, including its header and enclosing braces.

```
void outputDouble(double aNumber, const char label[])
{
    cout << label << aNumber << endl;
}
```

The method for the input object will prompt the user for an integer and read the number that the user enters. The reply that the input object returns in response to a message is the value that was read. There are two acceptable ways to implement the input object as a function: (1) the function can return a value, which is the integer that was read, or (2) it can use a reference argument whose value is assigned the integer that was read. By choosing the reference argument, we can reuse the code that we wrote earlier in this chapter, the function `inputInt()`.

The calculator object is different from the other objects in that it has no visible interface. The calculator object is implemented through `main()`.

```cpp
// Name: Convenience store owner
// Version: 2.0
// Purpose: Convert the price of an item in U.S. pennies per pound to
//    Canadian dollars per kilogram.
#include <iostream.h>
#include <iomanip.h>


//--------------------------- interfaces ---------------------------
double priceCanadian(int priceUS);
// Argument: priceUS - Price per pound of an item in US pennies.
// Returns: Price in Canadian dollars per kilogram for the item.

void inputInt(int& aNumber, const char prompt[]);
// Arguments:
//    aNumber - out - Integer entered by the user
//    prompt - Message displayed to the user
// Side effect: Prompts for and reads aNumber.

void outputDouble(double aNumber, const char label[]);
// Arguments:
//    aNumber - Number to be displayed
//    label - An explanation of the number which is displayed.
// Side effect: Displays aNumber on the screen followed by a newline
//    Numeric output is set to fixed decimal form with precision 2.
//------------------------- end of interfaces ---------------------------

//------------------- calculator object implementation ----------------------
void main()
{
   double dollarsPerKg;   // Item's cost in Canadian dollars per kilogram
   int penniesPerLb;      // Price in U.S. pennies per pound of an item

   inputInt(penniesPerLb,"Enter the item price in pennies per pound: ");
   dollarsPerKg = priceCanadian(penniesPerLb);
   outputDouble(dollarsPerKg,
         "The item price in Canadian dollars per kilogram is $");
}
//-------------- end of calculator object implementation -------------------

//------------------- computing object implementation ----------------------
```

```
double priceCanadian(int priceUS)
{
    const double kgPerLb = .45;              // Number of kilograms in a pound
    const double dollarsCanPerUS = 1.26;     // Number of Canadian dollars per
                                             //  U.S. dollar (exchange rate)
    const int penniesPerDollar = 100;        // Number of pennies in a U.S. dollar

    return priceUS/kgPerLb * dollarsCanPerUS/penniesPerDollar;
}
//--------------- end of computing object implementation ------------------

//-------------------- input object implementation ----------------------
void inputInt(int& aNumber, const char prompt[])
{
    cout << prompt;
    cin >> aNumber;
}
//--------------- end of input object implementation --------------------

//-------------------- output object implementation ----------------------
void outputDouble(double aNumber, const char label[])
{
    cout << setiosflags(ios::fixed) << setprecision(2)
         << label << aNumber << endl;
}
//--------------- end of output object implementation --------------------
```

Our new program is not quite as short as the old one, but you can tell which code belongs to which object. Later on, if we want to change the specifications again, the modifications will be easy to make. That's partly because we have separated the program into distinct and almost independent pieces. The objects do not interfere with each other's code. Hopefully a change in one object will not mean that code for another one must also be changed.

Redesigning and reimplementing the changemaker problem

As was the case with the original solution to the convenience store problem, the first solution to the changemaker problem did not prompt the user for input. That suggests one specification change: the user will be prompted for the amount to change. An additional specification that we can easily include is to have an introductory banner appear on the screen when the program begins execution.

Those two specification changes force us to modify the old design, but we will not settle for only those two. In the new design, we will show the communication that takes place among the various objects. In addition we will change the format of a message to the output object. A message to the output object must contain a number and a label to explain the meaning of the number. (Haven't we seen that somewhere before?)

The new changemaker input object can be just like the one used for the convenience store. Let's reuse it. The new changemaker output object, which is simpler than the old one, isn't going to be entirely new either. It is the same as the new convenience store output object, except that the explanation (label) will be printed after the number rather than before it. Let's use the convenience store output object for the changemaker.

How do the input object, the teller object, and the output object interact? First of all, the prompt can be known by the teller object. The interaction between the input object and the teller object in the changemaker design is identical to the interaction between the input object and the calculator object in the convenience store design. Good. That means we can even reuse the calculator object–input object communication lines from the convenience store owner design.

So what do we have so far? The teller object will begin by displaying a banner and asking the input object to get the amount of money to change. Everything has been pretty simple up to now. What happens next? In the old design, the computing object could compute an entire labeled sequence of values all at once. In the new design, the teller object will not be able to send the output object a message to display an entire sequence of numbers and their corresponding labels all at once. Instead, the teller object must send eight messages to the output object, one message for each denomination. Each message has the same format: output a single integer and a single label for that integer.

Since the output object can only accept a single number and corresponding label at one time, the computing object must be able to figure out one denomination count at a time. The computing object does not generate an entire sequence of values all at once. It computes only a single count for a single denomination. Each time the computing object computes a count for a denomination, it reduces the amount left to distribute accordingly. The teller object uses the computing object eight different times, once for each denomination.

All of this sounds more complicated than it really is. The effective change that we have made is to replace a sequence of values with a sequence of messages. We have simplified the computing object and the output object based on the idea that each should do one thing, rather than eight things, at a time. The teller object is more complicated, however. It must send eight simple messages to the output and computing objects rather than one message to the computing object and one message to the output object. Figure 3.16 illustrates our new design.

The new implementation of the changemaker design will clearly use functions. Should there be any other difference between the new program and the old one? To answer this question, let's take another look at the problem specifications. Here is the original statement of the problem:

Write a computer program that can take an amount and computes the count of bills and coins of each denomination required to sum to the amount.

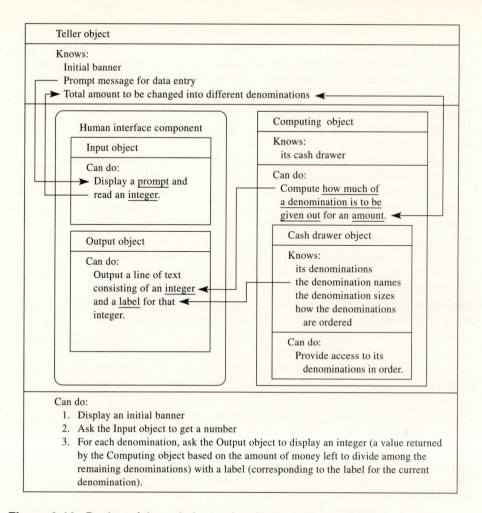

Figure 3.16 Design of the solution to the changemaker problem.

Recall the assumptions on which the original solution was based. One was that all currency was to be U.S. currency; another was that there were eight denominations ranging from $20 bills to pennies; a third was that the supply for each denomination was unlimited. Our final solution was explicitly tailored to those assumptions. It did not handle any generalities at all.

It is impossible to anticipate all of the likely uses for a program that solves this kind of problem. Our old program would fail on anything besides U.S. currency. What happens if the user wants to switch to pounds or francs from dollars? Right now, we do not have the tools to be able to create a truly generic solution. What we can do is make the program as general as possible in order to make future changes a little easier to implement. Problems change over time, and problem solutions must change with them.

The way we can now anticipate future changes is to give the functions that belong to the computing object generic names. For example, the name of the function that returns the number of $20 bills can be `countForDenom1()` rather than `countOfTwenties()`. This does not make the code more general in terms of how it executes, and it unfortunately makes the code harder to read. But it does remind us of possible future changes in specifications.

Our new program is significantly longer than the original one, but it offers several improvements. The objects are more clearly delineated by functions. Except for the global constant declarations that belong to the cash drawer object, the computing object and the output object do not share code.

As you read this program, compare it to the original changemaker program as well as to the latest convenience store program. There are several things to notice. Since the input objects for both problems behave exactly the same, the implementation of the input object from the convenience store program can be reused in this program. The output objects also behave the same except for the order in which the number and the label are displayed. We can look at the convenience store output object to see how we might implement the changemaker object.

The implementation of the cash drawer object is very similar to its original implementation. The difference is that in the new implementation, it consists of global definitions rather than definitions local to `main()`. By making the definitions global, each function thus has access to them. If they were local, they would have to be passed as arguments in the function calls. We did protect them against possible change by declaring all of the definitions that implement the cash drawer to be constant.

Finally, observe how little work is done in `main()`. The code of `main()` represents the behavior of the teller object. The teller object relies on the input object, the computing object, and the output object to do most of the substantial work.

```
// Name: The changemaker
// Version: 2.0
// Purpose: Determine the count of each denomination from twenty dollar bills
//    down through pennies that constitute a given monetary amount.

#include <iostream.h>

//---------------------------- interfaces ---------------------------
void inputInt(int& aNumber, const char prompt[]);
// Arguments:
//    aNumber - out - Integer entered by the user
//    prompt - Message displayed to the user
// Side effect: Prompts for and reads aNumber.

void outputLine(int aNumber, const char aString[]);
// Arguments:
//    aNumber - Integer to be displayed
```

```
//    aString - Message displayed to identify the output
// Side effect: Display a number and message followed by a newline.

void divMod(int numerator, int denominator, int& quotient, int& remainder);
// Arguments:
//    numerator, denominator - two integers
//       ASSUME: numerator >= 0; denominator > 0
//    quotient - out - The quotient of numerator/denominator
//    remainder - out - The remainder of numerator/denominator
// Side effect: Find the result of integer division of numerator/denominator.

int countForDenom1(int& amountLeft);
int countForDenom2(int& amountLeft);
int countForDenom3(int& amountLeft);
int countForDenom4(int& amountLeft);
int countForDenom5(int& amountLeft);
int countForDenom6(int& amountLeft);
int countForDenom7(int& amountLeft);
int countForDenom8(int& amountLeft);
// int countForDenomN(int& amountLeft)
//    Argument:
//    amountLeft - in - Amount from which to give out the Nth denomination
//                      (ASSUME: amountLeft >= 0.)
//               - out - Remainder of the amount after giving out the
//                       the Nth denomination
//    Returns: The count of the Nth denomination in theAmount
//    (Side effect: Reduce amountLeft by the amount of the Nth denomination)

//------------------------- end of interfaces -------------------------

//------------------ cash drawer object  implementation ------------------
const int denomValue1 = 2000;          // Number of pennies in $20.00
const char denomName1[] = "twenties";  // Name of $20.00 denomination
const int denomValue2 = 1000;          // Number of pennies in $10.00
const char denomName2[] = "tens";      // Name of $10.00 denomination
const int denomValue3 = 500;           // Number of pennies in $5.00
const char denomName3[] = "fives";     // Name of $5.00 denomination
const int denomValue4 = 100;           // Number of pennies in $1.00
const char denomName4[] = "ones";      // Name of $1.00 denomination
const int denomValue5 = 25;            // Number of pennies in $.25
const char denomName5[] = "quarters";  // Name of $.25 denomination
const int denomValue6 = 10;            // Number of pennies in $.10
const char denomName6[] = "dimes";     // Name of $.10 denomination
const int denomValue7 = 5;             // Number of pennies in $.05
const char denomName7[] = "nickels";   // Name of $.05 denomination
const int denomValue8 = 1;             // Number of pennies in $.01
```

```
const char denomName8[] = "pennies";    // Name of $.01 denomination
//-------------- end of  cash drawer object  implementation ----------------

//-------------------- teller object implementation ------------------------
void main( )
{
   cout << "Change Maker (version 2)\n\n";

   int amountLeftToChange;                // Amount left to be changed
   inputInt(amountLeftToChange, "Enter amount to be changed in pennies: ");

   outputLine(countForDenom1(amountLeftToChange), denomName1);
   outputLine(countForDenom2(amountLeftToChange), denomName2);
   outputLine(countForDenom3(amountLeftToChange), denomName3);
   outputLine(countForDenom4(amountLeftToChange), denomName4);
   outputLine(countForDenom5(amountLeftToChange), denomName5);
   outputLine(countForDenom6(amountLeftToChange), denomName6);
   outputLine(countForDenom7(amountLeftToChange), denomName7);
   outputLine(countForDenom8(amountLeftToChange), denomName8);
}
//---------------- end of teller object implementation --------------------

//--------------------- input object implementation -----------------------
void inputInt(int& aNumber, const char prompt[])
{
   cout << prompt;
   cin >> aNumber;
}
//------------------- end of input object implementation -------------------

//--------------------- output object implementation -----------------------
void outputLine(int aNumber, const char aString[])
{
   cout << aNumber << " " << aString << endl;
}
//------------------ end of output object implementation -------------------

//-------------------- computing object implementation --------------------
void divMod(int numerator, int denominator, int& quotient, int& remainder)
{
   quotient = numerator / denominator;
   remainder = numerator % denominator;
}


int countForDenom1(int& amountLeft)
{
```

```
    int result;        // Value to be returned
    divMod(amountLeft,denomValue1, result,amountLeft);
    return result;
}
int countForDenom2(int& amountLeft)
{

    int result;        // Value to be returned
    divMod(amountLeft,denomValue2, result,amountLeft);
    return result;
}

int countForDenom3(int& amountLeft)
{
    int result;        // Value to be returned
    divMod(amountLeft,denomValue3, result,amountLeft);
    return result;
}

int countForDenom4(int& amountLeft)
{
    int result;        // Value to be returned
    divMod(amountLeft,denomValue4, result,amountLeft);
    return result;
}

int countForDenom5(int& amountLeft)
{
    int result;        // Value to be returned
    divMod(amountLeft,denomValue5, result,amountLeft);
    return result;
}

int countForDenom6(int& amountLeft)
{
    int result;        // Value to be returned
    divMod(amountLeft,denomValue6, result,amountLeft);
    return result;
}

int countForDenom7(int& amountLeft)
{
    int result;        // Value to be returned
    divMod(amountLeft,denomValue7, result,amountLeft);
    return result;
}
```

```
int countForDenom8(int& amountLeft)
{
    int result;      // Value to be returned
    divMod(amountLeft,denomValue8, result,amountLeft);
    return result;
}
//---------------- end of computing object implementation ------------------
```

The most striking feature of this implementation is its length. There are eight functions to compute eight numbers. Although we combined their header documentations, those eight functions have separate declarations and definitions. We needed these eight functions to implement the computing object, which can compute only one value at a time. Another striking feature is the similarity of the countForDenom functions. They look almost identical. Surely C++ has some mechanism whereby we could get by with a single function. (We'll find out later that it does.)

The algorithm to determine the number for each denomination is based on integer division. Rather than code explicit integer division as part of each of the eight functions, that task was factored out into a separate function, the divMod() function from earlier in this chapter. This reflects an important use of functions, to separate out tasks that are common to different activities.

Each of the eight functions has a single reference argument and each returns a value. Why didn't we write them as procedures? If we had done that, this is how the body of main() might have looked:

```
{
    cout << "Change Maker (version 2)\n\n";
    int amountLeftToChange;  // Amount left to be changed
    int countToGive;         // Count of the current denomination to give out
    inputInt(amountLeftToChange, "Enter amount to be changed in pennies: ");

    countForDenom1(countToGive, amountLeftToChange);
    outputLine(countToGive, denomName1);
    countForDenom2(countToGive, amountLeftToChange);
    outputLine(countToGive, denomName2);
    countForDenom3(countToGive, amountLeftToChange);
    outputLine(countToGive, denomName3);
    countForDenom4(countToGive, amountLeftToChange);
    outputLine(countToGive, denomName4);
    countForDenom5(countToGive, amountLeftToChange);
    outputLine(countToGive, denomName5);
    countForDenom6(countToGive, amountLeftToChange);
    outputLine(countToGive, denomName6);
    countForDenom7(countToGive, amountLeftToChange);
    outputLine(countToGive, denomName7);
```

```
      countForDenom8(countToGive, amountLeftToChange);
      outputLine(countToGive, denomName8);
}
```

We designed our functions to return values based partly on this long version of `main()`. If the eight functions were instead procedures, there would be two reference arguments instead of one. As a result, there would have to be an extra variable declared in `main()` to represent the number for each denomination. (Each number was simply a function call in the real code.) This longer version of `main()` is more difficult to understand than the real version.

The penalty that we paid for our choice was that each of the eight functions not only returned a value but also had a side effect. We had to be especially careful to document the side effect in the function headers. Readers do not expect functions that return values to contain side effects.

Those eight functions that return the numbers of the denominations look almost identical. In reading the code, you get a feeling that the same thing is being done over and over, that there is a bunch of duplicate code. In the next three chapters, we will show you C++ programming tools that will allow replacement of those eight functions with a single function.

3.6   Using class libraries

There are many features that would be nice if they were in a language. Language designers decide somewhat arbitrarily at what point to leave things out. For example, modern FORTRAN has a complex number type because that language is used by engineers and mathematicians who require one; C and C++ do not. It is not easy to extend FORTRAN to include new types, but it is easy with C++. More than almost any other language, C++ is **extensible**.

Most extensions to C++ come as class libraries. A library is a collection of related code usually in the form of a header file and a binary file.[5] We have already been using an important extension to C++, the iostream library. Any program containing `cin` or `cout` uses that library. At the top of such a program you will likely find an include directive for the iostream library header file.

```
#include <iostream.h>
```

A sure sign that a program is using a standard extension of C++ is the `#include` with angle brackets.

Programmers can also create their own extensions to C++. One important programming technique is to think of what language features would be useful to

---

[5] We will use the term *binary file* rather than *object file* in this discussion to help you avoid any confusion over the two uses of the term *object*.

implement a design and then extend the language to include those features. For you, that is a glimpse into the future. You're not about to design a library like the iostream library any time soon. It is terribly complicated and has more features than you will probably learn about in a long time (if ever). Designing reliable general purpose libraries for wide distribution is an exacting art not to be attempted by the casual programmer and certainly not by the novice programmer.

But you will use libraries that you write and, more important, you will use libraries that other programmers write. The object-oriented era has seen some real trends developing among programmers. The unwritten rule of the programming culture used to be "real programmers write all their own code." The motto for the future is "real programmers use first-rate libraries whenever possible rather than generating their own code to do the same task."

What kinds of things are in libraries? When people talk about C++ libraries, they are talking about class libraries. A class is a programmer-defined type. If your design calls for rational number type objects, you will probably implement those rational number objects through a rational number class. If your program calls for a list type object, you will probably implement the list object through a list class. If your program calls for a changemaker type object, you may well implement that object through a changemaker class. That is another look into the future.

We are not going to tell you how to define a class now, but we can show you how to use classes. Throughout our discussion, remember that a class is a type for defining objects in the same way that built-in types like `int`, `float`, `double`, and `char` are used to define data objects. However, unlike the built-in types, most classes are used for defining objects that are not simply data objects. Most class type objects can do things. You can send messages to class type objects, and they can reply to those messages.

Class messages

Classes receive messages and reply to them through functions, which are special functions that are members of the class. We'll see how to define classes and their member functions in Chapter 7. But for the moment, let's content ourselves with knowing how to use them.

Whether you realize it or not, you've been using libraries, classes, and objects from the very first moment you began to program in C++. Remember that we said `cin` and `cout` are defined in the iostream library and that `cout` is a predefined object of a class type. That means you do not have to define `cout` yourself, because its definition has already been made. Although you do not need to know this in order to use `cout`, the name of the class type for `cout` is `ostream_withassign`. (Don't blame us for that name. We didn't make it up!) When you look in more detail at the iostream library, you will discover not only that you can send a wide range of messages to these objects but also that you can create new objects of a similar kind for your own use.

Since `cout` is a class type object, you ought to be able to send `cout` a message. Let's look again at that part of Chapter 2 where we discussed setting the field width on the next output statement. We pointed out that you could do it this way:

```
cout.width(8);
```

That expression represents the following message to `cout`: "Set the field width of the next output to 8." The `cout` part of the message is the name of the object receiving the message and the `width(8)` part is a function call. The name of the object receiving the message and the message itself are joined by a period. The ordinary syntax for sending a class type object a message is this:

nameOf-Object.message

You can send messages to `cin` as well as `cout`. Do you remember how to send `cin` a message using the ordinary (function) syntax? Suppose `ch` is a `char` variable. This statement contains a message to `cin` to get the next character from input and store it in `ch`.

```
cin.get(ch);
```

Exactly what kinds of messages you can send to `cin` and `cout` depend on how their class types are defined. If you have access to the class definition, then you have a good idea of what messages are possible to objects of that class type. You do not have to know the methods an object uses to respond to a message or what data the object uses. All you need to know are the forms that messages to an object of that class type will take.

In addition to the iostream library, which everyone uses, we will look at some simple libraries developed specifically for this book. Later on, we'll discuss how to develop libraries. Right now, our view will be that libraries are collections of classes for our use.

Two sample class libraries

Our first example of a class library provides an English-metric converter class. Here is the header file for that library.

```
#ifndef _ENGLISHMETRIC_H
#define _ENGLISHMETRIC_H

// Converts between English and metric measures
class EnglishMetricConverter {
public:
    double poundsToKilograms(double lb);  // Kilogram equivalent of lb pounds
```

```
   double KilogramsToPounds(double kg);    // Pound equivalent of kg kilograms
   double feetToMeters(double ft);         // Meter equivalent of ft feet
   double metersToFeet(double m);          // Foot equivalent of m meters
   double gallonsToLiters(double gal);     // Liter equivalent of gal gallons
   double litersToGallons(double l);       // Gallon equivalent of l liters
};

#endif
```

The important part of the header file is the definition of EnglishMetric-Converter. The definition starts with the keyword class and continues through the right brace and the semicolon near the bottom of the file. (Forget about the lines that begin with #. Until you start writing your own class libraries, they are of no interest.)

Inside the definition of the EnglishMetricConverter class are the prototypes for its member functions. Those prototypes tell what kinds of messages can be sent to an object of type EnglishMetricConverter. The actual definitions of the member functions normally appear in the binary file that is part of the library. The binary file is not a text file, so you can't read it to see the definitions of the member functions. The binary file is a black box, as was the compiled definition of function sqrt() in the math library. You don't know what the original source code looks like. Furthermore, you don't care. All you need to know is how to use the function—what the function expects as arguments and what guarantees it offers about the results it gives back.

And that's how class libraries work. All you need to know is how to use the class, not how an object does what it can do. You just need to know how to ask it to do what it can do. The member function prototypes and documentation should provide that information.

Let's see how to ask an EnglishMetricConverter object to do something. First, we need to define such an object. We'll use the following definitions for our examples:

```
EnglishMetricConverter translator; // Translates English-metric measures
double tankSize;                    // Gallon capacity of a water tank
double length;                      // Length of a swimming pool in meters
```

The three definitions create three objects. The last two, tankSize and length, are double data objects. The first one, translator, is an object, but it is definitely not a mere data object. It can do things.

Suppose we want to assign tankSize a gallon measure of a 1000 liter tank. We can send a message to the translator to make the following conversion:

```
tankSize = translator.litersToGallons(1000);
```

If length has been assigned a legitimate value, then this statement writes out that value in feet rather than meters.

```
cout << "Length of pool is " << translator.metersToFeet(length) << " feet";
```

Even though we said that the binary file containing the compiled definitions of the member functions is a black box, it is not too difficult to imagine how the definitions of the member functions of the `EnglishMetricConverter` class were originally coded. You could write them yourself if you knew the English-metric conversion factors and the syntax for defining member functions of a class. However, the next class library example we will give is a black box for sure. We'll start describing the class by suggesting a problem.

Suppose part of a programming problem requires creating a text document. In analyzing the problem, you decide that the document must appear as typeset page-by-page, with a header at the top of each page and page numbers at the bottom. Each line of text must be left-justified, with as many words as possible appearing on the line before dropping down to the next line. A word cannot be split over two lines unless there is not enough room for it on a single line. The entire text is organized into paragraphs and then pages.

Consider an object that can manage a document made of a sequence of pages. Start with a simple scenario. How might typesetting have been done 200 years ago? Think of a print shop of that time. Much of the work in a print shop might be accomplished by a typesetter, whose main responsibility is formatting the pages of the document. Part of the typesetter's initial work is setting up the mechanical page forms for the document, with a possible header (banner at the top of the page), margins, and page numbers at the bottom. As the text of the document becomes available, the typesetter inserts each piece of movable type for the text into its correct position on the page form.

We do not particularly care how the typesetter does the work, so we are not going to look very closely into the print shop. We really just want to tell the typesetter what to do, not how to do it. In particular, we want to be able to do the following:

- Tell the typesetter how the document is to be formatted (header, maximum line length, numbers of lines per page, number for the first page).

- Give the typesetter the numbers, characters, and strings of characters in the order in which they are to appear in the document.

We do not want to have to figure out where words begin and where they end. The typesetter can do that. We do not want to have to figure out when a word must drop to the next line because of lack of room on the current line, or where to finish off one page and start another, because the typesetter ought to be able to take care of all that too.

We will want to be able to give the typesetter special instructions that are not part of the text data. For example, we want to tell the typesetter when to start a new paragraph. Even though the typesetter will handle these details without our asking, we might want to ask the typesetter to format some part of the text in a style different from the original page forms. So additional special instructions might be related to ending the current word, to the current line, or the current page.

The typesetter takes care of the messy details of actually inserting the "movable type" characters into the mechanical page forms. Furthermore, we can leave it up to the typesetter to do any special cleanup at the end, such as putting a page number at the bottom of the last page and making sure the entire document is printed.

In the object-oriented world, the process we have just described is a collection of messages that we would like to send to an object that can format pages and documents. Wouldn't it be nice if we could just define a typesetter object in our code? Given an appropriate class, we could do just that. That's where a typesetter class library comes in handy.

We developed a typesetter class library just for this problem. The library provides a single class, which is named `TypeSetter`. The interface to the library is a single file, shown below. (The library as a whole consists of its interface and the binary code. There is a full discussion of the library's implementation in Chapter 13.)

```
#ifndef _TYPESETTER_H
#define _TYPESETTER_H

#include <iostream.h>

class Worder;
class Liner;
class Pager

// A Typesetter object formats text into pages.
//    Each line on the page has a fixed maximum length.
//    Each page has a fixed maximum number of lines.
//    Pages have optional headers at the top and page numbers at the bottom.
//       The header is on the top line of the page followed by a blank line and
//       then the first line of text.  Four lines follow the last line of text--
//       a blank line, a line with the page number, and two more blank lines.
//       A form feed character is placed at the end of each page.
//    Characters are divided into "words," where each word is a sequence of
//       non-whitespace characters.  Each word that is too long to fit on the
//       rest of the current line is wrapped to the next line. If a word is
//       longer than an entire line, then it is split at the end of the line
//       and continuted at the beginning of the next line.
//    Whitespace characters are translated to blanks or newlines as
//       appropriate. Adjacent whitespace characters are compressed into a
//       single blank (or newline where appropriate).
//    Pages are separated by ASCII formfeeds.

class TypeSetter {
public:
```

```
    enum { minPageNumber = 0, maxPageNumber = 10000, defaultPageNumber = 1,
           minLineLength = 10, maxLineLength = 255, defaultLineLength = 72,
           minLinesPerPage = 5, maxLinesPerPage = 100,
           defaultLinesPerPage = 55 };

    TypeSetter(int lineLength = defaultLineLength,
               int linesPerPage = defaultLinesPerPage,
               int pageNumber = defaultPageNumber,
               const char header[] = "", ostream& os = cout);
        // Creates a paged document in the stream os.
        //    header - is printed at the top of every page
        //            (truncated if necessary to the maximum line length)
        //    pageNumber - the page number for the first page
        //            (set to be in range minPageNumber - maxPageNumber)
        //    lineLength - maximum number of characters per line
        //            (set to be in range minLineLength - maxLineLength)
        //    linesPerPage - maximum number of text lines per page
        //            (set to be in range minLinesPerPage - maxLinesPerPage)
        // ASSUME: os is an open, valid output stream.
    ~TypeSetter();                      // Ends document, ending current page.
    void endWord();                     // Ends current word in the document
                                        //    and flushes it to current line.
    void endLine();                     // Ends current line and flushes it to os.
    void endParagraph();                // Ends current paragraph and flushes it to
                                        //    os.
    void endPage();                     // Ends current page, numbers it, and
                                        //    flushes it to os.

    void add(char aChar);               // Adds a character to the document.
    void add(const char aString[]);     // Adds a string to the document.

    // Output operators add characters, strings, ints, and doubles to the
    //    document.
    TypeSetter& operator<< (char aChar);
    TypeSetter& operator<< (const char aString[]);
    TypeSetter& operator<< (int anInt);
    TypeSetter& operator<< (double aDouble);

private:
    Worder* theWorder_;
    Liner* theLiner_;
    Pager* thePager_;

    enum {theBufSize_ = 25};
    char theBuf_[theBufSize_];
```

```
    TypeSetter& operator=(const TypeSetter&);
    TypeSetter(const TypeSetter&);
};

#endif
```

        Immediately before the `TypeSetter` class definition are three declarations of other classes that the `Typesetter` class uses. Their definitions are part of the implementation of the library, so you can not use them directly. All you can use is the `TypeSetter` class itself. We will concentrate on the part of the header that starts with `class TypeSetter` and ends with the right curly brace.

        The `TypeSetter` class definition looks more complicated than the definition of the `EnglishMetricConverter` class. Notice that it has two sections, the first one beginning with the keyword `public`, the second with the keyword `private`. Forget about the private section (which you can't access anyway). The public section is important. It contains the declarations of the member functions, and those declarations tell what kinds of things a `TypeSetter` can do—what kinds of messages can be sent to a `TypeSetter` object.

        The first member function of the `TypeSetter` class, which looks strange because it has no return type and its name is the same as the class itself, shows the different ways to create a `TypeSetter` type object. The equal signs that appear inside the formal argument list indicate default values for the formal arguments. If no actual argument is given, then the default value will be used instead.

        If you define the `TypeSetter` object `simple` in this manner, then `simple` will have all of the default page settings.

```
TypeSetter simple;   // simple has all default settings:
                     //    output goes to cout
                     //    header at the top of each page is blank
                     //    page numbering starts at 1
                     //    line length limited to 72 characters
                     //    lines per page limited to 55 lines
```

        By default, whenever information is inserted into `simple`, the results will be sent to `cout`. It is possible to create a disk file instead for the newly formatted document. If you decide to make a disk file, you are responsible for making sure that disk file is properly opened to receive input. (Appendix F in this book shows the syntax for creating and opening a text file.)

        Page numbers appear at the bottom of each page of the document. By default, the first page of the document for `simple` is numbered 1. Line lengths and the number of lines per page are also set by default to 72 characters and 55 lines respectively. It is possible to create a document with a different line lengths or different numbers of lines per page. But if the numbers you specify are too large, they will be changed to the maximum possible values. If they are too small, they will be changed to the minimum possible values.

The TypeSetter class allows you to specify the settings on the document, filling them in from left-to-right. The following definition creates a TypeSetter object named paper in which none of the default values are used. The identifier myDoc is the name of an output stream to which paper will send the document.

```
ofstream myDoc("Termpaper");  // Output stream which creates the new
                              //   text file named Termpaper.
TypeSetter paper(60, 70,1,"DRAFT",myDoc);
                              // paper has the following settings:
                              //  Maximum line length = 60 characters.
                              //  Lines of text per page = 70 characters.
                              //  Page numbering starts at 1.
                              //  DRAFT is the header at the top of each page.
                              //  Output goes to myDoc.
```

You can specify only some of the actual arguments for a TypeSetter if you wish, letting the default values provide the rest. To do so, fill in the ones you want to use starting with the first and going from left to right. For example, the definition below creates a document with lines limited to 15 characters and number of lines per page limited to 30 lines.

```
TypeSetter memo(15, 30);  // memo has default page settings except the
                          //   line is length limited to 15 characters and
                          //   lines per page are limited to 30 lines.
                          //  Page numbering begins at 1.
                          //  The header is empty.
                          //  Output goes to cout.
```

When a TypeSetter object is defined, it is initialized with all of the settings that determine the format of a page. The definition of an object creates and initializes it. When a TypeSetter object dies (when it leaves its lifetime), the document it represents is cleaned up. The last line is terminated, enough blank lines to fill to the bottom of the page follow it, and then a page number and two blank lines are placed at the bottom of the last page. That all happens because of the second member function with another funny name, ~Typesetter(). The nice thing about that function is that it guarantees the final cleanup. You do not call it; it works behind the scenes to do what has to be done.

There are four formatting messages you can send to simple, memo, and paper in the ordinary syntax: (1) endWord() to end the current word, (2) endLine() to end the current line, (3) endParagraph() to end the current paragraph, and (4) endPage() to end the current page. (Keep in mind that you never have to send a TypeSetter object any of these messages because a TypeSetter will do all of the formatting for you. But you can ask for special treatment such as ending the current paragraph at any given time during the preparation of the document.)

There are additional kinds of messages too, except they do not use the standard member function syntax. Those additional messages are output messages, and they use the output operator much the same way the output operator works with cout.

```
simple << "Hello\n";        // Inserts "Hello " into simple's document
simple << 'M' << 'a';       // Inserts 'M' and 'a' into simple's document

simple.endLine();           // Ends the current line in simple's document
simple << 3 + 45;           // Inserts 48 into simple's document

simple.endParagraph();      // Ends the current paragraph in simple's document
simple << "Hello      ";    // Inserts "Hello " into simple's document
simple << "Pa";             // Inserts "Pa" into simple's document
```

The output generated by the sequence of messages to simple is as shown in the box.

```
Hello Ma
48

Hello Pa
```

The following function illustrates the creation of a document through a Typesetter object. The document uses cout for its display. Page numbering starts at 1.

```
void billOfRights(int width, int height)
{
    TypeSetter article1(width,height,1,"Article 1");
                        // Creates a document to hold the first
                        //  amendment of US Constitution

    article1 << "Congress shall make no law respecting an establishment of "
            << "religion, or prohibiting the free exercise thereof; or "
            << "abridging the freedom of speech, or of the press; or "
            << "the right of the people peaceably to assemble, "
            << "and to petition the Government for a redress of "
            << "grievances.";
    article1.endParagraph();
    article1 << "Bill of Rights";
}
```

The output generated by the call billOfRights(20,10) is as follows.

```
Article 1

Congress shall make
no law respecting
an establishment of
religion, or
prohibiting the free
exercise thereof; or
abridging the
freedom of speech,
or of the press; or
the right of the


Page 1

Article 1

people peaceably to
assemble and to
petition the
Government for a
redress of
grievances.

Bill of Rights


Page 2
```

The methods a `TypeSetter` object uses to implement its behaviors are a real mystery, as are the methods that an output stream uses to implement its behaviors. But that is part of some of the pleasure of using class libraries. You do not have to know how they work. You just need to know what libraries can provide the object types for your designs.

3.7 ▮ Summary

What do functions offer that is special? What have you gained through learning how to use functions as a programming tool? Probably more that you realize. At the expense of introducing some new technical jargon, we can summarize the benefits of functions in four categories: (1) reuse and generalization; (2) modularization; (3) information hiding; and (4) object interfaces.

Reuse is the ability to use the same code in a variety of circumstances. Generalization is the ability to reuse code with different data or information and it is made possible through arguments. While it is possible to have reuse without generalization, most common behavior that must be implemented in code is not identical at all times. But the variations can be made through the use of arguments. A good example of reuse and generalization is the code in the changemaker program that does the division. The function `divMod()` is used for eight different computations by varying the actual arguments.

Modularization is the grouping together of variables, constants, and statements that perform a particular task. An example of modularization in the changemaker program is the function `inputInt()`. It is used only once; the program groups all of the implementation code for the input object together and sets it off from the environment in which it is used. In some situations, it easy to group the code that implements an object into a single function.

Information hiding is the restriction of variables and constants that appear in one part of the program so that they cannot be arbitrarily manipulated or even seen by code in another part of the program. Programmers try to enclose within a protecting scope variables and constants that are to be used only within that scope. They are not to be available to any other code. Examples of protected variables are local variables, since they are used only in the body of a function in which they are declared. Local variables cannot be altered without the permission of the function in which they are declared. In terms of object-oriented program development, information hiding means that the attributes of an object are private to that object. Those attributes cannot be accessed directly by other objects.

The interface to an object is the means by which we give information to an object, get information back from an object, and request the object to do the things that it can do. In short, it is the means by which we send messages to the object. For example, in the changemaker program, ask the input object to do what it does (get an integer) by calling its only function `inputInt()`. To get the output object to do what it can do, send it a message. Call the function `outputLine()`.

Those four benefits of using functions in C++ programs ought to be enough to satisfy programmers who have been implementing non–object-oriented designs for years. But for object-oriented programmers, functions are not just nice, they're necessary. The methods that objects use to implement their behaviors are function definitions. Messages that cause objects to do things are function calls.

Glossary

actual argument   An argument that appears in a function call.

automatic   An object defined in a block whose lifetime extends to the end of execution of that block.

block scope   The scope of a declaration made inside a block, extending from the declaration to the end of the innermost nested block containing the declaration.

body of a function   Statements to be executed when the function is called.

declaration   The introduction of an identifier into a program.

definition   A declaration that tells the meaning of the identifier.

extensible   Capable of defining new operators and new types.

file scope   The scope of a global declaration, extending from the declaration to the end of the file.

formal argument   An argument declared in the function header.

function declaration   A listing of a function by return type, name, and formal argument list.

function definition   A declaration of a function that includes the function body.

global   Declarations that are made outside any block (having file scope).

hidden   A declaration which has within its scope another declaration of the same name. An object which is hidden cannot be referred to directly by name. A declaration that is not hidden in its own scope is visible.

interface of a function   The function prototype and complete documentation on how to use the function.

lifetime   The time during program execution when memory is allocated to an object.

local   An object defined inside the body of a function.

message   A function call; objects interact by sending each other messages.

method   A function that determines what an object can do.

pass-by-reference argument   A formal argument that serves as a name for the actual argument during the execution of the function.

pass-by-value argument   A formal argument that is created and initialized by the value of the actual argument when execution of the function begins.

precondition of a function   An assumption that the function makes about its actual arguments.

procedure   A void function.

prototype   A function declaration that is not a definition.

return statement   A function statement that exits the function. If the function is not void, the return statement specifies what is to be returned.

scope of a declaration   The set of lines in a program where the name introduced by a declaration refers to the object or function being declared.

signature   A function prototype that does not include names for the formal arguments.

static lifetime   An object whose lifetime extends beyond the execution of the function in which it is defined.

visible   Not hidden.

void formal argument list   An empty argument list, symbolized by `()` or `(void)`, to indicate that the function has no arguments.

void function   A function that does not return a value (a procedure).

3.8 ▮ Exercises

1. Assume that the following program has been given:

```
#include <iostream.h>

double f(int y);                                    // Line 1

void main()                                         // Line 2
{                                                   // Line 3
    int x;                                          // Line 4
    cout << "Enter a number: ";                     // Line 5
    cin >> x;                                        // Line 6
    cout << "1/" << x << " = " << f(x) << endl;     // Line 7
}                                                   // Line 8

double f(int y)                                     // Line 9
{                                                   // Line 10
    return double(1) / y;                           // Line 11
}                                                   // Line 12
```

   a. Which line of the program contains a declaration for f()?
   b. Which line of the program contains an invocation (a call) of f()?
   c. Which lines of the program contain the definition for f()?
   d. What is the name of the formal argument for f()?
   e. What is an actual argument for f() in this program?

2. Suppose that the function g() has the following prototype:

```
int g(int x, int y, double z);
```

   For each of the following invocations of g(), indicate which actual arguments correspond to which formal arguments.
   a. g(1, 2, 3)
   b. g(1, 1 + 2, 1 + 3)
   c. g(x + 3, y + 7, 33 * sqrt(x))
   d. g(y, y, y)
   e. g(g(1, 2, 3), 2, 3)

3. The built-in math library contains many common mathematical functions, including these:

   fabs(x) is the absolute value of x

atan(x) is the inverse tangent of x
ceil(x) is the smallest integer that is greater than or equal to x
pow(x, y) is x raised to the power y

Write expressions that evaluate to the following:

a. The cube root of 75.9

b. The absolute value of x - y, where x and y are double data objects

c. 3 raised to the power 8

d. The real number π (*Hint*: the tangent of π/4 is 1. Use the inverse tangent of 1.)

e. x raised to the power y if y is positive and x raised to the power -y if y is negative

4. What are the values of the following expressions, which use functions in the built-in math library? (The compiler directive #include <math.h> is needed for a program that uses the math library.)

a. pow(11,7)

b. ceil(-2.79)

c. atan(5)

d. cos(.5)   // cos(x) is the cosine of x (in radians)

e. fabs(-5.4)

f. log10(10)   // log10(x) is the log base 10 of x

g. log(10)   // log(x) is the natural log of x

h. exp(1)   // exp(x) is the number *e* raised to the power x

5. Correct all of the syntax errors in the following function definition. Do not change any lines that do not contain syntax errors.

```
void badFunction(int x, y, double& z);
{
    int X = y + z;
    x /= 2;
    int X = 4;
    z -= 5;
    return x + z + 1;
}
```

6. Assume that the following function prototypes have been given:

```
void fct1(int x);
int fct2(int z);
void fct3( );
```

```
int fct4( );
double fct5(int x, int y, int z);
```

Which of the following are legal statements? For the ones that are not, indicate why they are not legal.

a. `fct1(25);`

b. `fct2(35);`

c. `int x = fct4;`

d. `int y = fct3(3) + fct4();`

e. `cout << fct1(5);`

f. `fct1(int 7);`

g. `fct1(7,8);`

h. `double z = fct5(3,4,5);`

i. `cout << fct5(fct1(3),2,3);`

j. `cout << fct5(3,4, fct5(3,4,5));`

7. Assume that the following function definition has been given:

```
double f(int x, double y)
{
    y = x - 1;
    x = x % 3;
    return x + y;
}
```

What output is generated by each of the following code fragments?

a.
```
double val = 2.5;
int num = 13;
double res = f(num,val);
cout << val << ' ' << num << ' ' << res << endl;
```

b.
```
int x = 12;
double y = 10.3;
cout << x << ' ' << y << ' ' << f(x,y) << endl;
```

c.
```
int y = 10;
double x = 2.6;
cout << x << ' ' << y << ' ' << f(y,x) << endl;
cout << x << ' ' << y << ' ' << f(x,y) << endl;
```

8. Assume that the following function definition has been given:

```
double g(int& x, double& y)
{
    y = x - 1;
```

```
    x = x % 3;
    return x + y;
}
```

What output is generated by each of the following code fragments?

a. ```
   double val = 2.5;
   int num = 13;
   double res = g(num,val);
   cout << val << ' ' << num << ' ' << res << endl;
   ```

b. ```
   int x = 12;
   double y = 10.3;
   cout << x << ' ' << y << ' ' << g(x,y) << endl;
   ```

c. ```
   int y = 10;
   double x = 2.6;
   cout << x << ' ' << y << ' ' << g(y,x) << endl;
   ```

9. Assume that the following function definitions have been given:

```
int h(int x)
{
    x += 4;
    return x + 4;
}

int k(int& x)
{
    x += 4;
    return x + 4;
}

int t(int& x)
{
    x += 4;
    return x + 4;
    x += 12;
}
```

What output is generated by each of the following code fragments?

a. ```
   int num = 10;
   cout << num << ' ' << h(num) << endl;
   cout << num << ' ' << k(num) << endl;
   cout << num << endl;
   ```

b. ```
   int count = 0;
   count = k(count);
   cout << count << endl;
   ```
   ```

```
count = t(count);
cout << count << endl;
```

c.
```
int count = 0;
cout << count << ' ' << k(count) << count << endl;
cout << t(count) << count << endl;
```

10. Assume that the following definitions for `firstFunction()` and `secondFunction()` have been given. For the segments of code in (a) through (d), trace each function call. For each trace:

- Indicate the values of the local identifiers (formal value arguments and local variables) at the end of the execution of the function.

- Indicate the values of the actual arguments immediately after the execution of the function call.

```
int firstFunction(int x, int y)
{
    int temp = 3;
    x = y - 4 + temp;
    temp = y - temp;
    return x + y + temp;
}

void secondFunction(int& x, int& y, int z)
{
    int temp;
    x = y + z;
    temp = x * y;
    y = y - temp + z;
}
```

a.
```
int amount = 12;
int count = 7;
amount += firstFunction(3,count);
```

b.
```
int amount;
int count = 7;
secondFunction(amount,count,5 + count);
```

c.
```
int x = 10;
int y = 4;
x += firstFunction(x,y);
y = firstFunction(y,x);
```

d.
```
int x;
int y = 7;
secondFunction(x,y,15);
secondFunction(y,x,5 + x);
```

11. Write the specifications of the interfaces of each of the described functions, including a prototype (a declaration) and appropriate header documentation to describe the arguments and to indicate what the function does.

   a. The function returns the number of meters for a measurement given in yards.

   b. The function returns the volume of a right circular cylinder. (The volume of a right circular cylinder of height h and radius r is $\pi r^2 h$.)

   c. The function prints a row of 20 asterisks, a blank line, a message, another blank line, and another row of 20 asterisks on the screen. The function has one argument, the message.

   d. The function has a single char argument. It prints the argument, a tab, the ASCII code of the argument, then a newline. Are there any limitations on the argument?

   e. The function takes three int reference arguments and performs a cyclic shift on them. The first argument gets the original value of the second, the second gets the original value of the third, and the third gets the original value of the first.

12. Define the functions described in the following:

   a. Exercise 11 (a)

   b. Exercise 11 (b)

   c. Exercise 11 (c)

   d. Exercise 11 (d)

   e. Exercise 11 (e)

13. Define two functions as follows. Write a separate declaration and appropriate header documentation for each function.

   a. The function takes the x- and y-coordinates of two points and returns the distance between them.

   b. The function takes a point and a line and returns the distance between the point and the line. The formula for the distance between the point (x_1, y_1) and the line given by the equation $Ax + By + C = 0$ is

$$\text{Distance} = \frac{Ax_1 + By_1 + C}{\sqrt{A^2 + B^2}}.$$

14. Define two functions as follows. Write a separate declaration and appropriate header documentation for each function.

   a. Carbon dating is based on the fact that the amount of carbon-14 in an artifact decreases over time. The carbon decay is exponential, according to the formula

$$A = A_0 e^{-kt},$$

where A is the amount of carbon-14 in the artifact after t years, assuming an initial amount of A_0, e is the base of the natural log, and k is the constant $(\ln 2)/5700$. Define a function that takes values for A_0 and t and returns A. Define a second function that determines the age of the artifact—that is, it takes A and A_0 and returns t. Your functions should use the built-in math library functions `exp()` and `log()`. The function `exp()` returns e raised to the power of its argument and the function `log()` returns the natural log of its argument.

b. It is easy to convert from a logarithm in base 10 to a logarithm in base 2 or between any base logarithms. The formula for converting from a log in base b to a log in base a is as follows:

$$\log_b x = \frac{\log_a x}{\log_a b}.$$

Write a `double` valued function named `logBase` with two arguments, an `int` a and a `double` x, which returns $\log_a x$, the log to the base a of x. Include in the header documentation the assumption that both arguments are positive.

Test `logBase()` using a driver program if necessary. (See the exercises in Chapter 2 for a discussion of driver programs.) The value of `logBase(2,16)` should be 4; the value of `logBase(3,27)` should be 3.

15. Define five functions as follows. Write a separate declaration and appropriate header documentation for each function.

a. Define a function that returns the net amount to be paid to an employee for a week's work, given the number of hours worked, the hourly pay rate, and the income tax rate. The paycheck is computed as the hours worked multiplied by the hourly pay rate minus the following deductions: social security tax (8.5 percent of the gross pay); income tax on gross pay; and union dues totaling $5.00. The social security rate and union dues are local constants.

b. Define a procedure that is almost identical to the one in part (a) except that this function computes both the net pay and the amount to pay for social security. (Both of these are arguments.)

c. Define a function that returns the monthly payment for a mortgage loan based on the amount of loan, the annual interest rate, and the number of years in which the loan will be paid back. The amount of monthly mortgage payment P for a loan of amount A with a monthly interest rate R to be paid back over a period of N months is given by the following formula:

$$P = \frac{AR}{1-(1+R)^{-N}}.$$

Remember to convert the annual rate to monthly rate and years to months in the function. This function can call `pow()` from the built-in math library to compute the exponentiation.

d. Define a function that gauges inflation. The function has two floating point arguments that represent the price of an item in 1985 and the price of the same item in 1995. It returns the percentage increase (or decrease) of the price of the item.

e. Define a function with three arguments instead of two as in part (d). The first two are floating point arguments that represent the price of an item at two different times. The third argument is an `int` that represents the number of weeks between the time the first price was observed and the time the second price was observed. The function should return the yearly rate of inflation of the price of that item. Does your function make any assumptions about the values of the actual arguments?

16. Define the following procedures that implement some behaviors of input and output objects. Write a separate declaration and appropriate header documentation for each one.

a. Define a procedure named `readTwoDoubles` that prompts for and reads two double values. It has three arguments, a prompt, the first number input, and the second one input.

b. Define a procedure named `outputFixed` that writes a label then a `double` formatted in fixed decimal notation. Arguments to the procedure are the label, the `double` value, and the number of digits to the right of the decimal to be printed. For example, the call `output-Fixed("Amount left = ", 23.4567e3, 2)` should generate the following output:

```
Amount left = 23456.70
```

The procedure should make sure the scientific flag is turned off before it generates output, and it should reset the fixed flag to go off before it quits execution.

17. a. Define a procedure named `inRange` that has three `int` arguments. The first two are passed by value and the third is passed by reference. In any call to `inRange()`, the first argument should be less than or

equal to the second. If the last argument is less than the first, the procedure should make it equal to the first. If the last argument is greater than the second, the procedure should make it equal to the second.

b. Define a procedure named split that has three arguments: x (a double pass-by-value argument); whole (an int reference argument); and fraction (a double reference argument). The function assigns the integer part of x to whole and the fractional remainder of x to fraction.

18. Assume that the following program has been given:

```
#include <iostream.h>
int x = 4;              // line 1
int y = 12;             // line 2

int f(int);             // line 3
int g(int);             // line 4

void main( )            // line 5
{
    int z = x;          // line 6
    if (x > 0) {        // line 7
        int y = 12;     // line 8
        cout << y;      // line 9
        x -= y;         // line 10
    }
    y = 14;             // line 11
    f(y);               // line 12
}

int f(int x)            // line 13
{
    int k = 10;         // line 14
    cout << x + 1;      // line 15
}

int g(int y)            // line 16
{
    cout << y;          // line 17
}
```

Answer each of the following in terms of the numbers of the lines.

a. What lines are in the scope of the declaration for x from line 1?

b. What lines are in the scope of the declaration for y from line 2?

c. What lines are in the scope of the declaration for f() from line 3?

d. What lines are in the scope of the declaration for g() from line 4?

e. What lines are in the scope of the declaration for z from line 6?

f. What lines are in the scope of the declaration for y from line 8?

g. What lines are in the scope of the argument x from line 13?

h. What lines are in the scope of the declaration for k from line 14?

i. Where is the declaration for x from line 1 hidden in its scope?

j. Where is the declaration for y from line 2 hidden in its scope?

19. Trace the calls to the following functions that have static local data objects:

a.
```
int f(int k)
{
    static int x = 7;
    x += k;
    return x;
}
```

What is output by the following code fragment? (Assume that the first statement contains the first call to f() that is executed in the program.)

```
cout << f(3) << endl;
cout << f(3) << endl;
cout << f(3) << ' ' << f(3) << endl;
```

b.
```
void ff( )
{
    int s = 0;
    static int t = 0;
    s++;
    t++;
    cout << "s = " << s << "\tt = " << t << endl;
}
```

What output is generated by execution of these three calls? (Assume that the first statement is the first call to ff() that is executed in the program.)

```
ff();
ff();
ff();
```

20. Define a function print() with a string type argument that prints the number of times it has been called, a period, two blanks, the string, and

finally a newline. For example, if `print()` has not been invoked previously, then the following code

```
print("First message");
print("Next message");
print("Final message");
```

generates the following output:

```
1.   First message
2.   Next message
3.   Final message
```

21. Suppose you have several programs with some objects doing the following things:

    a. Compute the square roots of numbers.

    b. Print a table of prime numbers.

    c. Request the user to enter a sequence of characters.

    d. Create a document in which the pages are formatted with 10 lines per page and 50 characters per line, and with page numbers at the bottom.

    What include directives should your programs have in order for all of these tasks to be accomplished easily? (Assume that the name of the header file for the definition of the `TypeSetter` class is `typesetter.H`.)

Programming Projects

22. Solve the following problem with a C++ program:

    A steel fabrication plant produces steel tanks that are in the shape of cylinders with hemispherical ends. In order to determine how much steel goes into a tank, the plant manager needs to compute the surface area of each tank based on its height and radius.

    Use the calculator model from the solution to the convenience store problem as a basis for your analysis and design. Assume the numbers input by the user will be integers (height and radius in inches). That means the input object for this new problem is identical to the input object for the convenience store problem.

Draw a picture of the design, being especially careful to draw arrows in order to show the information that is communicated among objects. Implement the solution with a C++ program. Your program should have one function for each of the following objects: the computing object, the input object, and the output object. The calculator should be implemented as `main()`.

In your implementation of the output object for this problem, use the function `outputFixed`, which was described in exercise 16 (b).

23. Suppose that the specifications on the previous problem have been changed so that the steel fabrication plant builds right cylindrical tanks with flat ends as well as tanks with hemispherical ends. Redesign the solution to that problem so that it can satisfy the new specification. The input object of your new solution must have expanded capabilities so that it can tell which kind of tank the customer is going to order.

24. Solve the following programming problems:

The Bagel Bakery sells bagels by the dozen and half-dozen, and by the single bagel. The price of a dozen bagels is $3.80; the price of a half-dozen bagels is $2.60; and a single bagel is 50¢. What is the cost of a single order of bagels?

a. Solve the problem as stated. Adopt the calculator model as a basis for your analysis and design. The input that the user is expected to enter is the exact number of bagels.

b. The specifications just changed as follows. A dozen bagels is actually a baker's dozen, which is 13 and not 12. Solve the problem with the new specifications.

c. Narrow down the specifications to be sure that the customer always gets the best price on an order, even with the potential result of getting more bagels than ordered. For example, if the customer orders 10 bagels, then the best price is going to be $3.80. Instead of 10 bagels, the customer receives 13. So the customer pays the minimum amount necessary to buy at least as many bagels as ordered.

25. Write a program to solve the following problem:

A mortgage loan officer of a bank needs to be able to determine the amount of payment on a loan based on the amount of the loan, the annual interest rate, and the number of years for the loan to be repaid.

You can adopt the calculator model as a basis for your analysis and design. The input that the user is expected to enter consists of the amount of the loan (an integer), the interest rate (a floating point number), and the number of years for the loan to be repaid (an integer). The input object should contain two different objects, one for integer input and one for floating point input. A message to the output object should contain the number to be output, the explanation or label for that number, and the precision of the numeric output. (See exercise 16b.)

Draw a picture of the design, including the information that is sent along with the messages and replies. Implement the solution with a C++ program. The computing object can be implemented by the function of exercise 15 (c). The input object requires two functions for implementation and the output object requires one. The calculator itself should be implemented as `main()`.

Chapter 4

Decision Behavior: Selections and Alternatives

I N the previous chapter we concentrated on implementing object behaviors as functions. In this chapter and the next, we will pay attention to what goes into those functions. An object's methods for implementing behaviors may be complicated. Objects often make decisions about how to do something based information that varies from time to time.

Many of the blocks of code that have looked at so far in this book consist of collections of statements to be executed in sequence. That is, the first statement in the block is executed first, the second statement next, the third statement next, and so on through the last statement. That sequence does not allow for executing some statements but not others, and it does not allow an object to make decisions to be made depending upon current values of particular attributes.

Selection statements are the most common tools that programmers use to enable (or disable) execution of some statements at runtime. The few examples of selection statements in the previous chapters involved the constructs `if` or `if/else`. A third kind of selection construct is provided by `switch` statements.

In this chapter, we will take a careful and deliberate look at selection statements, and through numerous examples, we will show when and how to use them. We will also tie selection statements and functions together in a powerful programming tool called recursion.

Selection statements allow us to write more complicated programs in order to solve problems more complicated than most of those that we have discussed at this point. This complication comes at a price, however. The more complicated the code, the more difficult it is to figure out whether or not it is correct. At the end of this chapter we will discuss some strategies for dealing with that problem.

4.1   `if` **and** `if/else` **selection statements**

Here is a short programming problem:

> A city income tax of 3 percent has been levied against all residents who make more than $20,000 per year. One object in a design model can compute the amount the person must pay in city income tax. Write a function to implement this object's behavior. The function has a single argument representing a person's annual income and it returns the amount the person must pay in city income tax.

How should the function work? It can use the following formula.

$$\text{tax} = \begin{cases} .03 * \text{salary} & \text{if salary} \geq 20000 \\ 0 & \text{otherwise} \end{cases}$$

The formula indicates that there are two different things to do based on the size of the salary: set the tax to 0 or set the tax as 3 percent of the salary. Here is one correct definition for a function that uses the formula. The argument `salary` is the value of the person's income.

```
float taxToPay(float salary)
{
    float tax = .0;          // Income tax to be paid
    if (salary >= 20000)
        tax = salary * .03;
    return tax;
}
```

In this definition, `tax` is initialized to 0. The statement following the declaration of `tax` is an `if` statement extending over two lines of code. When the `if` statement begins execution, `salary` is compared to 20000. If the value of `salary` is 20000 or more, the line that follows, `tax = salary * .03;` is executed. (This assignment statement is actually part of the `if` statement.) If the value of `salary` is less than 20000, the assignment statement is skipped. In either case, the final statement executed in the function is the `return` statement.

General forms of `if` and `if/else` statements

The function `taxToPay()` contains the simplest kind of selection statement. If the condition in parentheses is true, then a single simple statement is executed. The next example is only slightly more complicated. Suppose `first`, `second`, `small`, and `large` are `int`s. Here is a segment of code that assigns to `small` the smaller of the two values of `first` and `second` and assigns to `large` the larger of the two values.

```
small = first;
large = second;
if (first > second) {
    small = second;
    large = first;
}
```

The execution of this `if` statement is as follows. If the value of `small` is bigger than the value of `large`, then the entire block of two statements is executed. If it is not, then the entire block is skipped. (Recall that a block is the same as a compound statement. It ends with a right brace, not with a right brace followed by a semicolon.) The second `if` statement fits into the same general form as the first one.

```
if (condition)
  statement-T
```

The *condition* in this general form is a **Boolean expression**, which means it has a value of true or false. The condition must be enclosed in parentheses. The *statement-T* can be a simple statement or a compound statement.

C++ has an if/else statement in addition to the if statement. The else part of the if/else offers an alternative action to be executed when the condition is not true. Therefore an if/else statement contains two different possible branches that could be executed, depending on the value of the condition. Here is the general form of the if/else statement:

```
if (condition)
    statement-T
else
    statement-F
```

The execution behavior of an if/else statement is what you expect. If *condition* is true, then *statement-T* is executed and *statement-F* is skipped. If *condition* is false, then *statement-F* is executed and *statement-T* is skipped. Both *statement-T* and *statement-F* can be simple or compound statements.

A simple illustration of an if/else statement can be drawn from the city income tax problem in this section. We could have calculated tax using an if/else rather than an if. In that case, we would omit the initialization of tax to .0 and replace the if statement with the following code.

```
if (salary >= 20000)
    tax = salary * .03;
else
    tax = .0;
```

Now for a different example. This time we'll write a specification for a function and then write its definition. The function can be used to compute an employee's weekly paycheck based on an hourly pay rate and the number of hours the employee worked. The function also has a pass-by-reference argument to indicate whether or not overtime work was performed. Its type is bool, a new type that we will discuss carefully later in this chapter. The type name stands for "Boolean." There are two bool values: true and false.

```
void findPay(float hourlyWage, int hoursWorked, float& paycheck,
             bool& overtime);
// Arguments:
//    hourlyWage - Hourly pay rate for an employee.
//    hoursWorked - Number of hours that the employee claimed to work in a
//          single week.
//       ASSUME: hourlyWage >= 0; hoursWorked >= 0
//    paycheck - out - Amount of money the employee earns for the a week.
```

```
//    overtime - True if the employee worked overtime (more than 40 hours).
// Side effects:  Finds the amount of money an employee earns for a single
//    week's work.  The amount is computed as follows:
//       the number of hours worked * hourly wage for the first 40 hours
//            + 1.5 times the hourly wage for every hour worked over 40
```

The function `findPay()` must do two different things, depending on how many hours the employee worked. For each possibility, it must assign a value to `paycheck` and a value to `overtime`.

Here's a correct definition for `findPay()`:

```cpp
void findPay(float hourlyWage, int hoursWorked, float& paycheck,
             bool& overtime)
{
    if (hoursWorked <= 40) {
        paycheck = hoursWorked * hourlyWage;
        overtime = false;
    }
    else {
        paycheck = 40 * hourlyWage + (hoursWorked - 40) * 1.5 * hourlyWage;
        overtime = true;
    }
}
```

This function definition contains three sets of braces. The outer braces determine the body of the function. The two inner braces determine the compound statements described earlier in the discussion of the general form of an `if/else` as *statement-T* and *statement-F*.

Notice how semicolons are used in conjunction with braces and `else`s. If the statement to be executed for an `if` is a compound statement, then it is enclosed in curly braces. There is no semicolon between the ending right curly brace and the `else`. If the statement to be executed for an `if` is not a compound statement, then it is, of course, terminated by a semicolon. So a semicolon may or may not appear before an `else`, depending on whether or not the matching `if` statement is compound or simple.

Since C++ is a free-format language, the formatting of `if` and `if/else` statements does not matter to the compiler. But code is much easier to read when the statements belonging to the `if` and the `else` are indented. Those statements are actually part of the entire selection statement. In a sense, they are subordinate to the `if` and the `else`. The placement of the right curly brace in line with the `if` and the `else` is a common stylistic practice.

Nesting selection statements for multiple alternatives

The previous chapter contained a function that returned a letter grade of `'P'` or `'F'` based on a weighted average of test and exam scores. For an average that was less than 60, the function returned `'F'`. Otherwise, it returned `'P'`. But most students are used to receiving these letter grades: A, B, C, D, and F. A popular grade scale for these letters is a 10-point scale:

$90 \leq$ average	earns a letter grade of A
$80 \leq$ average < 90	earns a letter grade of B
$70 \leq$ average < 80	earns a letter grade of C
$60 \leq$ average < 70	earns a letter grade of D
average < 60	earns a letter grade of F

Is it difficult to write a segment of code to assign a letter grade based on a numeric grade using the ten-point scale? Not if you use a sequence of cascading `if/else` statements. Suppose `letterGrade` is a `char` and `average` is a `double`. The following code assigns `letterGrade` the letter corresponding to `average` based on a 10-point grading scale.

```
if (average >= 90.0)
    letterGrade = 'A';
else if (average >= 80.0)
    letterGrade = 'B';
else if (average >= 70.0)
    letterGrade = 'C';
else if (average >= 60.0)
    letterGrade = 'D';
else
    letterGrade = 'F';
```

The code executes as follows. Starting from the top, as soon as `average` satisfies one of the conditions in parentheses, `letterGrade` is assigned the corresponding letter and the remainder of the code is skipped. If none of the conditions are met, then `letterGrade` is assigned `'F'` as shown by the final `else`.

This entire code sequence is really an `if/else` statement in which the statement belonging to every `else`, except for the last one, is itself another `if/else` statement. In other words, the later `if/else`s are nested inside the earlier ones. The code could have been formatted differently to illustrate that structure. (The original formatting style is the most commonly used one, partly because the code does not tend to run off the right-hand side of the screen and partly because the alternatives are easier to read and compare if they are vertically aligned.)

```
if (average >= 90)
    letterGrade = 'A';
else
    if (average >= 80)
        letterGrade = 'B';
    else
        if (average >= 70)
            letterGrade = 'C';
        else
            if (average >= 60)
                letterGrade = 'D';
            else
                letterGrade = 'F';
```

Nesting one `if` or `if/else` inside another is a common programming practice. Sometimes the nesting is confusing and it can be hard to tell which `else` belongs to which `if`. Here's an illustration of what we mean.

Automobile insurance rates usually depend on the gender and the age of the driver. Suppose one insurance company has a rate structure according to the following table.

Age	Male	Female
Under 21	$800	$390
21 or older	$400	$370

How can we assign the correct premium due if the driver is male? Answering this question in English is easy. It's really just a matter of reading the chart.

> If the driver is male, then
>   If the driver is under 21,
>   the premium is $800
>   If the driver is 21 or older,
>   the premium is $400

Much of actual coding consists of translating this kind of description into C++ code. Let's do that now. Assume `gender` is a `char` corresponding to the driver's gender, `age` is an `int` corresponding to the driver's age, and that `premium` is a `double` corresponding to the driver's insurance premium. The following are two pieces of code that are supposed to be a translation of what we just described in English. The equals operator, `==`, tests to see if two items are the same. The Boolean expression `gender == 'M'` is true whenever the value of `gender` is 'M' and it is false when the value of `gender` is not 'M'.

```
if (gender == 'M')              if (gender == 'M')
   if (age < 21)                   if (age < 21)
      premium = 800.0;                premium = 800.0;
else                               else
   premium = 400.0;                   premium = 400.0;
```

The code on the left is identical to the code on the right except for the indentation. That means they are equivalent as far as the compiler is concerned. The indentation of the code on the left makes it look as if the `else` goes with the first `if`. The indentation of the code on the right makes it look as if the `else` goes with the second `if`. Which interpretation is correct? Does each piece of code translate the English description that we just gave? Or does each piece translate this description instead?

If the driver is male, then
If the driver is under 21,
the premium is $800
If the driver is female,
the premium is $400

This second way of looking at the code seems plausible. If we believe that the code corresponds to the second description, then the code is clearly incorrect. If the driver is a female, then the premium does not match the table.

In fact, both pieces of code correspond to the first (correct) description. This may tell you how C++ matches `if`s with `else`s. The `else` for each piece of code goes with the second `if`.

Not only is proper indentation useful in helping the reader understand nested selections, but so are appropriate comments. The comments should reflect the conditions under which the corresponding statement is executed.

```
if (gender == 'M')            // gender is male
   if (age < 21)              // gender is male and age < 21
      premium = 800.0;
   else                       // gender is male and age >= 21
      premium = 400.0;
```

The compiler does not pay attention to indentation or comments even though people usually do. Programmers must know the real C++ rule about matching `else`s with their corresponding `if`s. That rule is more difficult to state than it is to understand. An `else` corresponds to the nearest preceding `if` having the same block scope. If you ever read code that is not perfectly formatted, pay careful attention to the braces. Whenever an `if` is inside a block different from the one containing a following `else`, it is *not* the `if` that goes with that `else`.

For our example, many programmers would prefer to put a set of braces around the entire body of the first `if` statement. The braces emphasize the point that the `else` goes with the `if (age < 21)` rather than the `if (gender == 'M')`.

```
if (gender == 'M') {          // gender is male
   if (age < 21)              // gender is male and age < 21
      premium = 800.0;
   else                       // gender is male and age >= 21
      premium = 400.0;
}
```

4.2 ▌ Evaluating Boolean expressions

Boolean expressions, which control the execution of selection statements, usually contain **relational operators** or **equality operators**. The examples that you have seen so far have been pretty simple. They have all involved operators that compared the value of one data object to another. But the Boolean expressions can be much more complex, and in some unfortunate cases, not at all intuitive.

There are six operators that compare the values of data objects:

< (less than)
> (greater than)
<= (less than or equal to)
>= (greater than or equal to)
== (equal to)
!= (not equal to)

The first four operators (<, >, <=, and >=) are relational operators; the last two operators (== and !=) are equality operators.

Even though C++ usually ignores extra blanks and tabs, you cannot insert a blank between the < and = the less than or equal to operator, <=, any more than you can insert a blank or a tab into the middle of an identifier. Similarly, each of the operators >=, ==, and != must be written as exactly two characters, with no intervening whitespace.

Relational operators, which are used to determine whether or not one value is bigger than another, can be used with numeric operands such as double, float, int, and char. For example, the expressions 1 < 15, 15 <= 15, and 5 >= 5 are true. The expressions 10 > 15 and 3 >= 7 are false. It is possible to compare two numeric values even if their types are not the same. For example, suppose x is a float and i is an int. Then x < i is true if the value of x is less than the value of i (where the value of i is considered as a float) and false if the value of x is greater than or equal to the value of i.

The equality operators behave much as you would expect. If j is an int, then j == i is true if the values of i and j are the same and false if they are not the same. The operator != is the negation of ==. So j != i is true if the values of i and j are different and false if they are the same. Equality operators, just like relational operators, are used with numeric operands. Since real numbers are not guaranteed to have exact representations as floats or doubles, most programmers use equality operators only to determine if two integer values are the same or not the same. They do not use them to see if two floating point values are the same or not.

Boolean operators

Frequently, selection statements depend not on a single simple Boolean condition but on a compound condition. Consider the example from the last section on assignment of automobile insurance premiums based on age and gender. The following code makes an assignment to premium for a young male.

```
if ((age < 21) && (gender == 'M'))
   premium = 800.0;
```

The operator && is called the **logical AND operator**. It requires two Boolean operands. An expression of the form A && B is true if and only if both A and B are true. If A is false or B is false or if both of them are false, then A && B is false.

Two other operators can be used to make complex conditions from simple ones. One is the **logical OR operator** (||). An expression of the form A || B is false if and only if both A and B are false. If A is true or B is true or if both are true, then A || B is true. The other one, the **logical negation operator** (!), is a unary operator (it requires a single operand). The expression !A is true if A is false and it is false if A is true.

Numerous examples using of the logical operators can be shown. The following is a list of Boolean expressions written in both English and equivalent C++ code. As you read the list, assume that all data objects are ints or chars.

1. **English**: The temperature is above 90 or the humidity equals 90.
   C++: temperature > 90 || humidity == 90

2. **English**: The mathematical expression $a \geq b \geq c$.
   C++: a >= b && b >= c

3. **English**: It's not true that a and b are both 0.
   C++: !(a == 0 && b == 0)

4. **English**: The person's gender is not female and the age is less than 21.
   C++: gender != 'F' && age < 21

5. **English**: The character is an alphabetic character.
   C++: ch >= 'a' && ch <= 'z' || ch >= 'A' && ch <= 'Z'

6. **English:** *a* is not 0 and *a/b* equals *c*.
   C++: `a != 0 && a/b == c`

Each Boolean expression in this list involves relational or equality operators as well as logical operators. The expressions are not simple expressions, and the operations in each expression are evaluated one at a time. How can you tell the order in which they are evaluated? The answer lies in operator precedence.

Arithmetic operators have higher precedence than relational operators. That means, for example, that the expression `3 < x + 1` is equivalent to `3 < (x + 1)`. Relational and equality operators have higher precedence than the logical operators `&&` and `||`. Many programmers prefer to put in extra parentheses to make the code easier to read. For example, they would use this expression: `(a > b) && (b > c)` instead of the equivalent expression `a > b && b > c`.

The operator `!` has higher precedence than arithmetic, relational, and equality operators. That's why it appears outside the outer parentheses in the expression `!(a == 0 && b == 0)`. The operator `&&` has higher precedence than the operator `||`. For example, the expression

$$3 == 5 \ || \ 1 == 1 \ \&\& \ 1 == 2$$

is false. Here, the right-hand operand of `||` is the subexpression `1 == 1 && 1 == 2`, which evaluates to false. Since the left-hand operand of `||` also evaluates to false, the entire expression is false.

The precedence rules are summarized in the following list. The operators at the top of the list have higher precedence than the ones lower in the list.

Operator(s)	Meaning(s)
`!`	Logical negation
`*, /, %`	Multiplication, division, modulus
`+, -`	Addition, subtraction
`<, >, <=, >=`	Less than, greater than, less than or equal to, greater than or equal to
`==, !=`	Equal to, not equal to
`&&`	Logical and
`||`	Logical or

Many programmers do not bother to memorize all of the precedence rules. Instead, they use parentheses to determine the order of expression evaluation. That turns out to be a good programming practice. Often, extra parentheses make code easier to read and understand.

Complex Boolean expressions can sometimes be simplified or written in a form that is easier to understand. For example, the expression `!(a > 0)` can be simplified to `a <= 0`; the expression `!(b != a)` can be simplified to `b == a`; the expression `(A && B) && (A && C)` can be simplified to `A && B && C`.

Boolean expressions containing `!` along with `&&` or `||` can be rewritten according to the following rules, which are known as **DeMorgan's laws**:

- `!(A && B)` is equivalent to `!A || !B`.

- `!(A || B)` is equivalent to `!A && !B`.

When `!` is pulled inside the parentheses, it is applied to both operands, but `&&` is changed to `||` and `||` is changed to `&&`. Here are some sample applications of DeMorgan's laws.

Boolean expression	*Equivalent expression*
`!(a < 0 && b < 0)`	`a >= 0 || b >= 0`
`!(a > 0 || b < 0)`	`a <= 0 && b >= 0`
`!(a >= 0 && b <= 0 && c > 0)`	`a < 0 || b > 0 || c <= 0`
`!((a < b && b < c) || a != 0)`	`(a >= b || b >= c) && a == 0`
`!(a != 0 || b != 0 || c != 0)`	`a == 0 && b == 0 && c == 0`

The form in which a compound Boolean expression should be written depends on the particular coding situation. There is only one important guideline to follow: Make the Boolean expressions as easy for the reader to understand as possible.

Short-circuit Boolean evaluations

Suppose `a` and `b` are `int`s. Look at the following pair of selection statements:

```
if (a != 0 && (b/a > 3))        if ((b/a > 3) && a != 0)
    a = 4;                          a = 4;
```

In most circumstances these two statements execute exactly the same, but their runtime behavior is radically different when `a` is 0. The evaluation of the Boolean condition in the statement on the right begins with the integer division `b/a`. And if `a` is 0, that attempted evaluation aborts the code execution. The program crashes.

If `a` is 0 when the selection statement on the left is executed, the first thing that is evaluated is the Boolean condition `a != 0`. Since `a != 0` is false, there is no reason to continue. C++ knows that false "and" any other Boolean expression is false. Therefore there is no attempt made to evaluate the right-hand side of the `&&`. How fortunate. That means the expression `b/a` will not be evaluated, the condition is false, and so the statement `a = 4;` will be skipped.

Partial evaluation of a Boolean expression such as this one is called **short-cir-cuit evaluation**. Short-circuit evaluations are special language features of both C and C++. They are a convenience for the programmer, but they are not entirely necessary. For example, the last selection statement could be written safely as follows:

```
if (a != 0) {
    if (b/a > 3)
        a = 4;
}
```

The alternate form is more cumbersome in this case and can become even more complicated in more complex expressions.

Short-circuit Boolean evaluations work with the || operator as well as the && operator. The following example is analogous to our first one:

```
if (a == 0 || (b/a > 3))
    a = 4;
```

The evaluation of the entire Boolean condition proceeds from left to right. If a is 0, then the expression a == 0 is true. Since true "or" any Boolean is also true, there is no need to evaluate the right-hand side of the ||.

You cannot take advantage of short-circuit Boolean evaluations if you fail to pay attention to the operations that can have disastrous consequences. The advantage of using short-circuit Boolean evaluations is to save programs from disaster at execution time by checking first for the critical values. Do not attempt to evaluate an integer division without first making sure that the divisor is not 0.

Boolean types and integers

In all of our discussion so far, we have used the terms Boolean, true, and false as if they were C++ keywords. We think of Boolean as a type whose values are true and false. For almost all of your programming, that is an appropriate way to think. But this is not always the case.

New C++ compilers support a Boolean type called `bool`. A data object of type `bool` can have one of two values, `true` or `false`. The values `true` and `false` can be converted to integers. The value `true` converts to the integer 1; the value `false` converts to the integer 0. Conversely, the integer 0 converts to `false`. Every nonzero integer converts to `true`.

The new `bool` type can be used with the logical operators, `!`, `&&`, and `||`. The following tables summarize their use:

```
!true is false      true && true is true        true || true is true
!false is true      true && false is false       true || false is true
                    false && true is false       false || true is true
                    false && false is false      false || false is false
```

Older C++ compilers do not have a built-in Boolean type. Instead, they use integers to express true and false. False is `0`; true is `1`. The integer value of the Boolean expression `3 > 4` is `0`. The integer value of the Boolean expression `3 <= 4` is `1`. With the older compilers, the result of evaluating a relational or equality expression is thus `0` or `1`, depending on whether the expression is false or true. For a selection statement, as long as the Boolean condition is not `0`, the condition is considered to be true.

None of this really matters with respect to what we have discussed so far in this chapter. The fact that a C++ compiler may use the integers `0` and `1` rather than special values called `false` and `true` does not effect how you should code the ordinary selection statements based on relational or equality operators.

All C++ compilers will let you use an integer expression as a condition to control execution of a selection statement. So we need to give you a serious warning. All C++ compilers, whether they are new or not so new, will allow you to write code like this:

```
if (a = 6)
    b = 17;
```

even if you really meant to type this:

```
if (a == 6)
    b = 17;
```

Forgetting to put the second `=` in the `==` operator is a very common programmer error. The result is that rather than having the equality operator, you end up with the assignment operator. Many compilers will give you a warning message for that first selection statement, but all of them will compile it.

How does having an assignment expression as a selection condition make any sense to a compiler? The explanation is as follows. When the expression `a = 6` is evaluated, the resulting value is 6. The value of an assignment expression is the actual value that is assigned to the left-hand operand. The value 6 is an `int`. Since 6 is not 0, 6 is considered to be true. (Any integer that is not 0 is true.) So the statement `b = 17;`, which is the body of the selection, will be executed.

Evaluation of an assignment expression does have a side effect. When the expression `a = 6`, which is the selection statement condition, is evaluated the variable `a` is assigned the value 6. Programmers rarely desire such side effects in conditions. They are easy to overlook as a source of errors because their appearance is so subtle.

The logical operators !, &&, and || can be applied to integers as well as Booleans. Evaluations of integer expressions using these operators will not surprise you. The following summary shows how logical operators work with integer values.

$$!x = \begin{cases} 0 \text{ if } x \neq 0 \\ 1 \text{ if } x = 0 \end{cases} \qquad x \text{ \&\& } y = \begin{cases} 0 \text{ if } x = 0 \text{ or } y = 0 \\ 1 \text{ if } x \neq 0 \text{ or } y \neq 0 \end{cases} \qquad x \text{ || } y = \begin{cases} 0 \text{ if } x = 0 \text{ and } y = 0 \\ 1 \text{ if } x \neq 0 \text{ or } y \neq 0 \end{cases}$$

You will see much C++ code that uses ints rather than bools to represent Boolean type data objects. With that style of programming, the prototype of the function findPay(), which we defined earlier in this chapter, could be written as follows.

```
void findPay(float hourlyWage, int hoursWorked, float& paycheck,
          int& overtime);
```

The definition of findPay() would have to be changed as follows to accommodate substituting int for bool:

```
void findPay(float hourlyWage, int hoursWorked, float& paycheck,
          int& overtime)
{
    if (hoursWorked <= 40) {
        paycheck = hoursWorked * hourlyWage;
        overtime = 0;
    }
    else {
        paycheck = 40 * hourlyWage + (hoursWorked - 40) * 1.5 * hourlyWage;
        overtime = 1;          // Could assign any number but 0.
    }
}
```

4.3   Typedefs and enumerations

Older C++ compilers do not provide a special Boolean type. (We say older, but when we started writing this text, no compiler that we were using supported a built-in bool type.) But all C++ compilers will let you create your own Boolean type. If your compiler does not support a bool type, it is easy to create your own type via the following trio of statements:

```
typedef char bool;
const bool false = 0;
const bool true = 1;
```

The first statement is a **typedef,** a feature of C++ that allows a programmer to give a new name for a type. This typedef defines the symbol `bool` to be another name for the type `char`. The other two statements simply define two new constant data objects of the type `bool`, which is now another name for `char`.

A typedef introduces a new name to the compiler and gives a meaning to that name. But it is not the same as a definition for a variable or a constant. A typedef does not set aside memory for an object. It just introduces a synonym, or another name, for a type that the compiler already knows about.

Typedefs help make the notation in a program clean and easy to read. This is the general format for a simple typedef:

```
typedef type newTypeName
```

The definition of a typedef begins with the keyword `typedef`; *type* is a description of the type that is being named; *newTypeName* is the new type name.

It is possible to define a new name for any known type. For example, if you prefer the identifier `integer` to the name of the built-in type `int`, then make a typedef to define the identifier `integer` to mean the same as `int`.

```
typedef int integer;
```

With the definitions of `bool`, `true`, and `false`, we are able to use those three terms as we have been using them all along in this chapter. The following code illustrates what we mean.

```
bool flag;
bool error = false;
```

Why define `flag` as a `bool` and not as a `char`? The name `bool` suggests that the variables `flag` and `error` are going to be used as Boolean conditions. That serves as documentation for the code. See how `flag` and `error` are used in this example:

```
if (flag)
    x = y + 4;        // Assignment is made if flag is true
if (!error)
    salary *= 1.1;    // Assignment is made if error is false
if (flag || error)
    reportError();    // Call is made if flag or error are true
```

A typedef gives a new name for an old type. It is also possible to create entirely new types. We will now show you how to create an **enumeration type,** a programmer-defined integer type. Both typedefs and enumeration types are used to make programs easier to read, understand, and modify when necessary.

Enumeration types are particularly nice for directly relating code in a program to the situation that the program is trying to model. For example, let's assume that a program is supposed to model automobile traffic in a section of a city. At each intersection, the traffic is controlled by lights, which can be red, yellow, or green. We can use the numbers 0, 1, and 2 to represent the traffic light colors (if we just remember which number goes with which color), or we can define an enumeration type for traffic light colors:

```
enum TrafficLight {red, yellow, green};
```

The definition for an enumeration type contains the keyword enum, the name of the type, and a listing of all of the names of the values that a data object of that type can assume. The listing of values is important—remember that this is a new type with new values that have to be spelled out. The names of the type and the values are identifiers. Both the type name and value names must be constructed according to the C++ rules for legal identifiers. That is, they begin with a letter (or underscore) and contain only letters, underscores, and digit characters.

The listing of enumeration values is put inside braces. (That use of braces is different from their use in a compound statement.) The type definition is a statement and must end with a semicolon. Our example TrafficLight is the name of a new type. The identifiers red, yellow, and green are the names of the values that a data object of type TrafficLight can assume.

When an enumeration type is defined, the enumeration constants are assigned integer values. By default, the first constant listed is assigned the value 0, the second one is assigned the value 1, and so on. As we will see shortly, it is possible to assign enumeration values different integers from the defaults. The enumeration values are considered to be constant data objects.

The program with the TrafficLight enumeration type definition could use data objects like these to represent the status for various traffic lights.

```
TrafficLight east;                  // Color of light for eastbound traffic
TrafficLight west;                  // Color of light for westbound traffic
TrafficLight north;                 // Color of light for northbound traffic
TrafficLight south;                 // Color of light for southbound traffic
const TrafficLight stopLight = red;// red means stop!
```

Here is an if/else statement that could represent traffic light activity. (The statement for the final else is an error check. It calls a function errorCheck(), which presumably is declared in the program.)

```
if (west == red) {
   east = red;
   north = green;
   south = green;
}
```

```
else if (west == yellow || west == green) {
   east = yellow;
   north = red;
   south = red;
}
else // There is an error.
   errorCheck();
```

The advantage of using enumeration type declarations in selection statements like this is that programmers do not have to remember which numbers are assigned to which light colors, whether 0 means red or green. In fact, the numbers 0, 1, and 2 are completely irrelevant to the real-world problem. In this example, the identifiers themselves indicate the meaning of the selection statement.

Enumeration types can be used as function argument types. The following is a prototype for a function with two enumeration type arguments. The first is a value argument and the second is a reference argument.

```
int exampleFunction(TrafficLight x, TrafficLight& y);
```

With the typedef that we gave earlier for the identifier `integer`, we could have instead declared `exampleFunction()` as follows:

```
integer exampleFunction(TrafficLight x, TrafficLight& y);
```

It is also possible to have a function that returns an enumeration type value. The following prototype is an illustration:

```
TrafficLight anotherExample();
```

The function `anotherExample()` has no arguments. It returns a value of type `TrafficLight`.

Enumeration type definitions and typedefs follow the same scoping rules as function declarations. If you want several different functions to be able to know about an enumeration type or a typedef, then the enumeration type definition and typedefs should be global rather than local.

Some programmers use **anonymous enumeration types**—enumeration types having no type names—in order to create named integer constants. The enumeration type `TrafficLight` had a name, `TrafficLight`. Here is an anonymous enumeration type:

```
enum {low = 20, medium = 50, high = 100};
```

There is no name for this type, but there are values (`low`, `medium`, and `high`). Those values can be used like ordinary constants. They are initialized with special values in the enum definition. (Without those initializations, `low`, `medium`, and `high` would have the default values 0, 1, and 2 respectively.)

Enumeration values must be integers. You cannot define an enumeration type to create names for floating point literals.

4.4 ▌ `switch` **statements**

Nested `if/else` statements are one tool that a programmer can use for multiple alternatives. In this section, we will look at a similar tool, `switch` statements. The `switch` statements are not as versatile as nested `if/else` statements, but they do have the benefit of explicitly listing all of the possible cases that determine which actions are to be performed.

A `switch` statement is used to offer a list of alternative actions based on a single control expression. The listing associates each possible value of the expression with a collection of statements. Here is a `switch` statement that does exactly the same thing as the last `if/else` statement of the previous section:

```
switch (west) {
    case red:
        east = red;
        north = green;
        south = green;
        break;
    case yellow: case green:
        east = yellow;
        north = red;
        south = red;
        break;
    default:
        errorCheck();
        break;
}
```

The general form for a `switch` statement is as follows.

```
switch (controlExpression)
    statement
```

The *controlExpression* should be an expression that is **integer valued**, which means it should not be a floating point or a string but it can be an `int`, `char`, `bool`, enumeration type, etc. The *statement* is usually a block or compound statement, which begins with a left curly brace, {, and ends with a right curly brace, }.

The *statement* usually consists of several `case` labels, ordinary statements, `break` statements, and possibly a `default`. The words `case` and `default` are keywords that are used only with `switch` statements. The word `break` is also a keyword, and it is used to quit execution of the code inside the braces of the `switch` statement.

The possible values of the control expression are listed in the `case` labels. When the `switch` statement is executed, the control expression is evaluated. That value is compared to the values for the `case` labels, starting with the first one. As soon as the control expression value matches a `case` label value, the computer begins execution of the statements that follow the `case` label. When the `break` at the end of the statements for that `case` label is executed, the entire `switch` statement is exited.

If none of the `case` label values match the control expression, then the statements following the `default` label are executed. The `default` label is optional. Without it, if none of the `case` label values matched the control expression value, then none of the statements in the entire block would be executed.

The `break` statements at the end of the `case` label statements are essential. Without them, the `switch` statement would execute as follows: the control expression is evaluated, then, starting at the top, as soon as that value matches the value of a `case` label, the computer begins execution of all of the statements following the `case` label. That means the statements belonging to subsequent `case` labels are also executed. Usually, however, the programmer wants the `switch` statement to quit execution as soon as the statements associated with the matching case label are executed.

Omitting `break` statements from `switch` statements is a common programming error. In our example, the last `break` statement, which goes with the `default` label, is optional. However, many programmers place a `break` statement at the end just to stay in the habit of ending every label with a `break`.

The `case` labels in a `switch` statement are constant integer expressions. The control expression can be any integer valued expression. It need not necessarily be a simple variable. For example, test scores ranging from 0 thorough 100 can be expressed as letter grades on a 10-point scale. Suppose `testScore` is an `int` whose value is in that range, and suppose `letterGrade` is a `char`. The following `switch` statement assigns `letterGrade` the appropriate value according to `testScore`. (The `default` label could be replaced by `case` labels for values 5 through 0.)

```
switch (testScore / 10) {
    case 10:
    case 9: letterGrade = 'A'; break;
    case 8: letterGrade = 'B'; break;
    case 7: letterGrade = 'C'; break;
    case 6: letterGrade = 'D'; break;
    default: letterGrade = 'F'; break;
}
```

The statements for switch `case` labels are usually written on a single line as long as there are no more than two of them, including the `break`. This is one of the few situations in which it is stylistically acceptable (and common) to place two statements on a single line.

Surprise payoff: The changemaker becomes shorter

The last implementation of the changemaker solution was very long. It contained eight different functions, `countForDenom1()` through `countForDenom8()`, corresponding to eight different denomination sizes. And all of the functions looked almost identical, the only difference being the value of the denomination associated with each one.

By using a selection statement, we can replace those eight functions with a single function. The new function requires an additional argument to indicate which denomination is currently being computed. We wrote our new function with a `switch` statement to select action based on the value of the denomination. The following is the definition of our new function, `countForDenom()`, complete with header documentation.

```
int countForDenom(int thisDenomination, int& amountLeft)
// Arguments:
//    thisDenomination - A value in the range 1 through 8 corresponding
//       to the 8 different denominations. Values are ordered according to
//       denomination sizes: 1 corresponds to twenties and 8 corresponds to
//       pennies.
//    amountLeft - in - Amount from which to give out this denomination.
//                      ASSUME: amountLeft >= 0
//               - out - What is left of the amount after giving out
//                      this denomination
// Returns: Number of this denomination in theAmount.
// (Side effect: Reduce amountLeft by the amount of this denomination.)
{
    int result;                 // The result returned
    int denomValue;             // Value of this denomination
    switch (thisDenomination) {
        case 1: denomValue = denomValue1; break;
        case 2: denomValue = denomValue2; break;
        case 3: denomValue = denomValue3; break;
        case 4: denomValue = denomValue4; break;
        case 5: denomValue = denomValue5; break;
        case 6: denomValue = denomValue6; break;
        case 7: denomValue = denomValue7; break;
        case 8: denomValue = denomValue8; break;
    }
```

```
    divMod(amountLeft, denomValue, result, amountLeft);
    return result;
}
```

The body of `main()` is easily modified to accommodate the new function. The old sequence of eight calls can be replaced by this new sequence:

```
outputLine(countForDenom(1, amountLeftToChange), denomName1);
outputLine(countForDenom(2, amountLeftToChange), denomName2);
outputLine(countForDenom(3, amountLeftToChange), denomName3);
outputLine(countForDenom(4, amountLeftToChange), denomName4);
outputLine(countForDenom(5, amountLeftToChange), denomName5);
outputLine(countForDenom(6, amountLeftToChange), denomName6);
outputLine(countForDenom(7, amountLeftToChange), denomName7);
outputLine(countForDenom(8, amountLeftToChange), denomName8);
```

What have we gained by all of this? The entire changemaker program is now much shorter, but shorter code is not necessarily "better" than longer code. (Sometimes the opposite is true.) The real gain that we experience is that the function `countForDenom()` is more general than the eight original functions. We have written one general function to replace eight very specific functions. The new function argument provided that generality.

4.5 | The conditional operator: Providing shorthand for a simple `if/else`

Look at the following simple `if/else` statement. Assume that x and y are `int` variables.

```
if (x > y)
    x = 4;
else
    x = 7;
```

Both *statement-T* (executed if the condition is true) and *statement-F* (executed if the condition is false) are assignments to x. We could describe the value assigned to x as, "If x > y then the value is 4 else the value is 7."

This kind of programming construct is so common, that C and C++ provide a special operator called the **conditional operator** for an `if/else` shorthand. The conditional operator is the only operator for C++ that is ternary, which means it has three operands instead of two (for a binary operator) or one (for a unary operator). The operator itself uses two symbols, ? and : . The general form for a condition expression is as follows:

```
<condition> ? <expression-T> : <expression-F>
```

The `condition` is a Boolean condition equivalent to the condition for an `if/else`. The value of the entire expression is `expression-T` if the `condition` is true and `expression-F` if the `condition` is false.

The `if/else` above could be replaced by the following simple one-line statement:

```
x = (x > y) ? 4 : 7;
```

The parentheses are optional. We left them in to make the statement easier to read. (Many C++ programmers follow the same convention.) The precedence of the operators in the assignment statement is as follows:

>   highest
? :   next
=   lowest

A condition expression does not have to be part of an assignment statement. For example, the function `taxToPay()`, which we gave at the beginning of this chapter, could have been defined this way:

```
float taxToPay(flioat salary)
{
    return (salary >= 20000) ? salary * .03 : .0;
}
```

If you find the conditional operator awkward to use at this point, take comfort in the fact that you can always rely on an `if/else` instead. But be aware that the conditional operator is popular among some programmers. You are very likely to encounter the conditional operator again if you read any significant amount of C++ code.

4.6   Recursive functions

A **recursively defined function** (or simply a **recursive function**) is one whose definition contains a function call to itself. In this section, we will show you some simple recursive functions.

Exercise 25 (b) from Chapter 2 contained the following problem:

Suppose x is an int whose value is between 0 and 9999 inclusive and sum is an int. Write a segment of code that assigns to sum the sum of the digits of x.

The suggested solution required four variables, `onesDigit`, `tensDigit`, `hundredsDigit`, and `thousandsDigit` corresponding to the one's digit of x, the ten's digit of x, the hundred's digit of x, and the thousand's digit of x respectively. The four variables could be assigned values as follows. The sum of the digits is just the sum of the values of the four variables:

```
onesDigit = x % 10;
tensDigit = (x / 10) % 10;
hundredsDigit = ((x / 10) / 10) % 10;
thousandsDigit = (((x / 10) / 10) / 10) % 10;
```

This problem is not very difficult, but it becomes more so when x is allowed to have more than four digits. In fact, 32-bit C++ integers can have 10 digits. Does that mean we must have 10 different integer variables and 10 different assignment statements to find the digits?

The answer is no. There are several ways to approach the problem of computing the sum when x can be any nonnegative number. Let's look at this problem via an example calculation. Use 3412089 as the value of x. We need to find the sum of the digits in a seven-digit number.

Thinking recursively

To find the sum of the digits in 3412089, add 9 (the one's digit) to the sum of the rest of the digits—the digits in the number 3412089/10. We now have a new problem: finding the sum of the digits in 341208. But that's a six-digit number, so the sum of its digits ought to be easier to compute than the sum of digits in the original seven-digit number. To find the sum of the digits in 341208, add 8 (the one's digit) to the sum of the remaining digits—those in the number 341208/10. That's yet another problem, but with five digits instead of six. Finding the sum of the digits in a five-digit number is easier than finding the sum of the digits in a six-digit number. The process continues in this manner, reducing each problem to an easier one, until you run out of digits.

The sequence of problems to solve cascades as shown below. Each problem is reduced to the sum of the one's digit plus the sum of the remaining digits (the digits in the number divided by 10). We can stop finding these sums when the number is reduced to 0.

$$9 \; + \; \text{sum of digits in } 341208$$
$$8 \; + \; \text{sum of digits in } 34120$$
$$0 \; + \; \text{sum of digits in } 3412$$
$$2 \; + \; \text{sum of digits in } 341$$
$$1 \; + \; \text{sum of digits in } 34$$
$$4 \; + \; \text{sum of digits in } 3$$
$$3 \; + \; \text{sum of digits in } 0$$
$$0$$

There are two ways to implement this algorithm. One way is to use loops, which we will cover in the next chapter. The other way is to use a recursive function that has a nonnegative integer argument and returns the sum of its digits. The following is a suitable recursive function definition:

```
int sumOfDigits(int n)
// Argument: n - a nonnegative integer
// Returns: the sum of the digits in n.
{
    if (n == 0)          // There's only one digit, and it's 0
        return 0;
    else                 // Add the ones digit to the rest of the digits
        return (n % 10) + sumOfDigits(n / 10);
}
```

The return statement that is executed in the body of sumOfDigits() depends on the value of the argument. Execution of the first return statement, which occurs when the argument is 0, does not generate any function call. Execution of the second return statement, which occurs when the argument is not 0, generates a recursive function call. However, each time sumOfDigits() calls itself, it makes that call with a smaller actual argument. Eventually, the calls have to stop because at some point the actual argument for the call will be 0.

Recursive functions have two distinct characteristics:

1. The body of the function is controlled by a selection statement. At least one the alternatives does not contain a recursive call. The condition associated with that alternative is the exit condition.

2. At least one of the alternatives contains a recursive call. The new call, however, is on a smaller (easier) version of the problem than the problem of the current call.

Since our old model for tracing function calls is not particularly useful for recursive functions, we need a different approach. Let's evaluate the expression sumOfDigits(12783). We will substitute each call by the expression of the return statement using the call, and in each expression we will use the value of the actual argument:

```
sumOfDigits(12783)
   = 3 + sumOfDigits(1278)
   = 3 + ( 8 + sumOfDigits(127))
```

```
= 3 + ( 8 + (7 + sumOfDigits(12)))
= 3 + ( 8 + (7 + (2 + sumOfDigits(1)))))
= 3 + ( 8 + (7 + (2 + (1 + sumOfDigits(0))))))   // exit condition
= 3 + ( 8 + (7 + (2 + (1 + 0)))))
= 3 + ( 8 + (7 + (2 + 1)))
= 3 + ( 8 + (7 + 3))
= 3 + ( 8 + 10)
= 3 + 18
= 21
```

For our next examples, we will write two recursive functions, neither of which returns a value. Here's the programming problem: Write C++ code that will print a right triangle consisting of copies of a single character, with the same number of characters across (or down) each leg. The triangle should be a right triangle with one leg at the top and the other at the left (the hypotenuse runs from lower left to upper right). A triangle fitting that description in which the length of each leg is eight and the character is ' * ' looks like this:

This particular triangle actually contains eight different triangles, including the original triangle of height eight; the triangle of height seven that starts right after the first row of eight asterisks; the triangle of height six that begins after the second row of asterisks; and the last "triangle" of height one, which consists of a single asterisk. These observations lead us to an algorithm:

> To print a triangle of height n consisting of copies of the character ch
> > if n is positive
> > > first print a row of n copies of ch
> > > then print a triangle of height n - 1 consisting of copies of the character ch
> > if n is not positive, do nothing

Let's try to implement this algorithm as a C++ function. The function needs two arguments: the character to be printed and the height of the triangle. And it will not return any particular value, it will just print something. Here's a partial implementation of the function:

```
void printATriangle(int n, char ch)
{
   if (n > 0) {
      // code goes here          // First, print a row of length n.
      printATriangle(n - 1, ch);   // Then print a triangle height n - 1.
   }
}
```

It looks like we have one task left: we need to be able to print a row of n copies of ch. That is really easier than printing triangles, and we can use the same kind of thinking process that we used to solve the triangle problem. Let's see. We know how to print a single character:

```
cout << ch;
```

We know how to terminate a line:

```
cout << endl;
```

If we want to print eight characters in a row, we can print a single character, then finish by printing the rest of the row with seven characters. And to print the rest of the row with seven characters, we can print a single character followed by printing the rest of the row with six characters—a familiar story. But how can we end all of this? To print a row with one character, we can print a single character and then a print the rest of the row with no characters. To print a row with no characters, all we need to do is terminate the line.

The algorithm that captures this discussion can be easily described.

To print a row of n copies of the character ch:
      if n is 0
            terminate the line
      else
            print one copy of ch
            print a row with n - 1 copies of ch

The body for a recursive function that implements the algorithm is very simple to construct. We will name the function printARow(). The arguments to printARow() are a character and an integer. The function will work correctly only if the integer argument is not negative. A complete definition for print-ARow(), including documentation, is shown here:

```
void printARow(int n, char ch)
// Arguments:
//    ch - The character to be printed.
//    n - The number of copies of ch to appear on the row. (ASSUME: n >= 0)
// Side effect:  n copies of the character ch, followed by a newline are
```

```
//    printed.
{
    if (n == 0)                      // There are no characters to print. Finish off
        cout << endl;                //    with a newline.
    else {
        cout << ch;                  // Print one copy of the character.
        printARow(n - 1, ch);        // Finish printing with row of length n - 1.
    }
}
```

Let's see how the call `printARow(2,  '$')` could be translated directly into code:

```
// Replace for printARow(2,'$');
if (2 == 0)
    cout << endl;
else
    cout << '$';                                          // output: $
    // Replace for printARow(2 - 1, '$');
    if (1 == 0)
        cout << endl;
    else {
        cout << '$';                                      // output: $
        // Replace for printARow(1 - 1, '$')
        if (0 == 0)
            cout << endl;                                 // output: newline
        else;
            // END OF RECURSION. No code executed here
    }
}
```

The output generated by the call `printARow(2,'$')` is just what it is supposed to be, two dollar signs followed by a newline.

```
$$
```

Putting everything together is easy. The function `printATriangle()` calls `printARow()` to do all of the actual printing!

```
void printATriangle(int n, char ch)
// Arguments:
```

```
//   ch - The triangle consists of printed copies of ch.
//   n - The base and height of the triangle.
// Side effect: A right triangle of height n and base n  and consisting of
//   copies of the character is printed on the screen. If n is not
//   positive, nothing is printed.  The triangle is oriented with one leg
//   at the top and the other at the left.
{
   if (n > 0) {
      printARow(n, ch);              // Print a row of n characters.
      printATriangle(n - 1, ch);     // Then print a triangle of height n - 1.
   }
}
```

These two recursively defined functions are correct. Each function has an exit condition, and each successive recursive call is used to solve a smaller problem (print a shorter row or a smaller triangle). That does not *prove* correctness by any stretch of the imagination. But we can at least trace the code to become more convinced.

Let's trace the call printATriangle(3,'$'). Again, we'll use the same technique that we used to trace printARow.

```
// Replace for printATriangle(3,'$');
if (3 > 0) {
   printARow(3, '$');                                    // output: $$$
   // Replace for printATriangle(3 - 1, '$');
   if (2 > 0) {
      printARow(2, '$');                                 // output: $$
      // Replace for printATriangle(2 - 1, '$');
      if (1 > 0) {
         printARow(1, '$');                              // output: $
         // Replace for printATriangle(1 - 1, '$');
         if (0 > 0);
            // END OF RECURSION: no code executed here
      }
   }
}
```

The output from printATriangle(3,'$') looks just as it should.

```
$$$
$$
$
```

Sample use of recursion: error checking

Suppose that the user running the changemaker program enters the number -375 as the amount to change. Up to this point we have not anticipated negative numbers for input, but it is possible that the program might get one. What kind of results will the changemaker program generate for negative input? Most likely, the results will not be particularly useful. Detecting and handling erroneous user input is called **error checking**.

One responsibility that we can assign to the input object is to deal with erroneous input. At this point, let's not be too ambitious. We don't know enough about input streams to handle the problem of a user entering something that is not even a number. But with a simple selection statement, we can determine if the number that was entered is negative.

What should the input object do with a negative user entry? There are several choices.

1. Set the amount to a fixed value, for example 0 or 1.

2. Use the absolute value of the input number for the amount.

3. Exit the program immediately.

4. Remind the user that the input must be nonnegative, and then request a different entry.

5. Remind the user that the input must be nonnegative, and then request a different entry or allow the user to terminate execution of the program.

Some of these choices are better than others. Input error checking for good commercial programs is most likely the last choice. That's the hardest one to implement, however. But with recursive functions, it looks like the fourth choice is easy.

As long as we are redesigning the input object to enable some error checking, let's implement it by a function with a new name, `inputNonNegativeInt()`. Here is its definition and header documentation:

```
void inputNonNegativeInt(int& aNumber, const char prompt[])
// Arguments:
//   aNumber - out - The nonnegative integer entered by the user
//   prompt - Message displayed to the user
// Side effect: Prompts the user and reads a nonnegative value for aNumber
// Error check:  The user is prompted to continue entering numbers until a
//   nonnegative number is entered.
{
    cout << prompt;
    cin >> aNumber;
    if (aNumber < 0) {
        // Error check.  Request the user to enter another number.
```

```
        cout << "Your entry must not be a negative number."
            << "  Please reenter.\n" << endl;
        inputNonNegativeInt(aNumber,prompt);
    }
}
```

4.7   Testing: the evaluation part of the implementation process

The traces of `printATriangle()` and `printARow()` from the section on recursive functions are fairly convincing, but they do not constitute proof that the functions are correct. (A real proof of correctness would be based on mathematical induction.) Both of those functions are very small. But the real problem lies with larger pieces of code. Proving correctness of entire programs is almost always extremely difficult and for most practical purposes impossible. Most programmers rely on testing rather than mathematical proofs to find out if their code is incorrect. **Testing** a program means executing it with the intent of finding errors.

The implementation phase of the object-oriented development process consists of writing code, compiling it, and testing it. Testing is easy for novice programmers to overlook. It can be the most difficult part of implementation, the time when you find out what you have done wrong and when you reveal poor design decisions and defective code that does not do what it was designed to do.

Testing strategies

Programmers test programs and functions by executing them with various sets of input data and actual arguments in order to find errors in their code. **Exhaustive testing**, which means testing code with all possible input or values, is virtually impossible for almost all cases. (Think how difficult it would be to do exhaustive testing of the convenience store problem. You would have to run the program with *every* integer value!) Since exhaustive testing is impossible, programmers use other testing strategies to find defective code.

Finding a good set of input data to test a piece of code is not easy. What manageable collection of input data is most likely to uncover errors? That is usually a difficult question to answer. One method involves looking at the range of possible input values and picking test values that are at the ends of the range as well as in the middle. For example, the changemaker program expects input data to be nonnegative integers. One value that should be used for any test dataset to test the program is 0—the smallest acceptable input value.

If the code that you are testing contains selection statements, another important testing strategy can be used: **path testing**. To do path testing, a programmer creates a set of test data that will trace each possible path through the code. For example, if your code contains a `switch` statement with five different `cases` followed by an `if/else` with two branches, then there are at least 10 possible paths through the code. The first path is the first `case` with the `if` statement; the second is the first `case` with the `else` statement; the third is the second `case` with the `if` statement, ...; the tenth is the fifth `case` with the `else` statement.

Suppose you have written a C++ function to compute the price a roofing company customer must pay for shingles according to this pricing scenario:

A roofing company sells two grades of shingles. The price of a pack of shingles depends on the grade and the quantity that the customer purchases. Discount pricing breaks come at 20 packs and at 50 packs. A customer who buys fewer than 20 packs of shingles pays more per pack than a customer who buys at least 20 packs but fewer than 50 packs of the same grade shingles. A customer who buys at least 50 packs of the same grade shingles pays less per pack than either of the other two customers.

Your shingle-pricing function requires two arguments: one for the grade and one for the quantity. The grade is a `char` (say `'A'` or `'B'` for the actual argument). The quantity is a nonnegative `int`. You need to come up with a set of data to test the code.

Look first at the problem of testing all paths. There must be at least six possible paths through the body of the function. The number six comes from multiplying the number of grades (two grades) by the number of quantity pricing schemes (below 20 packs, at least 20 but less than 50, and 50 or more). Here are six sets of test data, one for each path:

Grade	Quantity
`'A'`	10
`'B'`	10
`'A'`	30
`'B'`	30
`'A'`	55
`'B'`	55

Is this test dataset likely to find an error in the code? Perhaps. But you can enhance the test data by including numbers on the discount break point boundaries. In addition to the six datasets above, you should include ones in which the quantities are 0, 19, 20, 49, and 50. The test dataset is expanded from six sets to 16.

In constructing the 16 datasets, the possibility that the shingle grade could be anything but `'A'` or `'B'` or that the number of packs of shingles could be negative was never considered. The function should also be executed with erroneous values, to test its error checking if it has any or how it behaves if it does not have error checking. This could add at least three new test datasets: `A` and –10, `C` and 10, and `C` and –10, for example.

Exhaustive testing is almost always impossible from a practical standpoint, and although is important to do some path testing, doing thorough path testing may also be impossible. So if you can not do it all, what kinds of testing does that leave you with?

Many programs have some boundary conditions. The changemaker, for example, was designed to work with positive input (or at least nonnegative input). A boundary condition for the changemaker is the input value 0. If you implemented the changemaker, testing your program with the value 0 is part of the implementation process.

Let's look at another example. Suppose that an automobile switches gears at the following rpm's: 1200, 2000, 3000, and 3500. Suppose also that your program contains a model of the automobile. At a minimum, your program should be tested with rpm values of 1200, 2000, 3000, and 3500. The boundary test values are the best initial candidates for detecting errors.

Regardless of your testing strategies and input data, you should always know how your program should respond to the input data ahead of time, and you should always look at the results of the testing when it is completed. It does no good to test a program if you do not know what the results are supposed to be. How can you figure out if the results are correct?

Module testing

A code **module** is a self-contained portion of code. It can mean a single function or a collection or library of related functions. It can also mean the implementation of an object. Module testing is especially important for object-oriented programming, which is centered on the creation of reusable designs and reusable code.

A single module can be used by many different programs. When a module is first created, the programmer cannot possibly anticipate all of its future uses. It is important that the module be correct for many different environments. That means it must be tested in a context that is independent of the original program for which the module was intended.

Suppose we look at the shingle-pricing function of the previous section as a module. It is easy to see how testing both that module and a program that uses it at the same time could get out of hand. The shingle-pricing function alone requires at least 16 separate test cases. If it is part of a reasonably complex program, then the number of test cases can be enormous. Just trying to figure out a single set of test data for a particular path through the entire program can become difficult.

Fortunately, the shingle-pricing function is easily tested apart from the eventual programs that might use it. Some development environments allow testing of single stand-alone functions. For those that do not, a driver program will do. (See exercise 21 from Chapter 2.) A **driver** is a program written specifically for testing a function. Drivers usually contain the function to be tested and `main()`. In order to test the function using a variety of arguments, `main()` usually consists of input statements (to get values for the actual arguments), a call to the function being tested, and output statements to indicate the results of the call.

The shingle-pricing function is not a particularly good example for module testing because it has such limited and specialized use. Modules that are reused are not usually so specialized. When you learn more advanced features of C++, you will see how modules can be packaged to be incorporated into a program. This does not mean cutting and pasting from one source code text file to another. It does not even mean recompiling the module. It means reusing the module much the same way as the iostream or math library is used, as a built-in part of the language.

4.8 ▊ Application example: navigational running lights

The following problem is based on one that was presented at the 1989 ACM Collegiate Programming Contest Finals.[1]

> An offshore oil rig in the Gulf of Mexico is on constant vigilance to make sure ships traveling at night do not come too close to its platform. Nighttime ship movements are tracked by electronic and visual means. Special care is taken it ensure that the electronic information is consistent with the visual sightings.

Problem analysis

Let's begin with some background information. Nighttime visual sightings of ships are made possible by their running lights, which all ships are required to display at night. Each ship has four running lights in strict configuration. One light is at the stern (the back), one is on the mast, and two are on either side of the bow (the front). Lights on the mast and stern are white. The light on the starboard side (right side) of the bow is green. The one on the port side (left side) of the bow is red. The maximum distance from which a ship can be sighted is 10 nautical miles.

Angles in naval practice are measured clockwise, beginning at 0° for due north. Due east is 90°, due south is 180°, and due west is 270°. Ranges of the running lights for a ship heading due north are shown in Fig. 4.1. The masthead light has a full 360° range, visible from any direction. The red running light on the port

---

[1] ACM stands for Association for Computing Machinery, the professional society for computer scientists. ACM sponsors a series of programming competitions for college students every year. During each contest, teams of students solve as many problems as they can in a 5-hour period. The culminating contest for the series is the ACM Contest Finals.

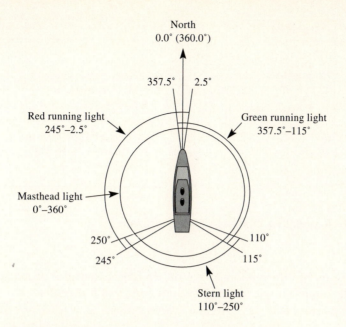

Figure 4.1 Running-light ranges for ship traveling due north.

side shines between 245° to 2.5°. The green running light on the starboard side shines between 357.5° to 115°. The stern light shines between 110° to 250°. The visible sectors of a ship's lights intersect.

What does it mean to confirm electronic and visual sightings? Imagine a crew member on the deck of the oil rig looking at the nighttime sea. The crew member can spot a traveling ship by its running lights, which appear in a certain order depending on the location of the ship relative to the oil rig and its bearing (its direction of travel). If the running lights appear to a crew member in a left-to-right order of green–masthead–red, then the ship is heading almost directly toward the rig, anywhere from 357.5° to 2.5° (−2.5° to 2.5°) relative to the rig.

What about the electronic information? With radar on board, the oil rig can find the location and bearing of any ship in the vicinity. If there is no radar, a crew member can send a radio message to a ship to determine its location and bearing.

We now have enough information to begin constructing a model. What are the objects that you would choose for such a model? We selected an oil rig as one object and a ship as another. Details of our model are provided in Fig. 4.2.

The oil rig knows its own location and the configuration of running lights on any ship that it sees. It can determine if its visual sightings are consistent with that ship's location and bearings. The ship itself knows and can report on its location and bearing.

Notice that we have kept the information in our model to a minimum. We did not include the ship's speed or tonnage as part of its attributes, even though those would be essential in almost any other navigation problem. We also did not

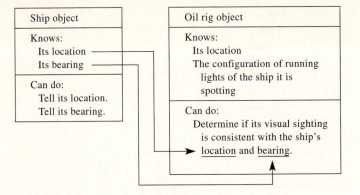

Figure 4.2 A model for the ship-sighting problem.

include any more information in the oil rig object than the problem called for. Keeping the model simple lets us focus only on what is essential.

Design of the solution

How does the oil rig object know if its visual sightings are consistent with the ship's location and bearing? That's a design issue. *What* an object does is analysis; *how* it does it is design.

The oil rig can find out the ship's location and bearing by sending it a message. From that information, the oil rig can compute what it should see and compare those values to the actual sightings. Suppose the oil rig has all of the information it needs. How does it compute?

Let's backtrack for a moment. How are locations measured? Nautical locations are typically given in terms of latitude and longitude. Angles are spherical angles. Latitude, longitude, and spherical angles are not particularly difficult to deal with, but we decided to simplify the problem by using nautical miles as units of measurement and pretending the earth is flat, or at least almost flat. A grid consisting of squares that are one nautical mile on a side is imposed over the entire picture. Locations for both ships and oil rigs are given in terms of their x- and y-coordinates. Figure 4.3 shows an oil rig at location (5.0, 2.0) and a ship at location (11.5, 5.5).

Given this data, which running lights should be visible to the oil rig? If the ship is heading directly away from the oil rig, then the masthead and stern lights are visible. If the ship's bearing is 315°, then the red and masthead lights are visible. The lights visible to the oil rig depend on the relative bearing from the ship to the oil rig, as shown in Fig. 4.4.

The oil rig confirmation method must perform several computations:

• Compute the relative bearing from the ship to the oil rig.

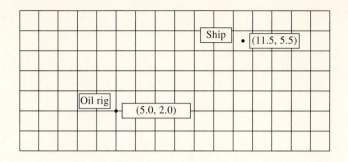

Figure 4.3 Oil rig and ship locations imposed on a grid of square nautical miles.

- Compute the configuration of the visible lights according to that relative bearing.

- Compare that computed configuration with the visible configuration that was actually sighted.

Since this is a lot of work for one object, we can create another object—a computer object—within the oil rig to do some of that work. In object-oriented parlance, the oil rig object *has-a* computer object. The oil rig will delegate to the computer object the work of figuring out the relative bearing and light configuration based on the ship's location and true bearing.

Has-a is an object-oriented term. Whenever object A contains an object of type B, we say, "A *has-a* B."

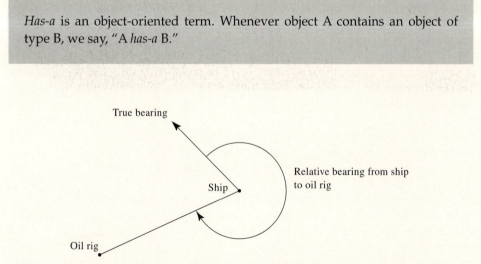

Figure 4.4 Relative bearing from the ship to the oil rig is the clockwise measure of the angle whose initial side is the fixed vector of the ship's true bearing and whose terminal side is the line segment connecting the ship and the oil rig.

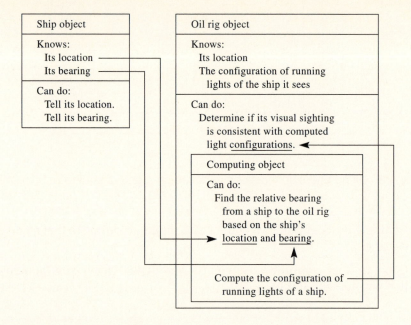

Figure 4.5 The design model of a solution to the oil rig problem.

Introducing new objects at the design level is a common practice in object-oriented development. It was not until we found out just how complicated the computation of the oil rig was that we decided to create a new object. Figure 4.5 illustrates our design.

That new object is the computing object. The interfaces of the two methods of the computing object can be described by the function prototypes and headers. Before the function prototypes, we'll make an enumeration type, Light, to indicate which light is observed.

```
enum Light {redRunning, greenRunning, masthead, stern, invisible};
void lightConfiguration (Light& left, Light& middle, Light& right,
                                   double x, double y);
// Arguments:
//   left -out- Leftmost visible light (invisible if none are visible)
//   middle -out- Middle visible light (invisible if less than 3 are visible)
//   right -out- Rightmost visible light (invisible if none are visible)
//   x - x-coordinate of location of sighting
//   y - y-coordinate of location of sighting
// Side effect: Computes the left-to-right light configuration of a ship as
//   sighted from (x,y).  The ship's location and bearing constitute the reply
```

```
//    of a message to the ship.  The results are based on the standard range
//    configurations for ships. (For  ship heading due north, masthead is
//    0 - 360; stern is 110 - 250; red is 245 - 2.5; green is 357.5  - 115).
//       If the ship is more than 10 nm away from (x/y), all lights
//    are invisible.  If only 2 lights are visible, middle is set to invisible.

double relativeBearing(double x, double y, double shipX, double shipY,
                       double trueBearing);
// Arguments:
//    (x,y) - (x,y) coordinates of a point relative to a square grid
//    (shipX,shipY) - (x,y) coordinates of a ship relative to a square grid
//    trueBearing - The bearing of the ship (measured from true north)
//                  ASSUME: 0 <= trueBearing < 360
// Returns - The relative bearing from the ship to the point (x,y).
```

The interface of the oil rig object is very simple compared to the interfaces of the computing object. The oil rig object has one method, which determines if what it sees and what it computes are consistent. The reply is either true or false. We will implement this method as a Boolean function.

```
bool consistentLightInfo();
// Returns: true if the configuration of running lights as sighted from the
//    oil rig match the configuration of running lights as computed from the
//    location and bearing of the ship
```

The implementation of the oil rig will conform to these prototypes. We haven't mentioned anything about a human interface component, and we have omitted further discussion of the ship object. We will leave both of these to you.

Partial implementation of the solution

We begin the implementation of the oil rig object with a global enumeration type definition. It describes the values of the running lights as seen from the oil rig.

```
enum Light{redRunning, greenRunning, masthead, stern, invisible};
```

The oil rig data includes its location on the grid and the light configuration of the ship as seen from the oil rig. How shall we package all of this together? Do we create five local data objects? Do we make them global? There's a tradeoff. If they are all local, then any functions that need their values in order to do work must have corresponding arguments for them. The interfaces for such functions could be unfortunately long. On the other hand, making this information global has two major drawbacks:

1. If the attributes are not hidden within a function or by some other means, they are available to any function belonging to another object. That allows the possibility of unintentional (or intentional) tinkering by other objects that have no business knowing that these attributes even exist.

2. The attributes may be implemented as global data objects. That has the potential of removing their usefulness in another programming context.

We decided to place the attributes for the oil rig object into the single function implementing its behavior, a convenient solution. Such a decision might be less easily made if the oil rig had two methods instead of one.

The fact that the computing object has two methods does not necessarily mean that the computing object is best implemented by two functions. In fact, we will use three: `lightConfiguration()`, `relativeBearing()`, and `nauticalAngle()`. The third function, `nauticalAngle()`, is a utility function that `relativeBearing()` uses. Its prototype is as follows:

```
double nauticalAngle(double fromX, double fromY, double toX, double toY);
// Arguments:
//    (fromX,fromY) - (x,y) coordinates of a point on a square grid
//    (toX,toY) - (x,y) coordinates of a point on a square grid
// Returns:  The degree measure of the angle that the vector from
//    (fromX,fromY) to (toX,toY) makes with the positive y-axis, measured
//    clockwise.  The value returned will be in the range from 0 up to but
//    excluding 360.  If the two points are the same, 0 is returned.
```

The complete implementation of the computing object is as follows. The computing object sends the ship object a message to determine the ship's location and bearing. (That message is a call to a function named `shipReport()`.)

```
//-------------------- computing object implementation---------------------
void lightConfiguration(Light& left, Light& middle, Light& right,
                        double x, double y)
{
   double xShip;       // x-coordinate of the ship's location
   double yShip;       // y-coordinate of the ship's location
   double bearing;     // Ship's bearing

   // Send the ship object a message to report its location and bearing.
   shipReport(xShip,yShip,bearing);

   // The default value for all lights is invisible.
   left = invisible;
   right = invisible;
   middle = invisible;
```

```
    // Find the configurations for ships within 10 nautical miles.
    if (distance(xShip,yShip,x,y) <= 10) {
        double angle = relativeBearing(xShip,yShip,x,y,bearing);  // Relative
                        // bearing from the ship to the oil rig platform
        if (angle > 357.5 || angle < 2.5) {
            left = greenRunning;
            middle = masthead;
            right = redRunning;
        }
        else if (angle >= 2.5 && angle < 110) {
            left = masthead;
            right = greenRunning;
        }
        else if (angle > 110 && angle < 115) {
            left = stern;
            middle = masthead;
            right = greenRunning;
        }
        else if (angle >= 115 && angle < 180) {
            left = stern;
            right = masthead;
        }
        else if (angle >= 180 && angle <= 245) {
            left = masthead;
            right = stern;
        }
        else if (angle > 245 && angle < 250) {
            left = redRunning;
            middle = masthead;
            right = stern;
        }
        else {// (angle >= 245 && angle <= 357.5)
            left = redRunning;
            right = masthead;
        }
    }
}
double relativeBearing(double fromX, double fromY,
                   double toX, double toY, double trueBearing)
{
    double alpha = nauticalAngle(fromX,fromY,toX,toY);
    if (alpha >= trueBearing)
    return alpha - trueBearing;
    return 360 + (alpha - trueBearing);
}
```

```
double nauticalAngle(double fromX, double fromY, double toX, double toY)
{
    if (fromX == toX)
        // The line connecting (fromX,fromY) and (toX,toY) is vertical.
        if (fromY <= toY)
            return .0;
        else
            return 180.0;
    else {
        // The line is not vertical. Compute its slope and its angle with
        //    the positive x-axis.
        double slope = (fromY - toY) / (fromX - toX);    // Slope of the line
                                      // connecting (fromX,fromY) and (toX,toY)
        double angle = atan(slope) * PI / 180;         // Angle of the
                                      //  line segment from (fromX,fromY) to
                                      //  (toX,toY) with the positive x-axis

        // Return the angle the line segment makes with the positive y-axis.
        if (slope >= 0 && fromX <= toX || slope < 0 && fromX <= toX)
            return 90 - angle;
        else
            return 270 - angle;
    }
}
//-------------------- end of computing object implementation --------------
```

The attributes of the oil rig object are implemented through data object definitions at the beginning of the function `consistentLightInfo()`. The details of how
those attributes get their values are left to the input object.

```
bool consistentLightInfo()
{
    //-------------------- oil rig object attributes ----------------------
    double xRig;          // x-coordinate of the oil rig's location
    double yRig;          // y-coordinate of the oil rig's location
    Light visibleLeft;    // Leftmost visible light (invisible if none are
                          //    visible)
    Light visibleMiddle;  // Middle visible light (invisible if less than 3 are
                          //    visible)
    Light visibleRight;   // Rightmost visible light (invisible if none are
                          //    visible)
    //------------------ end of oil rig object attributes ------------------

    Light shipLeft;       // Computed leftmost light (as seen by the oil rig)
    Light shipMiddle;     // Computed middle light (as seen by the oil rig)
    Light shipRight;      // Computed rightmost light (as seen by the oil rig)
```

```
// Send a message to the input object to get oil rig attributes.
getDataFor(xRig,yRig,visibleLeft,visibleMiddle,visibleRight);

// Send a message to the computer to determine the light configuration
//   based on the actual ship data that it receives.
lightConfiguration(shipLeft,shipMiddle,shipRight,xRig,yRig);

if (shipLeft == visibleLeft && shipMiddle == visibleMiddle
      && shipRight== visibleRight)
    return true;
  return false;
}
```

As you can see from the definition of `consistentLightInfo()`, the input object is implemented at least partially by the function `getDataFor()`. That function is responsible for obtaining proper values to the location of the oil rig and the configuration of lights that the oil rig is currently focusing on.

Some exercises at the end of this chapter are based on variations of this problem. When we solved this problem, we were frustrated by our inability to package the data for an oil rig into one neat place. Well, we did put the data inside the oil rig object's only method, but we realized this solution is not particularly nice for an object with several methods. Even though the computing object had no attributes, we would have preferred packaging its methods together, too. In Chapter 7, we will see how we can package all of the attributes and behaviors of an object into a single object.

4.9 ▌ Summary

This chapter focused on how objects make decisions. Let's restate that: This chapter focused on how to implement decision making in object methods. C++ provides three language features for decision making: `if`, `if/else`, and `switch`.

The selection constructs `if` and `if/else` use Boolean conditions to determine which decisions an object may make (which code in a method will be executed). Boolean and relational operators give a programmer tremendous flexibility in coding such conditions. An object can make a decision based on many different combinations of factors.

All general purpose languages have features that allow conditional execution of some code. Conditional execution was considered essential long before the term object-oriented appeared in the programming world. It is a concept that is fundamental to most algorithms.

The combination of conditional execution and of functions being able to call themselves provides another powerful programming tool: recursion. By using recursion, programmers are able to ensure repetition of execution of a segment of code according to the value of a certain condition rather than according to some predetermined, small number.

With these new, essential programming tools comes the ability to write programs that are more complicated than those written before. That is both a wonderful and terrible responsibility. It makes testing code to see if it is right or wrong more difficult and more crucial. Testing is an important—and mandatory—part of implementation.

Glossary

anonymous enumeration type An enumeration type that is defined without a type name.

Boolean expression An expression whose value can be interpreted as true or false.

conditional operator The ternary operator ? :. The expression A ? B : C evaluates to B if A is true and to C if A is not true.

DeMorgan's laws Two rules indicating how to distribute ! over && and ||. !(A && B) is equivalent to !A || !B and !(A || B) is equivalent to !A && !B.

driver A program written explicitly to test a function or module.

enumeration type A programmer-defined integer type.

equality operators One of the operators == and !=.

error checking The process of detecting and handling erroneous input data.

exhaustive testing Executing a program on all possible combinations of input values.

logical AND The operator &&. A && B is true if both operands are true and it is false otherwise.

logical negation The operator !. !A is false if A is true and true if A is false.

logical OR The operator ||. A || B is false if both operands are false and it is true otherwise.

module A self-contained portion of code.

path testing The process of executing a program with test data that will execute every possible combination of statements.

recursive function A function that calls itself.

relational operator One of the operators <, <= , > , and >=.

selection statement A statement specifying different code to be executed depending on the value of a condition.

short-circuit evaluation Partial evaluation of a Boolean expression. If A is false, B is not evaluated in A && B (the value of the expression is false). If A is true, B is not evaluated in A || B (the value of the expression is true).

testing The process of executing a program with the intent of detecting errors in the program.

typedef A language feature for giving a new name to an existing type.

4.10 ▌ Exercises

1. Consider the following code:

```
if (x > 10)
    y += x - 4;
else if (x < 0)
    y = x;
else
    y = 31;
```

   a. Which statement is executed if the value of x is 7?

   b. Which statement is executed if the value of x is 14?

   c. Which statement is executed if the value of x is -1?

2. Suppose that x and y are ints. Write if and if/else statements for the following:

   a. Increment x by 1 (increase the value of x by 1) if the value of y is 0.

   b. Increment x by 1 if the value of y is 0 and increment x by 2 if the value of y is not 0.

   c. Increment x by 1 if y is positive, increment x by 2 if y equals 0, and increment x by 3 if y is negative.

   d. Write a selection statement that sets y to 0 if both x and y are positive and does nothing if they are not both positive.

3. Suppose x, y, and z are ints. Write if and if/else statements for the following:

   a. Assign x the smaller of the values of y and z.

   b. Assign x the largest of the three values of x, y, and z.

   c. Assign x the value 50 if both x and y are within the range of 0 to 100.

   d. Assign x the value of 0 if the last two digits of x are even (or the last digit of x is even in the case where x has only one digit). Assume x is nonnegative.

   e. Increment x by 1 if y is between 0 and 5 inclusive, increment x by 2 if y is between 6 and 25 inclusive, and increment x by 3 if y is between 26 and 100 inclusive. Your code should not change x if the value of y is greater than 100 or if it is negative.

   f. Assign z the value 0 if the values of x and y satisfy the mathematical inequality $|x| < |y|$.

4. Simplify the following expressions:

   a. `a < b  && a <= b`

   b. `a <= b && a >= b`

c. a < b || a == b

d. !(a > 0)

e. !(a > 0 || !(c < 0))

f. !(a == 0 && b >= 0)

5. Each of the following code fragments is defective. Rewrite each fragment so that it is not defective.

   a. Reformat the following code so that its indentation reflects the structure of the code. The indentation should reveal which else goes with which if.

```
if (a < b) if (c < d) x = 1; else if (d < e) if (b < c) x = 2;
else if (a < e) if (b == c) x = 3;
```

   b. Correct the syntax errors in the following code fragment:

```
if (a < b) {
    a = b + 4;
    b = 0;
};
else
  if (a == 0 && c == a)
    b = 0;
```

6. Assume x, y and z are ints. Each of the following code fragments could result in a runtime error. Rewrite each fragment so that it cannot generate an error.

   a. `if (sqrt(x * y) > z)`
      `z += 2;`

   b. `if (0 < (x + y) / (x - 1) || x == 1)`
      `z += 2;`

7. Assume x and y are ints. What happens as result of execution of these selection statements?

   a. `x = 17;`
      `if (x = 0)`
      `y = 17;`

   b. `x = 0;`
      `if (x = 0)`
      `y = 17;`

8. For each function described, write not only its definition but also a separate declaration and header documentation.

   a. Define a procedure curveGrade() that has a single int reference argument representing a test grade. curveGrade() curves its argument as follows:

- If the grade is greater than 70, the curve is 5%.
- If the grade is greater than 40 but less than or equal to 70, the curve is 8%.
- If the grade is less than or equal to 40, the curve is 10%.

Is this grade curving scheme fair?

b. Define a function with a single `char` argument that returns the upper-case equivalent of the argument. If the argument is not an alphabetic character, then your function should return the value of the actual argument.

c. Define a function with a single `char` argument that returns true if the value of the argument can be used as a character in a simple C++ identifier.

9. Define functions as follows. For each function, write not only the definition but also a separate declaration and header documentation.

a. Define a Boolean valued function named `inOrder` that has three `double` arguments. The value `inOrder(x,y,z)` is true if and only if x, y, and z satisfy the mathematical inequality $x \leq y \leq z$.

b. Define the function named `orderThree` that has three `int` reference arguments and assigns the smallest value to the first one, the middle value to the second one, and the largest value to the last one.

10. Write the definition of a function named `insurancePremium` that has an `int` argument representing a person's age and a `char` argument representing that person's gender, with possible values 'f', 'F','m', or 'M'. `insurancePremium()` returns the insurance premium of a person with that `age` and `gender` according to the table in section 4.1.

a. Write the body of the function using nested `if` and `if/else` statements but no compound Boolean conditions.

b. Write the body of the function using compound Boolean conditions to control the selection statements.

11. Suppose that `temperature` is an `int` variable representing the temperature of an oven. Write a sequence of multiple `if/else` statements that output the phrases below based on temperature.

Value of temperature	Phrase to print
Not over 200	Too cold to cook.
Over 200 but not over 350	Oven is preheating.
Over 350 but not over 425	Put in the apple pie.
Over 425 but not over 500	Time to cook pizza.
Over 500	Call the fire department!

12. Assume `grade` is an `int` and its value is 78. The following code is supposed to generate output indicating the appropriate corresponding letter grade for `grade` based on a 10-point scale. What is the actual output generated in this case?

```
switch (grade / 10) {
    case 0: case 1: case 2: case 3: case 4: case 5: cout << "Grade is F\n";
    case 6: cout << "Grade is D\n";
    case 7: cout << "Grade is C\n";
    case 8: cout << "Grade is B\n"
    case 9: case 10: cout << "Grade is A\n";
    default: cout << "Grade " << grade << " is invalid\n";
}
```

Correct the code so that whenever the `grade` is greater than 100 or less than 0, an "invalid grade" error message is output. In your correction of the code fragment, use a switch statement to generate the valid grade messages, such as "Grade is C."

13. a. Make a definition for an enumeration type `Color` to represent the colors of the rainbow: violet, indigo, blue, green, yellow, orange, and red.

   b. Define a data object `hue` of type `Color`.

   c. Write a switch statement to write out the "value" of `hue`. For example, if the value of `hue` is `indigo`, then output from executing your switch statement should be:

   ```
   indigo
   ```

   d. Define an anonymous enumeration type with enumeration values named `capacity` (value is 100) and `bottomLine` (value is 5).

14. a. Make a definition for an enumeration type called `Rank` to represent the undergraduate classification for a university student (freshman, sophomore, junior, and senior).

   b. Define a variable `x` of type `Rank`. What happens when you try to execute this assignment statement?

   ```
   x = 1;
   ```

   c. What happens when you try to execute this assignment statement?

   ```
   x = Rank(1);
   ```

   d. Assume `predictedGPA` is a `double`. Write a multiple `if/else` statement controlled by the value of `x` (of type `Rank`) that assigns the value `3.5` to `predictedGPA` if `x` is a `freshman`, `2.5` to `predictedGPA` if `x` is a `sophomore`, `2.1` to `predictedGPA` if `x` is a `junior`, and `2.9` to `predictedGPA` if `x` is a `senior`.

e. Write a `switch` statement equivalent to the multiple `if/else` statement of part (d).

15. The function `changeId()` is designed to be part of a program that modifies personal identification numbers for bank customers. Write a correct definition for `changeId()`. Put a `switch` statement into the body of the function to assign the correct value to `number`.

```
void changeId(int& number);
// Argument:
//    number - in - An integer (ASSUME: number > 0)
//    number - out - All digits are the same as the original except the
//    one's digit, which is changed to 0, 1, or 2 as follows.
//       If the original one's digit is even, then it is changed to 1.
//       If the original one's digit is odd and less than 5, then it is
//       changed to 0.  If the original one's digit is odd and greater than
//       or equal to 5, then it is changed to 2.
//    Side effect: The value of the actual argument is changed to suit the
//    scheme described.  For example, if the original value is 3459,
//    then the new value is 3452.  If the original value is 3458, then
//    the new value is 3451.  If the original value is 3453, then the
//    new value is 3450.
```

16. Suppose that `x` and `y` are `doubles`, `ch` is a `char`, `go` is a `bool`, and `val` is a `TrafficLight` (an enumeration type defined in section 4.3). Rewrite the following code fragments to use `if/else` statements rather than conditional statements.

a. `return (x > 0) ? sqrt(x) : sin(x);`

b. `return ('A' <= ch && ch <= 'Z') ? ch - 'A' +'a' : ch;`

c. `go = (val == red || val == yellow) ? true : false;`

17. Explain in simple English what `mystery()` does. Trace the function call `mystery(3,7)`.

```
double mystery(double x, int y)
{
   if (y == 0)
      return 1;
   else if (y % 2 == 0) {
      double temp = mystery(x, y / 2);
      return temp * temp;
   }
   else
```

```
            return x * mystery(x, y - 1);
    }
```

18. Write a recursive function that takes a nonnegative integer n and returns the sum of the following sequence if n is odd

$$1^3 + 2^2 + 3^3 + 4^2 + 5^3 + \ldots + (n-1)^2 + n^3$$

or the sum of the following sequence if n is even

$$1^3 + 2^2 + 3^3 + 4^2 + 5^3 + \ldots + (n-1)^3 + n^2$$

19. Write a recursive function with a single `char` argument that prints a table of characters and their ASCII values for all `chars` bigger than or equal to the argument.

20. Write a recursive function with a single `int` argument that prints a sequence of characters from the value of its argument as follows: For each digit in the argument, the function prints * if the digit is even. If the digit is odd, the function prints the digit instead.

21. Write a recursive function named `reverse` with a single `int` argument that prints the digits of the argument in reverse order. For example,

```
reverse(2345) prints 5432
reverse(100562) prints 265001
```

22. Write an appropriate set of test data to determine if the function described in exercise 9 (b) is defective.

23. Define a function named `tenPointScaleGrade` that takes an integer between `0` and `100` and returns the corresponding letter grade based on a 10-point scale. Write a driver for `tenPointScaleGrade()`. What is an appropriate set of data that can be used to test the function?

24. Write an appropriate set of data to test a program solution to exercise 26.

Programming Projects

25. Reimplement the changemaker solution, substituting the eight functions returning the numbers for the different denominations into a single function as described in section 4.5.

26. The personal income tax tables for the state of North Carolina in 1989 were printed on the income tax form as follows.

| If the net taxable income is | | The tax is |
over	but not over	
-0-	$ 2,000	3% of net taxable income
$ 2,000	$ 4,000	$ 60 + 4% of the amount over $2,000
$ 4,000	$ 6,000	$140 + 5% of the amount over $4,000
$ 6,000	$10,000	$240 + 6% of the amount over $6,000
$10,000		$480 + 7% of the amount over $10,000

Write a program that can compute the income tax liability based on that table.

27. Complete the design and implementation of the oil rig problem of section 4.8. Test your problem with a set of input data for every possible light configuration. (There are seven of them, including the configuration of no visible lights.)

28. Members of the crew on an oil rig must be concerned about ships traveling in the vicinity of the oil rig for fear that the ships might collide with the rig platform. A variation on the oil rig problem is as follows. The oil rig can see the running lights of a ship and the ship can tell its location. Based on that information and its location, the oil rig will send a warning to the ship if it is possible that the ship may come within a quarter of a nautical mile of the oil platform.

    Analyze and design a solution to this version of the problem.

29. The original oil rig problem that was part of the ACM Programming Contest had nothing to do with oil rigs. It was concerned only with ships traveling at night: your ship and a different ship. Each ship knew its location, speed, and bearing at any given time. As a crew member on your ship, you were responsible for taking readings on your own and the other ship's locations, speeds, and bearings for two times, three minutes apart. If the distances between the ships decreased and the relative bearing from your ship to the other stayed almost the same (within 2°), then you were responsible for issuing a collision warning.

    Analyze and design a solution based on this version of the problem.

Chapter 5

Iteration Behavior: Loops

THE convenience store problem from Chapter 1 was modeled on a special purpose calculator that could power up, solve a single problem, and then power down. Wouldn't it be nice if that calculator could keep on solving problems rather than powering down after one single problem? The calculator object could send a message to the input object to get a number, a message to the computing object to figure out the answer, and a message to the output object to show the answer and then go through the same cycle all over again.

Objects can make decisions. Decisions are implemented in an object's methods as selection statements. Objects can also repeat or iterate actions. Iteration is implemented in an object's method either by recursion or by C++ **loops**, a feature that allows programmers to execute a particular set of statements over and over again. Repeated execution of the same set of statements is called **iteration**.

Both loops and selection statements are used to change the flow of control of execution from the ordinary sequential execution. A selection statement offers one or more branches. If the condition for a selection has one value, then one set of statements (one branch) is executed. If the condition has another value, then another set of statements (another branch) is executed, and so on. Selection statements permit one group of statements to be executed sometimes to the exclusion of another. Loops allow an entire group of statements to be executed multiple times.

We showed how to implement iteration in the previous chapter with recursive functions, which work quite well for both simple and complicated iterations. However, most programmers would have coded the iteration of the previous chapter with loops rather than recursive functions. What we did before with recursion, we will now do with loops. C++ has three kinds of loops: `while` loops, `do/while` loops, and `for` loops. This chapter will explain how to construct and use them.

As an application of loops, we will look at a new programming problem, starting with analysis and design and completing it through implementation. Although we will be constructing a brand new model, that does not mean we cannot incorporate components and objects from old models. (One of the goals of object-oriented programming is to reuse components and objects as much as possible.) In constructing the implementation of the new model, we will take a closer look at the input and output streams `cin` and `cout`.

5.1 ▌ The first loop structure: `while` **loops**

Let's begin by looking at a coding problem. Suppose x is an `int` that has been assigned a value. Find the sum of all odd integers that are positive and less than or equal to x. For example, if x is 10, the sum is $1 + 3 + 5 + 7 + 9$; if x is 9, the sum is $1 + 3 + 5 + 7 + 9$; if x is 1, the sum is 1; if x is 0 or negative, the (default) sum is 0.

The following code solves the problem.

```
// Find the sum of all odd positive integers less than or equal to x.
const int firstInt = 1;      // Smallest positive integer
int upperLimit = x;          // No integer greater than this is added
int oddSum = 0;              // Sum of consecutive odd integers added so far
int nextOdd = firstInt;      // Next integer to add to the sum

while (nextOdd <= upperLimit) {
    oddSum += nextOdd;
    nextOdd += 2;
}
```

The first four statements of the code define and assign values to the data objects that will be used to find the sum. Those statements are not actually a part of the loop. The code that starts with the keyword `while` and continues to the right brace is a `while` loop. Right after the keyword `while` is the **loop condition**, `nextOdd <= upperLimit`, which controls the execution of the body of the loop. The **body** of this `while` loop is a compound statement enclosed by the curly braces. The two statements in the body of the loop serve two different purposes. The first one adds an odd integer to the sum. The second prepares for the next execution of the loop. Figure 5.1 illustrates the terms in the loop.

The loop begins execution with evaluation of the loop condition, `nextOdd <= upperLimit`. If the condition is true (as it will be in the first evaluation whenever x is positive), the body of the loop is executed. The entire process then starts over again, beginning with the evaluation of the loop condition. On the other hand, if `nextOdd <= upperLimit` is evaluated to false, then the body of the loop is skipped, and loop execution is terminated.

We'll trace the execution of the loop for x with a value 9.

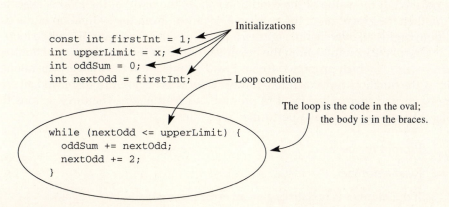

Figure 5.1 A `while` loop.

	nextOdd	oddSum	upperLimit (*same as* x)
Loop condition is first evaluated	1	0	9
Immediately after first iteration	3	1	9
Immediately after second iteration	5	4	9
Immediately after third iteration	7	9	9
Immediately after fourth iteration	9	16	9
Immediately after fifth iteration	11	25	9

The loop begins its sixth execution with evaluation of the loop condition. At that time, `nextOdd` is 11 and `upperLimit` is 9. The condition `nextOdd <= upperLimit` is now false and the loop execution terminates.

Notice that the loop body was constructed so that the loop condition would eventually become false. Eventually `nextOdd` becomes larger than `upperLimit` because every time the loop body is executed, `nextOdd` increases by 2. That's important. Otherwise, we would have an **infinite loop**, a loop whose execution does not stop.

Technically, a `while` loop looks like this:

```
while (condition)
    statement-L
```

The *condition* is the same sort of condition used for `if` statements. The *statement-L* is usually a compound statement although it can be a simple statement.

When a `while` loop begins execution, the condition is evaluated. If the value of the condition is false, the body of the loop is skipped—the execution of the loop is finished. If the value of the condition is true, the body of the loop is executed. And then the execution of the entire loop, starting from the evaluation of the condition, begins all over again. Figure 5.2 illustrates the execution of a while loop.

One of the examples from the previous chapter is the function `inputNonNegativeInt()`, which prompted for and read an integer. If the integer was nonnegative, the function quit execution. If the integer was negative, it displayed an error message, and then called itself to prompt and read again. The three actions that `inputNonNegativeInt()` performed were these:

1. Prompt the user.

2. Read a number.

3. If the number is negative, give an error message and begin again.

We can write a definition for `inputNonNegativeInt()` so that it uses a loop to do that repeated activity. The new implementation is fairly simple.

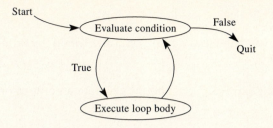

Figure 5.2 Trace of `while` loop execution.

```
void inputNonNegativeInt(int& aNumber, const char prompt[])
// Arguments:
//    aNumber - out - A nonnegative integer entered by the user
//    prompt - Message displayed to the user
// Side effect: Prompts the user and reads a nonnegative value for aNumber.
// Error check:  The user must continue to enter numbers until a nonnegative
//    number is entered.
{
    cout << prompt;
    cin >> aNumber;
    while (aNumber < 0) {
        // Error check.  Request the user to enter another number.
        cout << "Your entry must not be a negative number."
            << "  Please reenter.\n\n" << prompt;
        cin >> aNumber;
    }
}
```

Notice that aNumber has a legitimate user input value before the loop begins execution. The value of aNumber is the most recent number that the user entered. If that most recently entered number is negative (if the condition aNumber < 0 is true), the loop body is executed. Execution of the loop body displays an error message on the screen and an additional prompt for input. Another value is read for aNumber. This updates aNumber to be the new most recent number that the user entered. The loop condition is evaluated again, this time with that new user entry for the value of aNumber.

The function printARow() was also discussed in the previous chapter. That function has two pass-by-value arguments, an int and a char. Its purpose is to print a row of characters on the screen. The int argument indicates how many characters to print, and the char argument indicates which character is to be printed. A declaration of printARow() is as follows:

```
void printARow(int n, char ch);
// Arguments:
```

```
//    ch - Printable character
//    n - Nonnegative number
// Side effect:  n copies of the character ch, followed by a newline are
//    printed on the screen.
```

The call `printARow(5,'A')` should generate an output of five A's followed by a newline:

```
AAAAA
```

The old definition of `printARow()` used recursion to print the character. The new definition has a loop to print the character every time the loop body is executed.

```
void printARow(int n, char ch)
{
    int count = 0;         // Number of characters already printed
    while (count < n) {
        count += 1;
        cout << ch;
    }
    cout << endl;
}
```

This loop is controlled by the local variable `count`. A variable that appears in the loop condition in this manner is called a **loop control variable**. When the body of the loop is executed, `count` is incremented by 1 and `ch` is output. The order of execution of statements in the body of a loop is usually important, but, for this loop, that order is irrelevant.

It is important to recognize when this loop quits execution. Suppose n is 3 and ch is `'A'`. Beginning the first execution of the loop, no copies of `'A'` have been printed, and `count` is 0. Beginning the second execution of the loop, one copy of `'A'` has been printed, and `count` is 1.

Beginning the third execution of the loop, two copies of `'A'` have been printed, and `count` is 2. The first statement in that third iteration of the loop body, increments `count` to 3. Even though the condition `count < n` *would* evaluate to false immediately after execution of that increment statement, the condition is not evaluated until the loop body has finished execution. The statement `cout << ch;` is executed *before* the loop condition is checked for the final time.

The table following traces the execution of the loop from the very beginning. The loop step column tells what is evaluated and on which iteration of the loop the evaluation is occurring. The remaining columns show the status of the objects, expressions, and the output after the evaluations have occurred.

Loop step	count	n	count < n	Output generated so far
1. (count < n)	0	3	true	
1. count += 1;	1	3	true	
1. cout << ch;	1	3	true	A
2. (count < n)	1	3	true	
2. count += 1;	2	3	true	
2. cout << ch;	2	3	true	AA
3. (count < n)	2	3	true	
3. count += 1;	3	3	false	
3. cout << ch;	3	3	false	AAA
4. (count < n)	3	3	false	

The exit from the body of the loop is not simply done in the middle of the body when the loop control variable is changed. If the loop body were exited in the middle, that third 'A' would not be printed. Exit from the body of the loop occurs at the *end* of execution of the loop body. The condition is not checked until the entire body has completed execution.

5.2   Constructing loops: How to start, how to quit, and how to get to the next step

In the first example of this chapter, a loop calculated the sum of a sequence of numbers. That sequence consisted of all the odd numbers starting with 1 and going up through the largest odd number that did not exceed the upper limit. The loop in the second example of this chapter (from the function inputNonNegativeInt()) also processed a sequence of numbers. The sequence consisted of all of the integers input by the user up through the first nonnegative integer.

The third loop in this chapter (from the function printARow()) printed a row of characters. In a sense, that loop also processed a sequence of numbers. That sequence, which started with 1, was used only to count how many characters had been output. The variable count kept track of those numbers.

Not all loops process sequences of numbers. But in a real sense, every loop processes a sequence of something. Sometimes that sequence is obvious, as was the one for the function inputNonNegativeInt(). Sometimes the sequence is hidden in a counter, as it was in printARow(). Sometimes the sequence as just the "loop step" sequence, which counts how many times the body of the loop has been executed.

Processing a sequence is a problem that has infinite variations. Additional examples of processing sequences of numeric data include finding the average of a sequence of numbers, printing all positive items, and printing the numbers from smallest to largest.

Iterator objects

There are two parts to processing a sequence: (1) getting the items in the sequence, one at a time, and (2) doing whatever processing is necessary to each individual item. This section will concentrate on the first part. Being able to go through each item in a sequence is so important that we will make up a new object just to do that: an iterator on a sequence or an **iterator object** for short.

An iterator object knows its sequence. It can initialize itself to process the sequence from the start, it can access the next item in the sequence, and it can tell whether there are more items in the sequence. So the iterator object knows how to start and how to keep on going, and it knows when to quit. The iterator object is a design object whose implementation will be part of the loop code itself.

The first loop of this chapter found the sum of all positive odd integers less than or equal to the integer x. Let's take another look at that loop in terms its underlying sequence. This time we will document the code just to show how the first item in the sequence is accessed, how each subsequent item is accessed, and how to tell whether there are more items in the sequence. The iterator object is implemented by the code that is commented.

```cpp
// Find the sum of all odd positive integers less than or equal to x.
const int firstInt = 1;            // First item in the sequence
int upperLimit = x;
int oddSum = 0;
int nextOdd = firstInt;            // Get started

while (nextOdd <= upperLimit) {    // More to do?
    oddSum += nextOdd;
    nextOdd += 2;                  // Go to the next step
}
```

The iterator object can take many forms, depending on the nature of the sequence itself. Let's see how it is done in the function inputNonNegativeInt().

```cpp
void inputNonNegativeInt(int& aNumber, const char prompt[])
{
    cout << prompt;
    cin >> aNumber;                                     // Get started
    while (aNumber < 0) {                               // More to do?
        cout << "Your entry must not be a negative number."
             << "  Please reenter.\n\n" << prompt;
        cin >> aNumber;                                 // Go to the next step
    }
}
```

In both loops, the iterator object was implemented through the loop control variable. We won't always be able to implement the iterator object in exactly these forms. It is helpful to think of the iterator in terms of what it does rather than in terms of how it does it. What the iterator can do is described by three phrases:

- *startup*   Sets up the iterator to process the first item
- *next*   Gets the next item in the sequence
- *more*   True if there are more items, false if not

In our loops, the iterator's *startup* includes getting the first item (if there is a first item). The iterator's *more* checks to see if there are more items to be processed. The iterator's *next* gets the next item (if there is one). The general form of a while loop amounts to this:

```
initialize
startup          // Get the first item if there is a first item!
while (more) {
   process most recently accessed item
   next           // Get the next item, if there is a next item!
}
finalize
```

The code for *initialize* and *finalize* are for any initialization or wrap-up necessary to complete the entire procedure. Both of the first two examples of this chapter contained explicit initialization code. The first three definitions in the code to find the sum of odd numbers were initializations of the data objects that were not part of the sequence but were used in the loop. The very first prompt in the code for inputNonNegativeInt() was initialization code in the sense that it told the user to enter the first item in the sequence.

The function printARow() contained explicit finalization code. When the loop finishes execution, all of the necessary characters have been printed. The specifications called for printing the characters in row, followed by a newline. So the code necessary to finalize the task was the last statement in the body of the function: cout << endl; .

There are some significant variations to sequence processing and a few situations in which the ideas in this section will not work. There are also other situations in which the answers to the questions "What is the first item? What is each next item? Are there more items?" will not look exactly like the general form. But the answers to these questions will always appear in some form within the code that processes the sequence.

How to process each loop step

Knowing how to start, how to quit, and how to get to the next step will not reveal everything that is supposed to happen inside the body of the loop itself. The main problem that programmers are faced with is "Exactly how is the loop going to do what it is supposed to do? What does it mean to process data?"

Let's look at an example that will provide some insight into this problem. Determine the average of some positive integers, which are to be entered by the user. The last number that the user will enter is 0. The number 0 is a **sentinel value**, a number that signifies the end of input. The sentinel is not to be averaged in with the other integers. If the user enters 50 100 0, then the average is 75 rather than 50.

This problem clearly calls for processing a sequence of data, the sequence being the numbers entered by the user. The problem says to calculate the average of a sequence of numbers, which is the sum of the numbers in the sequence divided by the size of the sequence. The loop itself can process each number in the sequence by keeping a running sum and a running count of the numbers in the sequence. To process a number in the sequence means to add it to the running sum and to increment the running count by 1.

What makes this problem a candidate for a loop is that we can conceive of how to solve it in a step-by-step way. When the loop finishes execution, the running sum will be the sum of all numbers in the sequence that were processed and the running count will be how many numbers in the sequence were processed. In fact, we can make an even stronger statement than that. After each execution of the loop body, the running sum will be the sum of all numbers in the sequence that have been processed *so far* and the running count will be how many numbers in the sequence have been processed *so far*.

Let's set up five data objects for the problem: (1) the sentinel, (2) the average, (3) the running sum, (4) the running count, and (5) the most recently entered number. The sentinel for the sequence should be a constant. The loop itself will do all of the data processing (summing and counting). So before the loop begins execution, the running sum and the running count should be initialized to 0.

```
const int sentinel = 0;   // Sentinel for end of input
int x;                    // Number most recently entered by the user
int count = 0;            // Count of data numbers added so far
int sum = 0;              // Sum of data numbers added so far
double average;           // Average of all numbers entered
                          //    excluding the last one (the sentinel)
```

The initializations for sum and count are not the only preparation necessary for starting the processing. The first number in the sequence should have been accessed before the loop begins execution. (Access in this case means it should have been input.) We can use the old, familiar input object from the changemaker to do that input:

```
inputInt(x,"Enter a number. ");
```

What can we say about the data objects immediately before the loop begins execution? Certainly the following points are true.

1. sum is 0.

2. count is 0.

3. x is the number most recently entered by the user.

Statements such as these, which are true immediately before the loop is executed, are known as **loop preconditions**.

Keep in mind that processing involves both summing and counting. The processing takes place in the body of the loop itself. After each number is processed, the next number must be accessed (again, using inputInt()). At the end of every execution of the loop body, the following statements are true:

1. sum is the sum of all the numbers that have been added so far.

2. count is how many numbers have been added so far.

3. x is the number most recently entered by the user.

These last three statements are completely consistent with the loop preconditions. If the loop has not been executed at all, sum is 0, the same as the sum of all the numbers that have been added so far. Also, count is 0, the same as how many numbers have been processed so far. Statements such as these, which are true immediately before the loop is entered and at the end of every execution of the loop, are known as **loop invariants**. A loop invariant is true even immediately before the loop begins execution for the first time.

How can we tell if more numbers in the sequence must be processed? Certainly the sentinel value should not be processed, but all other numbers should be. Evaluation of the condition x != sentinel will reveal whether there is additional processing to be performed. Immediately after the loop completes execution, the last number entered by the user is the sentinel value—which means that the loop condition is false. So immediately after the loop completes execution, the following statements are true:

1. sum is the sum of all the numbers that have been added so far.

2. count is how many numbers have been added so far.

3. x is the number most recently entered by the user.

4. x is the sentinel and the loop condition is false.

The first three statements are the loop invariant that we had listed previously. Statements that are true immediately after the last execution of the loop are known as **loop postconditions**. Since all of the numbers in the sequence have been processed, sum is the total of all of those processed numbers and count is how many numbers were processed.

> After each execution of the loop, loop invariants describe what has happened in processing the sequence so far. And at the end of the entire execution of the loop, the invariants describe what has happened to the objects after the entire sequence has been processed.

Using loop invariants to construct correct loops

How can you capture the ideas of loop invariants in code? Our suggestion is to use the loop invariants to document the data object declarations and then to write the loop to be sure that the documentation is correct.

The following code finds the average of the sequence. It uses the function inputInt() from the changemaker to get the sequence numbers.

```
// Find the average of a sequence of numbers entered by the user. The
//    sequence is terminated by the sentinel value 0.
const int sentinel = 0;      // Sentinel value for end of input
int x;                       // Number most recently entered by the user
int count = 0;               // Count of numbers added so far
int sum = 0;                 // Sum of numbers added so far
double average;              // Average of all numbers entered
                             //    excluding the last one (the sentinel)

inputInt(x,"Enter a number. ");      // Get started
while (x != sentinel) {              // More processing?
   sum += x;                         //    Process ...
   count += 1;                       //    ...
   inputInt(x,"Enter a number. ");   //    Go to the next step
}

if (count > 0)                       // Finish processing
   average = (double(sum))/ count;
```

If the sequence of numbers entered by the user contains at least one number (besides the sentinel), then the concept of average makes sense. There is no assignment to average if no numbers except the sentinel are entered by the user. Because the problem specifications did not indicate how to handle that special case, that case is not covered in the code.

The computation of average is not part of the loop and needs to be done only once. Furthermore, that computation can be performed only after sum and count are calculated for the entire sequence. The computation therefore is part of the finalization code rather than part of the loop itself.

Good loop invariants are helpful in constructing correct loops. Before constructing a loop, ask yourself these questions about the objects involved:

1. What is true just as the loop starts?

2. What is true after the loop completes each step (after each execution of the body)?

3. What is true right after the loop is done?

The idea of a loop invariant is simply a clever scheme that somebody came up with to answer those three questions.

Many statements can be loop invariants. The important loop invariants—those that can help you construct loops—are the ones that describe the relationships among the data objects and what they represent in terms of what is actually happening when the code is executing. Even though the data objects themselves change from one execution of the loop body to the next, what they represent is the same.

Although it is not critical that you always directly identify important loop preconditions, postconditions, and invariants, it often helps you construct proper loops if you think about those things *before* you code. Show the loop invariants in the code by commenting the objects involved in the loop. The comments should describe what the objects represent and how they are related.

Let's put these new ideas to work by solving another problem: find the smallest number in a sequence. Here's the situation. The user will be prompted to enter a sequence of integers, which is terminated with 0. The number 0 is a sentinel and is not to be processed as a member of the sequence.

What are some useful data objects? How about `sentinel` and `x` exactly as they were in the previous problem? In fact, we can use exactly the same code for accessing the first number, indicating if there are more numbers, and accessing each subsequent number that we used for the previous problem. A new data object for this problem, `smallest`, will represent the smallest number in the sequence that has been processed.

In the previous problem of finding the average, the values `count` and `sum` were meaningful even in the situation where the user entered only the sentinel value and nothing else. In that special case, the sequence of actual data numbers was an empty sequence that had nothing in it. The value of `count` was 0, which means that the number of data values that was added was 0. That made sense. The value of `sum` was also 0, which also made sense. The sum of no numbers ought to be 0. The loop to compute `sum` and `count` was correct even for the case in which the input sequence was empty. (We did not try to find the average of the empty sequence, but that calculation of the average was not part of the loop.)

What does it mean to find the smallest number in a sequence of numbers if there aren't any numbers in the sequence? There is no obvious, reasonable answer to that question. What can we do? We can arbitrarily choose a number, say the sentinel, as the smallest. Or we can simply assume that the user will enter a sequence that contains at least one data number (a number besides the sentinel).

Suppose we make the latter assumption: the user will enter at least one data number. When the first data number is entered, we can assign to smallest the value of that first number, before the loop begins execution at all. The loop, which is designed to find the smallest number, will have the following invariant: smallest is the smallest data number (nonsentinel number) found so far in the sequence. Another invariant is the same as for the previous example: x is the number most recently entered. (It is either the sentinel, or it is the next number in the sequence to be processed.)

How will the code go? Before the loop is executed, the first number is entered and smallest is assigned its value. In the body of the loop, the number being processed should be compared to smallest. If the number being processed is smaller than the smallest seen so far, then the value of smallest needs to be changed to that number. At the end of the loop body, there should be another statement to get the next element in the sequence.

The entire solution can be written this way:

```
// Find the smallest number in a non-empty sequence which is terminated by
//   a sentinel value.
const int sentinel = 0;    // Sentinel value for end of input
int x;                     // Number most recently entered by the user
int smallest;              // Smallest data number found so far
inputInt(x,"Enter a number. ");      // Get started
smallest = x;
while (x != sentinel) {              // More data to process?
    if (smallest > x)
        smallest = x;
    inputInt(x,"Enter a number. ");  // Go to the next step
}
```

Let's change this problem slightly. Instead of finding just the smallest number in a sequence, we'll find the largest number also. The code is very similar to what we just wrote. We simply need a new data object, largest, that indicates the largest data number read so far.

```
// Find the smallest and largest numbers in a non-empty sequence which is
//    terminated by a sentinel value.
const int sentinel = 0;    // Sentinel value for end of input
int x;                     // Number most recently entered by the user
int smallest;              // Smallest data number found so far
int largest;               // Largest data number found so far

inputInt(x,"Enter a number. ");      // Get started
smallest = x;
```

```
largest = x;
while (x != sentinel) {                    // More data to process?
   if (smallest > x)
      smallest = x;
   if (largest < x)
      largest = x;
   inputInt(x,"Enter a number. ");   // Go to the next step
}
```

Notice that before the loop begins execution, `smallest` and `largest` are assigned values. They are both assigned the same number, which is the first number in the entire sequence. That makes sense. If the sequence had only one number, then that number would be both the smallest and the largest number in the sequence.

The next example uses the function `rand()`, which is defined in the general utility library built into C and C++. The header file for the general utilities library is `stdlib.h`. In order to use `rand()`, source code must have the following include directive.

```
#include <stdlib.h>
```

The function `rand()` has no arguments. Different calls to `rand()` return different "random" nonnegative integers.[1] The sequence generated by successive calls `rand()` can be used to generate another sequence of floating point numbers whose values lie between 0 and 1. The following expression, for example, calculates such a floating point number:

```
(rand() % 1000) / 1000.0
```

The remainder of dividing a number returned by `rand()` by 1000 is between 0 and 999 inclusive. Dividing that remainder by 1000.0 produces a number between 0 and 1.

Suppose we generate a finite sequence of such numbers—say, a sequence of 50,000 of them. How are they distributed? How many of those numbers are between 0 and .5? How many are greater than or equal to .5 but less than .75? How many are greater than .75? A loop can provide the answers.

```
int firstHalf = 0;       // Count of random numbers so far that are less
                         //    than .5
int thirdFourth = 0;     // Count of random numbers so far that are .5
                         //    or greater but less than .75
int count = 0;           // Total number of random numbers counted so far
```

---

[1] `rand()` is called a pseudo-random number generator. "Pseudo" because the numbers that it returns appear random.

```
while (count < 50000) {
   double x = (rand() % 1000) / 1000.0;
   if (x < .5)
      firstHalf += 1;
   else if (x < .75)
      thirdFourth += 1;
   count++;
}
```

The documentation of this code shows the important loop invariants. When the loop finally quits execution, the value of `count` is 50000. Can you guess approximate values for `firstHalf` and `thirdFourth`?

In Chapter 4, we used recursive function calls to perform iteration. How to start, how to stop, and how to continue to the next step are issues for iteration that are done through recursion as well as through loops. For performing iteration through recursion, they translate into the following:

- How to start is the initial call to the function.

- How to continue to the next step is the recursive call inside the function itself.

- How to quit is condition of the selection statement inside the body of the recursive function. The recursive call is part of the body of that selection statement. If the condition is false, the iteration stops.

The next example of a loop also uses the `rand()` function. Suppose that you are asked to find out how many random integers have to be generated by `rand()` before you find two in a row that differ by less than 10,000.

```
double oldRandom = rand();      // The next-to-last random number generated
double thisRandom = rand();     // The most recently generated random number
double delta = 10000;           // Are the last two random numbers this close?
int numberGenerated = 2;        // Number of random numbers generated so far
                                //   for this test
while (fabs(oldRandom - thisRandom) >= delta) {
   oldRandom = thisRandom;
   thisRandom = rand();
   numberGenerated += 1;
}
```

The two variables `oldRandom` and `thisRandom` keep track of the two most recent random numbers. Even though their initializations look the same, they are not the same value at all. Remember that rand() returns a new number every time it is called. The variable numberGenerated, which is used to count how many random numbers have been generated, is initialized to 2. After all, when its definition is executed, two random numbers have already been generated.

The loop condition is (fabs(oldRandom - thisRandom) >= delta). The function fabs() is part of the math library. It returns the absolute value of its argument. The condition is true if the last two random numbers differ by at least 10,000. It is false if they do not.

Notice how the body of the loop changes the values of oldRandom and this-Random to prepare for the next loop iteration. The variable oldRandom is used to store the most recent random number, while thisRandom is updated to the next random number. And, of course, numberGenerated is updated to reflect the fact that one more number was generated.

5.3 The second loop structure: do/while loops

Sometimes it is known ahead of time that a sequence has at least one item to be processed. In that case, the body of a while loop to process such a sequence is guaranteed to be executed at least once. The last loop from the previous section was an example of such a situation. As a programming convenience, C++ offers the do/while loop, an additional looping structure that ensures that the body of the loop is guaranteed to execute at least once.

For an example of a do/while loop, let's go back to the first problem in this chapter: finding the sum of nonnegative integers less than or equal to some number x. If we can assume that x is at least as large as 1, then that first loop can be replaced by the following code:

```
const int firstInt = 1;    // Smallest positive integer
int upperLimit = x;        // No integer greater than this is added
int oddSum = 0;            // Sum of consecutive odd integers added so far
int nextOdd = firstInt;    // Next integer to add to the sum

do {
   oddSum += nextOdd;
   nextOdd += 2;
} while (nextOdd <= upperLimit);
```

The body of a do/while loop is executed first, then the condition is evaluated. If the condition is not false, the entire process is repeated again. The iterator object is still sitting in this code in the following form:

- *startup*   int nextOdd = first;
- *next*   nextOdd += 2;
- *more*   (nextOdd <= upperLimit)

There is only one difference between a `do/while` loop and a `while` loop: in a `do/while` loop, the condition is evaluated at the end of the execution of the loop body rather than before the execution of the loop body. The general form of a `do/while` loop is as follows:

```
do
    statement-L
while (condition);
```

Figure 5.3 illustrates execution of a `do/while` loop. Of course, `statement-L`, which constitutes the body of the loop, can be a simple statement, but it is usually a compound statement. When it is compound, you will see a right closing brace immediately before the `while`.

As another illustration of `do/while` loops, let's go back to an old problem from the previous chapter, which was actually first introduced in Chapter 2. The problem is to find the sum of digits in a nonnegative integer.

The sum of digits in an integer is the last digit plus the sum of the rest of the digits. The sum of digits in 3456789 is 9 plus the sum of digits in 345678. Integer division is important here: the digit 9 is the remainder of 3456789 divided by 10 (3456789 % 10) and the number 345678 is the quotient of 3456789 divided by 10 (3456789/10). We can use the results of integer division to find a running sum of the digits and also to figure out what digits in the original number have not yet been added to the running sum.

How about constructing a loop to find this sum? If you look at this problem as processing a sequence (3456789, 345678, 34567, 3456, 345, 34, 3, 0), then you can figure out what constitutes the iterator object and go from there. You probably are not going to think in terms of sequences right off the bat, but you can think in terms of steps. So the important "sequence-processing" questions for this problem are how to start the first step, how to know when all the steps have been done, and how to get from one step to the next.

Three data objects will be useful for this problem. The first data object, `sum`, represents the sum of digits added so far (the running sum). The digits that have not yet been added into that running sum are those in the second data object, `restOfDigits`. The different values of `restOfDigits` will constitute the sequence that we outlined in the last paragraph. The descriptions for `sum` and

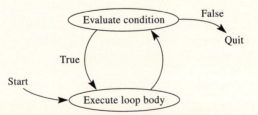

Figure 5.3 Trace of `do/while` loop execution.

`restOfDigits` are loop invariants. The third data object, `rightmostDigit`, represents the least significant digit of `restOfDigits`. That rightmost digit will be the next digit to be added to the sum.

To get started on the first step, set `sum` to 0 and `restOfDigits` to `number` (the number whose digits are to be summed). That gives the following definitions and initializations.

```
int sum = 0;                  // Sum of digits in the number added so far
int restOfDigits = number;    // Digits of the number which have not
                              //   yet been added
int rightmostDigit;           // Next digit to be added
```

How do you know when to quit? When the `restOfDigits` becomes 0, there is nothing left to sum. And to go from one step to the next, you must discard the least significant digit from `restOfDigits`.

Here is a summary of what the loop will do. Peel the rightmost digit off `restOfDigits` and add it to `sum`. After doing that, see if there are any digits left to add to the sum. If not, quit. If there are digits left, do the same thing over again. The idea is essentially captured by this algorithm.

> initialize `sum` to 0
> do
>> get the least significant digit (rightmost digit) of the `restOfDigits`
>> add the least significant digit to `sum`
>> peel that least significant digit off `restOfDigits`
> while there are still digits left to sum in `restOfDigits`

The body of the loop is not too difficult to code. The least significant digit (rightmost digit) of `restOfDigits` is `restOfDigits % 10`. To eliminate the least significant digit from `restOfDigits`, divide `restOfDigits` by `10`. The result of putting all of these ideas together in code is as follows:

```
int sum = 0;                  // Sum of digits in the number added so far
int restOfDigits = number;    // Digits of the number which have not
                              //   yet been added
int rightmostDigit;           // Next digit to be added

do {
   rightmostDigit = restOfDigits % 10;
   restOfDigits /= 10;
   sum += rightmostDigit;
} while (restOfDigits > 0);
```

By the way, this code is correct if `number` is nonnegative. Recall that the modulus operator, `%`, is useful only if the left-hand operand (the numerator) is nonnegative and the right-hand operand (the denominator) is strictly positive!

5.4 The third loop structure: `for` loops

You can write any loop as a `while` loop. In fact, if you put in the correct conditions, you can write any loop as a `do/while` loop. As was the case of `do/while` loops, `for` loops are provided by C++ as a matter of convenience rather than a matter of providing something extraordinary that cannot be accomplished easily otherwise.

Before discussing `for` loops, we will divert our attention to some new operators that are particularly nice to use with `for` loops. When you see them, you will begin to understand how C++ got its name.

Increment and decrement operators and the comma operator

Four new arithmetic operators are frequently used by C and C++ programmers: prefix `++`, postfix `++`, prefix `--`, and postfix `--`. The first two are **increment operators** because they increment their operands. The second two are **decrement operators** because they decrement their operands. They are so often used in conjunction with loops that we digress here to take a look at them.

All increment and decrement operators are unary operators, which means they have only one operand. (Most of the arithmetic operators that we have used, such as `+` and `*`, are binary operators, which means they require two operands.) The operand for each of the four new operators should be a numeric variable.

Unlike the other arithmetic operators, increment and decrement operators cause their operands to change—they generate side effects. Here is how the postfix `++` operator works. If `x` is a numeric variable, then evaluation of the expression `x++` does two things *in the order listed:*

1. The value of the expression is the current value of `x`.

2. The value of `x` is incremented by `1`.

The use of `++` as a prefix operator means that the `++` comes before the operand rather than after. Prefix `++` is similar to postfix `++`, except that the steps 1 and 2 are reversed. For example, suppose `x` is an `int` with value 8. Then the statement

```
cout << x++;
```

prints 8, and the value of `x` is changed to 9. If `y` has the value 6, then the statement

```
cout << ++y;
```

changes the value of `y` to 7 and then prints 7.

Here are some additional examples of the use of the increment operators:

```
int aNumber;                       // The value of aNumber is not meaningful
int count = 0;                     // count is 0
count++;                           // count is 1
aNumber = count++;                 // aNumber is 1, count is 2
aNumber = aNumber + 2 * count++;   // aNumber is 5, count is 3
++count;                           // count is 4
aNumber = ++count - 12;            // aNumber is -7, count is 5
if (count++ > 0)                   // count is 6
    aNumber++;                     // aNumber is -6
```

Both the prefix ++ and postfix ++ operators can be used in assignment statements, alone as single statements, or in expressions such as the condition in a selection or loop statement.

The prefix -- and postfix -- operators are analogous to the prefix ++ and postfix ++ operators. The difference is that the operand is decremented rather than incremented. The evaluation of x-- is as follows:

1. The value of the expression is the current value of x.

2. The value of x is decremented by 1.

Here are the same examples as before, only we have replaced increment by decrement and changed the initialization of count.

```
int aNumber;                       // The value of aNumber is not meaningful
int count = 8;                     // count is 8
count--;                           // count is 7
aNumber = count--;                 // aNumber is 7, count is 6
aNumber = aNumber + 2 * count--;   // aNumber is 19, count is 5
--count;                           // count is 4
aNumber = --count - 12;            // aNumber is -9, count is 3
if (count-- > 0)                   // count is 2
    aNumber--;                     // aNumber is -10
```

Commas appear frequently in C++ programs. So far, you have used them to separate items in lists, like lists of actual function arguments. For example, the function swap(), which we used to exchange the contents of two int variables, can be invoked this way:

```
swap(aNumber,count);
```

A comma separates the names of the two actual arguments that are part of that call to swap(). For this use, the comma is not an operator.

What happens if a comma is used to join expressions together into a single expression? In that situation, the comma is considered to be an operator. We have not yet used the comma operator in this book, but let's see how it works. Suppose i and j are two int variables. You can assign i the value 3 and j the value 7 with a comma expression statement as follows:

```
i = 3, j = 7;      // i gets 3 and j gets 7
```

The operands of the comma operator are expressions. A comma expression is evaluated from left to right. The value of a comma expression is the value of the rightmost operand.

The operands for the comma operator do not need to be assignment expressions. In fact, you are more likely to see the increment or decrement operators instead, as in this example:

```
i++, j--           // i is now 4; j is now 6
```

That example is a comma expression, not a comma expression statement. Even though the expression is probably more important for its side effects on i and j, it does have a value of 6.

Our final example will also use i and j, whose values at the beginning of evaluation of the expression are 4 and 6 respectively. The following example shows how the left-to-right evaluation effects the final values of the variables.

```
i++, j -= i        // i is now 5; j is now 1
```

We do not want to make a big deal out of the comma operator. It is a convenience, but hardly a necessity. But it is not hard to use and you are not likely to have difficulty with it.

Constructing `for` **loops**

Recall the function `printARow()`, which has two arguments, an integer n and a character ch. It prints a row of n copies of ch. Our most recent definition of `printARow()` used a `while` loop as follows:

```
int count = 0;
while (count < n) {
    count += 1;
    cout << ch;
}
```

This code looks like the following when a `for` loop replaces the `while` loop:

```
for (int count = 0; count < n; count++)
    cout << ch;
```

The variable `count` serves as the loop control variable for both loops. It represents the number of characters that have already been printed. In the `while` loop, `count` is defined and initialized outside of the loop, before the loop begins execution. In the `for` loop, `count` is defined and initialized in the loop itself. The same Boolean condition, `count < n`, controls loop execution for both loops. The body of the `while` loop contains two statements, one outputs the character and the other updates `count`. The body of the `for` loop consists of a single output statement. After the body of the `for` loop is executed, `count` is updated.

The general structure of a `for` loop is this:

```
for (initStatement; continueExpression; updateExpression)
   bodyStatement
```

Semicolons terminate the *initStatement* and separate *continueExpression* and the *continueExpression* from the *updateExpression*. There is no semicolon between the parentheses and the *bodyStatement*.

The execution of a `for` loop proceeds as follows:

1. The *initStatement* is executed when the loop first begins execution and not any time thereafter.

2. The *continueExpression* is evaluated.

   If *continueExpression* is false, the rest of the loop is skipped and execution of the loop is terminated.

   If *continueExpression* is true,

      3. The *bodyStatement* is executed

      4. The *updateExpression* is evaluated

      5. The process repeats, beginning with step 2.

The `for` loop execution is illustrated in Figure 5.4. The *initStatement* typically involves a definition and initialization or an assignment. This is not always the case, however. The *continueExpression* is a Boolean expression that is equivalent to the *condition* of a `while` loop. The *bodySatement*, which is the body of the `for` loop, may be a simple or compound statement.

The *initStatement* and the *updateExpression* inside the `for` loop parentheses usually have side-effects—they change some object in memory. The *continueExpression* may also have side effects (which is true also for `while` loops and `do/while` loops as well), although our first example does not.

The loop

```
for (int count= 0; count <n; count ++) cout <<ch;
```

fits the general `for` loop structure as follows:

```
int count = 1     is the     initStatement
count <= n        is the     continueExpression
```

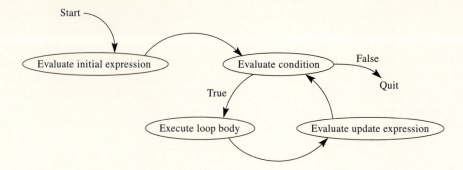

Figure 5.4 Trace of `for` loop execution.

```
count++            is the   updateExpression
cout << ch;        is the   bodyStatement
```

The update expression uses the postfix ++ operator. That expression could have been written in any of the following ways:

```
count++                 // Original expression
count = count + 1
count += 1
++count
```

How do *initStatement*, *continueExpression*, and *updateExpression* fit into the original scheme of sequence processing? The iterator object in our old loops was responsible for starting, checking if there are more items, and getting the next item. The iterator object is also part of a `for` loop. The *initStatement* corresponds to starting. The *continueExpression* corresponds to checking to see if there are more items to process. The *updateExpression* corresponds to getting the next item.[2]

In the last `for` loop, the loop "counted up," taking count from 0 through n. The following `for` loop accomplishes the same thing. It counts down rather than counting up, which means that count represents the number of remaining characters to be printed.

```
for (int count = n; count >0; count--)
    cout << ch;
```

Any `for` loop can be written as an equivalent `while` loop. The general form is translated in this fashion:

---

[2] There are many `for` loops that do not follow this convention. It is possible to put many different expressions into the statements and expressions that constitute the top of the `for` loop, including the entire body of the loop!

```
initStatement;
while (continueExpression) {
    bodyStatement
    updateExpression;
}
```

Any while loop can also be written as a for loop. The following for loop solves the first problem of this chapter, finding the sum of odd integers less than or equal to x.

```
int oddSum = 0;
for (int nextOdd = 1; nextOdd <= x; nextOdd += 2)
    oddSum += nextOdd;
```

By the way, this is not the only for loop that can solve this problem, but it clearly illustrates how a for loop works.

Our for loops examples so far have been controlled by integer variables. That is not our only option. The following loop computes the sum of square roots of real numbers, starting with .5 and going through 20.0 in increments of .5.

```
float sum = .0;
for (float x = .5; x < 20.1; x += .5)
    sum += sqrt(x);
```

Another problem that is easy to solve using a for loop should have a familiar ring. Find the number of digits in a nonnegative integer. Earlier in this chapter, we saw how to find the sum of the digits in a nonnegative integer. Figuring out how many digits the integer has ought to be at least as simple.

Let's use the same identifiers as before: number is the original nonnegative integer and restOfDigits is the digits in the number that have not yet been processed (processed in this problem means counted). The variable count will be the number of digits of number that have already been counted. The variable restOfDigits is the loop control variable.

Both count and restOfDigits can be defined before the loop is executed. The variable count can be initialized when it is declared. (This just makes the loop a little easier to understand. We could actually initialize count as part of the initStatement for the loop.)

```
int count = 0;        // Number of digits counted so far
int restOfDigits;     // Digits which haven't been counted so far
if (number == 0)
    count = 1;
else
    for (restOfDigits = number; restOfDigits > 0; restOfDigits /=  10)
        count++;
```

The loop for counting digits is a little tricky. We had to treat the number 0 as a special case in order to count it as a single-digit number. Let's trace the execution of the entire code. Assume that the value of number is 3097 before execution of the code.

number	count	restOfDigits	
3097	0		after execution of the code preceding the loop
3097	0	3097	after evaluation of *init*
3097	1	309	after 1st execution of *body* and *update*
3097	2	30	after 2nd execution of *body* and *update*
3097	3	3	after 3rd execution of *body* and *update*
3097	4	0	after 4th execution of *body* and *update*

It is easy to modify the previous example so that it not only counts the digits in the number but also finds the sum of the digits in the number. The body of the new for loop will be a compound statement rather than a simple statement. (In this new version, we dispensed with the variable rightmostDigit.)

```
int count = 0;        // Number of digits counted so far
int restOfDigits;     // Digits which haven't been counted
int sum = 0;          // Sum of digits added and counted so far
if (number == 0)
   count = 1;
else
   for (restOfDigits = number; restOfDigits > 0; restOfDigits /=  10) {
      count++;
      sum += restOfDigits % 10;   // Add the rightmost digit to the sum
   }
```

Don't take it for granted that this loop works. Trace it for yourself. (Even textbook authors can make a mistake.)

A for loop can have a definition and initialization of a data object as its *initStatement*. The scope of the declaration of that data object extends to the end of the block in which the for loop resides and not just to the end of the body of the loop. This means that the same data object cannot be redefined and reinitialized in a subsequent for loop appearing later in the same level of the same block. In order to use the same data object to control the second loop, make the second *initStatement* an assignment rather than a definition.

Our next example of a `for` loop is slightly more complicated than the previous ones. The problem that it solves is simple: generate a table of powers of two.

For the solution, we'll write a void function (a procedure) that could be part of an output object. The function has a single argument that tells how big the table is supposed to be.

```
void outputPowersOf2(int exponent)
// Argument: exponent - A nonnegative number
// Side effect: Outputs a table of powers of two from 2^0 to 2^exponent
{
    for(int i = 0, j = 1; i <= exponent; i++, j*= 2)
        cout << "2^" << i << " = " << j << endl;
}
```

Let's examine the `for` loop carefully. The *initStatement* consists of the definitions and initializations of two `int` variables. Ordinarily we prefer not to combine two definitions into a single expression, because that can make the definitions more difficult to understand and more difficult to document. However, in a `for` loop in which the loop control variables are easy-to-understand counters, such a programming style is common among C++ programmers. (Besides, we cannot string the two definitions together with a semicolon, because the semicolon would make the second definition part of the loop condition.)

The condition of the `for` loop is simple and similar to our previous examples. The body of the loop will be executed as long as `i <= exponent` is true. The *updateExpression* is an example of a comma expression. Both of the expressions `i++` and `j *= 2` are evaluated at the end of execution of the loop body. The comma allows us to update two different variables in a single update expression. We do not need—we are not allowed to put—a semicolon between the `i++` and the `j *= 2`.

Incidentally, the first comma, which separated the initialization of `i` from the initialization of `j`, was not the comma operator. It served as a list item separator. The second comma, appearing in the *updateExpression* to separate the update of `i` and the update of `j`, was the comma operator.

The output generated by the function call `outputPowersOf2(5)` is shown below.

```
2^0   = 1
2^1   = 2
2^2   = 4
2^3   = 8
2^4   = 16
2^5   = 32
```

5.5 Nested loops

A code fragment from the previous section had a `for` loop nested inside an `if/else` statement.

```
if (number == 0)
    count = 1;
else
    for (restOfDigits = number; restOfDigits > 0; restOfDigits /=  10)
        count++;
```

Nesting loops inside selections, selections inside loops, loops inside loops, and selections inside selections are common programming practices. In this section, we'll show you some examples of loops nested inside other loops.

Nested loops can be used to print triangles of characters. In the previous chapter, we used a pair of recursive functions to print those triangles. The function `printATriangle()` from that chapter has two arguments: the height of the triangle to be printed and the character that was to make up the triangle. The function call `printATriangle('+',6)` would generate this output:

```
++++++
+++++
++++
+++
++
+
```

Suppose we name `printATriangle()`'s formal arguments `ch` (the character to be printed) and `size` (the height of the triangle). Let's see how to redefine `printATriangle()` using nested loops instead of recursive function calls.

A triangle can be printed one row at a time. Think of those rows as numbered from the height of the triangle down to 1. Across each row, the characters are printed in columns. Think of the columns as numbered also, where the numbering goes from 1 up to the number of the row. The following algorithm for printing a triangle uses that description:

> for each row (where rows vary from the height of the triangle down to 1)
>   for each column of the row (where columns vary from 1 up to the
>   number of the row)
>   print the character (to fill in this column of this row)
>   finish this row

Here is an alternate definition for `printATriangle()` based on this algorithm:

```
void printATriangle(int size, char ch)
{
    for (int row = size; row > 0; row--) {
        for(int column = 0; column < row ; column++)
            cout << ch;
        cout << endl;
    }
}
```

The loop control variable for the outer loop is row. It represents the number of rows yet to be printed. Each iteration of the body of the outer loop prints a single row. At the beginning of execution of the function, there are size rows that have not yet been printed. When row has the value 0, then there are no more rows to print.

The loop control variable for the inner loop is column. It indicates the number of characters that have already been printed in this row. Each iteration of the body of the inner loop prints a single character. At the beginning of execution of the inner loop, no characters for that row have been printed, so column is initialized to 0. The length of the row is the value of row. When column has the same value as row, then there are no more characters to print in that row. After the inner loop is executed, the row is finished off with a newline.

Look at the values of row and column during the execution of the nested loops. Suppose size is 4. The pair of values for row and column is different for each character that is printed. Here is their sequence of values during the printing:

row	column	Character printed
4	0	first character in first row
4	1	second character in first row
4	2	third character in first row
4	3	fourth character in first row
4	4	the first newline
3	0	first character in second row
3	1	second character in second row
3	2	third character in second row
3	3	the second newline
2	0	first character in third row
2	1	second character in third row
2	2	the third newline
1	0	first character in fourth row
1	1	the final newline

One of the consequences of using nested loops is that some statements may be executed numerous times. For example, if `size` in `printATriangle()` were 80, then the body of the inner loop (the statement `cout << ch;`) would be executed a total of 3240 times. (3240 = 80 + 79 + ... + 2 + 1.) The number of executions of that assignment depends on how large `size` is. Going from `size` 4 to `size` 5 increases the number of executions from 10 to 15 while going from `size` 20 to `size` 21 increases the number of executions from 210 to 231. The total number of executions of the innermost statement is approximately proportional to the square of `size`.

Here is another problem that we can solve using nested loops. The user will be prompted to enter a sequence of positive integers, terminated by 0. For each integer entered except the sentinel, the proper factors of the integer will be printed. (A positive integer is a proper factor of the number x if it divides x and it is not 1 or x.) The general structure of the solution is as follows:

> prompt and read a number
> while that number is not the sentinel
> > for each integer between 2 and half the number, print it if it is a factor
> > prompt for and read the next number.

The smallest possible proper factor of any number is 2 (and 2 is a proper factor only of even numbers greater than 2). Also, there can be no proper factor of any number that is greater than half of the number. (Why?) So a check for possible factors must start at 2 and go no greater than half the number.

The resulting code is not foolproof. It fails if the user enters a negative number. The functions `inputInt()` and `outputLine()` are the same as those in the changemaker program.

```
int sentinel = 0;    // Sentinel value to terminate input
int x;               // Number most recently entered by the user

inputInt(x, "Enter a positive integer to factor or 0 to quit: ");

while (x != sentinel) {

    // testFactor iterates through possible proper factors
    for (int testFactor = 2; testFactor <= x / 2; testFactor++)
        if (x % testFactor == 0)
            outputLine(testFactor, " is a factor");

    inputInt(x, "Enter a positive integer to factor or 0 to quit: ");
}
```

5.6   Alternative loop constructions and the `break` statement

It's not too hard to read your own well-written code and understand what it does. But that doesn't mean you can read other programmers' code and be so sure. If your favorite looping construct is a `do`/`while` loop, you will definitely be in a small minority of C++ programmers—perhaps a minority of one.

If your favorite loop construct is a `while` loop, then you might be among those who first learned to program in Pascal. Or you may just believe that `for` loops are harder to understand just because they tend to be so short. But many C++ programmers use `for` loops almost exclusively. One reason for the popularity of `for` loops is that their code tends to be shorter and more compact than the equivalent `while` loop code. Some programmers take this to the limit by encompassing the entire body of the loop inside the parentheses. For example, the following `for` loop prints the integers from 1 to 9:

```
for(int i = 1; i < 10; cout << i++ << endl);
```

The loop to find the sum of all odd integers less than or equal to a particular integer x could be written in this abbreviated form:

```
for (int nextOdd = 1, sum = 0; nextOdd <= x; sum += nextOdd++, nextOdd++);
```

Look at the semicolons following the right parentheses for both of these loops. Each loop body is a null statement. Novice programmers may have to stare at these `for` loops just to figure out if their syntax is even legal.

In a `for` loop, it is possible to leave out any of the expressions inside the parentheses. We could have left out the *initStatement* in the loop that printed 1 through 9.

```
int i = 1;
for( ; i < 10; cout << i++ << endl);
```

Indeed, you can leave out all of the expressions inside the parentheses. The beginning of such a loop would look like this:

```
for( ; ; )
```

This is a potentially infinite loop because there is no *continueExpression* that would eventually evaluate to false to stop the loop execution. Who needs an infinite loop? Nobody. C++ provides a `break` statement as a way of bailing out a loop in addition to a `switch`.

Let's see how the `break` statement can be used to solve the following problem. Find the sum of numbers entered by the user. Stop when the user enters a negative number or as soon as 101 numbers have been entered, whichever comes first. First, we'll solve this problem using a simple `while` loop and no `break` statement.

```
int count = 1;        // Count of numbers entered so far
int sum = 0;          // Sum of nonnegative numbers added so far
int x;                // Number most recently entered by the user

inputInt(x,"Enter a number. (negative number quits)  ");
while (x >= 0 && count <= 100) {
    sum += x;
    count++;
    inputInt(x,"Enter a number. (negative number quits)  ");
}
```

The compound condition that controls execution of the loop body must meet two requirements in order to be true: (1) the most recently entered number cannot be negative and (2) no more than 100 integers can be entered. We could use a `break` statement instead of the compound condition. This code behaves exactly the same as the previous code. We changed the documentation on the variable x to reflect the fact that no input is performed before the loop begins execution.

```
int count = 0;    // Count of numbers entered so far
int sum = 0;      // Sum of nonnegative numbers entered so far
int x;            // Postcondition: Number most recently entered by the user

while (count < 100) {
    inputInt(x,"Enter a number. (negative number quits)  ");
    if (x < 0)
        break;
    sum += x;
    count++;
}
```

The differences between the loop with the `break` statement and the one without are subtle but significant. The loop with the `break` statement does not require an input statement prior to the first execution of the loop to make sure the loop condition will deal with legitimate data. Instead, the loop with the `break` statement relies on all input being performed in the body of the loop itself. When the user enters a negative number, the `break` statement is executed and the entire loop is exited.

How does the same problem look with a `for` loop instead? Here is one answer:

```
int x;        // Postcondition: Number most recently entered by the user
for(int count = 0, sum = 0; count < 100; sum += x, count++) {
    inputInt(x,"Enter a number. (negative number quits)  ");
```

```
   if (x < 0)
      break;
}
```

A break can be used only to exit a loop or a switch. It cannot be used in any other context.

It looks like break statements are wonderful, secret tools that only experienced programmers are allowed to use. Do we recommend that you use them also? Not necessarily. They tend to hide the loop exit conditions inside the body of the loop instead of displaying them right up front. The result may be code that is more difficult to read or debug. In addition, break statements have limited use in nested loops. Execution of a break statement inside an inner loop exits only that inner loop. It does not exit the outer loop. That can be an unfortunate surprise for some programmers.

If you do use break statements, don't let them be a crutch to avoid designing correct, easy-to-understand loops. Even with a break statement, you still ought to be able to identify loop invariants and use them to construct correct loops.

5.7 | Design modification: redesigning the calculator

The model of the special-purpose handheld calculator in the convenience store problem was designed so that the calculator powered itself on, did one problem, then shut itself down. Most calculators are not like that. Rather than shutting down after a single computation, they continue until the user decides to quit.

Loops make it easy to change the calculator so that it is able to do multiple computations. We will redesign the calculator object so that it can do several computations rather than a single one after it is powered on.

In our new model, the user will indicate if an additional computation is desired. The calculator somehow needs to be able to ask the user if it should continue with another computation or quit. In response to an appropriate prompt, the user can enter a single character, 'y' (for yes) or 'n' (for no).

Which object can do this new prompt and read? The most natural choice is the input object. It can already prompt for and read an integer. Certainly its capabilities can be expanded so that it can prompt for and read a character as well.

How about the calculator? What new things will it know? The calculator will know the user's last character response to quit or continue, and it will also know the appropriate prompt to be shown to the user. In order to figure out the user's continue or quit response, the calculator object can send a message to the input object to get a value for that character. Part of the message will be the prompt itself.

When the calculator turns itself on, it will now do four things:

1. Ask the input object to get a number.

2. Ask the computing object to calculate the answer based on the number.

3. Ask the output object to display the answer.

4. Ask the input object to get the user's quit/continue response.

The new convenience store design is shown in Fig. 5.5. The output object and the computing object are the same as they were before. Only the calculator and input objects have changed.

The new input object is easy to implement. It has one more method, which can be coded as a function that is very similar to inputInt().

```
void inputChar(char& aCharacter, const char prompt[])
// Arguments:
//    aCharacter - out - The non-whitespace character entered by the user
//    prompt - Message displayed to the user
// Side effect: Prompts for and reads non-whitespace character.
{
    cout << prompt;
    cin >> aCharacter;
}
```

The previous calculator was implemented by main(). We will use the same idea here. The new calculator implementation will be similar to the old main(), but this time it will contain a char data object for the user's response and a loop. The body of the loop will consist of the appropriate messages to the input object, the computing object, the output object, and then again the input object. The loop control variable is the user's quit-or-continue character response. This is the new main().

```
//------------------ calculator object implementation --------------------
void main()
{
    double dollarsPerKg;    // Item's cost in Canadian dollars per kilogram
    int penniesPerLb;       // Item's price in U.S. pennies per pound
```

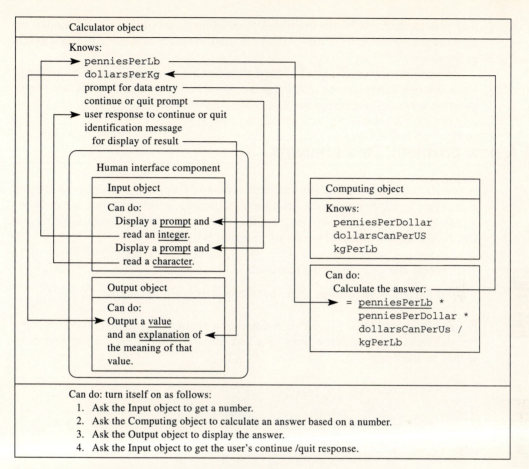

Figure 5.5 Redesign of the calculator of the convenience store solution. Now the calculator can perform multiple calculations on a single power up.

```
char response;          // User's quit or continue response

do {
    inputInt(penniesPerLb,"Enter the item price in pennies per pound: ");
    dollarsPerKg = priceCanadian(penniesPerLb);
    outputDouble(dollarsPerKg,
        "The item price in Canadian dollars per kilogram is $");
    inputChar(response, "Another computation? <y/n> ");
} while (response != 'n' && response != 'N');
}
//--------------- end of calculator object implementation ---------------
```

Notice how convenient a do/while loop is for this problem. You can assume that your uncle turns on the calculator to do at least one problem. And there is no sense in asking him if he wants to do a calculation before at least one calculation is performed.

We could have used a `while` loop instead of a `do/while` loop. But we would have to work harder not to query the user on whether or not an additional computation were desired before the first computation even started.

5.8   A new problem: Text analysis

A popular executable program available on many computing systems counts the number of words in a text file. Another one displays or echoes a text file on a terminal. We can write our own program that does both of those things. Given a text file, here is a description of what our program is to do:

1. echoes the text file on the terminal.

2. at the end of execution, tells how many words are in the file.

For this problem, a "word" is defined as a sequence of alphabetic characters. For example, here are some lines of a text file and the corresponding counts of words on the lines:

Line of text file	Count of words on that line
Isn't it nice.	4
one-at-a-time	4
abcd efg	2
R2D2	2
1234 5678	0

This book has not even mentioned text files before. Before plunging ahead with analysis and design of this problem, we ought to see what facilities C++ has for processing text files. C++ can process any input as a stream, whether it comes from a file on disk or from characters entered from the keyboard. You learned how to do some stream processing of `cin` in Chapter 2. Appendixes D, E, and F at the back of this book give some further information on stream processing. (But you do not need to read those appendixes to understand this section.)

A quick peek at `cin`

The input stream `cin` is an object associated with a particular sequence of characters. By default, `cin` is associated with the sequence of characters entered from the keyboard by the user. When the user presses a key, the character corresponding to that key enters the input stream.

One way to remove characters from the sequence is through the input operator, >>. If ch is a char variable, cin >> ch removes all characters from the input stream sequence up through and including the first non-whitespace character.[3] Recall that whitespace characters are blanks, tabs, newlines, and carriage returns. That first non-whitespace character is assigned to ch.

Suppose the input stream sequence looks like the following, where \t is a tab, \n is a newline, and the empty boxes are blanks.

\t		\n		I		h	a	v	e		1	2		c	a	t	s	.	\n		X	Z		\n

Execution of this series of input statements results in the values for ch shown in the comments.

```
cin >> ch;    // ch is 'I'
cin >> ch;    // ch is 'h'
cin >> ch;    // ch is 'a'
cin >> ch;    // ch is 'v'
cin >> ch;    // ch is 'e'
cin >> ch;    // ch is '1'
// The first 6 non-whitespace characters have been removed from the input
// sequence. The total number of characters removed is 12 (6 non-
// whitespace, 4 blanks, a tab, and a newline).
```

There are times when those whitespace characters are important, and your program needs to know the value of the next character in the input stream, not just the next non-whitespace character. How can you avoid just skipping the whitespace characters?

The input stream cin has a function named cin.get(). We explained how to use cin.get() back in Chapter 2, but here is a quick review of how cin.get() works. If ch is a char variable, cin.get(ch) extracts the next character from its input sequence and assigns that character to ch. No distinction between whitespace and non-whitespace characters is made.

Return to the old example of the input stream sequence.

\t		\n		I		h	a	v	e		1	2		c	a	t	s	.	\n		X	Z		\n

This series of calls to cin.get() results in the values for ch shown in the comments:

---

[3] It is possible to change cin so that extraction does not skip whitespace.

```
cin.get(ch);    // ch is '\t'
cin.get(ch);    // ch is ' '
cin.get(ch);    // ch is '\n'
cin.get(ch);    // ch is ' '
cin.get(ch);    // ch is 'I'
cin.get(ch);    // ch is ' '
```

Here's a problem for which `cin.get()` will be useful: echo a text file on the terminal. **Echoing** a text file on the terminal means displaying it on the terminal. We need to write code that will display the text file, character by character and line by line. Whitespace is important. What appears on the screen when the code implementing the object is executed are the characters in the text file itself—blanks, tabs, newlines, and all.

Most computing environments allow a user to redirect the input for a program so that it comes from a text file rather than from the terminal.[4] In this situation, the source of the characters for `cin` is the text file, not the characters entered by the user at the keyboard while the program is running. Output can also be redirected. It can be sent to the terminal, as usual, or it can be used to create or modify a file on disk. One of the special features of C++ streams is that they can be associated with different files and devices. Unless specified otherwise, however, by default both `cin` and `cout` are associated with the terminal.

Although there is no upper limit on the number of characters that the user can enter, text files are not infinite. The operating system knows where each text file starts and where it ends. The question is, how can your program determine when all the characters in a text file have been processed—when there are no more characters left in the input stream sequence?

Think of the operating system as placing a sentinel at the end of a file to mark the end. The sentinel does not belong to the file. It is simply a marker. So a text file can be thought of as a sequence of characters terminated by a sentinel that is not part of the sequence. The idea of a sequence that is terminated by a sentinel value is not new. We first saw that idea when we found the average of a sequence of numbers terminated by 0. That value 0 was not to be calculated as part of the average.

So a text file is a sequence of characters terminated by a sentinel value, which is not to be considered as an actual character in the file. An iterator object can be used to iterate over those characters. It can also tell if there are more characters in the file and get the next one if there are. We have implemented the iterator object with three different parts of loop code, the initialization part (*startup*), the condition part (*more?*), and the update part (*next*). But now we combine all of the behaviors of the iterator object into a single expression.

The expression `cin.get(ch)` does two different things, depending on how much of the input has been processed. If there is an additional character in the

---

[4] In UNIX and MS-DOS environments, if the name of the executable file is `myprog` and the name of the file from which you want the input to come is `text.in`, the following command will redirect the input for `myprog` to come from `text.in`.

```
myprog < text.in
```

input stream sequence, then `cin.get(ch)` places in `ch` the value of that character and it removes the character from the input stream sequence. In that case, the value of the expression `cin.get(ch)` when it is used as a condition of a selection statement or a loop is considered to be true. If there is not an additional character in the input stream, the value of the expression `cin.get(ch)` as a condition of a selection statement or a loop is considered to be false.

A simple loop that processes each character in the input stream can be structured like this:

```
while (cin.get(ch))
    statement to process ch
```

No additional input statement is necessary in the body of the loop or before the beginning of the loop execution. The evaluation of the condition controlling the loop does all the work.

This is exactly what happens in the execution of the loop.

1. If there are more characters remaining to be processed in the input stream sequence (in the text file)
   - `ch` is assigned the next character from the input stream sequence. That character has now been processed and it no longer remains in the input stream sequence.
   - The condition `cin.get(ch)` is considered to be true, so the loop body is executed.

2. If there are no more characters left to process in the input stream
   - The value of `ch` remains unchanged.
   - The condition `cin.get(ch)` is considered to be false, so the loop body is not executed.

Using the expression `cin >> ch` as a loop condition is similar to using `cin.get(ch)`, but the whitespace is skipped. The processing loop that skips whitespace is as follows:

```
while (cin >> ch)
    statement to process ch
```

You can probably predict the execution of the loop.

1. If there are more *non-whitespace* characters remaining to be processed in the input stream sequence (in the text file)
   - `ch` is assigned the next non-whitespace character remaining in the input stream sequence. That character has now been processed and it no longer remains in the sequence.

- The condition `cin >> ch` is considered to be true, so the body of the loop is executed.

2. If there are no more characters in the input stream sequence or if the only remaining characters are whitespace
   - The value of `ch` remains unchanged.
   - The condition `cin >> ch` is considered to be false, so the loop body is not executed.

Both `cin >> ch` and `cin.get(ch)` can be used as conditions for `if` statements as well as loops. The evaluations of `cin >> ch` and `cin.get(ch)` have side effects. Until now, we have not seen examples where such side effects are desired. But they are extremely important in processing input data. The only way that you can tell if there are no more characters remaining to be read in a file is to try to read one. If you cannot, then there are none left. If you can, then there was at least one left. In either case, the program will not crash.

An input stream goes into a **failed state** when an attempt to extract an item fails. Here are some situations that cause `cin` to go into a failed state.

- Evaluation of `cin.get(ch)` when there are no more characters in the input stream sequence.

- Evaluation of `cin >> ch` when all the remaining characters in the input stream sequence are whitespace or there are no more characters.

- For a numeric type variable x, evaluation of `cin >> x` when the first non-whitespace character is not a numeric character (a digit, a sign, or a period). For example, if x is an `int` and the next non-whitespace character in the input stream is `'A'`, then evaluation of `cin >> x` places `cin` in a failed state but it does *not* change the value of x.

When `cin` is in a failed state and the expression `cin` is the condition used to control the execution of a loop or the execution of a selection statement, then the condition is considered to be false. If `cin` is not in a failed state, then the condition is considered to be true.

We can put together all such information to write code that echoes a text file to the terminal. Assume that the input has been redirected to the text file and the output, as usual, is displayed on the screen. Here are two versions, both of them wonderfully short. Nothing should be extracted from the input stream prior to execution of the code.

```
// Version 1: a while loop and a condition with side effects
while (cin.get(ch))
    cout << ch;
```

```
// Version 2: a while loop and a condition without side effects
cin.get(ch);
```

```
while (cin) {
    cout << ch;
    cin.get(ch);
}
```

The first version is shorter, but it does have the feature that there is a side effect in the evaluation of the condition. Evaluation of the condition in the second version does not produce a side effect. For that reason, some programmers prefer the second version. Of course, you could also write a `for` loop to do the input processing.

```
// Version 3: a for loop version
for( ; cin.get(ch); )
    cout << ch;
```

The variations on the different loop constructs to process text files are almost endless.

Not all data in a text file or in the sequence of characters entered by the user will be treated strictly as character data. Many times we are interested in reading "numbers" rather than single characters. And a stream will go into a failed state if it tries to read a number and is unable to do so. If an input stream is in a failed state, then no more data can be extracted from its sequence unless the failed state is first cleared. For example, if `cin` is in a failed state because an attempt to read a numeric value failed, then any subsequent attempt to read any type of value will not succeed unless the stream is cleared. You can get `cin` to clear its failed state by sending it this message:

```
cin.clear();
```

If there are more characters in the input stream sequence, then clearing the failed state allows them to be read.

Modeling the text analyzer

Let's return to the original problem of this section, finding out how many words are in a text file. What model can we use as a basis for the analysis, design, and implementation of our solution? The old special-purpose handheld calculator, which we used for the convenience store problem, just does not seem to fit here. It is hard to imagine a calculator that shows text files on its display window. The teller model for the changemaker problem does not fit either. A brand new model is in order.

The input for this program will be a sequence of characters from a text file—a stream. The information contained in the stream can be thought of as flowing or being transferred from one place to another, like the transfer of information that takes place when a signal is sent through a cable to your television set. (When the television station is transmitting a movie, the movie itself is not going anywhere, but the information from the movie appears on your television set.)

A limitation of streams as they are implemented in C++ is that you cannot hook up one stream to another directly. In order for information from one stream to flow into another, you have to write the code to do it. The final code in the previous section did just that. It took the information from the input stream and placed it into the output stream.

Imagine this scenario for the input and output streams of our problem: The characters flow through a pipe, which represents an input stream connected to a file. Another pipe can be used to represent the output stream connected to a terminal. What we want to do is to build a bridge connecting the two pipes, so the characters can flow from the input stream pipe, across the bridge, and then into the output stream pipe.

A bridge can be an object in the text analyzer model that we will eventually create. The bridge object knows its input stream (incoming pipe) and its output stream (outgoing pipe). It can do one thing: transfer an item from the input stream to the output stream (see Fig. 5.6).

If the input stream is `cin` and the output stream is `cout`, only the following code is needed to implement the transfer of a single character by the bridge object:

```
cin.get(ch);
cout << ch;
```

The problem that we are solving needs more than a simple bridge, which by itself can only transfer a single character from one pipe to another. That takes care of the copy (echo) part of this problem. The other part of the problem is that the words in the stream have to be counted. The bridge transfers single characters, but the items that need to be counted are not single characters. They are words. That makes two different kinds of items that are important in this problem: characters and words.

Figure 5.7 illustrates a bridge and the pipes. The bridge appears as a conveyer belt, which transports characters from one pipe to another. The characters appear as blocks. The blocks come in two different heights. The ones containing alphabetic characters are over twice the height of the blocks containing nonalphabetic characters.

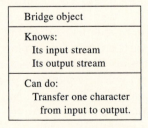

Bridge object

Knows:
    Its input stream
    Its output stream

Can do:
    Transfer one character
    from input to output.

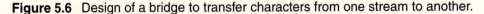

Figure 5.6 Design of a bridge to transfer characters from one stream to another.

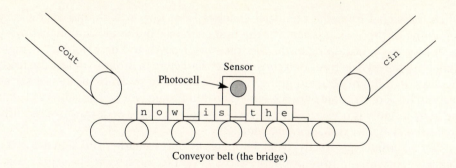

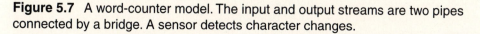

Conveyor belt (the bridge)

Figure 5.7 A word-counter model. The input and output streams are two pipes connected by a bridge. A sensor detects character changes.

Behind the conveyer belt, there is a sensor, whose job it is to count words as they are going by. A photocell, mounted on the front of the sensor, is able to determine the level of a character as it passes by (high level for alphabetic and low level for nonalphabetic).

The photocell is a kind of filter. The output of the photocell is illustrated in Fig. 5.8. As each character passes by, the photocell produces a high or low signal. The sequence of signals that the photocell produces for the characters in the diagram is the "square wave."

The square wave shows the transitions between alphabetic characters and nonalphabetic characters as they are being transported. The signals are the horizontal segments and the transitions are the vertical edges. Each vertical edge is either a leading edge, going from low to high, or a trailing edge, going from high to low. In the diagram, the leading edges occur in three places:

- At the beginning with the n in the word now

- Between the blank and the i in the word is

- Between the blank and the t in the word the

How does all of this help the sensor, which must count words? The sensor can count words just by counting the number of leading edges. A leading edge occurs

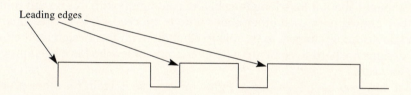

Figure 5.8 The square wave output of the sensor's photocell.

when the signal from the photocell changes from low to high and at the very beginning of processing whenever the first character in the file is alphabetic. So, except for at the beginning of the file, the sensor needs to know not just a single signal but the signals from two consecutive characters in order to detect the leading edge that might occur in going from one to the next. Think of the sensor as keeping track of the state of processing. The initial state is low. The state is high if the most recently processed character was alphabetic. It is low if the most recently processed character was nonalphabetic.

Let's summarize exactly what happens in our scenario. The signal for the character currently in front of the photocell is sent to the sensor. The sensor compares that signal to the one that was sent for the previous character. If the signal for the previous character was low (the sensor's state is low) and the signal for the current character is high, then the sensor increments a word counter. When the sensor quits processing a character, it sets its state to correspond to the level of that character. If that most recently processed character was nonalphabetic, the state is set to low. If it was alphabetic, the state is set to high.

What kind of model can we draw with our usual collection of boxes and arrows? The overall model, corresponding to the old calculator from the convenience store problem and the teller from the changemaker problem, is going to be a text analyzer object. It can turn itself on. It contains four objects: a bridge object, a sensor object, a photocell object, and an output object (to display the number of words).

The bridge object knows its streams. It can transmit a character from the input stream into the output stream. In the middle of this transmission, it will send a message to the sensor to analyze the character that is being transmitted.

The photocell object can tell if the level corresponding to a character is high or low. The sensor object knows its state (high or low) and it knows a word counter. It can do two things: analyze the current character and report the number of words that have been counted.

Only the photocell needs to know what constitutes a word. If the definition of a word changes (such as redefining a word so that it can contain hyphens and digits in addition to alphabetic characters), then only the photocell needs to be changed. The photocell is actually the only object that knows *what* is being counted. The sensor can still keep track of two different signals. The photocell illustrates a key principle of object-oriented design: Confine as much of the specific problem as possible to as few objects as possible, and make designs and write code that can be reused in other designs and programs.

The text analyzer problem was a difficult one to solve. (The authors of this book, thought about it for a long time before coming up with this design solution, and they argued with each other about how to proceed.) It is not reasonable to expect novice programmers to be able to come up with this design on their own. New designs are hard to come up with even for people who have been programming for years.

But now you have seen this design, you can use it again for other problems that involve stream processing. One of the design issues was especially important: sometimes it is useful to keep track of the last thing that was done as well as the current thing that is being done.

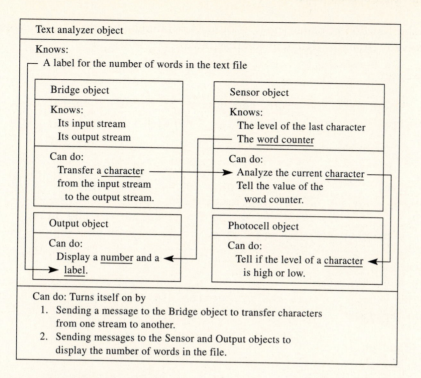

Figure 5.9 Text analyzer model.

Implementation of the text analyzer

The implementation of the solution to the text analyzer problem will be much easier to do than the design. We've looked at many of the hard issues. As usual, we will implement our solution using the somewhat elementary tools that we already know about.

There is one new thing here that we have not illustrated in a program before. The local variable processingState in the function sensor() is declared as a static local variable. Because it is a local variable, its scope is limited to the body of sensor(), but its lifetime endures for to the end of program execution. One thing the static declaration means is that processingState retains its value from one execution of sensor() to the next. Another is that processingState is initialized (with the value low) only one time, when sensor() begins execution for the first time.

Data objects that are static are initialized only once, and they are **persistent**, which means they keep their same values from the end of one call to the function in which they are declared to the beginning of the next call.

The function `outputLine()` should look familiar to you. We conveniently borrowed it from the changemaker program.

```
// Name: Text analyzer
// Version: 1.0
// Purpose: Echo a text file and count the number of words it contains. A
//    word is a maximal sequence of alphabetic characters.

#include <iostream.h>

enum Signal {low,high};       // Type of signal produced by the photocell
//------------------- sensor object implementation ------------------------
int wordCount = 0;            // Count of words found so far in the file
//-------------- sensor object implementation to be continued----------------
//------------------------- interfaces ---------------------------------
void sensor(char ch);
// argument: ch - Any character
// Side effect: The sensor updates the processing state to reflect the value
//    of the actual argument.

Signal photocell(char ch);
// Argument: ch - Any character
// Returns: high if ch is alphabetic and low if it is not alphabetic

void bridge();
// Side effect: Copies the input stream to the output stream counting the
//    number of words in the input stream. (A word is a maximal sequence of
//    alphabetic characters.)

void outputLine(int aNumber, const char message[]);
// Arguments:
//    aNumber - The integer to be displayed
//    message - Message displayed to identify the output
// Side effect: Display a number and a message followed by a newline.

//------------------ text analyzer object implementation --------------------
void main( )
{
   bridge();
   outputLine(wordCount, "\n\nThe number of words in the file is: ");
}
//-------------- end of text analyzer object implementation ------------------
//--------------------- photocell object implementation --------------------
Signal photocell(char ch)
{
   if (('A' <= ch && ch <= 'Z') || ('a' <= ch && ch <= 'z'))
      return high;
```

```
        else
            return low;
    }
    //------------------ end of photocell object implementation ----------------
    //-------------- continuation of sensor object implementation --------------
    void sensor(char ch)
    {
        static Signal processingState = low;    // Level of the most recently
                                                //    processed character
        Signal currentState = photocell(ch);    // Level of the character
                                                //    currently being processed

        if ((processingState == low) && (currentState == high))
            // Count the word. This is a leading edge.
            wordCount++;
        processingState = currentState;
    }
    //------------------ end of sensor object implementation --------------------
    //---------------------- bridge object implementation ----------------------
    void bridge()
    {
        char ch;                     // Next input character
        while (cin.get(ch)) {
            sensor(ch);
            cout << ch;
        }
    }
    //-------------------- end of bridge object implementation ------------------
    //---------------------- output object implementation ----------------------
    void outputLine(int aNumber, const char message[])
    {
        cout << message << aNumber << endl;
    }
    //-------------------- end of output object implementation ------------------
```

Observe in this program how the implementation of the sensor object is spread over two program entities: the global variable wordCount and the function sensor(). That is the best we can do for now, but later we will see how to encapsulate an object's data and methods into a single program entity.

5.9 ▌ Summary

Loops are a major tool that C++ programmers use to implement a method in which actions or code are repeated. C++ provides three loop constructs: while loops, do/while loops, and for loops. Each of these can be used for general-purpose loops.

In a sense, all loops process sequences of data. Whether or not an iterator object is explicitly coded and documented as a special object, it can iterate through that sequence. In an ordinary while loop, the iterator object prepares to access the sequence in initialization code that is before the actual loop. The iterator object appears in the loop condition where it determines whether there are more items in the sequence, and it appears in the body of the loop when it accesses the next item in the sequence.

Loop invariants are a useful tool in constructing correct loops. Problems that plague programmers at all levels of experience include loop conditions that are too complicated, having too many or too few loop iterations, improperly initialized loop variables, and improperly updated loop variables. Appropriate loop invariants help avoid all of those problems.

Loops (or recursion) and selection statements are fundamental control mechanisms in virtually all high-level computer languages. They are used in the implementation of methods for many different objects, a feature that makes them important for object-oriented programming.

Glossary

decrement operators Unary prefix and postfix operators, ++, which decrement their operands.

failed state (of an input stream) An input stream is in a failed state when the last attempted operation on the stream failed.

increment operators Unary prefix and postfix operators, ++, which increment their operands.

infinite loop A loop whose execution does not stop.

iteration Repeated execution of a set of statements.

iterator object An object which acts on a sequence as follows: it can get the first item, determine if there are more items, and get the next item.

loop A language feature allowing a collection of statements to be executed repeatedly.

loop condition A Boolean expression whose value determines if the loop body will be executed.

loop control variable A variable whose value is part of the loop condition expression.

loop invariant An assertion that is true immediately before the loop begins execution and immediately after every execution of the loop body.

loop postcondition An assertion that is true immediately after the loop completes execution.

loop precondition An assertion that is true immediately before the loop begins execution.

sentinel value A value signifying the end of a sequence of items.

5.10 ▮ Exercises

1. Assume that the following code is given:

```
int sentinel = -1;
int count = 0;
int sumSquare = 0;
int x;

inputInt(x, "Enter a number (-1 quits) ");

while (x != sentinel) {
    sumSquare += x * x;
    count++;
    inputInt(x, "Enter another number: ");
}
```

   a. What is the loop condition?

   b. What code constitutes the body of the loop?

   c. What are the values of sumSquare and count after the user enters the following input sequence?

      3   9   1   12   5   -1

   d. What is the value of x immediately after loop execution is completed?

2. Write comments for the data object definitions in the code of exercise 1 so that each comment is a loop invariant. Each comment should a true assertion about the data object immediately before the loop is executed and after each execution of the loop body.

3. Each of the following segments of code attempts to find the number of different factors of a positive integer x. For example, 3 has two factors (1 and 3), 6 has four factors (1, 2, 3, and 6), and 17 has two factors (1 and 17). Each segment of code is incorrect. For each one, tell why it is incorrect. Then, rewrite the code so that it is correct.

   a.
```
// ASSUME: x > 0
// At end of execution, factor is the number of factors of x.
int factors = 0;       // Number of factors of x found so far
int try = 1;           // Next possible factor of x
while (try <= x) {
    if (x % try == 0)
        factors++;
}
```

   b.
```
// ASSUME: x > 0
// At end of execution, factor is the number of factors of x.
```

```
int factors = 0;        // Number of factors of x found so far
int try = 1;            // Next possible factor of x
while (x % try == 0) {
    factors++;
    try += 1;
}
```

c.
```
// ASSUME: x > 0
// At end of execution, factor is the number of factors of x.
int factors = 1;        // Number of factors of x found so far
int try = 1;            // Next possible factor of x
while (try <= x) {
    if (x % try == 0)
        factors++;
    try++;
}
```

4. Each of the following segments of code is incorrect. For each one, tell why it does not always work as its documentation claims.

a.
```
// ASSUME: x >= 0.
// At end of execution, numDigits is the number of
//   digits of x.
int numDigits = 0;    // Number of digits counted so far
while (x > 0); {
    numDigits++;
    x /= 10;
}
```

b.
```
// ASSUME: x >= 0.
// At end of execution, numDigits is the number of
//   digits of x.
int numDigits = 0;    // Number of digits counted so far
while (x > 0) {
    numDigits++;
    x /= 10;
}
```

c.
```
// At end of execution, sum is the sum of all
//   positive integers less than 30.
int i = 1;
int sum = 0;
while (i <= 30) {
    sum += i;
    i++;
}
```

5. Fill in the blanks for each of the following code fragments so the execution of each will output 12 asterisks.

```
a. for(int i = _____; i <= 12; i++)
       cout << '*';

b. for (int j = 0; j < 3; j++)
       for (int i = ____; i > 10; i--)
           cout << '*';

c. int i = 5;
   while (i > _____ ) {
       cout << '*';
       i -= 1;
   }

d. int i = _____;
   do {
       cout << '*';
       i += 2;
   } while (i < 30);
```

6. Write `while` loops for each of the following tasks. For each loop, document the definitions of the data objects involved to show your loop invariants.

   a. Suppose x is an `int`. Write a loop that computes the product of the smallest 8 integers that are greater than x.

   b. Write a loop that prints all of the lowercase letters in the alphabet on a single line. The loop control variable should be a `char` that assumes values from `'a'` through `'z'`.

   c. Write a loop that counts how many of positive and negative numbers are in a sequence of integers entered by the user. (Call the function `inputInt()` to get each integer in the sequence.) The sequence is terminated by the number 0.

7. The loop for the new implementation of the calculator of the convenience store problem was a `do/while` loop. Replace the `do/while` loop with the equivalent `while` loop.

8. Write a function that prints out the ASCII table for printable non-white-space characters (ASCII values greater than 32 and less than 127). Write three different definitions of the function.

   a. The first definition uses a `while` loop with a `char` loop control variable defined and initialized to `' '` (blank). Stop as soon as the loop completes the output of `'~'`.

   b. The second definition uses a `for` loop that uses an `int` loop control variable initialized to 33 and going through the value 126.

   c. The third definition is for a recursive function. The recursive function version has a single argument, the next character to be printed (if it is between 32 and 127).

9. For each of the following loops, tell how many times the character '*' is written.

a.
```
int i = 0;
while (i <= 10) {
    int j = 0;
    while (j <  i ) {
        cout << '*';
        j++;
    }
    i++;
}
```

b.
```
int i = 0;
while (i <= 10) {
    int j = 0;
    while (++j <  i )
        cout << '*';
    i++;
}
```

c.
```
for (int i = 0; i < 6; i++)
    for (int k = 0; k < 6; k++)
        for (int m = 0; m < 6; m++)
            cout << '*'<< endl;
```

d.
```
for (int i = 0; i < 5; i++)
    for (int k = 0; k < i; k++)
        cout << '*';
```

10. Change the following loop structures:

a. The `while` loop from exercise 1 to a `do/while` loop.

b. The `while` loops from exercise 9 (a) to `for` loops.

c. The `for` loops from exercise 9 (c) to `while` loops.

d. The `while` loop from exercise 1 to a `for` loop.

11. Using nested loops, write four variations on `printATriangle()`.

a. The first variation results in this output for the call `printATriangle('*',5)`.

```
*
**
***
****
*****
```

b. The second variation results in this output for the call `printATriangle('*',5)`.

```
    *
   **
  ***
 ****
*****
```

c. The third variation results in this output for the call
`printATriangle('*',5).`

```
1      * * * * *
2       * * * *
3        * * *
4         * *
5          *
```

d. The final variation results in this output for the call
`printATriangle('*',5).`

```
        *
       * * *
      * * * * *
     * * * * * * *
    * * * * * * * *
```

12. The greatest common divisor of two positive integers is the largest integer that is a divisor of them both. The Euclidean algorithm is an efficient algorithm for finding the greatest common divisor. The algorithm can be summarized as follows: Assume that a and b are two `ints` with positive values. Now follow these steps:

a. Find the remainder of a ÷ b.

b. Assign a the value of b.

c. Assign b the value of the remainder.

d. If b is 0 then `quit`. a is the greatest common divisor.

e. Otherwise, go back to step 1 and repeat the entire process.

Define a function `gcd()` that returns an `int` and that has two `int` arguments. `gcd()` returns the greatest common divisor of its arguments. Document the declaration of `gcd()`. Be sure to state the assumptions on the values of the actual arguments.

13. Suppose that a company estimates the actual rate of depreciation on some of its equipment to be a certain percentage for the first year. They estimate that the rate of depreciation will decrease by 10% per year for every year thereafter. For example, if the first year's depreciation rate is 25%, then the second year's depreciation rate will be 22.5%, the third year's depreciation rate will be 20.25%, and so on.

Write a function that returns an `int` and has a single `float` argument indicating the percentage of depreciation in the first year. The function returns the number of years it takes for the equipment to lose at least half of its value.

14. Write a loop that counts how many times a character is the same as the previous one in a sequence of characters terminated by `'@'`. For example, if the sequence of characters beginning with the character `'a'` is

```
ab cd  effghaa@
```

then the number of characters that matched the preceding character is 3 (counting the third blank, the second `'f'`, and the third `'a'`). You may assume that the sequence of characters contains at least one character besides the sentinel value. Document the definitions in order to show the loop invariants.

15. How many lines of output do you think the following loop will generate? (This is actually a question about the accuracy of floating point representations.)

```
for (float x = 0; x != 10.0; x += .01)
    cout << "x = " << x << endl;
```

Test your hypothesis to see if you are correct. Make sure that you know how to stop the execution of an infinite loop before you run your program.

16. Test out the function `rand()` in the general utilities library using the loop that was at the end of section 5.2. How many numbers were less than .5? How many were greater than or equal to .5 but less than .75? How many were greater than or equal to .75?

17. Write a loop to find the two largest numbers in a sequence of integers.

a. Use the function `inputInt()` to get the numbers. Let the sequence be terminated by the sentinel value 0 (which is not a number in the sequence). Assume that the user will enter at least two numbers before the sentinel.

b. Use the function `inputInt()` to get the numbers. Whenever the user enters a number, query the user to determine if there are additional numbers. The sequence is terminated when the user responds `'N'` (for "no"). Assume that the user will enter at least two numbers before responding "no."

c. Use the function `rand()` to generate the sequence of numbers. Terminate the sequence when `rand()` returns a value that exceeds 2,000,000,000.

d. Use `rand()` to generate a sequence of 100 numbers.

e. Repeat part (a), but this time assume that the user may terminate the sequence after entering only one number. In that case, the two largest numbers are that single sequence value.

18. Write a loop to find the two smallest numbers in a sequence of integers. Follow parts (a) through (e) from the previous exercise.

19. A prime number is a positive integer greater than 1 whose only divisors are itself and 1. Examples of prime numbers are 2, 3, 5, 7, 11, 13, 17, 19, 23, 29, etc. Suppose n is an int and the value of n is greater than 1.

    a. Write a function called isPrime() with a single argument n of type int that returns true if n is prime and false if n is not prime.

    b. Write a loop that prints out all prime integers less than or equal to n.

20. Base 10 numbers that are in the range of 0 to 999 can be thought of as three-digit numbers from the sequence 000, 001, 002, ..., 010, 011, 012, ..., 100, 101, 102, 013, ... 998, 999. Base 10 numbers require 10 different digits. Base 2 numbers require only two digits, 0 and 1. The three-digit base 2 numbers are 000, 001, 010, 011, 100, 101, 110, and 111.

    Write nested for loops that will print out all of the four-digit base 2 numbers. The first number to print is 0000 and the last one is 1111. Format the output so that the numbers appear in a table with four numbers per line. The first line of output should be as follows:

    ```
    0000   0001   0010   0011
    ```

21. Write a function sumSeries() with a single argument n of type int that returns the sum of the series:

$$\frac{1}{1} + \frac{1}{2} + \ldots + \frac{1}{n^2}$$

    Hint: Start the summation beginning with the smallest term ($1/n^2$) rather than 1.

    Write a recursive version of the function and compare that to your original solution.

22. Define a function named savingsBalance that has arguments of a beginning balance of a savings account, an annual percentage interest rate, a compounding period (in days), and a number of days. It returns the balance that would be in the savings account after that many days given the interest rate and compounding period and assuming that no withdrawals were made.

Programming Projects

23. The ABC company assigns all of its employees identification numbers that are positive integers. All identification numbers have the property

that their least significant digit is either 1 or 0. In addition, the sum of the digits in each identification number is odd. Write a program that prompts the user to input possible identification numbers. The input is terminated when the user enters the sentinel number 0. For each number input, the output generated is the number and a label that tells whether or not the integer is a valid identification number. Use the model of the special-purpose calculator to design your solution. The structure of your solution should be similar to the structure of the newest version of the convenience store problem.

24. The Handrick family wanted to figure out whether their old clunker of a car could get decent gas mileage for their last trip. Every time they filled the tank, they jotted down the car's odometer reading as well as the number of gallons needed. In order to determine if the car was getting consistent mileage from one tank to another, they wanted to compute the following for each tank of gas:

a. The number of miles per gallon the car traveled on the last tank of gas.

b. The average number of miles per gallon the car traveled for the entire trip to that point.

   Design a solution to this problem. Your final code solution should generate a table of the following information for each tank of gas bought on the trip:

• Odometer reading

• Gallons of gas purchased

• Odometer reading for the previous gas purchase

• Number of miles per gallon on the previous tank of gas

• Number of miles per gallon the car has traveled on the entire trip

25. Do exercise 27 from the previous chapter. This time, instead of concentrating on your ship and a single other ship, consider a collection of ships in the area. Your ship can ask any ship in the area its location, bearing, and speed. Your ship knows its own location, speed, and bearing. Readings of locations, bearings, and speeds are taken every three minutes. If any other ship comes closer to your ship and has approximately the same relative bearing (within 2°) to your ship, then your ship must issue a collision warning.

26. Some text editors can determine if the parentheses in a text file are "balanced." Parentheses are balanced if two things are true: (1) The total number of left parentheses is the same as the total number of right parentheses; and (2) The total number of right parentheses counted thus far never exceeds the total number of left parentheses counted thus far in the file. The counting starts from the beginning of the file.

a. Suppose that you discover that your editor does not have that feature, so you need to create it. Write a program solution to this problem.

b. File streams are discussed in Appendix F of this book. Modify your program for part (a) so that it does not redirect input to come from the text file. Instead, it queries for the name of the text file and opens an input file stream to that text file. Use the following function for defining and opening an input file stream.

```
void openFile(ifstream& f)
{
    char nameOfFile[80];    // Name of the text file
    cout << "Name of text file to be analyzed --> ";
    cin >> nameOfFile;
    f.open(nameOfFile);
}
```

The function `openFile()`, must be invoked with an `ifstream` (type name for an input file stream). The code for defining an `ifstream` and subsequently opening it is as follows:

```
ifstream myFile;
openFile(myFile);
```

Your program must have the following include directive to use file streams.

```
#include <fstream.h>
```

c. Write a program that determines if the curly braces in a C++ program are balanced. Use your own program as a test input file.

27. Write a program that determines how many pairs of successive lines of a text file begin with the same character. Use `fstreams` as in exercise 26 (b), or redirect input from a text file to test your program.

28. Write a program that takes a text file and echoes all of its words to the terminal and places a single whitespace character (blank or newline) between consecutive words. Words consist of alphabetic characters only. Your program should write only five words on each line, separating words on a line by blanks. The box below on the left shows sample input and the box on the right shows the corresponding correct output.

```
Any person, rich, poor, young, or
old can go. Nobody will be denied
access!
```

```
Any person rich poor young
or old can go Nobody
will be denied access
```

29. Write a program that takes a text file and compresses it by removing adjacent duplicate characters. For example, if the text file contains the line

```
Did Jenny get the Mississippi maps from AAA?
```

then your program's corresponding output must be

```
Did Jeny get the Misisipi maps from A?
```

30. Suppose that a text file contains digit characters in addition to other characters such as alphabetic characters, punctuation characters, whitespace, and so on. Suppose also that you need to find the sum of all of the "numbers" in the file. For example, the numbers in this line

```
One and 2 and 260 and the 40th are on 23rd St
```

are 2, 260, 40, and 23 and their sum is 325. Write a program solution to this problem.

31. Many handheld calculators can do rational number arithmetic in addition to floating point arithmetic. Write a program that simulates such a calculator. The calculator user is expected to enter arithmetic problems such as the following:

```
3 1/4 - 2/5 + 7 8/9 =
45/19 * 16 / 25 =
6 1/3 + 2 3/4 - 5 7/9 + 12/17 - 5 =
```

Analyze the problem carefully to determine what the input object should do. Your final coded implementation should contain documentation indicating exactly what kinds of problems your calculator can solve.

Chapter 6

List Objects and Array-Based Implementations

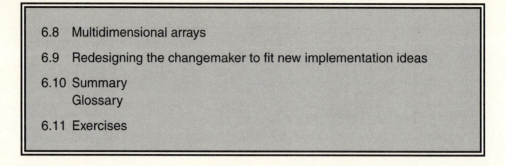

MANY programs—most programs—deal with sequences or lists in some form or another.[1] Both the changemaker and the convenience store programs, which were first introduced in Chapter 1, have lists. The changemaker program has a list of denomination names and sizes; the convenience store program computes a sequence of wholesale prices; and the text analyzer from Chapter 5 processes a sequence of characters.

An object's methods can use loops to process lists and sequences. The loops from the previous chapter were designed so that one item of a sequence could be examined at a time, then discarded as soon as it was examined. But many times items cannot be discarded in that fashion. Sometimes the lists themselves are objects that live during the entire execution of the program. The list items cannot simply be forgotten as they are processed. Good examples of this are easy to find. Consider a list of test grades for a class of 50 students. What kinds of behavior for that list are possible? How about sorting its grades? Or adjusting each grade according to some formula that depends on the values of the individual grades?

C++ has several tools for implementing lists. The new tool that we will introduce in this chapter is an array. An array can hold different items of the same type. Arrays are examples of C++ **aggregates**, which are objects capable of holding more than one item at a single time.

This chapter will be devoted to lists, and indexed lists in particular. We will discuss familiar list operations and illustrate how list data and list methods can be implemented with arrays and functions that manipulate arrays. While you read this chapter, it will be important for you to remember that arrays and lists are not the same thing. The design object under consideration here is a list. The array is simply a language tool.

At the end of the chapter, we will return to the changemaker problem. We will redesign some of its components as lists. And we will implement those lists using arrays.

---

[1] In this chapter, the terms *sequence* and *list* will be used interchangeably.

6.1   Implementing list objects with old programming tools

Let's look at a simplified version of the student test grades problem mentioned in the introduction above. An instructor must manage a list of all final examination grades for a class of five students. How can we implement a list-of-grades object using only tools from previous chapters of this text?

Here's one way to approach the problem. Define five `int` variables, each representing one of the five items in the list.

```
int item_0;    // First item in the list
int item_1;    // Second item in the list
int item_2;    // Third item in the list
int item_3;    // Fourth item in the list
int item_4;    // Fifth item in the list
```

Items in this list are indexed or numbered according to their names. In the tradition of C and C++ programming, we opted to make the indices start at 0 rather than 1. The index of `item_0` is 0, the index of `item_1` is 1, and so on. Each index tells the position of the item in the list. Any item can be accessed—i.e., looked at or changed—by its index.

We could have called the items in the list `item0`, `item1`, and so on. But the underscores are there to make a point. We wish the compiler could look at the two parts of the name that are separated by underscores as two different entities: a list and an index. Of course, the compiler will not look at these parts separately. The underscore is a legitimate character in an identifier name. But we anticipate a time when we will be able to separate the two parts. What we would really like is to use is something like `item_n`, where n is an integer variable.

Let's simplify the implementation problem for the time being by assuming `item_0`, `item_1`, `item_2`, `item_3`, and `item_4` are global variables. The function `lookAt()`, which returns the value of a list item according to its index, can use those variables directly without using them as arguments.

```
int lookAt(int index)
// Argument: index - Index of the item in the list (ASSUME: 0 <= index <= 4)
// Returns: The value of the item with the given index.
{
    switch (index) {
        case 0: return item_0;
        case 1: return item_1;
        case 2: return item_2;
        case 3: return item_3;
        case 4: return item_4;
    }
}
```

We will continue this implementation by defining `change()`, a function that takes an index and a new value and changes the list item with that index to the new value. The function `change()` allows us to assign a new value to one of the list items. Here is its definition:

```
void change(int index, int newValue)
// Arguments:
//    index -   Index of the item in the list (ASSUME: 0 <= index <= 4)
//    newValue - New value for the item
// Side effect: Changes the value of the item with the given index to the
//    new value.
{
    switch (index) {
        case 0: item_0 = newValue; return;
        case 1: item_1 = newValue; return;
        case 2: item_2 = newValue; return;
        case 3: item_3 = newValue; return;
        case 4: item_4 = newValue; return;
    }
}
```

How about curving up all of the test grades by 15 points? Our old friend the iterator object, which we defined in the previous chapter, comes in handy here. The iterator object can iterate through the items of the list. Since each item is indexed, the iterator needs a counter to go through the list indices. Indeed, the iterator object can be implemented as a simple loop with a counter to go through all of the indices of the list. This code will curve the test grades.

```
for (int i = 0; i < 5; i++)
    change(i,15 + lookAt(i));
```

Two different function calls are necessary to increment a list item, one call to `lookAt()` and one call to `change()`. The following is a different implementation of a list of five test grades. The new implementation allows us to change an item with a single function call rather than two. It also has a C++ feature that we have not discussed before: a function that returns an *object* rather than the value of an object.

```
int& item(int index)
// Argument: index - Index of the item in the list (ASSUME: 0 <= index <= 4)
// Returns: The object which is the list item with the given index
{
    static int item_0;      // First item in the list
    static int item_1;      // Second item in the list
    static int item_2;      // Third item in the list
    static int item_3;      // Fourth item in the list
```

```
    static int item_4;        // Fifth item in the list

    switch (index) {
        case 0: return item_0;
        case 1: return item_1;
        case 2: return item_2;
        case 3: return item_3;
        case 4: return item_4;
    }
}
```

The type `int&` is called a reference to an `int`. A function with a reference return type returns an object of that type instead of returning a value. The "value" returned by such a function is an object's lvalue instead of its rvalue. That is consistent with our notion of reference arguments. When a function with a reference argument is called, an object rather than a value is sent as the actual argument.

The keyword `static` appears as the first part of each definition of the list objects. Therefore the list objects are created when `item()` is first executed. They exist even while `item()` is not executing, and they do not die until the program finishes execution. Static in this situation is important. Remember, `item()` returns an object—a local data object to be precise. If that object dies when `item()` finishes execution, then that object will not be of much use to the calling code.

Code to increment each test score by 15 looks like this:

```
for (int i = 0; i < 5; i++)
    item(i) = 15 + item(i);
```

Since `item()` returns an object rather than a value, the function call `item(i)` can appear on the left-hand side of the assignment operator. The assignment statement

```
item(3) = 87;
```

changes the value of the static local object `item_3` to 87. The assignment statement

```
item(i) = 15 + item(i);
```

increments the value of the object returned by the call `item(i)` by 15.

Both of these implementations of a list of five grades are correct but not good implementations. The number five is small and easy to manage. Suppose the number of students were much larger, say 100 students. Using this kind of solution, we would have to define 100 variables, not just five. The switch statements for each function would need 100 cases rather than five. Nobody wants to read or write that kind of code.

As now set up, each function can deal with exactly one list. For the first implementation, the list is explicitly given by the collection of global variables, `item_0`, `item_1`, `item_2`, `item_3`, and `item_4`. In the second implementation, the list is explicitly coded as the collection of local static variables. If we are to have any reasonable hope of representing more than one list, those variables ought to be sent as arguments to the functions. As small as the number five is, we were too lazy to send a collection of five variables as arguments. Imagine how we would balk at sending 100 of them.

There is another drawback to these solutions. The items in the list are logically related in our heads but not in the program. At a minimum, we want to encapsulate the data objects of a list into a single object.

6.2   Arrays: The fundamentals

The variables `item_0`, `item_1`, `item_2`, `item_3`, and `item_4` from the last section represent items in a particular list. Even though the individual items have names, the list itself does not have a name. The only way to group the items is to give them similar names that might somehow reveal that they are related. We want to be able to think of those items as the things that make up a single list that we can refer to by a single name. An array is one tool that a C++ programmer can use to help do just that.

An array is composed of a sequence of objects, each one having a fixed position in the sequence. The sequence itself has a name, which is the name of the array. The objects, which are the items of the sequence, are called the **elements** of the array. Each array element has a **subscript** or index to indicate its position in the array.

> An array can be used to implement a list in which each item in the list has an index indicating its position in the list. Each item also corresponds to an element in the array. Each list index corresponds to an array subscript.

Defining and using array type data objects

The following definition creates an array of five `int`s. The name of the array is `grade`. The array itself can be used in an implementation of the list of grades that students made on their final examinations.

```
const int numGrades = 5;
int grade[numGrades];
```

The type `int` at the beginning of the definition of `grade` indicates that the array elements are data objects of type `int`. The `[]` at the end indicates `grade` is an array of `int`s rather than a single `int`. The `numGrades` inside the brackets indicates the number of elements in `grade`. (See Fig. 6.1.)

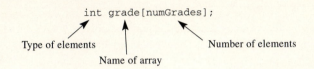

```
                        int grade[numGrades];
```

Type of elements   Number of elements

Name of array

Figure 6.1 Syntax for an array definition.

The subscripts of the elements of `grade` are 0, 1, 2, 3, and 4 (`numGrades - 1`). C++ always numbers its array elements starting with 0. The name of an array element is a two-part expression: the name of the array itself and the subscript of the element inside square brackets. The subscript is an integer expression that tells which element of the array is being referenced.

arrayName[elementSubscript]

The elements of `grade` are `grade[0]`, `grade[1]`, `grade[2]`, `grade[3]`, and `grade[4]`. Figure 6.2 illustrates how the elements of `grade` are stored in memory. (The question marks indicate that we simply do not know the values of the elements.)

Each element of `grade` is an `int` variable. Each element can be treated the same way an ordinary `int` variable is treated. If `grade` is used to implement a list of five grades, then we can treat each of the grades as a separate item. In the following sequence of statements, we assign each element of `grade` a value.

```
grade[0] = 78;
grade[1] = 94;
grade[2] = 30;
grade[3] = 65;
grade[4] = 84;
```

The results of making those five assignments are shown in Fig. 6.3. The question marks from Fig. 6.2 have been changed to the newly assigned values.

Some additional examples of assignments to array elements are as follows:

```
grade[3] = grade[3] + 8;      // The next-to-last grade is incremented by 8
grade[0] = grade[4];          // The first gets the value of the last one
cin >> grade[1];              // Read the second grade
for (int i = 0; i < numGrades; i++) // Curve each grade 15 points
   grade[i] = grade[i] + 15;
```

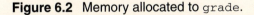

???	???	???	???	???

grade[0]   grade[1]   grade[2]   grade[3]   grade[4]

Figure 6.2 Memory allocated to `grade`.

78	94	30	65	84
grade[0]	grade[1]	grade[2]	grade[3]	grade[4]

Figure 6.3 The array grade after the sequence of assignments.

Does the loop look familiar? Look at the code from the previous section. Instead of item_0, we can use the notation grade[0]. Instead of the assignment item(i) = item(i) + 15, we can use grade[i] = grade[i] + 15. The parentheses, (), and the brackets, [], play identical roles for these two different list implementations.

Of course, we need not limit our use of array elements to input or assignment. Individual array elements can be used as actual function arguments and in arithmetic expressions. In short, they can be used wherever ordinary int type variables can be used.

```cpp
cout << grade[0];                       // Write the first grade
int i = (grade[0] + grade[1])/ 2;       // Average of the first two grades
double z = sqrt(grade[numGrades - 1]); // Square root of the last grade
```

Array syntax, a closer look

An array definition has the following form:

elementType arrayName[numberOfElements];

Here is the meaning of each part.

- *elementType* indicates which type the array elements will be. The type can be almost any type. It is possible to have an array of chars, an array of doubles, even an array in which every item is itself an array.

- *arrayName* is a valid C++ identifier.

- Brackets indicate that this is an array type object.

- *numberOfElements* is the number of elements in the array, a positive integer. It must be a literal, a const, or a constant expression whose value is known at compile time.

Here are some sample array definitions. One of them uses a literal integer to establish the number of array elements. The other uses a constant integer for the number of array elements.

```cpp
const int maxName = 30;    // Number of characters in a name limited to 30

double speed[10];          // Top speeds of 10 boats in a race
char aName[maxName];       // A person's name
```

The maximum number of characters that can be used to represent a person's name in `aName` is 30. The number of boats whose top speed can be represented by `speed` is 10.

The range of valid subscripts for any array depends on the number in the square brackets of its definition. The range of valid subscripts for `speed` is 0 through 9. The range of valid subscripts for `aName` is 0 through 29.

It is a mistake to try to access an element with a subscript greater than or equal to that number. Such an element does not even exist! The following code contains an error.

```
int x = 35;
aName[x] = 'k';        // Error! 35 is not a valid subscript for aName
```

The insidious thing about that pair of statements is that it may generate a runtime error. Or it may simply write over some information belonging to another object that has nothing to do with `aName` but whose memory location is near the memory location for `aName`. Runtime errors are bad enough; incorrect output is terrible.

It is the programmer's responsibility to be sure that array subscripts are in the correct range. If a subscript for an array element is negative or if it is bigger than or equal to the maximum declared size, the result is an error. The error may cause the program to abort (a runtime error) or it may cause the program to generate the incorrect results (a logic error).

Suppose that an array `a` is defined to have `N` elements. The range of valid subscripts for `a` will go from `0` through `N - 1`. The standard "idiom" for accessing all of the elements of `a` is a `for` loop:

```
for(i = 0; i < N; i++)
    // do something with a[i]
```

Arrays can be initialized when they are defined. The values initializing the individual array elements are written inside enclosing braces. In that situation, it is not necessary to tell the size of the array when it is defined because the compiler can figure out the number of elements by counting the number of values listed inside the braces.

Here are four examples of initialized array definitions:[2]

```
int measure[] = {2, 6, 1, 5, 0};    // measure has 5 elements
double x[] = {1.2, 3.1, -4.1};      // x has 3 elements
```

---

[2] Some compilers will not allow array initializations with braces in this fashion except for static or global arrays.

```
int tally[6] = {2, 1, 3};          // tally has 6 elements: 2 1 3 0 0 0
int score[100] = {0};              // score has 100 elements; all are 0
```

If the initialized array definition has a number within the brackets that is larger than the number of values listed in the braces, then the first elements of the array are initialized with the values in the braces and the remaining elements are initialized with 0. It is an error to put a number in the brackets that is smaller than the number of values listed in the braces.

The brace notation is valid only for initialization—only for the time when the array is defined. The brace notation is not valid for assignment or any other context. It cannot be used to create a "literal" array to send as an argument to a function.

Arrays as formal and actual arguments for functions

Suppose that the procedure f() has one formal argument, an array of doubles. There are four different ways to declare f(). As we first pointed out in Chapter 3, the two declarations where the argument is not named are signatures for f():

```
void f(double x[]);
void f(double[]);        // Signature style; formal argument is not named
```

or

```
void f(double* x);
void f(double*);         // Signature style; formal argument is not named
```

These declarations are completely equivalent. Each simply uses syntax that is different from but equivalent to the others. (Later in this text we will show you what the asterisk, *, really means in C++. The types double* and double[] are not the same unless you are talking about formal array arguments. For now, you should simply note that some programmers use the asterisk notation for formal array arguments.)

No mention of the number of array elements appears in the formal array argument. If you use the bracket notation for a formal array argument, the compiler will ignore any number inside the brackets.

Suppose the arrays num and val are defined in the following fashion:

```
double num[20];
double val[45];
```

Even though the number of elements of num and val are different, f() could take either array as an actual argument. Both of the following calls are valid.

```
f(num);
f(val);
```

The function `f()` has no way of knowing how many elements the actual array argument is supposed to contain. The programmer must guard against accessing an array element that is beyond the range of legitimate subscripts. One way to accomplish that is to make a function with an array argument have two arguments: an array and an integer to indicate the size of the array.

```
void g(double x[], int numElements);
```

In C and C++, array arguments are different from the other kinds of function arguments. Array arguments are *always passed by reference*, even though no `&` appears in the type of the formal array argument. Whatever changes occur to the formal argument `x` in the definition of `f()` also occur to the actual argument `num` in the call `f(num)`.

> Since arrays are always passed by reference, no array storage is allocated for a formal array argument when the function is called. That is why the number of array elements is not part of the formal array argument.

The function `makeZero()` assigns all of the elements of an array of `doubles` the value 0. The following is a prototype.

```
void makeZero(double array[], int numElements);
// Arguments:
//     array - Array of numbers
//     numElements - Number of elements in the array
// Side effect: Sets all the elements of array to 0.0.
```

The definition of `makeZero()` uses the second argument to indicate how many elements in the array are to be assigned 0. Note how the formal argument `numberOfElements` controls loop execution in the function definition.

```
void makeZero(double array[], int numElements)
{
    for(int i = 0; i < numElements; i++)
        array[i] = 0.0;
}
```

The following pair of function calls assigns all of the elements of `num` as well as `val` the value 0.0.

```
makeZero(num,20);    // All of the elements of num become 0.0
makeZero(val,45);    // All of the elements of val become 0.0
```

The fact that all arrays are automatically passed by reference presents a problem. One reason for using value arguments is to protect the actual arguments against any possible change or side effect that the function may create. Is such protection possible for arrays? The answer is yes.

C++ provides "read-only" array arguments. If the keyword const precedes the array type in the formal argument list, then the corresponding formal array argument is said to be passed by **constant reference**. Here is an example:

```
void g(const double x[]);      // Alternatively: void g(const double* x);
```

By using a constant formal reference argument, the elements of the actual argument can be examined while g() is executing, but they cannot be changed. Think of the const as modifying the term double. While g() is executing, x is considered to be an array of const double objects.

Objects that are constant cannot be changed. Statements such as this are not allowed in the definition of g().

```
x[0] = x[1];      // illegal in the definition of g(). x is a constant
                  //  reference argument.
```

Whenever you want a function to access the elements of an array without changing them, make the array argument type a const. If you want a function to be able to change the elements of an array, then do not use const to modify the argument type. In either case, do *not* use & in the argument type.

The function findMinPsn() returns the subscript of the smallest item in an array of doubles. It does not change the array. Here is a prototype for findMinPsn():

```
int findMinPsn(const double array[], int numElements);
// Arguments:
//     array - Array of numbers
//     numElements - Number of elements in the array
// Returns: The subscript of the smallest element in the array. If there
//    is more than one smallest element, the subscript of the first smallest
//    element is returned.
```

The definition of findMinPsn() uses the standard for loop mechanism to figure out the subscript of the smallest element.

```
int findMinPsn(const double array[], int numElements)
{
```

```
    int bestGuess = 0;                          // Best guess so far of the
                                                 //    subscript of the smallest item

    for (int i = 1; i < numElements; i++)
       if (array[bestGuess] > array[i])
          bestGuess = i;
    return bestGuess;
}
```

The syntax for invoking a function with a constant array formal argument is no different from the syntax for invoking a function with the default reference formal argument. Here are two invocations of findMinPsn(). They use the arrays of doubles num and val for actual arguments.

```
int where = findMinPsn(num,20);            // Subscript of smallest
                                           //    element of num
double smallValue = val[findMinPsn(val,45)]; // Smallest value of val
```

The first invocation for findMinPsn() is used to initialize an int. The second is used to initialize a double. Notice how findMinPsn() returns a subscript that is in the range of valid subscripts for an array as long as the second argument is no larger than the number of elements of the array.

The final example below shows how one might get some data into an array to begin with. After all, the numbers that are the values of the array elements do not just come out of thin air. The function readFromFile() reads integers from a text file into an array of ints. In order to work correctly, readFromFile() must be sent an open, valid input stream. (Appendixes D and F at the back of this book contain a description of how input streams work.)

```
void readFromFile(istream& in, int array[], int numElements, int& numRead)
// Arguments:
//    in - in\out - An open, valid stream
//    array - out - Numbers from in (in the order in which they appear)
//    numElements - Number of elements of array
//    numRead - out - Number of integers read into array
// Side effect: Reads integers from in until numElements have been read or
//    end-of-file is reached or a numeric read fails, whichever comes first.
//    If the a numeric read fails, the error flags are cleared from the
//    input stream.
{
   numRead = 0;
   while (numRead < numElements && in >> array[numRead])
      numRead++;
   if (!in.eof() && !in.bad())
      in.clear();
}
```

If the file `whole.txt` consists of a sequence of numbers, then the following code can be used to store up to 30 of those numbers in an array:

```
const int maxSize = 30;           // Maximum number of integers to store
int integer[maxSize];             // Holds the integers
int size = 0;                     // Number of integers stored

ifstream input("whole.txt");      // Integers are read from this file
readFromFile(input, integer, maxSize, size);
```

The effect of invoking `readFromFile()` is that up to a maximum of 30 integers will be read from `whole.txt` and stored in consecutive elements of `integer`, starting at `integer[0]`. In effect, `integer` represents a list of numbers. We'll use that kind of representation for lists later in this chapter.

Using arrays: Additional examples

Arrays are collections of objects. We already looked at a collection of grades when we defined the `grade` array earlier in this section.

```
const int numGrades = 5;          // Number of grades in a collection
int grade[numGrades];             // The grades
```

Recall that `for` loops are the standard mechanism that programmers use to process array elements. Suppose we want to find out how many of the grades were at least 60.

```
int passing = 0;                  // Number of passing grades found so far
for (int i = 0; i < numGrades; i++)// i goes through the array subscripts
   if (grade[i] >= 60)
      passing++;
```

Another example should have a familiar ring. This loop determines the highest grade among the five. We'll use the same variable `i` for the array subscripts. (Assume that `i` was just defined in the previous loop.)

```
int highest = grade[0];           // Highest grade found so far
for (i = 1; i < numGrades; i++)
   if (grade[i] > highest)
      highest = grade[i];
```

This segment of code computes the average of the grades. As before, it uses a loop to access the individual elements of the array.

```
   float average;                        // Average of the grades
   int sum = 0;                          // Sum of grades added so far
```

```
for (i = 0; i < numGrades; i++)
   sum += grade[i];
average = sum / float (numGrades);
```

In most of the remainder of this chapter, we'll use arrays to implement list type objects. Our collection of grades could be considered to be a fixed-size list containing numGrades items. But arrays need not be used simply for lists.

The next example has a different flavor. Instead of limiting ourselves to a collection of five grades, suppose we look at a collection of 1000 grades instead.

```
const int colSize = 1000;        // Size of a collection
int studentGrade[colSize];       // Collection of grades
```

Assuming that the studentGrades have already been assigned, let's now determine their distribution. That is, let's find the number of students who scored 0, the number who scored 1, the number who scored 2, and so on up to the number who scored 99 and 100. (We will not worry about grades that are negative or greater than 100.)

Let's keep track of the numbers of these grades in an array named tally, which is defined as follows:

```
const int range = 101;           // range of grades is 0 through 100
int tally[range] = {0};          // tally[i] is the number of students
                                 //    (counted so far) making a grade of i
```

Each of the 101 elements in tally from tally[0] through tally[100] is initialized to 0. This loop accomplishes the counting.

```
for(i = 0; i < colSize; i++)
   if (studentGrade[i] >= 0 && studentGrade[i] < range)
      tally[studentGrade[i]] += 1;    // Could use tally[studentGrade[i]]++
```

The if statement shows how the subscript of an array need not be limited to a simple literal such as 0 or 1 or to an int such as i. The subscript for tally is the value of an element of grade. For example, if studentGrade[729] is 65, then tally[65] will be incremented by 1.

6.3 ▍ List type objects

When Dr. Smith returned to campus after attending an extended conference, she listened to all of the messages that had been left on her answering machine in her absence. All of the callers had left their telephone numbers for her to return their calls. Some callers had left several messages at different times. Dr. Smith, always very conscientious, must now call everyone who left her a message.

The calls on the answering machine constitute one list of information. Dr. Smith makes a second list consisting of the telephone numbers of people who called her. With pencil and paper in hand, she listens to the original messages. As she listens to each message, she runs her finger down the list of numbers on the paper to see if the telephone number for the current message has already been written down. If it has not, she writes it at the end of list of numbers on paper.

Simple lists as design objects

What objects can be involved in solving the answering machine problem? The obvious choices include an input object, an output object, and a list object. By the time an entire program solution is designed, there may be many more. We'll concentrate on a list.

Consider the list to be an intelligent object that knows what Dr. Smith knows about the list and is able to do what she can do with it. Dr. Smith is out of the picture. This list knows its items and can find whether or not an item is already in the list and add an item to the end of the list. What a list knows and what it can do are the list's attributes and its behaviors.

We will fit one additional object into our design: an iterator object. An iterator object can be tied to a particular list or sequence—it is a "friend" of its list and knows it well. Since it is used to access the list items one at a time, the iterator object knows the item it is currently accessing. It can start up (prepare to process the list from the beginning), get the next item, and indicate whether or not there are additional items in the list.

Figure 6.4 does not dictate how the list and the iterator object must be implemented. If the list is to be implemented with an array, then its operations will be implemented as functions that manipulate the array. The iterator object may or may not be implemented as a separate object apart from the code that does the manipulations on the array. The array and the corresponding functions are implementation details that are not part of this design.

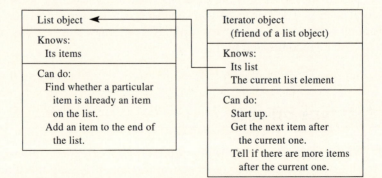

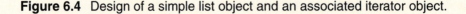
Figure 6.4 Design of a simple list object and an associated iterator object.

List methods and messages

What kinds of things can lists do? Almost every list can add an item and find out whether or not it contains a particular item. Many lists have additional capabilities. The things a list can do are its *methods*, which are performed when the appropriate messages are sent to the list.

We use the term *simple list* to describe a kind of list-type object. The items of a simple list are of one fixed type. A simple list has the following methods:

- Tell its current size, which is the number of items currently in the list. (That number can vary from zero up to the maximum capacity.)

- Tell its maximum capacity, which is largest number of items that the list is able to hold.

- Clear out all of its items, thus making itself empty.

- Add a new item at the end.

- Indicate whether an item is already present.

Dr. Smith's list is almost a simple list, but it has one restriction. It will add an item only if that item is not already in the list. Dr. Smith's telephone number contains no duplicates.

Suppose `list` is a simple list of integers. We can represent the messages that can be sent to `list` by actual C++ function prototypes.

- `int list_size();`   `// Number of items currently in`
                            `// the list`

- `int list_maxsize();`   `// Maximum number of items the`
                            `// list can hold`

- `void list_clear();`   `// Make the list empty`

- `void list_add(int);`   `// Add the int item to end of`
                            `// the list`

- `bool list_member(int);` `// Is the int item in the`
                            `// list?`

We do not need to know exactly how the methods corresponding to these prototypes are implemented in order to send messages to `list`. Here are some sample tasks and messages that can be sent to do those tasks. In all of the examples, *aNumber* is an integer.

Example 1: If `list` is not full, add another number to `list`.

```
if (list_size() < list_maxsize())
    list_add(aNumber);
```

Example 2: Get six integers and make *list* contain only those six integers for list items.

```
list_clear();
for (int i = 0; i < 6; i++){
    // code to get aNumber goes here
    list_add(aNumber);
}
```

Example 3: Get six integers as before, but now *list* should contain only those values with no duplicates.

```
list_clear();
for (int i = 0; i < 6; i++){
    // code to get aNumber goes here
    if (!list_member(aNumber))
        list_add(aNumber);
}
```

In order to access each item in the list, one at a time, we can expand our definition of *list* to include an iterator. Rather than make a separate iterator object outside the list, we'll put the iterator object methods as part of the list itself. These three prototypes will suffice.

```
• void list_setupIterator();    // Sets up the iterator so the next item
                                //    is the first list item
• bool list_more();             // Are there more items in the list?
• int list_next();              // Next item in the list if one exists
```

Example 4: With the new iterator methods, we are able to print the items in *list*, each on a separate line.

```
list_setupIterator();
while (list_more())
    cout << list_next() << endl;
```

Since *list* can tell how many items it contains (through a *list_size()* message), there is an alternative way to print out the *list* items:

```
list_setupIterator();
for (int i = 0; i < list_size(); i++)
    cout << list_next() << endl;
```

Let's go back to Dr. Smith's list. Suppose she writes down the telephone numbers on a lined notepad with line numbers at the left part of the lines. Each telephone number on the list corresponds to a line number on the paper, which indicates a particular position. A list in which each item in the list is in a numbered position is called an **indexed list**. The position of an item in such a list is its index.

We can expand our definition of the simple list type to make it into an indexed list. Let's add the following function prototype:

- `int& list_item(int);    // The item whose index is the int argument`

The `&` at the end of the return type indicates that `list_item()` returns the object at the given position, not just the value of the item. (The type `int&` is a reference type.) The message `list_item(i)` returns the item whose index is `i`. If the `list` positions begin at 0, then code to print each number on the list on a separate line can be as follows:

```
for (int i = 0; i < list_size(); i++)
    cout << list_item(i) << endl;
```

> *Example 5*: We can use the `list_item()` method to change the value of a `list` item. For example, suppose we want to change the first item to the telephone number 489-5269. This message is sufficient.
>
> `list_item(0) = 4895269;`

The "code" from this section illustrates messages to simple lists. It was real code in the sense that it adhered to C++ syntax. But we did not show how the methods were implemented in a program. We did not even show how the list items could be implemented. But, of course, you already know that list items can be implemented as array elements. The list methods can be implemented as functions with array arguments.

6.4 ▐ Array-based implementations of lists

Arrays and lists are not the same thing. A list is a design object, an array is a programming tool that can be used to represent a list. Functions that have array arguments can implement list behaviors.

Let's be specific about the exact representation of a list using an array. The array is where the list items can be held. If `a` is the name of an array that holds list items, then `a[0]` is where the first list item is stored, `a[1]` is where the second one is stored, `a[2]` is where the third one is stored, and so on. (See Fig. 6.5 for an illustration.)

The list will usually have fewer items than the array has elements. Think of the array as a large storage area. The list can then change size as items are added or removed. Since the size of the list may vary, we need not only an array to hold the list items but also an integer in order to tell how many of the array elements

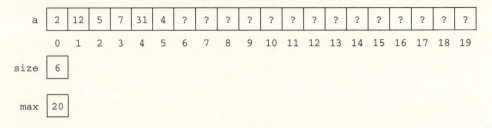

Figure 6.5 A list implemented with an array `a` and two integers `size` and `max`. The list items are 2, 12, 5, 7, 31, and 4. `a` holds the list items, `size` is the number of list items, and `max` is the number of elements of `a`.

are list items. We will thus make three different definitions in the code to implement the list data:

1. A constant integer indicating the maximum possible size of the list.

2. An array of that maximum size number of elements.

3. An integer telling how many items are in the list at any given time.[3]

The size of a list can range from 0 (representing an empty list) through the maximum possible capacity (representing a completely full list with no room to grow). The values of the list items are stored in the array at consecutive subscripts in the array starting at 0. The last list value is stored in the array at a subscript that is 1 less than the size of the list.

> The range of valid subscripts for items currently in a list implemented as an array is from 0 through the current list size − 1.

These three definitions can be used in the implementation of an indexed list of 100 integers or less. There are two restrictions on lists that are implemented via these definitions. Their items must be integers and the lists cannot contain more than 100 items.

```
const int maxList = 100;    // Maximum capacity of the list (maxList may be
                            //   global.)
```

---

[3] Lists that have fixed sizes can be implemented with just an array rather than an array and an `int` indicating the current list size.

```
int listItem[maxList];    // Holds the actual list items
int size = 0;             // The number of items in the list
                          //    0 <= size <= maxList
                          //    Items are stored in listItem[0] through
                          //    listItem[size - 1].
```

The initialization of the variable size to 0 implements the design operation *list_clear()*. That initialization is a very common programming practice. Lists are usually built when the program is executing. At the beginning of execution, such lists should be created as empty lists. Of course, it does not make any sense to say that the array is empty. There is always data in the array, even though the data may not represent a list when the array is defined.

List traversals

Assume now that an indexed list contains some items. Suppose we want to access each item in the list, starting with the first one. To do so, we can iterate through all of the items in the list, a process that is sometimes called a **traversal**. We have already shown you several examples of array traversals, so a traversal of a list implemented through an array should look familiar to you. A traversal of listItem can be coded in the following manner:

```
for (int i = 0; i < size; i++)
    access(listItem[i]);
```

In this code, access() stands for any function with a single int argument or for any statement that involves listItem[i]. The next loop will print all of the integers in the list starting with the first one. (It need not print out all of the elements of the array, since the printing stops when i is size rather than maxList.)

```
for (int i = 0; i < size; i++)
    cout << listItem[i] << endl;
```

With indexed lists implemented via arrays, the iterator object can go through the subscripts of the elements of the array that are list items. Almost all programmers use for loops rather than while loops to traverse arrays. The iterator object in that last loop goes from the first item in the indexed list through the last one. If the list is empty (if size is 0), the loop will not generate any output.

Adding an item to a list

The process of adding an item depends upon the kind of list it involved. If it is a simple list, such as Dr. Smith's telephone number list, new items are added at the end. (It would be pretty pointless for Dr. Smith to squeeze a new telephone number in between two other numbers.)

We can implement the method that a simple list uses to add an item to the end of a list as a function. The function needs three arguments: two for the list attributes (the array and the size) and one for the new item to be added. Both the array and the size arguments are reference arguments. After all, adding an item to a list does change the list. The new item argument can be a value argument.

```
void addToEnd(int item[], int& size, int newItem)
// Arguments:
//    item - in - Holds a simple list of items
//         - out - If not full to start with, holds the original items with
//                 the new item added to the end
//    size - in - Number of items in the list before the attempted add
//           ASSUME: 0 <= size <= number of elements of item
//         - out - Number of items in the list after the attempted add
//    newItem - A number
// Side effect: If there is room for an additional list item, newItem is
//    added to the end of the list.
{
    if (size < maxList) {
        item[size] = newItem;
        size++;
    }
}
```

Although `addToEnd()` implements a simple list add method, not all lists are simple. An **ordered list** is one whose items occur in order of their values. The telephone directory for any town or city is a good example. If such a list were not ordered alphabetically by surnames, it would be almost impossible to find a particular name.

One of the easiest ways an ordered, indexed list can maintain its order is to insert every new element into its correct position. Items are not just added to the beginning or the end of a list. Usually, they are inserted somewhere in the middle. How do lists squeeze in new items? Some items already in the list will have to shift position to make room for the new item.

Let's look at that shifting process in the context of a real-life situation. Suppose that each seat in a row of theater seats is numbered, starting with the number 0, and that the first 12 of those seats are occupied but the remaining ones are empty. (In other words, seats numbered 0 through 11 are occupied and seats 12 and above are not.) A person entering the theater wants to sit in a particular seat among the people already seated in that row. If the chosen seat is seat 12, there is no problem. The newcomer can simply sit in seat 12 and no one will have to move. On the other hand, if the chosen seat has a number less than 12, then some of the people already seated will have to move in order to accommodate the newcomer. A shifting process will occur.

Now the whole insertion problem boils down to a single question: "How do the people who are already seated shift to make room for the newcomer?" Let's assume that the seat chosen by the newcomer is seat 9. Then the person in seat 11 moves to seat 12, the person in seat 10 moves to seat 11, and the person in seat 9 moves to seat 10. The moving has to be done in that order. If the person in seat 9 were to move and sit down before the person in seat 10 moved, then someone would end up sitting in someone else's lap. (And that would create a terribly uncomfortable situation.)

Look at Fig. 6.6, which illustrates the entire shifting process. The row has 18 seats, numbered from 0 through 17. The maximum possible size of a list of seated people is 18. Seats numbered 0 through 11 are occupied (indicated by shaded rectangles). So the current size of the list of people already seated is 12.

The newcomer selects seat 9. The people in seats 11 through 9 shift, and then the newcomer sits down. This means that seats 0 thorough 12 are now occupied and that the size of the list of seated people is 13.

The theater scenario describes an insertion algorithm for an indexed list implemented with an array. The row corresponds to the array and the seats correspond to the individual array elements. To insert an item in a particular position in an indexed list, the items at the end of the list must be shifted over one position each. Each corresponding array element must be shifted over one subscript, beginning with the element at the subscript `size - 1`.

We know how to shift. All that we must do now is determine where the new item belongs. We will combine looking for that insertion position with the shifting process itself.

Let's start with the last item of the list. If that item is larger than the new one to be inserted, we shift it over one, because we know it will have to move anyway to accommodate the new element. We then move to the next-to-last item. If it is larger than the new one to be inserted, we shift it over also, to make room for the new item. We continue in this manner, starting with the last item as the current item.

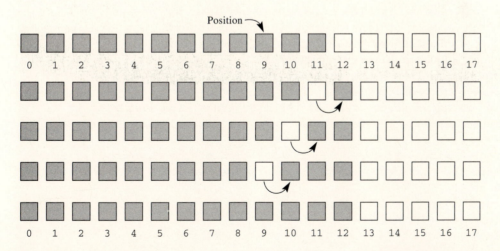

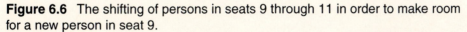

Figure 6.6 The shifting of persons in seats 9 through 11 in order to make room for a new person in seat 9.

Let's summarize our shifting process. If there is a current item and if the new item is less than the current item,

1. Shift the current item over one position.

2. Make the current list item the one immediately before the one that was just shifted and repeat.

When the new item is greater than or equal to the current list item or when there is no current list item, stop shifting and put the new item into the now "empty" position.

The function `insert()` implements an insertion of a new item into a list that is already sorted in ascending order. It requires two pieces of information: the list itself and the new item to be inserted. The representation of the list data (items and size) is a pair of arguments to `insert()`. The new item is an additional argument. This `insert()` makes the assumption that the list is not full (`size < maxList`). No matter where in the list the insertion is supposed to take place, when the new item is inserted, the size of the list is incremented by 1.

```
void insert(int item[], int& size, int newItem)
// Arguments:
//   item- in - Holds list items sorted in ascending order before a new
//              item is inserted.
//              ASSUME: The list is not full.
//        - out - Holds list items after the new item is inserted.
//   size - in - Number of list items prior to insertion.
//              ASSUME: 0 <= size < number of elements of item
//        - out - Number of list items after the insertion
//   newItem - A new item to be inserted in the list
// Side effect: The new item is inserted into the ordered list in its proper
//   position relative to the rest of the list items. The list size is
//   incremented by 1.
{
    int current = size - 1;          // Position of the current list item
    // Look for the correct position to insert the new item, shifting item as
    //   you go.
    while (current >= 0 && item[current] > newItem) {
        item[current + 1] = item[current];
        current--;
    }
    // The new item goes one past the current position.
    item[current + 1] = newItem;
```

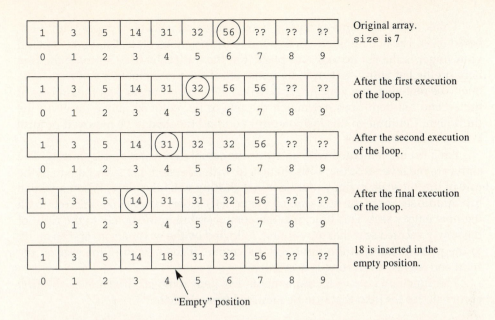

Figure 6.7 Insertion of 18 into the ordered list 1, 3, 5, 14, 31, 32, 56. The circled item is the one currently being examined. The "empty" position is after the current position.

```
        size++;
}
```

Figure 6.7 traces what happens to the array during the execution of insert() when an original list of seven items consists of 1, 3, 5, 14, 31, 32, and 56, the new item to be inserted is the number 18.

A programmer who uses insert() is responsible for making sure that it is called only when the array and the size do not represent a full list.

Removing an item from a list

The method for adding items to a list depends on what kind of list it is. The method for removing items also depends on what kind of list it is. A special kind of list called a stack will add and remove items only from one end (called the top of the stack). Another special kind of list called a queue adds items to the back but removes them from the front. Many other lists, however, can remove items from anywhere inside the list—they can remove items according to their values rather than according to their positions.

If a list can remove items according to their values, then any remove message has to indicate the value of the item to be removed. The list will have to search its items to find the one to be removed. Finding such an item in the list is easy.

Think of the list items as having been written on a sheet of paper with numbered lines. The line numbers correspond to the positions of the list items. Pretend your finger is the list iterator and place it at the top of the list. Compare the first item on the list with the item to be removed. If the first item does not match the one to be removed, run your finger down to the second one. Repeat the process. If the second list item does not match the one to be removed, move down to the third item. Continue in this fashion until you find the item to be removed or until you run out of list items.

For a list implemented with an array, the actual removal requires shifting. The shifts are the reverse of the shifts that occur with insertion. Let's refer again to the row of theater seats to figure out how that shifting will take place. When a person in a middle seat or in the first seat (on the far left) leaves, others may shift left to fill the now empty seat. This time, it is the person sitting immediately to the right of the newly vacated seat that moves first, followed by the next person, and so on up to the person sitting at the right end. Of course, if the person in the seat on the right end leaves, no shifting is necessary.

The function `remove()` implements list item removal. It removes the first occurrence of the item that is to be removed from the list.

```
void remove(int item[], int& size, int itemToGo)
// Arguments:
//    item - in - Holds list items before an item is removed
//    item - out - Holds list items after the removal is attempted
//    size - in - Number of items in the list before the attempted removal
//              ASSUME: 0 <= size <= number of elements of item.
//         - out - Number of items in the list after the attempted removal
//    itemToGo - the item to be removed
// Side effect: If itemToGo is in the list, its first occurrence is removed
///    from the list. Each list item past itemToGo is moved to the next
//     smaller position and the list size is decremented by 1.
{
   int psn = 0;                              // Position of next list item
                                             //   to compare to itemToGo
   while (psn < size && item[psn] != itemToGo)  // Look for itemToGo in the
      psn++;                                 //   list.
   if (psn < size) {                         // If itemToGo is in the list,
      for (int i = psn; i < size - 1; i++)   //    shift back all list items
         item[i] = item[i + 1];              //       after the itemToGo.
      size--;                                //    Decrement the list size.
   }
}
```

Figure 6.8 traces the execution of `remove()` when the original list of seven items consists of 3, 5, 1, 32, 56, 14, and 31. The item to be removed is 56.

In case you think that the list has a duplicate value at the end, keep in mind that Fig. 6.8 shows pictures of the array, not the list. Yes, the number 31 is the value

3	5	1	32	56	14	31	??	??	??
0	1	2	3	4	5	6	7	8	9

Original array.
size is 7

3	5	1	32	14	14	31	??	??	??
0	1	2	3	4	5	6	7	8	9

After the first execution
of the loop.

3	5	1	32	14	31	31	??	??	??
0	1	2	3	4	5	6	7	8	9

After the final execution of
the loop and the assignment
size is 6

Figure 6.8 Removing the item 56 from the list 3, 5, 1, 32, 56, 14, 31.

of both of the array elements item[5] and item[6], but the number of items in the list is 6. The actual list items are 3, 5, 1, 32, 14, and 31, which occur as the array elements item[0] through item[5]. The value of item[6] is completely irrelevant to the actual list.

Using arrays and functions to implement list objects: Sample code

Let's see how we can use a list in a program. The following definitions implement the attributes for a list:

```
const int capacity = 20;    // Maximum number of items the list can hold
int myItem[capacity];       // Holds the list items
int currentSize = 0;        // Number of items currently in the list
```

These three definitions do not indicate anything about what kind of list this is. We can control what kind of list it is (simple, ordered, or whatever) by the functions we will invoke to do the list operations. For this example, we will use the operations appropriate for an ordered list. And that means when we add a new item to a list, we will use insert() rather than addToEnd().

The initialization of currentSize to 0 initializes the list is as an empty list. Suppose we want to add a few items to the list. This code adds 15, 81, 10, 13, and 9 to the list.

```
insert(myItem, currentSize, 15);    // The list is: 15
insert(myItem, currentSize, 81);    // The list is: 15, 81
insert(myItem, currentSize, 10);    // The list is: 10, 15, 81
insert(myItem, currentSize, 13);    // The list is: 10, 13, 15, 81
insert(myItem, currentSize, 9);     // The list is: 9, 10, 13, 15, 81
```

We then print out the list and its current size:

```
cout << "List items:";
for (int i = 0; i < currentSize; i++)
```

```
        cout << ' ' << myItem[i];
    cout <<"\nNumber of items in the list: " << currentSize << endl;
```

The output generated by execution of the code is shown in the box below.

```
List items: 9 10 13 15 81
Number of items in the list: 5
```

Suppose we want to create another list with the same items as the ones in this list, but in reverse order. We need a new array and a new size.

```
int reverse[capacity];      // Holds items of a list
int revSize = 0;            // Number of items currently in the list
```

We now need to fill the new array with the items from the original list. There is more than a single way to do this. The following code traverses the original list from end to beginning, using addToEnd() to add each item from the original list to the new list.

```
for (int i = size - 1; i >= 0; i--)
    addToEnd(reverse, revSize, myItem[i]);
```

The items in the reversed list are 81, 15, 13, 10, and 9.

Of course, we can remove an item from a list using remove(). The first invocation of remove() will remove item 13 from the original sorted list. The second invocation does not change the list since the item to be removed does not belong to the list.

```
remove(myItem, currentSize, 13);      // The list is: 9, 10, 15, 81
                                      //    currentSize is 4
remove(myItem, currentSize, 27);      // The list is: 9, 10, 15, 81
                                      //    currentSize is still 4
```

With the functions addToEnd(), insert(), and remove(), managing a list can be an easy process. In object-oriented terminology, managing a list means sending it messages to add an item to the end or to insert or remove an item. At least for now, the function invocations are the ways we send the list messages.

6.5   Sorting and searching

Ordered lists do not need to sort themselves—they are already sorted. Many lists are not ordered, but they may sort their items when necessary. The list of test scores is an example of an unordered list. To find the median test score (the number in the middle of the sorted sequence) or to see how the scores are distributed, the unordered list of test scores can first sort itself. (Think how hard it could be to compute that median number if the test scores were not sorted.)

Sorting is something that everybody knows how to do. A sorting process should not be difficult to describe. We'll look at only one way to sort a list, using a method that you have probably used many times outside the world of computers.

Insertion sorts

Imagine this situation. You have written some names and addresses on index cards and placed them into a box. How would you go about sorting the box of cards according to the names?

Think about rearranging the box of cards, starting from the front. Leave the first card in the box at the front. If the second card belongs after the first, leave it after the first. Otherwise, put it before the first. To put the third card in the correct place, check to see where it belongs relative to the two in the front. Then insert it into the proper position relative to those first two. Insert the fourth card into its correct position relative to the first three in the same manner. Then insert the fifth card, the sixth card, and so on until each card has been inserted into its correct position relative to those that have already been placed.

Throughout this entire process, the box of cards is divided in two parts: the front part is a sorted list of cards; the back part consists of the cards that have not been inserted into their correct relative positions in the sorted part. The fundamental operation in this sorting process consists of two steps:

1. Get the next card remaining in the back part of the box.

2. Insert that card into its correct position in the sorted front part.

Every time you insert a card into the front part, the front part grows by one card and the back part decreases by one. That's good. Since the sorted list and the remaining unsorted cards occupy the same box, the sorted list will have room to grow by one as long a card is removed from the unsorted back of the box. This sorting algorithm is called an **insertion sort**. Each card is inserted into its correct position into a sorted list.

Figure 6.9 illustrates how the sorting proceeds with a box of five cards. The cards in the box that are shaded are the front, sorted part of the list. The cards in the box that are not shaded are the ones that remain to be inserted into the sorted part.

It may be a little hard to imagine the cards in the box constituting an indexed list. The positions of the cards are not actually numbered. (Most boxes do not have special numbered grooves, each of which can hold a single card.) But we can use an indexed list to simulate the cards in the box. The index of a card can mark its relative position, with the first card having an index 0, the second card having index 1, and so on. The payoff in using an indexed list to model the box of cards is that you already know a way to implement an indexed list.

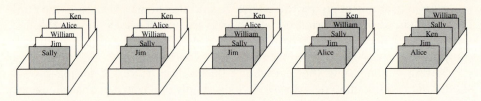

Figure 6.9   Sorting a collection of index cards.

The insertion sort algorithm has only one difficult part: inserting the next item into the sorted front part of the list. But think about the front part of the list as constituting another list—a sorted list at that. We know how to insert an item into a sorted list simply by using the function `insert()`. The first part of the insertion sort algorithm consists of getting the next item. But that's pretty easy. All we have to do is go through the list items, one at a time, starting with the one next to the front, a process that probably can be implemented with a simple loop.

The function `insertionSort()` implements an insertion sort on a list of integers.

```
void insertionSort(int item[], int size)
// Arguments:
//    item - in - Holds list items prior to sorting
//    item - out - Holds list items after sorting
//    size - Number of items in the list
//          ASSUME: 0 <= size <= number of elements of item.
// Side effect: The list items are sorted in ascending order.
{
    int sortedSize = 1;    // Size of the sorted part of the list.
                           //    The sorted list contains one item initially,
                           //    the item at the front of the list.
    // For each next item, starting right after the first one, insert it
    //    into the sorted front part.
    for (int i = 1; i < size; i++)
      insert(item, sortedSize, item[i]);
}
```

There are many different algorithms for sorting lists. We used this one because it is a natural technique. And besides, we could reuse old code, the function `insert()`, to implement it.

We could have defined `insertionSort()` without using `insert()`. The insertion algorithm in this case is coded directly into the function definition. This is what the new definition looks like:

```
void insertionSort(int item[], int size)
// Version 2
{
```

```
    for (int i = 1; i < size; i++) {        // The list items before position
                                            //    i - 1 are already sorted
        int nextItem = item[i];             // Next item to put into the sorted
                                            //    part

        for (int j = i - 1; j >= 0          // Find the correct location of
                && item[j] > nextItem; j--) //    nextItem; shift the items in the
            item[j + 1] = item[j];          //    sorted part as you are looking
        item[j + 1] = nextItem;             // Put nextItem into its position in
    }                                       //    the sorted front part
}
```

Linear searches

Suppose we need to know whether or not a particular item is in a list. When we removed an item in the list, we had to find out not only whether the item was in the list, but also where it was. We needed to search the list for the location of the item. That's what this section is all about.

Do you remember how searching was done in the definition of the function remove()? Starting from the beginning, the search went through the list items one at a time until the item was found or there were no more items in the list to look at. That searching algorithm is called a **linear search**.

A linear search is easily implemented as a function, linearSearch(). The function takes a list and an item and returns the position of the first instance of the item in the list. By position, we mean the subscript of the item in the array holding the list items. If the item is not in the list, linearSearch() returns -1.

```
int linearSearch (const int item[], int size, int itemToFind)
// Arguments:
//    item - Hold list items.
//    size - The size of the list.
//           ASSUME: 0 <= size <= number of elements of item.
//    itemToFind - A number to search for in the list.
// Returns: The item subscript of the first occurrence of itemToFind. If
//    itemToFind is not a list item, -1 is returned.
{
    for (int i = 0; i < size; i++)      // Look for the item
        if (item[i] == itemToFind)      //    If you find it,
            return i;                   //       return its subscript
    return -1;                          // The item is not in the list
}
```

A more efficient linear search is possible for sorted lists. The search can begin at the front of the list but it may quit early when it starts finding list items that are bigger than the one it is searching for. In that case, there is no need to search the list from that point on—the item is too small to be found among the bigger items at the end.

The function `linearSearchOrderedList()` implements the search method. Its definition is similar to the definition of `linearSearch()`. The `if` statement in the body of the loop of the original linear search is changed to an `if/else` statement.

```
int linearSearchOrderedList (const int item[], int size, int itemToFind)
{
    for (int i = 0; i < size; i++) {      // Look for the item
        if (item[i] == itemToFind)        //    If you find it
            return i;                     //        return its subscript
        else if (item[i] > itemToFind)    //    If the remaining items are too
            return -1;                    //        big, quit looking
    }
    return -1;                            //  The item is bigger than all the
                                          //    items in the list
}
```

Binary searches

How do you find the queen of hearts in a shuffled deck of cards? Start at the beginning and stop when you have found it or when you have run through all of the cards. Starting at the beginning of a list and quitting when you have found the item or when you have run through all of the items in the list may be the only surefire way to find an item. On the other hand, if you know something about how the items in the list are organized, you might go about searching in a more intelligent way. When you are looking for "John Smith" in the telephone directory, do you start at the beginning of the directory? Of course not. You use the fact that the directory is sorted to look for the number.

Suppose a list keeps its items in ascending order and you want to find a particular item in the list. Rather than starting at the beginning of the list, compare the item you are looking for to the item which is in the middle of the list. If there is a match, then you can quit looking. Of course, if the middle list item does not match the one you are looking for, you cannot stop here. If the item you are looking for is greater than the middle list item, then it cannot be in the first half of the list. It has to be in the second half. If it is less than the middle list item, then it must be in the first half of the list. So start your search all over again, this time limiting the part of the list in which to search for the item to half of the original list.

To continue searching for the item, compare it to the list item that is in the middle of the only part of the list that the item could possibly be (the first or last half of the list). Once again, if the item you are looking for does not match the middle one of that part, you can eliminate half of the remaining space to search. If you continue in this manner, eventually one of two things will happen. Either you will find a match or you will run out of any more places to look—you will have eliminated all of the search space. This search algorithm is called a **binary search**.

Figures 6.10 through 6.13 illustrate how you can use a binary search technique to find the number 46 in a sorted list of numbers. Start the search with the entire list, which begins at subscript 0 and ends at subscript 26.

The number 46 is larger than the middle number of the list, which is 21. For the second attempt to find 46, narrow the search space down to the last half of the list. That means for the second guess, the part of the list to search for 46 are the items with subscripts beginning at 14 and ending at 26. There is no need to look at the item with subscript 13 again. You already know that it is smaller than 46. Figure 6.11 shows how the search space has been reduced to half of its original size.

Now look at the middle item in the last half of the list. Its subscript is 20 (the average of 14 and 26), and its value is 71. Since the middle item, 71, is larger than the search item, 46, you can narrow down the search space once again. By now you know that if 46 is in the list, it must have a subscript that is in the range of 14 through 19. Again, you have eliminated half of the remaining search space. See Figure 6.12.

The middle item of the new search space is at subscript 16, which is halfway between subscript 14 and subscript 19. The value of that middle item is 41, which is smaller than the number you are searching for, 46. So you can narrow the search space for the next guess down to the items with subscripts in the range 17 to 19. See Figure 6.13.

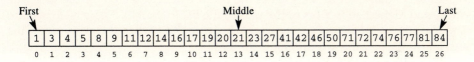

Figure 6.10 Beginning of a binary search for the number 46.

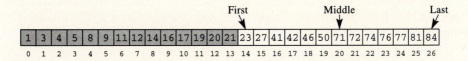

Figure 6.11 Continuing the binary search for the number 46. The first half of the original search space has been eliminated by the initial comparison.

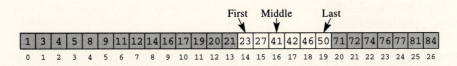

Figure 6.12 Continuing the binary search for the number 46. The last quarter of the original search space has been eliminated by the second comparison.

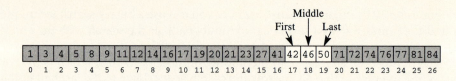

Figure 6.13 Continuing the binary search for the number 46. The search space is down to the only three items. 46 matches the middle item.

Look at the middle item in the list that begins at subscript 17 and ends at 19. Its value is 46, which matches the number you are looking for. Finally, there is success on the fourth comparison. The search is over. The entire search took you only four guesses. The number of comparisons that would have been made in the most efficient linear search would have been 19.

If the item that you were searching for had been 45 instead of 46, then your search would have gone through two more iterations. The next would have kept the first subscript of the search space at 17 and put the last subscript at 17. The final iteration would have kept the first subscript at 17 and put the last subscript at 16. That means there would be nowhere remaining to look.

The function binarySearch() implements the binary search algorithm. The arguments for binarySearch() are a list of integers, an item to search for, and two numbers that indicate the part of the list in which to search for the item (the lowest and highest subscripts of the part of the list to search). There is no need to send the size of the list as an argument, because the part of the array to do the search is limited by the low and high subscripts.

binarySearch() is recursive. Each time it is called, it first checks to see if there is any search space. If the lowest subscript of the search space is larger than the highest, then there is nowhere else left to look and the function returns –1, indicating an unsuccessful search. If there is a search space, however, the item to search is compared to the middle item of the search space. If the item to search does not match the middle item, then the search starts all over again, this time in either the first half of the search space or the second half of the search space.

```
int binarySearch (const int item[], int itemToFind, int low, int high)
// Arguments:
//    item - Holds items of a list.
//          ASSUME: The list items are in ascending order.
//    itemToFind - A number to find in the list.
//    low - The smallest subscript of the part of the array to search.
//          ASSUME: low >= 0
//    high - The largest subscript of the part of the array to search.
//          ASSUME: high <= largest subscript of a list item
// Returns: A subscript of itemToFind in item's list. If itemToFind is not a
//    list item, -1 is returned.
```

```
{
    if (low > high)                    // If there's no place to look
       return -1;                      //    return -1 for no success.
    else {
       int middle = (high + low) / 2;  // Middle subscript of search space
       if (item[middle] == itemToFind) // If the item to find matches the
          return middle;               //    middle one, quit looking.
       else if (item[middle] > itemToFind)// If the item to find is less than
                                       //    the middle one, look in the first
                                       //    half of the search space.
          return binarySearch(item,itemToFind,low,middle - 1);
       else                            // If the item to find is larger than
                                       //    the middle one, look in the last
                                       //    half of the search space.
          return binarySearch(item,itemToFind,middle + 1,high);
    }
}
```

To use `binarySearch()` to find an item in a list, you must indicate which part of the list to search. If you want to search the entire list, the part of the list to search begins at subscript 0 and ends at the subscript that is one less than the size of the list. For example, suppose the ordered list is implemented as follows:

```
const int maxCap = 500;        // Maximum list capacity
int myOrderedList[maxCap];     // Holds items of an ordered list
int mySize = 0;                // Size of the ordered list
```

Assume that the list is maintained as an ordered list (as the name array suggests). For example, we could insert items as follows:

```
insert(myOrderedList, mySize, 30);  // list is: 30
insert(myOrderedList, mySize, 41);  // list is: 30, 41
insert(myOrderedList, mySize, 15);  // list is: 15, 30, 41
insert(myOrderedList, mySize, 23);  // list is: 15, 23, 30, 41
insert(myOrderedList, mySize, 5);   // list is: 5, 15, 23, 30, 41
insert(myOrderedList, mySize, 610); // list is: 5, 15, 23, 30, 41, 610
insert(myOrderedList, mySize, 58);  // list is: 5, 15, 23, 30, 41, 58, 610
```

To search for a the number 41 in the list, this call to `binarySearch()` will suffice.

```
binarySearch(myOrderedList, 41, 0, mySize - 1)
```

The initial call to `binarySearch()` must include the smallest and largest subscripts of the search space. After that, the function itself takes care of determining the search space.

> A binary search provides an efficient way to search for an item in an ordered list. It cannot be used to find an item in an unordered list.

Since a linear search algorithm is simpler than a binary search algorithm, there ought to be some good reason for bothering to code a binary search instead a linear search. And there is. Suppose you are using a linear search to find an item in a list of 1000 items. You may end up looking at every item in the list before you are through. And increasing the size of the list by a factor of 2 (from 1000 to 2000) potentially doubles the number of items you need compare.

You will not encounter that problem with a binary search. If you double the size of a list, then you do not need to look at twice as many items as before. You need to look at only one additional item. That makes sense. Whenever you compare a list item to the item you are searching for, you will either find a match or eliminate half of the items as possible matches.

A binary search is much more efficient than a linear search and usually takes much less time.[4] For all of the programs that novice programmers write, it is rare when efficiency is an issue. The lists are usually short. The number of searches is small. Searching efficiency is important when lists are very large and when there are many searches to be performed. That's when a binary search can pay off handsomely.

Application: Searching in databases

The items in many lists are not simple names or numbers. For example, a list of contributors to a charity would probably contain the names of the contributors as well as the amount each had given. Each name and corresponding amount constitutes a single, composite entry in the list.

Lists of composite objects are often called databases. Maintaining databases is an activity that has been around for as long as people have kept written records. You can think of a database as an object that can do many things: print its entries, sort its entries, tell how many entries it contains, and so on. Although the variety of potential operations is extensive, virtually all databases are able to do three common operations: add an entry, remove an entry, and find an entry according to a certain key.

Imagine that you own a hardware store that keeps track of the items it sells according to their bar codes and prices. (You would probably keep more information on each item than that, such as a description of the item and how many of that

---

[4] A measure of the amount of work required to execute an algorithm is the computational complexity of the algorithm. A linear search has a computational complexity proportional to the number of items in the list. A binary search has computational complexity proportional to the log of the size of the list.

item is in stock. But we will settle for a simpler illustration.) The hardware store inventory is a list. Each item on the list consists of two pieces of information, a bar code and a price.

If you know how to maintain a list of simple items with an array, it is easy to maintain a list of composite items with **parallel arrays**. We will use parallel arrays for the inventory list, one to hold the bar codes and one to hold the prices.

```
const int maxInventory = 1000;    // Maximum number of items inventoried
int barCode[maxInventory];        // Item bar codes
float price[maxInventory];        // Item prices (positive numbers)
int size = 0;                     // Size of inventory list
```

The two arrays barCode and price can be managed as parallel arrays. That means the elements in the two arrays are in one-to-one correspondence with each other: price[0] is the price of the item whose bar code is barCode[0]; price[1] is the price of the item whose bar code is barCode[1]; and so on.

Parallel arrays used to implement a single list must be manipulated in a parallel fashion. If an element of barCode is moved, then the corresponding element of price is moved in the identical way. If a new number is inserted into barCode, then the corresponding price must be inserted into price at the same position. If a number is removed from barCode, then the corresponding price must be removed from price. If barCode is sorted, the elements in price must be moved to maintain the relationship that the item whose bar code is barCode[i] has price[i] as its price for every valid subscript i.

Your hardware store's inventory is a database. Each entry in the inventory consists of a bar code (the key) and a price (the value). The inventory must have methods to add entries, remove entries, and find the price of an item according to its bar code. Since finding the price of an item according to its bar code could be such a frequently performed operation, we will focus almost all of our attention to that method.

If the inventory is sorted according to bar codes, then the method for finding the price of an item can use a binary search. Before we plunge ahead to the definition of the method, we first need to decide what the inventory will do if it is told to find the price of an item that does not exist. The inventory could return a flag to indicate the item is not there. Or it could simply return a value that could not possibly be a price.

We decided on that latter option. If the inventory cannot find an item, it will return a negative number for the price of the item. The function find() implements the inventory's search method.

```
float find(const int key[], const float value[], int size, int findKey)
// Arguments:
//    key - Holds database keys
//    value - Holds database values.
//          ASSUME: All values are nonnegative; key and value have the same
```

```
//                      number of elements.
//    size - Number of items in the database
//           ASSUME: 0 <= size <= number of elements of key
//    findKey - key of item to search in the database
// Returns: The value of the item with the given key. If no such item
//    exists, -1.0 is returned.
{
    int psn = binarySearch(key, findKey, 0, size - 1);

    if (psn >= 0)
        return value[psn];
    else
        return -1.0;
}
```

Removing an item from the inventory can also be based on a binary search. The `remove()` definition shows how the two arrays that hold the database items must be manipulated in parallel.

```
void remove(int key[], float value[], int& size, int keyToGo)
// Arguments:
//    key - in\out - Holds database keys before\after attempted remove.
//                (Keys are in ascending order.)
//    value - in\out - Holds database values before\after attempted remove.
//    size - in\out - Number of database items before\after attempted remove.
//    keyToGo - Key of the item to be removed.
// Side effect: If an item whose key is keyToGo is in the inventory, it is
//    removed. Otherwise, the inventory remains unchanged.
{
    int psn = binarySearch(key, keyToGo, 0, size - 1); // location of the item
                                                        //  to be removed

    if (psn >= 0) {                          // Is this a legitimate location?
        for(int i = psn; i < size - 1; i++) { //   If so, shift the keys and
            key[i] = key[i + 1];             //    the values.
            value[i] = value[i + 1];
        }
        size--;
    }
}
```

We leave it as an exercise for you to implement the method to add a new item. But keep in mind that `remove()` and `find()` work appropriately only if the database is sorted to begin with. So the add method should add new items in their appropriate positions relative to the rest of items.

6.6 ▌ Strings: Implementation tool for names and phrases

Most lists are not simply lists of numbers. Recall Dr. Smith and her problem. Suppose she wants to know the names of people who called as well as their telephone numbers. That seems a reasonable enough desire. Instead of a list of numbers, Dr. Smith needs a list of names and numbers. We know how to keep track of the numbers. What about the names?

Before considering lists of names, we should figure out what a single name is. In a very fundamental sense, any name or any word is a list of characters. Sentences and phrases are also lists of characters. And computer programs, including the ones we have generated here, use lists of characters. Every string literal (sequence of characters enclosed in double quotes) is a list of characters.

A **string** is a list of characters. There are different ways to implement strings in C++. In this chapter, we will show you how to implement them using arrays of characters. Here is a typical trio of definitions to create two string variables.

```
const int maxLen = 50;   // Size of array to hold a string of characters
char aString[maxLen];    // A string of characters
char aName[maxLen];      // A string representing a name
```

The definition of `aString` is simply an ordinary array definition. The elements of the array are `char`s. Each element can be accessed in the usual fashion, using `aString` (the name of the array) and an integer subscript in the range of 0 through 49.

C++ relies on certain string programming conventions. The string literal `"abc"` refers to an array of four characters: `'a'`, `'b'`, `'c'`, and `'\0'`. (See Fig. 6.14.) That last character, which is the escape sequence `'\0'`, is the ASCII **null character**. C++ uses the null character as a sentinel value to mark the end of a string. An array of characters with the null character terminator is called a **C-string.**

The programmer is responsible for making sure that arrays of characters terminate with the null character. Some of the built-in facilities provided by C++ for string handling make that task easy.

Strings implemented as arrays can be initialized when they are defined. The initialization does not require the braces for ordinary array initialization. Instead, the array of characters can be initialized with a string literal.[5]

```
char myNiece[] = "Sabrina";
char prompt[] = "Enter a positive whole number: ";
```

The number of elements created for `myNiece` is eight, one for each letter and one for the terminating null character. Just as for arrays of `int`s or `double`s, this

---

[5] Some compilers will not allow string initializations with literal strings except for static or global arrays.

'a'	'b'	'c'	'\0'

Figure 6.14 Array representation of "abc".

's'	'a'	'b'	'r'	'i'	'n'	'a'	'\0'
0	1	2	3	4	5	6	7

Figure 6.15 Array representation of `myNiece`.

technique works only for initialization. As you will discover in the next section, C-string variables cannot be assigned string literal values.

C-strings can be arguments to functions or procedures. Since they are arrays, C-string arguments are automatically passed by reference. If the programmer wants to prohibit the actual argument from change, then the formal argument should be passed by constant reference. The following prototypes of the two functions `f()` and `g()` have string arguments, one passed by reference, the other passed by constant reference.

```
void f(char* string);                // string is passed by reference
void f(char string[]);               // Same as: void f(char* string);
void g(const char* string);          // string is passed by constant reference
void g(const char string[]);         // Same as: void g(const char* string);
```

Functions with string type arguments are not new to you. We first saw them back in Chapter 3 (where functions were formally introduced). Recall the prototype for `inputInt()`, which was a method for the changemaker input object. It looked as follows (the second formal argument, `prompt`, is a string type):

```
void inputInt(int& aNumber, const char prompt[]);
```

Built-in string handling library

Strings such as `aName` and `aString` may represent names or phrases, but you cannot treat those names as single entities. You cannot do wholesale C-string assignments. You cannot compare C-strings directly using < or <= to find out which would come first in a dictionary or a telephone directory. C-strings are not what we call first class variables. You cannot do simple assignments and comparisons such as these:

```
aString = aName;          // illegal!
aString = "hello";        // illegal!
```

```
if (aName != "Helen")        // not illegal, but probably not what you expect
    ...
```

Later on, we will show you how to remedy this situation by creating your own `String` type that acts like a first class type for which the operators =, ==, !=, and <= can be used in a natural manner. For now, we are stuck with C-strings, simple arrays of characters and the primitive operations that C++ automatically provides for handling them.

C and C++ have a built-in string library to handle strings such as `aName` and string literals. The library header file, `string.h`, must be #included in any program that uses the library routines. The string arguments for the string library functions are C-strings terminated by null characters.

To facilitate assignment, the string library contains the function `strcpy()`. It has two string arguments. The first argument is passed by reference and the second argument is passed by constant reference. Calling `strcpy()` generates a side effect on the first argument—it changes the first argument. This call assigns the string literal `"John"` to `aName`.

```
strcpy(aName, "John");
```

The function `strcpy()` also works with a pair of string variables for actual arguments. To assign `aString` the value of `aName`, invoke `strcpy()` in the following manner:

```
strcpy(aString, aName);
```

Execution of that call to `strcpy()` is equivalent to execution of the following code:

```
for (int i = 0; aName[i] != '\0'; i++)
    aString[i] = aName[i];       // Copy each character of aName to aString.
aString[i] = '\0';               // Copy the null character to aString.
```

Since `strcpy()` has no way of knowing how much memory was allocated to its first argument, you must be careful in using it. If the number of characters in the second argument is too large to be accommodated by the first argument, then **string overflow** will occur as it does in the following code:

```
char a[3];          // a has only 3 elements.
strcpy(a, "xyz");   // Equivalent to: a[0] = 'x', a[1] = 'y',
                    //                a[2] = 'z', a[4] = '\0';
```

Four characters are copied to the elements of `a`. Unfortunately, `a` has only three elements. So the final character, `'\0'`, is copied to a region of memory that is not reserved for `a`.

The function `strlen()` takes a string argument and returns the number of characters in the argument that precede the terminating null character. Since `strlen()` does not change its actual argument, it is safe to use.

Here are some sample calls to `strlen()` and the results of those calls.

```
int value;
value = strlen("Helen");    // value gets 5
strcpy(aName, "John");
value = strlen(aName);      // value gets 4
value = strlen("");         // value gets 0
```

The argument in the last call to `strlen()` is the **null string**, `""`. The null string begins with the terminating null character `'\0'`. We sometimes say that the null string "contains no characters."

The function `strcmp()` compares strings. It is a substitute for the relational operators <, <=, >, and >=, and the equality operators, == and !=. The arguments for `strcmp()` are two pass-by-constant-reference strings.

The function `strcmp()` compares its two arguments to see if they are in "lex-icographic" order. It scans the two strings character by character, beginning with the first character. It quits as soon as it detects two corresponding characters that are different or as it detects the terminating null character. If the corresponding characters match up through the terminating character, then `strcmp()` returns 0. The two strings are the same. If the last character scanned in the first string has an ASCII code less than the last character scanned in the second, `strcmp()` returns a negative integer.[6] Otherwise, `strcmp()` returns a positive integer.

Suppose `first` and `second` are strings. The results of using `strcmp()` to compare `first` and `second` are summarized in the following table:

Value of `strcmp(first,second)`	Interpretation
0	`first` and `second` are the same up through the terminating `'\0'`.
<0	The last scanned character of `first` is less than that of `second`.
>0	The last scanned character of `first` is greater than that of `second`.

Here are some examples of the results of calls to `strcmp()`.

---

[6] If the character set on the machine for which the code is written is not ASCII, then the comparison will be made according to the machine's character code rather than ASCII code.

Call	Result
strcmp("John", "Mary")	Negative
strcmp("Mary", "John")	Positive
strcmp("Mary", "Mary")	0
strcmp("John", "Jo")	Positive

Suppose aString and bString are two string variables defined to be of maximum length maxLen. Suppose also that aString and bString are legitimate C-strings. The following code can be used to swap aString and bString whenever aString is "bigger than" bString. It uses a buffer, a temporary array to hold the elements of one of the arrays.

```
if (strcmp(aString,bString) > 0) {
    char temp[maxLen];                // Temporary holding buffer
    strcpy(temp, aString);
    strcpy(aString, bString);
    strcpy(bString, temp);
}
```

There are many more functions in the string library. The functions strcpy(), strlen(), and strcmp() are perhaps the most useful.

String input and output

String values can be input and output from streams. The following statement outputs five characters 'H', 'e', 'l', 'l', and 'o' into the stream cout. (The terminating null character is not output.)

```
cout << "Hello";
```

It is the programmer's responsibility to be sure that each variable string array contains the null character as one of its elements. The null character tells C++ when to stop inserting characters from this array into the output stream.

Input of string values is a little trickier than output. Suppose that the user enters this sequence of characters.

```
John
Mary Ann
```

Suppose also that these two statements are executed.

```
cin >> aName;      // Puts "John" in aName
cin >> aString;    // Puts "Mary" in aString
```

The string "John" will be placed in aName. Figure 6.16 illustrates the memory that is allocated to aName. When the aName is read, C++ automatically inserts the null character to denote the end of the important characters in aName. The remaining 45 characters after the '\0' are not changed.

The string "Mary" will be placed in aString. Whenever a string is read using the input operator >>, leading whitespace characters are skipped. So the newline in the input stream between the 'n' in John and the 'M' in Mary is skipped. The entire sequence of non-whitespace characters after the newline is placed in the string variable. This placement of input characters stops when the first whitespace character is encountered. In this case, that first whitespace is the blank between Mary and Ann on the second line.

Input statements like cin >> aName; are not particularly safe to execute. If you hold the X key down for 60 copies of the character 'X' before entering return, then C++ will attempt to assign 61 characters to aName (60 'X's plus the null character). This generates a string overflow, which likely will abort execution of the program. You should not allow access to elements beyond what was allocated for the array.

This discussion points out two problems with reading strings using the input operator in this simple manner: (1) It is not safe; and (2) it will not get an entire string of characters off a single line of input if that line contains blanks or other whitespace characters.

Here is one technique you can use to work around these two problems. Input stream objects such as cin can do many things, including inserting data into objects. The type istream is a built-in class type for C++; cin is an istream. One of the behaviors that an istream object can do is to get a line of input. The following statement represents a message to cin to get a line of up to 49 characters and store the resulting string into aName:

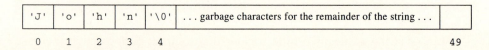

| 'J' | 'o' | 'h' | 'n' | '\0' | . . . garbage characters for the remainder of the string . . . | |
| 0 | 1 | 2 | 3 | 4 | | 49 |

Figure 6.16 Memory allocated to aName.

```
cin.getline(aName,50,'\n');
```

The statement works as follows. All of the unprocessed characters up to and including the first occurrence of a newline or the first 49 characters, whichever comes first, are read from input. Those characters, except the newline, are assigned to aName. The terminating null character is assigned to aName at the end of those characters. (The reason only 49 characters are processed from input is to leave room for the terminating null character.)

In order to use cin.getline() for reading strings, you need to be sure that no dangling newline is left in the input stream from the previous input operation. This can happen if you have just read into a numeric variable—the newline is still left over after the numeric characters are processed. To get rid of that dangling newline after a numeric read, use cin.ignore(). The following statement discards at most 80 characters up through the first occurrence of the newline. Unless the input lines are more than 80 characters long, the following statement will get rid of that dangling newline.

```
cin.ignore(80,'\n');
```

If x is a numeric variable and st is a string, be sure to flush the dangling newline from the input stream after reading x and before reading st. The following trio of statements illustrates how that can be accomplished.

```
cin >> x;
cin.ignore(80,'\n');
cin.getline(st,80,'\n');
```

For a more thorough discussion of how to use input and output streams with strings and other types of data, refer to Appendixes D, E, and F at the end of this book.

6.7 Lists of names

Now that we know how to represent a name, can we represent an indexed list of names? An array of C-strings will help. Here's the idea. Suppose all names on the list will be shorter than 50 characters long and suppose the list will contain no more than 100 names. This collection of definitions (along with appropriate functions, of course) gives an array implementation of a list of names.

```
const int maxName = 50;      // Names have fewer than this many characters
const int maxList = 100;     // Lists have no more than this many items
```

```
typedef char nameType[maxName];    // nameType is a type -- type array of
                                   //   char with maxName elements


nameType roll[maxList];        // Holds a list of up to maxList names
int size = 0;                  // Number of names on the list
```

Recall that a typedef introduces the name of a new type to the compiler. Programmers use typedefs so they can replace complicated type names with simple names. The following typedef

```
typedef char nameType[maxName];
```

tells the compiler to consider nameType to be a type for an array of maxName characters. It is a type for an array of strings.

The general format for a typedef of an array type is as follows:

```
typedef arrayElementType newTypeName[numberOfElements]
```

The array typedef requires a bracket and the number of elements of the array, just as an array object definition requires a bracket and number of elements. As before, *newTypeName* is the name of the type that is being defined.

Most of the types that we have used so far in this text have been simple, built-in types such as int and char. In Chapter 4, we introduced programmer-defined enumeration types. In this chapter, we introduced array types. Array types are more complicated than simple types and enumeration types. Typedefs are particularly useful for complicated types such as array types.

Additional examples of array typedefs are given below.

```
typedef int integerArray[100];   // integerArray is a type for an array
                                 //   of 100 int elements
typedef char stName[25];         // stName is a type for an array of
                                 //   25 char elements
```

After a typedef is made, an object of that newly named type can be defined. The new type name can be used like a built-in type name. The definitions of these data objects could follow the typedefs above.

```
    integerArray numberList;   // numberList is an array of 100 ints
    stName surname;            // surname is an array of 25 chars
    stName classRoll[30];      // classRoll is an array of 30 stNames
    integerArray table[50];    // table is an array of integerArrays
```

Arrays of C-strings

As we saw previously, the following pair of statements defines nameType to be a synonym for an array of characters type (type char[50]).

```
const int maxName = 50;
typedef char nameType[maxName];
```

These definitions create an array of 100 elements in which each element is an array of characters.

```
const int maxList = 100;
nameType guest[maxList];
int size = 0;
```

We could have defined `guest` without the convenient `nameType` typedef. This is the syntax we could have used:

```
char guest[maxList][maxName];   // Alternate definition for guest
```

With either definition for `guest`, the data objects `maxList`, `guest`, and `size` implement the attributes of a design object that is a list of names. The individual names on the list can be referenced as follows:

```
guest[0]          // First name on the list (if the list isn't empty)
guest[2]          // Third name on the list (if there is a third one)
guest[size - 1]   // Last name on the list (if the list isn't empty)
```

We can think of `guest` as an array in which each element is a `nameType`. Or we can think of `guest` as a **two-dimensional array** in which each element is of type `char`. To better understand the two dimensions, look at the alternate definition for `guest` that would be made if the typedef for `nameType` did not exist.

```
char guest[maxList][maxName];   // Alternate definition for guest
```

The arrays that we discussed at the beginning of this chapter were one-dimensional arrays. Every element of a one-dimensional array is referenced by the name of the array and one subscript. Every element of a two-dimensional array is referenced by a the name of the array and two subscripts. You can refer to an individual character in `guest` by using two different subscripts, the first subscript to tell which name and the second subscript to tell which character in that name.

Keep in mind that array subscripting starts at 0. The following expressions are some of the characters of the two-dimensional array `guest`.

```
guest[2][5]         // Sixth character of the third guest name
guest[0][0]         // First character of the first guest name
guest[size - 1][3]  // Fourth character of the last guest name
```

The number in the first bracket tells which string; the number in the second tells which character in the string. Figure 6.17 illustrates how `guest` is stored in memory.

	0	1	2	3	4	5	6	7	8	9	10	. . .	49
0	'J'	'a'	'n'	'e'	' '	'S'	'm'	'i'	't'	'h'	'\0'		
1	'M'	'a'	'r'	'y'	' '	'D'	'o'	'e'	'\0'				
2	'K'	'i'	'm'	' '	'P'	'a'	'g'	'e'	'\0'				
size													
.													
.													
.													
99													

Figure 6.17 Using `guest` to hold the names Jane Smith, Mary Doe, and Kim Page. The size of the list is 3.

Keep in mind that the array `guest` and the integer `size` can be used as attributes for a list of names. The behaviors of the list can be implemented by functions with arguments that are arrays of C-strings.

Arrays of C-strings as function arguments

Let's now look at an example of a declaration of a function that has an array of `nameType` elements as a formal argument. It does not look very different from the kinds of declarations we have shown before.

```
void insert(nameType name[], int& size, const char newName[]);
```

Recall that the definition for `nameType` says that an object of type `nameType` is a string that is an array of `maxName` characters. The maximum string length is important. The compiler does not care how many strings are in an argument that is an array of strings. It does care how many characters are in the individual strings that constitute the array elements.

The length of the string elements can be conveyed through a typedef as in the original declaration of `insert()`. Without a typedef, the length must be part of the formal array argument description. We could declare `insert()` in this fashion:

```
// alternative declaration
void insert(char name[][maxName], int& size, const char newName[]);
```

The alternative declaration of `insert()` does not use the typedef. The type for the formal argument `name` *must* include `maxName`, the maximum length of the string elements, in the second pair of brackets. No other numbers need appear in any other brackets in either function declaration. (Numbers inside the first brackets are ignored by the compiler.)

For each declaration of `insert()`, the formal argument `name` is an array of strings that can hold `maxName` characters apiece. The array is passed by reference.

From a design standpoint, lists of names are not different from lists of numbers. It is just that the items in a list of names are names and the items in lists of numbers are numbers. Operations on the two kinds of lists are identical. Methods to define the operations on lists of names are implemented as functions that manipulate strings rather than numbers.

The function `insert()` can put a name in its proper position into an ordered list of names. Lists of names are represented by a pair of arguments—an array and an `int` indicating the size of the list. This is consistent with the representation of a list of numbers via an array and an `int`.

The following is the definition for the new `insert()`. Note that the documentation is almost identical to the documentation for the original function `insert()`, which had an array of ints as an argument.

```
void insert(nameType name[], int& size, const char newName[])
// Arguments:
//    name - in - Holds list names sorted in ascending order before a new
//                name is inserted.
//                ASSUME: The list is not full.
//          - out - Holds list names after the new name is inserted.
//    size - in - Number of list items prior to insertion.
//                ASSUME: 0 <= size < maximum list capacity
//          - out - Number of list items after the insertion
//    newName - A new name to be inserted in the list
//                ASSUME: length(newName) < number of elements in nameType.
// Side effect: The new item is inserted into the ordered list in its proper
//    position relative to the rest of the list items. The list size is
//    incremented by 1.
{
   int current = size - 1;              // Position of the current list item

   while (current >= 0 && strcmp(name[current], newName) > 0) {
      strcpy(name[current + 1], name[current]);
      current--;
   }
   strcpy(name[current + 1], newName);
   size++;
}
```

We have named two different functions `insert()`. It is not an error to have two different functions with the same name as long as their argument lists are different. Having two different functions with the same name is called overloading. We will discuss this topic in more detail in the next chapter.

The function `insert()` was used to change a list. Functions that need to use lists of names without changing them are a little tricky. The function `isMember()` is an example. It determines whether or not a particular name is in a list of names.

```
bool isMember(const char name[][maxName], int size, const char st[])
// Arguments:
//    name - Holds list names
//    size - Number of list names
//    st - A name
// Returns: true if st is in the list, false otherwise
{
    for (int i = 0; i < size; i++)
        if (strcmp(name[i], st) == 0)
            return true;
    return false;
}
```

When you want to pass an array of strings by constant reference (as in the case of `isMember()`), do not rely on the typedef for the string type. With the typedef, the `const` does not protect the individual characters in any of the strings from being changed. That is an idiosyncrasy of typedefs that you will be able to work around as you learn more programming tools.

6.8 Multidimensional Arrays

Arrays of almost any type element are possible. A **multidimensional array** is an array whose elements are themselves arrays. There can be three-, four-, and larger dimensional arrays. The elements of a three-dimensional array are two-dimensional arrays. The elements of a four-dimensional array are three-dimensional arrays.

In this section, we will concentrate on multidimensional arrays that are not necessarily arrays of strings. Our first example is a two-dimensional array with `double` elements. We can model a mathematical matrix, which is simply a rectangular table of numbers with the following definition:

```
double matrix[3][5];   // A matrix with 3 rows and 5 columns
```

The definition of `matrix` is a two-dimensional array definition. You can tell it is a two-dimensional array because of the pair of square brackets. Unlike a list of names, in which each element in the list is usually thought of as a single entity, a matrix is rarely thought of as a list. It is a table of numbers.

The definition of `matrix` creates a table consisting of 3 rows and 5 columns. The number of rows in the table is the number in the first pair of brackets and the number of columns in the table is the number in the last pair of brackets. Each row is actually an array of 5 `doubles`.

Each number in the `matrix` can be accessed individually by giving its row and column subscript. The name of the element in the upper-left corner of the `matrix` is `matrix[0][0]`. The name of the last number in the `matrix` is `matrix[2][4]`.

It may be tempting to use the syntax `matrix[1,2]` to get the third number in the second row. Unfortunately, that does not work in C++. The value of the expression `1,2` is `2`. That is the comma operator at work. So the expression `matrix[1,2]` is the same as `matrix[2]`, which is an array of five `doubles`!

The following are assignments to individual array elements. Figure 6.18 shows `matrix` after all the assignments have been executed.

```
// Assign elements across the first row
matrix[0][0] = 0.0;
matrix[0][1] = 12.3;
matrix[0][2] = 5.4;
matrix[0][3] = -6.0;
matrix[0][4] = 7.2;

// Assign elements across the second row
matrix[1][0] = 5.1;
matrix[1][1] = 3.6;
matrix[1][2] = -2.0;
matrix[1][3] = 10.1;
matrix[1][4] = 6.8;

// Assign elements across the third row
matrix[2][0] = 1.1;
matrix[2][1] = 0.0;
matrix[2][2] = 3.1;
matrix[2][3] = 4.4;
matrix[2][4] = 5.5;
```

Programmers can define arrays of many dimensions, with a pair of brackets and a positive constant integer expression for each dimension. Here is an example of a three-dimensional array definition:

	0	1	2	3	4
0	0.0	12.3	5.4	-6.0	7.2
1	5.1	3.6	-2.0	10.1	6.8
2	1.1	0.0	3.1	4.4	5.5

Figure 6.18 The two-dimensional array `matrix`. Row subscripts are on the left, column subscripts are on top.

```
int reservation[6][10][4];
```

Multidimensional arrays can be initialized when they are defined. The initialization of a two-dimensional array of `doubles` can be done through nested braces:

```
int val[3][2] = {{1,5}, {2,7}, {3,-1}};
char names[][5] = {"Alan", "John", "Joan", "Kim"};
```

In the first bracket, the size is optional; in the remaining brackets, the size is required.

Multidimensional arrays can also be initialized merely by listing all of their elements without the extra braces on the inside. In that case, all of the sizes must be listed within the brackets. The definition and initialization of `val` could have been done in any one of the following three ways. They are all equivalent.

```
int val[3][2] = {1, 5, 2, 7, 3, -1};
int val[3][2] = {{1, 5}, {2, 7}, {3, -1}};
int val[ ][2] = {{1, 5}, {2, 7}, {3, -1}};
```

The prototype of a function that has a multidimensional array as a formal argument must describe that argument with brackets to indicate the sizes of all of the dimensions except the first. Those sizes must be constant integer expressions. The following prototypes are for functions that could take two- and three-dimensional arrays as actual arguments:

```
double f(const double x[][5]);    // Two dimensional array argument
void g(int x[][10][4]);           // Three-dimensional array argument
```

The function `f()` could take `matrix` as an actual argument. The function `g()` could take `reservation` as an actual argument.

The function `makeNonNegative()` defined below has two arguments, a two-dimensional array of `doubles` and an `int` telling how many rows are in the array. It sets all of the negative elements to 0.0.

```
void makeNonNegative(double m[][5], int numberOfRows)
{
```

```
    for (int i = 0; i < numberOfRows; i++)
        for (int j = 0; j < 5; j++)
            if (m[i][j] < 0.0)
                m[i][j] = 0.0;
}
```

The definition of `makeNonNegative()` accesses each element in the two-dimensional array using nested `for` loops. That is standard multidimensional array programming. The more dimensions in the array, the deeper the loop nesting.

The function `print()` writes out all the elements in a two-dimensional array of `doubles`. Notice that its formal array argument is a constant reference argument.

```
void print(const double m[][5], int numberOfRows)
{
    cout << setiosflags(ios :: scientific) << setprecision(3);
    for (int i = 0; i < numberOfRows; i++) {
        for (int j = 0; j < 5; j++)
            cout << setw(10) << m[i][j];
        cout << endl;
    }
    cout << resetiosflags(ios :: scientific);
}
```

The calls to `makeNonNegative()` and `print()` look just as you would expect. `matrix` is an appropriate argument to each of them.

```
makeNonNegative(matrix,3); // Makes negative elements 0
print(matrix,3);           // Prints a table of elements
```

Our discussion has focused on the mechanics of handling multidimensional arrays. Let's now see how they can be used outside the world of mathematics. For example, have you ever used a table showing distances between major cities or points of interest on a highway map? That kind of table could be nicely represented by a two-dimensional array.

Three- or higher-dimensional arrays are easy to imagine also. For example, the values of items in a warehouse in which merchandise is stored on floors, aisles, shelves, and perhaps shelf partitions could be represented by a four-dimensional array. The definition of `warehouse` that follows creates a four-dimensional array to represent the values of the contents of each partition of a warehouse with 3 floors, 10 aisles for each floor, 6 shelves for each aisle, and 5 partitions for each shelf.

```
float warehouse[3][10][6][5];
```

We could let our imagination run wild at this point, but we need to keep in mind how easy it is to make arrays that are impossibly large. For example, `warehouse` has 900 elements ($3 \times 10 \times 6 \times 5$). If the warehouse to be modeled has 3 floors, 20 aisles for each floor, 6 shelves for each aisle, and 50 partitions for each shelf, the four-dimensional array to represent the values of the contents of each partition would have 18,000 elements.

6.9   Redesigning the changemaker to fit new implementation ideas

It has been a while since we have referred to the changemaker (the problem asking us to figure out the number of bills and coins of each denomination from $20 bills down to pennies required to sum to a certain amount).

It would be helpful now to review what we did in Chapter 3. That old implementation has eight `int` constants (`denomValue1` through `denomValue8`) and eight character string constants (`denomName1` through `denomName8`). Those certainly look like lists. The computing object from that design also had eight methods (`countForDenom1()` through `countForDenom8()`). Some of that code in that old solution was similar to the list implementations we discussed at the beginning of this chapter before we introduced arrays. We now have better implementation tools. Let's take another crack at designing the changemaker solution to use the new tools.

Going back and modifying a design after a program has been coded illustrates a central part of object-oriented programming. Designs are not fixed. Thinking of implementation often gives rise to ideas that lead to an improved design and vice versa. (It is natural to be inhibited in your designs if you don't have any idea of how to implement them.) Once you have begun implementation, you can go back and reanalyze or redesign to take advantage of what you learn when you code. You can and you should go back to modify old analyses and designs whenever you figure out new information or learn new tools that can improve the design.

Our original changemaker design had five objects: a teller object, an input object, an output object, a computing object, and a cash drawer. The cash drawer was what made this problem somewhat unique. A cash drawer holds various denominations. It knows its denominations by name (such as `"quarters"`) and value (such as `25`). It can give access to its denominations in order.

A cash drawer is a list of eight denomination names and values. When the computing object calculates the answers, it creates another list of denomination names and counts. When the teller sends a message to the output object to print the answer, the output object uses that second list for the answers.

Take a closer look at the two different lists of denominations, the cash drawer and the list created by the computing object. The cash drawer list needs to know only the name and the value of each denomination. The list created by the computing object needs to know only the name and the count of each denomination to be returned. These are different but related types of lists. So we will combine them into a single type of list, a list of denominations. Each item in a list of denominations has all three attributes: a name, a value, and a count. Figure 6.19 illustrates the new design.

As it currently stands, our problem assumes that the cash drawer always has enough of each denomination to make "perfect change." The computing object can always return exactly what it is supposed to return. It will never have to resort to giving out four quarters rather than a dollar bill because the cash drawer will never run out of dollar bills. It has an endless supply of each denomination.

Our cash drawer is not a very realistic model. Most cash drawers do not have an infinite capacity. Aside from that, our cash drawer resembles a real-life cash drawer. The count for each item represents how many pieces of that denomination (bills or coins) are in the cash drawer. By having a slightly more complicated denomination list than the original perfect cash drawer actually needs, we have planned ahead for possible future modifications in the problem statement. And we have also improved reuse, because we used the very same generalization in the cash drawer and the output of the computing object.

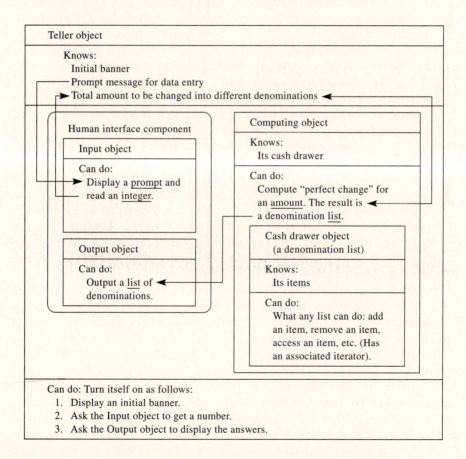

Figure 6.19 The redesign of the changemaker solution to use lists.

In the new design, the teller object does not know things that it does not need to know. It does not know the details of the representation of the cash drawer or of how a collection of change to be returned is represented. That is good. In general, programmers should try to minimize what one object needs to know about the representation of information belonging to another component.

The output object knows that it must display a list containing the name and count of every item in it. It has two ways of doing this. It can ask each item what its name and count are, and then display only those values. Or it can ask the list to display itself. We will choose the former. That way the output object itself can take care of such things as formatting as well as exactly what information is to be displayed. This decision of having the output object ask for values and displaying them goes along with the principle that objects should know as little as possible about the representation of information belonging to another object. The item in a list does not need to know how it should be displayed or even which part of the item should be displayed.

In our first design of the changemaker, we might have had a list in mind when we were thinking about a cash drawer. But if we did, that idea did not show up officially in the design. In fact, the old code actually implemented two lists. The implementations were very noncompact and awkward. The cash drawer was implemented as 16 different data objects. Half of those data objects were constant integers (for the values) and the other half were constant strings (for the names). Details of the implementation were spread throughout the code.

The implementation of the new design solution is much cleaner than the old version. The cash drawer now becomes three parallel arrays, one for the denomination values, one for the names, and one for the counts. (We included the count array in the current cash drawer to make the program look like the design and to anticipate new specifications). All three of the arrays are global. We cannot quite get away from that yet. Since the cash drawer list does not change during execution (in this version of the problem), the arrays are constants. Since the size of the list of cash drawer items is fixed, it is a global constant, too.

The list of denominations created by the computing object is implemented via a single function and three parallel arrays (for value, name, and count). We could have eliminated the names and the values since they will be the same names and values that the cash drawer has. But we included those two arrays to emphasize that the computing object creates a list of denominations. The computing object list is separate from the cash drawer list. The teller object will ask the computing object to create a list. Its arrays are not constant.

In our old solutions from Chapter 3, we relied on eight different functions to calculate the values. In Chapter 4, we replaced the eight functions with a single function with an index argument to indicate which denomination count was being computed. For both solutions, however, the teller object asked the computing object for the list item and then sent it as part of a message to the output object. We now place the responsibility of iterating through the list with the output object. The new teller object asks the input object for a number, asks the computing object to compute the answer for that number, and then asks the output object to print out the answer.

The structure of our new solution is similar to the old code from Chapter 3. Of course, the new solution is much shorter. We present the new version in its entirety, documentation and all. The implementation of the input object is the same. The output object requires a new function that can output a list. The computing object methods still use the old `divMod()` routine to calculate the quotient and remainder for an integer division. The function `compute_changeFor()` replaces the eight functions of the Chapter 3 version to compute the count of each denomination.

```
// Name: The changemaker
// Version: 4.0
// Purpose: Determine the count of each denomination from twenty dollar bills
//    down through pennies that constitute a given monetary amount.

#include <iostream.h>
#include <string.h>

const int slots = 8;            // Number of cash drawer slots (denominations)
const int maxName = 9;          // Maximum size of a denomination name

typedef char denName[maxName];  // Denomination name type

//------------------- cash drawer object implementation --------------------
const int cashDrawer_denomValue[slots] = {2000,1000,500,100,25,10,5,1};
const denName cashDrawer_denomName[slots] = {"twenties", "tens", "fives",
                    "ones", "quarters", "dimes", "nickels", "pennies"};
int cashDrawer_denomCount[slots];
//---------------- end of  cash drawer object implementation -----------------

//--------------------- computing object implementation --------------------
int compute_denomCount[slots];
denName compute_denomName[slots];
int compute_denomValue[slots];
//------------ computing object implementation to be continued --------------

//------------------------------ interfaces --------------------------------

void inputInt(int& aNumber, const char prompt[]);
// Arguments:
//    aNumber - out - The integer entered by the user
//    prompt - Message displayed to the user
// Side effect: Prompts for and reads aNumber.

void outputChange();
// Side effect: Output the list of denominations by name and count
//    whose total value is to be returned to a customer
```

```
void outputLine(int aNumber, const char aString[]);
// Arguments:
//   aNumber - The integer to be displayed
//   aString - Message displayed to identify the output
// Side effect: Display a number then a message then a newline.


void compute_changeFor(int amount);
// Argument:
//   amount - The amount of money to make change for
//              ASSUME: amount >= 0
// Side effect: For each subscript i, compute_denomCount[i] is the count and
//   compute_denomName[i] is the name of denomination i to constitute
//   the given amount.  The sum of the values of all the counts is amount.


void divMod(int numerator, int denominator, int& quotient, int& remainder);
// Arguments:
//   numerator, denominator - two integers
//      ASSUME: numerator >= 0; denominator > 0
//   quotient - out - The quotient of numerator/denominator
//   remainder - out - The remainder of numerator/denominator
// Side effect: Find the result of integer division of numerator/denominator.


//------------------------- end of interfaces -----------------------------

//------------------- teller object implementation ------------------------
void main( )
{
   cout << "Change Maker (version 4)\n\n";

   int amountToChange;          //  Amount of money to be changed

   inputInt(amountToChange, "Enter amount to be changed in pennies: ");
   compute_changeFor(amountToChange);
   outputChange();
}
//---------------- end of teller object implementation ---------------------

//--------------------- input object implementation ------------------------
void inputInt(int& aNumber, const char prompt[])
{
   cout << prompt;
   cin >> aNumber;
}
//------------------ end of input object implementation --------------------

//--------------------- output object implementation -----------------------
```

```
void outputLine(int aNumber, const char aString[])
{
    cout << aNumber << " " << aString << endl;
}
void outputChange()
{
    for (int i = 0; i < slots; i++)
        outputLine(compute_denomCount[i], compute_denomName[i]);
}
//----------------- end of output object implementation --------------------

//-------------------- computing object implementation ---------------------
void divMod(int numerator, int denominator, int& quotient, int& remainder)
{
    quotient = numerator / denominator;
    remainder = numerator % denominator;
}

void compute_changeFor(int amount)
{
    for (int i = 0; i < slots; i++) {
        // Count out the change, decreasing the amount as the change is counted.
        divMod(amount, cashDrawer_denomValue[i], compute_denomCount[i], amount);
        strcpy(compute_denomName[i],cashDrawer_denomName[i]);
    }
}
//--------------end of computing object implementation ---------------------
```

We are not through with the changemaker yet. We did not really use some of the arrays in its program solution (such as `cashDrawer_denomCount`), but we can foresee a time in which those arrays may be helpful. And we decided to put underscores in names in anticipation of being able to use the different parts separated by underscores as different entities.

Look for the changemaker problem in later chapters. We will use it to illustrate some fundamental object-oriented programming ideas.

6.10 ▌ Summary

Most solutions to programming problems involve lists in one guise or another. List type objects are common in both object-oriented analyses and object-oriented designs. Most of this chapter was devoted to discussing what list type objects can do and how to implement a list in code. Our implementations were all array-based.

Arrays are by no means unique to C++. Almost all high-level languages have arrays. Arrays are indexed, aggregate objects. They consist of many elements of the same type. Each element of a one-dimensional array is accessed by the name of the array and the subscript of the item. Multidimensional array elements require multiple subscripts.

Unlike some other high-level languages, C++ treats array-type function arguments in a special way. Formal array arguments are reference arguments by default. Other types of arguments are value by default. In order to protect an actual array argument from suffering unwanted side effects, an array can be passed by constant reference.

Character strings can be implemented as arrays of characters. In order to use the special built-in C++ facilities for handling strings, programmers must adhere to one convention: The characters of the string represented by an array of characters must terminate with the null character.

Databases are lists of composite, related elements. In addition to being able to do the simple list operations, databases usually have methods to sort their items according to some ordering criteria. They also search for items based on keys. Since databases are so prevalent, sorting and searching algorithms are an important part of the discipline of computer science.

Through all of our discussions, we have tried to impress on you that lists and arrays are not the same thing. We have used the term list to refer to a design object. The code implementation of a list in this chapter consists of many things: an array to hold the list items (parallel arrays in the case of databases), an integer to indicate the number of array elements that represent actual list items, and functions for the list behaviors. For most of the list implementations of this chapter, the functions had at least two arguments: the array and its integer size. Those arguments allowed us to let the same function be a method for more than a single list. We are not required to duplicate code in order to implement the same behavior for another, similar list.

We are not entirely satisfied with our array-based list implementations. Although such implementations are the best that many high-level languages can offer, we expect C++ to be better. What we are looking for is a way to package the array, the size, and all of the functions for the list methods into a single C++ code object. And that's what the next chapter is all about.

Glossary

aggregate   A single object consisting of a collection of objects.

binary search   A search on an ordered list in which the first place to look is the middle of the list. If the middle item is larger than the item being searched, a binary search is performed on the first half of the list. If the middle item is smaller than the item being searched, a binary search is performed on the last half of the list.

constant reference   A formal reference argument for which the function cannot change the corresponding actual argument.

C-string   A `char` array in which the characters of interest are the ones preceding the first null character in the array.

element (of an array) One of the objects constituting the array's collection of objects.

indexed list A list consisting of items in numbered positions.

insertion sort A list-sorting technique. The list is considered to be in two parts: (1) the part that is sorted and (2) the part that is not sorted. The main step of an insertion sort consists of inserting the first item from the unsorted part into its correct position in the sorted part.

linear search A sequential search of a list that starts from the beginning, going through each list item until the item being searched is found or until it is known that the item is not in the list.

multidimensional array An array whose elements themselves are arrays.

null character The character '\0', used to terminate a string.

null string An array of characters whose first character is '\0'.

ordered list A list which keeps its items in ascending (or descending) order.

parallel arrays Arrays used to represent different data for composite items in the same list.

string A list of characters.

string overflow Any attempt to place a character past the end the array allocated for a string.

subscript The number indicating the position of an element of an array. Subscripts begin at 0.

traversal One-at-a-time access of every element in a list, beginning with the first item.

two-dimensional array An array of arrays (every element has two subscripts).

6.11 Exercises

1. Assume the following definitions have been given.

```
int x[30];
const int max = 45;
float y[max];
float z;
```

   a. How many elements does the array x have?

   b. What is the subscript of the first element of x?

   c. Write a statement that assigns the value 7 to the first element of x.

   d. What is the largest valid subscript of x? What is the smallest valid subscript?

   e. What type of elements does y have?

   f. What is the subscript of the last element of y?

g. Write a statement that increases the value of the last element of y by 20%.

h. Write a statement that assigns the sum of the first three elements of y to z.

i. Write a loop that doubles the value of each element of y.

2. Write array-based definitions and initializations to implement the attributes (data) for the following objects. For the list type objects, you will need three different definitions: for the maximum list capacity, for the list items, and for the current list size.

a. A list of all daily low temperature readings to be taken in Yellowstone National Park for next year.

b. A list of SAT scores for incoming university freshmen. The university limits freshman enrollment to 3,000 students.

c. A point (x,y) in the real plane, initialized to the value (2.3, 5.41).

d. A line from a text file in which no line has more than 80 characters.

e. The first name of your maternal grandmother.

f. A list of towns on the travel itinerary of a rural health care nurse in Pennsylvania. The nurse visits no more than 10 towns for any given trip and town names are limited to 20 characters or less.

g. A list of names and ages of students in a computer science class. The class size is limited to 50 students.

h. A table of distances between pairs of 20 different cities.

3. Arrays can be initialized when they are defined by listing out the values of their elements in braces.

a. Define and initialize an array x of 10 ints in which each element is the same as its subscript (x[0] is 0, x[1] is 1, ..., x[9] is 9).

b. Define an array of 10 ints. Write a loop to assign each array element the value 0.

c. Define and initialize an array of 100 ints so that each array element has the value 0.

4. All of the following code fragments are defective. Some of the fragments have syntax errors. Other fragments are syntactically correct, but their execution could cause runtime errors. Explain the defects for each fragment.

a. `int max = 20;`
   `int array[max];`

b. `int other[4] = {5, 1, 1, 0, 0};`

c. `int x[4];`
   `x[4] = 0;`

   d. `double vec[20];`

      `makeZero(vec,30);`   `// makeZero() was defined in`
                                 `// Section 6.2`

   e.
```
void f(const int x[])
{
    if (x[0] < 0)
        x[0] = 0;
}
```

   f.
```
int y[5];
y = {1, 2, 3, 4, 5};
```

   g.
```
char message[] = "Hello, Paul";
message = "Goodbye";
```

   h.
```
const char firstMonth[] = "january";
firstMonth[0] = 'J';
```

   i.
```
char lastName[] = "Jones";
lastName[strlen(lastName)] = 's';
```

   j.
```
double display[3][4];
display[1,2] = 2.34;
```

5. Write the definition for the function `findMaxPsn()`, which is declared as follows:

```
int findMaxPsn(double array[], int numberOfElements);
// Arguments:
//    array - an array of numbers
//    numberOfElements - the number of elements in the array
// Returns: The subscript of the largest element in the array. If there
//    is more than one largest element, the subscript of the first such
//    element is returned.
```

6. Write prototypes for each of the following procedure descriptions.

   a. A procedure with three formal arguments, an array of `int`s, an array of `double`s, and an `int` which is passed by value. Both arrays are modified by the procedure.

   b. A procedure with two formal `int` array arguments, the first one is not modified by the procedure but the second one is.

   c. A procedure with a string argument that is not changed by the procedure.

   d. A procedure with a two-dimensional array of `double`s for a formal argument. The procedure can be called with the following array as an actual argument:

```
double anArray[5][10];
```

The procedure will not change its argument.

e. A procedure with a formal argument that is an array of strings, each of maximum length 80. The procedure will change some of the strings in the actual argument.

7. You have been given the following definitions to implement attributes for a list whose items are prices in a catalogue:

```
const int maxList = 500;
float price[maxList];
int size = 0;
```

Write a segment of code for each of the described operations.

a. Set each price on the list to 100.0.

b. Add the price 27.93 to the end of the list if the list is not full.

c. Remove the last price from the end of the list.

d. Increase each price on the list by 10%.

e. Find the smallest price on the list.

f. Find the largest price on the list.

g. Print all prices on the list, starting with the last one and going back to the first.

h. Delete the last 20% of the prices on the list.

i. Delete the first item on the list, if it has one.

8. Suppose *list* is a simple list with an iterator, as described in section 6.3. Write segments of code for each of these operations. Use *only* the operations that are described in section 6.3. Do not assume the *list* is implemented as an array. (You do not need to know anything about the implementation of the list data in order to use the *list* operations.)

a. Print every other item in *list*, beginning with the first item.

b. Find the sum of the positive items in *list*.

c. Keep adding copies of the value 0 to the end of *list* until *list* has no room for additional members.

d. Find out whether the items in *list* are in ascending order.

e. Assume that *list* can contain twice as many items as it currently contains. Modify *list* so that an entire copy of *list* is duplicated at the end of *list*. For example, if *list* is

```
1  4  9  3  7
```

then your code should modify *list* so that it is

```
1  4  9  3  7  1  4  9  3  7
```

9. Look at the implementation of the function with prototype `int&`
`item(int index)` from section 6.1. (It is the last function in that section.) Why are there no `break` statements inside the `switch` statement?
(This question has nothing to do with arrays or lists.)

10. Suppose that the attributes for a list of integers are implemented as an
array of `int`s named `a` and an `int` named `size`. Suppose also that the
list contains the following elements.

```
2  7  3  1  8  9  4
```

What are the elements in the list after each of the following segments of
code is executed? (Assume that the segments of code are independent.
In other words, immediately before *each* segment of code is executed,
assume that the list items are as shown above.)

a.
```
for(int i = 0; i < size; i++)
    a[i] += i + 1;
```

b.
```
for(int i = 0; i < size - 1; i++)
    a[i] += a[i + 1];
```

c.
```
for(int i = size - 2; i >= 0; i--)
    a[i] += a[i + 1];
```

d.
```
for(int i = 0; i < size - 1; i++)
    a[i] = a[i + 1];
size--;
```

e.
```
for(int i = size - 2; i >= 0; i--)
    a[i] = a[i + 1];
size--;
```

f.
```
for(int i = size - 1; i > 0; i--)
    a[i] = a[i - 1];
size++;
a[0] = 5;
```

g.
```
for(int i = 1; i < size; i++)
    a[i] = a[i - 1];
size++;
a[0] = 5;
```

h.
```
for (int i = 0; i < size / 2; i++)
    swap(a[i], a[size - i - 1]);   // swap() exchanges
                                    // the contents of
                                    // its two int
                                    // arguments
```

i.
```
for (int i = 0; i < size; i++)
    swap(a[i], a[size - i - 1]);
```

11. Write a function that can be used by a list of integers to remove *all* occurrences of a particular item from the list. A prototype and documentation for the function are as follows:

```
bool removeAll(int a[], int& size, int x);
// Arguments:
//    a - in - Holds a list of numbers
//    a - out - Holds the list of numbers after all occurrences of x
//              are removed
//    size - in - The number of items in the list before the removal.
//              ASSUME: 0 <= size <= number of elements of a
//    size - out - The number of items in the list after the removal
//    x - the item to remove
// Returns: true if the removal was successful (the list contained at
//    least one copy of x) and false if it was not successful (the list
//    contained no copies of x).
// Side effect: Elements of a are shifted left for each removal of x; size
//    is decremented by the number of removals.
```

12. Write a function that sorts a list of integers, removing duplicate values in the process. For example, if the list is

    3   18   4   18   17   24   9   17   9

    then after execution of the function, the list is

    3   4   9   17   18   24

    Your function should use an array of integers and an integer size as arguments.

13. Define a procedure named duplicate with two arguments representing data for a list of integers. Any list that is no more than half full can use duplicate() to duplicate all its items. Suppose the list items are as follows before duplicate() is called.

    1   4   9   3   7

    Then after duplicate() is called, the list items are

    1   1   4   4   9   9   3   3   7   7

    Define duplicate() so that no shifts are necessary. (*Hint:* Start duplicating from the end of the list rather than the beginning.)

14. Write typedefs for each of the following type descriptions.

a. `medString`   (a type for a string with a maximum length of 25 characters)

b. `vector`   (a type for an array of 3 `double`s)

c. `matrix`   (a type for a two-dimensional array of `float`s with 3 rows and 4 columns)

15. Use the typedefs from the previous question to do the following.

a. Write the prototype for a function that has a formal argument of type `medString`.

b. Write an appropriate prototype for the function `f()`, which is invoked in the following code. The second formal argument for `f()` should be a value argument.

```
vector v = {7.8, 3, 5.6};
f(v, v[2]);
```

c. Write an appropriate prototype for the function `g()`, which is invoked in the following code. The second formal argument for `g()` should be a reference argument.

```
matrix m;
g(m, m[2][1]);
```

16. Given the following definitions.

```
char one[12];
char two[] = "Susan Jones";
char three[12] = "";
```

a. What is the value of `three[0]`?

b. What is the value of `two[0]`?

c. Write a single statement that assigns `one` the string value `""` (the null string).

d. Write a single statement that prints the length of `two`.

e. Write a loop that assigns `one` the value `"xxx"`. (Don't use `strcpy()`.)

f. Write a statement that exchanges the values of `one` and `three` if the string represented by `one` is less than the string represented by `three`.

17. Use the identifier `city` as the name of the major array for this problem.

a. Make a typedef and then define an array of strings (`city`) and an `int` to implement the data for a list of up to 100 city names in which each city name has at most 80 characters.

b. Write a loop that can be used by an input object to read the city names from `cin`. Assume that the user will never enter more than 80 characters on a line of input (including the newline). Add to the list all city names the user enters up to at most 100 names or until the user enters the null string, whichever comes first.

c. Does the code for part (b) change if it is known ahead of time that the user will not enter any names with embedded blanks, such as St. Louis or Hong Kong?

d. Do part (b) again, only this time the input will come from an `ifstream` named `inf`, which has been opened to a text file on disk. Each line in the file is a city name. (See Appendixes D and F at the end of this book.)

18. Use `city` as defined in the previous problem. Define an array of `ints` named `population` that can hold the populations of the cities in `city`.

a. Write a loop that can be used by an input object to read the city names and their populations from `cin`. Input will come in pairs of lines, in which the first line in each pair is the name of the city and the second line is the population of that city.

b. Assume that the user will never enter more than 80 characters on a line of input (including the newline). Add to the list all city names and populations that the user enters up to at most 100 names and populations or until the user enters the null string for a city name, whichever comes first.

c. Do part (a) again. This time assume that the input will come from an `ifstream` named `inf`, which has been opened to a text file on disk.

19. Write procedures for each of the following.

a. Change all of the lowercase alphabetic characters of a C-string to uppercase.

b. Change the first letter of every word in a C-string to uppercase. Consider a word to be a sequence of alphabetic characters. The first character in a word must be the first character in the string or be preceded by a nonalphabetic character. The last character must be followed by a nonalphabetic character or be at the end of the string.

c. Remove all of the blanks in a C-string.

d. Strip all leading blanks and trailing blanks from the C-string. (A leading blank comes before the first nonblank character; a trailing blank comes after the last nonblank character but before the terminating null character.)

e. Reverse the characters in a C-string. For example, if the value of a string is `"Hello"`, then the procedure would make it `"olleH"`.

20. The string library has a function `strncpy()` with three arguments, a target string `t`, a source string `s` that is passed by constant reference, and an int `n`. It copies at most the first `n` characters from `s` into `t`. It quits copying from `s` as soon as the null character of `s` has been copied or as soon as `n` characters have been copied, whichever comes first. If only `m` characters are copied, where `m < n`, then `m - n` null characters are placed in `t` following the first `n` characters. For example, assume `t` is defined as follow:

    ```
    char t[30];
    ```

    Here are two results of calling `strncpy()`:

    ```
    strncpy(t,"Mary Ann",6) // t is "Mary A"
    strncpy(t, "John", 8)   // t is "John", but t[4] through t[7] are '\0'
    ```

    Write a function `myCopy()` that behaves the same as `strncpy()`.

21. Suppose `nameType` is a C-string variable that represents a person's first and last name, where the format is *last-name, first-name*. Write a function called `firstNameFirst()` that takes such a string and rewrites it to be in the format `first-name last-name`. For example, if `aName` is `"Smith, Martha"` then `firstNameFirst(aName)` changes `aName` to `"Martha Smith"`.

    a. Write the function based on the assumption that all actual arguments are defined with a maximum of 50 characters.

    b. Write the function with no assumption on the maximum sizes of the actual argument. Your function can make the assumption that both names consist of only alphabetic characters, each is at least one character long, and a comma and a single blank separate the last name from the first name. (This problem is actually not as easy as it looks. Remember that you cannot create a temporary string buffer without knowing its length ahead of time. That means you cannot define an array like

    ```
    char buffer[x];
    ```

    where the value of `x` may differ from one execution of the function to another.)

22. Write a definition of an array for a matrix of real numbers with four rows and four columns.

    a. Write a segment of code that makes the array represent the zero matrix.

    b. The identity matrix is the matrix with ones positioned on the main diagonal and zeros everywhere else. In other words, it has a 1 in the first row and first column position, in the second row and second column position, in the third row and third column position, and in the fourth row and fourth column position. All of the elements in the remaining 12 array positions are 0. Write a function that takes an argument that is a matrix and changes it into the identity matrix.

c. Write a function sum() with three two-dimensional array arguments A, B, and C, representing three matrices with four rows and four columns. Your function must assign to C the matrix sum of A and B. It should not change either A or B.

d. Write a function multiply() similar to sum() of part (c) that assigns the matrix product of A and B to C.

23. A popular sorting technique presented in many introductory programming textbooks is called a selection sort. Here's how it works to sort the items in a list. First look through the list for the smallest item and then swap it with the first item in the list. Then look through the list, starting with the second item to find the next smallest item. Swap it with the second list item. The nth step continues this twofold process.

   Write a function that takes a list of strings and sorts them using a selection sort technique. Your code should use two nested loops. The outer loop iterates through every item in the list starting with the first and ending with the next-to-last in order to fill every position correctly. The inner loop searches the remainder of the list for the smallest item.

24. Make suitable definitions for parallel array implementations of data for a grade roster for a math class. The grade roster is a list in which each item in the list corresponds to a description of a student in the class. The description consists of a name (a string of no more than 25 characters), a social security number, and a letter grade for the class. Limit the size of the class to a maximum of 100 students.

25. Suppose you are given a telephone directory list, with each item consisting of a name and a telephone number. The directory is sorted in ascending order by name.

a. Write definitions of parallel arrays that can be used to implement the telephone directory data.

b. Write a function to search for the a name in the telephone directory and to return the corresponding telephone number. If the name is not in the directory, the function should return the number -1. Use a linear search technique.

c. Write a function that does the same as (b) except that it uses a binary search instead of a linear search.

26. The following question may amuse you. (Don't worry if you can't answer it now. It will be much easier to understand after you have more experience with reference types.) Look at the following function definition:

```
int& minimum(int& x, int& y)
{
    if (x < y)
        return x;
    return y;
}
```

Will this code compile? If so, what do you think happens when the following code is executed?

```
int a = 34;
int b = 78;
minimum(a,b) = 31;
```

Programming Projects

27. Modify the changemaker so that the cash drawer contains fixed counts of each denomination. When the teller gets to work, it will display a banner and then ask the input object to get those counts. The denomination list created by the computer should not have any count that is greater than the count of the corresponding denomination in the cash drawer. In the event there is still money left to pay after all of the change has been given out, the teller should tell the output object to display a message to that effect, indicating how much is left to pay.

28. How could the list of the denominations output by the changemaker be modified to allow the program user to make restrictions on what is to be returned? For example, the user might ask that no bills be returned or that at least two quarters be returned. Don't worry about how the input object could get this information. Instead, tell how that information could be used by the computing object to create its list of denominations. This is actually a two-part question.

    a. How should the restrictions be represented?

    b. Assuming your answer to the above is correct, how would the computing object use that information to compute its denomination list?

    Implement your answers to both of these questions with C++ code.

29. Dr. Smith wants to be able to perform some statistical analyses on the grades that her students made on their final examination. In particular, she wants to figure out the mean (the average), the median (the middle grade or the average of the two middle grades after they are sorted), and the modes (the grades having the greatest frequency). Solve this problem for her.

    Analyze this problem in terms of four different objects: a list of grades, an input object, an output object, and a report generator which makes sure the statistical analyses are done. For this part of the problem, draw an OOA diagram that shows each of the objects. Your diagram should be similar to the OOA diagrams in Chapter 1.

Design a solution for Dr. Smith's problem. Remember that the design should be a refinement of the analysis. Pay careful attention to the design of the list of grades. It is not a simple list; it can sort itself and find its mean, median, and modes. For this part of the problem, make a design diagram such as the changemaker design of this chapter. Implement your design with a C++ program.

30. A hardware store keeps an inventory of plumbing supplies by bar code number and price. The store clerks frequently must add new items to the inventory, change the prices of items, remove items, and find the price of an item based on its bar code.

    Analyze and design a solution in terms of four different objects: a list of bar codes and prices, an input object, an output object, and a menu object. The menu displays an initial banner, asks the input object to get the inventory from a file, shows the choices, asks the list to do whatever the user selected, and quits. Draw a design diagram to illustrate the objects, what they know, what they can do, and how they communicate with each other. Implement the design with a C++ program.

31. Solve the following programming problem.

    Given a polynomial with integer coefficients, factor it into a product of linear factors with rational roots and a polynomial with no rational roots.

    Use a handheld calculator as a model for your solution. What does the input object need to be able to do? Are there any restrictions about the input? What about the output object? In what form will it display the results?

    The computing object is the difficult object to design. It should keep track of the rational roots that have been determined as well as the coefficients of the polynomial that has not yet been factored into linear factors. A major part of the design requires devising an algorithm that the computing object can use to find those roots and the factors.

    Hint: Rational root of the polynomial $a_n x^n + a_{n-1} x^{n-1} + \ldots + a_1 x + a_0$, where all of the coefficients are integers, are of the form a/b, where a is a divisor of a_0 and b is a divisor of a_n. So it is easy to generate a finite list of all possible rational roots. (You will want a pair of lists, one for the numerators and one for the denominators of the possible roots.) Synthetic division is a useful algorithm for testing a root candidate. If a candidate r is indeed a root, synthetic division also shows the coefficients of polynomial when $(x - r)$ is factored out.

Chapter 7

Producing Objects Through Classes

WHY is this chapter so important? Why are people who already know C but want to learn C++ likely to read Chapter 1 and then skip directly to this one? The answer lies in the importance of two goals of object-oriented programming that make it a superior software development technique: (1) modularization, or how the code is organized, and (2) reusability of the code. In most object-oriented programming languages, the principle feature by which these two goals are achieved is through classes.

Object-oriented programming grew out of the tradition of structured programming. In structured programming, the approach to solving a problem is to consider the entire problem as one big task that must be divided into small tasks. The language tools that are necessary for structured programming are the ones that we discussed in Chapters 2 through 6. Until this point, we have written our programs using traditional code, even when the designs of the solutions were object-oriented. With this introduction to classes, we can begin to write object-oriented code as well.

We have always had objects in our designs. That has never been an issue, and our programs have used the design objects to organize their code. What we haven't seen so clearly is the connection between objects and their implementations. When we introduced programming in this book, we relied strictly on comments to show how design objects were implemented. And when we covered functions, we were able to capture some of an object's behavior in a new way. In Chapter 6, we emphasized using both data and functions to implement objects. But throughout those previous chapters, our objects were obvious only in the design. Code corresponding to an object had to be bracketed with explanatory comments to show how the objects lived in the code. That will not always be necessary from now on. Most of the major objects of interest in our solutions will be implemented as classes.

We have one word of warning. Classes are a C++ language tool. Classes will not always correspond perfectly to some of the objects in our designs. Not every object in a design is going to be a class. Not every use of a class in the source code will necessarily correspond to objects in the design. We will use classes and structs, their related counterparts, as data aggregates. We will also use classes for **data abstraction**, a process that wraps together and provides clean interfaces for a related set of tasks and data. Our primary focus in this chapter will be on creating classes as types for the major objects in our object-oriented designs.

7.1 Simple objects: Structs

Objects are characterized by two things: their attributes and their behaviors. Most of the objects in our designs have had both attributes and behaviors. Some objects can be very complex, and some can be very simple. Before we get into complicated objects, let us look at a few simple ones. We will begin with a date object.

An object that represents a date must have three attributes: a day, a month, and a year. It is not obvious that a date object has any special behavior. So we can say that it has no behavior, or at least it has only "minimal" behavior.[1] To use a date in a program, all we need to implement are the date's attributes. We can do that by defining three integer type data objects: one for the day, one for the month, and one for the year. In any program using such an implementation, the programmer must be careful to treat those three integers logically as a single entity. It would be nice to have a type of data object that could represent all of the three date attributes at the same time. With a type like that, a programmer could keep track of a single data object for a date rather than three separate ones.

C++ allows programmers to define their own types, as do most high-level languages. We defined new types in the past when we created our own enumeration types. Enumeration types are simple integer types. They are not complex enough for our new date example. So we will use a C++ language feature called a **struct** to make a new type.

Struct type definitions and simple operations

The following is a struct type definition of a date type. This definition tells the compiler the name of a new type, `DateStruct`. The three parts to this struct—called the **members** of the struct—are day, month, and year.

```
struct DateStruct {
    int day;
    int month;
    int year;
};
```

[1] We are stretching our words here a little. We say that our example is of an object that has no behavior, but in fact almost all objects have some behavior. Most can set the values of their attributes and tell what some of those values are.

A struct definition starts with the keyword `struct` and then a name. Declarations of the members of the struct appear inside curly braces. Notice the semicolon that follows the right brace. Another time when we have seen a semicolon after a right brace is at the end of an enumeration type definition.[2]

A struct type is a type of data aggregate. An aggregate groups different data together into a single type. An array type is also a data aggregate. The data for an array are homogeneous—all elements for a single array are of the same type. Data for a struct can be heterogeneous. The members of a struct can be different types.

The `DateStruct` definition does not create a variable. It defines a type. The identifier `DateStruct` can be used to define variables the same way the predefined types `double` and `int` can. The following are definitions of data objects of type `DateStruct`:

```
DateStruct today;
DateStruct birthday;
```

The members of `today` are ordinary `int` variables, with not so ordinary names. The names of the members of a struct object come in two parts, one part is the object name and the other part is the member name. The two parts of the name are separated by a period.

```
objectName.memberName
```

The members of `today` are `today.day`, `today.month`, and `today.year`. Since `today.day`, `today.month`, and `today.year` are actually `int` type variables, they can be treated like any other `int` variable. Here is some code that uses `today`:

```
today.day = 12;
today.month = 1;
today.year = 1996;                      // today is January 12, 1996

cout << today.month << '/' << today.day << '/' << today.year << endl;

today.day++;                            // today is now January 13, 1996
```

The three assignment statements above can be used to assign values to `today`. However, we could have defined and initialized a `DateStruct` object in a single statement, in much the same way we can define and initialize `int`s or other numeric types. The syntax is somewhat different, partly because a full initialization of a `DateStruct` requires three numbers rather than one. Here is a definition and initialization of a new `DateStruct` variable, `tomorrow`. The initialization of a

---

[2] It is possible to declare a struct or a class without defining it, much the same way as it is possible to declare a function without defining it. A declaration of `DateStruct` that is not a definition omits the curly braces: `struct DateStruct;`

struct is similar to the initialization of an array. The member values are listed, in order, inside a pair of braces.

```
DateStruct tomorrow = {14,1,1996};      // tomorrow is January 14, 1996
```

As with arrays, the brace notation is for initialization only. It cannot be used for assignments.

It is possible to invent all sorts of complicated types by combining structs that have struct members, structs that have array members, and arrays whose elements are structs. The following declarations include an array of structs. They could be used in an implementation of a list of dates.

```
const int maxCalendar = 40;           // Maximum size of appointment list
DateStruct appointment[maxCalendar];  // Appointment dates
int size = 0;                         // There are no appointments yet.
```

The syntax for accessing any date on the appointment list is simple. If the list is not empty, the first date on the list is `appointment[0]`, the second date, if there is one, is `appointment[1]`, and the last date on the list is `appointment[size - 1]`.

What about the day of the first date on the list? The syntax is easy to figure out here, also. Since the first date on the list is a struct type object, a member of that struct object follows the same naming convention of any member of a struct object. The day of the first date on the list is the name of the first date (`appointment[0]`) followed by a period, followed by the name of the member (`day`). So the day of the first date on the list is

```
appointment[0].day                   // Day of the first appointment
```

The following code defines a struct type to group the attributes for a list of appointments under a single name. The attributes are the dates on the appointment list and the number of dates on the list.

```
struct DateList {
   DateStruct appointment[maxCalendar];
   int size;
};
```

A `DateList` data object can be defined like this:

```
DateList calendar;
```

These statements assign data to `calendar`:

```
calendar.size = 0;                    // There are no appointments yet.
calendar.appointment[0].day = 5;      // This and the next 3 lines
calendar.appointment[0].month = 1;    //    establish a first
```

```
calendar.appointment[0].year = 1995;  //   appointment.
calendar.size++;
```

We will not mention any behaviors to go with a date yet, but lists of dates are a different matter. Lists can do things. Suppose we want to use `DateList` in an implementation of a simple list of dates. One thing a simple list can do is add an item to the end of its list of items. (This is consistent with how we used simple lists in the previous chapter.) We will write a function for the date list behavior.

Structs as arguments and return values

Functions can have struct type arguments and can return struct type values. This function is the "add-to-end" method for a list of dates. As the documentation indicates, it works only if the list is not full when the add is attempted.

```
void addToEnd(DateList& aList, const DateStruct& newDate)
// Arguments:
//   aList - in - Data for a list of dates
//               The list is not full. (aList.size < maxCalendar)
//            out - List data after newDate is added to the end
//   newDate - A date
// Side effect: newDate is placed at the end of aList, whose size is
//   incremented by 1.
{
   aList.appointment[aList.size] = newDate;
   aList.size++;
}
```

The `addToEnd()` definition illustrates several interesting things. Look at the formal argument declaration that represents list data (the declaration for `aList`). That first argument is passed by reference. Even though arrays are automatically passed by reference (bypassing the need for the `&`), structs are not. When a struct is passed by value, a copy of the entire struct, *including all elements of any array members it may have*, is sent to the function. The entire struct, including its array members as well as all others, is duplicated somewhere in memory. The function works with that duplicate copy rather than the actual argument. In order for the function to modify the actual argument, the argument must be passed by reference. Therefore the `&` is absolutely necessary for `addToEnd()` to change the list data.

The `DateStruct` argument for `addToEnd()` is passed by constant reference. It could also have been passed by value, with the same resulting effect. However, as we just observed, when a struct is passed by value, a copy of the struct is made in memory. Unless we need a duplicate copy instead of the original, this duplication may be an inefficient use of computer time and resources. In order to avoid that duplication but still have access to the data of the actual argument, we have used a constant reference for the formal argument. With this kind of formal argument, the actual argument is not duplicated. So `addToEnd()` has access to the data of the actual argument corresponding to `newDate`. It is prevented from changing that data by the `const` modifier.

Look at the first assignment in the function body. You can make a wholesale assignment of one struct to another without referring to any of the members. It is not necessary to copy one `int` member at a time. In the assignment statement, all of the data from the struct `newDate` is copied over into the struct `aList.appointment[aList.size]`.

For an additional illustration, consider this definition:

```
DateList anotherList;
```

In order to copy all of the information from `calendar` into `anotherList`, a single assignment will do.

```
anotherList = calendar;
```

You cannot make an assignment like that with ordinary arrays. But you can with structs. In that sense, structs act like "ordinary variables" while arrays have to be treated differently. Arrays are not first class variables. They have to be treated specially. Structs can be treated just like `int`s or `double`s or other standard built-in simple types, at least as far as argument passing, return values from functions, and assignment are concerned.

The following function has a `DateStruct` argument as well as a `DateStruct` return type. It returns a value that represents the last day of the month of a particular date.

```
DateStruct lastDayOfMonth(const DateStruct& aDate)
// Argument: aDate - An actual date
// Returns: The last day of the month of aDate
{
    DateStruct lastDay = aDate;          // Date to be returned

    switch (aDate.month) {
        case 1: case 3: case 5: case 7: case 8: case 10: case 12:
        // January, March, May, July, August, October, December
            lastDay.day = 31; break;
        case 4: case 6: case 9: case 11:
        // April, June, September, November
            lastDay.day = 30; break;
        case 2:
        // February.
            //    Take care of leap years. Leap years are divisible by
            //    4 but not divisible by 100 unless they are divisible by 400.
            if (aDate.year % 4 == 0 && aDate.year % 100 > 0
                || aDate.year % 400 == 0)
```

```
            lastDay.day = 29;
        else
            lastDay.day = 28; break;
    }

    return lastDay;
}
```

7.2 ▮ Implementing objects with behaviors: Classes

Early in the previous section, we decided that a date object has attributes but nothing beyond minimal behavior. Just what is that minimal behavior? Let's specify both the attributes and behavior of a date object as follows.

Object type: Date
    Knows:
        Its day
        Its month
        Its year
    Can do:
        Initialize itself as a particular date
        Tell what its day is
        Tell what its month is
        Tell what its year is
        Advance to the next date

C++ allows us to encapsulate an object's attributes and its behaviors into a single type by creating a **class** type. Once we make a class type definition, we can create as many objects of that type as we wish. Each object will have its own attributes and its own behaviors, whose characteristics are spelled out by the class definition.

Class type definitions

A **class definition** contains the declarations of members of the class. The following definition tells the programmer all that is necessary in order to declare and use an object of the type `Date`. It mimics the design of the date object that we just outlined. The definition of a class begins with the keyword `class` and then the name of the class. As with a struct, declarations of the class members appear in the curly braces that follow the name of the class.

```
// A simple date type
class Date {
public:
    // Constructor
    Date(int d, int m, int y);  // Initializes Date to day d, month m, year y
                                // ASSUME: m/d/y is a valid date.

    // Functions to access data individually
    int theDay() const;         // Day of this date
    int theMonth() const;       // Month of this date
    int theYear() const;        // Year of this date

    // A function to change the Date
    void advance();             // Changes the date to the next day

private:
    // Data
    int day_;                   // Date's day
    int month_;                 // Date's month
    int year_;                  // Date's year
};
```

Date is the name of a class type. Date has three **data members**: day_, month_, and year_. They represent the attributes of the date design object. In this book, we will follow the popular C++ programming convention of making the names of data members of a class end in underscores.

Date also has five **member functions**: Date(), theDay(), theMonth(), theYear(), and advance(). Member functions are also called **methods**. They implement the behaviors of the date design object.

The definition of Date wraps methods and data together as a single unit. There are many questions to answer about that definition:

- Where are the member functions defined?

- What is the strange looking member function Date()? It has no return type and its name is the same as the name of the class.

- What does const mean when it appears at the end of a of member function declaration?

- How can you define and use a Date type *object*?

- What do the words private and public mean?

When we answer each of these questions, we will not be looking at new and fundamental things about objects. Instead, we will make a foray into C++ syntax and conventions that C++ programmers use in making choices about how to write actual code.

Member function definitions

The class member functions are declared within the class definition itself. The definition for `Date` contains only the prototypes and not the definitions for its member functions. Indeed, that is what you can expect since the class definition just specifies the interface of the class. The class definition spells out *what* the class does, not *how* the class does it.

Member functions `theDay()`, `theMonth()`, and `theYear()` are "accessor" functions in that they simply tell the values of the attributes. The prototypes for these three functions end with the keyword `const`, indicating that these are **const member functions**. Member functions that are const do not change the data members of the class.[3]

The class methods are usually defined outside the class definition.[4] The definition for `theDay()` is as follows:

```
int Date :: theDay() const
{
    return day_;
}
```

It is possible to have an ordinary function named `theDay` or a function named `theDay` that belongs to another class. If the definition of `theDay()` is a member of the `Date` class, it must tell the compiler that this definition is for the member of `Date` as opposed to an ordinary function or a member of another class.

The **scope resolution operator**, `::`, designates the class to which the function belongs. The name of the class followed by the scope resolution operator qualify the name of the member function so that the compiler can tell which function named `theDay` is being defined (the one belonging to `Date`). The most common format in which the scope resolution operator appears is this:

className :: *memberFunctionName*

In the definition of a member function, the notation `Date :: theDay` says that the name of the function being defined is `theDay`, and it is a member of the `Date` class. The word `const` in the function header is a promise by the programmer who writes the definition that this function will not change any of the data members of the class.

The body of `theDay()` contains a reference to the identifier `day_`. In this situation, `day_` refers to the class data member named `day_`. A member function can refer to any data or function member of the same class directly by name. It does

[3] It is possible to declare a member function const and still have it change a data member. The definition of such a function requires a trick that is beyond the scope of this chapter.

[4] It is possible to put the definition of a member function inside the class definition. Such a definition is said to be inline. We discuss inline functions later in this book.

not need to use the scope resolution operator.[5] All members of a class, including data members as well as member functions, have **class scope**, which means their names can be referred to directly inside the definitions of all of the member functions for that class.

The definitions of the remaining accessor member functions theMonth() and theYear() are very similar to the definition of theDay().

```
int Date :: theMonth() const
{
    return month_;
}
int Date :: theYear() const
{
    return year_;
}
```

The definition of advance() takes some work. It advances a Date to represent the date of the following day.

```
void Date :: advance()
{
    day_ += 1;                          // advance the day
    switch (month_) {
        case 1: case 3: case 5: case 7: case 8: case 10:
        // January, March, May, July, August, October
            if (day_ == 32) {
                day_ = 1;
                month_ += 1;
            } break;
        case 12:
        // December
            if (day_ == 32) {
                day_ = 1;
                month_ = 1;
                year_ += 1;
            } break;
        case 4: case 6: case 9: case 11:
        // April, June, September, November
            if (day_ == 31) {
                day_ = 1;
                month_ += 1;
            } break;
```

[5] The exception is when the member function has a formal argument or a local variable that has the same name as the name of the class member.

```
    case 2:
    // February
        if (day_ > 29 || day_ == 29 && ( year_ % 4 > 0 || year_ % 100 == 0)
                                    && year_ % 400 > 0 ) {
            day_ = 1;
            month_ = 3;
        } break;
    }
}
```

The definition of advance() is tedious because of the different number of days in different months and because of leap years. (A leap year is divisible by 4 but not divisible by 100 unless it is also divisible by 400.)

Constructors

The first member function declared in the Date definition, Date(), is special. It is called a **constructor** for the class. A constructor is a member function that is automatically called when a new object of that class type is created. One purpose of the constructor is to initialize an object.

A class constructor declaration is characterized by two things:

1. A constructor has no return type (not even void).

2. A constructor has the same name as the class itself.

Any member function that satisfies these two conditions is a constructor. Constructors are the only member functions with the same name as the class itself.

The definition for the Date constructor can be written as follows:

```
Date :: Date(int d, int m, int y) : day_(d), month_(m), year_(y)
{ }
```

Let's pick apart the syntax of the constructor definition to see what everything means. There is no return type at the beginning of the constructor definition. However, since the constructor is a member of the Date class, it requires the Date:: qualifier before its name in the header.

A constructor has an argument list, as does every C++ function. The argument list for the Date constructor has three int type arguments. But what is the code in the header that starts after the end of the argument list, beginning with the colon, :?

The part right after the colon is called an **initialization list**, a list specifying the initial values for objects that are its members. In this case, day_ is to be initialized with the value of d, month_ is to be initialized with the value of m, and year_ is to be initialized with the value of y.

For our example, the initialization list does all the work for this constructor. However, the constructor is still a function, so its definition must have a body. Of

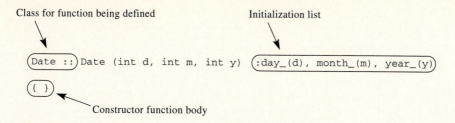

Figure 7.1 Constructor definition with an initalization list.

course, all function bodies start with a left brace, {, and end with a right brace, }.
But in this `Date` constructor, the body does not contain any code. Figure 7.1 illustrates the syntax for a constructor definition.

The body of a constructor may contain additional code. As an alternative to an
initialization list, we could have defined our constructor in this fashion, with
exactly the same result in this case.

```
Date :: Date(int d, int m, int y)
{
    day_ = d;
    month_ = m;
    year_ = y;
}
```

Whether you choose to use an initialization list, as in the first definition, or
make the assignments in the body of the function itself, as in the second, is often a
matter of personal taste. Sometimes, as we shall see later in this book, an initialization list is necessary.

Defining and using class type objects

The definition of a `Date` type object is similar to the definition of any type of
object. The following are several examples of different object definitions. The first
one defines an `int`, using a form of initialization that we mentioned in Chapter 2
but have not shown since then.[6]

```
int x(0);                          // Equivalent to: int x = 0;
Date holiday(4,7,1995);            // holiday is July 4, 1995
Date today(10,1,1994);             // today is January 10, 1994
const Date christmas96(25,12,1996); // christmas96 is December 25, 1996
```

---

[6] This style of initialization of built-in types may not be acceptable to all compilers.

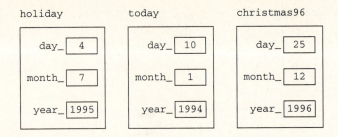

Figure 7.2 Instances of Date: holiday, today, and Christmas96.

The last three definitions create Date objects. The first one, holiday, is a variable initialized to represent July 4, 1995. The value of its day_ is 4, the value of its month_ is 7 (for July), and the value of its year_ is 1995. The second object, today, is initialized to represent January 10, 1994. The final definition creates a constant object representing Christmas Day 1996. In object-oriented programming terminology, an object of class type is called an **instance of a class**. So holiday, today, and christmas96, are instances of Date.

For the current version of the Date class, it is necessary to specify how the data members are to be initialized when Date type objects are created. Later we will show you some examples of how to change the definition of the Date class to avoid explicitly having to provide that kind of information.

The way to modify a Date object is through an assignment. To make today represent Christmas Day 1996, the following assignment statement will do:

```
today = christmas96;
```

Since christmas96 is a constant object, the following attempted assignment is not legal. The compiler should flag it as an error.

```
christmas96 = today;        // illegal! christmas96 is a const
```

This assignment makes today represent April Fools' Day 1997. On the right-hand side of the assignment operator is a literal Date value.

```
today = Date(1,4,1997);   // today is April 1, 1997
```

Instead of changing today, suppose we just want to know what year its value represents. To do that, we'll send a message to today to tell us its year. Sending a **message** to a class type object means calling a member function of that object's class. The following statement initializes an int data object as the value of today's year.

```
int num = today.theYear();
```

A call to a member function of a class must be qualified by the name of an object.[7] The following format may be used to call a member function:

nameOfObject.nameOfFunction(actualArgumentList)

The period plays the same role that it does when we refer to a member of a struct. With a member function call, however, the member we are referring to is a function rather than a data member. The notation can be explained in terms of sending an object a message.

- *nameOfObject* is the name of the object which is receiving the message.

- *nameOfFunction(actualArgumentList)* is the message.

A Date type object knows how to advance to the next day. For example, suppose today represents April 1, 1997. Then this code is a message to today asking it to represent the date of the following day:

```
today.advance();    // today is now April 2, 1997
```

Since christmas96 is a const, it cannot be assigned a new value. But it is possible to send it messages to tell what its day, month, or year are. This segment of code represents two different messages to christmas96:

```
cout << "Christmas day is December " << christmas96.theDay()
     << ", " << christmas96.theYear() << endl;
```

The output is shown below.

```
Christmas day is December 25, 1996
```

The constness of christmas96 limits the member functions that can be invoked with christmas96 to the const member functions. The member function advance() is not const. It changes the data members. If we attempt to send christmas96 an advance message, we will get a syntax error.

```
christmas96.advance();    // illegal! christmas96 is const and advance() is
                          //    a non-const member function
```

---

[7] There are two exceptions to this statement. The qualifier is omitted when a call to a member function is made inside the body of another member function. It may also be omitted when a static member function is called.

Only const member functions can be invoked through const objects. It is illegal to invoke a non-const member function with a const instance of the class.

The definition of `Date::theYear()` (and in fact each member function of `Date`) contains a subtlety that you may of overlooked when we first talked about member function definitions.

```
int Date :: theYear() const
{
    return year_;    // Return the year_ data member of this object
}
```

We have created three `Date` type objects: `holiday`, `today`, and `christmas96`. Each one has a member named `year_`. The three `year_`s are different. When the function `theYear()` is invoked, which `year_` does the function return? It returns *the `year_` member of the object for which the function was invoked*. The object that receives the message is the one that responds. That's why a call to `theYear()` requires the name of an object. The period merely separates the object name from the member function name.

Though C++ translators vary in detail, you can think of all of them as first translating C++ code into C code. A C++ member function is translated into an ordinary C function that has one more formal argument than the member function. An invocation of a C++ member function is translated as an ordinary C function call. The object for which the member function is invoked is translated as the first actual argument of the C function call. For example,

`christmas96.theDay()`   gets translated to   `theDay(christmas96)`

Comparing private and public members

A class can have members that are **private** and members that are **public**. The data members of `Date` (`day_`, `month_`, and `year_`) are private. The function members (`Date()`, `theDay()`, `theMonth()`, `theYear()`, and `advance()`) are public. Private members are listed under the heading `private:`. Public members are listed under the heading `public:`.

Private and public refer to class member **access control**. If a member of a class is private, then the only code that can access that member is the code belonging to a member function.[8] On the other hand, any code that knows about an object of a class type can access any of that object's public members.

The public part of the class definition is the **interface of the class**, the part of a class definition that tells how the class can be used. If you follow good design guidelines, that interface consists almost entirely of function declarations. The interface specifies exactly what kinds of messages can be sent to an object of that class type. (Go back to the definition of the `TypeSetter` class in Chapter 3 to see just how important the interface is. The interface shows everything a client needs to know about a class in order to use it.) Data members are almost never public. That's why they have the funny-looking names with the underscores, to emphasize that they are not for general use.

Keep in mind that private members cannot be accessed in `main()`. Suppose that the object `holiday` is defined as a global variable or simply local to `main()` or to any ordinary function. What we are about to say is true for any of those circumstances. Since the member `year_` is private to `Date`, the code in `main()` cannot reference `holiday.year_` directly. All of the following statements are illegal:

```
holiday.year_ = 1990;             // illegal! Can't access a private member.
cout << holiday.year_ << endl;    // illegal! Can't access a private member.
holiday.year_++;                  // illegal! Can't access a private member.
```

Not only is the code in `main()` unable to change `holiday.year_`, it cannot even look at it directly. The only way to find out the value of `holiday.year_` is to ask `holiday` what its year is. It does so by invoking the public member function `theYear()`. The illegal output statement in that last segment of code can be replaced by this legal statement:

```
cout << holiday.theYear() << endl;    // legal
```

If you have had considerable programming experience, the rationale for having public and private members may be clear. If you have not, then you may be scratching your head asking "Why bother? Wouldn't it be easier to have everything public? Then you could do away with those three functions `theDay()`, `theMonth()`, and `theYear()`. Less code, less bother."

There has to be a good reason to have public and private members. And C++ programmers have in fact adopted conventions indicating whether a certain member of a class should be public or private. They usually make all data members of a class private and most member functions public. Some member functions are made private if those functions simply do internal manipulations or bookkeeping operations that do not need to be apparent outside the class.

By having private members, the class itself has complete control over how these members are represented and how they are changed. In the case of the `Date` class, those private members cannot be changed individually. The entire `Date`

---

[8] The exception to this is functions and classes that are *friends*, a topic we'll discuss in the next chapter.

object can be changed through assignment to another `Date`, but the individual data members cannot be tinkered with as individual `int`s.

Back in Chapter 1 when we first mentioned objects, we talked about objects as intelligent beings having attributes and behaviors. We have been able to implement objects in code through data objects and functions as well as comments to show the relationship between the design and the code. But objects can also do things for themselves.

Until now, we have not had any programming language tools to capture this new idea. But now we can use classes. What a class object knows are the data members of the class. A class object can keep its data members out of the interfering hands of other code simply by making them private.

How can you ask an object do something? Send it a message. A message is a request made to an object. The request is merely a call to a member function of the object. What the member function returns and the side effects are the object's response to the message.

Let's focus again on structs. We did not mention at the time we presented them that structs can have member functions and they can have private as well as public members. Most C++ programmers use structs only to group data together into a single type. They do not have to, but they generally do follow that convention. In a class definition, unless specified otherwise, a member is private. The default access control for classes is private. The exact opposite of that is true for structs. The default access control for structs is public. Unless specified otherwise, a member of a struct is public.

The definition of a class (or a struct) shows the interface of the class. That is analogous to the declaration of a function. The interface of a class is completely specified if it contains all of the documentation and declarations necessary for a programmer to understand how the class can be properly used.

While it is possible for the definition of a member function to be placed inside the actual definition of the class, we will avoid doing so. The reason is that there is no need to show implementation of a member function. A user of a class should not need to know *how* a class does something.

Talking the language of OOP and C++

This short glossary relates ideas of OOP and C++ classes. The examples are based on the following definition:

```
Date today;
```

OOP	C++
object	An instance of a class (a variable or constant that is of a class type). *Example:* `today`
method	A member function of a class. *Example:* `Date :: advance()`
attribute	A data member of a class type object. *Example:* `today.year_`
message-send	A call to a member function of a class. The receiving object is the one whose name qualifies the function name in the call. *Example:* `today.theYear()`
message-reply	The value returned by the function called in a message-send. *Example:* `y = today.theyear()`, which saves the message reply as the value of `y`.
interface	The messages to which an object can respond. *Example:* The public portion of `Date`

7.3   A simple list class with an array data member

The behavior that we attributed to a `Date` object was almost minimal, a characteristic that makes a `Date` object unusual in that respect. Most objects do not have minimal behavior. Instead, they do things that are part of how they are conceptualized. We have seen many examples of objects with behaviors, including the computing object of the convenience store problem and the cash drawer of the changemaker.

Another object with more than just minimal behavior is the simple list, a subject discussed in Chapter 6. The description below constitutes a quick analysis of a simple list.

Object type: Simple list
>   Knows:
>   Its items
>   How many elements are currently in its list
>   Can do:
>   Initialize itself as an empty list
>   Tell its maximum capacity
>   Tell how many items it currently contains
>   Clear out all of its items to make itself empty
>   Add an item to the end
>   Tell if a particular value is an item in its list

Suppose we want to design a simple list of integers. We can specify such a design by defining a `SimpleList` class. What a simple list knows constitutes the data members of the class. What it can do constitutes the function members of the class. They are the class methods. As before, we will make the data members of `SimpleList` private and the function members public.

```cpp
// A simple list of integers
class SimpleList {
public:
    // Constructor
    SimpleList();                       // Constructs an empty list.

    // These methods change the list
    void clear();                       // Makes the list empty.
    void add(int newItem);              // Adds newItem to the list.
                                        // ASSUME: The list is not full.

    // These methods tell information about the list
    bool member(int anItem) const;      // True if anItem is a list member.
    int maximumCapacity() const;        // Maximum possible list size.
    int currentSize() const;            // Number of items currently in the list.

private:
    // List data
    enum {maxSize_ = 100};              // Maximum size of the list
    int item_[maxSize_];                // List items
    int size_;                          // Number of items currently in the list
};
```

Observe that the member functions `clear()` and `add()` change the `SimpleList` data. The member functions `member()`, `maximumCapacity()`, and `currentSize()` do not change any data so they are declared as const functions.

Encapsulation of data in a single object

Before going to its member functions, we turn our attention to the `SimpleList`
data members. In the previous chapter, we implemented list data with definitions
of three different data objects: a constant integer for the maximum capacity (the
number of array elements), an array, and an integer size to indicate how many
array elements represented list items. The `SimpleList` class encapsulates all of
the data for a single list in a single object.

The `SimpleList` class definition includes an anonymous enumeration type
to establish the value of the maximum capacity of the list. Within the class, the
enumeration type makes the name `maxSize_` another name for the value 100. We
did not use a constant integer to establish the number of array elements because of
a limitation of the language. C++ does not allow us to initialize a const inside a
class definition.

It is possible to define a constant integer outside a class or as a static class
member, then use it to declare an array inside the class. But that would separate
the list data into two different objects, one containing the items and the current
size and the other containing the maximum capacity. The anonymous enumeration type solves the problem of making the number of array elements private
to the class. The enumeration type makes it possible to declare the array data
member item using `maxSize_` to tell the compiler the number of array elements.

The definition of the enumeration type inside the definition of `SimpleList`
illustrates two issues that are important to programmers: encapsulation and information hiding. **Encapsulation** means keeping together data and functions that
belong together. We defined the enumeration type inside the definition of the
`SimpleList` class in order to encapsulate all of the data for a simple list inside a
single object. **Information hiding** means keeping the interface of the class separate from the details of its implementation. Information known by the class alone
should not be known by other code. That is why we made the enumeration type
definition private instead of public.

The implementation of the `SimpleList` type is complete when the member
functions have been defined.

```
SimpleList :: SimpleList() : size_(0)
{ }

void SimpleList :: clear()
{
    size_ = 0;
}

void SimpleList :: add(int newItem)
{
    item_[size_] = newItem;
    size_++;
}
```

```
bool SimpleList :: member(int anItem) const
{
    for (int i = 0; i < size_; i++)
        if (item_[i] == anItem)
            return true;
    return false;
}
int SimpleList :: maximumCapacity() const
{
    return maxSize_;
}
int SimpleList :: currentSize() const
{
    return size_;
}
```

SimpleList **type objects**

We can create a SimpleList object with a single definition.

```
SimpleList list;                 // list is initialized to empty
```

Notice how this code differs from the definitions of Date type objects. For a Date definition, we had to supply integers that were the initial values of the data members of the object. The constructor of a SimpleList, however, has no arguments. No actual arguments can be supplied when a SimpleList object is defined.

Here are some messages to list:

```
list.add(34);                    // list is now: 34
list.add(27);                    // list is now: 34, 27
list.add(345);                   // list is now: 34, 27, 345
list.add(58);                    // list is now: 34, 27, 345, 58
```

Figure 7.3 illustrates the list data after the sequence of add messages just given.

Both add() and clear() are capable of changing a SimpleList.

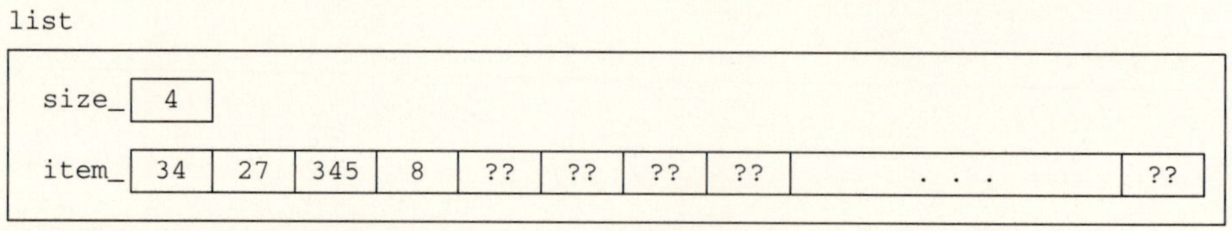

list

size_	4								
item_	34	27	345	8	??	??	??	??	. . . ??

Figure 7.3 Data for list, SimpleList that represents 34, 27, 345, 8.

```
int x = list.currentSize();    // x is initialized to 4
if (list.member(27))
   x++;                        // x is incremented to 5
list.clear();                  // list is now empty
x = list.currentSize();        // x is now 0
```

Figure 7.4 illustrates the `list` data after the `clear` message.

We did not try to add any item to the list by accessing the array data member directly. Indeed, we could not have. The only access we have to list information, either to change it or even to see it, is through the member functions. To find out what the size of the list is, we send the list a message.

How does the class implementation of a simple list compare with our old implementation of a simple list from the previous chapter? Let's review some of the old code that we used in that chapter. The way that we described the behavior of a simple list was through some pseudo-code function prototypes:

```
int list_size();        // Number of items currently in the list
int list_maxsize();     // Maximum number of items the list can hold
void list_clear();      // Make the list empty
void list_add(int);     // Add the int item to end of the list
bool list_member(int);  // Is the int item in the list?
```

If we wanted to translate these behaviors directly to a C++ implementation using an array and an `int` for the list size, we could use these global data object declarations:

```
const int maxList = 100;
int list_item[maxList];
int list_size = 0;
```

The following is a comparison between the implementation of a list via the global data objects `list_item` and `list_size` and the implementation using a `SimpleList` object. On the left is a definition for `list_clear()`, one of the functions with the old-style implementation of the list behavior. On the right is `SimpleList::clear()`, one of the functions with the class-style implementation of the list behavior. Following that are some messages to the list. (Unless the array

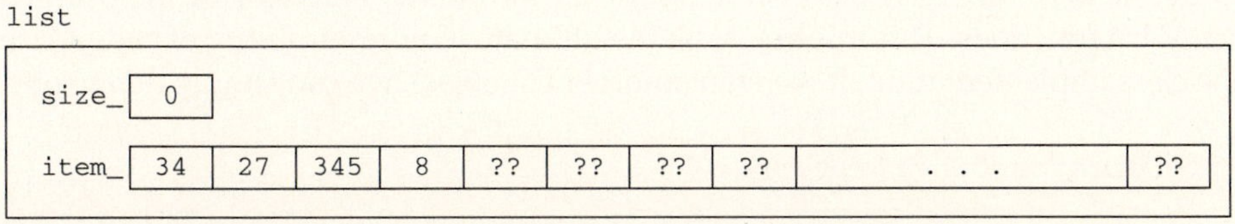

Figure 7.4 Data for `list`, after invocation of `list.clear()`.

list_item and integer list_size are global, the array implementation is impossible.)

Old style—array implementation	New style—class implementation
(using global list_item, list_size)	(using the SimpleList object named list)

```
void list_clear()                    void SimpleList::clear()
{                                    {
    list_size = 0;                       size_ = 0;
}                                    }
```

```
// Ask the list for its current size. Then ask it to make itself empty.
```

```
int x = list_size;                   int x = list.currentSize();
list_clear();                        list.clear();
```

```
// Read in five integers and ask the list to add them to its items.
```

```
int aNumber;                         int aNumber;
for (int i = 0; i < 5; i++){          for (int i = 0; i < 5; i++){
    cin >> aNumber;                      cin >> aNumber;
    list_add(aNumber);                   list.add(aNumber);
}                                    }
```

The code for the two implementations is almost identical. The underscores on the left turned into periods on the right. The question remains: "What have we bought with classes that we couldn't have in the old implementation?"

The answer is more than expected. One thing is for certain. With the old array implementation, it is possible to have only a single list object. Using the array implementation, if we want another simple list in our program, we would have to define another array and another integer for the size. Even worse, we would have to define an entire new set of functions that mimic the behavior of the original array-list functions. This might just be the ultimate in nonreusability of code. With the class implementation, if we want another list object, we can simply define one.

```
SimpleList anotherList;
```

The new SimpleList object, anotherList, has all of the same kinds of attributes and behaviors of list. A class does not limit us to a single object.

Indeed, a class provides us with an easy way to produce as many objects as we wish. We can even assign one `SimpleList` to another. Consider this code:

```
anotherList.add(55);          // anotherList is now: 55
anotherList.add(78);          // anotherList is now: 55, 78
anotherList.add(15);          // anotherList is now: 55, 78, 15
list = anotherList;           // list is now: 55, 78, 15
```

Even though a `SimpleList` contains an array, it isn't used like one. Wholesale assignments like this are possible. In this assignment, all of the data for `anotherList` is copied into `list`. See Fig. 7.5.

We did recognize in the previous chapter that if we implement lists through arrays, then we need to include those arrays as arguments to the functions that implement list behaviors. That overcomes the problem of needing a separate function for each list object. But it creates two additional problems. First, the list is an argument, so the functions have a layer of complexity that class member function syntax avoids. By using a function with arguments, we lose sense of the actual behavior of objects. Second, the list is not encapsulated into a single type. The code for implementing the behavior of a list is completely separate from the code for implementing the attributes of a list.

There is even more to class implementations of objects than what we just said. One of the best things about classes is that they function as the mechanism that C++ uses to support inheritance. For now, think about inheritance as the ability to create new types of objects based on old types. You can reuse old code directly, without modifying it, to create new types from it. The new types inherit the characteristics of the old ones. That's part of the tip of an iceberg that makes C++ popular. Inheritance makes code really reusable.

We have not mentioned inheritance before, even though inheritance is considered to be absolutely essential to object-oriented programming. We have been

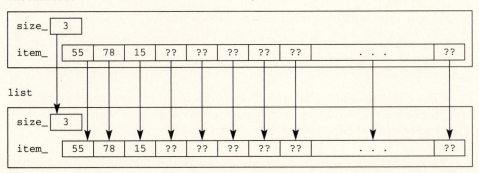

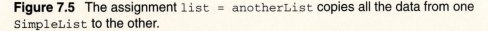

Figure 7.5 The assignment `list = anotherList` copies all the data from one `SimpleList` to the other.

busy for the past six chapters talking about things that are also essential for object-oriented program development. What we are beginning to see with classes are things crucial for implementing more complex designs and language features that provide very strong reusability support.

A simple list with an iterator

The `SimpleList` class is well-named. A `SimpleList` object has very limited list behavior. It can say whether a particular integer is a list member, but it cannot go through its list members one at a time and indicate what those members are.

How have we dealt with this problem in the past? The previous chapter was all about lists, so we know we have at least one solution. In that chapter as well as the chapter before it, we designed an object just to be able to give us access to individual list items—an iterator.

Let's review what an iterator object is all about through the following scenario. A list has been written on a sheet of paper. You run your finger down the list of items, looking at each item one at a time. Or, for an alternative scenario, think of the list as appearing in a spreadsheet on your computer. Imagine pressing the return key or down arrow key in succession in order to scan the list items. In both scenarios, you are able to look at each list item starting with the first item. And you know when there are no more list items left to look at.

An iterator object gives one-at-a-time access to list items. The iterator knows about a list, and it has a cursor to run through the positions in the list. In the first scenario, the iterator's cursor is analogous to your finger. In the second, the iterator's cursor is the cursor that belongs to the spreadsheet. An iterator object has behaviors as well as attributes. It can set itself to point to the beginning of the list. It can get the next item in the list, if a next item exists. And it can tell if there are more items in the list.

How can we incorporate an iterator into a simple list? There are several options, all of which are reasonable choices.

- The iterator is an object that is separate from the list.

- The list has an iterator object as one of its members. (We have already seen an example of one object that contained another object. The computing object of the changemaker contained a cash drawer object.)

- The attributes and behaviors of the iterator object are integrated into the list so that the iterator is actually part of the list itself rather than a separate object that happens to reside within the list.

We decided to go with that last option, integrating the attributes and behaviors of an iterator directly into the simple list. The new class, `SimpleListWith-Iterator`, has all of the data and methods of both a simple list and an iterator.

```
// A simple list of integers with an iterator.
class SimpleListWithIterator {
public:
    // Constructor
    SimpleListWithIterator();           // Constructs an empty list

    void clear();                       // Makes the list empty.
    void add(int newItem);              // Adds newItem to the list.
                                        // ASSUME: The list is not full.

    bool member(int anItem) const;      // Is anItem a list member?
    int maximumCapacity() const;        // Maximum possible list size.
    int currentSize() const;            // Number of items currently in the list.

    // Iterator behaviors
    void setIterator();                 // Set the iterator to the list beginning.
    int next();                         // The next item.
                                        // ASSUME: There is a next item.
    bool more() const;                  // Are there more items?

private:
    enum {maxSize_ = 100};
    int item_[maxSize_];
    int size_;
    int cursor_;                        // Iterator attribute—the cursor
};
```

Look at the declarations of the `SimpleListWithIterator` member functions. Except for the constructor and the iterator, they are identical to those of `SimpleList`. Until we learn about inheritance, we will have to content ourselves with duplicating the definitions of those member functions.

The definitions of the member functions of `SimpleListWithIterator` should make it clear to you why the scope resolution operator is important. The prefix `SimpleListWithIterator::` for each definition says that these definitions go with the `SimpleListWithIterator` class rather than the `SimpleList` class.

```
SimpleListWithIterator :: SimpleListWithIterator() : size_(0)
{ }

void SimpleListWithIterator :: clear()
{
    size_ = 0;
}


void SimpleListWithIterator :: add(int newItem)
```

```
      item_[size_] = newItem;
      size_++;
   }


   bool SimpleListWithIterator :: member(int anItem) const
   {
      for (int i = 0; i < size_; i++)
         if (item_[i] == anItem)
            return true;
      return false;
   }


   int SimpleListWithIterator :: maximumCapacity() const
   {
      return maxSize_;
   }


   int SimpleListWithIterator :: currentSize() const
   {
      return size_;
   }
```

You may be puzzling over the definition of the `SimpleListWithIterator` constructor. Why doesn't it set the data member `cursor_` to 0? The specification of the class says that when a `SimpleListWithIterator` is constructed, the cursor is in an undefined state. That does not mean the implementation is required to set the value randomly. It simply means that we cannot rely on the cursor having any particular value. The practical effect of the specification is that we must call `setIterator()` before we start iterating through the list with `next()`.

Specifications are derived from designs. They determine the interface of a class. The interface represents a contract or promise from the implementor of the class to potential clients or users. The specification tells the clients what they can count on about the behavior of objects of that class type. The specification also determines what the implementor is free to accomplish by whatever means she sees fit—what the clients cannot count on.

C++ class definitions usually reveal too much information to the client of the class—they show the private declarations. That's why it is important to have clear comments that tell the client what is in the official interface. A client with any sense will pretend to be unaware of any other information in the class definition.

Here are the definitions for the member functions implementing the iterator behaviors. The cursor for the iterator is hidden in the private section of the class. After all, only the iterator needs to have access to the cursor. And only those methods associated with the iterator will need the cursor.

```
void SimpleListWithIterator :: setIterator()
{
   cursor_ = 0;
}


int SimpleListWithIterator :: next()
{
   return item_[cursor_++];
}


bool SimpleListWithIterator :: more() const
{
   if (cursor_ < size_)            // We could use this code instead of the
      return true;                 // if/else:
   else                            //    return (cursor_ < size_);
      return false;
}
```

Look carefully at the definition of next(). It returns the item pointed to by the cursor (the element of item_ whose subscript is cursor_). It also advances the cursor to point to the next item. That is exactly what makes the iterator capable of traveling through the list items.

The interface for SimpleListWithIterator—the public section of the class definition—tells how a SimpleListWithIterator object can be used. If you write client code that defines and uses a SimpleListWithIterator object, you must pay attention to the following restrictions.

1. Don't ask the SimpleListWithIterator object to add a new item when it is full.

2. Don't ask the SimpleListWithIterator object if there are more items without previously having asked it to set the iterator to the beginning of the list.

3. Don't ask the SimpleListWithIterator object to tell what its next item is without finding out if there actually is a next item.

Those warnings should be easy enough to follow. Let's now look at some sample code. Consider the following definitions:

```
SimpleListWithIterator myList;        // myList is empty
SimpleListWithIterator yourList;      // yourList is empty
```

```
int max = myList.maximumCapacity();     // max is 100
for (int i = 0; i < max; i++)           // After the loop is executed, myList
    myList.add(i * 3);                  //  is:  0, 3, 6, 9, ..., 297

yourList.add(17);                       // yourList is: 17
yourList.add(25);                       // yourList is: 17, 25
myList.setIterator();
if (myList.more())
    yourList.add(myList.next());        // yourList is: 17, 25, 0

yourList.setIterator();
while (yourList.more())
    cout << yourList.next();            // Output: 17, 25, 0
```

A `SimpleListWithIterator` can be used as a function argument. Consider the following function, which takes two `SimpleListWithIterator` objects and makes the second one contain only the items from the first one which are even.

```
void takeEvens(SimpleListWithIterator& one, SimpleListWithIterator& two)
// Arguments:
//    one - A simple list with an iterator
//    two - out - Consists of all of the items in one which are even
// Side Effect: The original items in two are removed. The even items of one
//    are copied into two.
{
    two.clear();                        // Make two an empty list

    one.setIterator();                  // Prepare to access one's items
    while (one.more()) {                // While there are more items to access
        int x = one.next();            //   x is one's next item
        if (x % 2 == 0)                 //   If x is even
            two.add(x);                 //       add it to two
    }
}
```

See what happens with this call.

```
takeEvens(myList, yourList);            // yourList is: 0, 6, 12, ..., 294
```

The definition of `takeEvens()` illustrates a point that we want to emphasize with respect to class type arguments. The second formal argument, `two`, must be a reference argument because the corresponding actual argument is supposed to change. Remember that even though a `SimpleListWithIterator` object has an array member, it is definitely not an array. It is an instance of a class. And classes, even those with array members, are not automatically passed by reference.

The first formal argument, `one`, is also a class type argument. We made it a reference argument. If we had made it a pass-by-value argument instead, any invocation of `takeEvens()` would create a local object for the formal argument, initializing it with the corresponding actual argument. Think what that means. A temporary `SimpleListWithIterator` object would be created and initialized by all of the data associated with the actual argument. That data includes an array of 100 `int`s as well as two other `int`s for the size and the cursor.

Rather than create a new, temporary `SimpleListWithIterator` object, we simply pass that first argument by reference. This effectively passes the address of an object (which is small) rather than the value of an object (which, in this case, is large).

> When you define a function with a formal class type argument, make the formal argument a reference argument. If the function is not supposed to change the corresponding actual argument, make the formal argument a const reference argument.

An unfortunate consequence to our decision to include the iterator as part of the list is that it is impossible to iterate over a const `SimpleListWithIterator`. Thus, we could not have the first formal argument type be `const SimpleListWithIterator&`. There are some ways around this. But the most elegant way to deal with the problem involves keeping the iterator as a separate object outside the class itself. We will discuss that strategy in Chapter 12.

7.4 ▍ Constructors revisited

A class constructor is a special member function used to initialize the data members of instances of the class. Creating an object of a class type requires two actions: allocating space for the object and constructing the object within that space. In short, constructing an object involves initializing the data members of the object. The purpose of most constructors is to make sure the initialization creates an object that is a legitimate instance of the class. However, a constructor is a function, complete with argument list and a function body. So it can do more than just initialize class members.

The constructor for a `SimpleList` initializes the list as an empty list. The constructor for a `Date` initializes all of its data members . Here again is that definition of the `Date` class. `Date` has one constructor, which is a public member of the class.

```
class Date {
public:
    Date(int d, int m, int y); // Initializes Date to day d, month m, year y.
```

```
   int theDay() const;        // Day of this date.
   int theMonth() const;      // Month of this date.
   int theYear() const;       // Year of this date.
   void advance();            // Advances this date to the following day.

private:
   int day_;
   int month_;
   int year_;
};
```

In order to create a new `Date` object, it is necessary to fill in the actual expressions that correspond to the formal arguments of the constructor. With a `Date` class definition such as this one, it is impossible to create a new instance of a `Date` without telling explicitly which three integer values will be used to initialize the new object. In that respect, a `Date` is far different from an `int`. You can create an `int` without explicitly initializing it.

All of this may be of trivial consequence for the `Date` class. But it may not. Both of these definitions are illegal.

```
Date yesterday;            // illegal! Must be initialized with 3 ints
Date arrayOfDates[100];    // illegal! All 100 Dates must be initialized
                           //            with 3 ints
```

When a `Date` object is created, a constructor is automatically called. Think of how the compiler can make that call take place. Since the constructor is a function with three arguments, a definition for a `Date` type object must somehow show three actual values for those arguments.

The definitions of `yesterday` and `arrayOfDates` lacked information to tell what those actual arguments to the constructor are. The definition of `yesterday` requires one call to the constructor, but the illegal "definition" does not specify the actual arguments. The illegal definition `arrayOfDates` is more complicated yet, since it would involve 100 calls to the constructor, creating a different object for each array element.

There is a reasonable way around this roadblock. In addition to its current constructor, the `Date` class needs a **null constructor**, a class constructor that requires no arguments. Before we can show you how to incorporate a null constructor into the current version of the `Date` class, we first need to explain another feature of C++, overloaded functions.

Overloaded functions

We have alluded to *constructors* for a class rather than *the* constructor for a class—emphasis on the plural. So a class can have more than a single constructor. Let's change the definition of the `Date` class so that it has two constructors rather than one. The first constructor will be the original constructor with three arguments.

The second constructor will be the null constructor. It will not have any arguments. Of course, both constructors must be named `Date`, which is the same as the name of the class.

```
class Date {
public:
    Date(int d, int m, int y);          // Original 3-argument constructor
    Date();                             // Null constructor
    int theDay() const;
    int theMonth() const;
    int theYear() const;
    void advance();
private:
    int day_;
    int month_;
    int year_;
};
```

The definition of a null constructor may have no initialization list and an empty body, in which case it truly performs no explicit initialization. Or the definition of a null constructor may have some initialization code. The single constructor for the `SimpleList` is a null constructor, and it does contain initialization code. We'll put in some initialization code for `Date`'s new null constructor so that a new object created when this constructor is called will contain legitimate data.

Since the purpose of the constructor is to give a new object legitimate data, we need to decide which date we want a new object to represent. That choice is arbitrary. We happen to like the last day of the twentieth century, December 31, 2000.

The definitions for the two constructors can be written in the following way:

```
// Original constructor
Date :: Date(int d, int m, int y) : day_(d), month_(m), year_(y)
{ }

// Null constructor
Date :: Date() : day_(31), month_(12), year_(2000)
{ }
```

How can the compiler tell the difference between these two constructors? How does it know which one is being called? The compiler looks at the signatures of the constructors to decide which one should be called when a `Date` type object is created. (Recall that the signature of a function is the function declaration without names of the formal arguments.) In our example, if a `Date` type object is defined with three arguments, the original constructor is called. If a `Date` type object is defined with no arguments, the null constructor is called.

Given the new definition for the `Date` class, here are three valid definitions for `Date` objects. For the first instance, the original constructor is called. In the second, the null constructor is called. In the third, the null constructor is called for the 100 objects that are the elements of the array. That third declaration is possible only because the null constructor is declared in the new version of the Date class.

```
Date hisBirthDate(3,5,1954);    // hisBirthDate is April 3, 1954
Date someDay;                   // someDay is December 31, 2000
Date goodDays[100];             // 100 Dates representing December 31, 2000
```

> The definition of an instance of a class that has a null constructor must *not* contain empty parentheses after the name of the object.
>
> ```
> Date someday();    // Wrong!  This does not create a
>                    // Date object.
>                    //   This is considered to be a
>                    //   function prototype.
> ```
>
> The compiler treats this code as a declaration of a function named someday, which returns a Date and has no arguments!

Other functions besides constructors can have the same names, too. It is possible to have several member functions of the same class with the same name. It is also possible for several different functions that are not even part of a class to have the same name. **Function overloading** means defining two different functions with the same name and in the same scope.

The constructors in the Date class are overloaded, since there are two of them. The following two functions are also overloaded and not part of any class. They have file scope rather than class scope. The first function exchanges the contents of two integer arguments and the second function exchanges the contents of two floating point arguments.

```
void swap(int& x, int& y);
void swap(double& x, double& y);
```

The two functions differ only in the types of arguments. The first swap() has int arguments and the second swap() has double arguments.

How does the compiler know when to use the first swap() and when to use the second? It uses **argument matching**, a process that compares the actual arguments one by one with the corresponding formal arguments. The compiler looks at the actual arguments in the call to swap(). If they are int arguments, the compiler calls the first swap(). If they are double arguments, the compiler calls the second swap().[9] This is illustrated by the following code:

---

[9] If both of the actual arguments are neither int nor double, then the compiler has a list of obscure rules governing "odd" cases in order to determine which function to call.

```
int i = 27;
int j = 35;
double z = .98;
double w = 12.1;
swap(i,j);          // swap(int&, int&) is called
swap(z,w);          // swap(double&, double&) is called
```

The argument lists distinguish between two functions with the same name. Two overloaded functions can have different return types, but the return types alone are not enough to distinguish them. If two functions are overloaded, their formal argument lists must differ in the number of arguments or the types of arguments or both.

Default arguments

It is possible to rewrite the definition of the Date class so that is has a single constructor declaration that can do the work of the two different declarations. With the appropriate constructor declaration, the following four kinds of definitions for Date objects are legal:

```
Date hisBirthDate(3,5,1954);    // hisBirthDate is April 3, 1954
Date someDay;                   // someDay is December 31, 2000
Date anotherDay(3,8);           // anotherDay is August 3, 2000
Date yetAnother(15);            // yetAnother is December 15, 2000
```

The number of arguments in these definitions varies from none (for someDay) through three (for hisBirthDate). So the Date class must have the equivalent at least four constructors: one with no arguments, one with a single argument, one with two arguments, and one with three arguments. The way C++ accomplishes this in a single constructor declaration is through **default arguments**. A function with default arguments automatically supplies values for missing actual arguments in calls to the function.[10]

The comments accompanying the last four definitions indicate that the default arguments for a Date constructor are 31 for the first argument (corresponding to the day), 12 for the second argument (corresponding the month), and 2000 for the third argument (corresponding to the year). Here is a new definition for the Date class, which has a constructor with default arguments capable of handling those last four object definitions.

```
class Date {
public:
```

---

[10] A constructor with all default arguments ought to serve as a null constructor. That is not true for all C++ compilers. In order to make an array of Dates, we may also have to declare two constructors. One is the null constructor (which would initialize the data members with the old default argument values) and another is a constructor that requires at least one actual argument.

```
    Date(int d = 31, int m = 12, int y = 2000);  // Constructs a date with
                                    //    default values 31 (day), 12 (month), and
                                    //    2000 (year).
                                    //    ASSUME: m/d/y is a valid date.
    int theDay() const;             // Day of this date.
    int theMonth() const;           // Month of this date.
    int theYear() const;            // Year of this date.
    void advance();                 // Advances this date to the following day.
private:
    int day_;
    int month_;
    int year_;
};
```

This latest version of the Date class has only one constructor declaration. The three constructor arguments have the default values 31, 12, and 2000. The definition of the new constructor is absolutely identical to the definition of the original three-argument Date constructor.

```
Date :: Date(int d, int m, int y) : day_(d), month_(m), year_(y)
{ }
```

The default values do not show up in the argument list in the constructor definition. They appear only in the declaration.

When the Date object named yetAnother is created with the definition

```
Date yetAnother(15);              // yetAnother is December 15, 2000
```

the constructor itself supplies the missing actual arguments. The definition of yetAnother supplies only one actual argument, 15. The constructor supplies the value 12 for the second actual argument and 2000 for the third actual argument.

The first actual argument corresponds to the first formal argument, counting from the left. If we run out of actual arguments and there are still unmatched formal arguments, then the default values of the formal arguments are used. If a Date type object is created with one actual argument, then that argument is used to initialize its day_. The default arguments are used to initialize its month_ and year_. If a Date type object is created with two actual arguments, then the first actual argument is used to initialize its day_ and the second one is used to initialize its month_. If a default argument is used to initialize the object's day_, then default arguments must be used to initialize the object's month_ and the year_ also.

For some compilers, the constructor in the latest version of the Date class merely provides a shorthand way of declaring and defining four different constructors. For those compilers, the latest version of the Date class is almost completely equivalent to the following definition:

```
class Date {
public:
    Date(int d, int m, int y);
    Date(int d, int m);        // year initialized to 2000
    Date(int d);               // year initialized to 2000, month to 12
    Date();                    // year initialized to 2000, month to 12, day to 31
    int theDay() const;
    int theMonth() const;
    int theYear() const;
    void advance();
private:
    int day_;
    int month_;
    int year_;
};
```

The only difference between this version and the default argument version is that with the default arguments, only one constructor must be defined and with the four-constructor version, four constructors must be. Those default arguments provide some shorthand, indeed. They also make reuse of the implementation code easier. Suppose we want different default initialization values. Instead of modifying four constructor definitions, we would need to change only declaration. Furthermore, the actual definition of the constructor with the default values remains the same no matter what those default values are declared to be in the class definition.

One word of caution is in order. If a constructor has all default arguments, then there cannot be an additional constructor with no arguments. No C++ compiler accepts these two declarations in the same class.

```
// These cannot both be declared in Date. The first declaration
//   includes the null constructor.
Date(int d = 1, int m = 1, int y = 2000);
Date();
```

If you think about it carefully enough, it should be clear why both declarations cannot be made. Which constructor would be called when an object is created with no actual arguments? The compiler has no way of knowing. That's why that pair of declarations is illegal.

Default arguments for a constructor (or any function) must be at the end of the argument list. If a function has one default argument, it must be the last one. If it has two, they must be the last two. It is not legal for one of the arguments to be a default argument and a later one not to be a default argument. For example, this is not a valid constructor declaration:

```
Date(int d = 1, int m = 2, int y);   // illegal! y is not a default
```

> Default arguments come at the end of a formal argument list. A nondefault formal argument may not be placed after a default formal argument in the function declaration.

As a final note, just as it is possible to overload ordinary functions (functions with file scope), it is also possible for ordinary functions to have default arguments. Those functions must satisfy the same restriction that class member functions must satisfy. Any default arguments must be at the end of the argument list rather than in the middle or the beginning. Also, if the function has a separate declaration, then the default values appear in the declaration and not in the definition.

Here are two examples of function declarations which have default arguments. Following their declarations are sample calls to them.

```
void promptAndRead(int& aNumber, const char message[] = "");
double slope(double x1, double y1, double x2 = .0, double y2 = .0);
promptAndRead(age, "Enter your age ");

promptAndRead(next);                    // Same as: promptAndRead(next,"");

double z = slope(1.2, 3.4, 5.5, 6.0);
cout << slope(x,y);                     // Same as: cout << slope(x,y,.0,.0);
```

What happens when there isn't any constructor?

Let's rephrase that question. "What happens when a class type object is created for a class that has no constructor?" In truth, there is no such situation. A class always has a constructor, even if the programmer never bothered to write one. If a class has no explicitly written constructor, then C++ automatically provides a **default constructor**. The default constructor is a null constructor because it has no arguments. If a class does have at least one explicitly declared constructor, then C++ does not provide a default constructor.

Let's go back to the beginning of this chapter when we discussed structs. We did not include a constructor in the definition of the `DateStruct`. In fact, we did not even mention the existence of member functions in that first section. We used structs as aggregates, simply to group data together and nothing else. However, recall what we said about the difference between classes and structs. Programmers generally use structs to group different data into a single type (to implement object attributes). They use classes to implement objects with attributes and behaviors. What we just said describes a convention of C++ programming. As far as a C++ compiler is concerned, the only difference between classes and structs is that unless indicated otherwise, a member of a struct is public and a member of a class is private. A programmer who bothers to do so can write a constructor or any other member function for a struct.

Since the `DateStruct` has no explicitly written constructor, the language automatically provides a default constructor. What does a default constructor do to initialize the members of the class or struct? If the member is itself another class type, then a constructor for that other class will be called. If the member is a built-in type such as an `int`, then there might not be initialization with a special value. That means the value of that `int` member may be garbage until some attempt is made to give it a legitimate value. There is no guarantee about what happens. Some compilers will initialize with specific values, some will not.

7.5 ▐ A class with string data

In the previous chapter, we created a typedef, `nameType`, for a C-string. Typedefs provide a naming mechanism. They do not create new types. Classes are used to create new types. Occasionally, programmers define classes to use in place of built-in types. We will create a new class just to represent people's names. We will use this class instead of the old typedef.

The definition of the class `Name`, a very simple class, is shown below. A `Name` type object can be created from a C-string (array of characters). Its value can be converted to a string value, and it can print itself.

```
// Type for representing a person's name with 49 characters or less.
class Name {
public:
   Name(const char n[] = "");        // Creates a name from n, using at most
                                      //   the first 50 characters from n, up to
                                      //   and including the terminating '\0'.
   void copyToString(char target[]); // Copies the characters of the name to
                                      //   target.
                                      // ASSUME: target array >= 50 elements.
   void print() const;               // Prints the name to cout.
private:
   enum {maxName_ = 50};
   char name_[maxName_];
};
```

The definitions of the member functions are straightforward. The constructor makes sure that no overflow can occur as characters from the argument are copied into the array data member.

```
Name :: Name(const char n[])
{
```

```
      for(int i = 0; i < maxName_ - 1 && n[i] != '\0'; i++)
         name_[i] = n[i];
      name_[i] = '\0';
}

void Name :: copyToString(char target[])
{
   strcpy(target, name_);
}

void Name :: print() const
{
   cout << name_;
}
```

The following code illustrates how the new type can be used:

```
Name charles("Chuck");              // charles' name_ is "Chuck"
Name deborah("Deb");                // deborah's name_ is "Deb"
char cString[50] = "Bill";          // cString is "Bill"
Name anonymous;                     // anonymous' name_ is ""
anonymous.copyToString(cString);    // cString is ""
anonymous = deborah;                // anonymous' name_ is "Deb"
anonymous = Name("Hannah");         // anonymous' name_ is "Hannah"
```

The last assignment used an explicit invocation of the Name constructor to create a temporary Name, which could then be assigned to anonymous. Names can be assigned values directly, but strings cannot.

This next segment of code produces output, which is shown in the box that follows.

```
cout << "charles' name is ";
charles.print();
cout "\ndeborah's name is ";
deborah.print();
cout "\nThe anonymous name is ";
anonymous.print();
```

```
charles' name is Chuck
deborah's name is Deb
The anonymous name is Hannah
```

7.6 ■ Classes with class type member data

Our next example models a simple checking account. The account has two attributes: an owner and a balance. It can do what all checking accounts do—deposit money and write checks—and it can tell what its balance is and the name of its owner. The name of the new class is CheckingAccount.

The owner of a checking account will be a name—make that a Name, with a capital N. We can use the Name class that we just constructed in the previous section. So one of the members of the class will be a Name type. In object-oriented lingo, we say that a CheckingAccount *has-a* Name.

Here is the definition of a CheckingAccount class:

```
// A simple checking account type. Each account has an owner and a balance.
class CheckingAccount {
public:
    CheckingAccount(const char n[] = "", float b = 0);
                                    // Creates a checking account with an owner
                                    //   named n and beginning balance b.
                                    // ASSUME: length of n < 50; b >= 0.

    float theBalance() const;       // The account balance
    Name theOwner() const;          // Name of the account owner
    void deposit(float amt);        // Credits the balance with amt.
                                    // ASSUME: amt >= 0.
    void writeCheck(float amt);     // If the current balance is >= amt, amt is
                                    //   debited from the balance, else nothing
                                    //   nothing is changed.
                                    // ASSUME: amt >= 0.
private:
    float balance_;
    Name owner_;
};
```

Let's look at the CheckingAccount constructor first. There are two different ways to write the constructor. We'll use an initialization list, and then we'll show how it could be written without an initialization list.

```
CheckingAccount :: CheckingAccount(const char n[], float b) :
                                    balance_(b), owner_(n)
{ }
```

The initialization list form initializes the member owner_ by using the argument n. Recall that a Name can be constructed from a C-string. The Name construc-

tor shows how that is done. Indeed, the compiler will invoke the `Name` constructor
to initialize `owner_` from n.

We can also assign a value to `owner_` inside the body of the `Checking-
Account` constructor. The assignment statement uses an invocation of the `Name`
constructor to create a temporary `Name` to be assigned to `owner_`. The following
definition is an alternative to the first `CheckingAccount` constructor definition.

```
// Alternative definition for the constructor.
CheckingAccount :: CheckingAccount(const char n[], float b) : balance_(b),
{
    owner_ = Name(n);   // Create a temporary Name from n; assign it to owner_.
}
```

Here are the definitions of the remaining `CheckingAccount` member functions. The member function `theOwner()` returns a `Name` that is a copy of the value
of `owner_`.

```
Name CheckingAccount :: theOwner() const
{
    return owner_;
}


float CheckingAccount :: theBalance() const
{
    return balance_;
}


void CheckingAccount :: deposit(float amt)
{
    balance_ += amt;
}


void CheckingAccount :: writeCheck(float amt)
{
    if (balance_ >= amt)
        balance_ -= amt;
}
```

We'll define a couple of `CheckingAccount` objects to show how the class can
be used. The `CheckingAccount` constructor has a default argument. It serves as a
null constructor, a constructor that can create an object from a C-string, and a constructor that can create an object from a C-string and a `float`.

```
CheckingAccount hisAcct("Jim");      // hisAcct's owner is Jim; it has
                                     //  a zero balance
```

```
CheckingAccount herAcct("Jan", 500); // herAcct's owner is Jan; it has a
                                     //   balance of $500
```

The documentation for the class says that any client code using the CheckingAccount class is responsible for making sure that no account is initialized with a negative balance and that the check and deposit amounts are nonnegative. Furthermore, before a request to write a check is made, it is probably a good idea to make sure that there is enough money in the account to write the check.

```
hisAcct.deposit(65.50);                // hisAcct balance is $65.50
if (herAcct.theBalance() >= 34.95)
   herAcct.writeCheck(34.95);          // herAcct balance is $465.05
hisAcct.deposit(75);                   // hisAcct balance is $140.50
```

If we send a message to herAcct to write a check for more than the balance, then nothing happens.

```
herAcct.writeCheck(400.0);             // herAcct balance is $65.05
herAcct.writeCheck(80.0);              // herAcct balance is not big enough
                                       //   to write a check for $80.00
```

The next segment of code shows how the member functions theOwner() and theBalance() can be used to output the values of the checking account attributes.

```
cout << setiosflags(ios::fixed) << setprecision(2);
cout << "Account of ";
hisAcct.theOwner().print();
cout << " has a balance of $" << hisAcct.theBalance() << endl;

cout << "Account of ";
herAcct.theOwner().print();
cout << " has a balance of $" << herAcct.theBalance() << endl;
```

The output generated by those last two statements is as follows.

```
Account of Jim has a balance of $140.50
Account of Jan has a balance of $465.05
```

In order to print the name of the owner of the checking account, we must pay attention to the fact that theOwner() returns a Name, not a string. The syntax for printing the name requires using two methods of two different classes, theOwner() and print().

7.7 An inventory table class

Here's a new problem to work on, or at least one that is almost new. We'll tackle the following problem, which we introduced briefly in the Chapter 6.

> A hardware store keeps track of the items it sells according to their bar codes and prices. Maintain that inventory so that new items can be added, old items can be removed, and prices for individual items can be changed.

Let's step back for a minute. Look at the problem from the standpoint of the clerk who is going to use the program. The clerk wants to be able to inventory items based on their bar codes. What kinds of things could the clerk expect? Here are some reasonable ideas. Items will be identified by their bar codes. Two different items ought to have two different bar codes. The clerk needs to be able to update the inventory by adding new items, removing old ones, and changing the prices on some. How the entire inventory will be maintained inside the computer is not the clerk's concern.

What about the objects that are part of the solution to the problem? What *types* of objects are going to be useful? Clearly one type of object is needed to represent a single hardware store item. And another type of object will be needed for the inventory itself. The inventory is a special kind of list in which items are identified according to their unique lookup keys (bar codes in this example). Such a list is often called a lookup table. The lookup table for this problem will be capable of modification.

There is a lot of flexibility in how we might continue the analysis. Throughout our analysis and design, we are going to make decisions based partly on our need to illustrate some language features and partly on the need to solve the problem as we have viewed it.

In a real hardware store, there is much information about each type of item that the store owner and the customers probably find useful. Examples of such information include a description of the item, the quantity of that item currently in stock, the date the item was last ordered, a bar code identifier for the item, the current price of the item, and so on. We are not going to use all of those for the item attributes. Two simple attributes, the bar code and the price, will suffice for our hardware items. The behavior of a hardware item is minimal—so minimal that in our design we can think ahead to the implementation of a hardware item type as a struct rather than a class. So we will design our hardware item type to be a data object type.

Now for the inventory itself. A list of bar codes and corresponding prices is shown in Fig. 7.6. To find an item in the table, look for its bar code. The bar codes are the lookup keys. Two different items cannot have the same key, and the same item cannot appear twice in the table.

Notice that we have not mentioned anything about how the inventory table is ordered. This is not a concern for the clerk, nor is it a concern for us at this point either. Indeed the table will take care of its own ordering.

Bar code	Price
01383467	12.87
49001345	.68
11105431	7.79
30991457	234.50
. . .	. . .

Figure 7.6 Lookup table configuration. The bar codes are keys.

What about the table's attributes? The table ought to know its items at the very least. It will know its size, too. We will incorporate an iterator object into the table. The iterator has a cursor into the list of hardware items. So the table will know the iterator's cursor. The table will be able to set that cursor to the beginning of the list of hardware items, get the next item, and tell if there are additional items. The iterator allows the table to tell what its items are, one at a time, starting with the first item.

What about behaviors that are not iterator behaviors? An inventory table should be able to initialize itself as an empty table with no items and tell whether or not it is full (whether there is any room for expansion). In order to be of any use in the hardware store, an inventory table will be able to find out whether or not it contains an item with a particular bar code. If it can find an item with that bar code, the table will to be able to remove it from its inventory, look up its price, or change its price. If no item with that bar code is in the table, the table will to be able to add a new item with that bar code and a specified price.

The following box is our analysis so far of the inventory table.

Object type: Inventory table of items with different bar codes
    Knows:
        Its items
        How many items are currently in its inventory
        Its cursor (an iterator attribute)
    Can do:
        Initialize itself as an inventory table with no items
        Tell whether or not it is full
        Add an item to the inventory
        Remove an item from the inventory according to its bar code
        Find the price of an item in the inventory according to its bar code
        Set the iterator to start at the beginning of the list
            (iterator behavior)
        Tell the next item in the inventory (iterator behavior)
        Tell if there are additional inventory items (iterator behavior)

At this point, we can specify the interface of hardware item objects and inventory table objects. In fact, we can actually write that design in code, as struct and class definitions. Coding of member functions must come later when the class is implemented.

Design specification—a class definition

Let's start with the definition of the `HardwareItem` type. We already decided to make the `HardwareItem` a struct. So its definition shows two data members for its attributes, `barCode` and `price`.

```
// Item in a hardware store, identified by its unique bar code
struct HardwareItem {
    int barCode;            // Bar code for the hardware item
    float price;            // Price of the item.  (price >= 0.0)
};
```

We can complete the design of the inventory table by writing its class definition and accompanying documentation. The documentation, which is essential, makes the definition of the `InventoryTable` class somewhat long. However, the class definition is the place where full documentation that describes how to use an object of this class type belongs. In particular, notice that an `InventoryTable` maintains a table for which the hardware items have nonnegative prices. Programmers who use the `InventoryTable` class and fail to observe that convention could corrupt their `InventoryTable` objects.

A class definition serves two different purposes: (1) to be source code for the compiler and (2) to show the design of the class through specifications of its interface. The interface is the common boundary between the class and the client code that uses an `InventoryTable` object. The definition shows the class what it has to be able to do, and it shows the client code what it should expect the class to be able to do.

```
// Description of an inventory of hardware store items.  The key for each
//   item is its bar code.  The value for each item is its price.  Bar codes
//   are unique; prices are nonnegative.
class InventoryTable {
public:
    InventoryTable();                   // Creates an empty inventory.

    bool isFull() const;                // Is the inventory at maximum
                                        //    capacity?
    double find(int code) const;        // The price of the item with code
                                        //    for its key.  If no such item
                                        //    exists, -1 is returned.
    void update(int code, float newPrice);// If an item with code for its
                                        //    key is in the inventory, its
```

```
                                              //    price becomes newPrice. If no
                                              //     such item exists, no changes.
                                              // ASSUME: newPrice >= 0.0.
       void add(int code, float price);       // If the inventory is not full and
                                              //   no item with code for its key is
                                              //   in the inventory, an item with
                                              //   the given code and price is
                                              //   added.  Otherwise the
                                              //   inventory is unchanged.
                                              // ASSUME: price >= 0.0.
       void remove(int code);                 // If the inventory contains an item
                                              //   with the given code (key), it is
                                              //   removed. Otherwise the
                                              //   inventory is unchanged.


       // The iterator
       void setIterator();                    // Sets the iterator to the beginning
                                              //    of the inventory.
       const HardwareItem& next();            // The next item.
                                              //     ASSUME: there is a next item.
       bool more() const;                     // Is there another item?

private:
    enum {maxInventory_ = 5000};
    HardwareItem inventory_[maxInventory_];
    int size_;
    int cursor_;
    int position(int code) const;
};
```

Before we get into the definitions of the member functions of the inventory table, we need to rethink its organization. We have already decided that the table will not contain two entries with the same bar code. The ordering of the individual items in the table is another matter, and the decision we have made for this implementation is arbitrary. The table will not be ordered. That makes inserting a new item into the table an easy task. But it also means that in order to find a particular item, we may have to look at every item in the table before we find it (or before we find that it is not in the table). We will leave it to you as an exercise to rewrite the definitions of the class methods so that the items are ordered and so that searching takes advantage of that ordering.

Implementation of the `InventoryTable` class

The `InventoryTable` class definition is both a design for the class as well as a part of the implementation. The definitions of the member function complete the implementation. We'll write those definitions starting with the simplest ones.

The constructor will set `size_` to 0. That is identical to the constructor for the `SimpleList` class. The constructors for both the `SimpleList` class and the `InventoryTable` class are null constructors, since they have no arguments.

```
InventoryTable :: InventoryTable() : size_(0)
{ }
```

The definition of `isFull()` is easy to write. The definition relies on `maxInventory_` as well as the value of `size_`, which are both private.

```
bool InventoryTable :: isFull() const
{
    return (size_ == maxInventory_);
}
```

If we were to write code that creates and uses an `InventoryTable` type object, would we need to know anything about the class other than what is in the public section? Would we need to know that the inventory items are maintained in an array? No. All we must know is what messages can be sent to an `InventoryTable`, how to send them, and what to expect as a result. The actual position of any particular `HardwareItem` in the inventory is of no interest to us. We do not want to have to instruct the `InventoryTable` where to insert or where to remove an item. All we need to do is tell the `InventoryTable` what we want to be inserted and removed. The `InventoryTable` takes care of where.

In light of that, we have hidden the gritty bookkeeping details about the positions of items in the inventory (or the positions of where they should be) inside the class methods for `find()`, `update()`, `add()`, and `remove()`. All of those methods use code that searches the inventory for the location of a particular bar code. In the case of `add()`, the search must be done to find out whether or not the item is already in the inventory. The inventory table does not allow duplicate bar codes.

By defining the member function `position()`, we can avoid duplication of the searching code in the definitions for `find()`, `update()`, `add()`, and `remove()`. Because it is useful only for the inner workings of the class itself, `position()` is a private member function. Since a programmer who creates and uses an `InventoryTable` object does not need to know about the array implementation or item positions, `position()` provides no useful behavior outside the definitions for the class methods.

```
int InventoryTable :: position(int code) const
// Returns: The position of the item in the inventory with code for its key,
//    if it exists.  Otherwise, size_ is returned.
{
    int i;                           // Array subscript
    for (i = 0; i < size_; i++)
        if (inventory_[i].barCode == code)
            return i;                // Here is the item, return its subscript
```

```
    return size_;                       // The item is not in the inventory
}
```

See how easy it is to write the definitions of the rest of the member functions
now that we have position(). Each member function begins the same way, by
defining a local variable to serve as the location of the item whose bar code matches the one it is sent. Each one then calls position() to figure out whether and
where an item is in the inventory.

```
double InventoryTable :: find(int code) const
{
    int i = position(code);             // Location of the item with this
                                        //    code for its key
    if (i < size_)                      // If the item is in the inventory
        return inventory_[i].price;     //    return its price
    return -1.0;                        // Otherwise, return -1
}


void InventoryTable :: update(int code, float newPrice)
{
    int i = position(code);               // Location of the item with this
                                          //    code for its key
    if (i < size_)                        // If the item is in the inventory
        inventory_[i].price = newPrice;   //    update its price
}


void InventoryTable :: add(int code, float price)
{
    int i = position(code);               // Location of the item with this
                                          //    code for its key
    if (i == size_ && !isFull()) {        // If the item is not in the inventory
        inventory_[size_].barCode = code; //    and the table is not full,
        inventory_[size_].price = price;  //       add the new item
        size_++;
    }
}


void InventoryTable :: remove(int code)
{
    int i = position(code);                 // Location of the item with this
                                            //    code for its key
    if (i < size_) {                        // If the item is in the inventory
        for (int j = i; j < size_ - 1; j++) //    remove it
            inventory_[j] = inventory_[j + 1];
        size_--;
    }
}
```

The last three member functions for the `InventoryTable` class are all iterator behaviors. The cursor for the iterator is hidden in the private section of the `InventoryTable` class. After all, only the iterator needs to have access to the cursor.

```cpp
void InventoryTable :: setIterator()
{
    cursor_ = 0;
}

const HardwareItem& InventoryTable :: next()
{
    return inventory_[cursor_++];
}

bool InventoryTable :: more() const
{
    return (cursor_ < size_);
}
```

Look at the return type for `next()`. It is a **constant reference type**. Reference comes from `&` and constant comes from `const`. To say that `next()` returns a reference type means `next()` returns an object—the name of an object, to be precise. But the `const` part says that you cannot use that name to change the object. You can use the name just to look at the object. That is similar to passing an array to a function by constant reference. The function can look at the array, but it cannot change any of its elements.

The object that `next()` returns is the element of the `HardwareItem` array member of the `InventoryTable`, which has `cursor_` for its index. If `stock` is the name of an `InventoryTable`, then `stock.next()` is another name for an element of `stock`'s array. Rather than create a new, temporary `HardwareItem` and return that temporary, `next()` simply returns the name of a `HardwareItem` that already exists. Returning constant reference types from functions is a very common C++ programming practice.

If you define a function which returns a reference type (a type ending in `&`), be careful about selecting the object to be returned. A reference type gives another name for an object, and objects have lifetimes. If your function returns an object whose lifetime is only the time of execution of the function, then the reference to it will be of little value to the calling code—the object will die before it can be used.

Objects that do not die when functions returning them quit execution include the following:

- Global objects

- Static objects

- Objects that are part of an instance of a class with suitable lifetime

- Reference arguments to the functions

   Do not define a function that returns a reference type (constant or otherwise) as returning a local, nonstatic object or a formal value argument.

Using an `InventoryTable` object

This sequence of statements shows how an `InventoryTable` object can be used by a client program. The sequence creates an `InventoryTable` object named `stock`. Then it sends `stock` messages to `add()`, `update()`, `find()`, and `remove()`.

```
InventoryTable stock;           // Creates an empty inventory
stock.add(3042,7.68);           // The inventory has one item
stock.add(7909,8.74);           // The inventory has two items
stock.add(1009,.65);            // The inventory has three items
if (stock.find(3101) < 0.0)
   stock.add(3101,1.00);        // The inventory has four items
```

Figure 7.7 shows the `stock` data at this point.

Here are three additional messages to `stock`. The second message, which is a request to remove an item that is not in the inventory, results in no change.

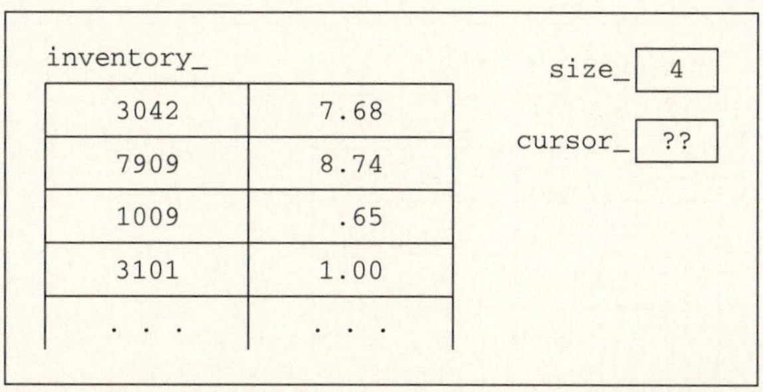

Figure 7.7 The `stock` data after four successive `add` messages.

```
stock.update(1009,3.75);    // Changes the price of item with bar code 1009
stock.remove(1000);         // Does not change the table
stock.remove(7909);         // Removes the item with bar code 7909
```

Figure 7.8 illustrates the `stock`'s new view of its inventory and member data. If we look merely at the inventory array and not at the size, then we might believe that the inventory contains two copies of the item with bar code 3101 and price 1.00. But the size indicates that the second copy of this item is not actually in the inventory. The inventory includes only the first three items.

As another example of client code that uses an `InventoryTable`, the function `averagePrice()` computes the average price of the items in an `Inventory-Table`. It returns 0 if the inventory is empty.

```
double averagePrice(InventoryTable& t)
{
   double sum = 0.0;            // Sum of prices added so far
   int i = 0;                   // Count of items added so far

   t.setIterator();            // Set the iterator to the beginning
   while (t.more()) {          // Find the total price and total number
      i++;                     //   of items in the inventory.
      sum += t.next().price;
   }
   if (i > 0)                   // if the inventory was not empty,
      return sum/i;            //    return the average price.
   return 0.0;                 // Otherwise, return 0.
}
```

The argument type for `averagePrice()` is `InventoryTable&`. We would like to make the argument a value argument or at least a constant reference argument. After all, `averagePrice()` should not change the actual `InventoryTable`.

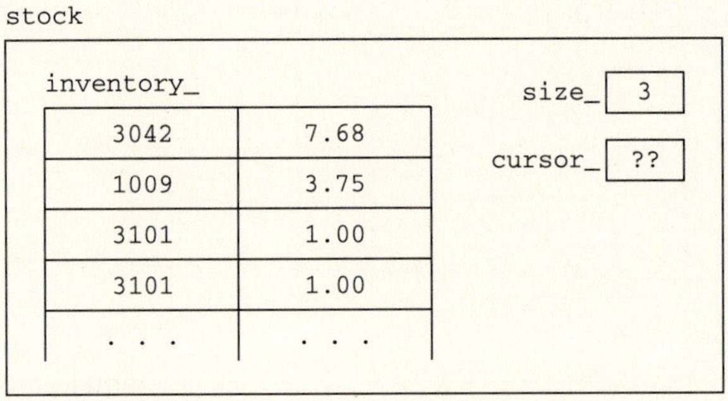

stock

inventory_		size_	3
3042	7.68	cursor_	??
1009	3.75		
3101	1.00		
3101	1.00		
. . .	. . .		

Figure 7.8 The `stock` data after `update` and `remove` messages.

We could not make the argument a constant reference argument because of the iterator. A non-const member function cannot be invoked on a const object (the formal argument in this case). So what would happen if the argument were passed by value instead of reference? In that case, a new object would be created and initialized by the value of the actual argument whenever the function is invoked. That means an entire `InventoryTable`, including its array member with 5,000 elements, would be created and initialized with the actual argument. That amounts to a duplication of a large amount of memory.

The body of the loop in the definition of `averagePrice()` may appear strange to you. The last statement in the body is this:

```
sum += t.next().price;
```

Remember that `t.next()` is the name of a `HardwareItem`. The price, of course, is `t.next().price`. The periods in that expression associate left to right. In other words, the expression is the same as `(t.next()).price`.

Our implementation of the `InventoryTable` class is not particularly efficient. If a `find()` message is sent immediately before an `update()`, then the `InventoryTable` methods will make two calls in a row to `position()`. The first is for the `find()`, the second is for the `update()`. That is an inefficiency that many programmers would find unpleasant if not intolerable. We'll show how to change the implementation of `position()` to solve that double-call problem in the exercises at the end of this chapter.

> Keep in mind that efficiency is not the first concern you should have when designing an object and implementing your design in code. It is much more important to write correct code. As a beginning programmer, focus first on writing code that works.

7.8   The changemaker revised—with classes

We are about to make some big changes in a solution to the old changemaker problem. The original problem statement from Chapter 1 was as follows.

> Write a computer program that can take an amount and computes the count of bills and coins of each denomination required to sum to the amount.

We have been alluding to the remaking of the changemaker solution since the beginning of the book. Indeed, we have already made two substantial revisions over the code that was in Chapter 1. In our original analysis and design, we came up with five different objects: (1) an input object, (2) an output object, (3) a cash drawer object, (4) a computing object, and (5) a teller object. In that first solution, the only way a reader could recognize the connection between the objects in the design and the objects in the program was through comments in the code. The second version (from Chapter 3), refined some of the connections between design objects and code objects. In that chapter, we implemented the behaviors of some of the objects as functions. Each function definition was a method that an object used for one of its behaviors.

The object that gives the changemaker solution its unique flavor is the cash drawer, the object that helped us devise the original algorithm that determined how the money should be given out. In Chapter 6, we recognized that the cash drawer object was actually a list of denominations of U.S. currency. Since that version of the changemaker problem dealt with denominations of $20 bills and smaller, the currency list (the list of denominations in U.S. currency) contained only eight denominations. (We gave up on $2 bills, Susan B. Anthony dollar coins, and 50-cent pieces.) The currency list was implemented in the previous chapter by two parallel arrays, one for the value of each of the eight denominations and one for the name of each denomination.

In the version of the changemaker that we are about to present, the cash drawer's attribute is still a currency list. But the cash drawer is no longer going to have minimal behavior. It will be able to do things. In the past, the only thing the cash drawer did was to give access to its denominations. The computing object did all of the work, with the help of the cash drawer, of course. The cash drawer was actually a part of the computing object.

Redesigning the cash drawer to have behaviors

Suppose we allow the cash drawer itself to do what the computing object was able to do in the past: compute perfect change. When we make that design modification, the computing object is left with no useful behavior. The computing object perhaps could receive a message to do a computation, then pass it on to the cash drawer to do the actual work. But that does not really make much sense. Why not just do away with the computing object altogether? The design would be simpler. And the code could be simpler too. With that decision, Figure 7.9 becomes the basis for our new design.

The fact that the cash drawer is still a currency list is apparent in the design. But what are the denomination items in the currency list? Even though they did not show up in this design, we can still think of denominations as objects. Each denomination object would have three attributes: a value, a name, and an amount. The value is the monetary value of that denomination in the smallest unit of measurement for the currency. The value of the denomination representing a quarter is 25; the name of that denomination is `"quarters."` If the cash drawer has a limited capacity, then it must know how many of each denomination it contains, the number of bills or coins of that denomination are actually in the cash drawer. That number is the denomination's amount.

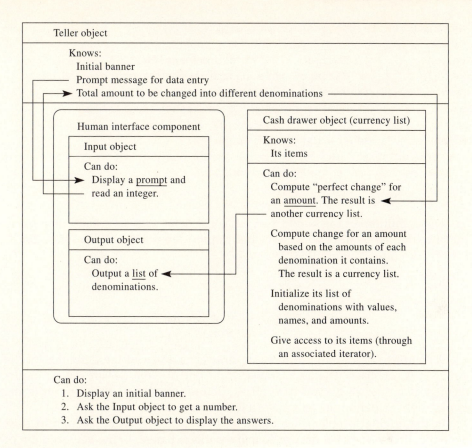

Figure 7.9 The new changemaker solution. Computations are done by the cash drawer.

The attributes and behaviors of a denomination can be described by a struct, `Denomination`. The fact that we decided upon a struct was somewhat arbitrary. We made that choice partly because the behavior of the denomination objects can be minimal. And the struct type seemed like the simplest implementation of such an object.

Even though a `Denomination` object does not have any explicit behaviors, we wrote a `Denomination` constructor. While we would prefer that any code that creates a `Denomination` object be forced to specify at least its value and its name, we wrote the `Denomination` constructor with all default arguments, so that it can be used as a null constructor. This decision makes it possible to have an array of `Denominations`. (In order to have an array of struct or class type elements, the struct or class must have a null constructor or a default constructor.)

```
// Denomination in a cash drawer.  The denomination is identified by its name,
//   its value (in terms of a unit such as pennies), and the number of pieces
```

```
//    of this denomination in the cash drawer slot.
struct Denomination {
    enum {maxNameLen = 9};   // Maximum size of a name string.
    int value;               // Value of this Denomination in units.
    char name[maxNameLen];   // Name of this Denomination.
    int amount;              // Number of this Denomination available.

    Denomination(int v = 1, const char n[] = "pennies", int a = 0);
    // Initializes value, name, and amount with v, n, and a respectively.
    //    ( v >= 0, a >= 0, n is a string of length <= 8)
};
```

The definition for the `Denomination` constructor uses an initialization list to initialize the `value` and `amount`. The body of the definition initializes the `name`.

```
Denomination::Denomination(int v, const char n[], int a): value(v),amount(a)
{
    strcpy(name, n);
}
```

A complete description of the cash drawer is given in the definition of the `CurrencyList` class. The cash drawer from our original design can be implemented as a `CurrencyList` type object. Before we plunge ahead to write the `CurrencyList` definition, let's make a few observations.

In the original problem, we assumed that there would be enough of each denomination in the cash drawer to make perfect change. In the new solution of the problem, we will have two different kinds of currency lists instead of a single cash drawer. In one kind of currency list, the amounts of the denominations are irrelevant. In the other, the amounts are important. The first kind can be used to create a cash drawer with an unlimited supply of each denomination—a perfect cash drawer. The second kind of currency list can be used to create a cash drawer with limited amounts. The amount of each denomination in such a cash drawer restricts what can be given out in response to a request to make change.

That second kind of currency list, in which the amounts of the available denominations matter, will be important when the computing object returns the change. The change will be an instance of `CurrencyList`, with the amounts indicating how much of each denomination is used to constitute the total amount of money to change.

Where do the amounts come from and how do they influence the creation of a `CurrencyList` object? The responsibility of figuring out those amounts belongs to the code that creates `CurrencyList` object. If that code does not specify any amounts, then the `CurrencyList` object that is being created will assume that the amounts are meaningless. In that situation, the only kind of change the `CurrencyList` object should be asked to make is perfect change. But if the code that creates a `CurrencyList` object does know the amounts, then those amounts

must be communicated to a constructor when the object is created. A cash drawer
that is implemented as a `CurrencyList` with amounts can be asked not only to
compute perfect change, as if there were enough of each denomination to do so, but
also to make exact change if that is possible with the amounts it currently contains.

There will be two different `CurrencyList` constructors, one for each kind of
currency list. The first constructor will be used to create a `CurrencyList` with the
eight denomination values and names, as was done for all of the previous solutions to this problem. The other constructor will be used to create a `Currency-`
`List` with the eight denomination values, names, and amounts. Any code that
defines that latter type of `CurrencyList` object must send enough numbers to
initialize each of the different denomination counts.

```
// A list of the eight denominations that make up U.S. currency: $20 bills,
//    $10 bills, $5 bills, $1 bills, quarters, dimes, nickels, and pennies.
class CurrencyList {
public:
    CurrencyList ( );    // Initializes the name and value of each denomination
                         // All amounts are set to 0.
    CurrencyList (const int amt[]);
                         // Initializes the name and value of each denomination
                         //    Amounts are initialized by the elements of amt.
                         //    (The first element is the amount of $20s, the
                         //    second is the amount of $10s, etc.)
                         // ASSUME: amt has 8 elements; all are nonnegative.


    // Iterator
    void setIterator();         // Sets the iterator to the list beginning.
    const Denomination& next(); // The next Denomination.
                                //    ASSUME: there is a next Denomination.
    bool more() const;          // True if there are additional Denominations

    CurrencyList perfectChange(int amountToChange) const;
        // Returns: An optimal currency list whose total value is amountToChange
        //    For each Denomination in the return list, the total value of the
        //    smaller Denominations is less than the value of that Denomination.
        // ASSUME: amountToChange >= 0
    CurrencyList change(int amountToChange, bool& success);
        // Returns: If possible, the optimal currency list in which the total
        //    value of its items is amountToChange and in which the amount of
        //    each denomination does not exceed its amount in this list.
        // Side effects:  If is possible to make change, the amount of each
        //    Denomination returned is deducted from the amount of the
        //    corresponding Denomination in this list.
        // (success - out - Was it possible to make change?)
        // ASSUME: The cash drawer list has been assigned amounts for each
        //    Denomination; amountToChange >= 0.
```

```
private:
   enum {size_ = 8};
   Denomination denom_[size_];
   int cursor_;
};
```

Implementation of the `CurrencyList` class

The definition of the `CurrencyList` class spells out the exact design of a `Currency-List` object. We will go through the methods of the `CurrencyList` one at a time, starting from the top. The first two members of the class are the constructors. The following definitions suffice:

```
CurrencyList :: CurrencyList( )
{
   int denVal[size_] = {2000,1000,500,100,25,10,5,1};
   char denName[size_][Denomination::maxNameLen]= {"twenties", "tens",
                "fives", "ones", "quarters", "dimes", "nickels", "pennies"};
   for (int i = 0; i < size_; i++)
      denom_[i] = Denomination(denVal[i],denName[i]);
}

CurrencyList :: CurrencyList(const int amt[])
{
   int denVal[size_] = {2000,1000,500,100,25,10,5,1};
   char denName[size_][Denomination::maxNameLen]= {"twenties", "tens",
                "fives", "ones", "quarters", "dimes", "nickels", "pennies"};
   for (int i = 0; i < size_; i++)
      denom_[i] = Denomination(denVal[i],denName[i],amt[i]);
}
```

The definitions of the local arrays `denName` and `denVal` are also initializations. `denName` is an array of strings. The length of each string is the enumeration value `maxNameLen`, which was defined in `Denomination`. That is why it appears as `Denomination::maxNameLen`.

Look at the assignment statements in the bodies of the loops. The right-hand sides of those assignments are calls to the constructors to create temporary `Denomination` type objects whose values can be assigned to the left-hand operands. In the loop of the null constructor, `denom_[i]` is assigned a `Denomination` with value of `denVal[i]`, name of `denName[i]`, and `amount` the default value 0.

The iterator declarations follow the constructor declarations. We chose to incorporate the iterator object within the `CurrencyList` class itself. The iterator object uses the data member `cursor_` for its bookkeeping.

```
void CurrencyList :: setIterator()
{
```

```
        cursor_ = 0;
}
const Denomination& CurrencyList :: next()
{
        return denom_[cursor_++];
}
bool CurrencyList :: more() const
{
        return cursor_ < size_;
}
```

The definition of the method for perfectChange() is very similar to the computing object method in the previous two changemaker solutions. It relies on the function divMod(), which performs integer division. (We defined divMod() in Chapter 3.) The divMod() function has four arguments. The first two, which are passed by value, represent a numerator and a denominator. The last two, which are passed by reference, represent the quotient and remainder that result from dividing the denominator into the numerator.

```
CurrencyList CurrencyList :: perfectChange(int amountToChange) const
{
        int amt[size_];                         // Amount of each Denomination to return
        for (int i = 0; i < size_; i++)
            divMod(amountToChange, denom_[i].value, amt[i], amountToChange);
        return CurrencyList(amt);
}
```

The local array named amt is used to create a new CurrencyList. The loop assigns it values through successive calls to divMod(). So amt[0] will be assigned the number of $20 bills to return, amt[1] will be assigned the amount of $10 bills to return, and so on through amt[7], which will be assigned the number of pennies to return. Then amt is used as the argument to the CurrencyList constructor, which is called explicitly in order to create the return value.

Since perfectChange() does not alter the values of any of the data belonging to a CurrencyList, it is a const member function. That is not true for change(). A change() message should be sent only to a cash drawer for which the denomination amounts are meaningful. When a change() message is sent, one of two things will happen: (1) the cash drawer will be unable to make the amount of change requested, in which case it will set a success flag to false or (2) the cash drawer will make the change and deduct the amount of each denomination making up the change from their corresponding amounts in the cash drawer.

```
CurrencyList CurrencyList :: change(int amountToChange, bool& success)
{
        int amt[size_];                         // Number of each Denomination to return
        for (int i = 0; i < size_; i++) {
```

```
        divMod(amountToChange, denom_[i].value, amt[i], amountToChange);
          // Guard against taking more for a Denomination than is available.
        if (amt[i] > denom_[i].amount) {
            amountToChange += (amt[i] - denom_[i].amount) * denom_[i].value;
            amt[i] = denom_[i].amount;
        }
    }
    if (amountToChange == 0)              // There was enough of each denomination
        success = true;                   //   to make change.
    else {
        success = false;                  // There wasn't enough in the currency
        for (i = 0; i < size_; i++)       //   list to make change.  Put back into
            denom_[i].amount += amt[i];   //   the list what had been taken out in
    }                                     //   trying to make change.
    return CurrencyList(amt);
}
```

How are the `Denomination` and `CurrencyList` classes to be used in the new changemaker implementation? Here is one version of a new program that uses the new declarations. This version relies on a library to supply the implementation of the `CurrencyList`.

```
// Name: The changemaker
// Version: 4.0
// Purpose: Determine the count of each denomination from twenty dollar bills
//    down through pennies that constitute a given monetary amount.

#include <iostream.h>
#include "currency.h"

//------------------------------ interfaces --------------------------------
void inputInt(int& aNumber, const char prompt[]);
// Arguments:
//    aNumber - out - The integer entered by the user
//    prompt - Message displayed to the user
// Side effect: Prompts for and reads aNumber.

void outputChange(CurrencyList& list);
// Argument: list - A list of Denominations of a particular currency
// Side effect: Output each item in the list by name and amount on a separate
//    line.

void outputDenom(const Denomination& denomination);
// Argument: denomination - A denomination
// Side effect: Display the amount and the name of the denomination followed
//    by a newline.
//-------------------------- end of interfaces -----------------------------
```

```
//------------------ teller object implementation ------------------------
void main()
{
    cout << "Change Maker (version 4)\n\n";

    CurrencyList cashDrawer;       // The cash drawer
    int amountToChange;            // Amount of money to be changed

    inputInt(amountToChange, "Enter amount to be changed in pennies: ");

    CurrencyList theAnswer = cashDrawer.perfectChange(amountToChange);
    outputChange(theAnswer);
}
//--------------- end of teller object implementation ----------------------

//-------------------- input object implementation ------------------------
void inputInt(int& aNumber, const char prompt[])
{
    cout << prompt;
    cin >> aNumber;
}
//----------------- end of input object implementation --------------------

//------------------- output object implementation -----------------------
void outputDenom(const Denomination& denomination)
{
    cout << denomination.amount << " " << denomination.name << endl;
}

void outputChange(CurrencyList& list)
{
    list.setIterator();
    while (list.more())
        outputDenom(list.next());
}
//----------------- end of output object implementation --------------------
```

This solution of the changemaker problem makes only perfect change. It does not use an ordinary, imperfect cash drawer to make ordinary change. (We will leave it as an exercise to you to write a program that can make ordinary change.) And as you can see, a large amount of code seems to be missing. Where are the declarations for `Denomination` and `CurrencyList`? Where are their class methods defined? Where is the definition for `divMod()`? And what is that strange-looking include directive directly below the include directive for the iostream library?

The complete answers to these questions will come in the next section. Suffice it to say for now that the code that implements the new classes can be organized into a library that this program and other programs will be able to use. The include directives in this program say that it will use libraries that are not physically part of the source code file containing the program.

7.9 Organization of program source code and libraries

Construction of classes can require an extensive amount of code. Indeed, reimplementing the changemaker solution to use classes for the cash drawer object instead of ordinary arrays and functions required a significant amount of additional code. Your immediate question is probably "What did we gain?" And your second question may be "If the amount of source code increases when objects are implemented with classes, how can that code be organized in order for us to be able to manage large programs?" The answers to these two questions are related.

The current functionality of this version of the changemaker program (what the program can do) is no greater than that of the previous version. However, it is easy to look ahead to a couple of features that could enhance that functionality. If we ever need a cash drawer that has only a limited supply of denominations, the code to implement one already exists. It is not the CurrencyList class that will need to be changed in order to take advantage of its additional capability. It is the programs that use the CurrencyList class that will need to be changed. Those programs are CurrencyList clients. The definition of the CurrencyList class and the definitions of its member functions will be the same for the current version of the changemaker program as well as any different version of the program that incorporates the additional capability. Two different programs could share the same code.

Of course, large numbers of programs share code all the time. Whenever a program uses iostreams or the math library, it uses code that is used by countless other programs as well. That's hardly news. But just how do you use those libraries? For the iostream and math libraries, the answer is simple: Put two include directives at the top of the program source file.

```
#include <iostream.h>
#include <math.h>
```

Each of those libraries consists of at least two files. One of the files for a library is a header file. The header file for the iostream library is called iostream.h; for the math library, it is called math.h. Header files are text files. The include directive in your program source code tells the compiler to look at the header file whose name is in brackets to get the declarations contained in that header file. It is as if the text of the header file were actually placed into the program source file at the point of the include directive. A library consists not only of a header file but also of one or more object files. Object files are not text files. They are binary files. Their names end in .o rather than .h. The object files contain the actual binary code that the execution of a program can use.

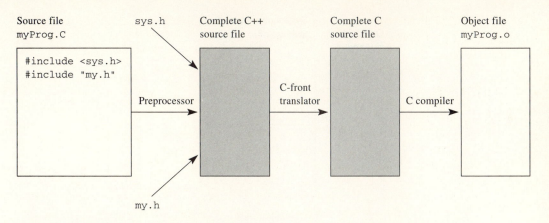

Figure 7.10 Translation phase of a compilation process. The shaded boxes represent temporary files.

Recall how executable files are created from source files. A compile command used to create an executable invokes a compiler and then a linker. A complete compilation of a source file containing a program involves two major phases: a translation phase and a linking phase.

The translation phase has several steps. In the first step, the part of the compiler called a **preprocessor** creates a temporary file that contains the program source code as well as the text of the header files that the original source code file included. Many compilers have **C-front translators** that convert the output of the preprocessor into C code. The C code translation is followed by a C compile into object code. Figure 7.10 illustrates the entire translation process. There are variations on this sequence of translations, such as a possible intermediate translation into assembler code. In any case, the entire sequence of translation steps creates an object file.

The final translation is followed by the linkage phase. The linker uses the object file created through the translations together with any library code to create an executable file. (Executable files tend to be very large, in part because the linker incorporates much of the code from the library files into the final executable file.)

The linker usually knows how to find the system binary files without being told specifically where to look.[11] Object files that a program uses that are not system files are a different story. How the linker is told where and what they are depends on the system being used. If you are using a PC or a Macintosh, those nonsystem object files are typically kept in some project directory or folder. If you are working on a UNIX system, then the names of the object files must be incorporated into a compile command.

---

[11] On UNIX systems, programmers usually have to tell the linker where to find the math library code by putting the option -lm in the compile command.

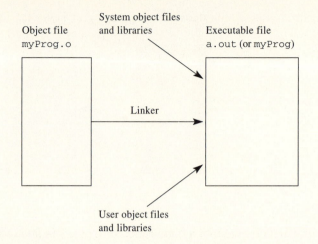

Figure 7.11 Linking phase of a compilation process.

Think of the entire process of creating an executable from a source file as consisting of two essential phases: a translation phase and a linking phase. The header files included in your program source file are used only for the translation phases. It makes no sense to try to compile them. Header files do not create object files. Object files are not used in the translation phase. Object files are used only in the linking phase. It makes no sense to include them in any source code file.

You can see what is in the header files for your compiler's libraries. Where those header files reside varies from one system to another. They are typically somewhere in a directory or folder that is associated with the compiler. You will have to investigate your particular system to find them. Once you do, you can examine them with the same editor that you use to create your program source files. Don't be surprised if the header files are difficult to understand. Their documentation will be minimal at best. And they will contain some advanced features of C++ with which you are probably unfamiliar.

What about the libraries that you create, the libraries that do not come with the system? What about the library that implements the cash drawer and denomination objects? When you create that library, you will write it in two different files: a header file and a source code file that will be used to create an object file. The header file contains the definitions for the `Denomination` class and the `CurrencyList` class, but it does not contain anything else for those classes but documentation. You must document the header file, since the header file is your library's interface. In order for your library to have a naming scheme that is consistent with the rest of the C++ world, the name of your header file should end in `.h` or `.H` (or some minor variation thereof).

The following is the general format of the header file for the changemaker library. We have left out the code that belongs inside the actual definitions for the sake of brevity. You should include in your library headers the fully documented class and struct definitions.

```
#ifndef _CURRENCY_H
#define _CURRENCY_H

struct Denomination {
    // All members are declared here, as well as the enum.
};

class CurrencyList {
    // All data members and member functions are declared here.  The
    //    private anonymous enum declaration goes here also.
};

#endif
```

Header files typically have three lines of code in them that are not part of any of the ordinary C++ code. They are the first two lines in the header file and the last line, and they begin with a pound sign, #.

```
#ifndef   _CURRENCY_H
#define   _CURRENCY_H
...
#endif
```

These three lines are for the preprocessor, which uses them to avoid putting the same definitions in a program more than once. (Remember that while it is acceptable to make a declaration more than once, nothing can be defined more than once. And this header file does contain class definitions.)

How is it even possible to get duplicate definitions in a program that includes header files? Suppose that the header file outer.h has an include directive for the header file inner.h, and your program has at least two include directives, one for outer.h and the other for inner.h. Then the text for inner.h is considered to be part of the text for outer.h, and the texts of both of them are considered to be part of the program source file. So the definitions in inner.h appear in the program two times, once through inclusion in outer.h and the other for inclusion in the program. With the three lines beginning with #, however, the preprocessor is told that if it has seen this code before—this code being defined by _CURRENCY_H, for example—then the code should not be used a second time. Typically program-mers make up names like _CURRENCY_H that resemble the name of the header file. One convention is to begin with an underscore, put the name in all capital letters, and replace all the periods with underscores.

The header file for our library contains the class definitions. Class definitions contain the *declarations* of member functions rather than their definitions. Member function definitions are written in a different file.[12] Since a file with member function definitions contains code that will actually be compiled, the name of the files containing those definitions must conform to the naming convention of C++ source code files. The suffix on the name of the source code file must end in .C, .cpp, or whatever convention is necessary for the system in which the code is to be compiled. Most programmers stick to a naming scheme that they can remember. If the header file for the changemaker library is currency.h, then it is natural to name the corresponding source code with a similar name, such as currency.C.

The file currency.C contains all of the member function definitions. It may also contain other C++ code, such as the definition of the utility function divMod(). Recall that divMod() was originally part of a method of the computing object. The methods of the cash drawer objects will use divMod() in the newest version.

So what does currency.C look like? Just like a program that uses the change-maker library, the top of currency.C file should contain an include directive for currency.h. The definitions of all of the member functions, utility functions, and any other useful constants, types, and objects follow. We have left the bodies of those definitions out for brevity, but of course, they do belong in this file.

```
#include "currency.h"
#include <string.h>

// Definitions for utility functions:
//      void divMod(int num, int den, int& quo, int& rem) {...}

// Definitions of Denomination constructor:
//      Denomination(int v, nameType n, int a) {...}
// Definitions of CurrencyList member functions:
//      CurrencyList :: CurrencyList( ) {...}
//      CurrencyList :: CurrencyList(const int amt[]) {...}
//      void CurrencyList :: setIterator() {...}
//      Denomination CurrencyList :: next() {...}
//      bool CurrencyList :: more() const {...}
//      CurrencyList CurrencyList::perfectChange(int amt) const {...}
//      CurrencyList CurrencyList::change(int amt, bool& success) {...}
```

Notice the difference between the two include directives at the top of the file currency.C. The name of the header file currency.h is enclosed in quotes. The name of the header file string.h is in angled brackets. Names of system header files must go in angled brackets and names of custom header files must go in quotes.

---

[12] This is true unless the definition is inline or a template.

The source code for the system libraries is seldom available. Instead, those libraries come with a text header file and one or more object files (which were created from the original source files). Programmers can share their own libraries the same way. That means library source files can be compiled into object files. These files cannot be used alone to generate executables since they do not contain `main()`. Creating `currency.o` from `currency.C` in a UNIX environment may be done as follows:

```
CC -c currency.C
```

The `-c` compiler option tells the compiler not to make an executable file. The compilation stops at the end of the translation phase, so no linking will be attempted. The output generated by the compiler is the object file `currency.o`.

When a program source file using the changemaker library is compiled, the code from `currency.C` does not need to be recompiled. Instead, `currency.o` needs merely to be linked to the program file in order for an executable file to be created. On a UNIX system, a compile command such as the following is what is required to generate an executable from `currency.o` and a program source file named `myProg.C`.

```
CC -o myProg myProg.C currency.o
```

The `-o` compiler option tells the compiler to name the executable file `myProg`. In addition the specification of `currency.o` at the end of the command tells the linker to go to the file `currency.o` in order to find the user-created object code.

7.10   Sharing constant class data

In the program that uses the `CurrencyList` class, there were two different instances of `CurrencyLists`: the cash drawer and the `CurrencyList` that was returned by the cash drawer responding to a `perfectChange()` message. For any program that uses a `CurrencyList` class, a new instance of a `CurrencyList` is generated every time change is made, whether it is perfect change or just change from an imperfect cash drawer.

All `CurrencyList` objects have some information in common. In this section, we will see what that information is and how two or more `CurrencyList` objects can share that common information. Rather than each object having its own copy of the information, all of them will share a single copy.

Recall that a `CurrencyList` knows each denomination in its list. Even though the amounts of the denominations might change, the names and values do not change. This is true no matter what any particular instance of `CurrencyList` does. The names and values are fixed entities. In addition, those names and values are exactly the same from one instance of a `CurrencyList` to another. According to the way the `CurrencyList` class is now defined, each `CurrencyList` object has its own copy of the denomination names and each will have its own copy of the values. In order to avoid this inefficiency of duplicate copies, we will introduce an additional feature of C++, **static class members**, class members shared by all instances of the class.

Before we go further, a warning is in order. C++ has only 48 keywords, some of them appearing in two different contexts with totally different meanings. Our previous use of the keyword `static` was to qualify local variables and constants. For some compilers, it is necessary to define arrays as static in order to initialize them. A static local variable in a function has a lifetime that extends beyond the execution of the function to the end of execution of the entire program. The use of the keyword `static` in class definitions has a different meaning from those altogether. A static class member is one that is shared by objects of that class type. Rather than an object having its own copy of the static class member, it shares a single copy with all of the other objects of that type. We will make a new definition of the `CurrencyList` class so that the denomination names and values are static.

Static data members can be shared. Does it make any sense to have static function members also? The answer to that question is yes, although it may be more difficult for you now to anticipate the possible benefits of static member functions. The member function in the `CurrencyList` class that has exactly the same side effects and returns exactly the same thing independent of any particular `CurrencyList` object is `perfectChange()`. We will make `perfectChange()` a static function in the new definition.

What must we do to make the names and values of the denominations and the member function `perfectChange()` into static members? One of the data members from the last definition of a `CurrencyList` was an array of denominations. In the new definition, we will break that array into three parallel arrays: one for the names, one for the values, and one for the amounts. Only the names and values can be shared among all `CurrencyList` objects. Those names and values will be in static constant member arrays. The amounts cannot be in a static array. Different `CurrencyList` objects are likely to have different amounts.

Other than making three arrays for the list of denominations (one for the amounts, one for the names, and one for the values) and qualifying the names, values, and the member function declaration of `perfectChange()` with the keyword `static`, the new `CurrencyList` definition will look almost identical to the previous version.

```
class CurrencyList {
public:
    CurrencyList ();
    CurrencyList (const int amt[]);
    void setIterator();
    Denomination next();
    bool more() const;
    static CurrencyList perfectChange(int amountToChange);
    CurrencyList change(int amountToChange, bool& success);
```

```
private:
    enum {size_ = 8};
    static const int value_[size_];
    static const char name_[size_][Denomination::maxNameLen];
    int amount_[size_];
    int cursor_;
};
```

The place to put this new `CurrencyList` definition (and its missing documentation) is in the header file for the currency list library. The definition for the `Denomination` class belongs there also. The class member definitions, including initialization for the static constant arrays, belong in the implementation file for the library.

Since `value_` and `name_` are static constant arrays, they cannot be treated like ordinary array members such as `amount_`. They need special initialization as follows. This initialization code is placed in the same file as the member function definitions. Notice that the keyword `static` is not written in the definitions. It must not be written there. (It will not necessarily produce a compiler error. Instead the compiler will give it a completely different meaning.)

```
const int CurrencyList :: value_[CurrencyList::size_] =
                                {2000, 1000, 500, 100, 25, 10, 5, 1};
const char CurrencyList ::name_[CurrencyList::size_][Denomination::maxNameLen]
            = {"twenties", "tens", "fives", "ones",
                    "quarters", "dimes", "nickels", "pennies"};
```

How do the class methods change as a result of the new definition? One thing to think about is how the constructors fit into the new definition. Remember that a constructor is called when a new instance of the class is created. Constructors frequently serve to initialize the data class members. However, we have already initialized the static arrays, `name_` and `value_`. (It makes no sense to reinitialize them whenever a new `CurrencyList` is created. Indeed C++ does not permit it. The arrays are constant, after all.) So the only array that remains to be initialized by the constructors is the `amount_` array.

```
CurrencyList :: CurrencyList ( )
{
    for (int i = 0; i < size_; i++)
        amount_[i] = 0;
}


CurrencyList :: CurrencyList (const int amt[])
{
    for (int i = 0; i < size_; i++)
        amount_[i] = amt[i];
}
```

The default constructor could just forget the amount_, assuming that any instance of the CurrencyList being created with that constructor will never make anything but perfect change. However, we have chosen in this version to assign 0s to all of those amounts. This is partly in anticipation of features that we might want to add in the future. It is also partly in remembrance of the previous CurrencyList null constructor. That constructor did not have to initialize the amount of each denomination to 0 since that initialization was taken care of by the default value of the Denomination constructor.

It is not absolutely necessary for the null CurrencyList constructor to initialize those amounts. With the non-null constructor there is no choice. That constructor must initialize each amount from the corresponding element the actual array argument. But just like the null constructor, the other constructor does not initialize the names or values.

How do the remaining methods for this new version of the CurrencyList class change? Here is the definition for next(), which is part of the iterator. Since our new definition no longer contains an array of Denominations, next() cannot merely return an element of an array as it did in the previous version. Instead, next() must return a Denomination value that is obtained through an explicit call to the Denomination constructor. That call sends the three elements in the three parallel arrays to create the appropriate return value.

```
Denomination CurrencyList :: next()
{
    Denomination d(value_[cursor_], name_[cursor_], amount_[cursor_]);
    cursor_++;
    return d;
}
```

The methods for setIterator() and more() involve only the cursor_. They remain absolutely identical from the previous CurrencyList class to this new one.

In the previous version of the CurrencyList class, the methods for perfectChange() and change() create their return values through explicit calls to the CurrencyList constructor. They can do it again in the new version. Here is the definition for the new perfectChange(). By the way, notice that perfectChange() is no longer a const function. Static member functions cannot be declared const.

```
CurrencyList CurrencyList :: perfectChange(int amountToChange)
{
    int amt[size_];
    for (int i = 0; i < size_; i++)
        divMod(amountToChange, value_[i], amt[i], amountToChange);
    return CurrencyList(amt);
}
```

We leave it as an exercise for you to write the definitions of the other member functions. The only remaining question is how to use the new class definitions. There is not much to tell here. The new definition can be used in exactly the same way as the previous one. So the most recent program source file will work exactly the same way with the new `CurrencyList` definition as it did with the previous one.

There is an extra bonus with the new definition besides the new efficiency. Recall that `perfectChange()` is independent of any particular instance of a `CurrencyList`. It behaves the same no matter which `CurrencyList` object is used to invoke it. Since it is independent from any class instance, it can be invoked in a program source code completely separate from any instance of a `CurrencyList`. It does not have to be. You can still invoke it through a particular instance in the usual fashion. Here are two examples of its invocation:

```
// The next line is legal even though no CurrencyList object exists yet.
outputChange(CurrencyList::perfectChange(1783));

CurrencyList aCashDrawer;
...
outputChange(aCashDrawer.perfectChange(1783));
```

These two calls to `outputChange` generate identical output. In the first example, an anonymous `perfectChange()` message produced a `CurrencyList`. The syntax for making a call to `perfectChange()` without using an object requires the class name, `CurrencyList`, and the scope resolution operator, `::`. In the second call, a message to an instance of a `CurrencyList` (the object named `aCashDrawer`) produced the `CurrencyList` for the output object to display.

There is much more to classes than what we have covered. But this chapter pushes you one giant step closer to being able to write object-oriented code. In subsequent chapters, we will use this same changemaker problem to illustrate some features of C++ that are in the language specifically to support creation of object-oriented code.

7.11 Summary

When you define a class in C++, you are defining a new type of object. An object is an instance of a class. The attributes of an object are the data members of the class. The methods of an object are the member functions. The function prototypes in the class definition show the forms of messages to the object.

Classes have special member functions called constructors. One purpose of a class constructor is to ensure that objects are initialized properly when they are created. Whenever a class or struct type object is created, a constructor for that

object is automatically called. Which constructor is called depends on the argument list that is given in the object definition. If the class has no programmer-defined constructor, then C++ provides a default constructor.

Design is reflected in the interface of a class. The interface should be stable with respect to differences in implementation. C++ incorporates all of the necessary facilities for programmers to create well-designed classes. It is up to the designer of a class, however, to make sure that the class is useful.

A class designer could choose to make all class members public. The C++ language allows a class to have public data. However, public class data are a rarity. That is partly due to fundamental object-oriented principles. Objects know their own attributes, they can do things, and they alone can tinker with their attributes. One of the essential tenets of software engineering is information hiding. Only the object should have access to its own data. Only the object should know how its methods can do what they do. Such information should be hidden from all other objects. If we want an object to do something, we send it a message. The object itself can control exactly what it will do, what if any change to its data it will perform, and how that change is implemented.

There is more to object-oriented programming than classes. Good object-oriented code is extensible and reusable. Good code comes from good design. Designing classes is the focus of the next chapter. We know about classes. How can we design them effectively?

Glossary

access control   Specifies which code can access class (or struct) members. Any attempt to reference a class member that violates the declared access restrictions is a syntax error.

argument matching   The compiler's process of comparing actual arguments with formal arguments to determine which overloaded function to call.

C-front translator   A feature of some C++ compilers that translates C++ into C code.

class   A type consisting of data and functions. Classes are the major feature of C++ that support modularization and reuse.

class definition   A class declaration that contains the declarations for its members.

class scope   The code in which a class member can be referred to directly by name. Class scope includes the class definition and the definitions of the member functions of the class.

const member function   A member function of a class that can be invoked through const objects. Const member functions are declared with the keyword `const`, and they do not change member data. (Also called constant member functions.)

constant reference type   A name for an object, which cannot be used to change the object.

constructor   A class member function with same name as the class, used for ini-

tializing instances of the class. Whenever an instance of a class is created, a constructor is automatically called.

data abstraction Wrapping a related set of tasks and data together into a single type. Data abstraction is a description of data in terms of its behavior (what you can do with or to it) and not in terms of its representation in the computer.

data member A member of a class that is an object. (Also called an *instance variable*.)

default argument A formal function argument that has a default value. The default value is used for any call to the function which fails to supply a corresponding actual argument.

default constructor A constructor automatically supplied by C++ when no constructor is declared in the class definition.

encapsulation Keeping together data and functions that belong together. A class encapsulates the data and functions (attributes and behaviors) of objects in a single type.

function overloading Defining different functions with the same name but within the same scope.

information hiding Separating the interface of a class from the details of its implementation.

initialization list A list in the definition of a constructor specifying the initial values for objects which are class members.

instance of a class A class type object.

interface of a class The public section of a class definition. The interface spells out the messages to which an instance of the class can respond.

member An object or function belonging to a class or struct, declared in the definition of the class or struct.

member function A member of a class which is a function. (Also called a method.)

message (to an object) A call to a member function of a class.

method A member function of a class.

null constructor A constructor that requires no arguments.

preprocessor The part of a C++ compiler that takes creates a temporary file containing program source code as well as the text of the header files that the original source code file included.

private Access specification for a class (struct) member. Only class members have access to private members of the class. (The exception to this is friends, which are discussed in Chapter 8.) The default access for members of a class is private.

public Access specification for a class (struct) member. Public members can be accessed by any code. The default access for members of a struct is public.

scope resolution operator The operator : :, used to specify the class to which a function or object belongs. It is used most frequently in the definitions of member functions.

static class member A class member shared by all instances of the class.

struct A data type consisting of data and possibly functions. Structs are most often used to group related data objects together into a single data object.

7.12 ▐ Exercises

1. The definition of `Toy` is as follows:

```
struct Toy {
    float price;        // Purchase price of a toy
    bool isNew;         // Is this a new toy?
    char kind[40];      // Description of the toy.
};
```

   a. What are the names of the members of `Toy`?

   b. Define a variable `x` of type `Toy`.

   c. Write a segment of code that makes `x` represent a new basketball with a price $35.99.

   d. Define a variable `y` of type `Toy`, initializing it to represent a used pair of skis costing $60.00.

   e. Write a segment of code that increases the price of `x` by 10% if `x` is a new toy.

2. Assume that the following definitions have been given:

```
struct DateStruct {
    int day;        // Day of a Date      ASSUME: 1 <= day <= 31
    int month;      // Month of a Date    ASSUME: 1 <= month <= 12
    int year;       // Year of a Date     ASSUME: 0 <= year <= 2100
};

struct Student {
    char name[40];          // Student's name
    DateStruct birthDate;   // Date of student's birth
    int grade[5];           // Student's test grades
};

DateStruct today;       // Today's date
Student joeCollege;     // College student
double average;         // Average of 5 test grades
```

   a. Write a statement that makes `today`'s month represent February.

   b. Write a statement that makes `joeCollege`'s name be `"John Little"`.

   c. Write a statement that makes `joeCollege`'s `birthDate` the same as `today`.

   d. Write a statement that prints the month `joeCollege` was born.

   e. Write code that assigns `average` the average of `joeCollege`'s five test grades.

f. Write code that outputs the first five characters of `joeCollege`'s name. (If `joeCollege`'s `name` does not contain five characters, only the characters of the `name` should be output.)

3. Consider these definitions in addition to the ones in the previous exercise.

```
struct ClassRoll {
    Student roll[50];    // Currently enrolled students in the class
    int testsGiven;      // Number of tests students have taken
    int size;            // Number of students currently enrolled
};

ClassRoll math101;       // Class roll information for Math 101
```

a. Suppose `math101.size` is 25. What is the name of the last student enrolled in `math101`?

b. How many students are currently enrolled in `math101`?

c. What is the first grade of the first student currently enrolled in `math101`?

d. During which year was the second student currently enrolled in `math101` born?

e. Assume that at least one test has been given in `math101`. Write a segment of code that assigns the test average of the last student enrolled in `math101` to `average`.

f. Define a `double` function `classAverage()` with a formal argument of type `ClassRoll` that returns the overall average of the grades of all tests given to the students in the `ClassRoll`.

4. Write struct definitions for the following types.

a. A pair of dice. The values on the face of a die range from 1 through 6.

b. Cartesian coordinates of a point (x,y) in the real plane. The coordinates x and y are real numbers.

c. An ordinary playing card. The cards are identified by suit (club, diamond, heart, spade) and face value (ace, two, …, ten, jack, queen, king). To represent a suit type, make an enumeration definition before making the struct definition for the card. Represent the face values as integers (1 through 13).

d. Using the struct definition for part (c), define a data object that could represent the cards in a deck of 52 playing cards.

e. An automobile license plate. Information on the plate is the "number" (at most 10 characters), the state (2 characters), and the year.

f. A telephone directory entry. The entry consists of a person's name (at most 40 characters) and a seven-digit telephone number.

5. Use the `Date` class definition from section 7.2.

   a. Define three instances of `Date`, `firstDay`, `midTerm`, and `lastDay`. Initialize them to August 23, 1996, October 12, 1996, and December 7, 1996 respectively.

   b. Assign `firstDay` the date September 6, 1996.

   c. Write a statement to print `lastDay` in the form mm/dd/yy.

   d. Write a statement that is a message to `lastDay` to advance to the following day.

   e. Write a statement to change the `year_` member of `lastDay` to 2000.

   f. Write a segment of code that prints `lastDay` in the usual form:

      ```
      <Month> <day>, <year>
      ```

      where `<Month>` is the name of the month and both `<day>` and `<year>` are integers.

   g. Define a function with two `Date` arguments. The function returns `true` if the two actual arguments represent the same date.

   h. Write a function with a single `Date` argument. The function returns the `Date` that is one week later than the actual argument. *Hint*: Use `advance()`.

6. Consider the following definitions of two instances of `Date`.

   ```
   Date anyday;
   const Date special(31, 3, 1995);
   ```

   Explain the mistakes in each of the following lines of code.

   a. `cin >> anyday.day_;`

   b. `special.advance();`

   c. `cout << special.month_;`

   d. `anyday.theYear() = 1995;`

   e. `special = Date(3, 4, 1989);`

7. Consider the following definitions.

```
class Student {
public:
    Student(char n[] = "Sam", int g = 1000);
        // Creates a student with name n and SAT score g.
        // ASSUME: n is a C-string with length < 40; 400 <= g <= 1600
```

```
    const char* theName() const;    // Student's name
    int theScore() const;           // Student's SAT score
    void retake(int newScore);      // Changes the SAT score to newScore
                                    // ASSUME: 400 <= newScore <= 1600

private:
    enum {maxName_ = 40};
    char name_[maxName_];
    int score_;
};

Student joan("Joan", 1150);
Student x;
```

    a. What is the value of `joan.score_`?

    b. Write a statement that outputs `x.name_`, a blank, then `x.score_`.

    c. Write a statement that makes `joan`'s SAT score 1220.

    d. Define `sam` as a `Student` with name `"Sam"` and SAT score 1000.

    e. Write a statement that makes `joan`'s SAT score drop 20 points.

    f. Declare a function `f()` that has a single reference argument of type `Student`. The function `f()` changes the `score_` of the actual argument.

    g. Declare a function `g()` that has a single argument of type `Student` but does not change the actual argument. Do not make the formal argument a value argument.

  8. Consider the following definition of a class to represent a ship:

```
class Ship {
public:
    Ship(float s = 4.5, float b = 0, float x = 33, float y = 78);
       // Creates a ship traveling at speed s (nautical miles per hour),
       //    bearing b (degrees), at latitude x and longitude y (degrees).
    float speed() const;        // Ship speed (nautical miles per hour)
    float bearing() const;      // Ship direction
    float latitude() const;     // Latitude of location (degrees)
    float longitude() const;    // Longitude of location (degrees)

    void changeSpeed(float s);  // Change speed to s (nautical miles per
                                //    hour)
    void turn(float b);         // Change direction to b (degrees)
    void cruise(int min);       // Travel at current bearing and speed
                                //    for m minutes.
```

```
private:
    float speed_;
    float bearing_;
    float latitute_;
    float longitude_;
};
```

```
Ship ladyBug;
```

a. Which of the member functions of Ship cannot be invoked with const Ship objects?

b. Write a message to ladyBug to increase her speed 50%.

c. Write a segment of code for ladyBug to cruise for 3 hours and then to stop.

d. Write a message to ladyBug to reverse her direction of travel.

e. Write the definition for the Ship constructor.

9. Define a class named StoreComputer that can be used to create a computing object for the convenience store problem first described in Chapter 1. The design of the computing object specified a single attribute, the U.S. to Canadian dollar exchange rate. The computing object had one behavior: change a price in U.S. currency to an amount in Canadian currency.

   The StoreComputer class should have a single data member, which represents the exchange rate. It should have two member functions. One is a constructor and the other does the computation. Make the constructor have a single floating point argument with default value 1.26. The argument provides the initial value for the data member. Define both member functions.

10. Use the Date class definition given in this chapter.

    a. Define a function named earlier with two Date type arguments. The function should return true if the first Date occurs before the second Date and false otherwise.

    b. Define a function named daysTilChristmas with a single Date type argument. The function should return the number of days that will occur from the Date of the argument until the next Christmas day (December 25).

    c. Define a function named daysFrom with two Date type arguments. The function should return the number of days from the first argument until the date of the second argument. For example, daysFrom(Date(1,2,1999),Date(1,4,1999)) is 2. Write full header documentation for your function, including any assumptions that the function makes about the values of the arguments.

11. Consider the following design description of a car object.

<u>Object Type</u>: car
   <u>Knows:</u>
      The capacity of its gas tank
      The number of miles per gallon it can travel
      The amount of gas in its tank
   <u>Can do:</u>
      Drive a given number of miles or until its tank is empty, whichever
        comes first
      Fill its gas tank
      Tell the capacity of its gas tank
      Tell the number of miles per gallon it can travel
      Tell the amount of gas in its tank

Define a class named `Car` for this design. Make all of the data members private and all of the function members public. Define a constructor for `Car` that can initialize a `Car` with a given tank capacity, miles per gallon, and a full gas tank. Define all of the member functions.

12. Define classes for both of the following types of objects.

   a. A pair of dice:

<u>Object Type</u>: pair of dice
   <u>Knows:</u>
      The value on each face (1 - 6)
   <u>Can do:</u>
      Roll for new face values
      Tell the value on each face

Initialize a pair of dice to the value 1 on each face. Write the definitions for the member functions. *Hint*: The expression `rand() % 6 + 1` gives a "random number" between 1 and 6 inclusive. `rand()` is defined in the library `stdlib.h`.

   b. A deck of 52 playing cards.

<u>Object Type</u>: deck of playing cards
   <u>Knows:</u>
      Its cards
      How many cards have been dealt
      Which cards have been dealt

Can do:
    Shuffle
    Deal a card off the top of the deck
    Tell how many cards have been dealt

Use the enum and struct definitions from exercise 4 (c) to define a
`Card` type. Define a constructor that can create a sorted deck of cards.
Define the member functions. Shuffling can be done by selecting a
card for each subscript i as follows: pick a random number n between
i and 51—use n = rand() % (52 - i) + i. Exchange the cards
at subscripts n and i.

13. Consider the following design description of a clock object.

Object Type: clock
    Knows:
        Its hour (0 through 24)
        Its minute (0 through 59)
        Its second (0 through 59)
    Can do:
        Make a 1 second tick
        Tell its hour
        Tell its minute
        Tell its second

Define a class named `Clock` for this design. Make all of the data members private and all of the function members public.

a. Define two constructors for `Clock`, one with no arguments that initializes a clock time to noon and another with three arguments for the
   hour, minute, and second respectively.

b. Complete the `Clock` implementation by defining all of the member
   functions.

c. Define an instance of a `Clock` named `alarmClock`, with the initial
   time of 6:30 A.M. Define a second instance named `watch` with time initialized to noon. Define a third instance named `timer` initialized to
   9:00 P.M. (Do you need to modify your documentation or your code to
   accommodate the difference between AM and PM?)

d. Define a function `setAhead()` that has two arguments, a `Clock` and
   an int (assumed nonnegative). `setAhead()` changes the time on the

`Clock` argument by setting it ahead by the amount of seconds given by the value of the `int`.

e. Write the definition of a function named `sooner()` with two `Clock` type arguments. The function should return true if the first argument is a `Clock` whose time of day occurs before the time of day of the second `Clock` argument and false otherwise.

14. Consider the following design description of a borrower from a university library.

Object Type: borrower
    Knows:
        Name (at most 50 characters)
        Telephone number
        Amount owed to the library
    Can do:
        Tell the telephone number
        Tell the amount owed
        Copy the name to a C-string
        Credit or debit a given amount toward the amount owed

---

Define a class named `Borrower` for this design. Make all of the data members private and all of the function members public.

a. Define a single constructor for `Borrower` with three default arguments corresponding to the three data members. Make the default values the null string for the name, 0 for the telephone number, and 0 for the amount owed.

b. Complete the `Borrower` implementation by defining all of the member functions.

c. Define a class named `SimpleListOfBorrowers`, modeled after the `SimpleList` class of section 7.3, in which the elements of the array member are `Borrowers`.

15. Implement the `EnglishMetricConverter` class that was defined in section 3.6 of Chapter 3. You will have to look up all the conversion factors between English and metric measures. Two ways to include the conversion factors into the class are given in parts (a) and (b) below.

a. Implement the class so that the conversion factors are local static data objects in the corresponding member functions.

b. Redefine the class so that there is a private section with six constant integer data objects. Put a null constructor in the public section. The

An Introduction to Object-Oriented Design in C++

definition of the null constructor must use an initialization list to provide the constants with their appropriate values.

Warning: It is tempting to "define" the constant integers inside the class definition. But you can only *declare* integers inside the class definition: you cannot define them there. This means that you cannot initialize class data members inside the class definitions, whether they are constant or variable. The only way you can initialize constant data members that are not static is through an initialization list. (It is also tempting to declare an anonymous enumeration type with values for each of the conversion factors. Unfortunately, enumeration types are integer types, and the conversion factors are floating point values.)

c. Implement the `EnglishMetricConverter` class as a library. Put the class definition in a separate header file. Test your library by writing a short program that creates an `EnglishMetricConverter` class object and sends it a variety of messages.

16. Assume that the following definitions of a class and two objects have been given:

```
class Counter {
public:
    Counter (int x);          // Initializes the counter value to x.
    void increment();         // Increments the counter value by 1.
    void decrement();         // Decrements the counter value by 1.
    int value() const;        // The value of the counter.
private:
    int val_;
};


Counter myCount(3);
Counter fourCount(4);
```

Which of the following segments of code are legal? For each illegal code segment, tell why it is illegal. For each that is legal, explain what it does.

a. `myCount.increment();`

b. `if (myCount.val_ < 10)`
     `myCount.increment();`

c. `fourCount = myCount;`

d. `Counter yourCount;`

e. `Counter arrayOfCounters[20];`

f. `void f(Counter x)`
   `{`
       `x.increment();`
   `}`

```
g. void g(Counter& y)
   {
       y.decrement();
   }

h. void h(const Counter& z)
   {
       z.increment();
   }
```

17. The version of the `InventoryTable` in this chapter does not maintain its bar codes and prices in ascending order. Make new definitions for the member functions `add()`, `find()`, and `remove()` so that the items are maintained in order of ascending bar codes.

18. The `InventoryTable` implementation in this chapter was not particularly efficient. For example, suppose a clerk always looks up an item before trying to change it. If the item is in the inventory, then changing it involves another search for the item. The `find()`-`change()` sequence results in two different searches for the same item.

    One way to avoid the duplication of search effort is for the `InventoryTable` to keep track of its most recently accessed item. It can keep an extra integer in the private section to be the index of the most recently accessed item. If `table` is an `InventoryTable` that contains an item with bar code 12100, then this code would require only a single search rather than three separate searches.

    ```
    if (table.find(12100) > 0)
        table.update(12100, table.find(12100) * 1.1);
    ```

    a. Write an alternate definition for the `InventoryTable` using the extra private integer to represent the most recently accessed item. Then implement all of the functions again, taking advantage of the new representation to make the definitions more efficient.

    b. Do the same as part (a) but define the member functions so that the inventory is always in sorted order according to bar codes. Keep in mind that an `add` operation is likely to be preceded by a `find` operation.

19. The `CurrencyList` client program in this chapter uses a cash drawer that does not change throughout execution of the program. It is a perfect cash drawer.

    a. Redesign and recode the input object for that solution so that the cash drawer object can be created with real amounts. The input object must be able to get a list of eight initial amounts from the user in order to stock the cash drawer with its initial amounts of all of the denominations.

b. Implement the program for part (a) as source code in one file and the `CurrencyList` and `Denomination` classes in a separate library. Compile the library. Then compile and execute the program to see if it does what you want.

c. The current version of the `CurrencyList` class does not allow the cash drawer (a `CurrencyList`) to be replenished (except through a fairly complicated sequence of assignments). Write a `CurrencyList` class definition in which the `CurrencyList` has an additional method. With the new method, the client code will be able to put more of a given currency into a `CurrencyList`. Write the definition of the new method. Think carefully about how you will design the new method. What arguments will it require?

20. The following definition for a `Book` class uses the class `Name`, which was defined in section 7.5.

```
class Book {
public:
   Book(const char t[] = "", const char a[] = "");
    // Creates a book with title t and author a.
    // ASSUME: t and a are valid C-strings, length(t) < 50, length(a) < 50.

   Name theAuthor() const;        // Book's author
   Name theTitle() const;         // Book's title

   static int numberOfBooks();    // Total number of books created

private:
   Name title_;
   Name author_;
   static int total_;
};
```

a. Define the constructor for `Book`. The private member `total_` keeps track of the total number of `Book` objects that have been created. So the constructor should increment `total_` as well as initialize `author_` and `title_` according to the actual arguments.

b. Write the definitions of the static class members.

c. Write the definitions of the nonstatic member functions.

d. Create a C++ library for the `Book` class. Put the definition of the class into a header file named `book.H` and member definitions into an implementation file.

e. What output will the following program generate?

```
#include <iostream.h>
#include "book.H"

void f(const char t[], const char a[]);

void main()
{
    Book novel("Tom Sawyer", "Mark Twain");
    Book documentary("Silent Spring", "Rachel Carson");
    cout << "There are " << Book :: numberOfBooks() << " books:\n";
    novel.theTitle().print();
    cout << endl;
    documentary.theTitle().print();

    Book array[20];
    cout << "\n\nThere are now " << Book :: numberOfBooks() << " books.\n";

    f("Raney", "Clyde Edgerton");
    cout << "There are finally " << Book :: numberOfBooks() << " books.\n";
}


void f(const char t[], const char a[])
{
    Book b(t,a);
    cout << "\nf: ";
    b.theTitle().print();
    cout << endl;
}
```

A defect of the Book class is that the constructor increments the total number of books when a new book is created, but nothing decrements that total when a Book object leaves its lifetime. In Chapter 9, we will see how to remedy this problem by defining a special member function called a destructor. A constructor is called when an object is born; a destructor is called when an object dies.

Programming projects

21. Analyze, design, and implement a solution to the following problem.

    The Math 101 teacher needs to maintain information on each student currently enrolled in the class. The relevant information for each student consists of the student's name, test scores (up to 5), final exam grade, and letter grade for the course. All students in the class will have the same number of test scores.

a. One type of object in your solution will be a student type. Define a student struct type. Make a constructor for this type that is capable of using all default arguments.

b. The other type of object in your solution will be used for the class roll. Analyze the class roll object as follows.

<u>Object Type:</u> Class roll
    <u>Knows:</u>
        Its students
        Its maximum length
        Its current size
        The number of tests that have been recorded
        Whether or not the grades for the final exam have been recorded
    <u>Can do:</u>
        Add a student
        Remove a student
        Find a student
        Update a student's test grade
        Update a student's final exam grade
        Update the total number of test grades
        Update whether the final exam has been recorded
        Record the final letter grade for a student based on the percentage
           of the total grade devoted to the test average and the percentage
           devoted to the final exam.
        Show the first student (iterator behavior)
        Show the next student after the current one (iterator behavior)
        Tell if there are more students

When you write the definition for the class roll, document it carefully. Be sure to show what the member functions assume.

c. Implement the student and class roll types in a library.

d. Design the rest of the solution to this problem. Implement your design then test it to see if your solution is correct.

22. The definition of the `InventoryTable` class was only one part of the solution to the original inventory maintenance problem. Analyze and design a solution to the entire problem. Design the user interface so that the user can select the appropriate `InventoryTable` message (`add()`, `remove()`, `find()`, etc.) from a menu of choices. Both the input object

and the output object will be much more complicated than any that have appeared in this text.

Construct your solution over at least three files. Two of those files should be the `InventoryTable` library. One file will be the main program source file. Depending on the design of the user interface, you may opt for an additional library.

23. The "Game of Life" was designed by mathematician John Conway to illustrate population growth. The game is actually a simulation, and it can be described as follows.

The game is played out on a rectangular grid of squares. Each square, which has eight neighboring squares, is considered to be alive or dead. A play of the game means a change from one configuration of the grid to the next as follows. If a square has exactly three living neighbors in the current configuration, then it comes to life for the next configuration. If a living square has exactly two or exactly three living neighbors in the current configuration, then it survives to the next configuration. Otherwise, it dies for the next configuration.

The idea behind a play of the game is this. Each configuration represents a generation. Organisms in one generation will reproduce a new organism for the next if there are the right number of them in the right places (in a position that has exactly three living neighbors). But an organism will die off if it is overcrowded (with four or more living neighbors) or if there are not enough living neighbors (fewer than two) to sustain it.

a. Write a class definition that is capable of representing the grid.

Object Type: grid
   Knows:
      The values of its squares (living or dead)
      Its dimensions
   Can do:
      Initialize itself with a given configuration of live squares or with a
         default configuration of four live squares in the middle of the grid
      Tell how many squares are alive
      Make a single play, changing from one configuration to the next
      Tell its current configuration

b. Write a simulation for the game. The input object should have two behaviors, get the initial positions of the live squares and find out whether or not the user wants to see the next configuration. The output object should be able to show a configuration. The game itself should create the grid and then repeatedly ask the output object to display the grid, ask the grid to change to its next configuration, and ask the input object to see if the user wants to see another configuration. It can quit when the user says no.

24. Design a class to represent a game of tic-tac-toe. Look at the design outlined in the previous problem to get an idea of what kinds of attributes the game should have. And then decide the behaviors. Here are some questions you should ask yourself about the design.

   - What kinds of messages should one be able to send to a the game to make a play?
   - What kinds of message responses should the game have?
   - Will the game allow players to keep on playing after a win?
   - Will the game allow a player to have two turns in a row?
   - Will the game be able to report what its grid looks like?
   - How will the game signal when it is over?
   - Will players be able to erase the marks on the grid and start over?
   - Can the game keep track of how many games each player has won and how many games ended in a draw?
   - Can the game tell when it will result in a draw before all of the squares are filled in?

Chapter 8

First Class Objects

Chapter Contents

THE first data types presented in this book were primitive numeric types. We saw how to do arithmetic with them and how to assign them values, read them from input, and write them to output. Learning about some of this was easy. C++ arithmetic looks much like arithmetic in the "real world." The sum of the values of the `int` data objects x and y is x + y; the sum of two variables x and y in an algebraic expression is $x + y$. C++ kept that familiar addition notation with its built-in arithmetic operators, +, -, *, and /. Assignment, input, and output operations do not have a real-world counterparts. These "computer-world" operations are so fundamental for data manipulations that they have their own operator symbols: =, >>, and <<. We are able to do what we want to do with numeric types, and the notation for doing so is convenient and natural. For that reason, the primitive, built-in numeric types are **first class types**.

Can you remember the first time you encountered types that were not first class? Here's a clue. Take a look at Chapter 6. If a and b are arrays of ints, even if they are the same length, you cannot use the notation a + b. You cannot make the assignment a = b. You cannot even do simple assignment on arrays of characters, or C-strings. Chapter 6 was full of nasty surprises. If s is a C-string, the assignment s = "Sam" will not compile. It is possible to use strcpy(s, "Sam"), provided s has at least four elements. That is not an ideal solution. The strcpy() notation is awkward, and strcpy() is not even safe.

The Date type from Chapter 7 is not first class. If today and laborDay are two Date type objects, the expression today == laborDay will not compile. Indeed, using the current definition of the Date class, there is no simple way to see if two Dates are the same. And you certainly cannot use today < laborDay to see if today occurs before laborDay.

This chapter is about creating your own first class types. In those cases where the type has operations that are normally expressed using symbols such as + and ==, we will show you how to use that familiar notation on your types. First class types do not have surprises. They behave in a predictable manner. First class types are good examples of reusable code.

Much of our work will concentrate on two major examples: a rational number type and a vector type. As we go through these examples, we will look at some powerful features of C++ that support object-oriented programming and ease of object use.

8.1 ▌ A numerical example: Rational numbers

The primitive numeric types int and double are useful for representing mathematical integers or real numbers. Occasionally, that is not sufficient. Neither of those types provide ways of performing exact arithmetic on numeric data that have fractional parts. Although doubles represent numbers with fractional parts, their representations are only approximations. And although integer arithmetic is exact, ints represent whole numbers. In this section, we will create a rational number type that incorporates the exactness of ints and the fractional characteristics of doubles.

In mathematics, a rational number is any real number that can be expressed as a quotient of two integers. Examples of rational numbers are $\frac{1}{2}$, $\frac{12}{5}$, and $-\frac{19}{14}$. Integers are rational numbers, since any integer can be written as itself over 1. So the numbers $2 = \frac{2}{1}$, $0 = \frac{0}{1}$, and $-5 = -\frac{5}{1}$ are integers as well as rational numbers. Some numbers are not rational, including $\sqrt{2}$, π, and e (the base of natural logarithms). If your mathematics background is shaky, don't worry. It is only the rational numbers we are after.

Take a closer look at rational numbers from a mathematical viewpoint. What types of data are required for rational numbers? What types of operations are defined on that data? A complete description of both the data and the operations that a type requires is called an **abstract data type**, or **ADT** for short.[1] We're talking at the design level here, not the coding level. The process of defining a new type in code is a two-step process. First define the abstract data type as a design type, and then implement the abstract data type as a class—a first-class class.

An ADT is the result of the process of abstraction applied to a data type (or a family of related types). A data type is a collection of values and operations, for example, integers and integer operations. A (nonabstract) concrete data type consists of a representation (as bit patterns, in the case of computer data types) of the data and a set of operations on the data representations (the bit patterns).

For example, consider a very simple data type with values represented by the bytes: 00000000 and 00000001. The operations are defined as follows: $!x = 1-x, x\&y = x*y, x|y = x+y-x*y$.

Abstracting from the specific bit patterns in the representation, we could describe the data type this way: There are exactly two values, call them A and B. The operations !, &, and | behave as follows:

$!A=B$	&	A B	|	A B
$!B=A$	A	A A	A	A B
	B	A B	B	B B

In programming terminology, an abstract data type is a specification for a class.

Designing a rational number ADT to be implemented as a class requires making decisions about both data and operations. For the data, we will use a traditional representation of rational numbers as pairs of integers—numerators and denominators. To figure out what operations on rationals are necessary, consider how mathematicians perform arithmetic on rational numbers and how they compare them.

Right away, we have some ideas that can be encapsulated into a class. A class for a rational number ADT must implement a rational number representation—a pair of integers will suffice. It must also provide five arithmetic operations (addition, subtraction, multiplication, division, and negation) and six comparison operations (less than, less than or equal to, greater than, greater than or equal to, equal to, and not equal to).

---

[1] ADT is the computer science term for a mathematical idea called an algebraic structure. An algebraic structure consists of a domain of objects and operations that can be performed on those objects.

Is there anything else the class must be able to do to implement the rational number ADT? The only operations that we have discussed are the real-world operations. What about the computer-world operations? In the computer world, programmers define and initialize rational number objects. They make rational number assignments. They input and output rational values. They treat rational numbers as real numbers. So the computer-world operations that are part of the rational number ADT include definitions and initializations, assignments, input and output operations, and a conversion from rationals to reals.

We will define a new class, `Rational`, so that it implements the rational number ADT as we just described it. Our eventual goal is to create the new class so that it is a first class implementation of the ADT. To do so, we will define the arithmetic operators +, −, *, and / so that they can be used in the ordinary fashion with `Rational` type operands. We will also define the input, output, and assignment operators so that they can be used with `Rational` operands the same as they are used with the built-in primitive numeric types. When we say "used the same way," we mean it. We will adhere closely to the "first class objects don't have surprises rule," making the `Rational` type behave like a built-in numeric type.

One feature of C++ that lets programmers use old syntax in a new context is called **operator overloading**. Much of the rest of this section will be devoted to operator overloading. First we'll show you how to do it and then we'll show you how to do it well.

Operator overloading

An operator is a symbol. C++ has more than 40 operators. The operator precedence table in the Appendix C shows most of them. They include symbols such as !=, =, and + as well as some that you probably do not think of as operators. For example, [], (), and the type cast int() are C++ operators.

Overloading a function means having two different definitions for that function name. Overloading an operator means having two different definitions for that operator. C++ treats operators as special kinds of functions. **Operator functions** can be called with the ordinary function call syntax. They can also be called with the ordinary operator use syntax.

> It is possible to define operator functions only if they are members of classes (or structs) or if they have class, struct, or enumerated type arguments. Overloading an operator with only built-in type arguments is not allowed.

It is not necessary to overload operators in order to implement the rational number ADT as a class. Operator overloading is never necessary. It merely provides notational convenience, not functionality that cannot be achieved with what you already know. We say "merely," but the convenience is substantial and important. With properly overloaded operators, we can use notation in our program that is the same as standard real-world notation. Operator overloading helps us to define the rational number class as a first class type.

The name of an overloaded operator has the following form:

```
operator<operator-symbol>
```

The name of the overloaded addition operator is operator+; the name of the overloaded equality operator function is operator==; the name of the overloaded subscript operator is operator[].

We will illustrate overloading operators with the Rational class. The following Rational class definition that follows is only a skeleton. (Warning: Not only will we complete the definition later, but we will also make some changes in the early prototypes.)

In the Rational class definition, we maintain the practice introduced in Chapter 7 of passing class type arguments by constant reference rather than passing by value. This has nothing to do with overloaded operators but simply carries on the tradition introduced in the previous chapter.

```
// The Rational number type, version 1.0
class Rational {
public:
    Rational(int n = 0, int d = 1);          // Constructs the rational number n/d
                                             // ASSUME: d != 0

    Rational operator+ (const Rational& r);
    // Other arithmetic operators go here.

    bool operator!= (const Rational& r);
    // Other comparison operators go here.

    // Modified assignment operators go here.
    // I/O operators go here.
    // A convert to double value goes here.

private:
    int num_;
    int denom_;
    void reduce();
};
```

The constructor part of this definition is simple. Since it has two default arguments, the constructor can be used with zero, one, or two actual arguments to define Rational type objects. Zero actual arguments constructs the rational number 0. One actual argument constructs a rational number that is an integer (the same as the argument). Two actual arguments constructs a rational number with the first argument as its numerator and the second one as its denominator.

```
Rational r;        // r is 0
Rational s(5);     // s is 5
Rational t(2,3);   // t is 2/3
```

The constructor is convenient not only for initializing new `Rational` objects but also for being able to express `Rational` type values. Given this definition of the `Rational` class, the expression `Rational(-7,9)` is the value representing –7/9. The following assignment has a literal `Rational` value as its right-hand operand.

```
r = Rational(-7,9);    // r is assigned the Rational value -7/9
```

The constructor is actually more powerful than the assignment statement illustrates. We'll see what this means when we try to add `Rational`s and `int`s. Let's turn our attention to the definition of `operator+`.

```
Rational Rational :: operator+(const Rational& r)
{
    Rational result;
    result.num_ = r.num_ * denom_ + r.denom_ * num_;
    result.denom_ = denom_ * r.denom_;
    result.reduce();
    return result;
}
```

The function's name is preceded by `Rational::`, indicating that this operator function, `operator+()`, is a member function of the `Rational` class (as opposed to a member of no class or of some other class). The `Rational` return type for the function means that the value resulting from adding two `Rational` values will be a `Rational` value. The private function `reduce()`, which is called in the body of the definition, keeps the magnitudes of the `num_` and `denom_` as small as possible.

The overloaded addition operator can be used as an ordinary member function, or it can be used in its symbolic form. First let's use the operator function as an ordinary member function. This expression is a call to `t.operator+()`.

```
t.operator+(s)    // t is 2/3; s is 5; the value of the expression is 17/3
```

The name of the operator function is not an ordinary identifier because it contains the symbol +. But the rest of the addition expression looks like an ordinary member function call. The instance of the `Rational` class for which the member operator function is invoked is t. The argument to the function is s. The result is the Rational value that represents the sum of the values of t and s.

One of the purposes of overloading + is to have a natural syntax for expressing Rational addition. But the function call notation is far from natural. The usual notation for addition is the infix notation in which the + symbol appears between its two operands. This is the alternate and preferred way to find the sum of t and s.

```
t + s      // t is 2/3; s is 5; the value of the expression is 17/3
```

That's more like it. The left-hand operand of the newly overloaded + is the Rational object t. The right-hand operand is the Rational value s. This is how all overloaded infix operators that are class members work. The left-hand operand is the instance of the class for which the function is called. The right-hand operand is the member function's actual argument.

Surprisingly, we can also write this expression.

```
t + 3      // t is 2/3; the value of this expression is 11/3
```

The symbol 3 is a literal int and t is a Rational. How can the compiler make sense out of the expression t + 3? Think about it this way. Expressions t + 3 and t.operator+(3) are equivalent. Even though t.operator+() is a function with a Rational argument rather than an int argument, the compiler does not simply give up and complain about a mismatch between the formal and actual argument types. Instead, it converts the actual argument, the value 3, to a Rational value. To do the conversion, the compiler creates a temporary Rational object from the int value 3. That temporary Rational object is used as the actual argument to t.operator+().

The compiler is able to create a temporary Rational object from 3 because the Rational class contains a constructor with a single int argument. The compiler simply makes the call Rational(3) to create the temporary object. A constructor that can take a single different type argument and create an object out of that different type serves as a **conversion constructor**, converting from one type to another.

The process that the compiler goes through of obtaining a Rational value out of an integer is called **implicit type conversion**. It is a type conversion because one type of value is created from a different type. It is implicit because it is done by the compiler rather than the programmer. Without a Rational constructor that is able to initialize a Rational object out of an int value, the conversion would be impossible.[2]

---

[2] The expression t.operator+(3,4) is not valid, even though it is possible to construct a Rational from two ints. In this situation, the compiler first detects that the number of arguments to the operator function is not correct.

Constructors are used to initialize objects. This initialization can occur to named objects which are defined through specific declarations. An example is

```
Rational r(3,8);
```

The constructor can be called explicitly, as it is in

```
r = Rational(1,2);        // Explicit call to Rational(1,2)
```

The constructor will also be called implicitly (by the compiler) for necessary type conversions. In the first statement, the compiler makes the call `Rational(3)` to create the value assigned to `r`. In the second, the compiler makes the call `Rational(5)` to create an argument for `operator+`.

```
r = 3;                    // The compiler calls Rational(3)
r = r + 5;                // The compiler calls Rational(5)
```

In the real world, rational number addition is commutative. In other words, if *x/y* and *z/w* are rational numbers, then *x/y* + *z/w* equals *z/w* + *x/y*. What about adding `t` and `3` in the reverse order so that `3` is the left-hand operand and `t` is the right-hand operand? If the expression `t + 3` makes sense, surely `3 + t` ought to make sense too. More than that, `3 + t` ought to represent the same value as `t + 3`. Unfortunately, `3 + t` is not a legitimate expression with the current version of the `Rational` class. The left-hand operand determines which `operator+` function is called. While it makes sense to call the function `t.operator+()`, there is no function `3.operator+()`. Since `3` is an `int` and C++ does not treat built-in types as classes, the notation `3.operator+()` does not even make sense.

As we just overloaded it, + is not a commutative operator. It is possible to have a `Rational` on the left side of the + and an `int` on the right side. But it is not possible to have an `int` on the left and a `Rational` on the right. This is a serious lack of symmetry. The same lack of symmetry will occur with the current version the overloaded operator `!=`. The expression `t != 0` is syntactically correct. But `0 != t` is not valid.

Our attempt to make `Rational` into a first class type has not been very successful so far. It is not that we have failed to overload + and `!=` but that we have failed to overload those operators so that they behave on mixed `int`s and `Rational`s the same way they behave on mixed primitive numeric types. We are now stuck with a `Rational` definition that is not very useful. It violates the principle that "first class objects don't have surprises."

Friends

Let's take another shot at overloading +. This time we'll do it right. We'll define the operator function `operator+()` as a **friend** of the `Rational` class rather than a member. The word `friend` is a keyword in C++. It is used only in the context of classes.

A friend of a class can be either a function or another class. If the friend is a function, then the definition of the friend function can refer to any private member of the class. A friend that is a function is *not* a member of the class. If the friend is another class, then the definitions of the member functions of the friend class can refer to the private members of the original class.

> Friends have access to private members. Any class that has friends is open to corruption by those friends. A class must choose its friends wisely.

The designation of friend is made within the original class. A function that is not a class member is incapable of being a friend of the class without explicit permission from the class. The definition of a friend function will make no mention of the friendship. A function can be a friend of many classes.

The situation of friends that are classes is the same. In order for class F to be a friend of class C, then class C must designate F as a friend. It is impossible for class F to declare itself as a friend of C just as it is impossible for a function to define itself as a friend of a class.

Our new definition of the `Rational` class does not declare any friend classes. But it declares plenty of friend functions, all of which are operator functions. We've made the documentation as brief as possible in order to make the definition easy to read. Compare the declaration of the overloaded `operator+()` in the previous version to its declaration in the following improved version:

```
class Rational {
public:
    Rational(int n = 0, int d = 1);          // Constructs the Rational number n/d
                                             // ASSUME: d != 0

    // Arithmetic operators.
    Rational operator-() const;              // unary -
    friend Rational operator+ (const Rational& r, const Rational& s);
    friend Rational operator- (const Rational& r, const Rational& s);
    friend Rational operator* (const Rational& r, const Rational& s);
    friend Rational operator/ (const Rational& r, const Rational& s);
                                                        // ASSUME: s != 0


    // Comparison operators.
    friend bool operator<  (const Rational& r, const Rational& s);
    friend bool operator<= (const Rational& r, const Rational& s);
    friend bool operator>  (const Rational& r, const Rational& s);
    friend bool operator>= (const Rational& r, const Rational& s);
    friend bool operator== (const Rational& r, const Rational& s);
```

```
    friend bool operator!= (const Rational& r, const Rational& s);

    // I/O operators.
    friend ostream& operator<< (ostream& out, const Rational& r);
        // Inserts a rational number in the form n/d into out.
    friend istream& operator>> (istream& in, Rational& r);
        // Extracts items of the form n/d from in.
        // r is assigned the value Rational(n,d).

    // Modified assignment operators.
    Rational& operator+= (const Rational& r);
    Rational& operator-= (const Rational& r);
    Rational& operator*= (const Rational& r);
    Rational& operator/= (const Rational& r);          // ASSUME: r != 0

    // Conversion to a double
    double doubleVal() const;        // Floating point value of this Rational

private:
    int num_;
    int denom_;
    void reduce();
};
```

Even though a friend of a class is not a member of a class, it must be declared inside the class definition. The declaration of `operator+()` which is inside the `Rational` class definition is as follows:

```
    friend Rational operator+(const Rational& r, const Rational& s);
```

The friend `operator+()` differs from the old member function `operator+()` of the original version in two respects. The member function version had only one argument. In that version, the left-hand operand for + was the instance of the class for which `operator+()` was invoked and the right-hand operand was the actual argument. In the new friend function version, the first actual argument is the left-hand operand and the second actual argument is the right-hand operand.

Since `operator+()` is not a member of the `Rational` class, its definition does not use the modifier `Rational::` in front of its name. And although friendship is declared inside the class definition, the word `friend` does not appear in the definition of `operator+()`. But since `operator+()` is a friend of the `Rational` class, its definition can access num_s and denom_s of the arguments and of any local `Rational` objects.

```
    Rational operator+(const Rational& r, const Rational& s)
    {
        Rational result;
```

```
        result.num_ = r.num_ * s.denom_ + r.denom_ * s.num_;
        result.denom_ = r.denom_ * s.denom_;
        result.reduce();
        return result;
}
```

Of course, `operator+()` can be used with function style notation. This operator function has two arguments. Since it is not a member function, the function style call to the new version of `operator+()` has a different syntax from the original member version. It is not invoked through an instance of the `Rational` class, and it requires two `Rational` type values rather than a single value for arguments.

```
Rational t(3,4);       // t is 3/4
Rational s(5,8);       // s is 5/8
operator+(t,s)         // value is 11/8
operator+(t,3)         // value is 15/4
operator+(3,t)         // value is 15/4
```

In both of the last two expressions, the compiler converts the literal value 3 to a `Rational` in order to match the corresponding formal argument type. There is nothing special about the first argument to the overloaded `operator+()` that distinguishes it from the second argument. The actual arguments can be anything that the compiler can convert to `Rational` values.

What about using the symbol notation for addition? You should be able to guess this on your own. The addition expressions above can be replaced by these alternative ones:

```
// Assume t is 3/4 and s is 5/8.
t + s                   // value is 11/8
t + 3                   // value is 15/4
3 + t                   // value is 15/4
```

The symbol notation is one with which we are very familiar. The left-hand operand for the operator is the first actual argument to the `operator+()` function. The right-hand operand is the second actual argument.

A benefit of using the symbol notation that we mentioned briefly before is the ability to make complicated arithmetic expressions. The symbols conform to the precedence and associativity rules for built-in type operands. The following is a legal expression:

```
3 + s + Rational(5,9) + t
```

For the curious, this would be the equivalent function style notation. It is not very pretty, but it is legal. It certainly does not fit into our idea of a first class `Rational` type.

```
operator+(operator+(operator+(Rational(3),s),Rational(5,9)),t)
```

It is difficult to overemphasize the importance of C++ type conversions. Without a `Rational` constructor that has a single `int` argument (a conversion constructor), the compiler would be unable to convert an `int` to a `Rational`. That would make it necessary to overload addition two more times, one addition with `Rational` and `int` arguments and another one with `int` and `Rational` arguments.

The remaining binary arithmetic operators are similar to +. Their definitions are different of course. But the `Rational` class declares all of them to be friends rather than members. The same reason for making addition a friend rather than a member can be applied to all arithmetic operators. We should be able to evaluate expressions like `t - 3`, `t * 3`, and `t / 3`. We should also be able to evaluate expressions like `3 - t`, `3 * t`, and `3 / t`. The easiest way to make sure these symmetric operations are possible is to declare the corresponding overloaded operators as friends.

The negation operator is a unary operator rather than a binary operator—it has one operand rather than two. Negation is usually called unary minus. It is not declared as a friend, because no implicit type conversion is necessary. (The expression `-3` will not be converted to `-Rational(3)` because unary minus is an operation that is already defined on `int`s.)

Since it is a member of the `Rational` class, the unary `operator-()` requires `Rational::` in its definition's header.

```
Rational Rational :: operator-() const
{
    return Rational(-num_,denom_);
}
```

Notice that unary minus does not have any arguments. Its single operand is the `Rational` instance for which it is invoked.

The comparison operators are straightforward. The return type for comparison operators is `bool` rather than `Rational`. The declaration for `operator==()` that appears inside the `Rational` class definition is as follows:

```
friend bool operator== (const Rational& r, const Rational& s);
```

The definition for `operator==()` is easy to write, if you simply keep in mind that there are infinitely many ways to represent a single rational number. (Remember that ½ can also be represented as ²⁄₄, ³⁄₆, ⁴⁄₈ and so on.)

```
bool operator== (const Rational& r, const Rational& s)
{
    return (r.num_ * s.denom_ == r.denom_ * s.num_);
}
```

The symbol == can now be used with Rational operands the same way it can be used with primitive numeric operands. This code illustrates using both the equality operator and the addition operator.

```
if (s == r + t)
    s = 3 + r;
```

The code behaves exactly as might be predicted. C++ maintains the normal precedence of the overloaded == and +. For the sample code, that means r + t is evaluated and then its result is compared to s. Furthermore, 3 + r is evaluated before the result is assigned to s. Additional parentheses are not required. The operator + has precedence over the operator == as well as the operator =.

All of the relational and equality operators, !=, ==, <, <=, >, and >= are friends. Again, the justification is for symmetry in using mixed Rational and non-Rational operands. Certainly the following expressions should be valid: t < 3, t <= 3, t > 3, t >= 3, and t == 3. And so should these: 3 < t, 3 <= t, 3 > t, 3 >= t, and 3 == t.

Computer-world operations: Input, output, and assignment

The operations that we have discussed so far correspond to real-world operations. The computer-world operations have their own complexities. Input, output, simple assignments, and modified assignments all belong to the computer-world. These operations do not have the same symmetry as the real-world operations. For example, suppose x is an int variable. The assignment expression x += 3 is legitimate, but 3 += x is nonsense. And while it might be fine to insert the value of x into cout like this: cout << x, it does not make any sense to insert the value of cout into x like this: x << cout. Does that mean input, output, and assignment will be members and not friends? Not necessarily. Input and output operators will be friends. Assignment and modified assignment operators will be members.

Why are input, >>, and output, <<, friends? The reason is because the left-hand operand for each of those is a stream, not a Rational. The left-hand operand for input is an input stream such as cin. The left-hand operand for output is an output stream such as cout. If input and output were members of the Rational class, then their left-hand operands would have to be Rationals. What a terrible surprise that would be—overloaded operators whose use is inconsistent with their use for all other data types. In that situation, we would be forced to remember syntax that is both special and unusual for the input and output of `Rational` types.

Operator functions that return objects rather than object values

The operator functions for input, output, and assignments do not return values of objects as the arithmetic operators did. They return objects instead. And that is one additional complex issue in its own right. Here is a declaration for the output operator that appears inside the definition of the `Rational` class:

```
friend ostream& operator<< (ostream& out, const Rational& r);
```

When operator `<<` is properly implemented, it will be possible to insert the `Rational` object r into the output stream `cout` by executing this statement:

```
cout << r;
```

There are two occurrences of the reference type `ostream&` in the prototype for the overloaded `operator<<()` function. An `ostream` is a type for an output stream. (See the Appendix E in this book for a discussion of `ostream`s.) The stream `cout` is an instance of an output stream and an object of type `ostream`.[3] The evaluation of the expression `cout << "Hello"` results in a side effect—the stream `cout` is changed via the insertion of the literal string `"Hello"`. Since an output stream changes when any value is inserted, the `ostream` argument to `operator<<()` must be a reference argument.

What about the return type for `operator<<()`? To understand why `ostream&` must be the return type as well, look at this sequence of insertions into `cout`. This is the kind of output statement that was introduced back in Chapter 2.

```
cout << "Answer is: " << x << " or " << y;
```

This compound output expression, which is a cascading of simple output expressions, is evaluated in stages. The first stage is the evaluation of this simple expression:

```
cout << "Answer is:"
```

Obviously `cout << "Answer is:"` is not void since it is the left-hand operand of the next insertion operation, `<< x`. Furthermore, in order to be able to insert x into what is produced by the evaluation of `cout << "Answer is"`, the value of the expression must be `cout` itself. So evaluation of `cout << "Answer is:"` yields an object, not simply the value of an object.

[3] Technically, `cout` is an output stream "with assign," which means its type is inherited from the `ostream` type. It can do everything that an `ostream` can do.

Keep in mind that our aim in overloading `operator<<` is to make the use of `<<` consistent with its use with built-in types. If `r` is a `Rational`, then the following compound output statement ought to be valid:

```
cout << r << " is the answer." << endl;
```

If the value of `cout << r` is `cout`, then both `" is the answer."` and `endl` can be subsequently inserted into `cout`. Of course, `cout << r` can be written with the operator function notation like this: `operator<<(cout,r)`. In fact, the entire compound output expression can even be written in this "unnatural" manner:

```
operator<<(cout,r) << " is the answer." << endl;
```

The last statement should remove any doubt about the appropriate return type for the overloaded `operator<<()`.

A function that returns an object rather than the value of an object must have a reference return type. The reference return type for an output stream is `ostream&`. Here is an appropriate definition for `operator<<()`:

```
ostream& operator<<(ostream& out, const Rational& r)
{
    out << r.num_ << '/' << r.denom_;
    return out;
}
```

Notice that the overloaded `operator<<()` returns the same stream that is the actual argument. Not returning the same stream as the left-hand operand would disallow compound output statements. Well, it would not disallow them, but the results could be a disaster.

We designed the overloaded input operator, `operator>>()`, to extract a sequence of characters in the form *integer1/integer2* from an input stream. Its first argument is an `istream&`. Since `cin` is a kind of istream, `cin` can be used with `>>` to extract a `Rational`. The second argument is the `Rational` object whose value is to change as a result of the extraction. Both arguments are reference arguments because both will change as a result of the input operation.

```
istream& operator>> (istream& in, Rational& r)
{
    int num;                    // Numerator to be read
    int den;                    // Denominator to be read
    char slash;                 // / character between num and den
    in >> num >> slash >> den;
    r = Rational(num,den);
    return in;
}
```

The input operator also returns a reference to a stream. The reason is the same as before. The sequence of input operations in the statement

```
cin >> x >> y >> z;
```

can be grouped as

```
((cin >> x) >> y) >> z;
```

The value of the expression `cin >> x` is `cin`. That is why `cin >> x >> y` makes sense.

The following code illustrates how output and input work with `Rational` operands and the predefined streams `cin` and `cout`.

```
Rational r;
Rational s;
cout << "Enter two fractions: ";
cin >> r >> s;
cout << "The sum of " << r << " and " << s << " is: " << r + s << endl;
cout << "The product of " << r << " and " << s << "is: " << r * s << endl;
```

If the user enters the characters ⅜ and ¹⁷/₁₂ in response to the prompts, the output generated by execution of the code is shown in the box below.

```
Enter two fractions: 3/8 17/12
The sum of 3/8 and 17/12 is: 43/24
The product of 3/8 and 17/12 is: 17/32
```

Overloading assignment operators

The assignment operators of the `Rational` class are both the easiest and the most difficult operators to explain. The simple assignment operator, =, is the easiest. You do not have to overload = for the `Rational` class because it is overloaded correctly by default. If r and s are `Rational` objects, then the side effect of evaluating r = s is that the numerator of r is assigned the numerator of s and the denominator of r is assigned the denominator of s. By default, C++ does **memberwise assignment** for class or struct type operands, assigning each data member of the right-hand operand to the corresponding one of the left.

```
r = s;   // has the effect of:
         //   { r.num_ = s.num_;
         //     r.denom_ = s.denom_;}
```

Simple assignment for `Rationals` works similar to simple assignment to primitive numeric types, thanks to the default behavior supplied by the compiler. However, no default definition of the modified assignment operator `+=` is supplied. Without explicit overloading of `+=`, the assignment `r += s` is not accepted by the compiler.

The C++ programming convention of overloading modified assignment operators is to make them members rather than friends. If an operator is a binary operator and if the left-hand operand is the object that changes as a result of the operation, then the operator should be a member of the class. If `r` and `s` are `Rational` type objects, then evaluation of the expression `r += s` should result in a side effect. The object `r` should change.

The declaration of `operator+=()` that appears inside the `Rational` class definition shows it to be a class member. There are two operands for `+=`. The right-hand operand corresponds to the formal argument `a`. The left-hand operand is the instance of the class for which the operator function is defined.

```
Rational& operator+= (const Rational& r);
```

The return types for assignment operator functions are reference return types. That is another C++ programming convention. The result of evaluating an assignment expression is an object. The result is not void and it is not simply the value of an object. The result is the object that is the left-hand operand of the assignment operator.

Consider what the overloaded `operator+=()` must do. It has a single argument, which is the right-hand operand. It returns a reference to a `Rational` object. That reference is the object for which `operator+=()` is invoked—it is the operator's left-hand operand. That's different from what we saw in the definition for the output operator, `<<`. For the output operator, the object that was returned was the first argument. In the case of the overloaded assignments operators, however, the object that is returned is the object for which the assignment operator function is invoked.

The object returned by `operator+=()` is not part of the formal argument list. What is the name of that object? How can it be referred to in the body of that definition? How can any object refer to itself in a member function?

The answers to these questions lie in the C++ keyword `this`, which has meaning only inside definitions of member functions. When you send a message to an object, you must specify which object is receiving the message. That is another way of saying that in order to call a member function of a class, the name of the instance of the class is part of the call.[4] In the body of the member function, the expression `*this` refers to the object that is receiving the message. The notation may look strange to you now, but it will soon become familiar.

The asterisk, `*`, is part of the notation of pointers, and `this` is a pointer. A pointer is a variable whose value represents the address of an object. Inside the

---

[4] The exception is calling a constructor or a static member function of a class.

body of the definition of a member function, `this` is a variable whose value is the address of the object for which the member function is invoked. The expression `*this` indicates the actual object for which the member function is invoked.

The definition of += follows below. Notice how `*this` is used in the return statement. It is the object that will be the left-hand operand of the operator += .

```
Rational& Rational :: operator+= (const Rational & r)
{
    num_ = r.num_ * denom_ + r.denom_ * num_;
    denom_ *= r.denom_;
    reduce();
    return *this;
}
```

It is possible to use `*this` explicitly in the definition of a member function before the return statement. The expression `r.num_ * denom_ + r.denom_ * num_` in the body of `operator+=()` is actually shorthand for the following notation:

```
r.num_ * (*this).denom_ + r.denom_ * (*this).num_
```

While the explanation of member functions, `this`, and reference return types may seem complicated, the use of the modified assignment operators is simple. Modified assignment operators can be used with `Rationals` the same way they are for primitive numeric types, with equivalent results. If `r`, `s`, and `t` are `Rational` objects, then these assignments make sense.

```
// Assume r is 3/4, s is 2/5, and t is -5/8
r += s + t;    // equivalent to r = r + (s + t); r is 21/40
t += s += r;   // assignments go right-to-left like this: s += r; t += s;
               //    r is 21/40, s is 37/40, t is 3/10
```

Of course, the assignment 3 += t does not make sense. Nor should it. If x is an `int`, then this assignment makes no sense either: 3 += x. Overloading `operator+=()` as a member function makes the symbol notation for += consistent with its use with primitive numeric types.

Sample uses of `Rational` objects

We leave you with the task of completing the implementation for the `Rational` class. Follow the examples from this section to complete the definitions of the operator functions. The only other detail that remains are the definitions for `doubleVal()` and the private member function, `reduce()`.

A natural organization scheme for your code is to package it into a library. The header file for the library should contain the class definition. The implementation file for the library would contain all of the function definitions.

Is what we have defined a first class implementation of the rational number ADT? It comes awfully close. Look at how the following code uses the new class. First we'll create some `Rational` objects:

```
Rational r;            // r is 0/1
Rational s(2);         // s is 2/1
Rational t(3,4);       // t is 3/4
```

And now some assignment statements:

```
s -= t;                // s is 5/4
t = s / t * 3;         // t is 5
r += Rational(2,5);    // r is 2/5
s -= t / r + 5;        // s is -65/4
```

We can use `Rational` values in control statements. The comparison expression `(1 > t)` in the `if` statement below requires the same implicit conversion on the part of the compiler that the addition `t + 3` required earlier. Since the overloaded `operator>()` is defined for `Rational` operands, the compiler creates a temporary `Rational` from the `int` value 1 to serve as the left-hand operand for `>`.

```
if (1 > t)             // r is 2/5
    s = 1 / r;         // s is 5/2
```

In the code that follows, the compiler makes an implicit call to the `Rational` constructor to make the assignment `r = 8`. The simple assignment operator, which is overloaded by default, requires that the left-hand operand be assigned a value of the same type. And in this assignment, the `Rational` constructor supplies the compiler with the code to figure out that `Rational` type value from an `int` type value.

```
r = 8;                     // r is 8/1
while (r > s) {
    cout << r << ' ';
    r -= Rational(3,2);    // r is decremented by 3/2
}
```

The output generated by the loop is as follows:

```
8/1 13/2 5/1 7/2
```

The expression `Rational(3,2)` in the body of the loop is an explicit call to the `Rational` constructor to return a temporary `Rational` object initialized with the values 3 and 2. The temporary `Rational` object represents the number ³⁄₂.

Of course, the `Rational` constructor and `doubleVal()` member function allow us to mix primitive numeric types such ints together with `Rational`s in the same expression.

```
r = Rational(17,9);               // r is 9/8
double x = r.doubleVal() * 4.5;   // x is 8.5
int z = r.doubleVal() + 6;        // z is 7
```

Instead of writing the `doubleVal()` member function, could we have overloaded the type cast operator `double()`? The answer is no, assuming we want to keep the rest of the `Rational` class definition as it is. If there were a `double` type cast, the expression `t + 3`, where t is a `Rational` object, would be ambiguous. Should the compiler create a temporary `Rational` from 3 to add to t using the overloaded `Rational::operator+()`? Or should the compiler use the double type cast `Rational::double()` to create a double value from t to add to 3 using the built-in operator +?

8.2 ▎ A second example: Three-dimensional vectors

A three-dimensional vector, $v = (x,y,z)$, consists of three real number components, x, y, and z. A first class three-dimensional vector class can be a nice addition to a collection of mathematics and engineering program tools. We will create such a class, our first step being to decide on an abstract vector data type. What operations should a vector type support?

Vectors belong to the world of mathematics. Typical mathematical operations on vectors include the following. (Here, $v_1 = (x_1,y_1,z_1)$ and $v_2 = (x_2,y_2,z_2)$ are three-dimensional vectors and a is a real number.)

1. Addition: $\quad v_1+v_2=(x_1+x_2,y_1+y_2,z_1+z_2)$

2. Subtraction: $\quad v_1-v_2=(x_1-x_2,y_1-y_2,z_1-z_2)$

3. Unary minus: $\quad -v_1 = (-x_1,-y_1,-z_1)$

4. Scalar product: $\quad av_1 = (ax_1,ay_1,az_1)$

5. Dot product: $\quad v_1 \cdot v_2 = x_1x_2 + y_1y_2 + z_1z_2$

6. Magnitude: $\quad |v_1| = \sqrt{x_1^2 + y_1^2 + z_1^2}$

Two of the six mathematical operations, dot product and magnitude, result in real numbers. The other four result in vectors. We will include all of these operations in our three-dimensional vector ADT.

While it does not make any sense to compare two vectors to determine which is larger, it does make sense to test them for equality. (Two vectors are equal if they have the same components in the same order.) Our three-dimensional vector ADT will have equality and inequality operations.

What vector operations are important in the computer world? Surely input and output operations and assignments. Are there more? Think of vectors as arrays for a moment. Programmers can access an array element by the name of the array and the subscript of the element. We will define our vectors so that their individual components can be accessed. They can be examined, and they can be changed.

The three-dimensional vector ADT that was just described is implemented with the `Vector3D` class. Its definition spells out the operations that it allows:

```
// 3-dimensional vectors with real components
class Vector3D {
public:
    Vector3D(double x = 0, double y = 0, double z = 0); // Constructs (x,y,z)

    // Comparisons. (Two vectors are equal if their components match.)
    friend bool operator==(const Vector3D& v, const Vector3D& w);
    friend bool operator!=(const Vector3D& v, const Vector3D& w);

    // Addition, subtraction, and unary minus.
    friend Vector3D operator+(const Vector3D& v, const Vector3D& w);
    friend Vector3D operator-(const Vector3D& v, const Vector3D& w);
    Vector3D operator-() const;

    // Dot product and scalar product.
    friend double operator*(const Vector3D& v, const Vector3D& w);
    friend Vector3D operator*(double a, const Vector3D& w);

    // Magnitude
    double magnitude() const;

    // Subscripting: access to individual components
    double& operator[](int i);        // ASSUME: i is 0, 1, 2
    double operator[](int i) const;   // ASSUME: i is 0, 1, 2

    // Input and output
    friend istream& operator>>(istream& in, Vector3D& v);
            // Inputs data in the form (x,y,z), where x, y, z are numeric.
    friend ostream& operator<<(ostream& out, const Vector3D& v);
            // Outputs data in the form (x,y,z).

private:
    enum {dimension_ = 3};
    double component_[dimension_];
};
```

`Vector3D` has a constructor with default arguments. That automatically provides a null constructor. The null constructor, which we will define for every class unless we have a special reason not to do so, creates the zero vector.

`Vector3D` has no overloaded assignment operator, `=`. We decided that the default assignment operator provided by C++ for all class types would suffice. Suppose `v` and `w` are vectors. The assignment `v = w` copies each of the elements of `w.component_` to the corresponding element of `v.component_`. That convenience is missing from ordinary arrays that are not members of a class or struct. Arrays cannot be assigned in that fashion. Classes that contain array members can.

Stylistic decisions: Friends or members?

Vectors are quite different from rational numbers. The only mathematical operation that mixes numeric and vector type operands is scalar multiplication. It is not necessary to define addition, subtraction, or comparisons as friends of `Vector3D` in order to allow different types of left-hand and right-hand operands. We could have defined those function operators as members instead. We chose to make them friends rather than members as a matter of programming style. A binary operator that does not change its left-hand operand is usually declared as a friend of the class rather than a member.

Scalar multiplication, `operator*(double, const Vector3D&)`, is declared as a friend. We could not make it a member since its left-hand operand is a `double` and not an instance of `Vector3D`. This is the same reason for declaring the input and output operators as friends rather than members. Their left-hand operands are streams, not vectors.

The only operator functions that are members of `Vector3D` are the unary minus operator and the subscript operators. Unary operators, such as unary minus, are typically defined as members. There is no real reason for making them friends. The only operand for an overloaded unary operator is an instance of the class for which it is defined.

We had no choice in declaring the subscript operators as members rather than friends. The syntax rules of C++ do not allow four particular operators to be friends. They must be class members. The subscript operator, `[]`, is one of the four. The assignment operator, `=`, is another. We'll see how and why to define it in the next chapter. The third operator is the member access operator, `->`. We will discuss its syntax and use in the next chapter. And the fourth operator that must be a member function rather than a friend is the function call operator, `()`.

Most C++ programmers use the following style guidelines for deciding whether to make an overloaded operator a friend or a member of a class.

An overloaded operator function should be a friend of the class if

• The operator is a binary operator and the left-hand operand is not an instance of the class.

- The operator is a binary operator and you want to allow the left-hand operand not to be an instance of the class.

An overloaded operator function should be a member of the class if

- The operator is a binary operator, the left-hand operand is an instance of the class, and the operator generates a side effect on its left-hand operand.

  or

- The operator is a unary operator.

For most operators, these guidelines are stylistic guidelines. However, the operators =, [], (), and ->, cannot be declared as friends.

The number of formal arguments of an operator function depends on whether it is declared as a friend function or a member function. If it is a friend, it has as many formal arguments as the operator has operands. That is, if it is a binary operator, then the friend operator function has two arguments. If it is a unary operator, then the friend operator function has one operand.

A unary operator function that is a class member has no formal arguments. A binary operator function that is a class member has one formal argument. In each case, the object for which the operator function is invoked—the leftmost operand using the operator symbol syntax—serves as an operand.

Overloading multiplication twice

The `Vector3D` class overloads the multiplication operator twice, once for the scalar product and once for the dot product. It is possible for a class to overload the multiplication operator function with two different definitions as long as the arguments to the operator functions are different types.[5]

The dot product requires two vectors and computes a number. The scalar product requires a number and a vector and computes a vector. The definitions for the dot and scalar product are as follows. They both use multiplication on `double` types for their computations.

```
// Dot product
double operator*(const Vector3D& v, const Vector3D& w)
{
```

[5] This assumes both operator functions are friends or both operator functions are members.

```
        double returnVal = 0.0;
        for (int i = 0; i < Vector3D::dimension_; i++)
            returnVal += v.component_[i] * w.component_[i];
        return returnVal;
}
// Scalar product
Vector3D operator*(double a, const Vector3D& v)
{
    Vector3D temp(v);       // temp is a copy of v
    for (int i = 0; i < Vector3D::dimension_; i++)
        temp.component_[i] *= a;
    return temp;
}
```

The return value for the scalar product is a `Vector3D`. The scalar product definition creates a local `Vector3D` object, `temp`, using the built-in **copy constructor**. A copy constructor creates a new object from another object of the same type. If a class definition does not contain a declaration for a copy constructor, then C++ automatically defines one. In the scalar product definition, the built-in copy constructor creates a new `Vector3D` object and initializes it with the data of the actual argument.

Definitions of both the dot and scalar products use the `dimension_` enumeration value to terminate execution of the loop. `dimension_` is not a member of `Vector3D`, but it is defined in the `Vector3D` definition. So it can be used by a friend function with the prefix `Vector3D::`. Remember that the overloaded multiplications functions are not members, they are friends. Friend functions cannot refer to class identifiers without indicating in which class they are declared.

Except for the overloaded subscript operators, the definitions of the remaining mathematics operators and the comparison operators are straightforward. The following code illustrates the use of some of the vector operations.

```
Vector3D v(3,2,1.0);        // v is (3.0,2.0,1.0)
Vector3D w(1.1,-4.5,8);     // w is (1.1,-4.5,8.0)

Vector3D z;                 // z is (0.0,0.0,0.0);
double x = v * w;           // x is 2.3

double a = 0.2;             // a is .2
z = a * v;                  // z is (.6,.4,.2)

if (z != v - 3.5 * v)       // true
    w = -w;                 // w is (-1.1,4.5,-8.0)
```

Deciding how input and output operations should behave is a design decision described in the class definition documentation. When a `Vector3D` is inserted into a stream, the output generated looks like a mathematical representation: (x,y,z), where x, y, and z are the vector's components.

```
ostream& operator<<(ostream& out, const Vector3D& v)
{
    out << '(';
    for (int i = 0; i < Vector3D::dimension_ - 1; i++)
        out << v.component_[i] << ',';
    out << v.component_[i] << ')';
    return out;
}
```

We leave it as an exercise to write the definitions for the input operator. The following code illustrates a mix of `Vector3D` operations. Assume `v` and `w` are `Vector3D` objects as defined earlier.

```
cout << "Enter a vector in the form (x,y,z): ";
cin >> v;
cout << "Enter another vector: ";
cin >> w;
cout << "\nDot product of " << v << " and " << w
     << " is: " << v * w << endl;
cout << "Scalar product of 3.5 and " << v << " is " << 3.5 * v << endl;
```

If `cout` is set to fixed decimal format with precision 1, then the output generated by execution of the code is shown below. (User input is in italics.)

```
Enter a vector in the form (x,y,z): (3,4,5)
Enter another vector: (-6.1,7,8)

Dot product of (3,4,5) and (6.1,7,8) is: 86.3
Scalar product of 3.5 and (3,4,5) is (10.5,14,17.5)
```

Overloading the subscript operators

We designed the `Vector3D` class so that a vector's components can be accessed with the same syntax as ordinary array element syntax. If `v` is a `Vector3D` object, then `v[0]` references its first component, `v[1]` its second, and `v[2]` its third.

We must admit, when we first saw an overloaded subscript operator, it looked strange. (Well, all of the operator functions looked strange, but this one was especially so.) That is probably because we were not used to thinking of `[]` as an operator. When we thought of operators, we thought of the ordinary infix operators such as +, *, or even =. But `[]` is an operator in C++. As a matter of fact, so is the function call operator, `()`. The unusual thing about `[]` is that one of its operands appears between the characters `[` and `]` which make up its symbol.

Before we define the overloaded subscript operators, let's take a closer look at their declarations in the `Vector3D` definition:

```
double& operator[](int i);
double operator[](int i) const;
```

It looks like we have two overloaded subscript operators, not just one. So what is going on? The answer is actually simple. The const subscript operator can be used with a const `Vector3D`. The non-const subscript operator can be used with a non-const `Vector3D`.

> It is possible to have two member functions with exactly the same signature if one of them is a const member function and the other is not. When the function is invoked with a const object, the const version is invoked. When the function is invoked with a non-const object, the non-const version is invoked.

For non-const version, the return type `double&`, indicates that the "value" to be returned by the function is not a value at all. It is an object, a `double` type data object. That is exactly how the return types for the overloaded input and output operators are declared. Those operator functions return objects, not values. In particular, the input and output operators return the streams that are the first actual arguments.

Unless it is declared to be const, an object returned by a function can be used like any variable object of that type. Since the non-const overloaded subscript operator returns a `double` object, that object can be used like any `double`. Its value can be used like an ordinary `double` value. The object returned can even be assigned a new value.

Which `double` object will the non-const `operator[]` return? It cannot be a local object, because any local would go out of its lifetime when the operator function finished execution. It has to be some other `double`. The obvious place to look is in the class data. The class has a single piece of data, `component_`, a private array. Here is our definition of the non-const `operator[]`.

```
double& Vector3D :: operator[](int i)
{
    if (i < 0 || i >= dimension_) {
        cerr << "Subscript range error";
        exit(1);
    }
    return component_[i];
}
```

Here is the definition of the const version. It has *exactly* the same body as the non-const version.

```
double Vector3D :: operator[](int i) const
{
   if (i < 0 || i >= dimension_) {
      cerr << "Subscript range error";
      exit(1);
   }
   return component_[i];
}
```

Both definitions begin with an error check. We'll focus on that error check in the next section. For now, let's concentrate on the return statements. The `double` *object* that the non-const subscript operator returns is an element of `component_`. The `double` *value* that the const subscript operator returns is the value of an element of `component_`.

The following code demonstrates how easy it is to subscript a `Vector3D` type object. The syntax is simple array syntax, even though a `Vector3D` is definitely not an array.

```
Vector3D v(5.2, 4, 6.1);    // v is (5.2,4.0,6.1)
const Vector3D c(1,2.2,3);  // c is (1.0,2.2,3.0)

cout << v[2];               // output: 6.1           {non-const [] is invoked}
v[1] = 35.4;                // v is (5.2,35.4,6.1) (non-const [] is invoked)

cout << c[1];               // output: 2.2           (const [] is invoked)
```

Since `v` is not a constant object, the expression `v[1]` invokes the non-const subscript operator. Since `c` is a constant object, the expression `c[1]` invokes the const subscript operator. The following statements are illegal:

```
cout << v.component_[2];    // illegal! component_ is private
v.component_[1] = 35.4;     // illegal! component_ is private
```

Although `v.component_` is an array, it cannot be accessed outside the class or its friends as an array. The `component_` member of `Vector3D` is private. That is actually fortunate. The legal syntax is simpler, more natural, and easier to use than the illegal struct-member syntax.

Since `c` was declared as a constant, the following statement is also illegal.

```
c[1] = 5.1;                          // illegal! c[1] does not return an object
```

Remember that `c[1]` is a call to the const overloaded subscript operator, which returns a value, not an object. And only objects can be assigned values.

Simple error checking using `exit()` and `cerr`

The `Vector3D` class gives a programmer access to its private data through the subscript operator. That can be a dangerous gift. In Chapter 6, we discussed how arrays are not safe. C++ does not provide any automatic error checking on array subscripts. If a programmer attempts to reference an element with an illegal subscript (beyond the bounds of the array), then different behaviors could result, depending on exactly what memory location was referenced. The program could terminate abnormally (in other words, it could crash). The program could also be left in an "illegal" state with corrupted data.

The error check that is part of the subscript operator definition is known as bounds checking. If a programmer uses an illegal subscript for a `Vector3D` object (anything but 0, 1, or 2), the program terminates with an error message. The error check does not leave the program in an illegal state. It does not attempt to fix the error by guessing what should happen.

The error checking code in the subscript operator definition has two parts. The first is an insertion of an error message into `cerr`.

```
cerr << "Subscript range error";
```

C++ has four predefined streams: `cin`, `cout`, `clog`, and `cerr`. The stream `cerr` is an output stream. It is typically used to record error information. By default, `cerr` displays output on the terminal. Output for `cerr` can be redirected to a disk file instead. (Redirection is an operating system notion. How to do redirection varies from one operating system to another.)

The second part of the error check is a call to the function `exit()`, which is defined in `stdlib.h`. In order to make a call to `exit()`, a program must have an include directive as follows:

```
#include <stdlib.h>
```

This is the signature for `exit()`:

```
void exit(int)
```

The `int` argument for `exit()` is a return code for the operating system. Think of a program as a function called by the operating system. The function `main()` returns an integer value, which is used to convey information to the operating system, particularly if the program is viewed in some larger context. The convention is that 0 is an indication of no errors. Anything but 0 is used to convey errors or in some cases, a special nonerror status.

Normal program termination occurs when the last statement in `main()` is executed. The operating system needs to do several things after a program finishes such as flushing buffers and closing files. The call to `exit()` ensures that work is done even though the program termination is not done in `main()`.

When `exit()` is called, the program terminates. There is no return to `main()`—the program simply quits execution. Before it terminates the program, however, `exit()` flushes all buffers, closes all files, and does the necessary cleanup for global and other static objects. In our error check, the `cerr` buffer will be flushed, thus writing the error message to the terminal or to a file, depending on whether `cerr` was redirected to a disk file.

8.3   Designing first class types

When do you design a first class type? How do you design a first class type? C++ programmers are frequently faced with these questions. Let's look at the "when" question first.

You design a first class type when you need it and you don't have it and you can't find it anywhere else. First class types are tools that are as important to C++ programmers as electric drills and power saws are to carpenters. Yes, you can get along without them. But having them makes many tasks so much easier. If you are designing a class that you alone intend to use and then only once, you may be able to afford the risks associated with using a type that is not first class. But object-oriented programming is not about writing code for a one-time limited use. It is about writing code that is reusable. Our general advice is this: if you are designing a class, take the care to design and implement it as a first class type.

How do you go about designing first class types? How do you decide what does and what does not go in? How will you implement it?

Two principles guide the design and implementation of first class types:

1. Design principle: Include at least a minimal set of operations that all users would reasonably expect from the type.

2. Implementation principle: Create no surprises. Implement the type so it behaves in a predictable manner.

Keep in mind that the designer of a class is responsible for making the chores of the user of a class straightforward.

Deciding what goes into a class is what constructing abstract data types is all about. The notion of an abstract data type was adopted by computer scientists to provide a framework for determining what constitutes a type. An ADT gives a programmer the organization for figuring out the essential attributes and behaviors that a type should exhibit.

Mathematically based ADTs such as the rational number ADT and the three-dimensional vector ADT are designed from two perspectives: a real-world perspective and a computer-world perspective. A mathematically based ADT ought to include a complete set of operations corresponding to the complete set of real-world operations. For example, any rational number ADT that leaves out division or comparison will not be a first class design. Not all mathematically based ADTs will include four arithmetic operators and six comparison operators. What would the operation <= mean in a vector ADT? While we could make some guesses, there is no natural answer to that question.

Nonmathematically based ADTs are often more difficult to create than those that are mathematically based. Some of these nonmathematical ADTs do not have obvious real-world counterparts. (We'll concentrate on two such nonmathematical ADTs in the next chapter.) Others, such as an ADT for a telephone directory, come out of an everyday, real-world context. To figure out the operations for a telephone directory ADT, you must rely heavily on your previous personal experience with telephone directories. Surely any good telephone directory ADT should support these operations: finding a number, adding a new entry, and removing a defunct one. That may not be all, so it is important to think very carefully about how you and other programmers might want to use a telephone directory class. No, you cannot anticipate every use. (Inheritance allows you to design classes without knowing the future.) But you can include the functionality that you are certain that most users need.

What computer-world operations should be included in a mathematically based ADT? Think about the nonmathematical operations on primitive, built-in numeric data. The following computer-world operations should be considered:

- Input and output

- Conversions between primitive types and the ADT type

- Representation of literal values

- Assignment

- Initialization

The importance of these operations is not limited just to mathematically based ADTs. They are important for all ADTs.

Operations on first class types should mimic their real-world or computer-world counterparts as closely as possible. We wanted to make operations not only safe but also natural. For the examples of this chapter, we concentrated most of our efforts on overloading operators. Occasionally we were limited by the constraints of the language. For example, the Rational class could not overload type casting in place of declaring its doubleVal() member function.

Overloading operators made sense for the Rational and Vector3D classes. But suppose we are implementing the telephone directory class. Does it make sense to implement a telephone directory class by overloading operators? Probably not. What would it mean to multiply two telephone directories? What would + or – mean? (We could think of a couple of alternatives.) As a general rule, operators should be overloaded only when the user would not have to guess what the operator means in a given context. There are frequent occasions when member or even friend functions that are not operators are the best choices for implementation of the operations specified in the ADT.

There are hosts of issues to decide with every new type. We've tried to give you some basic guidelines. But we realize that as a newcomer to C++, you may initially find it difficult to design and implement first class types. Eventually, if you program long enough, you will come to appreciate the work that you do to create those first class types. The payback will be well worth the investment.

8.4 ▌ Efficiency issues: Inlining

A complaint leveled against C++ classes—member and friend functions in particular—is that the overhead of invoking a friend or member function may be too high for the trivial amount of work that the function does. Overhead in this context means time.

The `Rational` class provides two classic examples of what we mean. Unary minus, `operator-()`, is a member of the `Rational` class and multiplication, `operator*()`, is a friend. We can write both definitions as simple one-liners:

```
Rational Rational :: operator-()
{
    return Rational(-num_, denom_);
}
Rational operator*(const Rational& r, const Rational& s)
{
    return Rational(r.num_ * s.num_, r.denom_ * s.denom_);
}
```

The overhead of invoking a simple function can sometimes be avoided by defining (and declaring) the function **inline**. Inlining is a request to the compiler to treat the function in a special way. If it honors the request, the compiler will substitute each invocation of the function by the function body, replacing the formal arguments in the body by the actual arguments of the invocation. If the inline function is a member of a class, the compiler will qualify all class members in the body by the name of the object for which the function is invoked.

If all of that sounds confusing, realize that our original function-tracing mechanism from Chapter 3 worked just like inlining. To trace a function, we can substitute the code of the function body for the function call. We can then replace the formal pass-by-reference arguments by the actual arguments and the formal pass-by-value arguments as local objects initialized by the values of the actual arguments.

Here is an illustration of how inlining works in the context of the `Rational` class. Suppose the unary `operator-()` and `operator*()` are both inline and a, b, and c are `Rational` objects. Consider these statements:

```
c = -a;
cout << b * c;
```

If the compiler honors the inline requests, then it will expand the code to this:

```
c = Rational(-a.num_, a.denom_);
cout << Rational(a.num_ * b.num_, a.denom_ * b.denom_);
```

The private-public protection mechanism does not break down here. After all, it is the compiler that expands the code, not the programmer.

The syntax for requesting that a function be inline is simple. For a friend function, place the keyword `inline` in front of its return type. In the `Rational` class definition, this means changing the declaration of friend `operator*()` to this:

```
// Declaration of operator*() inside the Rational class definition
friend inline Rational operator* (const Rational& r, const Rational& s);
```

The definition of `operator*()` requires the `inline` specifier as well.

```
inline Rational operator*(const Rational& r, const Rational& s)
{
    return Rational(r.num_ * s.num_, r.denom_ * s.denom_);
}
```

It is possible to define inline functions that are neither members nor friends of classes. The following function `disc()` is a simple example. The first line is a function prototype. The definition is next.

```
inline double disc(double a, double b, double c);    // prototype

inline double disc(double a, double b, double c)    // definition
{
    return b * b - 4 * a * c;
}
```

What about inline member functions? They are declared as inline within the class definition. For example, the unary `operator-()` can be declared in the `Rational` class definition this way:

```
// Declaration of operator-() inside the Rational class definition
inline Rational operator-() const;
```

The definition of `operator-()`, which appears outside the `Rational` class definition, requires the inline specifier.

```
inline Rational operator-() const
{
    return Rational(-num_, denom_);
}
```

There is a simple and popular alternative to declaring a member function inline and then defining it later. Define the function inside the class definition itself. In that case, the `inline` keyword specifier is not used.

```
// Definition of operator-() inside the Rational class definition.
Rational operator-() const {return Rational(-num_, denom_);}
```

Inlining member functions is done only for very short functions. Occasionally you may see class definitions in which every member function is inline, including the constructors. Refer to the simple `Date` class that appeared in Chapter 7. This is what its definition would look like if all of its methods except `advance()` were inline:

```
class Date {
public:
    // Constructor
    Date(int d, int m, int y) : day_(d), month_(m), year_(y) { }
    int theDay() const      {return day_;}
    int theMonth() const    {return month_;}
    int theYear() const     {return year_;}
    void advance();
private:
    int day_;
    int month_;
    int year_;
};
```

Keep in mind that inlining amounts to a request to the compiler. Compilers have their own rules to determine whether to honor the request. Those rules differ from compiler to compiler. In general, compilers will not expand functions inline that are more than a couple of lines long or functions with complicated control structures or recursive calls.

In the situation where the compiler will expand inline, the resulting code may be significantly more efficient, especially if the function is invoked many times. But there are penalties for inlining. Under some circumstances the inlined expansions are actually less efficient to execute. Also, inline expansions may result in a substantial amount of code generation and consequently require more memory to store and execute.

The final drawback to inline functions is a matter of hiding the details of a method from the programmer who uses it. When a function that is part of a library is declared inline, its definition must appear in the header file for the library. It cannot be hidden within the object code for the implementation. Whenever code invoking an inline function is compiled, the inlined function must also be recompiled.

8.5   Summary

The syntax for defining and using classes is an important part of C++. Like most good ideas, classes can be used well or used poorly, or even misused. You will be able to use classes well in your designs and programs if you keep in mind several ideas about how classes are supposed to be used.

A class is often the best way to encapsulate the data and functions that together implement a type of object. So far we have emphasized this "grouping together" use of classes, which benefits organization of code and helps match the organization of code to a design developed in terms of objects.

An additional use of classes is to separate interfaces from implementations. Remember that in problem analysis, we discover (or invent) objects in order to devise a solution for the problem. The design phase of program development specifies the interfaces to classes. The interface of an object tells how the object can be used. The interface to a class is the set of public members and friends, together with a description of what they do (not how they do it). For classes representing design objects, the interface expresses what the objects can do.

Data abstraction is a traditional design technique that emphasizes specifying the interfaces to the types of data mentioned in the problem analysis. Thanks to mathematicians and computer scientists, there is a sizable collection of well-known and generally useful ADTs that can be called upon in program development. Examples include such ideas as rational and complex numbers, strings, stacks, and queues.

We have used data abstraction in our object-oriented program development. By creating ADTs, we have been able methodically to figure out the characteristics of objects in our designs. C++ and other object-oriented programming languages support object-oriented program development through features like classes, inheritance, class hierarchies, and polymorphism. Such features aid in implementing ADTs.

One of the benefits of object-oriented program development is reuse of designs and code. The major reason for creating first class types is to foster that reuse. First class types are not necessarily bound to special applications or special problems. They are general-purpose programming tools that are usable in a variety of contexts.

Glossary

abstract data type (ADT)   A complete description of the data and operations that a type requires. The description is independent of any computer implementation.

`cerr`   A built-in output stream. Output is flushed as soon as it is inserted to `cerr`. By default, output appears on the terminal.

conversion constructor   A constructor that can construct an object from an object of a different type.

copy constructor   A constructor that creates a new object from another object of the same type.

exit() A function from the built-in libraries that immediately halts program execution when invoked.

first class type A type that exhibits expected behaviors in the same sense as the built-in numeric types. A user-defined first class type supports all of the familiar type operations in a natural way (using built-in operators when possible) including assignment, equality, inequality, input, and output operations.

friend A function not belonging to a class but having access to all of the class members. A class can be a friend of another class, in which case its member functions are friends of the other class.

implicit type conversion The automatic conversion by the compiler from one type of value to another.

inline A request to the compiler to substitute each invocation of the function by the body of the function using the appropriate argument substitutions.

memberwise assignment The default assignment for classes. Each member of the left-hand operand is assigned the corresponding member of the right-hand operand.

operator function A built-in operator used as a function. The name of an operator function is of the form operator<*symbol*>, where *symbol* is the symbol for that operator.

operator overloading The definition of a built-in operator to use class or enumeration type objects as operands.

this (keyword used only in the definitions of member functions) A variable whose value is the address of the object for which the member function is being invoked.

8.6 Exercises

1. Suppose that the class Example is defined as follows.

```
class Example {
public:
    Example(int x = 2);
    friend Example operator+(const Example& x, const Example& y);
    friend bool operator>(const Example& x, const Example& y);
private:
    int stuff_;
};
```

Which of the following code fragments is legal?

a. Example one;
   cout << one + one << endl;

b. Example two;
   Example three(3);
   Example four = two + three;

```
c. if (Example(5) > Example(6))
      cout << 17;
```

```
d. if (Example(5) <= Example(6))
      cout << 18;
```

```
e. Example seven(7);
   seven = seven + 12;
```

```
f. Example eight(8);
   eight = Example(8) + 5;
```

```
g. Example nine(9);
   nine += 5;
```

2. Write the definitions for the remaining operators of the `Rational` class that were not defined in the text.

   a. Write the definitions for the overloaded arithmetic operators, subtraction and division. Multiplication was defined in the discussion on inlining in section 8.4. Define multiplication so that it is not inline.

   b. Write the definitions for the overloaded comparison and equality operators, `<`, `<=`, `>`, `>=`, and `!=`. (The operator `==` was defined in the text.)

   c. Write the definitions for the overloaded modified assignment operators, `-=`, `*=`, and `/=`. (The operator `+=` was defined in the text.)

3. Two member functions of the `Rational` class were not defined in the text. They must be defined in order to complete the class implementation.

   a. Write the definition for the function `Rational::doubleVal()`.

   b. Write the definition for the function `Rational::reduce()`. The algorithm for `reduce()` should be reasonably efficient. *Hint*: Recall how you reduced fractions when you were in elementary school. You found the greatest common divisor of the numerator and denominator and divided each by that greatest common divisor. The greatest common divisor of two integers is efficiently computed using the Euclidean algorithm (see exercise 12 in Chapter 5). In implementing the `reduce()` method, you may incorporate the Euclidean algorithm directly into the definition `reduce()`. Or you may define `gcd()` as a separate, global function that `reduce()` calls.

   c. Organize the entire `Rational` class as a library. Put the class definition into a header file and the member and friend function definitions into a `.C` file (an implementation file). If you use `gcd()` from part (b) to implement `reduce()`, then put its definition into the implementation file also.

4. The following problem illustrates a common oversight that all-too-human programmers can make. Given:

```
Rational r(8/9);
```

What are the values of r.num_ and r.denom_?

5. Suppose that r is defined as follows:

```
Rational r(12,36);
```

a. What is the value of the expression r.doubleVal()?

b. If r is defined in main() (or anywhere outside the Rational class member or friend definitions), is the expression r.reduce() valid? If so, what happens when it is evaluated? If not, explain why it is not valid.

c. Is the expression (r/4).doubleVal() syntactically correct? If it is, what is its value? If it is not, explain why not.

6. Consider these declarations of overloaded input and output operators:

```
ostream& operator<<(ostream& out, const Rational& r);
istream& operator>>(istream& in, Rational& r);
```

a. Explain why the second argument to operator<<() is a const Rational&.

b. Explain why the second argument to operator>>() is a non-const Rational&.

7. See the Name class from section 7.5 of Chapter 7. Replace the declaration of the member function print() with a declaration for an overloaded output operator. Declare an overloaded input operator. Define both overloaded operators.

8. Modify the Date class definition from Chapter 7.

a. Include the prototype for the overloaded less than operator, <. Write its definition.

b. Include the prototype for the remaining relational operators, <=, >, and >=. Write their definitions.

c. Include the prototypes for the equality operators, == and !=. Write their definitions.

d. Test your version of the Date class with its overloaded relational operators and equality operators. What results do they give for the following comparison expressions?

```
Date(12,2,1987) < Date( 2,3,1987)
Date(12,12,1990) < Date(1,2,1991)
Date(1,2,1234) == Date(1,2,1234)
Date(12,12,1998) >= Date(4,7,1998)
```

e. Explain your rationale for making the new operators members or friends.

9. The Date class defined in Chapter 7 is not a first class type. The previous exercise required overloading the relational and equality operators for Date. However input and output are also important operators for any first class type.

    a. Include the prototype for the overloaded output operator, <<. Write its definition.

    b. Include the prototype for the overloaded input operator, >>. What input format does your version of this operator expect? Document the prototype to include a description of that format. Write the definition of operator>>().

10. The previous two exercises involved creating a first class Date type with just the minimal set of operations to make it first class. This exercise is not necessary to make the Date class truly first class, but it does show how a class may be enhanced to provide more than the minimal functionality.

    a. Include the prototype for an overloaded addition operator with a Date, and an int for operands. If today is a Date representing November 16, 1995, then today + 20 is a Date representing 20 days after today, or December 6, 1995.

    b. Include a prototype for still another overloaded addition operator with an int, and a Date for operands. (The operands for this addition operator are in the reverse order of the operands for the original addition operator.) The behavior of the new addition operator mimics the behavior of the first one. That is, if today represents November 16, 1995, then 20 + today also represents December 6, 1995.

    c. Are two overloaded addition operators necessary to accomplish the Date-int addition? Why or why not?

11. Operators can be overloaded if they have at least one enumerated (only for some compilers), class, or struct type argument. Assume that you are given the enumerated type Color defined as follows:

    ```
    enum Color {red, yellow, green};
    ```

    Write a definition for the overloaded output operator, <<, with the following signature. (Notice that the operator function is not a friend, since Color is not a class.)

    ```
    ostream& operator<<(ostream&, Color);
    ```

12. Redesign and redefine the overloaded output operator for the Rational class so that it can output a Rational in mixed number format. Assume you are given the following code:

```
Rational r(6,3);
Rational s(30,12);
Rational t(-7,-3);
Rational u(12,-8);
Rational v(3,5);
cout << r << '\n' << s << '\n' << t << '\n' << u << '\n' << v << endl;
```

The output generated by execution of the code is as follows:

```
2
2 1/2
2 1/3
-1 1/2
3/5
```

13. List all of the functions declared in the definitions of the Rational or Vector3D classes that are invoked in the execution of the code below. Include implicit invocations by the compiler for type conversions.

    a. `Rational x(1,4);`

    b. `Rational y;`

    c. `y += Rational(3,4) + Rational(2);`

    d. `Vector3D v;`

    e. `Vector3D w(1,2,3);`

    f. `v = v + w - 3.6 * w;`

    g. `v = -(3.6 * w);`

14. The Rational class did not use an overloaded type cast operator to convert a Rational value to a floating point value. The declaration for such a type cast in the Rational class definition would be as follows:

```
operator double() const;
```

The return type for an overloaded type cast operator is not necessary.

    a. Write the definition for the overloaded double type cast operator.

    b. Explain what your compiler does when it attempts to compile the following code:

```
Rational v(3,4);
v = 3 + v;
```

Can you understand the nature of the compiler's complaint?

15. First class types are usually implemented via libraries. The header file for the library contains the class definition. The implementation file contains the definitions of the member functions and the friend functions.

   a. Create a class library that implements the rational number ADT.

   b. Create a class library that implements the three-dimensional vector ADT.

   c. Create two new class libraries for the rational number and three-dimensional vector ADTs. This time, write all of the functions inline.

16. Why didn't we name the vector class `3DVector`? It does seem to be a nicer name.

17. The documentation on the overloaded extraction operator for `Vector3D` indicates that the input must be in the strict format `(x,y,z)`.

   a. Rewrite the documentation so that `operator>>()` can accept any of the following formatting styles:

   ```
   (x,y,z)
    x y z
    x, y, z
   ```

   b. Define `operator>>()` to conform to the new specifications.

18. Another mathematical operation on three-dimensional vectors is the cross product. If $v_1 = (x_1, y_1, z_1)$ and $v_2 = (x_2, y_2, z_2)$ are three-dimensional vectors, then the cross product of v_1 and v_2 is a vector v defined as follows.

$$v = (y_1 z_2 - z_1 y_2, z_1 x_2 - x_1 z_2, x_1 y_2 - y_1 x_2)$$

   a. Redesign the vector ADT so that the cross product is one of its operations.

   b. Redefine the `Vector3D` class so that it implements the cross product operation. Is it possible to overload multiplication for the cross product?

Programming Projects

19. Two-dimensional vectors can be thought of as points in the real plane. The coordinates for a point p in the plane can be expressed in terms of the familiar Cartesian coordinate system:

$p = (x,y)$, where x is the x-coordinate, y is the y-coordinate

The coordinates for a point p can be expressed in terms of a polar coordinate system:

p = (r,Θ), where r is the distance from the point to the origin and Θ is the angle that the line segment connecting the point and the origin make with the positive x-axis.

a. Design and implement a first class `Vector2D` class for points whose coordinates are expressed in a Cartesian coordinate system.

b. Design and implement a first class `Polar2D` class for points whose coordinates are expressed in a polar coordinate system.

c. Write a `Vector2D` constructor that constructs a point in the Cartesian coordinate system from its polar coordinates.

d. Write a `Polar2D` constructor that constructs a point in the polar coordinate system from its Cartesian coordinates.

e. Test your implementations to see that the conversions between the two class types are correct.

20. Design and implement a simulation of a handheld calculator that does rational arithmetic.

Chapter 9

Storage Management for Objects

THE previous chapter was about designing, constructing, and using tools. This chapter is also, as we continue to concentrate on first class types. Part of our emphasis will be on developing abstract data types to guide the design; part will be on overloading operators to take advantage of familiar C++ operator syntax; and part will be on using first class types.

Most of the objects we have discussed so far in this book are created through their definitions. Unless they are global or static, those objects die when the block in which they are defined finishes execution. In this chapter, we will discuss a different way to create objects and subsequently to destroy them. The mechanism we will use is pointers.

Pointers are powerful tools that are an essential part of all programming toolkits. We have mentioned pointers in the past, but that's about it. In this chapter we will show you what a pointer is. We'll discuss pointer syntax and how to use pointers to create and destroy objects. Pointers can be wonderful, but poor use of powerful tools can create terrible mistakes. We will show you how to avoid those mistakes by adopting careful programming habits.

To illustrate using pointers and classes with pointer members, we will design and implement two new data types: a string type and an extensible array type. The `String` class and the `ExtArray` class are models that you can follow when you create your own pointer-based classes.

It is difficult to overemphasize the importance of pointers and their counterparts, references. When you read code written by experienced C++ programmers, you will find liberal use of pointers throughout. As you become a more experienced programmer, you will become much more fluent in reading such code as well as in writing your own pointer-based code.

9.1   Pointers

You are familiar with many built-in types, `int`, `char`, and `double` to name a few. And you know how to create your own types through enumerations and class definitions. Now we want to introduce **pointer** types, which are used to represent addresses of objects.

Early in this book we mentioned that data objects could be characterized by name, type, value, and address. The address of an object is its location in memory. The type of an object tells how the information stored at the address of that object is to be interpreted as a value. For example, the information stored at the address of an `int` type data object is a value that is an `int`. The information stored at the address of a `double` type data object is a value that is a `double`. The information stored at the address of a pointer type data object is a value that is an address of a particular type of object. A pointer value is an address.

Suppose `p` is a pointer type data object whose value is the address of an object named x—the rvalue of `p` is the lvalue of x. This means that we can refer to that object by x, as we have done in the past. Or we can refer to that object through `p`. That gives the potential for changing the value of the object via `p`, since `p` knows where the information for the object is located.

The importance of pointers is not to provide alternative access to objects that already have names. One of the most important tools that they provide is the ability to create new objects at execution time. Through pointers, programs can create new objects on the fly.

Pointers and aliases

The following two simple definitions look quite similar. But they create two very different types of data objects.

```
double x;
double* p;
```

The first data object, x, is of type double. The second data object, p, is of type double*. The type double* is called pointer-to-double and it represents an address of a data object of type double. The variable p is a pointer variable or **pointer data object**. When the value of p is the address of an actual double type object, then we say that "p points to that object." The object is called p's **referent**. Figure 9.1 illustrates the relationship between p and the double type data object whose value is 21.3 and which is pointed to by p.

You can create pointers to any defined types. The types int* (pointer-to-int) and char* (pointer-to-char) are examples. Given the Rational class from the previous chapter, the type Rational* (pointer-to-Rational) is another example of a pointer type.

Suppose s is of type int* and t is of type Rational*. Even though the values of s and t are machine addresses, they are not the addresses of the same types of objects. The types int* and Rational* are not compatible. Neither are the types int* and double*. These assignments are illegal.

```
s = t;   // illegal!!  s is of type int*, t is of type Rational*
p = s;   // illegal!!  s is of type int*, p is of type double*
```

Now let's focus on legal code. The pointer-to-double p is capable of pointing to a double type object. A question still remains: How do pointer variables get legitimate object address values? There are several answers to be considered. One way to make sure that a pointer points to an actual object is to assign it the address of an object by using the **address-of operator**, &.

The address-of operator & is a unary prefix operator. To say & is unary means it has one operand (as opposed to a binary operator like +, which has two operands); to say & is a prefix operator means it is written before its operand (as

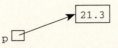

Figure 9.1 A pointer and its referent.

opposed to after its operand, like the postfix increment operator ++). The value of the expression &x is the address of the object x. The address-of operator can be used to find addresses of objects of built-in types such as `double` as well as programmer-defined types such as `Rational`.

Assume that p and x have been declared as pointer-to-double and `double` respectively and that the following statements are executed:

```
x = 4.8;       // x is 4.8
p = &x;        // p is the address of x
```

Figure 9.2 illustrates the resulting relationship between p and x. The value of the pointer p is the address of x. But just what is the address of x? That answer differs from machine to machine and from one execution of the code to the next. For example, the last time we executed that last segment of code on our system, we obtained the following lvalues (addresses) and rvalues (values) of p and x:

Address of p (lvalue)	Value of p (rvalue)	Address of x (lvalue)	Value of x (rvalue)
102770D8	10277A30	10277A30	4.8

The number 10277A30 is a hexadecimal machine address for the computer we happened to be using at the time. The number itself is not very informative, is it? That is why we use the arrow notation in our figures. Rather than show a real address, we use the arrow from a pointer to an object to indicate that the value of the pointer is the address of the object at the arrowhead.

Let's look closer at the assignments to x and p. The `double` data object with the value 4.8 can be referred to by the name x. Or it can be referred to by the expression *p (pronounced "star p"). The symbol * in *p has nothing to do with multiplication. In the context of pointers, * is a unary prefix operator, called the **dereference operator** or the **indirection operator**. The notation *p indicates the object whose address is stored in p—p's referent. The two expressions x and *&x mean exactly the same thing.

Pointers can be used to name objects. The `double` data object in Fig. 9.2 has two different names, x and *p. Alternate names for the same object are **aliases**.

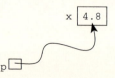

Figure 9.2 The pointer p points to the object x.

Pointers can create aliases. In our example, `*p` can be used in exactly the same way as x. The following assignment is legal.

```
*p = 3.1;                  // the value of x is now 3.1
```

The value of x changes, even though the assignment statement made no mention of the name x.

Here are some additional examples of pointer initializations and assignments. (Assume p has been defined as before, a pointer-to-`double`.) The code illustrates the connection between pointers and aliasing.

```
double xDouble = 7.4;    // xDouble is 7.4
int iInt = 3;            // iInt is 3
int jInt = 5;            // jInt is 5

double* p = &xDouble;    // p points to xDouble; *p and xDouble are aliases
int* q = &iInt;          // q points to iInt; *q and iInt are aliases
int* r = q;              // r and q point to the same object, iInt; so *r,
                         //    *q, and iInt are aliases, too
```

The results of executing the code are illustrated in Fig. 9.3. Note how r and q point to the same object, iInt.

Now let's make an assignment to `*r`.

```
*r = 7;                    // iInt is 7
```

The assignment to `*r` changes the value of iInt and the value of `*q`. The reason is obvious. The int data object whose value changes has three different names: iInt, `*q`, and `*r`. (See Fig. 9.4.)

It's not necessary to limit the use of pointers to simple assignments. The following code mixes assignments, addition, and output statements. As you read the code, look for aliasing.

```
// iInt is 7, xDouble is 7.4, q points to iInt, p points to xDouble
jInt = 8;
r = &jInt;                 // r now points to jInt
```

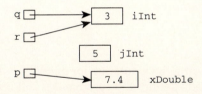

Figure 9.3 The status of the objects after the code initializations and assignments.

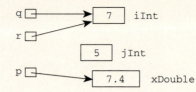

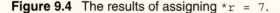

Figure 9.4 The results of assigning *r = 7.

```
cout << jInt <<endl;
*r += 5;                    // jInt is incremented by 5 (jInt becomes 13)
cout << jInt << endl;
cout << iInt + jInt + int(xDouble) << endl;
cout << *r + *q + int(*p) << endl;
```

The output that is generated by execution of the code is shown in the box that follows.

```
8
13
27
27
```

The notation for declaring and using pointers can be confusing. For example, this code defines two `int` variables:

```
int k, t;        // k and t are two int variables
```

However, the same paradigm cannot be used to define two pointer variables. Consider this code:

```
int*  kp, tp;    // kp is a pointer-to-int, tp is an int
```

The `*` associates with `kp` and not `tp`. While `kp` is a pointer-to-int type, `tp` is only an `int` type. If you want to declare two pointer types on the same line, put the asterisk in front of each name.

```
int *kp, *tp;    // kp is a pointer-to-int, tp is a pointer-to-int
```

As an alternative to using the `*` notation for defining pointers, you can make a typedef. The following code defines the variables `kp` and `tp` to be of type pointer-to-int.

```
typedef int* ptrToInt;
ptrToInt kp, tp;
```

Whitespace in pointer code is sometimes irrelevant, just as whitespace in arithmetic expressions is sometimes irrelevant. For example, the blanks in the expression 3 + 4 are helpful for reading. But 3 + 4 could just as easily have been written as 3 +4, 3+ 4, or with no whitespace at all, 3+4. While we used `double*` for pointer-to-`double`, we could have declared p in any of the following ways:

```
double* p;   or   double * p;   or   double *p;   or   double*p;
```

The address-of operator and the dereference operator can be written immediately before their operands. Or whitespace can be embedded between the operators and their operands. The address of x can be written in either of the following ways:

```
&x      or    & x
```

The object pointed to by p can be written in either of the following ways:

```
*p      or    * p
```

Pointers to class types

It is possible to create a pointer to any defined type. Consider the `Rational` and `Date` class definitions from the previous two chapters. Here are two pointer data objects. One is a pointer-to-`Rational` and the other is a pointer-to-`Date`.

```
Rational* rp;            // rp is pointer-to-Rational
Date* dp;                // dp is pointer-to-Date

Rational fraction(1,5);  // fraction is 1/5
Date today(14,9,1994);   // today is September 14, 1994

rp = &fraction;          // *rp is an alias for fraction
dp = &today;             // *dp is an alias for today
```

With these last two assignments, `*rp` can be used wherever `fraction` is used and `*dp` can be used wherever `today` is used. That gives the following notational equivalencies:

`(*rp).num_`	*is equivalent to*	`fraction.num_`
`(*rp).doubleVal()`	*is equivalent to*	`fraction.doubleVal()`
`(*dp).theDay()`	*is equivalent to*	`today.theDay()`

The parentheses are necessary. The class member access operator . has precedence over the dereference operator *. The notation `*rp.num_` means `*(rp.num_)`. For that expression to be valid, `rp.num_` would have to be a pointer, which it is not.

Since `*rp` is a `Rational` object, we can use it in conjunction with the operators overloaded in the `Rational` class. The following code illustrates the use of some of those operators. The initial value of `*rp` represents the fraction 1/5.

```
cout << *rp << endl;              // output: 1/5
*rp += Rational(3,4);             // *rp is 19/20
cout << *rp + *rp << endl;        // output: 19/10
*rp = Rational(3,5) / (*rp + 1);  // *rp is 4/13
```

C++ has a convenient and popular notation for pointers to classes and class members. The notation `rp->num_` indicates the `num_` member of the `Rational` object pointed to by `rp`. The operator `->` is used only with pointers to class or struct objects. Its left operand is a pointer to a class, and its right operand is a member of the class.

`rp->num_`	*is equivalent to*	`(*rp).num_`
`rp->doubleVal()`	*is equivalent to*	`(*rp).doubleVal()`
`dp->theDay()`	*is equivalent to*	`(*dp).theDay()`

Of the two class member notations, `->` is the more commonly used.

Let's try out the `->` operator notation in some code. These two examples use the `Rational` class and the `Date` class.

```
if (dp->theDay() == 1)
    cout << "First day of the month" << endl;
while (rp->doubleVal() < 1000)
    *rp *= 2;
```

Pointers to class types are very common in C++ programs. As you read more sophisticated C++ code, you will become well-accustomed to using pointers instead of explicitly named objects.

Dynamic object creation and destruction: `new` and `delete`

When the compiler translates source code, it makes sure that enough memory will be set aside for all of the objects whose definitions might be executed when the program runs. In that sense, objects that are defined through definitions in the program's code are allocated space at compile time. More precisely, the amount of memory to be allocated to those objects—their storage requirement—is known at compile time.

Other objects, which are not allocated any space at compile time, may be created when a program executes. These are dynamically created objects, or **dynamic objects** for short. The memory in which they reside is not allocated to them until runtime, a process called **dynamic memory allocation**. Whether or not a dynamic object will be created during program execution is not known by the compiler. Not only that, exactly how much space might be required by a dynamic object may also be unknown by the compiler. Whether a dynamic object is created and exactly how much space will be allocated to the object will not be known until the program is executing.

All of the objects that we have coded so far in this text are allocated memory at compile time. A dynamically created object, whose memory is allocated at runtime, requires pointers. With that background, let's define some pointer variables.

```
char* cp;
char* cq;
Rational* rp;
```

Since they were not explicitly initialized, cp, cq, and rp now have values that are meaningless. We could simply assign them the addresses of already created objects. However, it is possible to create new char and Rational type objects and assign the addresses of the new objects to the pointers. The process for making this happen is twofold:

1. Create the object.

2. Store the address of that object as the value of a pointer.

The keyword new is the name of an operator used to create objects dynamically. new is a unary operator whose operand is a *type* rather than an object. A new expression allocates memory for and creates an object of the given type. The value of the expression is the location or address of the newly created object.[1]

Here is how new can be used to create a char type object:

```
cp = new char;
```

Now cp points to the newly created char object. Figure 9.5 illustrates the three pointer variables cp, cq, and rp immediately after the new char object is created. The *only* way that char object can be accessed is through the only name it currently has, *cp. That is why new often appears on the right side of an assignment expression. The left side of the assignment is a pointer variable. The expres-

---

[1] If space for a new object is not available, the value of the new expression is null.

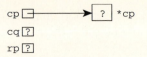

Figure 9.5 A new object , *cp, is created after cp, cq, and rp are defined.

sion assigns the address of the dynamically created object to the pointer variable, thereby giving access to the object.

It is possible to play pointer games with newly created char and Rational type objects. We could make these assignments:

```
cq = cp;
*cq = 'A';
rp = new Rational(3,5);
```

Notice how the Rational object is created. The new operator allocates memory, invoking a constructor for whatever type object is created. Which constructor is invoked depends upon the actual arguments inside the parentheses—the actual arguments for the call to the constructor. Figure 9.6 shows how the picture changes with that last segment of code.

Of course, you can treat *cq, *cp, and *rp as ordinary char and Rational objects now. The code for doing so should not be surprising.

```
Rational f(5);              // f is 5/1
f += *rp + 1;               // f is 33/5
cout << rp->doubleVal();    // output:  0.6
cout << *cq << *cp;         // output:  AA
```

Even though cp already points to an object, we can reassign it to point to a new one. The old one does not go away. So what do you suppose happens with this pair of statements?

```
cq = new char('B');
cp = cq;
```

The first statement creates a char data object initialized to 'B' and pointed to by cq. The second assignment, cp = cq, makes *cp an additional name for the

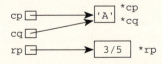

Figure 9.6 cq is assigned the value of cp. rp is assigned the address of a dynamically created Rational.

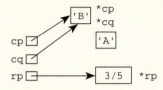

Figure 9.7 The `char` object with value `'A'` is no longer accessible.

new `char` data object. The older `char` data object whose value is `'A'` still exists. But it does not have any name. That old `char` data object cannot be accessed. (See Fig. 9.7.)

The term **lost memory** means dynamically allocated memory to which there is no access. A **memory leak** is program behavior that produces lost memory. Two different problems are associated with memory leaks. Lost memory may contain important information; there is no way to get that information. Memory that is lost is no longer available to the program as it is executing.

As long as the program is executing, that lost memory is taking up space that could be used for something else. That may not be of any consequence. But it has potential to be a serious problem if the total amount of memory lost becomes large. In such a situation, a program may run out of memory.

Reassigning pointers is one way to have a memory leak, but it is not the only way. Memory leaks can also occur if the only access to an object is a pointer variable that goes out of scope. The lifetime for a dynamically created object extends from the time it is created to the time it is explicitly destroyed. If the object is not destroyed, its lifetime extends to the end of the execution of the program. That is quite different from the lifetime of an automatic object, which exists from the time of execution of its definition until it goes out of scope at the end of the block in which it is defined.

Suppose `p` is a pointer that is a local variable pointing to the object `*p`. Suppose also that `p` is the only access to `*p`. When `p` goes out of scope at the end of execution of the block in which it is defined, the object whose name *was* `*p` still exists. But now, there is no way to access that object. That inaccessible object is lost memory.

How do you recapture lost memory? You do not. You prevent it from becoming lost in the first place. If a dynamically created object is no longer needed, then it can be destroyed so long as there is still a pointer to it. Just as creation of an object requires allocation of memory for the object, destruction of the object involves **deallocation** of that memory. The operator `delete` is a unary operator with a pointer operand. It destroys the object pointed to by the pointer variable, deallocating the memory for that object. When memory is deallocated, it is freed up to be used for other purposes.

Suppose object `*cp` is no longer needed. The following statement deallocates the memory that was allocated for the object:

```
delete cp;   // deallocates memory for *cp, the object pointed to by cp
```

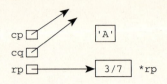

Figure 9.8 The results of deleting `cp`.

The object pointed to by both `cp` and `cq` has been destroyed. The memory that had been allocated to that object is now available for some other use. No, you do not have control over exactly how it is used. You should not try to access the now nonexistent object through `cp` or `cq`. Instead, you should think of the values of `cp` and `cq` as **dangling pointers**, which means the memory they point to has been deallocated.

Null pointers

It is an error to use a pointer to access an object that does not exist. But how can you tell when the value of a pointer is not the address of an object? C++ programmers have a convention just to handle that problem. They use a special value called the **null pointer**, a legitimate pointer value that is known *not* to represent the address of an object.

```
cp = 0;        // cp is now the null pointer
cq = 0;        // cq is now the null pointer
```

The result of those last two assignments is illustrated in Fig. 9.9.

C++ converts the token 0 as the null pointer when it is assigned or compared to a pointer type data object. Any type of pointer variable can be assigned the null pointer value. Any type of pointer can be compared to the null pointer.

If you should try to delete a null pointer, nothing happens.

```
cp = 0;        // cp is a null pointer
delete cp;     // nothing occurs
```

Deleting a pointer that is not null does not change the pointer itself. It changes the pointer's referent—what it points to. That makes pointer code dangerous in its

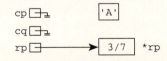

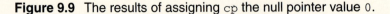

Figure 9.9 The results of assigning `cp` the null pointer value 0.

own special way. The only dangers we have discussed so far are aliasing and memory leaks. But an insidious problem for both beginning programmers and experienced programmers is assuming that a pointer value is the address of an actual object.

> The token 0 can mean several things, including the integer literal 0, the floating point literal 0.0, or the null pointer. How it is interpreted depends on where it is used. When 0 is used as the value of a pointer (in assignments or comparisons), it is interpreted as the null pointer. So the Boolean expression
>
> ```
> (cp != 0)
> ```
>
> can be interpreted as "cp is not the null pointer." But cp can also be used as a Boolean expression, without comparing it directly to 0 (the null pointer). The expression
>
> ```
> (cp)
> ```
>
> is true if cp is not the null pointer and false if cp is the null pointer.
>
> Many programmers prefer to use the token NULL instead of 0 to represent the null pointer. NULL is defined in the standard library. The include directive
>
> ```
> #include <stdlib.h>
> ```
>
> makes NULL available to your code. The following two assignment statements are equivalent:
>
> ```
> cp = 0;      // 0 is the token for a null pointer
> cp = NULL;   // NULL is the token for a null pointer
> ```

Let's look at those assignments of the null pointer to cp and cq once again:

```
cp = 0;      // cp is now the null pointer
cq = 0;      // cq is now the null pointer
```

After the assignments, neither cp nor cq point to actual objects. The pointer ip, whose definition is below, may not point to an actual object either.

```
int* ip;
```

If ip, cp, and cq do not point to actual objects, what happens if we use them as if they did? What happens if the following assignments are made?

```
*ip = 21;
*cp = 'X';
*cq = 'Y';
```

Our best prediction is a disaster that is likely to happen with the first assignment. If not, the second assignment will almost surely fail—and the third assignment is irrelevant (it wouldn't even have a chance to execute).

The disasters come from trying to assign values to objects that do not exist. In the expression `*ip = 21`, the value 21 is assigned to the object whose address is the value of `ip`. But `ip` was never explicitly initialized, so you can assume the worst: `ip`'s value is an address of memory that is not available to your program, or an address of memory that does not even exist, or an address of memory already used by your program for something else important. Who can say? The first two scenarios generate runtime errors. The third scenario may generate a runtime error or just clobber important information.

There are numerous kinds of pointer errors, and it is often difficult to predict when an error will occur. It is possible to get different results each time a program with faulty pointer code is executed, depending on factors such as initial values and how much and where dynamically allocated memory is located. Some errors, like memory leaks, may produce no ill effects. It is often difficult to look at code and determine that it may be faulty. This is especially true in the case where two different pointers in two physically separate pieces of code have the same referent. What appears as proper use of one pointer may result in corruption of the other.

Attempting to dereference an improper pointer value (one that does not point to an actual object) may be a disaster even if you do not try to assign a value to a nonexistent object. Sometimes the result will be a runtime error; sometimes it will be bizarre data; sometimes the data will look legitimate but be faulty. The potential for a nasty error is very high.

Among the more common results of pointer misuse are operating system errors that arise from illegal memory references. The kinds of errors an operating system reports and how it describes them varies from system to system. UNIX systems may produce "segmentation faults." Microcomputers, in which memory is not well protected against abuse, often require rebooting. Macintosh systems may display bombs and illegal address messages. Windows systems may destroy active windows and display restart messages. In the worst case, part of the operating system could be corrupted. What a mess!

A discipline that many programmers use to avoid using nonexistent objects is assigning the null pointer to uninitialized pointers and pointers that have been deleted. If `cp` were initialized to null (or initialized to a legitimate pointer value) and if it were set to null whenever `*cp` was destroyed, then comparing the value of `cp` to null indicates whether or not `cp` points to an actual object. The following selection statement could avoid an error in the assignment to `*cp`:

```
if (cp != 0)          or equivalently    if (cp)
    *cp = 21;                                 *cp = 21;
```

Unfortunately, no such simple test can be used to determine `ip` if it has never been assigned a value. Similarly, if `*cp` and `*cq` are aliases and then `cp` is deleted and set to null, no simple test can be used to determine that `cq` points to an object that has been deallocated.

If you maintain the discipline of making sure that every pointer either points to an actual object or is null before you attempt to use its value, then you will not fall into the pit of using memory that was not allocated. But there is one other problem with using pointers that is difficult to guard against, running out of memory.

The `delete` and `new` operators have symmetric syntax. To create a new `Rational` object and assign its address to `rp`, use

```
rp = new Rational;
```

To destroy the object, you must delete a pointer to that object. The `delete` does not change the value of the pointer and it does not destroy the pointer. Instead, it destroys the pointer's referent. (Deleting a null pointer does nothing.)

It is wise programming practice to set a pointer to null after deleting it. That is one way to avoid the serious dangling pointer problem.

```
delete rp;
rp = 0;
```

Storage allocated though `new` must be explicitly deallocated through `delete`. The lifetime of a dynamically created object is from the time the object is created to the time it is explicitly destroyed (via deleting a pointer to it).

Using `new` and `delete` to create and destroy class type objects

We will go back now to the definition of the `SimpleList` class of Chapter 7. `SimpleList` implements a very simple list type which does not have very sophisticated operations. Here is its definition.

```
class SimpleList {
public:
    SimpleList();              // Constructs an empty list.
    void clear();              // Makes the list empty.
    void add(int newItem);     // Adds newItem to the end of the list.
                               // ASSUME: the list is not full.
```

```
   bool member(int anItem) const;   // Is anItem a list member?
   int maximumCapacity() const;     // Maximum possible list size.
   int currentSize() const;         // Number of items currently in the list.

private:
   enum {maxSize_ = 100};
   int item_[maxSize_];
   int size_;
};
```

The following code creates a `SimpleList` that contains the numbers 5, 7, and 4. The new list object is pointed to by `myList`.

```
SimpleList* myList = new SimpleList;   // myList points to a SimpleList
myList->add(5);
myList->add(7);
myList->add(4);
```

We can continue to use `myList` for other operations as well. For example, we could output the maximum capacity and the current size of the object pointed to by `myList` as follows:

```
cout << "Maximum capacity: " << myList->maximumCapacity() << endl;
cout << "Current size: " << myList->currentSize() << endl;
cout << "Growing room: "
        << myList->maximumCapacity() - myList->currentSize() << endl;
```

The output of the code is shown in the box.

```
    Maximum capacity: 100
    Current size: 3
    Growing room: 97
```

We invoke the `SimpleList` member functions `member()` and `add()` to add a new item to the list if it is not already in the list.

```
if (!myList->member(25))     // 25 is not a list member
   myList->add(25);          //    so add 25 to the list
if (!myList->member(7))      // 7 is a list member, skip the if body
   myList->add(7);           //    statement
```

Now let's see what happens when we create another `SimpleList` pointer. This time, we will define the pointer, and then assign it to point to another dynamically created `SimpleList` type object.

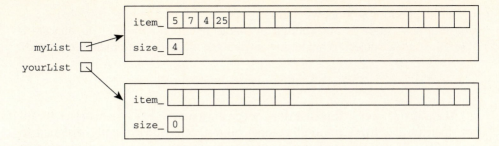

Figure 9.10 Dynamically allocated memory referenced by `myList` and `yourList`.

```
SimpleList* yourList;         // Creates a pointer
yourList = new SimpleList;    // Creates a new object pointed to by yourList
```

Figure 9.10 illustrates the memory that has been dynamically allocated. It might make you a little more careful about avoiding memory leaks.

Of course, if you simply assign `yourList` as follows, without deleting it, you generate a serious memory leak.

```
yourList = myList;            // Memory leak!
```

The entire 100 element array as well as the `int` that were data members of the original `SimpleList` pointed to by `yourList` can no longer be used. Furthermore, they occupy memory that could be of potential use at another time during program execution. While just the loss of that memory may not be very significant, the loss of many such pieces of memory may be. To avoid the memory leak caused by the assignment to `yourList`, delete `yourList`.

```
delete yourList;      // Destroy *yourList, thus deallocating memory
yourList = 0;         // Avoid dangling pointer problems
```

Then, if you want both `yourList` and `myList` to point to the same `SimpleList`, you can make an assignment to `yourList`.

```
yourList = myList;    // No memory leak if yourList was just deleted
```

9.2   Dealing with failures: `exit()` and `assert()`

One of the revolutions in computer hardware has been the relatively recent availability of large amounts of memory. Cheap memory at that. But while memory is abundant and inexpensive, it is not infinite. It is possible for a program to attempt to create more objects than the available memory can accommodate.

In the previous section, we defined `yourList` to be a pointer-to-`SimpleList` type. Suppose there is not enough available memory remaining to allocate a `SimpleList` type object. What happens when the following statement is executed?

```
yourList = new SimpleList;  // Not enough memory? new returns 0.
```

The `new` operator in this case does not create a new `SimpleList` object. It cannot. Instead, it returns the null pointer value that is subsequently assigned to `yourList`. To determine if a new object was created, compare the value of `yourList` to the null pointer.

```
if (yourList == 0) {
    // yourList is the null pointer
    cerr << "Out of memory";
    exit(1);
}
```

The selection statement is a simple error check. It sends a message to `cerr` to indicate the nature of the error. And then it terminates the program, cleaning up as it goes. The call to `exit()` is possible if the code contains the following include directive:

```
#include <stdlib.h>
```

Another popular program development technique uses a different built-in library. It requires this include directive:

```
#include <assert.h>
```

Programmers use `assert` for program development and debugging. Let's see how we might use it. Replace that last assignment and `if` statement with the following code:

```
yourList = new SimpleList;   // Try to create a new SimpleList.
assert(yourList != 0);       // Was there enough memory to create one?
```

Think of `assert` as a function that has a single Boolean type condition for an argument. The function behaves as follows.[2]

- If the condition is true (here, if `yourList` is not the null pointer), then nothing happens.

---

[2] `assert` is usually implemented as a macro. The advantage of using it is that it is easy to arrange that the assert statements are treated merely as comments and generate no code at all.

- If the condition is false (here, if `yourList` is the null pointer), then the program halts execution and prints a message on the terminal that tells which line in the file contained the `assert`.

Suppose that the name of the source code file containing the code is `aProg.C` and that the number of the line in the program containing the `assert` is 57. Suppose also that `new` returned a null pointer, making the assert condition false. The exact message that assert reports may vary among different programming environments, but this format is typical:

```
Assertion failed: yourList != 0, file aProg.C, line 57
```

Of course, if there are several asserts in the program, then the line number indicates which one triggered the message.

9.3 █ References

You already know about references. We first discussed them in Chapter 3 in the context of functions and reference arguments. A **reference** to an object is an alias for that object. Pointers can also be used for aliases. So references and pointers have much in common. But they are not the same.

Let's review how reference types work for formal function arguments. Consider the following definitions, one for a function named `inc()` and one for a global variable named `y`:

```
void inc(double& x)
{
    x += 1;
}
double y = 4;            // y is global
```

What exactly happens when `inc(y)` is executed? A new name for a `double` object, a reference to `double`, is created. The type `double&` is a reference type. Reference types are used as aliases for other objects. When `inc(y)` is executed, the formal argument x, which is type `double&`, becomes an alias for the global variable y. There is only one `double` object. Its global name is y, but it is referred to as x when executing the body of `inc(y)`.

What we have just explained should be old news to you. But let's take a closer look at reference types. Although they are used almost exclusively for reference arguments and return types, it is also possible to define variables or constants that are references.

```
int n;              // n is an ordinary int variable
int& b = n;         // b is a reference to n
```

The variable b is a reference to an object of type int. Rather than being the name of a new data object, b is simply a new name for an old data object, n— b is an alias for n. Any changes that occur to the object named b automatically occur also to n and vice versa. After all, it has two names, but there is only one int data object. So with an assignment of 37 to b

```
b = 37;
```

the value of n also becomes 37. Figure 9.11 illustrates what we mean.

Unlike pointers, when they are defined references must be initialized to be names of objects that already exist. Also unlike pointers, references cannot be assigned as aliases of different objects after they have been defined.

Suppose we throw in the following definition in addition to the others:

```
const int& c = n;   // c is a constant reference to n and cannot be used to
                    //   change the value of n
```

The constant c is a reference to n also. So c, b, and n are three different names for the same int type data object. But c is a constant reference—it cannot be used to change the value of the object. In particular, c cannot be used on the left side of an assignment and c cannot be used as an actual argument corresponding to a formal, nonconstant reference argument.

The symbol & means different things depending on where it is used.

1. When placed in front of its operand, & is the address of operator.

2. When it appears after a type name, & makes the type a reference type.

3. As a binary operator, & is the bitwise AND operator.

The symbol * means different things depending on where it is used also.

1. When placed in front of its operand, * is the dereference operator.

2. When it appears after a type name, * makes the type a pointer type.

3. As a binary operator, * means multiplication.

An understanding of reference types makes clear how reference arguments and reference return values work. Take a look at two more examples:

n 37 b

Figure 9.11 n and b are two different names for the same object.

```
void f(const Rational& k);
Rational& g(Rational& m);
```

When `f()` is invoked, a const reference corresponding to the formal argument `k` is created and initialized with the actual argument. During execution of the function, `k` is an alias for the actual argument—it is simply another name for the actual argument. Since `k` is a const reference argument, `k` cannot be used inside the body of `f()` to change the actual argument.

When `g()` is called, `g()` returns a reference to a `Rational` type object. So if `r` is a `Rational`, then `g(r)` is a name for an object; `g(r)` can be used as an lvalue on the left side of an assignment. The following statements are valid:

```
// r is a Rational variable object.
g(r) = Rational(17);
g(r) += Rational(5,9);
```

Suppose C++ did not have reference types. Could pointer types be used to create "reference arguments"? The answer is yes. C does not have reference types. C uses pointers to substitute for references. The function `increment()` is very similar to `inc()`.

```
void increment(double* x)
{
    *x = *x + 1;               // alternatively, *x += 1;
}
```

The argument to `increment()` is of type `double*`. In order to initialize the formal argument properly, the actual argument should be an address. `increment()` adds 1 to the contents of the `double` object pointed to by the formal argument `x`. The address of the actual argument is necessary to initialize `x`. The following is a proper call to `increment()`:

```
increment(&y);
```

When this call is executed, a local pointer-to-`double` corresponding to the formal argument `x` is created and initialized with the value of the actual argument— the pointer `x` is initialized with the address of `y`. Since `x` is the name of a pointer, it must be dereferenced in order to access the `double` that it points to. During the execution of `increment(&y)`, `*x` is an alias for `y`.

The functions `inc()` and `increment()` illustrate some of the reasons why C++ programmers prefer to use reference types instead of pointer types for formal arguments. The function `inc()` is easier to understand and easier to use than `increment()`. Formal reference type arguments are not dereferenced inside the function body; formal pointer type arguments must be dereferenced. Actual arguments corresponding to formal reference type arguments are objects. Actual arguments corresponding to formal pointer type arguments must be addresses of objects. An additional complication that our examples do not show occurs when functions with pointer type arguments invoke themselves or other functions with pointer type arguments. The initial invocation is made with the address of the actual argument. Second and subsequent invocations are made with the pointer alone—those calls are made without the address-of operator, &. If this sounds confusing, be glad that C++ has reference types. They provide a consistent and simple way of dealing with functions with pass-by-reference arguments.

The essential difference between references and pointers is this: references are lvalues and pointers are rvalues that can provide lvalues by being dereferenced. References must be initialized with the names of the objects they reference. They cannot be reassigned as aliases to different objects. Pointers need not be initialized. They can be reassigned different addresses.

When should you use a pointer and when should you use a reference? The general advice is use a reference whenever you can and use a pointer whenever a reference is inadequate.

You cannot use a reference in the following situations:

1. When you want to have null as a pointer value. (A reference cannot be null; it must always reference a real object.)

2. When you want to change which object is the referent. (A reference is tied to the same object throughout its lifetime.)

References rather than pointers are commonly used for formal function arguments and return types (except in the case where the function can use null as an argument or can return a null value).

9.4 ■ Dynamic array creation

It seems like pointers are more trouble than they are worth. Instead of defining a pointer to an `int`, why not simply define an `int` instead and get rid of the pointer? The pointer just complicates the code.

While pointers-to-`int`s may not be particularly useful, pointers to more complicated types are a different story. We'll begin with an example. Suppose a program manages mailing addresses. The programmer can define a C-string type with this code:

```
const int maxSize = 25;
typedef char mailingAddress[maxSize];
```

The size of `mailingAddress` may be sufficient for most mailing address. But some mailing addresses are much longer; 25 characters will be completely inadequate. One way to attack the problem is to initialize `maxSize` with a larger number, say 50 or 100 or even 1,000. That may be one approach, but what should be the maximum size? It is hard to tell. If the maximum size is too small, we are back where we started. If it is too large, then the program may not be able to accommodate a long enough list of mailing addresses for its intended application.

So we are stuck with two possibilities: `maxSize` is small enough to allow implementing a list of mailing addresses but not large enough to allow the entire mailing address for everything on the list; or `maxSize` is large enough to allow full mailing addresses but too large to allow a long enough list of mailing addresses. Ideally, the size of a mailing address could be allowed to vary from one address to the next. Only long mailing addresses would be allocated large amounts of memory. Shorter ones would be allocated only the amount of memory they need.

Delaying decisions about how much memory should be allocated to an array until execution time can be accomplished through dynamic memory allocation and object creation. We need pointers to arrays for that.

Determining array size at execution time

The type `int*` is a pointer-to-int. But an `int*` data object can also point to an array of integers rather than simply a single `int`. A pointer to an array of integers points to an element of the array—the value of the pointer is the address of the array element. The type `int` is no different from other types in that regard. A `char*` can be a pointer to a C-string, a `double*` can be a pointer to an array of doubles, a `Rational*` can be a pointer to an array of `Rational`s.

The operator `new` is used for dynamic creation of array objects as well as nonarray objects. The expression `new double` allocates enough space for and creates a single `double`. The expression `new double[30]` allocates enough space for and creates an array of 30 `double`s. To create an array, the operand for `new` is the type of array element followed by the number of elements in the array in brackets. The number of array elements can be any integer expression. It does not have to be a constant.

```
new elementType[integerExpression]    // Creates an array with
                                      //    integerExpression elements of
                                      //    type elementType
```

In the code that follows, a is of type `int*` and n is an `int` variable. The last assignment creates an array of `int`s and assigns to a the address of the first element of the array. Figure 9.12 illustrates this new array.

```
int* a;
int n;
n = 20;
a = new int[n];
```

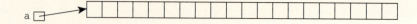

Figure 9.12 Type a points to an array of 20 `int`s.

Using arrays that have been dynamically created is easier than you may anticipate. Pointers to those arrays do not have to be explicitly dereferenced using the * operator. Instead, those pointers can be treated almost exactly the same as the names of the arrays. The following code assigns the value 16 to the first element of the array pointed to by a, and it assigns 31 to the second element.

```
a[0] = 16;      // Equivalent to *a = 16
a[1] = 31;      // Equivalent to *(a + 1) = 31
```

That second comment indicates that a[1] and *(a + 1) mean the same thing. This is an illustration of "pointer arithmetic." One example of pointer arithmetic is adding an integer to a pointer. You can guess, quite correctly, that a[5] and *(a + 5) mean the same thing too. When a points to an array, the lvalues *a, *(a + 1), *(a + 2), and so on are the successive elements in the array. C++ computes the value of a + 1 by adding the size of the array element to the address of the array, not by adding the number 1—the increment is based on the type of the pointer.

We can also dynamically allocate C-strings. The following code provides an example:

```
char* firstName;                          // Creates a pointer-to-char.
firstName = new char[strlen("Rex") + 1];  // Allocates an array of char.
strcpy(firstName,"Rex");                  // Copies "Rex" into the new
                                          //    array.
```

The second line allocates just enough memory for an array of characters to hold the characters 'R', 'e', 'x', plus one more for '\0'. The terminating null character is necessary if we want the array to be a proper C-string. The result of the last segment of code is illustrated by Fig. 9.13.

The mailing address problem can be solved with dynamically created arrays. Suppose buffer is the name of a C-string whose value represents a single mailing address. Suppose also that mail is of type char*. This code creates a new C-string with just the number of elements necessary to represent the mailing address currently in buffer.

```
mail = new char[strlen(buffer) + 1];
```

The expression strlen(buffer) is the number of characters in the buffer string before its terminating null character. For mail to have enough elements to hold buffer's characters as well as a terminating null character, the size of the array allocated is strlen(buffer) + 1.

You can now use mail as the name of the newly created array, without derefer-

Figure 9.13 `firstName` points to an array of four `char`s.

encing it. To copy the information in `buffer` to the newly created array, use `strcpy()`. The copy is safe because `mail` has exactly enough elements to hold all of the characters in `buffer` up through the first occurrence of the terminating `'\0'`.

```
strcpy(mail, buffer);
```

Keep in mind that `mail` now acts like an ordinary name for an array of characters; `mail[0]` is the name of the first character, `mail[1]` is the name of the second, and so on.

The built-in character handling library with header file `ctype.h` has a function `toupper()`, which has a `char` argument and returns the uppercase equivalent of that argument. If the argument is not a lowercase character, then the function returns the value of the argument. The following code is an illustration of its use:

```
#include <ctype.h>

char ch = 'a';
ch = toupper(ch);      // ch is now 'A'
ch = toupper('b');     // ch is now 'B'
ch = toupper('Q');     // ch is now 'Q'
```

This code uses `toupper()` to convert all of the letters in `mail`'s array to uppercase.

```
int len = strlen(mail);
for (int i = 0; i < len; i++)
   mail[i] = toupper(mail[i]);
```

Of course, we could translate that segment to a function definition. The function `uppercase()` takes a string of characters and turns all of the lowercase alphabetic characters into their uppercase equivalent. Its definition looks much like the code segment:

```
void uppercase(char s[])
{
   int len = strlen(s);                 // Use strlen to find out how many
   for (int i = 0; i < len; i++)        //   characters must be scanned.
     s[i] = toupper(s[i]);
}
```

The function `uppercase()` could be declared in any of the following ways:

```
void uppercase(char* s);
void uppercase(char s[]);
void uppercase(char*);      // Signature of uppercase().
void uppercase(char[]);     // Alternate uppercase() signature.
```

That's not all; `uppercase()` can be invoked with a pointer argument or an array argument. Suppose `mail` is defined as before and `name` is defined in this manner.

```
char name[] = "Lynn Barber";
```

Then both of these statements are valid invocations of `uppercase()`.

```
uppercase(name);    // name changes to "LYNN BARBER"
uppercase(mail);    // Lowercase mail characters are changed to uppercase
```

Creating arrays on the fly with `new []` is a very common programming practice. But whenever an object is dynamically created, whether it is an array type of object or not, there is a potential for a memory leak when the only pointer to that object goes out of scope or is assigned another value. C++ provides a way to destroy dynamically created arrays with the `delete []` operator.

By using `delete []` with a pointer to an array that was dynamically allocated, all of the memory that was set aside to hold the array elements is deallocated. The following statement destroys the array that was created for the mailing address.

```
delete [] mail;
```

The brackets are necessary when deleting a pointer to an array.[3] Don't put the number of elements of the array inside the brackets, because C++ keeps track of how much memory was allocated in the first place.

The rule about whether to use `delete` or `delete []` when destroying dynamically creating objects is clear:

- Use `delete` if the object was created with `new` (with no brackets).
- Use `delete[]` if the object was created with `new []`.

[3] Some compilers do not detect when `delete` is used instead of `delete []` when deallocating memory for an array. But the result could be a disaster, including obscure memory leaks. The language specifies that `delete []` must be used for arrays.

The definition of the function `reverse()` illustrates using `delete[]` to deallocate a C-string. The `delete []` prevents the memory leak, which would occur when the function quits execution and the local pointer `backward` goes out of scope.

```
void reverse(char word[])
// Argument: word - A valid C-string
// Side effect: Reverses the characters in word.
{
    int n = strlen(word);                 // Number of word characters (less the
                                          //    null character)
    char* backward = new char[n + 1];     // Buffer to hold the characters in word
                                          //    in reverse order

    for(int i = 0; i < n; i++)            // Copy the characters from word to
        backward[i] = word[n - i - 1];    //    backward in reverse order
    backward[n] = '\0';

    strcpy(word, backward);
    delete [] backward;                   // Avoid a memory leak when backward
                                          //    goes out of scope
}
```

The connection between pointers and arrays

Is an array simply a pointer? Although arrays and pointers seem to behave almost the same, the answer is no. There are subtle differences between arrays and pointers. Consider the following definitions:

```
char* cp;
char* cq;
char array[30];
cp = new char[30];
cq = new char;
```

The type of `cp` is `char*`; the type of `array` is `char[30]`. Those two types, `char*` and `char[30]`, are not the same. For the definition of `cp`, the compiler sets aside space for a pointer—enough space to represent a single machine address. Whether the object at that address is the first character in an array of 30 characters, the first character in an array of 1,000 characters, or simply a character is not part of the definition of `cp`. For the definition of `array`, the compiler sets aside enough space for an array of 30 characters. In addition, the compiler associates `array` with the address of the first character in that array.

Pointers differ from arrays in another respect. The name of an array is an lvalue that cannot be modified. That means `array` cannot be associated with the address of any character except the address of its first element, the address originally specified by the compiler. In effect, `array` cannot be the left-hand operand of an assignment. The following statement is illegal:

```
array = cp;        // illegal
```

On the other hand, `cp` and `cq` are modifiable lvalues. They can appear on the left side of assignment expressions. These assignments are legal:

```
cq = array;        // legal. cq points to the first element of array.
cp = cq;           // legal
```

Even though pointer and array types are not the same, C++ builds in conversions between them. The compiler can convert `array` to a pointer to its first element. The expression `*array` is syntactically legal, and its value is the same as `array[0]`. The compiler can also convert `cp` to the name of an array of characters. That is why the expressions `cp[0]` and `cp[10]` are syntactically legal. Of course, `cp[10]` makes logical sense only if `cp` points to the first character in an array of at least 11 characters.

What happens when arrays are passed as arguments to functions? Recall that these two function declarations are equivalent:

```
void f(char x[]);      equivalent to      void f(char* x);
```

C++ considers the formal argument `x` to be of type pointer-to-`char`. When `f(array)` is executed, C++ converts the value of the actual argument, `array`, to a pointer value—the address of the first element of `array` to be precise. That address is used to initialize the formal argument. So `*x` becomes another name for `array[0]`. Inside the body of the function, `x` can be used with pointer or array syntax. A simple assignment like `x[3] = 'A'` can be used to change an element of the array that `x` points to, an element of `array`. That is why array type arguments are always passed by reference, even though the syntax for a formal array argument looks like pass-by-value syntax.

Why can't you define an array the same as you can declare a formal array argument, such as: `int item[]`?

An array must be initialized to a specific number of elements. In the formal argument declaration, you are not initializing. The initialization takes place only when the actual argument is passed. Even then, the compiler does not treat that initialization as initializing an array. Instead, the compiler treats that initialization as creating an alias to the actual array argument.

To force the actual array elements to remain fixed, the programmer must specify that the formal argument points to constant values. The pointer argument must point to a constant object. The type `const char*` is called pointer-to-const-char. The pointer is not constant. What it points to, however, is. These two function prototypes are also equivalent:

```
void g(const char x[]);    equivalent to    void g(const char* x);
```

The type `const char*` says that what the pointer points to is to be treated as a constant. (It does not say that the value of the pointer—the address—is a constant.) So the function `g()` may not change what the actual pointer argument points to, whether it is a single character or an array of characters.

The syntax for pointers to constants and constant pointers can be confusing. These definitions of pointers illustrate the use of constants and pointers.

```
const T* p;        // p is a pointer to a constant T

T* const p;        // p is a constant pointer to a T

const T* const p;  // p is a constant pointer to a constant T
```

9.5   First class strings

C++ does not have a built-in string type, but it does have a string library. And C++ supports C-style strings, which are simply arrays of characters with `'\0'` terminators. But arrays are not first class types. In this section, we will create a better string type, a first class string type. We will begin our work by discussing a string ADT.

You can probably think of several possible string operations just from considering the string library functions. The string library functions that are perhaps the most useful are `strcpy()`, `strcmp()`, and `strlen()`. Another useful string library function is `strcat()`, which takes two C-string arguments and copies the characters of the last argument to the end of the first one.

While the string library functions are valuable, they are not as nice as the operations on built-in numeric types. Suppose s and t are two objects. Isn't the notation s = t more natural to use than `strcpy(s,t)`? That's not all; `strcpy()`

is not a safe operation. It is possible to copy more characters than there are elements in the target string. As far as comparisons are concerned, the expressions `s < t` and `s == t` look more natural than `strcmp(s,t) < 0` and `strcmp(s,t) == 0`. Our string ADT will have at least these operations: `=`, `==`, `!=`, `<`, `<=`, `>`, and `>=`. To provide the functionality of `strlen()`, our string ADT will have a length operation as well.

As a programmer, what other things might you want a new string type to accommodate? How about initializing a string when it is defined? You certainly ought to be able to initialize a string with an array of characters. In addition, you ought to be able to initialize a string with another string. Those two kinds of creations and initializations will be part of our string ADT. Creating a string from an array of characters gives conversion in one direction. Our string ADT will include conversion in the other direction too. We'll be able to convert a string value to an array of characters.

Input and output are essential computer-world operations just like assignment. A type that fails to support input and output operations is not a first class type. Input and output operations will be part of our string ADT.

We've made our way through the easy decisions. What other operations should our string ADT support? At this point we have some real choices and hard decisions. We could make our string ADT "fat," so that it includes everything that anyone could ever think of doing with strings. Or we could leave out some of that functionality, concentrating our efforts on a simple interface that is easy to understand. There is a tradeoff. We are going to compromise to include just a little more functionality than absolutely necessary for a first class string type but still keep the interface of the `String` class fairly simple.

Strings consist of characters. For some applications, programmers must be able to access individual characters within a string. The array bracket notation provides that access for ordinary arrays. If `s` is an array of characters and `i` an appropriately sized `int`, then `s[i]` is a character in `s`. The brackets are the symbol for the subscript operator. We decided to provide a subscript operator in our string ADT. That will allow a programmer to look at a particular character in a string without converting its value to an array of characters. In addition, the subscript operator will allow a programmer to change a single character in a string without making an entire string reassignment.

The final functionality that our string ADT will provide is the ability to attach one string value onto the end of another. This operation, called concatenation, is the result of "adding" one string to another. In the C++ domain of numbers, addition is accomplished by two different operators, `+` and `+=`. Our string ADT will include two concatenation operations, `+` and `+=`.

The description of the string ADT is sufficient to generate most of a `String` class definition. The only data member of the new class will be a pointer-to-`char`. An array to hold the string characters will be dynamically allocated when a `String` object is created. That alone is enough to introduce at least one new language feature into this class. And it will make coding member functions a little trickier. But the payback will be well worth the effort.

```
// A first class string type
class String {
public:
    // Constructors and destructor
    String(const char s[] = "");  // Constructs a deep copy of a C-string.
                                  //   ASSUME: s is a valid C-string.
    String(const String& s);      // Constructs a deep copy of s.
    ~String();                    // Deallocates String memory.

    // Assignment operators
    String& operator= (const String& rhs);   // Assigns a deep copy of rhs.
    String& operator+= (const String& rhs);  // Adds a deep copy of rhs on the
                                              //   end of this string.

    char& operator[](int i);          // The element at subscript i.
                                      // ASSUME: i < length of the string
    char operator[](int i) const;     // The element at subscript i.
                                      // ASSUME: i < length of the string

    int length() const;              // Number of string characters.
    const char* charString( ) const; // C-String equivalent value.
    // Comparison operators
    friend bool operator== (const String& s, const String& t);
    friend bool operator!= (const String& s, const String& t);
    friend bool operator<  (const String& s, const String& t);
    friend bool operator<= (const String& s, const String& t);
    friend bool operator>  (const String& s, const String& t);
    friend bool operator>= (const String& s, const String& t);

    friend ostream& operator<<(ostream& out, const String& s);
            // Writes the C-string equivalent to out.
    friend istream& operator>> (istream& in, String & s);
            // Reads at most 999 characters up to the next newline from
            //   from in. The newline is extracted but not assigned.
    friend String operator+(const String& s, const String& t);
            // A deep copy of s with a deep copy of t appended to the end.
private:
    char* info_;
};
```

Constructors of classes with dynamically created member data

The first two member functions of the `String` class are constructors. One constructor will be called whenever a new `String` object is created. The first one,
`String(const char s[] = "")`, is actually two functions in one. It is a null con-

structor. And since it has a formal argument that is a `char[]` (an array of characters), it is a conversion constructor, creating a `String` from a C-style string.

The documentation for each constructor indicates that they make **deep copies** of their arguments. This is what that means for the first constructor (the C-string conversion constructor). The argument is an address. The constructor makes a copy of what is at that address rather than simply copy the address. The constructor will create a new array and copy the elements of the array argument to the new array.

Whenever a new object is created, part of the task of the constructor for that object is to make sure that the new object has all of the resources it needs. In particular, the C-string conversion constructor makes sure that enough memory is allocated for the new object.

```
String:: String(const char s[])
{
    info_ = new char[strlen(s) + 1];      // Leave room for the '\0'.
    strcpy(info_, s);                      // Copy from s to info.
}
```

An array of characters will be dynamically created whenever a new `String` type object is constructed. The array is pointed to by the private member `info_`. The number of elements in the array depends on the argument to the constructor. For our implementation, the array has exactly enough elements to hold the characters of the argument up through the first occurrence of the terminating null character, `'\0'`. That convenient representation allows the `String` methods to manipulate the newly created array by using functions in the built-in string library.

The constructor for creating a `String` from a C-style string uses the string library twice. The first use of the library, `strlen(s) + 1`, is to determine the number of elements that must be allocated for the array. (The new array must have one more element than the string length of the argument in order to have room for the terminating `'\0'`.) The other use of the string library, `strcpy(info_,s)`, is to assign the argument to the newly created array.

The second constructor, `String(const String& s)`, is a **copy constructor**. It constructs a new `String` as a copy of an already existing `String`. Any constructor that creates a new object from an object of the same type is called a copy constructor.

The copy constructor makes a deep copy of its argument, too. In this case, a new array is created. Its elements are initialized with the values of the elements of the array associated with the actual `String` argument.

```
String:: String(const String& s)
{
    info_ = new char[strlen(s.info_) + 1]; // Allocate memory for the copy.
    strcpy(info_, s.info_);                 // Copy the argument's characters.
}
```

Notice that the argument type for the copy constructor is `const  String&` instead of `String`. The argument for the copy constructor *must* be a reference type. The `const` modifier in front of the reference argument type prohibits the constructor from modifying the object it is copying. It also allows making a copy of a constant object.

It is easy to recognize a copy constructor in the definition of a class that declares one. If `X` is the name of a class, then the copy constructor is the only constructor with a single argument whose type is a reference to `X`. To find the copy constructor for the class `X`, look for this signature:

```
X(const X&)        // Copy constructor signature for a class named X
```

Every class has a copy constructor. If a copy constructor is not explicitly declared in the class definition, C++ automatically provides one. Such a copy constructor makes a member-by-member copy from the argument to the object being created. If an object of a type exists, it is always possible to create a new object of the same type by using the existing one.[4]

Until this point, we have been content not to make our own copy constructors. The copy constructors automatically provided by C++ behaved correctly. But until this point, we have not defined any class that had pointer members either.

When are constructors called? Suppose that `s` is a `String` type object.

1. A constructor is called when a new object is defined.

```
String t(s);          // Copy constructor
String u("Hello");    // C-string conversion constructor
String v;             // Null constructor; v.info_ is ""
```

2. A constructor is called when a new object is dynamically created.

```
String* p = new String(s);    // Copy constructor:
                              //  p->info_ is a copy of s.info_
String* q = new String("Bye");// C-string constructor
                              //   q->info_ is "Bye"
String* r = new String;       // Null constructor
                              //   r->info_ is ""
```

3. A constructor is called when a function with a formal value argument is invoked. When a function with a formal const reference argument is

---

[4] There is one exception. If a copy constructor is defined as a private member of a class, then it may not be possible to create a new object of the class using an existing one.

invoked using an actual argument that is not an object of the same type, a conversion constructor that can create an object out of the actual argument is called (assuming, of course, that such a constructor exists).

```
void f(String x);
void g(const String& x);
...
f(s);         // Formal argument x created via copy constructor
f("Hello");   // Formal argument x created via C-string constructor
g(s);         // NO constructor is called; x is a reference for s.
g("Hello");   // Formal argument x created via C-string constructor
```

4. A copy constructor may be called when a function that returns a value (rather than a void function or a function that returns an object) completes execution. This is compiler dependent—the compiler will call the copy constructor if necessary. The compiler creates a temporary object to hold the value that is returned.

```
String g()
{
    String temp;   // Null constructor
    ...
    return temp;   // May have an implicit copy constructor
                   //   call, String(temp)
}
```

5. A constructor is called by the compiler when it must create a temporary object in order to evaluate an expression.

```
if (s == "abc")   // Compiler makes a temporary String, calling
    ...           //   a conversions constructor, String("abc")
t = String(w);    // Compiler makes a temporary String copy of
                  //   w, calling the copy constructor, String(w)
```

The `String` arguments for the overloaded `String` operators are either of type `String&` or of type `const String&`. For the operator functions, we could have used `String` arguments wherever `const String&` arguments appeared. But doing so would have created some inefficiency that is very easy to avoid.

Both `String&` and `const String&` are reference types. When a function with a reference type argument is called with an actual `String` argument, no new object corresponding to the actual argument is created. If a function with a value argument of type `String` is called, then a new `String` object corresponding to the actual argument is created. The compiler will call one of the `String` constructors to create that object. Both constructors dynamically create a new array of characters and then copy characters from the actual argument into the array. When an actual argument needs only to be looked at and not changed, the allocation and subsequent copying can be a waste of time and memory.

We used `const Rational&` type formal arguments rather than value arguments for the functions declared in the `Rational` class definition. The gain in efficiency was not very spectacular in that case. When a new `Rational` object is made, no new array is created. Instead, only two integers are copied for the data of the new object.

Although we could have used pass-by-value `String` type arguments for the operator functions, the `String` copy constructor could not have a value argument. That has nothing to do with whether or not the actual argument is changed. It has everything to do with the creation of new objects for formal value arguments. To make a new object from a `String` value, the `String` copy constructor is called. If the `String` copy constructor had a formal value argument, the copy constructor would have to call itself to create the object for the formal argument. And of course, when the copy constructor calls itself, another new `String` object for the formal argument of that next call would be created and initialized—using the copy constructor, of course! The process has no way of stopping. The ultimate effect would be infinite recursion. The formal argument for the `String` copy constructor and for all copy constructors must be a reference type.

Destructors

Both of the constructors for the `String` class dynamically create arrays of characters. Dynamic object creation has a potential of resulting in memory leaks when `String` type objects are destroyed or when they go out of scope. To prevent those memory leaks, a `String` object must have some method for deallocating the memory that was allocated to its character array.

It is possible to define a member function whose sole purpose is to destroy the array. That function could be called immediately before a `String` object goes out of scope to deallocate its array while it could still be accessed. If a `String` object itself was created through a pointer of type `String*`, then that member function could be called immediately before a pointer pointing to the object is deleted.

If the function that deallocates the array is an ordinary `String` class member function, then the programmer must make an explicit call to that function with the instance of the class that is going out of existence. That puts a burden on the programmer to write the calls for objects that are created in the code. Keep in mind that `String` objects can be created through a variety of mechanisms including an ordinary definition of a `String` object, dynamically creating a `String` object through the `new` operator, calling a function with a `String` pass-by-value argument, calling a function that returns a `String` value, and evaluating an expression that requires a temporary `String` object in order to perform the evaluation.

Let's focus on temporary objects for a moment. Temporary objects are created by the compiler. Their creation and subsequent death are not explicitly written in the code, so it is easy to forget about them—they are somewhat like local variables that are not declared. Temporary objects do not have names, but they are objects, nevertheless. And whenever any `String` object is created, whether it is temporary or not, a `String` constructor is invoked and memory for an array is dynamically allocated. Explicitly invoking a member function that deallocates memory through a temporary `String` object may be impossible. How can a programmer invoke a member function for an instance of a class that has no name?

The C++ solution to this problem is the **destructor**, a special member function that is automatically invoked by the compiler whenever any instance of that class dies. Those instances include temporary objects, objects defined through declarations or formal arguments, and dynamically created objects that go out of existence when pointers to them are deleted. The programmer does not invoke the destructor explicitly.[5] Instead, the compiler invokes the destructor, much the same as it invokes a constructor when a new object is created.

A class can have several constructors, but it can have only one destructor. The name of the destructor is the tilde symbol ~ followed by the name of the class. The destructor has no return type and it has no arguments. The destructor declaration that appears in the definition of a class named X is this:

```
~X();   // Destructor
```

The destructor for the `String` class is the member function `~String()`. The purpose of the `String` class destructor is to destroy the array pointed to by the member `info_`, deallocating the memory for the array.

```
String :: ~String( )
{
    delete [] info_;    // Deallocate the array.
}
```

Let's see how the constructors and destructors for the `String` class might be invoked in some sample code. We will illustrate their use with the function `example()`, whose definition is as follows:

```
void example(String x)
{
   // Creation of x invokes the copy constructor.

   String r("Ann");            // Conversion constructor; r.info_ is "Ann"
   String s;                   // Conversion constructor; s.info_ is ""
   String t(r);                // Copy constructor; t.info_ is "Ann"
   String* pt;                 // No constructor: pt is not a String
   pt = new String("Bob");     // Conversion constructor; pt->info_ is "Bob"
   String* qt = new String(r); // Copy constructor; qt->info_ is "Ann"
```

---

[5] Under some circumstances, the destructor for a class can be called explicitly. The syntax for doing so is unusual.

```
// Fig. 9.14 illustrates dynamically allocated memory at this time.

delete pt;      // Destructor is invoked for *pt.
qt = 0;         // Memory leak: the old *qt and qt->info_ are lost memory!
}               // Destructor is called for r, s, and t.
                // Destructor is called for argument x at this time.
```

Suppose that the call example("Linda") is executed. That function call is valid because the compiler knows how to initialize the formal String argument from the literal value "Linda". The String conversion constructor, which initializes an object from a C-string, tells it how.

The documentation inside the body of example() describes some of the dynamically allocated memory. Notice the differences among r, r.info_, and pt. They are all distinct types: r is a String, r.info_ is a pointer-to-char, and pt is a pointer-to-String.

Figure 9.14 shows the objects that are dynamically created and the relations among them prior to execution of delete pt. All of the boxes that have arrows pointing to them represent dynamically allocated memory.

When example("Linda") finishes execution, r, s, t, and x go out of scope. The compiler invokes the destructor for these String objects. The pointers pt and qt are a different story.

The destructor is automatically invoked when a pointer to a dynamically created String is deleted. The expression delete pt has two consequences:

- The destructor for *pt is called.

- The memory allocated for *pt is deallocated.

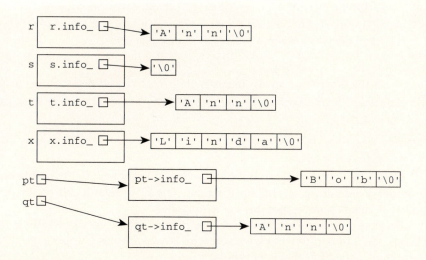

Figure 9.14   Illustration of objects created in the function invocation
example ("Linda").

The destructor for `*pt` deletes `pt->info_`. The array allocated for `pt->info_` is destroyed and its memory is deallocated. Without the operation `delete pt`, both the dynamically created `String`, `*pt`, and the dynamically created array, `pt->info_`, could have become lost memory.

The destructor for a dynamically created `String` *will not be invoked just because a pointer to the* `String` *is reassigned or goes out of scope.* The function `example()` creates a memory leak by assigning `qt` the null pointer before deleting it. It could have created an additional memory leak by failing to delete `pt`.

The following are three versions of syntax for the `new` operator:

1. `new type`
   allocates memory for and creates a single object of the given `type` via the null constructor.

2. `new type(arg-list)`
   allocates memory for and creates a single object of the given `type` via the constructor that can take `arg-list` for arguments.

3. `new type[N]`
   allocates memory for an array of `N` objects of the given `type` and creates those objects via calls to the null constructor.

The `delete` operator syntax has two forms:

1. `delete pointer`
   calls the destructor for `*pointer` and deallocates the memory allocated for `*pointer`. (To be used when `pointer` points to a single object rather than an array of objects.)

2. `delete [] pointer`
   calls the destructor on all elements of `*pointer` and deallocates the array allocated for `*pointer`. (To be used when `pointer` points to an array of objects.)

Destructors are so important that if a class does not explicitly define one, C++ provides a default destructor for the class. The C++ default destructor does not, however, delete pointer members of the class.

Because of their recursive nature, destructors can be very powerful features of classes. We'll illustrate what we mean with two examples. Suppose another class, `Y`, contains a member that is of type `String`.

```
class Y {
    . . .
```

```
    String st;
    ...
};
```

When an object of type `Y` goes out of scope or is destroyed, the destructor for `Y` will automatically be invoked for that object. Since that object contains a `String` member, invocation of the destructor for the `Y` type object automatically invokes the destructor its `String` member `st`.

The default destructor for an array automatically invokes the destructor for each element when the array goes out of scope or, in the case of a dynamically created array, when a pointer to the array is deleted. For example, suppose `aPtr` is defined as follows:

```
String* aPtr = new String[50];
```

Then `aPtr[0]` through `aPtr[49]` are `String` type objects that can be manipulated with any of the `String` operations. This code generates 50 copies of `"abc"` for the array elements.[6]

```
for (int i = 0; i < 50; i++)
    aPtr[i] = "abc";
```

The `delete []` operator is necessary to deallocate all of the memory for the array, including all 50 copies of `"abc"`. When `delete []` is used, the array destructor automatically supplied by C++ is invoked. In turn, the default array destructor automatically invokes the destructor on each of the array's elements. In Fig. 9.15, the memory allocated for all of the objects inside the box with dashed borders would be deallocated by the following delete operation:

```
delete [] aPtr;
```

We are satisfied with the constructors and destructors for the `String` class. They do exactly what they need to do, no more and no less. But destructors and constructors are functions, and their code is like code in any other member functions. Constructors may do things besides allocate memory and initialize data members. Destructors may do other things besides delete pointers. Constructors and destructors may contain input and output statements. They may call other member functions or functions that are not members of a class. Good constructors and destructors do not contain foolish code. But there are circumstances under which such things as output statements or changes to nonmember data might be useful in a constructor or destructor.

Examples of constructors and destructors that do not limit their activities to simple assignments or managing dynamically allocated memory are easy to

---

[6] The code works correctly if the assignment operator has been overloaded to make a copy of the array associated with the `String` argument.

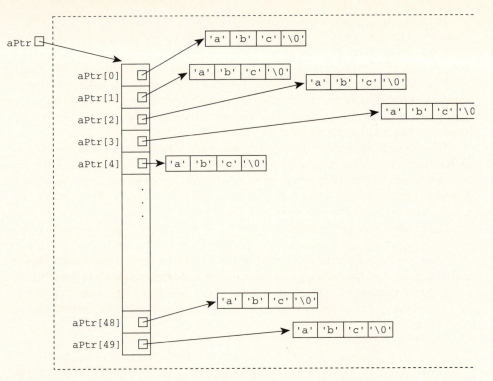

Figure 9.15 The array of `String`s pointed to by `aPtr`. All objects inside the box with dashed borders were dynamically created.

imagine. Suppose a class has a data member that is to be initialized by data in some file on disk. A constructor for that class may prompt the user to enter the name of the file in order to determine which data will be used for this object. A destructor may close that file.

A debugging trick that some programmers use to understand how many times certain class type objects are created is to place output statements in the constructors and destructors. Whenever an object is defined, the constructor's output statement is executed. The constructor's output statement would be executed whenever a temporary object is created. Whenever an object is destroyed, the output statement for the destructor would be executed. An exercise at the end of this chapter illustrates tracing object lifetimes through constructor and destructor output statements.

Overloading assignment for classes with pointer members

The `Rational` class did not overload the assignment operator. It didn't need to. Assignment was overloaded appropriately by default. The same was true for all of the classes that we have discussed prior to introducing the `String` class. That includes the `InventoryTable` class of Chapter 7, which may be surprising since

`InventoryTable` has a member that is an array. Assignment for all of those classes worked exactly as we would have hoped. The data members of the left-hand
operand are assigned the values of the corresponding data members of the right-
hand operand. For the `Rational` class, assignment simply copies the values of the
`num_` and `denom_` of the right-hand operand to the `num_` and `denom_` of the left-
hand operand. For the `InventoryTable` class, assignment copies the data members from the right-hand operand to the left-hand operand, including the entire
array member with all of the individual elements.

Pointers and arrays are very closely related, but they are not the same. Classes
with array members are different from classes with pointer members. That difference becomes dramatic in simple assignment. When one pointer is assigned the
value of another, then both of them point to the same memory. Assigning pointer
values (addresses) instead of copying what they point to is called **shallow copying**.

When an instance of a class with pointer members is assigned another
instance of the same class, it could be a disaster if assignment did a shallow copy,
assigning only the pointer values instead of what they point to. This is especially
true if the class has a destructor which always deallocates memory. Should one of
the objects go out of scope before the other, the destructor would be invoked for
that first object, leaving an invalid address as the value of the pointer member of
the remaining object.

*When a class contains a member which is a pointer, it should also contain an over-
loaded assignment operator.* In order to make assignment for `String`s behave the
same as assignment for ordinary type objects, we will define the overloaded
assignment very carefully.

```
String& String::operator= (const String& rhs)
{
    if (this != &rhs) {                        // Cover the case of s = s.
       delete [] info_;                        // Deallocate the old buffer.
       info_ = new char[strlen(rhs.info_) +1];// Allocate memory for a new one.
       strcpy(info_, rhs.info_);               // Copy the characters from the
    }                                          //  right side to the left.
    return *this;                              // Return this object.
}
```

There are two things to explain about this definition: (1) how to trace the code
and (2) why the code looks more complicated than it needs to be for most situations.

Recall that `this` is a keyword that can be used only in definitions of class
member functions. It is the name of a pointer to the instance of the class for which
the member function is invoked. We used `this` once before, with the overloaded
`+=` operator of the `Rational` class.

To trace the definition of `operator=()` for the `String` class, suppose `s`
and `t` are two `String` objects. Rewrite the assignment `s = t` with this syntax,
`s.operator=(t)`. The function notation makes it obvious that `s` is the instance of
the class for which assignment is invoked. The pointer `this` in the definition of
`operator=()` is of type `String*`. In the function `s.operator=()`, `this` is a pointer to `s`; `*this` and `s` are the same object—the value of `this` is the address of `s`.

In the assignment s = t, the argument for s.operator=() is t. The formal argument rhs is an alias for t, so the value of &rhs is the address of t. The condition this != &rhs is true if and only if the address of s (the instance of the String class for which the function is invoked) and the address of t (the actual argument) are not the same. In other words, this != &rhs is true if and only if s and t are not the same object. If the assignment were s = s instead of s = t, the if statement would prevent any change from occurring to s. In particular, it prevents destroying an array and subsequently referencing the memory that was just deallocated. The results of referencing deallocated memory may be of no consequence (if you're lucky), or it could result in a mess.

If the two assignment operands s and t are not the same, then the left-hand operand, s, will be changed. The if block destroys the array pointed to by s.info_. It dynamically creates a new array with just enough elements to accommodate the array pointed to by t.info_, the pointer member of the right operand. Finally, it copies all of the characters from the array of the right-hand operand to the array of the left-hand operand.

The last statement in the definition of the overloaded assignment will be executed every time an assignment is made. It returns the object to which this points—the instance of the class for which the overloaded assignment operator is invoked. In other words, the last statement in the definition of the overloaded assignment returns the object that is the left-hand operand of the assignment operator.

So now you are asking yourself "What silly programmer would ever write an assignment like s = s? Why go to all of this trouble of making sure a pointer is not blown away by a delete when nobody is ever going to write s = s?" Remember that one goal in defining a String class is to be able to have a first class string type. Any programmer, even a silly one, ought to be able to use String type objects in a natural manner. If x is an int variable, then the assignment x = x does no harm. So the assignment s = s should not do any harm either. A type that wipes out a program just through a simple assignment like s = s is hardly first class.

But there is more. How about most programmers, who would not think about writing s = s in their code? Consider the programmers who define pointers-to-Strings. If ps and qs are of type pointer-to-String, then the assignment *ps = *qs does not look so silly. It's quite possible that ps and qs point to the same String at the time the assignment is evaluated. Putting the if statement in the definition of the overloaded assignment to prevent inadvertent deallocation of the character array looks like a pretty good idea after all. If ps and qs point to the same String, the destruction, creation, and copy code that constitutes the body of the if would not be executed for the assignment *ps = *qs.

Initialization vs. Assignment

An object can receive a value using an equal sign (=) in two different ways: ordinary assignment and initialization. Initialization occurs when the object is created for the first time. When an object is created, it has a location and a value. Initialization establishes a value for a newly created object—it occurs only once. Assignment allows you to change the value of an existing object.

C++ recognizes by context when assignment and when initialization are called for. It follows these rules:

1. Initialization occurs when an actual function argument object is associated with a formal function argument. The formal argument is initialized with the actual argument's value.

2. Initialization occurs when a nonvoid function returns the value of an object. The temporary object automatically created by the compiler in the calling code is initialized with the returned value.

3. In the definition of an object, initialization occurs either with an explicitly specified value or a default (which may not specify a particular value at all). One of a variety of syntaxes for specifying an initial value in a declaration uses the = sign. Do not confuse that with assignment.

C++ provides default assignment operators and copy constructors for classes that do not specifically declare them. The default assignment operator does a memberwise assignment and the default copy constructor does a memberwise copy. The assignment operator is used when a class variable is assigned a value. The copy constructor is used whenever a variable is initialized with another variable of the same type.

In most cases the assignment operator and copy constructor are similarly defined.

Unlike the assignment operator, which fails to change anything for the assignment s = s, the modified assignment operator, +=, will change s for s += s. The modified assignment operator concatenates a copy of the string of the right-hand operand to the string of the left-hand operand. So in the evaluation of s += s, the number of characters for s will almost double. The definition of += must allocate an array with enough elements to hold the characters for both its left and right operands.

```
String& String :: operator+= (const String& s)
{
    char* temp = new char[strlen(info_) + strlen(s.info_) + 1]; // Create a new
                            // array to hold the two string arrays.
    strcpy(temp,info_);     // Copy the characters from this array into temp.
    strcat(temp,s.info_);   // Then copy the characters of s.info_ into temp.
```

```
    delete [] info_;          // Replace the old value for info_ by temp.
    info_ = temp;
    return *this;
}
```

There are many definitions of the overloaded += that are correct. We just wrote the one that we thought would be easy to trace. Notice that in this code, one new array is created and another one is destroyed. When the function stops execution, the pointer temp goes out of scope. But the newly created array is still pointed to by the info_ member of the left-hand operand of +=.

Overloading assignment makes it easy to overload concatenation (addition). Here is one way to write the definition of the overloaded + operator:

```
String operator+ (const String& s, const String& t)
{
    String temp(s);     // temp is a copy of s.
    temp += t;          // Add t to the end of temp.
    return temp;
}
```

We will leave it to you to define the member function length(). It is an easy one. You can use the strlen() function in the string library to do all of the real work. The definitions for the overloaded comparison operators are simple to write. You can rely on the string library for the definitions of those operators, also.

Overloading [] and explicit C-string type casts

The subscript operator, [], can be overloaded for the String class in the same way it was overloaded for the Vector3D class discussed in the previous chapter. The return type is char&, a reference to a char. The operator generates an alias for one of the characters in the String object's array of characters. That alias is an lvalue, so it can appear on either side of an assignment statement.

```
char& String::operator[](int i)
{
    return info_[i];
}
```

The const version of the overloaded subscript operator returns a char rather than a char&. It is the subscript operator that will be invoked for String objects that are const.

```
char String :: operator[](int i) const
{
    return info_[i];
}
```

The following code illustrates some of the power of overloading `[]`. The first statement allocates an array of eight characters for s. The last statement assigns `'\0'` to s[3]. That assignment does not change the size of the array. It does shorten the string represented by s.

```
String s("Goodbye");    // Conversion constructor; s.info_ allocated 8
                        //    elements in order to hold "Goodbye".
char ch = s[3];         // ch is initialized with 'd'
s[0] = 'F';             // s.info_ is "Foodbye"
s[3] = s[4];            // s.info_ is "Foobbye"
s[3] = '\0';            // s.info_ is "Foo"
```

We had to make a design decision before writing down the subscript operator method. Should we perform a safe string bounds check or not? We did the error check for the `Vector3D` class, partly to illustrate simple error checking. But for the `String` class, we deliberately omitted a similar error check. Again, our rationale was partly to illustrate what may happen as a result of that design decision. (You may well have chosen a different decision.)

What happens if the assignment s[10] = 'X' is executed? Just as it is a mistake with ordinary arrays to assign a position beyond the elements allocated to the array, it also is a mistake to do so with `String`s. The code in the overloaded operator `[]` does not prevent access beyond what was dynamically allocated for the `String`. The programmer who uses the `String` class has responsibility for using the overloaded `[]` appropriately. And of course, that is possible because `String` contains the member function `length()`.

The `String` class provides a mechanism to convert a C-string (char* or const char* types) value to a `String` type value through a constructor. What about converting in the other direction, from a `String` to a C-string. That is done with the member function `charString()`. It returns the C-string equivalent of a `String`, the `String` object's info_ member. For that reason, `charString()` can be used as an "explicit type cast," obtaining a C-string from a `String`.

So `charString()` will return a pointer. But returning a value of a pointer member of a class is tricky—`charString()` must avoid returning the value of the info_ member without assuring that value cannot be used to corrupt the `String` data. Here is what we mean by corrupting the data with a pointer. Suppose that s is a `String` and p is a char* with the same value as s.info_. The assignment p[0] = 'X' would change s.info_[0] to 'X'—p and s point to the same memory! The pointer p breaks the protection mechanism that private access provides for s.info_; the character string represented by s can be changed through manipulation of p.

We could opt for `charString()` to create a copy of the array pointed to by the info_ member, then return a pointer to that copy. That decision causes two problems. First, the `charString()` method would have to create a new array and then copy the characters from one array to another. Second, and more important, the dynamic creation of an additional array may result in an eventual memory leak. We bypassed both problems by requiring that `charString()` return a const char* rather than a char*.

```
const char* String :: charString() const
{
    return info_;
}
```

Take a closer look at the return type; it is `const char*`, not simply `char*`. The `const` in front of the `char*` says that the value to be returned is a pointer to a constant. In Chapter 6 and the end of section 9.4, we discussed the use of `const` with constant array types of formal function arguments. Consider this prototype:

```
void f(const char* x);   // equivalent to void f(const char x[]);
```

The `const` in front of the formal argument prevents the elements of the corresponding actual array argument in a call to `f()` from being changed. The formal argument references a constant array, and the compiler protects that constant array data while `f()` executes. Inside the body of `f()`, this expression is illegal: `x[0] = 'A'`. That is not all. Inside the body of `f()`, this expression is also illegal: `char* p = x`. The compiler will not let you get around the "constness" of the argument by defining a pointer and manipulating the array data through the pointer in this way.

The value returned by `charString()` can be used by a function with a `const char*` argument. The value can be assigned to a data object of type `const char*`. But the value returned by `charString()` cannot be assigned to an ordinary `char*` variable. Suppose `p` is of type `char*`, and `s` is a `String`. The following assignment would be illegal:

```
p = s.charString();   // Illegal use of const char* type assignment
                      //   to a non-const object, p
```

What can you do with the return value? It is possible to make a declaration like this:

```
const char* q = s.charString();
```

However, programmers would not often use the return value from `charString()` to initialize a pointer. Most of the utility of that return value comes from temporary use. The discussion that follows illustrates the temporary use.

Overloading input and output operators

Given the member function `charString()`, the definition of the overloaded `String` output operator is almost trivial to write.

```
ostream& operator<<(ostream& out, const String& s)
{
```

```
    out << s.charString();
    return out;
}
```

The definition above points out why our decision not to have the `charString()` definition allocate memory with a new array was a good one. Code such as the `operator<<()` definition, which uses the `charString()` return value, does not need to perform any deallocation to avoid a memory leak.

Reading `String` data from an input stream is not quite as easy as writing one to an output stream. Our efforts will be satisfactory for now, but certainly not perfect. In the next chapter, after we discuss string streams, we can write a better definition for the overloaded `String` input operator.

For now we will place constraints on the behavior for extracting a `String` from a stream. First, we will insist that all of the characters for the `String` must be on the same line of the stream, occurring before the next newline. In addition, we will limit the number of characters to be removed to 999. (The number 999 is an overly generous number that we selected somewhat arbitrarily. It has no special significance.) If there are more than 999 characters pending in the input stream before the first newline, then those additional characters will remain in the stream.

```
istream& operator>> (istream& in, String& s)
{
    char buffer[1000];                  // Buffer to store the stream characters
    in.getline(buffer,1000,'\n');       // Remove up to 999 characters from in,
                                        //   up to and including first occurrence
                                        //   of '\n'.  Store all but '\n' in the
                                        //   buffer; terminate the buffer with '\0'.
    s = String(buffer);                 // Create a new String from the buffer and
                                        //   assign it to s.

    return in;
}
```

By defining `buffer` as an array of characters rather than a pointer-to-`char`, we did not have to use `new` to create an array or `delete` to destroy an array at the end of the function. The compiler takes care of the creation and destruction of automatic variables.

The stream member function `getline()` has three arguments. The last one is a default argument with default value of `'\n'`. The execution of `in.getline(buffer,1000,'\n')` has the effect of removing at most 999 characters up to and including the first newline from the stream. All of those characters except the newline are stored in `buffer`. That leaves enough room in `buffer` for the `'\0'`, which is placed at the end of the newly stored characters.

The `String` argument is assigned a new value at the end of the function. The explicit constructor call `String(buffer)` initializes a temporary object created by the compiler. That temporary object becomes the right-hand operand for the assignment operator.

Sample code using Strings

Let's see how Strings can be used. We will begin by defining some String objects, including an array of Strings:

```
String student("John Brown");      // Conversion constructor
String mathTeacher("Helen Smith"); // Conversion constructor
const String month("May");         // Conversion constructor
String name[30];                   // Null constructor (30 times)
String physicsTeacher(mathTeacher); // Copy constructor
```

The definitions create 34 String objects. The array name accounts for 30 of them.

The object student was initialized to represent "John Brown". The next statement changes student to represent "Ann".

```
student = "Ann";
```

That assignment statement is more complicated than it looks. It involves the String conversion constructor as well as the String assignment operator. Remember that a function with a formal value or const reference argument can be invoked with an actual argument that is an object of the same type, an object of a different type, or simply a value. If the actual argument is a different type object or if it is a value, then the compiler must create a temporary object for the formal argument. It does so by calling a conversion constructor that can create an object using the original actual argument. This assumes, of course, that such a conversion constructor exists.

Look at that last assignment statement again. The C-string "Ann" is the actual argument to the String assignment operator, whose formal argument type is const String&. "Ann" is not a String, but the compiler can make a temporary String from "Ann", and that is precisely what it does.

We should be able to predict what happens with the next statement.

```
student += " Jones";
```

The C-string " Jones" is appended to the end of student's C-string. That concatenation involved two function calls. One was to the operator +=. The other was a call by the compiler to the String conversion constructor in order to create a temporary String object from " Jones".

We can assign String values to elements of name, the array of 30 Strings. The following code uses the overloaded assignment operator to do just that:

```
name[0] = "Jane Smith";// Conversion constructor is called
name[1] = mathTeacher; // No constructor is called; mathTeacher is a String
name[2] = student;     // No constructor is called; student is a String
name[3] = month;       // No constructor is called; month is a String
```

We can also read `String` values from `cin` or any open, valid input stream. The next loop prompts for and reads four elements of `name`.

```
for (int i = 4; i < 8; i++) {
    cout << "Enter a name: ";
    cin >> name[i];
}
```

The box that follows shows the terminal screen as a result of executing that last loop. The user's entries appear in italics.

```
Enter a name: Ann Rogers
Enter a name: Pat Ryan
Enter a name: Candace Young
Enter a name: Brian Rudolph
```

The array has four new values ranging from `"Ann  Rogers"` for `name[4]` through `"Brian Rudolph"` for `name[7]`. We can print all of them using the overloaded output operator.

```
for (i = 0; i < 8; i++)
    cout << "Name " << i << " is: " << name[i] << endl;
```

The output generated by that last segment of code is shown in the following box.

```
Name 0 is: Jane Smith
Name 1 is: Helen Smith
Name 2 is: John Brown
Name 3 is: May
Name 4 is: Ann Rogers
Name 5 is: Pat Ryan
Name 6 is: Candace Young
Name 7 is: Brian Rudolph
```

We can change or examine a character in a `String` by using overloaded subscript operators. The next segment of code changes `student` to `"Amy Jones"` and `name[3]` to `"Fay"`.

```
student[1] = 'm';
student[2] = 'y';
name[3][0] = 'F';
```

String has two overloaded subscript operators, one for Strings, which are const, and one for Strings, which are not. The const version returns a char; the nonconst version returns a char&. That last segment of code invoked the nonconst version.

The following statement uses the const subscript operator because month, the object for which [] is applied, is a const.

```
char ch = month[1];        // ch is 'a'
```

The compiler will not allow month[1] on the left side of an assignment expression. After all, month[1] is a char value, not a reference to a char object like student[1].

We left the implementation of the relational and equality operators as an exercise. But we assume now that all of them have been defined correctly. The following segment of code finds the "smallest" value among the first eight elements of name.

```
String smallest(name[0]);
for (i = 0; i < 8; i++)
   if (name[i] < smallest)
      smallest = name[i];
```

After execution of that loop, smallest represents "Ann Rogers". We could print out smallest directly, using the output operator. But the following code will also print smallest.

```
cout << smallest.charString() << endl;
```

The equality operator is useful in determining if a particular value is among the elements of name. This code finds the subscript of the element of name representing "Pat Ryan".

```
int subscript = -1;
for (i = 0; i < 8; i++)
   if ("Pat Ryan" == name[i]) {
      subscript = i;
      break;
   }
```

Let's turn our attention to pointer variables. Consider the following definitions:

```
String* p;
String* q = new String(month);        // q->info_ is "May"
```

At this time, p does not point to an object but q does. The copy constructor is invoked when q is initialized. So q->info_ and month.info_ point to two different C-strings, each with the value "May". The following assignment makes p point to a String representing "June".

```
p = new String("June");               // p->info_ is "June"
```

Remember that p can point to an element in an array of Strings as well as just a single String. The following code deallocates all the memory for p's referent and then creates an array of Strings, assigning the address of the first element to p.

```
delete p;
p = new String[50];
```

The array pointed to by p can be used in the same manner as name. The following code assigns the first eight elements of name to p.

```
for (i = 0; i < 8; i++)
   p[i] = name[i];
```

Keep in mind that each p[i] and each name[i] is a String. The last loop invoked the String assignment operator eight times.

While the elements of name are first class types, name itself is an array and not a first class type—name cannot be used alone on the left side of an assignment operator or the right side of an input or output operator. When name was defined, the compiler did invoke the String constructor to create each element. Similarly, when name goes out of scope, the compiler invokes the String destructor for each element.

When p was defined, it was not explicitly initialized. No call was made to the String constructor. However, when a new array of Strings was created and its address assigned to p, the compiler invoked the String constructor to create each element. When p goes out of scope, the String destructor will not be invoked. If we delete p, however, then the String destructor will be invoked for each element of p's array. The following statement deallocates all of the memory that was allocated to p's array.

```
delete [] p;
```

The examples that we have just given illustrate how the new String type is first class in the same sense that the built-in numeric types are first class. We will continue to use Strings through the remainder of the book. Look for more examples in later chapters.

9.6 ▌ Extensible arrays

One of the criticisms leveled at arrays is that they are of fixed sizes. When an array is defined, the compiler uses the number of elements specified in the definition to determine how much memory to set aside for the array. Even if the array is created through a pointer and the `new` operator, the amount of memory dynamically allocated for the array is fixed.

In this section, we will create an extensible array type to implement arrays that can expand or shrink when needed. Extensible arrays are programming tools much the same as strings are. While rational numbers and three-dimensional vectors have an existence outside of the world of computers, extensible arrays and strings do not. In developing an abstract data type for an extensible array, we will focus our entire attention on the computing world operations. We will look at the question "What operations do programmers expect from arrays?"

Perhaps we should rephrase that question to "What operations would programmers like to have for arrays?" To come up with some answers, go back to your earlier C++ learning experiences. Recall the time you discovered arrays. What were your disappointments? We remember several of our own. For one, assignment does not work. If a and b are arrays, the assignment a = b is illegal. If a and b are pointers, the assignment a = b merely assigns a new address to a. It does not assign any array elements.

Assignment is not the only operation that ordinary arrays do not support. Output and input are others. If a is an array, the expression cout << a does not write out the elements of a as you might have desired. The expression cin >> a is downright illegal.

Elements of an ordinary array are accessed through their subscripts. But if a is an array with 50 elements and the expression a[55] = 3 is evaluated, a does not expand to accommodate the new element. Instead, an error occurs.

Our extensible array ADT will not suffer from those shortcomings. We will be able to assign, read, and write them. We will also be able to access elements beyond their current bounds and to make them grow or shrink. Those are the essential features that characterize our extensible arrays.

The `ExtArray` class definition

Under what conditions should an extensible array change its size? That is a design decision that will be incorporated into an extensible array ADT and subsequently into an `ExtArray` class. We chose the following:

- The extensible array will grow (or shrink) when the user specifically sends it a message to resize itself. The message includes a value for the new size.

- The extensible array will grow (or shrink) when it is assigned another extensible array. Its new size will be the size of whatever it was assigned.

- The extensible array will grow (or shrink) when it is read from a stream. Its new size will be the number of values read.

- The extensible array will grow when the user tries to access an element whose subscript is too large for any of the current valid array subscripts.

   It is too early to focus on how the `ExtArray` methods will be defined. But we need to ask ourselves how these array behaviors will appear to the person who uses one. For example, if an array expands, will it initialize the new elements to any particular value? Also, what happens when an array resizes itself?
   For our design, we decided that each array would have a "blank" element value. When an array expands, it will fill in the new unspecified element values with the blank value. When an array contracts, it will shrink the end down to the last element that is not a blank value.
   The definition of the class `ExtArray` provides a specification for the extensible array ADT just described.

```
// An extensible array of integers, which expands as needed.
//   (For all operations that create or expand the array, an error will
//   occur if available memory is inadequate.)
class ExtArray {
public:
   ExtArray(int sz = 10, int bv = 0);        // Creates an array of sz elements
                                             //    initialized to bv.
                                             // ASSUME: sz >= 0
   ExtArray(const ExtArray& a);              // Creates a deep copy of a.
   ExtArray& operator=(const ExtArray& a);   // Assigns a deep copy of a.
   ~ExtArray();                              // Deallocates array memory.

   int size() const;           // Number of array elements.
   void resize(int n);         // Changes number of array elements to n. If
                               //    n < old size, elements at the end are
                               //    truncated. If old size < n, new  elements
                               //    are put at the end and assigned the blank
                               //    value.
                               //    ASSUME: n >= 0
   int& operator[](int i);     // Element at subscript i. If i > size, the
                               //    array expands to accommodate the
                               //    subscript; the blank value initializes
                               //    other new elements.
                               //    ASSUME: i >= 0
   int operator[](int i) const;// Element at subscript i.
                               //    ASSUME: i >= 0 && i < size
   friend istream& operator>>(istream& in, ExtArray& a);
      // Extracts a sequence of integers from in and assigns them to a,
      //   beginning with the first element. Extraction stops when the
```

```
        //   first attempted input of an integer fails. The array size is the
        //   number of integers extracted.
    friend ostream& operator<<(ostream& out, const ExtArray& a);
        // Inserts the elements of a into out, beginning with the first. Blanks
        //   are written between consecutive elements.

private:
    int* array_;
    int bufSize_;
    int blank_;
};
```

The first constructor creates an ExtArray with a default size and a default blank value. Its definition allows the user to create an ExtArray with no elements (which occurs if the actual argument for size is 0). In that case, the array_ pointer member is assigned the null pointer.

```
ExtArray :: ExtArray(int sz, int bv) : bufSize_(sz), blank_(bv)
{
    if (bufSize_ > 0) {              // If there is a buffer to create,
        array_ = new int[bufSize_]; //   allocate new memory,
        for (int i = 0; i < sz; i++) //   copy blanks into all array elements.
            array_[i] = blank_;
    }
    else
        array_ = 0;                 // Else, make the array null.
}
```

The copy constructor makes a deep copy of its argument. A new array is allocated and the elements of the array of the actual argument are copied to the new array.

```
ExtArray :: ExtArray(const ExtArray& a) :  bufSize_(a.bufSize_),
                                           blank_(a.blank_)

{
    if (bufSize_ > 0) {                      // If there is a buffer to create,
        array_ = new int[bufSize_];          //   allocate new memory,
        for (int i = 0; i < bufSize_; i++)   //   copy elements from the
            array_[i] = a.array_[i];         //     argument to the new array.
    }
    else
        array_ = 0;                          // Else, make the array null.
}
```

The overloaded assignment operator makes a deep copy of the right-hand operand. Its definition is similar to the definition of the String class overloaded assignment.

```
ExtArray& ExtArray :: operator= (const ExtArray& rhs)
{
   if (this != &rhs) {                    // Protect against assignments like x = x.
      delete [] array_;                   //   Deallocate this array memory.
      bufSize_ = rhs.bufSize_;
      blank_ = rhs.blank_;
      if (bufSize_ > 0) {                 //  If there's a buffer to create,
         array_ = new int[bufSize_];      //    allocate new memory,
         for (int i = 0; i < bufSize_; i++) //  copy elements from the
            array_[i] = rhs.array_[i];    //    rhs array to this array.
      }
   }
   return *this;
}
```

The ExtArray destructor deallocates the memory allocated to the array. Classes with dynamically allocated memory typically have destructors that perform the deallocation.

```
ExtArray :: ~ExtArray()
{
   delete [] array_;                      // Deallocate the array memory
}
```

You can understand some of how an ExtArray manages its data by reading the constructor and overloaded assignment definitions. They use new to allocate memory for the array_ member. The assignment operator as well as the destructor use delete to deallocate memory that is no longer needed.

Making an extensible array grow or shrink

The operations besides assignment that make an extensible array change size are resizing, subscripting, and extraction. A resize message requires an argument to indicate the number of elements for the new array.

```
void ExtArray :: resize(int n)
{
   int* p = 0;
   if (n > 0) {                           // If the new size is not 0:
      p = new int[n];                     //   Make a new array of n elements.
      for (int i = 0; i < n                //   Fill the new array with elements
               && i < bufSize_; i++)      //     of array_.
```

```
            p[i] = array_[i];
        for (; i < n; i++)           //    Fill in any remaining elements
            p[i] = blank_;           //        with blanks.
    }
    delete [] array_;                // Deallocate array_ memory.
    array_ = p;                      // Set array_ to the new array.
    bufSize_ = n;                    // Set bufSize_ to the new size.
}
```

A `resize` message explicitly determines the array size. Subscripting on non-const `ExtArray`s is different. When an array element beyond the current bounds of the array is accessed, the array will grow as large as necessary to make the subscript a valid subscript.

```
int& ExtArray :: operator[](int i)
{
    if (i >= bufSize_) {                    // If the subscript is too large:
        int* p = new int[i + 1];            //    Make a new array.
        for (int j = 0; j < bufSize_; j++) //    Copy array_ elements to the new
            p[j] = array_[j];               //        array.
        for (; j < i; j++)                  //    Fill in remaining elements of
            p[j] = blank_;                  //        the new array with blanks.
        delete [] array_;                   //    Deallocate array_ memory.
        array_ = p;                         //    Set array_ to the new array.
        bufSize_ = i + 1;                   //    Set bufSize_ to the new size.
    }
    return array_[i];
}
```

Of course, subscripting a `const ExtArray` object beyond its current bounds is an error. The const version of the subscript operator is easy to define.

```
int ExtArray::operator[](int i) const
{
    return array_[i];
}
```

The extraction operator has the potential for changing the size of the array. Whenever an extensible array is read, its old elements are discarded and new ones are assigned. How many new ones to assign is again a design decision. Our overloaded input operator extracts integers from a stream and assigns them to the extensible array. The process continues until an attempt to extract fails.

```
istream& operator>>(istream& in, ExtArray& a)
{
    int i = 0;                  // Subscript of the next element to read.
    while (in >> a[i])          // Read numbers into the array. (The array
```

```
      i++;                          //    expands as needed.)
    a.resize(i);                    // Resize the array to clean out old data.
    if (!in.eof() && !in.bad())     // If characters remain in the input stream,
      in.clear();                   //    clear error flags for subsequent reading.

    return in;
}
```

The extraction operator relies heavily upon the subscript operator to expand the array when the array runs out of room to store new data. At some point, the attempted extraction may fail because there is a non-whitespace character in the input stream that is not a part of an integer. In that case, `in.clear()` restores the stream to allow additional extractions of other data. Extraction may also fail because no additional characters remain in the input stream (end-of-file was reached). In that case, no restoration is attempted.

The `size()` operation and the overloaded insertion operator do not change the array. Their definitions are straightforward:

```
int ExtArray :: size() const
{
    return bufSize_;
}

ostream& operator<<(ostream& out, const ExtArray& a)
{
    for(int i = 0; i < a.bufSize_; i++)
        out << a[i] << ' ';                          // The const subscript operator
    return out;                                      //  is invoked since a is const.
}
```

Using the `ExtArray` class

Now that we have done all of this work, let's see how `ExtArray` objects can be used. We will begin with some definitions:

```
ExtArray pos(20,-1);      // pos has 20 elements, all are -1
ExtArray a;               // a has 10 elements, all are 0
ExtArray b(50);           // b has 50 elements, all are 0
```

The definitions establish the initial sizes for each of the extensible arrays. All of their elements are initialized with their own blank values.

Subscripting beyond the bounds of a increases its number of elements.

```
for (int i = 3; i < 12; i++)    // a is increased to 12 elements:
    a[i] = 3 * i;               //    0 0 0 9 12 15 18 21 24 27 30 33
```

Of course, we can specifically resize a, and then we can print out those values as follows:

```
a.resize(8);              // a has 8 elements
cout << a << endl;
a.resize(10);             // a has 10 elements
cout << a << endl;
```

The output below is generated by that code.

```
0 0 0 9 12 15 18 21
0 0 0 9 12 15 18 21 0 0
```

Resizing down truncates the array, leaving its nontruncated elements intact. Resizing up, does not change the original elements. It does add blanks on the end.

Input can also change the size of an array. Recall that the ExtArray named pos was created with 20 elements. Its blank value is -1. Consider the following code:

```
// Read some numbers into pos.
cout << "Enter data. <q quits>: ";
cin >> pos;
cout << "Number of elements of array: " << pos.size()
        << "\nArray elements are: " << pos << endl;
pos[10] = 300;
cout << "After assigning 300 at subscript 10:\n"
        << "   Number of elements of array: " << pos.size()
        << "\n   Array elements are: " << pos << endl;
```

The box below shows the output generated by execution of the code. (User input appears in italics.)

```
Enter data. <q quits>: 2 5 12 16 20 9 8 q
Number of elements of array: 7
Array elements are: 2 5 12 16 20 9 8
After assigning 300 at subscript 10:
    Number of elements of array: 11
    Array elements are: 2 5 12 16 20 9 8 -1 -1 -1 300
```

Since we have concentrated so much of our efforts in this chapter on pointers, we will look at some ExtArrays created through pointers.

```
ExtArray* ptr = new ExtArray(8,0);     // *ptr has 8 elements, blank is 0
ptr->resize(25);                       // *ptr has 25 elements
(*ptr)[28] = 155;                      // *ptr has 29 elements
(*ptr)[15] = 300;                      // *ptr still has 29 elements

ExtArray* aOfA = new ExtArray[7];      // aOfA points to an array of 7
                                       //  ExtArrays, each with 10 elements
                                       //  and blank value 0
aOfA[3] = pos;                         // (overloaded ExtArray::operator=)
aOfA[3][5] = 27;                       // (overloaded ExtArray::operator[])
```

The assignment aOfA[3] = pos does not use the overloaded subscript operator. That is because aOfA is a *pointer* to an ExtArray; it is not an ExtArray. However, aOfA[3] is an ExtArray. So the expression aOfA[3] = pos does invoke the overloaded ExtArray assignment operator.

The final assignment, aOfA[3][5] = 27, invokes the overloaded subscript operator. The element aOfA[3] is an ExtArray and can be subscripted. aOfA[3][5] is the element of aOfA[3] with subscript 5.

9.7 | Implementation standards for classes with pointers data

Both String and ExtArray are first class types. They are general-purpose programming tools just like the Rational and Vector3D classes of the previous chapter. They can be used in a variety of contexts—they were not designed to fit specific problems.

Suppose you have designed an abstract data type for a first class type, and now it is time for implementation. Our initial efforts at creating first class types focused on making their operations mimic their real-world or computer-world counterparts. We wanted to make operations natural. For the examples of this chapter, we concentrated most of our efforts on overloading operators.

The natural use of first class types is one thing. But it is not the only important issue in implementing first class types or even types that are not first class. Remember the guiding implementation principle, no surprises. The user of a class does not want to worry about details. The user does not want to worry about whether an operation that ought to be safe is safe. Your class should be well behaved. It should not contain land mines.

Both the String and ExtArray classes offered plenty of land mine opportunities. They include the usual pointer pitfalls: memory leaks, corruption of data through aliasing, premature deallocation of memory, and referencing deallocated memory. All classes with pointer members have potential for disaster. Disciplined C++ programmers protect against those disasters by adhering to the following convention: for every class with pointer members, define a copy constructor, an overloaded assignment operator, and a destructor.

Why didn't we define a copy constructor, a destructor, or an overloaded assignment operator with the `Rational` class? We could have, just to adhere to a discipline of defining them for every class. But C++ provides them by default. The default copy constructor and assignment operator simply make memberwise copies and assignments of one object to another. That kind of memberwise activity is exactly what is needed for most classes without pointer members.

C++ programming convention: if a class has a member that is a pointer, then that class should have the following:

1. A copy constructor

2. A destructor

3. An overloaded assignment operator

There is more to implementing first class types than following the three conventions for classes with pointers. There is more than simply overloading operators. Our `String` class implementation provided most of the functionality that we designed into the string ADT. And the implementation did follow the no-surprise principle. But there are some issues we did not mention. Those are efficiency issues. For example, we used `'\0'` terminated strings. That decision allowed us to use the built-in string library to do all of the string manipulations. But was it a good decision? What happens whenever the length must be computed? The computation is carried out by `strlen()`, which starts at the beginning of the array of characters and looks at each character until it reaches `'\0'`.

Is there another option with the `String` class? We could have put an extra `int` data member into the private section to represent the length. The member function `length()` could simply return its value. With that `int` data member, it would not be necessary to terminate the character arrays with `'\0'` (unless, of course, we insisted on relying on the string library for some of the method code).

The current implementation of the string abstract data type may be inefficient in other ways too. Consider the constructors and the assignment operators. In all of those methods, new memory is dynamically allocated. The method for the overloaded + allocates memory several times. Take another look at its current definition. This time we annotated it.

```
String operator+ (const String& s, const String& t)
{
    String temp(s); // Copy constructor allocates for temp->info_ then
                    //    copies s->info_ to temp->info_ one character at a
                    //    time
```

```
    temp += t;        // += allocates for a buffer, then copies s->info_ and
                      //   t->info_ into the buffer one character at a time
    return temp;      // Copy constructor creates a temporary String and
                      //   copies temp->info_ one character at a time to the
                      //   newly allocated memory
}
```

If u and v are Strings, evaluation of u + v results in three allocations of memory for arrays of characters, each followed by subsequent character-by-character copying. Assigning u + v to another String results in an additional allocation and subsequent copying. That's a lot of work.

There are other ways to implement the string abstract data type to avoid excessive allocation and copying. A popular alternate implementation of a string ADT allows some Strings to share pointer values and thus point to the same memory. That decision requires some bookkeeping to ensure that memory is not deallocated when it is still in use. A description of how to implement such a string type is one of the programming projects at the end of this chapter.

9.8   Summary

This chapter has focused much of its attention on syntax and on the inner workings of C++ in supporting first class types and dynamically allocated memory. We looked especially long at overloading operators and defining constructors and destructors. Overloading operators promotes natural notations for real-world and computer-world operations. C++ creates and destroys objects in ways that programmers can specify when they define class constructors and destructors.

Much of the power of C++ comes from using classes with pointer members as well from using pointers to objects. Almost all C++ programs written by experienced programmers use pointers. Pointers are necessary for dynamic object creation. Such objects are important in situations where the programmer cannot anticipate so completely the data that the program will be required to handle.

The syntax of pointers comes partly out of C syntax and partly out of the newer C++ syntax. The operator new, which is an operator in C++ but not in C, is used to create new objects. The creation both allocates space for the new object and constructs the new object in that space. The operator delete is the counterpart to new. It deallocates memory that was allocated for an object, and it does the necessary cleanup work specified by the class destructor.

Much of your learning process at this point will be devoted to learning new pointer and class syntax. As you develop new skills, you will also begin to more fully appreciate the benefits of good design and good implementation. When your skills become second nature, you will be able to place your attention on the more intriguing and challenging parts of object-oriented solution development, the analyses and the designs.

Glossary

address-of operator (&) A prefix operator that returns the address of its operand.

alias An alternate name for an object.

`assert()` A function which halts execution of the program if its Boolean argument is false. In that case, it prints a diagnostic message identifying the name and line number of the source code file of its invocation.

copy constructor A constructor that constructs a new object from another object of the same type.

dangling pointer A pointer that is not null but whose value is not the address of an object.

deallocation Releasing of dynamically allocated memory, freeing it for alternate use by the program. Deallocation is done with the operator `delete`.

deep copy A copy of a pointer's referent. A deep copy does not create an alias of an object; a shallow copy does.

`delete` The operator that deallocates dynamically allocated memory.

dereference operator (*) A prefix operator with a pointer operand that returns the pointer's referent.

destructor A special member function that is called whenever an object of that type goes out of existence.

dynamic memory allocation Runtime allocation of memory for an object. Allocation is done with the operator `new`.

dynamic object An object whose memory is allocated at runtime rather than compile time.

indirection operator *See* dereference operator.

lost memory Dynamically allocated memory to which there is no access.

memory leak Program behavior that produces lost memory.

`new` The operator that dynamically allocates memory for a new object.

null pointer A legitimate pointer value known not to represent the address of an object.

pointer The address of an object.

pointer data object A data object whose value is the address of another object. (The rvalue of the pointer is the lvalue of the object.)

reference A type which used to represent a name for an object. A reference to an object is an alias for the object.

referent The value of a pointer is the address of the pointer's referent.

shallow copy A copy of a pointer value. *See* deep copy.

9.9 Exercises

1. What output is generated by each of the following code fragments?

    a. `int* p = new int;`
       `*p = 4;`

```
    int* q = p;
    cout << *q;
```

b.
```
int x = 35;
int& y = x;
int* p = &x;
x++;
cout << x << ' ' << y << ' ' << *p;
```

c.
```
int x = 17;
int& y = x;
y++;
x++;
cout << x << ' ' << y;
```

d.
```
int* p = new int[5];
p[0] = 3;
p[1] = 4;
cout << *p << endl << p[0];
```

e.
```
Rational r(3,4);          Rational* p = &r;
double x = p->doubleVal();
cout << *p << ' ' << x;
```

f.
```
int x = 35;
int& y = x;
cout << x++ << ' ' << y;
```

2. In exercise 1 (d), explain the relationships among p, *p, &p[0], and p[0].

3. What are the errors in each of the following code fragments?

a.
```
int* p;
int x = 32767;
p* = x;
```

b.
```
int x = 35;
int& y = &x;
```

c.
```
int* p = new int;
double* q;
q = p;
```

d.
```
int x = 17;
int* p = x;
*p = 17;
```

e.
```
int x = 17;
int& r;
r = x;
```

    f. `int* p = new int;`
       `int& q = p;`

    g. `int* p = new int[5];`
       `int* q = new int[4];`
       `q = p;`

4. Consider the following definitions involving the `Rational` class (from Chapter 8).

```
Rational *rp, *sp, *tp;
Rational fraction(1,2);
```

    a. Write an assignment that makes `fraction` and `*rp` aliases.

    b. Write a statement that dynamically creates a new `Rational` object with value 5 and assigns the address of that new object to `sp`.

    c. Write a statement that dynamically creates an array of 50 `Rationals` and assigns the address of the first element of the array to `tp`.

    d. With the array in part (c), write a segment of code that assigns the first element of the array the rational number 5/2 and the second element the number -7/9.

    e. With the array in part (c), write a segment of code that outputs the first 20 elements.

    f. With the array in part (c), write a loop that increments every element of the array by the value 5/21.

5. In the previous problem, why were the three pointers `rp`, `sp`, and `tp` defined as

```
Rational *rp, *sp, *tp;
```

rather than this?

```
Rational* rp, sp, tp;
```

Was it just a matter of style, or do the two definitions create different types of objects?

6. This problem uses the class `InventoryTable`, which was defined in Chapter 7. Given the definition:

```
InventoryTable* inv;
```

    a. Write a statement that dynamically creates a new `InventoryTable` and assigns its address to `inv`.

    b. Write four statements that are `add` messages to the new `Inventory-Table`. Use the `->` operator. Add the items with the following data:

Barcode	Price
1211	$12.58
1011	$ .79
3200	$ .04
1515	$ 1.11

   c. Write a statement that updates the price of the item with barcode 1011 to $.81. Use the -> operator.

   d. Write a statement that removes the item with barcode 1515 from the InventoryTable. Use the -> operator.

   e. Write statements to iterate through the InventoryTable, printing the bar codes and prices as it does the iteration. Use the -> operator.

7. Write a new definition for the class InventoryTable from Chapter 7. Change InventoryTable::find() so that it returns a const Hard-wareItem* rather than a float. Assume inv is a pointer to an InventoryTable as in exercise 6 and x is a float. Write a segment of code to assign x the price of the item in the InventoryTable with barcode 1211.

8. Suppose prototypes for functions f() and g() are as follows.

```
ExtArray& f(const ExtArray& n, ExtArray m);
String g(const String& v);
int h(int i);
```

List all of the functions declared in either the ExtArray or String class definitions that may be called in the execution of the code in (a) through (p).

   a. ExtArray x(10,1000);

   b. ExtArray y = x;

   c. ExtArray z(y);

   d. ExtArray& ref = z;

   e. String c("abcd");

   f. String* pt;

   g. String* ptr = new String(c);

   h. cout << x << String("abc") << endl;

   i. f(x,ExtArray(3,12));

   j. f(x, y);

   k. c = g("abc");

   l. cout << g("xyz" + c);

```
m.h(x[55]);
```

```
n. x[35] += c.length();
```

```
o. delete ptr;
```

```
p. ExtArray* a[30];
```

9. A difficult part of the previous question was figuring out when constructors and destructors are called. The following exercise might help you determine when that happens.

a. Code the constructors and destructor of the String class so that each one contains an appropriate temporary output statement as follows:

```
cout << "Call to String null/C-string constructor." << endl;
cout << "Call to String copy constructor." << endl;
cout << "Call to String destructor." << endl;
```

Write a dummy main().

```
void main()
{
    cout << "Executing a definition." << endl;
    String automatic[5];
    cout << "Dynamic array creation. " << endl;
    String* dyna = new String[5];

    cout << "**** Destruction of dynamic String array." << endl;
    delete [] dyna;

    cout << "**** Destruction of automatic array." << endl;
}
```

Run your program and look at the results. How many times is a constructor called? How many times is the destructor called?

b. Suppose the function fun() is defined as follows.

```
String fun(String w)
{
    return String(w);
}
```

Rewrite main() from part (a).

```
void main()
{
    String a("abc");
```

```
        String b;
        b = fun(a);
        cout << b << endl;
    }
```

Which constructors are called and which code generates those calls? How many times is a destructor called?

c. Redo part (b) by changing the argument to `fun()` to a reference argument

```
String fun(String& w);
```

How many times is a constructor called?

d. Redo part (c) by redefining `fun()` to return a reference to a `String`.

```
String& fun(String& w)
{
    return w;
}
```

e. Code all of the members of the `ExtArray` class so that they contain output statements to indicate when they are being invoked and which member is being invoked. Write a dummy `main()` to include all of the statements in the previous problem that contained either an `ExtArray` or a pointer or reference to an `ExtArray`. Look at the results of executing the code to determine if your answers are correct.

10. Complete the implementation of the `String` class by defining `String::length()` and all of the overloaded comparison operators.

11. Suppose that the following definitions are given:

```
ExtArray x;
ExtArray* p;
```

a. Write a statement that dynamically creates a new `ExtArray` with 20 elements and blank value -1 and assigns its address to p.

b. Assign the value `2 * i` to each element `x[i]`, where i ranges from 0 through 22.

c. Assign `2 * i` to each element of p's referent, where i ranges from 0 through 22.

d. Write a statement that prints the size of p's referent to an output stream named `out`.

e. Write a statement that resizes p's referent to have 16 elements.

12. Redefine the `ExtArray` class so that instead of setting the size of the buffer to the value of a "too large" subscript, make the buffer twice the size necessary to accommodate the new subscript. What are the benefits of making that design decision? What are the drawbacks?

13. Reimplement the `SimpleListWithIterator` class from Chapter 7 using a pointer to a dynamically allocated array (its buffer) instead of an array data member. The new implementation should provide exactly the same functionality as the original version, except, of course, it cannot indicate the maximum capacity.

    A list object must keep track of its items, the number of items, the amount of room it has to store items (its buffer size), and the iterator's cursor. When the list does not have enough room to add a new item in its current buffer, it allocates a new array. The new buffer should have as much room as the old one plus room for 10 additional items. The class data can be defined as follows:

```
enum {extra_ = 10}; // Amount of extra room when a new buffer must be
                    //    allocated for the list items
int* item_;         // Points to the buffer holding the list items.
int size_;          // Number of items in the list
int bufSize_;       // Size of the buffer to hold list items
int cursor_;        // Iterator's cursor
```

14. Modify the `String` class to be a `Word` class, where a "word" is a sequence of alphabetic characters. Redefine the comparison operators so that the ordering on `Word` objects is not case sensitive, making `Word("abc") < Word("Bc")` even though `strcmp("abc","Bc")` is positive. Modify not only the comparison operations but also the input operation of the original `String` class for the new `Word` class. Modify the C-string conversion constructor to avoid constructing `Word`s containing nonalphabetic characters.

15. Reimplement the `String` class so that it does not use `'\0'` terminated strings. Instead, it has an `int` data member in the private section that indicates the current number of elements in the array allocated for the `String`.

Programming Projects

16. An efficient first class implementation of the string ADT does not require allocation of new memory whenever a string is assigned or copied. Instead the class allows different objects representing the same C-string to share data through "reference counting." Define the class `RefString` for that purpose.

    The definition of `RefString` class is similar to the definition of the

`String` class except there are two data members instead of one, a `char*` named `data_` and an `int*` named `count_`. The pointer `data_` points to a C-string. The pointer `count_` points to an integer, which is the reference counter. The purpose of `count_` is to keep track of the number of different `RefString` objects that have `data_` members pointing to the same C-string as this object's `data_`.

The `RefString` null constructor (the constructor with a default C-string argument) initializes `data_` the same way the `String` constructor initialized its `info_`. It dynamically allocates an `int` with value 1 and assigns its address to `count_`. The `RefString` copy constructor does not allocate any new memory. Instead, it initializes `data_` and `count_` with the values of the argument's `data` and `count_`. It then increments `*count_` by 1.

The assignment operator, which is somewhat complicated, does the following:

- If the objects on the left and right sides of the assignment are equal, or if the `data_` pointers of the two objects are equal, then no changes are made.
- Otherwise, the left-hand object relinquishes its old value and a new value is assigned. To relinquish the old value:
  If `*count_` is 1, then `data_` and `count_` are deleted.

  If `*count_` is greater than 1, then `*count_` is decremented by 1.

- The assignment of a new value works just like the copy constructor. That is, `data_` and `count_` are assigned the values of the argument's `data_` and `count_`. Then `*count_` is incremented by 1.

The overloaded non-const subscript operator behaves exactly the same as the overloaded non-const subscript operator on the `String` class if `*count_` is 1. Otherwise,

- `*count_` is decremented by 1,
- A new C-string is allocated, its address assigned to `data_`, and the original C-string is copied to `*data_`
- A new `int` with the value 1 is dynamically allocated for `count_`. After that, subscript behaves just like the overloaded subscript of the `String` class.

The destructor deletes `data_` and `count_` only if `*count_` is 1. Otherwise, it does not delete either member, but it decrements `*count_` by 1.

a. Implement the `RefString` class so that its public interface is identical to the public interface of the `String` class (except, of course, the identifier `String` is changed everywhere to `RefString`.) The behaviors of `RefString` and `String` should look identical, even though their methods are not.

b. (This is a variation on exercise 8.) Put a statement into the `RefString` destructor to output `*data_` and `*count_` before doing anything else. What output is generated by the following block of code?

```
{
    RefString a("abc");
    RefString b(a);
    RefString* p = new RefString(a);
    RefString* q;

    q = *p;
    delete p;
    a[1] = 'x';
    delete q;
}
```

c. Define `RefString` so that all of the member and friend functions that have simple one- or two-line definitions are declared inline.

17. Define a first class type for sets of nonnegative integers. The operations for a set-of-integer ADT are as follows.

- union   The union of sets A and B, $A \cup B$, is the set of all elements that belong to at least one of A and B.

- intersection   The intersection of sets A and B, $A \cap B$, is the set of all elements that belong to both A and B.

- difference   The difference of sets A and B, $A - B$, is the set of elements that belong to A but do not belong to B.

- membership   The number x is a member of the set A if x is an element of A.

- comparisons   The set A is a subset of the set B if and only if every element of A is an element of B.

                  The set A equals the set B if and only if A is a subset of B and B is a subset of A.

                  The set A is a proper subset of the set B if and only if A is a subset of B and A is does not equal B.

- cardinality   The cardinality of A is the number of elements of A.

The set ADT should include the empty set as a special set. (The empty set contains no elements.) Which computer-world operations should the ADT support?

a. Implement the set ADT as a class named `Set`. `Set` should have two data members, both of which are private. One is an `int`, which is the largest potential member of the set. The other is a pointer to an array of `bool` to be used as follows: the nth element of the array is false if n is not a member of the set and true if n is a member of the set.

Declare overloaded operators: `*` for intersection, `-` for set difference, `<` for proper subset, `<=` for subset, `==` for equality, and `!=` for inequality. Overload `+` twice, once for set union and once for adding a new element to the set. Declare nonoperator functions for membership and cardinality. Declare functions for computer-world operations.

Declare a copy constructor as well as a constructor with a `const int*` argument `val` with default value 0 and an `int` argument n with default value 0. That constructor initializes a `Set` with the first n non-negative elements of the array pointed to by `val`. Declare also an assignment operator and a destructor.

b. Discuss your rationale for deciding which computer-world operations the `Set` type supports.

c. Discuss your rationale for making the overloaded operators members or friends.

d. Discuss how your solution represents the empty set. What are the benefits of your design?

e. The specifications require at least two constructors. Discuss other potential constructors.

Chapter 10

Inheritance and Reuse

Chapter Contents

ONE of the major goals of object-oriented program development is reuse— reuse of analysis, reuse of designs, and reuse of both interfaces and implementations of code. One of the most important features of C++ for supporting reuse is **inheritance**, creating new classes out of existing ones. This does not mean changing the source code of existing classes to incorporate some new behavior or attribute. It means using existing classes as is and creating new classes for which only the new behavior and attributes must be included. The new classes will have the capability of the base classes as well as the additional new features.

One reason for creating first class types such as those discussed in the previous two chapters is to have code that could be reused in a variety of situations. Our examples of first class types were quite general. Although generic types are common to many situations, most applications require types that are designed for that particular application. With inheritance, it is possible to tailor old classes to meet the new application needs.

Tailoring generic types is not the only benefit of inheritance. C++ inheritance allows programmers to build a hierarchy of classes that are part of a central theme, a very powerful organizational tool for both developers and users of classes. Developers can design new classes based on a common, expected collection of attributes and behaviors inherited from old classes. Users of classes can rely on consistency of behaviors and attributes of classes in the same class hierarchy.

With new language features comes new syntax. In C++, new features often entail new uses of familiar keywords. Some of our efforts will be directed toward explaining new syntax. But most of our efforts will be directed toward showing you how to take advantage of inheritance in designing and coding solutions.

The process of writing code for the future without knowing what the future will require is a major software engineering problem that inheritance addresses. We will show how C++ uses inheritance to organize its stream classes. We will finish the chapter by changing the solution of the changemaker (from Chapter 1) to take advantage of inheritance. In doing so, we will develop a solution to a new problem that is a generalization of the simple changemaker.

10.1 Incremental programming: Extending an existing class

Inheritance is an important mechanism for reuse. The most straightforward example of how inheritance contributes to reuse is a case that extends an existing class. Consider the `String` class from the previous chapter. Here, for convenient reference, is the interface code for the class:

```
class String {
public:
   String(const char s[] = "");   // Constructs a deep copy of a C-string.
                                  // ASSUME: s is a valid C-string.
   String(const String& s);       // Constructs a deep copy of s.
   ~String();                     // Deallocates string memory.
   String& operator= (const String& rhs);   // Assigns a deep copy of rhs.
   String& operator+= (const String& rhs);  // Adds a deep copy of rhs to the
                                            //   end of this string.

   char& operator[](int i);         // The element at subscript i.
                                    // ASSUME: i < length of the string
   char operator[](int i) const;    // The element at subscript i.
                                    // ASSUME: i < length of the string
   int length() const;              // Number of string characters.
   const char* charString( ) const; // C-String equivalent value.

   // Comparison operators
   friend bool operator== (const String& s, const String& t);
   friend bool operator!= (const String& s, const String& t);
   friend bool operator<  (const String& s, const String& t);
   friend bool operator<= (const String& s, const String& t);
   friend bool operator>  (const String& s, const String& t);
   friend bool operator>= (const String& s, const String& t);

   friend ostream& operator<<(ostream& out, const String& s);
            // Writes the C-string equivalent to out.
   friend istream& operator>> (istream& in, String & s);
            // Reads at most 999 characters up to the next newline from
            //   from in. The newline is extracted but not assigned.
   friend String operator+(const String& s, const String& t);
            // A deep copy of s with a deep copy of t appended to the end.

private:
   char* info_;
};
```

There are two overloaded subscript operators for the String class. This is how they are defined:

```
char& String :: operator[](int i)
{
   return info_[i];
}
char String :: operator[](int i) const
{
   return info_[i];
}
```

There is no bounds checking in this code. There is no prediction about what happens if the subscript is not in the appropriate range. It is left to the user of the class to refrain from attempting to refer to a position past the end of underlying string.

Deriving a new class from the base class String

Suppose that we have come into possession of the String class, finding it to our liking except that we would prefer to have operator[] handle bounds checking. Here is where inheritance can be of help. We will create a new class, based on String, which remedies the omission in the behavior of operator[]. We will call our new class BCString (Bounds-Checked String).

```
// Bounds-Checked string class
// Any attempt to subscript past the length of the string results in an error.
class BCString : public String {
public:
    // Constructors, destructor, and assignment -- never inherited
    BCString(const char s[] = "");              // Constructs from a C-string
                                                //   ASSUME: s is a valid C-string

    BCString(const BCString& bcs);              // Constructs a deep copy of bcs
    ~BCString();                                // Deallocates string memory
    BCString& operator= (const BCString& rhs);// Assigns a deep copy of rhs

    // Remaining operators -- inherited, but modified behavior wanted
    BCString& operator+= (const BCString& rhs);   // Appends a deep copy of rhs
                                                  //   to the end of this string
    char& operator[] (int i);        // Character at subscript i; if i < 0 or
                                     //   i > length, exit() is invoked
    char operator[] (int i) const ;  // Character at subscript i; if i < 0 or
                                     //   i > length, exit() is invoked
    int length() const;              // Length of the string
    friend BCString operator+(const BCString& b, const BCString& c);
             // Returns the concatenation of b and c.

    friend istream& operator>> (istream& in, BCString & bc);
             // Reads at most 999 characters up to the next newline from
             //   from in. The newline is extracted but not assigned.
private:
    int length_;
};
```

The BCString class definition contains something new. Look at the top line, beginning with the keyword class. The definition begins like this:

```
class BCString : public String {
```

The part of this line between BCString and the left brace is called an **inheritance list**. It clues us in to the fact that BCString is a **derived class**, one that is defined as an extension of another class, String. The class String is a **base class**, a class from which other classes such as BCString are derived.

BCString is an example of **incremental programming**, the process of creating new types by enhancing old ones. The larger and more complex the base class from which a derived class inherits, the greater the benefit. There are many new ideas and new language features associated with inheritance to be introduced in this chapter and the next. This first example introduces us to a number of the new features. Let's look at a few of them in more detail. And don't worry if not everything about inheritance becomes clear in the next few paragraphs. We'll look at many examples after this.

A derived class (BCString) inherits the members of the base class (String). That means the members of a derived class include all of those members declared in its own definition as well as members declared in the definition of the base class from which it was derived. Data and function members of a base class are inherited by any class derived from it. Figure 10.1 illustrates the data members of a String and a BCString representing "Hello".

In principle any class can become a base class as the result of having a class derived from it. In practice it takes even more experience and skill to create a class that is useful as a base class than it does to create a class that is useful.

The BCString class is a clear case where it is natural to expect that the newly derived class is just like the base class String except for including bounds checking of subscript references. This idea of a derived class being *just like* its base class *except* for some change is quite important for understanding inheritance at the design level. Think for a moment about a specification for the String class. It mentions what a String object knows and can do. But it also leaves some things unspecified. For example, the specification may be very precise about what happens when the subscript operator is applied to a String object with a subscript that is nonnegative and less than the length of the C-string data; but the specification may be silent about what will happen if the subscript is out of range. BCString meets all the specifications of the base class, but it adds constraints on behaviors that are unspecified in the base class.

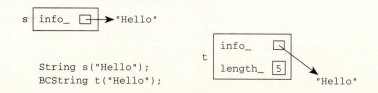

```
String s("Hello");
BCString t("Hello");
```

Figure 10.1 String and BCString objects for "Hello".

A derived class **inherits the interface** of the base class if it meets all the specifications of the base class, differing only in specifying what is left unspecified in the base or in adding new members that do not overturn any of the base class specifications. In that case, we say each derived class object *is-a* base class object too.

The main reason that our BCString implementation is as long as it is, is that we want BCString objects to be just as first class as String objects. We also want constructors, a destructor, and an assignment operator. These special member functions are an exception to the inheritance of members from the base class. A derived class will not inherit the constructors, destructor, or assignment operator from a base class.

To say that constructors, assignment, and destructor are not inherited does not mean they do not exist if the derived class does not declare them. C++ provides a default null constructor for any class with no declared constructor and a default copy constructor for a class that does not explicitly declare one. It also provides a default assignment operator and a default destructor. There is absolutely no guarantee—or, for that matter, no reason even to suspect—that the C++ defaults will behave in any way as the corresponding base class member functions. The base class behaviors are not inherited for these special member functions.

Defining derived member functions by letting the base members do the work

Since a derived class usually has more data members than a base class (the length_ member is an example), the constructors and the destructor and assignment operator of the base class will in the general case not be fully correct. Fortunately, C++ provides a way to add to the behavior of a base class function without having to rewrite the base class function in its entirety. A derived class function may call a base class function and add to its behavior incrementally, if that is suitable. Indeed all the noninherited member functions of the BCString class except the destructor and length() explicitly call the similar functions of the String class and add to the base class behavior.

The initialization list of the BCString constructor that has a C-string argument contains the expression String(s), an explicit call to the corresponding String constructor. That String constructor can initialize the BCString data member info_, which is inherited from String.

```
BCString :: BCString(const char s[]) : String(s), length_(strlen(s))
{ }
```

The length_ member, which is not inherited, is initialized separately in the list. The BCString copy constructor is similar. Its initialization list calls the String copy constructor, and it initializes length_ separately.

```
BCString :: BCString(const BCString& bcs) : String(bcs), length_(bcs.length_)
{ }
```

The destructor is particularly easy to define. Its body is empty, but that does not mean that nothing happens when a BCString goes out of existence. C++ automatically calls the base class destructor, ~String(), even if it is not mentioned in the derived class destructor definition.

```
BCString :: ~BCString()
{ }
```

Now for the two assignment operators. The first is the ordinary simple assignment operator; the second is a modified assignment operator. Both of them use new syntax when they invoke the corresponding assignment operators in the base class. Let's look at BCString::operator=:

```
BCString& BCString :: operator= (const BCString& rhs)
{
    String::operator=(rhs);         // Line 1 -- call to base class assignment
    length_ = rhs.length_;          // Line 2 -- ordinary int assignment
    return *this;
}
```

The symbol :: is the scope resolution operator. It is used to specify exactly which function is invoked. In the body of the definition of any member function of the BCString class,

String::operator=	means the assignment operator for the String class.
operator=	means the assignment operator for the BCString class.

The definition of the BCString class assignment operator takes advantage of all the hard work done by the String class assignment operator, String::operator=. Line 1 of the definition is a call to the base class assignment operator. The base class version does all of the appropriate memory allocation and assignment to info_. Line 2 of the definition is much more simple. It merely assigns the length_ data member of the right hand side operand (rhs) to this operand (the BCString for which the assignment operator is invoked).

We warned you that there would be some different-looking syntax. It appears again in the definition of modified assignment operator, operator+=. This definition looks almost like the last one. Only this time the function `String::opera-tor+=` is going to be invoked.

```
BCString& BCString :: operator+= (const BCString& rhs)
{
    String::operator+=(rhs);
    length_ += rhs.length_;
    return *this;
}
```

The two subscript operator functions are next. We defined them using that same technique of calling the corresponding subscript operator functions for the base class.

```
char& BCString :: operator[](int i)
{
    if (0 <= i && i < length_)
        return String::operator[](i);    // calls char& String::operator[]()
    else
        exit(1);
}
char BCString :: operator[](int i) const
{
    if (0 <= i && i < length_)
        return String::operator[](i);   // calls char String::operator[]() const
    else
        exit(1);
}
```

It is really the subscript operator that tempted us to derive a new class from `String`. Each one invokes the standard function `exit()` to halt execution if the subscript is too small (less than 0) or too large (greater than or equal to `length_`).

Reuse instead of starting from scratch

You might find yourself thinking that it would be much easier to reuse the `String` class code by simply editing the definitions of the subscript operators. There is certainly a good deal more code (and effort) in the definition and implementation of `BCString` than merely adding to the definition of subscripting. But it is very common not to have access to the source code of a library class. So even if it were easier to modify the source code, that would not be an option in many cases. In addition, even when source code is in principle available, it is often a bad idea to modify it rather than derive from it. When a new version of the `String` class is made available, code that uses the `BCString` class will be able to take advantage of the new `String` class by being relinked but without having to be recompiled. (And you will not have to be constantly editing your source code to keep it up to date.)

One of the promises of object-oriented programming is easy reusability of code. One of the problems of a traditional approach to programming is the idea that you must begin from scratch every time. If there is well-written, reliable code that is nearly suitable, it is almost always better to enhance it rather than to write your own not-so-reliable code.

Another reason for deriving a class is to improve or change some of the implementation of function members but not the behavior in the specification. The `length()` function of `BCString` is more efficient than the `length()` function of the base class `String`. The derived class version simply returns the value of the data member `length_`. The base class version counts the characters of a C-string each time it is called. Both versions will return the same result, but the `BCString` version will be faster.

```
int BCString :: length() const
{
    return length_;
}
```

Substituting a derived class for a base class

The definitions of the `BCString` assignment operators called the base class versions using a variation of the ordinary function call syntax. The actual argument for each was a `BCString` and not a `String`. That illustrates one feature of inheritance in C++: *it is always syntactically legal to pass a publicly derived class object as an argument to a function expecting a base class object*. Of course, the correctness of the resulting behavior depends upon the programmer who created the derived class to adhere to the expected standard of *is-a* inheritance that we just described. We relied on the compiler allowing this substitution whenever we called `String` base class functions with `BCString` objects as arguments.

When a derived class object is assigned to or passed by value as argument for a base class object, the result might not be what you hoped for; **slicing** will occur. In general, a derived class object will have more data members than its base class objects. `BCString` objects have an additional `int` data member called `length_`. When a `BCString` is passed as argument to a function expecting a `String` object, the compiler will not complain, but it will slice off the extra data members of the derived class object and use only the members inherited from the base class for the base class variable. When references or pointers to base arguments are involved as in the interface to the constructors and assignment operators of `String`, slicing does not occur. As we will see later on, this fact is one of the reasons that references and pointers are so important in C++ object-oriented programming.

BCString has only two friend declarations, one for the overloaded + operator and the other for the overloaded >> operator. It is not necessary to overload the comparison operators or the output operator. The base class overloads will suffice. Consider this code:

```
BCString john("John");
BCString mary("Mary");
if (john < mary)
    cout << "Comparison is OK" << endl;
```

The operator < was overloaded for String arguments. But since a BCString *is-a* String, the comparison works as expected. The function operator<() that takes String arguments will also work with BCString arguments. It needs only the info_ members to make the comparison.

As for operator +, we had to overload it in order for the member length_ to be correct. Here is one definition for that overloaded operator:

```
BCString operator+(const BCString& b, const BCString& c)
{
    BCString ret(b);   // Create a return value out of the first argument.
    ret += c;          // Use the BCString += operator.
    return ret;
}
```

The input operator had to be defined for BCStrings because of length_ also. The String version of the input operator and the BCString assignment operator do most of the work of overloading the BCString input operator.

```
istream& operator>>(istream& in, BCString& bc)
{
    String s;                          // Temporary string for getting the input.
    in >> s;                           // String input operator.
    bc = BCString(s.charString()); // Assign bc a BCString constructed from
                                       //    the temporary String's C-string.
    return in;
}
```

The overloaded input operator used the charString() member inherited from String. It could not use the info_ member because info_ was declared private in the base class. Even though the operator function is a friend of BCString, info_ is not accessible to it—info_ is a member of BCString, but it is not accessible even to the member functions of BCString.

10.2 ▐ Single inheritance: Designing a class hierarchy

Suppose that you have just become part of a software production team that is developing an adventure computer game that is still very much in the analysis stage. The software production team is wrestling with game scenarios. Every possible setting ranging from medieval castles, to the sewers in Paris, to space stations in different galaxies is under hot contention. While some of the team members are spending all of their energies dealing with exotic scenario decisions, you have to start producing code. Your boss wants a working prototype very soon.

One of the benefits of object-oriented development is that it is possible to make a working prototype long before the analysis of the problem is complete. That's not all. Code from the prototype can be reused for the final solution. Your task is to write code that can be reused, even though you cannot anticipate the decisions that will be the eventual outcome of the ongoing analysis and design of the game. How can you program for the future? How can you reuse from the past? Part of the object-oriented answer to those questions is inheritance.

Adventure games typically take players through a labyrinth of passageways, rooms, or edifices. Getting from one part of the labyrinth to another often means going through a door. Your responsibility as a software production team member is designing and implementing the doors. Your initial task is to decide what characteristics are common to all doors—what characteristic does an object have that tells you that the object is a door.

Let's try to devise a solution, starting with a simple door design. Every door is in one of two states: open or shut. A door knows its state. A door can tell whether it is open or shut. When a new door is created, initially it will be shut. (That initialization decision is arbitrary. The door could just as easily have been initialized as open.) A door can close itself. In anticipation of developments in classes that might be derived from a door class, we allow for the possibility that something could prevent a door from being able to open itself: A door can open itself, if that is possible. Here is the design that we just outlined.

Object Type: Door
    <u>Knows:</u>
        Its open or shut status
    <u>Can do:</u>
        Initialize itself to a shut door
        Open itself, if possible
        Close itself
        Tell whether or not it is open

We have made some decisions that constrain what classes derived from the base class `Door` will be able to do. The base class does not specify any dimensions for the door opening. So we certainly can add dimensions (height and width) in a derived class, if we wish. But our design does specify that doors will be either open or shut. That innocuous decision makes it unlikely that any derived class will have partially open doors. If we anticipate that need for partially open doors, we may want to redesign our base class `Door`. We have also, somewhat arbitrarily, not allowed for the possibility of a door being unable to close itself. That decision too may be reconsidered. Often we do not have a really good grasp on what should be ruled in and what should be ruled out and what should be left unspecified when a class is first designed for a specific use.

Good base classes grow over time as the result of experience, thoughtful reflection, and redesign.

Defining a base class

The design of our door is so simple that its class implementation will be almost trivial to write. Remember that this is just the design for a generic door. It is not complicated enough to represent doors with locks or doors that require special contortions on the part of the players to open or close them.

The simple, generic `Door` class will serve as a base to derive more sophisticated and complicated doors. In the `Door` class definition, you'll see a new C++ keyword, `protected`.

```
// A generic door class
class Door {
public:
    Door();                   // Constructs a shut door.
    bool isOpen() const;      // Is the door open?
    void open();              // Opens the door, if possible.
    void close();             // Shuts the door.
protected:
    bool shut_;
};
```

The member function definitions for the `Door` class are very easy to code. The fact that `Door` will be used as a base class from which other classes will be derived does not change how its member functions are coded.

```
Door :: Door() : shut_(true)
{ }
```

```
bool Door :: isOpen() const
{
    return !shut_;
}

void Door :: open()
{
    shut_ = false;              // By default, it is always possible to open.
}

void Door :: close()
{
    shut_ = true;
}
```

Derived classes and access control

There are two distinct ways that a class may be used. First, a class may be used by instantiation, declaring an object to be an instance of the class. Second, a class may be used by inheritance, as a base class from which other classes are derived. Creating a class that is well-suited for inheritance use requires additional skills and language features beyond those needed for instantiation use. One set of features concerns accessibility of members of a class.

Friends and member functions of a class that is derived from a base class have access to the members declared within the derived class. That's not surprising. But members of the derived class that are inherited from a base class are not always accessible to friends and member functions of the derived class. The inherited members of the derived class that are accessible are the ones that were declared as public or protected members of the base class.

Every derived class has two sets of members:

- Members that it declares
- Members inherited from the base class

It is not always possible for a derived class or a friend of a derived class to access the members inherited from the base class.

Friends and members of a derived class do *not* have access to the inherited members of the class that were declared private members of the base class. (That is why the overloaded + operator for BCString could not access a BCString's info_ member. The String class declared info_ as private.) Nonfriend functions outside the scope of a class have no access to the private or protected members of the class.

The keyword `protected` is used in the context of inheritance. It describes how class members can be accessed. C++ provides three ways to control access to class members: public, private, and protected. You already know what public and private mean. Everyone has access to public members. Only member functions and friends of a class have access to private members.

Member functions and friends of a derived class have no access to inherited members of the class that were declared private in the base class. A member declared as **protected** in a base class is accessible to the base class and its friends as well as to classes derived from the base and their friends. Access to protected members is denied to everyone else. Protected is a compromise between public and private.

The picture is slightly more complicated than we have just outlined. But before we spell it all out, let's look at a concrete example of a derived class. Access to class members depends on whether the member is inherited, how the member is declared in the first place, and what kind of inheritance is involved.

For an adventure game, many doors must be much more complicated than the simple `Door` type. But each will be a kind of door. The next type of door we will consider is a door with a lock—a lockable door. A lockable door *is a* door. So it knows and can do everything a door can do. But a lockable door knows more and can do more than a simple door. A lockable door knows whether or not it is locked. It knows how to unlock and lock itself. It can tell whether or not it is unlocked. Lockable doors are created as doors that are shut and locked. A lockable door cannot open itself unless it is unlocked.

Object Type: Lockable door
   Knows:
      Its open or shut status
      Its locked or unlocked status
   Can do:
      Initialize itself to a shut, locked door
      Open itself, if it is not locked
      Close itself
      Tell whether or not it is open
      Lock itself
      Unlock itself
      Tell whether or not it is unlocked

At this point, we could plunge ahead and define a `LockableDoor` class from scratch. We could even save ourselves some typing effort by copying the definition for the `Door` class, modifying some of the member function declarations, and adding new members. That's easy enough with this simple example, but we can actually do better than cutting, pasting, and modifying. We will leave the Door class as it is, building the LockableDoor from the Door base class. Code reuse means just that—*reusing the code without rewriting or modifying it, or even seeing it!*

In order to derive a new class from a base class, you need to have the source code containing the definition of the base class. You do not need the source code containing the definitions of the member functions of the base class— you do not need to see those member function definitions. But you will need to see the specifications for the public and protected member functions in order to make sure your derived class meets the specifications. And that means that the programmer responsible for the base class must write clear and precise specifications.

It is common practice to keep the definition of a class in a header file (whose name ends in .h or .H) and to keep the definitions of its member functions in a .C file. To compile the derived class definition, you need the header file of the base class. In order to link and execute the new code, however, you need the .o file produced from the .C file containing the definitions of the base class member functions.

Here's how the LockableDoor class reuses the code from the Door class:

```
// A lockable door class
class LockableDoor : public Door {
public:
    LockableDoor();            // Constructs a locked, shut door.
    bool isLocked() const;     // Is the door locked?
    void open();               // Opens the door if it is not locked.
    void lock();               // Locks the door.
    void unlock();             // Unlocks the door.
protected:
    bool locked_;
};
```

The LockableDoor definition looks pretty slim compared to its design that was outlined in the box. Where is there any mention of the open or shut status in the definition? What about the lockable door's abilities to close itself or to tell whether or not it is open? Even though the base class members shut_, isOpen(), and close() are not declared in the LockableDoor definition, they are members of the LockableDoor class. They are inherited from Door. The LockableDoor class thus has two data members, shut_ and locked_ as

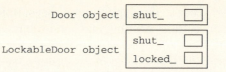

Door object   shut_ ☐

LockableDoor object   shut_ ☐
                       locked_ ☐

Figure 10.2 Memory allocation for `Door` and `LockableDoor` objects.

illustrated in Fig. 10.2. `LockableDoor` has seven member functions: its constructor, `isLocked()`, `open()`, `lock()`, `unlock()`, `isOpen()`, and `close()`.

The inheritance list of `LockableDoor`, which appears at the top of its definition, indicates that `LockableDoor` is derived from `Door`. The `LockableDoor` inheritance list contains only a single item:

`public Door`

An inheritance list looks similar to the initialization lists that we have used for class constructor definitions. Each list is introduced with a colon, `:`. An inheritance list appears between the colon and a beginning brace, `{`. In the case of an inheritance list, the beginning brace encloses the remainder of the class definition. In the case of an initialization list, the beginning brace encloses the remainder of the constructor definition.

Let's return to the issue of access. An inheritance list specifies the base classes from which a new class is derived and how the members of the base classes can be accessed as members of the derived class. So each item in an inheritance list consists of two parts: an access control specifier keyword, `public`, `protected`, or `private`, and a base class name. Those access control specifiers have the following meaning:

- **Public inheritance** means public members of the base class are public members of the derived class and protected members of the base class are protected members of the derived class.

- **Protected inheritance** means public and protected members of the base class are protected members of the derived class.

- **Private inheritance** means public and protected members of the base class are private members of the derived class.

Remember that in any case, even though private members of a base class are members of the derived class, they are not accessible to the members or friends of a derived class.

Figure 10.3 illustrates what the access specifiers mean for base classes and their derived classes. The headings for the rows indicate the member access specified in the base class. The column labels indicate the access specified in the inheritance list of the derived class.

A class can be derived from more than one base class, a process known as **multiple inheritance**. Each base class must appear in the inheritance list that is

Kind of inheritance

		public	protected	private
Accessibility in base class	public	public	protected	private
	protected	protected	protected	private
	private	*prohibited*	*prohibited*	*prohibited*
	prohibited	*prohibited*	*prohibited*	*prohibited*

Accessibility in derived class

Where a class member is accessible	Accessibility of member
Everywhere	`public`
Members and friends of the class Members and friends of derived classes	`protected`
Members and friends of the class	`private`
Nowhere	*prohibited*

Figure 10.3 Members of a base class are considered members of a derived class. Access to these members depends on whether they are private, public, or protected in the base class and whether the base class is inherited with public, protected, or private access by the derived class. Private members of a base class are not accessible at all within a derived class. Within the derived class, access to private members of a base class is prohibited.

part of the definition of the derived class. If a base class is not specified as public or protected, then it is assumed to be private.

Definitions of member functions of derived classes

The definitions of the members of `LockableDoor` contain some this new inheritance syntax. Let's start with the constructor. It uses an initialization list to initialize its members. Part of that initialization list is a call to the `Door` constructor.

```
LockableDoor :: LockableDoor() : Door(), locked_(true)
{ }
```

The call to the `Door` constructor, which appears in the initialization list, has no actual arguments. (It cannot. The `Door` constructor has no formal arguments.) That call effectively initializes the data member `shut_` to true. Recall that `shut_` is a member of `LockableDoor` by virtue of the fact that it is a member of `Door`. The data member `locked_` is not inherited from `Door`. It is initialized to true in the second part of the initialization list.

The call to the `Door` constructor is a convenience whose usefulness is not apparent in this simple example. However, if a class has a complicated constructor, the value of being able to initialize part of a derived class through a call to the constructor of a base class could result in reuse of a significant portion of the code. The `BCString` class provided a good example of this convenience. The base class `String` constructors did all of the hard work, but that was more than a simple convenience. If the base class contains private members, a call to a base class constructor may be the only way to initialize those private members. *If a constructor to a base class is not explicitly called when a derived class object is created, the compiler will implicitly call a constructor to the base class when the derived class object is created.*

The definitions for `isLocked()`, `lock()`, and `unlock()` are simple. They do not employ any special features of inheritance.

```
bool LockableDoor :: isLocked() const
{
    return locked_;
}

void LockableDoor :: lock()
{
    locked_ = true;
}

void LockableDoor :: unlock()
{
    locked_ = false;
}
```

The members `isOpen()` and `close()` are inherited from `Door`. They have the same meaning for `LockableDoor` type objects as for `Door` type objects. Those member functions are not redeclared in the `LockableDoor` class. The member function `open()` is different. It will be given a new definition for the derived class, `LockableDoor`. A function declared in a derived class is said to **hide** any function with the same name that is declared in a base class. `LockableDoor::open()` hides `Door::open()`.

A method declared in a derived class hides all of the methods of the base class that have the same name. When a function in a derived class has the same name as a function in a base class, *all* functions in the base class with that name are hidden, even the ones with different signatures. You cannot invoke any of the corresponding base class methods of that name by sending an ordinary message to the derived class object. With hiding, the compiler will not try to match the actual argument list with any of the base class members of that name. The compiler limits itself to looking only at the derived class members of that name.

```
class Base {
public:
    void f(int x)      {cout << "Base::f(int)" << endl;}
    void f(double x)   {cout << "Base::f(double)" << endl;}
    void f()           {cout << "Base::f()" << endl;}
};

class Derived : public Base {
public:
    // Derived::f() hides three members of Base
    void f(char x)     {cout << "Derived::f(char)" << endl;}
};

Derived d;
Base b;
d.f(125);          // output: Derived::f(char)
b.f(125);          // output: Base::f(int)
d.f(59.87);        // output: Derived::f(char)

b.f(59.87);        // output: Base::f(double)
d.f();             // illegal! Base::f() is hidden.
```

Hiding in this manner is generally considered to be poor programming practice. We will show you a better technique of dealing with hiding in Chapter 11.

Let's analyze more carefully how we want lockable doors to open themselves. A lockable door will be able to open itself only if it is unlocked to begin with. Users who want lockable doors to open must be sure those doors are unlocked in order for an open message to do any good.

Here is the new definition for open() as a member of the LockableDoor class, which hides its base class definition:

```
void LockableDoor :: open()
{
   if (!locked_)
      Door :: open();        // could have used:  shut_ = false;
}
```

This definition illustrates an important feature of C++. Even though a function can hide its definition in the base class, the inherited function from the base class can still be invoked by member functions of the derived class.

If a lockable door is not locked, then it opens the same way a door opens. There is no need to rewrite the code to open a door. All that is necessary is an invocation to the inherited function, `Door::open()`. The prefix `Door::` on the front of the inherited function name specifies that the `open()` function that is to be called is the one for the class `Door` as opposed to the one for the class `LockableDoor`. Without that prefix, the call in the selection statement would be to `LockableDoor::open()`, which in turn would call `LockableDoor::open()`, which in turn would call `LockableDoor::open()`, and so on. (That is "infinite recursion.") The prefix `Door::` is necessary to tell the compiler that it is `Door`'s `open()` member function that is being called rather than `LockableDoor`'s `open()` member function. Keep in mind that `::` is the scope resolution operator. It is used to indicate which class an identifier such as a function name refers to.

The following code illustrates the use of `LockableDoor` objects and `Door` objects. The comments accompanying the code show the status of the data members after execution of each statement.

```
Door generic;          // generic.shut_ is true
LockableDoor bathDoor; // bathDoor.shut_ and bathDoor.locked_ are true

generic.open();        // generic.shut is false
bathDoor.lock();       // bathDoor.shut_ and bathDoor.locked_ are true
bathDoor.open();       // bathDoor.shut_  and bathDoor.locked_ are still
                       //    true
if (!bathDoor.isOpen())
   bathDoor.unlock();  // bathDoor.shut_ is true; bathDoor.locked_ is false
```

Using a derived class as a base for additional classes

There are many different kinds of locks. Some lockable doors have hook-and-eye locks, some have keyed locks, some have combination locks. And if you stretch your imagination (which is necessary for any decent adventure game), you can think of more exotic kinds of locks. The door that was the entry to Ali Baba's cave required a password, "open sesame."

We can use `LockableDoor` as a base class to derive specialized lockable doors. We will restrict our attention to two new types of lockable doors: one with a combination lock and one requiring a password. Figure 10.4 shows the **class hierarchy** that we will develop. A class hierarchy consists of a base class and all classes derived either directly or indirectly from it.

The class hierarchy shows that `LockableDoor` is derived from `Door` and that `PasswordDoor` and `CombinationLockDoor` are derived from `LockableDoor`. The class `Door` is a direct base of `LockableDoor` and an indirect base of `PasswordDoor` and `CombinationLockDoor`.

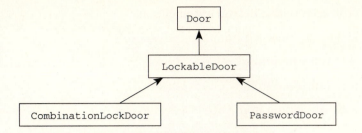

Figure 10.4 The hierarchy of classes derived from `Door`.

In order to unlock a combination lock, you must know the correct combination. How to define the `CombinationLockDoor` class to embody that idea is a design decision. What is the combination for a given door? How do you send a door a message to unlock itself? We chose to fix the lock combination when a `CombinationLockDoor` object is created. That combination can be an argument to a member function that unlocks the door. If no combination is specified either when the door is created or when it is sent an unlock message, a default value is assumed.

Ordinary combination locks in a hardware store have combinations that are sequences of three integers such as "30-0-15". We decided on a simpler model. The combinations for our locks will be single integers. This is the `CombinationLock-Door` definition:

```
// A combination lock door
// Combinations are single integers
class CombinationLockDoor : public LockableDoor {
public:
    CombinationLockDoor (int c = 0); // Constructs a door with combination c
    void unlock(int c = 0);          // Attempts to unlock the door using
                                     //   combination c. Does nothing if c
                                     //   is not the correct combination.
protected:
    int combination_;
};
```

It is not necessary to specify that `CombinationLockDoor` is derived from `Door` since `LockableDoor` is derived from `Door` and `CombinationLockDoor` is derived from `LockableDoor`. Thus `CombinationLockDoor` contains the following members:

- `combination_` (declared in `CombinationLockDoor`)

- `locked_` (inherited from `LockableDoor`)

- `shut_` (inherited from `Door`)

- A constructor with a default argument
- `isLocked()` (inherited from `LockableDoor`)
- `open()` (inherited from `LockableDoor`)
- `lock()` (inherited from `LockableDoor`)
- `close()` (inherited from `Door`)
- `unlock()`, with a default argument, and which hides `Lockable-Door::unlock()`
- `isOpen()` (inherited from `Door`)

The `CombinationLockDoor` constructor creates a locked door with a particular combination. The combination is the actual argument in the definition of a `CombinationLockDoor` object. If the object is defined with no argument, then the combination for its lock is the default number, 0.

```
CombinationLockDoor :: CombinationLockDoor (int c) : LockableDoor(),
                                                  combination_(c)
{ }
```

When a new `CombinationLockDoor` is created, the `LockableDoor` constructor is called. Since the `LockableDoor` constructor was defined to call the `Door` constructor, then the `Door` constructor will also be called. C++ constructs classes starting with the base class and working its way out through the levels of derived classes. Although this order is immaterial for `CombinationLockDoor`, the member `shut_` is initialized first, then `locked_`, and finally `combination_`.

The default argument in the constructor effectively gives `CombinationLock-Door` two different constructors. The default argument for `unlock()` effectively gives two member functions called `unlock`. Of course, only one definition is required. This is another example of hiding. `CombinationDoor::unlock()` hides `LockableDoor::unlock()`.

```
void CombinationLockDoor :: unlock(int c)
{
    if (c == combination_)
        LockableDoor::unlock();        // could use: locked_ = false;
}
```

This code contains another example of a call to a member function of a base class from within the definition of a member function of a derived class. That call is made only if the combination matches the actual argument, if there is one. If there is no actual argument, then the `CombinationLockDoor` object will not be unlocked unless its combination is 0. Notice that if a `CombinationLockDoor` object has a combination of 0, then it behaves almost exactly like a `LockableDoor` object. It responds to messages in exactly the same fashion.

Here is some code to illustrate the use of `CombinationLockDoor` objects:

```
CombinationLockDoor gymLocker(3016);       // gymLocker combination is 3016
                                           //  gymLocker is locked and shut
CombinationLockDoor simple;                // simple combination is 0
                                           //  simple is locked and shut
gymLocker.unlock(3016);                    // gymLocker is now unlocked
simple.unlock(20);                         // simple is still locked--20 is
                                           //  the wrong combination

CombinationLockDoor myLocker(gymLocker);// myLocker combination is 3016
                                           //  myLocker is unlocked and shut
```

Notice how `myLocker` was created from `gymLocker`. Every class has a copy constructor, whether it declares one explicitly or not. When none is declared (as in the case of `CombinationLockDoor`), the default copy constructor provided by C++ is used. That default copy constructor creates a new `CombinationLockDoor` by making a memberwise copy of each data member. So `myLocker` was created with the data of `gymLocker`, including the current value for `gymLocker.locked_`.

Classes with class type members

`PasswordDoor`, which is derived from the `LockableDoor` class, is almost identical to the `CombinationLockDoor` class. Instead of an `int` type `combination_`, a `PasswordDoor` will have a `String` type `password_` as a member. For this situation, we say a `PasswordDoor` *has-a* `String`.

It is at this time that creating `String` as a first class type will pay off. The implementation of `PasswordDoor` can be much shorter than if we had decided to make `password_` of type `char*`.

```
// A lockable door that requires a password to unlock
class PasswordDoor : public LockableDoor {
public:
    PasswordDoor(const char c[] = ""); // Creates a door with password c
    void unlock(const char c[] = "");  // Attempts to unlock the door using
                                       //  password c.  Does nothing if c
                                       //  is not the correct password.
protected:
    String password_;
};
```

The definitions for the `PasswordDoor` and `CombinationLockDoor` constructors are identical except that the identifiers `CombinationLockDoor` and `combination_` are replaced by the identifiers `PasswordDoor` and `password_`. It is really that simple. But what you may not see from first looking at these definitions is quite complicated.

If we go back to the `String` definition, we will see a `String` constructor that creates a `String` from a C-string. The `String` constructor allows us to construct the `PasswordDoor`'s `password_` out of a C-string also. All we need to do is invoke the `String` constructor in the initialization list of the `PasswordDoor` constructor.

```
PasswordDoor :: PasswordDoor(const char c[]) : LockableDoor(),
                                               password_(c)
{ }

void PasswordDoor :: unlock(const char c[])
{
    if (c == password_)
        locked_ = false;
}
```

When a `PasswordDoor` object is created through this constructor, the `LockableDoor` and `Door` constructors are called. The `String` constructor is also called, with the argument to the `PasswordDoor` constructor for an actual argument. There is more, too. Let's consider the following definitions and assignments:

```
PasswordDoor x("open sesame");          // C-string constructor
PasswordDoor y("hello");                // C-string constructor
PasswordDoor z(x);                      // copy constructor
PasswordDoor* p = new PasswordDoor(y);  // copy constructor
y = z;                                  // default assignment
delete p;                               // default destructor
```

Even though a member of the `PasswordDoor` class is a class type object with dynamically allocated memory, we do not have to worry about premature deallocation of that memory or a memory leak. The `String` class definition eliminated those problems.

The definition for z calls the `PasswordDoor` copy constructor. Remember that every class has a copy constructor. Since none was declared in the `PasswordDoor` class definition, the copy constructor for the class is provided by C++ by default. What may be surprising is that the default `PasswordDoor` copy constructor calls the `String` copy constructor in order to initialize the `String` type data member. That default behavior is designed into C++. Whenever a class has a default copy constructor, that default copy constructor invokes the copy constructors for any members of the class that are themselves of a class type.

Default assignments and default destructors work the same way as the default copy constructor. Since no overloaded assignment and no destructor were specifically declared in the `PasswordDoor` class, C++ provides a default assignment and a default destructor. The default assignment uses the assignment for the `String` class in order to assign to the `password_` member. The default destructor uses the destructor for the `String` class in order to destroy the `password_` member.

When a `PasswordDoor` object is assigned another `PasswordDoor`, the overloaded `String` assignment operator is put to work. And when a `PasswordDoor` object goes out of existence, the `PasswordDoor` destructor will be called. The `PasswordDoor` destructor is a default destructor, just as the `PasswordDoor` copy constructor is a default copy constructor and the `PasswordDoor` assignment is the default overloaded assignment. The default destructor calls the `String` destructor to get rid of the `String` data member. Whew. That's a significant amount of stuff going on behind the scenes. We don't even have to worry about writing special code just to see that it happens for two reasons:

1. We implemented the `String` as a first class type with appropriate constructors including a copy constructor, overloaded assignment, and a destructor to do dynamic memory management.

2. C++ was designed so that the default copy constructors, overloaded assignments, and destructors call the copy constructors, overloaded assignments, and destructors for any members of a class that are themselves class type objects.

Creating `String` as a first class type pays off handsomely here. We need not worry about the low-level details of memory management. We took care of those details long ago.

What is the order of calling constructors and destructors for derived classes and base classes? Suppose that class D is derived from class B:

When an object of type D is created, the base class portion and the class members of B are constructed before the code in the body of D's constructor is executed. The following is the order of that construction, regardless of the order in the initialization list for D's constructor.

1. The constructor of B is called.

2. If B is derived from another class, then its constructor is called.

3. If B contains class type members, then their constructors are called.

4. If D contains class type members, then their constructors are called.

5. The body of the constructor of D is executed.

> Construction is in BMD (base-member-derived) order.
> Objects are destructed in exactly the reverse order of their construction. That is, the members of D that are of class types are destructed first. The base class portion is destructed last.
> Destruction is in DMB (derived-member-base) order.

A class with pointer members generally needs a destructor to delete those pointer members. However, if its members are class objects instead of pointers, then the destructors for those class objects are automatically called when the object goes out of existence. This occurs when the class has a default destructor supplied by C++. It also happens when the class has an explicit destructor provided by the programmer.

Type compatibility between base classes and derived classes

The types Door and LockableDoor are not the same. Neither are the types LockableDoor and CombinationLockDoor. C++ will not perform certain operations such as assignment among incompatible types unless it knows how to make one type of object from another.

If two class type objects are of different types, it is possible to assign one to another if there is an appropriate constructor or type cast to inform the compiler how to convert from one type of object to another. The story on derived types is different from that. An object of a base class type can always be assigned the value of a derived class.

Assignment is one operation in which derived types are automatically converted to base types. Argument passing is another. Consider the following declarations:

```
void f(Door d);
void h(Door& d);
void s(const LockableDoor& k);

Door myDoor;
LockableDoor keyedDoor;
PasswordDoor caveDoor("open sesame");
```

The following code is thus legal:

```
f(keyedDoor);
h(caveDoor);
```

```
s(caveDoor);
keyedDoor = caveDoor;
myDoor = caveDoor;
```

The following code, however, is not legal:

```
s(myDoor);              // illegal
keyedDoor = myDoor;     // illegal
```

The compiler can always convert a value from a publicly derived class type to the base class type value by ignoring the members of the derived class that are not also members of the base class.[1] It slices off the members of the derived class that are not members of the base.

The essential rule to remember is as follows. From the compiler's point of view: *Anywhere a base class object is acceptable, an object of a publicly derived class is also acceptable.* However, it is up to the class designers and implementers to make sure that objects of a derived class type really do respect the interface specification of the base class.

When a derived class object is on the right side of an assignment to a base class object, only the members of the derived class that belong to the base class type are assigned to the base class object. The same holds true when a derived class value is an actual argument to a function that has a value argument of the base type.

Pointers and references to a certain type follow the same compatibility rules as the type. The value of a pointer or a reference to a derived class can be treated as a pointer or reference to a base class. The opposite of that is not true. The value of a pointer or reference to a base class cannot be treated as a pointer or reference to a derived class.

Pointers to objects are addresses. The address of a derived class object can be treated as the address of a base class object. The one-way compatibility for pointers and references explain why the function invocations h(caveDoor) and s(caveDoor) are legal but s(myDoor) is illegal. As you will find out in Chapter 11, pointers are of special importance in class hierarchies.

10.3   Multiple inheritance

The inheritance we have been discussing to this point is single inheritance. Each derived class has had a single direct base class. But a class can be derived directly from many classes. Each direct base class appears in the inheritance list of the derived class.

We'll illustrate with an example. A clock radio is a clock. A clock radio is a radio. Clocks and radios share few things, if any, in common. We will design a

---

[1] In cases of protected inheritance, derived class values can be converted to the base class type within member and friend functions of the derived class. In cases of private inheritance, derived class values can be converted to the base class type within member functions of the derived class.

ClockRadio as a class derived from two classes, a Clock class and a Radio class. Our Clock class is as follows:

```
// A simple clock class
class Clock {
public:
   Clock(int hh = 24, int mm = 0, int ss = 0);  // Constructs a 24-hour Clock
                                                 //    with time hh:mm:ss

   int hour() const;                             // Hour of time
   int minute() const;                           // Minute of time
   int second() const;                           // Second of time
   void setNext();                               // Advance the time by 1 second
   void reset(int hh, int mm, int ss);           // Time becomes hh:mm:ss
protected:
   int hour_;
   int minute_;
   int second_;
};
```

The Radio class is also very simple. (No AM-FM here. We're just going for the bare essentials.)

```
// A simple radio class
class Radio {
public:
   Radio(double n = 99., bool play = false);  // Constructs a Radio tuned to
                                              //    frequency n and turned on if
                                              //    play is true, off if play is
                                              //    false
   double frequency() const;                  // Frequency on the dial
   bool isOn() const;                         // True when the radio is on
   void flipSwitch();                         // Switches the radio from off/on
                                              //    to on/off
   void changeDial(double n);                 // Frequency is reset to n
protected:
   double frequency_;
   bool on_;
};
```

With these definitions, we can define a simple ClockRadio as follows:

```
// A simple clock radio class
class ClockRadio : public Clock, public Radio {
public:
   ClockRadio (int hh = 24, int mm = 0, int ss = 0, double n = 99.,
              bool play = false);
```

```
                // Constructs a ClockRadio with time hh:mm:ss, tuned to frequency n,
                //   and turned off if play is false and on if play is true.
};
```

The ClockRadio is a pure merging of the two classes Clock and Radio. Figure 10.5 illustrates the relationship among the three classes. Except for its constructor, the ClockRadio class has no other members than those of the two base classes combined. Its constructor calls the Clock and Radio constructors.

```
ClockRadio :: ClockRadio (int hh, int mm, int ss, double n, bool on)
                    : Clock(hh,mm,ss), Radio(n,on)
{ }
```

Notice how the colon, :, is used in two different contexts. It indicates the start of an inheritance list in a class definition. It is also indicates the start of an initialization list in a constructor definition.

As sparse as its definition appears, a ClockRadio has five data members: hour_, minute_, and second_ (inherited from Clock) and frequency_ and on_ (inherited from Radio). A ClockRadio has nine member functions in addition to its constructor. Member functions hour(), minute(), second(), reset(), and setNext() are inherited from Clock. Member functions dial(), isOn(), changeDial(), and flipSwitch() are inherited from Radio.

The following sample code shows how ClockRadio objects can be created and used:

```
ClockRadio mine(5,16,1,91.5,true);  // mine: time is 5:16:01, radio is tuned
                                    //   to 91.5 and turned on
ClockRadio yours;                   // yours: time is midnight, radio is
                                    //   tuned to 99.0 and turned off
ClockRadio hers(12,5,19);           // hers: time is 12:05:19, radio is
                                    //   tuned to 99.0 and turned off

mine.setNext();                     // mine: time is 5:16:02
mine.flipSwitch();                  // mine: radio is switched off
cout << hers.hour()
        << ':' << hers.minute();    // output is 12:5
```

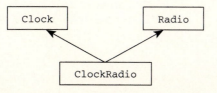

Figure 10.5 Multiple inheritance: ClockRadio is derived from Radio and Clock.

```
hers.flipSwitch();                    // hers: radio is switched on

yours = mine;                         // yours: time is 15:16:02, radio is
                                      //    tuned to 91.5 and turned off
mine = ClockRadio();                  // mine: time is midnight, radio is
                                      //    tuned to 99.0 and turned off

yours.changeDial(100.2);              // yours: radio is tuned to 100.2
yours.reset(3,17,0);                  // yours: time is 3:17:00
```

We have been very careful in our choices of the base classes. `Clock` and `Radio` do not have any members with the same names. In particular, they do not have any public member functions with the same name. However, it is possible to derive a class from two base classes that do have members with the same name. When that occurs, there is potential for **ambiguity**, which means the compiler is unable to determine which member with that name is being referred to. The programmer might not think reference to that name is ambiguous. But the compiler does. Anything the compiler sees as ambiguous, it will refuse to compile. Ambiguity is one reason why multiple inheritance must be used judiciously, if at all.

Ambiguity resolution

Let's approach this topic with a look at the common wristwatch. Wristwatches used to be very simple. They had hour and minute hands. Some had second hands. The fancy wristwatches had calendars that would advance automatically. We can build a fancy wristwatch out of a `Clock` and a `Calendar`. The `Calendar` class definition is as follows.

```
// A simple calendar
class Calendar {
public:
   Calendar(int dd = 1, int mm = 1, int yy = 1996);
                             // Constructs a calendar beginning on day
                             //    dd, month mm, and year yy
   int day() const;          // Current day of the calendar date
   int month() const;        // Current month of the calendar date
   int year() const;         // Current year of the calendar date
   void setNext();           // Advances the calendar one day
   void reset(int d, int m, int y); // Resets the calendar date to m/d/y
protected:
   int day_;
   int month_;
   int year_;
};
```

`Calendar` and `Clock` have two member functions with the same name: `reset()` and `setNext()`. `CalendarWatch` will hide the inherited function `setNext()`.

```
// A combination watch and calendar
class CalendarWatch : public Clock, public Calendar {
public:
   CalendarWatch(int day = 1, int mo = 1, int year = 1996,
                 int hour = 12, int min = 0, int sec = 0);
                           // Constructs a calendar watch initialized to date
                           //    mo/day/year and time hour:min:sec.
   void setNext();         // Advances the time by 1 second
};
```

The definition of the `CalendarWatch` constructor looks similar to the definition of the `ClockRadio` constructor.

```
CalendarWatch ::CalendarWatch (int day, int mo, int year,
                               int hour, int min, int sec) :
                               Clock(hour,min,sec), Calendar(day,mo,year)
{ }
```

We do not need to rewrite the algorithm for setting the time ahead one second and setting the date ahead one day in order to define `setNext()`. The `Calendar-Watch` method `setNext()` invokes the inherited versions of `setNext()`.

```
void CalendarWatch :: setNext()
{
   if (hour_ == 23 && minute_ == 59 && second_ == 59)
     Calendar::setNext();
   Clock::setNext();
}
```

Here is some sample code that uses the new `CalendarWatch` class:

```
CalendarWatch bill(12,4,1996);             // date: 4/12/1996   time: 12:00:00
CalendarWatch mac(1,1,1998,23,59,59);      // date: 1/1/1998    time: 23:59:59
CalendarWatch don(31,12,1995,23,59,58);    // date: 12/31/1995  time: 23:59:58

bill.setNext();                            // date: 4/12/1996   time: 12:00:01
mac.setNext();                             // date: 1/2/1998    time: 24:00:00
don.setNext();                             // date: 12/31/1995  time: 23:59:59
don.setNext();                             // date: 1/1/1996    time: 24:00:00
```

The code above is all valid code. The calls to `setNext()` are, of course, to the member function of `CalendarWatch`, which hides both inherited members of that name. The following code, however, is not valid:

```
bill.reset(3,8,89);    // illegal
```

Which `reset()` is being invoked? Is it `Clock::reset()`? Is it `Calendar::reset()`? We might guess from the arguments that the programmer intends to invoke `Calendar::reset()`. But the compiler cannot make such a guess. There is an ambiguity that the compiler is unable to resolve. When the compiler detects an ambiguity, it will not compile the code.

There are two solutions to the ambiguity problem. One is for `CalendarWatch` to hide the inherited `reset()` functions in much the same way it hides `set-Next()`. The other is to force the user of the class to specify which `reset()` is being invoked.

Here is the syntax for that latter option. It is quite ungainly.

```
bill.Calendar::reset(3,8,89);      // bill's date is now 8/3/89
bill.Clock::reset(4,17,30);        // bill's time is now 4:17:30
```

This example points out a serious danger of multiple inheritance. Any carelessness in the definition of the derived class can result in some unpleasant surprises for the user of the class.

> We generally recommend against using multiple inheritance. If you do use it, be careful to hide any member functions of the base classes with the same names, even if they have different signatures.[2]

Is-a and *has-a* relationships

Public inheritance is often described as implementing *is-a* (or is-a-kind-of) relationships. A `PasswordDoor` *is-a* `LockableDoor`. A `LockableDoor` *is-a* `Door`. A `CalendarWatch` *is-a* `Clock`, and a `CalendarWatch` *is-a* `Calendar`.

We can describe the relationships a little further. A `Door` is a general type of object. A `PasswordDoor` is a special kind of `Door`. In terms of C++ inheritance schemes, a base class is a generalization of a concept. A derived class is a specialization of that generalization. A `CalendarWatch` is a special kind of `Clock`. It is also a special kind of a more general class, `Calendar`.

Let's return to the `PasswordDoor` class for a moment. A `PasswordDoor` has a data member named `password_`. That data member is a `String`. So a `PasswordDoor` *has-a* `String`. Since `PasswordDoor` does not inherit from `String`, a `PasswordDoor` is not a `String`. A class containing a member of another class

---

[2] The compiler considers it an ambiguity even when the two functions of different base classes have the same name but different argument lists. That turns out not to be a case of overloading, as we might wish.

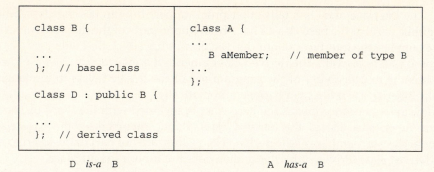

```
class B {                      class A {
                               ...
...                              B aMember;    // member of type B
};  // base class              ...
                               };
class D : public B {

...
};  // derived class
```

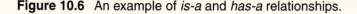

        D *is-a* B   A *has-a* B

Figure 10.6 An example of *is-a* and *has-a* relationships.

demonstrates a *has-a* relationship. *Has-a* relationships are often used to represent the parts of a compound object. Figure 10.6 illustrates the difference between *is-a* and *has-a* relationships.

Both *is-a* and *has-a* relationships are an important part of code organization and reuse in C++. Sometimes it is better to abandon one organization scheme and adopt the other. The class CalendarWatch is a prime example. A CalendarWatch *is-a* Calendar and a CalendarWatch *is-a* Clock. Multiple inheritance is best used for merging disjoint, independent classes, and Calendar and a Clock are two classes that are almost disjoint. However, both classes have functions named reset with identical signatures. While it is possible for CalendarWatch to hide both base class functions, it is not clear what a new CalendarWatch::reset() should do. There is not obvious and natural answer.

Think of redesigning a CalendarWatch as a special kind of Clock that *has-a* Calendar. After all, most people consider calendar watches primarily as watches. That redesign avoids the problem of dealing with the multiple resets. The language issues surrounding multiple inheritance are so complicated that it should be used only for very special situations—primarily for merging classes that have neither functions nor data in common.

Private inheritance

All cases of inheritance from our previous code have been examples of public inheritance, where the keyword public is used in the inheritance lists to specify the access of the base class. So public base class members are public in the derived class and protected base class members are protected in the derived class. The PasswordDoor class used the LockableDoor's open method rather than define its own open. Both the PasswordDoor and the LockableDoor used the Door's close method rather than define their own versions. Those are prime examples of code reuse.

Public inheritance is often called **inheritance of the interface**. Recall that the interface of a class consists of the documentation and the public part of its definition. The interface of a class tells other programmers how to use the class. Since the public parts of the base classes have been public parts of the derived classes in our examples, the interfaces of our derived classes have included the interfaces of the base classes as well. The derived class inherits the interface of the base class. But it is the responsibility of the programmer of the derived class to implement public inheritance; it does not happen automatically.

Private inheritance means the base class is specified with the word `private` in the inheritance list of the derived class. Public members of the base class become private members of the derived class—they are not part of the interface of the derived class. Private inheritance then does not inherit the interface.

The public and protected members of a privately inherited base class are considered to be private members of the derived class. As such, they can be used or invoked by friends and member functions of the derived class. They become part of the implementation of the derived class rather than its interface. Private inheritance is called **inheritance of the implementation**.

Why would you ever want to use private inheritance? The answer is when you want to implement a class as a kind of other class, where the "kind-of" is only an implementation detail that the user of the class need not know about.

Here is one situation in which private inheritance, inheritance of implementation, may be desirable. Consider a set of people. Sets do not contain duplicates. A set of people is not ordered in any apparent fashion. (Who would naturally be the first person? The one named Aaron, or the oldest one, or who?) A set is not an indexed list. A set is not an ordered, indexed list.

Standard set operations include such things as membership (determining if an element belongs to a set), union (combining the elements of two sets), intersection (finding the elements common to two sets), and creating a singleton set (a set with only a single, specified element). We could define a `Set` class and implement all of these methods as well as the set attributes from scratch.

But let's return to lists for a minute. We have already implemented some indexed lists. Suppose `List` is a class for an indexed list. Even though a set is not a list, the methods for a `Set` could invoke some of the methods of `List` to do their work. `Set` needs `List` only to implement some of its attributes and some of its own methods. The users of a `Set` have no need to know that `Set` uses `List` methods. `List` methods should not be available as `Set` methods. The `Set` class can be derived from the `List` class specifying private access.

```
class Set : private List {
...
};
```

Private inheritance is used to hide the interface of the base class from users of a derived class. If it is not reasonable to think of one class type as being a special kind of another class type, but it helpful to use the methods and data of the other class in defining the first class, then private inheritance may be a good coding choice.

An alternative to private inheritance in the `Set` class definition is to design the `Set` so it *has-a* `List` rather than *is-a* `List`. That means making `List` a private member of the `Set` class rather than deriving a `Set` from a `List`.

```
class Set {
   List theList_;
   ...
};
```

Most of the examples of inheritance in this book are examples of public inheritance. In Chapter 12, we give a full example of private inheritance.

10.4 ▍ Inheritance as an organizational tool

In addition to reuse, another use of inheritance is to organize collections of code and design information. This is particularly convenient when dealing with very large collections of code, not the small snippets usually seen in textbooks (including this one).

Although a complete example is too large for this book, we can illustrate what we mean with description of a more modest example. The popular C++ compilers that are available for PCs and Macintosh computers come with extensive graphical user interface (GUI) libraries. Our example is modeled on those GUI libraries.

GUIs are based on some sort of windowing mechanism. One of the basic types in GUI libraries is a general window type. There are many special kinds of windows. A window type is naturally a base class for specialized window types.

Our simple example has a `Window` base class. Three classes are often derived from a `Window` base:

1. `ScrollableWindow`. A scrollable window is a window with a scroll mechanism (usually a scroll bar at the side) to show different portions of the item being displayed in the window in case the window is too small to show the entire item at once.

2. `Dialogue`. A dialogue is a window in which questions can be displayed to the user and in which the user can respond with simple answers. A simple dialogue window contains a single message and yes and no buttons for the user's response.

3. `Menu`. A menu is a window that gives the user a selection of items from which to choose. Popular menu styles include pull-down menus and pop-up menus that disappear from the screen as soon as the user selects an option.

The `ScrollableWindow` class is derived from the `Window` class. It also serves as a base class for a special kind of scrollable window, the `TextEditWindow` class. A `TextEditWindow` is a `ScrollableWindow` in which the user can enter and edit text. Modern word processors rely on text edit windows for presentation of their documents.

Our example is very small. But in a real GUI class library, there are dozens of different kinds of special windows. There are special windows that are derived from other special windows. The inheritance levels can go deep, depending on the design of the library. The overwhelming complexity of a real GUI class library requires that the library be organized so that it can be readily used. Keep in mind that those libraries were built just for others to use.

A good GUI library is not merely an arbitrary collection of features. Through the library's organization, the user knows what behavior to expect from the different classes. The user need not look at all classes in order to find a class with particular features. The class hierarchy tells the user where to find a class. It also is important for expressing the relationships among classes. Without this kind of class hierarchy created through inheritance, the user could be lost in a tangle of classes. Looking for a special class could be like looking for a book in a library in which the books are scattered on the floor.

So far, we have described our example in terms of simple inheritance only. We can expand the example to include multiple inheritance as well. Recall that ostream is the name of an output stream class. It is part of the stream library built into C++. Our example contains a new class derived from the built-in ostream class. The new class, PagedStream, is an output stream consisting of text organized in page-sized units. PagedStream is derived from the base class ostream.

One reason for creating a PagedStream is to display its text in a window. The natural way to display the text is one page at a time. Our example has a Window class and a PagedStream class. They are disjoint, independent classes. We can merge them into a single class, a MoreWindow. Figure 10.7 shows the Window class hierarchy so far.

A MoreWindow is both a Window and a PagedStream. It displays the text of the PagedStream on a window one page at a time. (We named it a MoreWindow after the UNIX command, more. The more command is used to scroll through a text file one screen at a time.) Although we will not give a specification of the MoreWindow class, we will say that a MoreWindow tailors its display size and font to the size of the page of the PagedStream.

Large software projects can benefit significantly from inheritance. By using inheritance, program developers can spread the coding over a long period of time

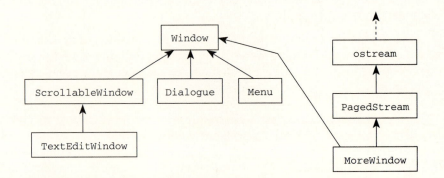

Figure 10.7 The hierarchy of a windowing scheme with multiple inheritance.

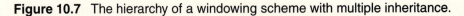

and many programmers. This amortization of effort pays off for the users of a class hierarchy also. A user who understands the `Window` class will have an easier time learning how to use a `ScrollableWindow` and a `MoreWindow` than a user who does not. The class hierarchy provides a logical structure for users to understand the use and functionality of a large collection of code.

10.5   C++ streams: Built-in inheritance

You are quite familiar with the input and output stream objects `cin` and `cout`. When you first encountered `cin` and `cout`, you did not think of them as instances of classes. You simply used them without worrying about how they were defined. But exactly what type are they? How are they like file streams? How are C++ stream types organized?

Let's back up for a moment. Input often consists of a sequence of characters from a file or entered by the user through an input device such as a keyboard. The characters are held in memory in a buffer (an array of characters) until they are processed. (See Fig. 10.8.) An output sequence works in the reverse manner. Output characters are generated by a program and held in a buffer until they are flushed to a file or some output device such as a terminal screen.

C++ performs input and output operations via streams. The stream type object associated with an input or output sequence of characters has methods that can process those sequences. But such processing is a very complicated task. The stream processing features of C++ are organized into a hierarchy of classes. We do not plan to go into complete discussions of the I/O stream classes. But we will tell you some of the things you can expect to find in those classes. (For additional discussion of the functionality and use of streams, refer to Appendixes D, E, and F at the back of this book.)

The I/O stream class hierarchy

As you learned long ago, in order to use C++ I/O streams, your source file must contain the include directive:

```
#include <iostream.h>
```

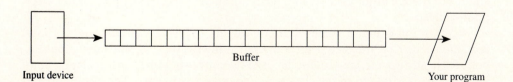

Buffer

Input device

Your program

Figure 10.8 Input characters are held temporarily in a buffer.

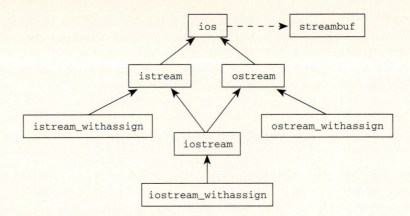

Figure 10.9   The I/O stream class hierarchy.

The iostream library contains the class definitions for the stream class hierarchy illustrated in Figure 10.9.

The class `streambuf`, provides a buffer, an array of characters, to hold the characters in the input/output sequence. `streambuf` is a low-level class which maintains the current position in that sequence.

The base class at the top of the I/O stream class hierarchy is the input/output specification class, `ios`. It has a `streambuf` pointer. The functionality of `ios` is relegated to two different areas: the state of the stream and format settings.

You have seen the identifier `ios` before. Recall that the output of floating point data can be scientific or fixed.

```
cout << setiosflags(ios::fixed);
...
cout << resetiosflags(ios::fixed) << setiosflags(ios::scientific);
```

The argument `ios::fixed` indicates that `ios` is the name of a class with an enumerated value named `fixed`. The `ios` class is responsible for maintaining information about the state of the stream. For example, `ios` can report on whether end of file was detected, and it is also responsible for maintaining stream format information. In addition, `ios` can change formatting of output by doing such things as specifying scientific or fixed floating point output and setting precision and it can change input formats by specifying such things as skipping or not skipping whitespace.

Keep in mind that a stream buffer contains sequences of characters. Those sequences must be translated to and from numeric type values (`int`, `double`, pointers to strings, etc.) in order to be used by your program. The translating abilities of streams come from the classes `ostream` and `istream`. The output operator, `<<`, and the input operator, `>>`, are defined in `ostream` and `istream`, which are derived from `ios`.

What about `cin` and `cout`? Both are stream objects; `cin` is of type `istream_withassign` and `cout` is of type `ostream_withassign`. The modifier `withassign` describes the fact that an assignment operator is overloaded for those class types. Figure 10.9 shows how the different input and output stream types are related.

The class `iostream` is an example of multiple inheritance in the I/O stream class hierarchy. It is a merging of the two classes `istream` and `ostream`. The merging allows creation of a stream object that can be used for both input and output.

File streams

In order for streams to process disk files, your source code must contain this include directive:

```
#include <fstream.h>
```

File streams are also part of the stream class hierarchy. Formatting and state information is maintained by `ios`. Translation is provided by `istream` and `ostream`, and `ifstream` and `ofstream` objects have the same capabilities. How do they relate to the input/output class hierarchy? Given their common functionality with `cout` and `cin`, `ifstream` and `ofstream` classes also are derived from `ios`, `istream`, and `ostream`. Figure 10.10 shows the part of the stream class hierarchy that includes `ifstream` and `ofstream`.

Notice how the `streambuf` class is a base for the `filebuf` class. File streams use pointers to `filebuf` objects. The stream class hierarchy, which is becoming complicated, is illustrated with an abbreviated picture.[3] We show you this hierarchy

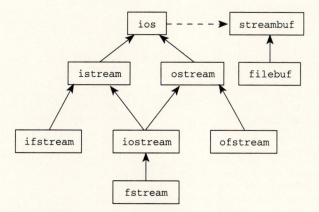

Figure 10.10 The file stream class hierarchy.

[3] Compilers may use an intermediate class for file handling that is derived from `ios`. The intermediate class is inherited by `ifstream`, `ofstream`, and `fstream`.

to impress upon you how the functionality for input and output processing is organized and shared among many classes.

String streams

Every stream type object is associated with a buffer. For input and output streams, the buffer serves as a temporary holding area for characters as they await translation to variable input or flushing to an output device or file. Stream buffers are arrays of characters. C++ has several classes that allow the programmer to treat a stream buffer as both an array and a stream. These streams are called **string streams**. In order to use a string stream, the source file must contain the following directive:

```
#include <strstream.h>
```

A string stream has all of the translation capabilities that are defined in the `istream` or `ostream` classes. The difference between an output string stream and an ordinary output stream is that the output goes to a buffer rather than a file or an output device. The difference between an input string stream and an ordinary input stream is that input comes from a buffer rather than an input file or device.

The stream classes for string streams are `strstream`, `ostrstream`, and `istrstream`. They fit into the stream class hierarchy much the same way as file streams. Instead of having a pointer to a `filebuf`, a string stream object has a pointer to a `strstreambuf`. (See Fig. 10.11.)

An output string stream is of type `ostrstream`. It has all of the functionality of an `ostream`, plus a little more. It can return the pointer to its buffer. A string stream buffer can be treated like an ordinary C-style string. The following code illustrates the use of an `ostrstream` and its overloaded output operator.

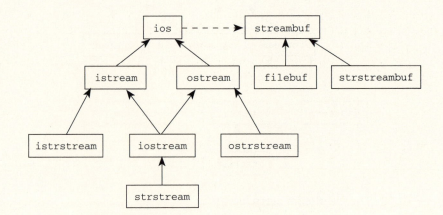

Figure 10.11 The string stream class hierarchy.

```
ostrstream os;           // creates an ostrstream with an "unlimited" buffer
char * p;                // an ordinary C-style array pointer
int x = 1234;
int y = 12;

os << "The sum is " << x + y << ends;  // ends inserts '\0'
p = new char[strlen(os.str()) + 1];    // os.str() returns a pointer to the
                                       //   buffer
strcpy(p,os.str());                    // p points to "The sum is 1246"
char* q = os.str();                    // q points to the stream buffer
```

The insertion of ends into a string stream is somewhat analogous to the insertion of endl into an output stream. The insertion of ends into the string stream puts the terminating null character into the buffer.

String streams can be used in conjunction with I/O streams. A string stream can provide an unlimited buffer to store a line of characters extracted from an input stream. It is not necessary to know how many characters are in the line before extracting them from the input stream. A string stream buffer can adjust its length dynamically as needed, depending on the length of the line. We'll use that idea to finish some work on the String class, which we developed in the previous chapter.

The String class overloads >>. The overloaded input operator reads a line from an istream into the String. All of the remaining characters in the istream before the first newline are stored in the String. Those characters as well as the newline are extracted from the istream.

At the time we defined the String class, we promised that we could redefine that overloaded input operator so that the length of a line of input was irrelevant to the overloading. In our old definition of, we made a very generous allowance for the length. We assumed no line of input would be more than 999 characters long. With our new definition, we make no assumption on the length.

Recall that the String class contains one data member, info_, which is of type char*. The overloaded input operator must change info_ to point to a string of characters read from an input stream. The new definition of operator>>() has two streams: an istream (the formal argument and return object) and an ostrstream, a temporary buffer for holding the line of characters.

```
istream& operator>>(istream& in,  String& s)
{
   char ch;                 // Last character read from in
   ostrstream line;         // Characters from a line of in
   in.get(ch);
   while (in && ch != '\n') { // Store characters from in up to but not
      line << ch;            //   including the first newline in line.
      in.get(ch);
   }
```

```
    line << ends;                   // Insert the terminating null character.
    delete [] s.info_;
    s.info_ = line.str();
    return in;
}
```

You may question the assignment of `line.str()` to `s.info_` in the definition. If the buffer for `line` is the array for `s`, there is potential for disaster. But an `ostrstream` relinquishes ownership of its array buffer when the member function `str()` is called. The responsibility for eventually deleting that buffer lies with the code that calls `str()`. Of course, we designed the `String` class to delete `info_` arrays that are no longer used. So the assignment of `line.str()` to `s.info_` will eventually result in the deletion of that array.

> Redefining the base class `String` input operator does not force us to redefine the derived class `BCString` input operator, even though the `BCString` version relies on the `String` version. Nor do we have to recompile the `BCString` input operator. We do need to recompile whatever file contains the new `String` input operator definition. And then we must relink any program that uses the `String` input operator directly or indirectly.
>
> If you supply a library containing the `String` input operator, a change in the operator definition only requires you to distribute a new `.o` file to your customers.

Suppose we know that a C-style string contains character representations of some numeric data such as this:

```
123  45 67
```

We can use a string stream to translate those characters into their corresponding numeric values. The following code illustrates how:

```
int x,y,z;                      // Creates three integer variables
istrstream is("123  45 67");    // Creates an istrstream whose buffer
                                //   is "123 45 67"

is >> x >> y >> z;              // x is 123; y is 45; z is 67
```

The input operator for the `istrstream` works much the same way as the input operator for `cin`. Successive data can be extracted. Whitespace is skipped by default.

Notice the difference between the definitions we have made for `ostrstreams` and `istrstreams`.

```
ostrstream line;
istrstream is("123  45  67");
```

The definition of `line` indicates that `ostrstream` has a null constructor, a constructor with no actual arguments. When an `ostrstream` is defined with no actual arguments, memory will be dynamically allocated as needed to store inserted characters. The amount allocated may change as additional data are inserted into the `ostrstream`.

The definition of `is` indicates that there is an `istrstream` constructor with an argument that is a C-string. The memory for an `istrstream` object's buffer does not change but remains fixed. There are two `istrstream` constructors. Both require arguments. The other constructor requires a `char*` and an `int`. It constructs an `istrstream` using an existing buffer at the specified area of memory of the specified fixed length.

Deriving your own classes from built-in stream classes

The stream class hierarchy provides not only a large amount of code that can be used for input and output but also a large collection of classes that the programmer can use to derive additional classes. In this section, we will show you how to derive a special class from a stream class, a class for creating "log files."

A log file is an output file stream. It opens as an ordinary empty output file stream, making its name out of the current system date. A file that is created as a result of creating a log file object in a program will have a banner at the top and a closing trailer at the bottom. Between the top banner and closing trailer will appear the data inserted into the stream.

The definition of a `LogFile` class is deceptively simple.

```
class LogFile : public ofstream {
public:
    LogFile();    // Creates a file named after the day it is created.
                  //   The top of the file contains a banner with the date.
    ~LogFile();   // Puts a trailer on the end of the file.
};
```

The definitions of the `LogFile` constructor and destructor require several built-in libraries. We used the following include directives for system libraries in our implementation:

```
#include <strstream.h>
#include <fstream.h>
#include <sys/types.h>
#include <time.h>
```

Classes provide a much cleaner way than those library calls to get services. It is common to provide class wrappers for system library types and functions.

Most operating systems provide libraries to access the system time and system date. These libraries may vary greatly from one operating system to another. The code that we show in this book is the code that we wrote for our system. In order for you to develop similar code for your system, you will very likely need to modify all of our code that contains any reference to the special system library functions and types.

In our `Logfile` constructor, the system functions and types are `time_t`, `time`, `tm*`, `localtime()`. These identifiers were defined in our `sys/types.h` header file. The function `dateNow()` gets the current date from the system.

```
// System dependent code. NOT PORTABLE.
void dateNow(int& month, int& day, int& year)
{
    time_t* clock = new time_t;    // time_t is a system type
    time(clock);                   // time() is a system function
    tm* date = localtime(clock);   // tm is a system type, localtime() is
                                   //    a system function
    month = date->tm_mon + 1;      // type tm is a struct with 3 members,
    day = date->tm_day;            //    tm_mon, tm_day, tm_year
    year = date->tm_year;
}
```

`Logfile` member functions that must be defined are the constructor and destructor. We wrote a utility function, `LogFileName()`, that the constructor will use to create the name of a file out of the character representation of three integers (representing a month, day, and year). The definition of `LogFileName()` uses an `ostrstream` to translate integers into their character representations.

```
char* LogFileName(int m, int d, int y)
// Returns a character string with the character representation of m.d.y.log.
//    For example, if m is 3, d is 20, and y is 94, returns "3.20.94.log".
{
    ostrstream nmstream;
    nmstream << m << '.' << d << '.' << y << ".log";
    return nmstream.str();
}
```

The `Logfile` constructor and destructor must use `this`. Recall that `this` is a pointer used in member function definitions to point to the current object (the

object for which the member function is currently invoked). That means `*this` is
another name for the current object and `this->open()` is another name for the
current object's `open()` function.[4]

```
LogFile :: LogFile()
{
    int month, day, year;
    dateNow(month, day, year);
    this->open(LogFileName(month,day,year));
                        // open() is inherited from ofstream. It has a default
                        //    string argument and it associates the stream with
                        //    a file of that name.

    *this << "*** Start of Log -- ";    // writes the top banner
    *this << month << '/' << day << '/' << year << " ***\n" << endl;

}


LogFile :: ~LogFile()
{
    *this << "\n*** End of Log ***" << endl; // Write the trailer to the file.
}
```

The constructor opens the `Logfile` by tying it to a disk file with the name
computed from the system date. It inserts the banner into the stream. The destructor writes the trailer on the file by inserting it into the stream. After the destructor
is called, the `Logfile` is automatically closed.

The following function creates and uses a `Logfile` object. The `Logfile` goes
out of existence when the function quits execution.

```
void demo()
{
    LogFile myLog;
    myLog << "1 + 1 = " <<  1 + 1 << endl;
    myLog << "2 + 2 = " <<  2 + 2 << endl;
    myLog << "1 + 2 = " <<  1 + 2 << endl;
}
```

Figure 10.12 shows the file that results from calling `demo()` on January 13,
1995. The name of the file is `1.13.1995.log`.

---

[4] In the `Logfile` constructor body, we could have used

`open(LogFileName(month,day,year));`

instead of

`this->open(LogFileName(month,day,year);`

We chose the latter because `open()` is part of the interface of the base class `ofstream`. It does not
appear explicitly in the interface of `Logfile`.

```
*** Start of Log -- 1/13/95 ***

1 + 1 = 2
2 + 2 = 4
1 + 2 = 3


*** End of Log ***
```

Figure 10.12 The file named `1.13.1995.log` created as result of calling `demo()`.

10.6 Changing the changemaker solution to incorporate inheritance

We've been modifying the original solution to the changemaker problem, first introduced in Chapter 1, throughout this book in order to take advantage of the features of C++ as they were presented. We originally chose this problem because it was a simple one that everyone could solve. But we anticipated a time when it would no longer be so simple. Making change for dollars and cents is easy, at least for people living in the United States or Canada. Suppose you had to make change for French francs, Polish zlotys, or Russian rubles? Hmmm . . . the changemaker problem could take a nasty turn.

How can you tailor the changemaker solution to work with Polish currency? You need to know the names and relative values of the different Polish coins and bills. What is their relationship to a zloty? Is a zloty the smallest unit of Polish currency much like the penny is the smallest unit of U.S. currency? Or is a zloty more like a U.S. dollar? You can ferret out the answers to these questions from encyclopedias, reference librarians, the Internet, Polish friends, or numerous other sources. But once you know the answers, making change for Polish currency is not much different from making change for U.S. currency.

Coins and bills that make up a currency can be ordered according to their values. Each currency has a smallest unit from which to measure the value of each coin and bill. That smallest unit in U.S currency is a penny; in Spanish currency, the unit is a peseta; in Italian currency, the unit is a centesimi. The values of the coins and bills of a currency are multiples of the unit.

The fact that the changemaker problem deals with money has forced our attention toward currencies. But many systems of measurement besides currency measurements are based on units. For example, the unit of British linear measurement is an inch. The unit of British weight measurement is an ounce. The unit for time measurement is a second. We use the term Basic Unit Measurement System to describe currency systems and other unit-based measurement systems. Figure 10.13 shows three Basic Unit Measure Systems: U.S. currency, British length, and time.

U.S. currency unit = penny		British length unit = inch		Time unit = second	
item	**value**	**item**	**value**	**item**	**value**
penny	1	inch	1	second	1
nickel	5	foot	12	minute	60
dime	10	yard	36	hour	3600
quarter	25	rod	198	day	86400
dollar	100	furlong	7920	week	604800
$5 bill	500	mile	63360		
$10 bill	1000				
$20 bill	2000				

Figure 10.13 Basic unit measurement systems.

Breaking down a number of pennies into the different bills and coins is just like breaking down a total number of seconds into weeks, days, hours, minutes, and seconds. The algorithm for doing each of those tasks is the same. What differs are the number of measures (eight for our version of U.S. currency as opposed to five for time) and the values of the different measures in terms of their corresponding units.

A general basic unit measurement class

In our new solution to the changemaker problem, we decided to define a class that could represent a unit-based system of measures. The only unit measurement system used by the changemaker problem in its original form is the U.S. currency system consisting of coins—penny (the unit), nickel, dime, and quarter—and bills—$1, $5, $10, and $20. Our new class will provide much greater functionality than the CurrencyList from Chapter 7.

The name of the new class is MeasureSystem. Much of the design of the class came from our old design of a CurrencyList. Each MeasureSystem has a list of measures. Each measure has a name and a value in terms of the unit for that system.

MeasureSystem can represent any system of measures in which the value of every measure is a multiple of some unit measure. Other examples we have mentioned are the British length measure system (with an inch unit) and a time measure system (with a second unit). Another example is the metric liquid measure system. If we take as the unit measure the milliliter, then other measures in that system include centiliter (10 milliliters), deciliter (100 milliliters), liter (1,000 milliliters), decaliter (10,000 milliliters), and hectoliter(100,000 milliliters).

The original changemaker solution made perfect change for given amounts. There were no limitations on the number of each denomination available. The cash drawer had an unlimited supply of each denomination. The customer who received the change could not make special requests such as "Include at least 6 quarters," or "Don't give me any $10 bills." A customer at a lumber store who is buying strip molding may want to make similar requests: "Give me at least 3 20-foot pieces" or "I don't want anything under 8 feet."

The MeasureSystem method change() provides the functionality of the old changemaker solution. A change message must include the amount to change. And it may optionally include a restriction on the limits of each measure available (corresponding to the amount of each denomination in the cash drawer), a minimum number and maximum amount of each measure to be included in the return value. The MeasureSystem will do the best it can under the restrictions of the request, but it will not return a total value greater than the amount in the change message.

Before defining the MeasureSystem class, we wrote in a typedef for a constant C-string type. That is simply a naming convenience.

```cpp
typedef const char* kstring;     // type synonym for constant strings
// Basic Unit Measurement System
class MeasureSystem {
public:
   MeasureSystem(int s, kstring n[], const int v[]);
                     // Constructs a system with s measures.
                     //    Measure i has name n[i] and value v[i].
                     //    The measures must be arranged in
                     //    ascending order of values -- the unit
                     //    is the first measure (index 0).
                     // ASSUME: arrays n and v have s elements.
   int unitVal(const int list[]) const;
                     // Returns the total value of list in terms
                     //    of the basic unit.  The ith item in the
                     //    list corresponds to the ith measure.
                     // ASSUME: the number of list elements equals
                     //    the number of measures in the system.
   int* change(int a,
            const int* limit = 0,
            const int* minNum = 0,
            const int* maxNum = 0) const;
                     // Returns an optimal list of counts of each
                     //    measure whose total value is as close to
                     //    a as possible without exceeding a.
                     // arguments:
                     //    a: a non-negative amount
                     //    limits: the limitation on the number of
                     //       each measure in the MeasureSystem
                     //    minNum: each count returned is at least
                     //       as great as the corresponding minNum,
                     //       if possible, with priority going to
```

```
                     //      the lower indexed minNums.
                     //   maxNum: each count returned is not
                     //     larger than the corresponding maxNum,
                     //     if that maxNum is NOT negative.
                     // ASSUME: for limits, minNum, and maxNum: if the
                     //   pointer is not 0, it points to an array with
                     //   exactly as many elements as the number of
                     //   measures in the system.

    kstring name(int i) const; // Name of measure i
                               //   ASSUME: 0 <= i < number of measures
    int value(int i) const;    // Value of measure i
                               //   ASSUME: 0 <= i < number of measures
    int size( ) const;         // Number of measures in the system

protected:
    const int size_;
    kstring* names_;
    const int* values_;

private:
    MeasureSystem(const MeasureSystem &);                    // No copying allowed.
    MeasureSystem& operator=(const MeasureSystem &);    // No assignment
                                                         //   allowed.
};
```

The interface for MeasureSystem specifies that each instance be constructed with correct information to describe a single system of measures. The number of measures is the constructor's first argument. This number must be the same as the number of names and the number of values. The names correspond to the values. The names and values must be arranged so that the values appear in increasing order. The first measure should correspond to the unit, whose value is 1. It is the responsibility of the user of a class to be sure that the list of names and the list of values corresponding to those names satisfies those constraints.

One thing that you will notice about MeasureSystem is the declarations of a copy constructor and an assignment operator in the private section. If a class has a privately declared member function, then only the class methods and friends of the class can invoke those methods. MeasureSystem has no friends. By declaring the copy constructor and assignment operator as private, we have prohibited any code not belonging to MeasureSystem from making a copy of or assigning the MeasureSystem.

MeasureSystem has a single public constructor. It is not a null constructor. No system of measures can be created without an appropriate set of initial names and values. The lack of a null constructor prohibits having an array of MeasureSystem type objects, but that is not a concern to us.

```
MeasureSystem :: MeasureSystem(int s, kstring n[], const int v[]) :
                             size_(s), names_(n), values_(v)
{ }
```

A MeasureSystem will not change any of its measure's names or values. Rather than create new arrays of strings and ints for the measure names and values, we assigned the pointer valued actual arguments to the pointer data members of the class. The const in the formal argument declaration notifies the compiler so that it can help enforce this decision.

The change method is the most complicated function in the MeasureSystem class. Its arguments are an original amount of units a to be subdivided among the available measures, and three optional arrays of integers, limit, minNum, and maxNum. The return value is an array of integers, where each integer corresponds to one of the measures. In our old changemaker terminology, the amount a is the total value to be changed. The return array has elements as follows. The element at subscript 0 is the number of units (pennies) to be returned. The last element is the number of the largest measure ($20 bills) to be returned. The return value is computed according to the default arguments limit, minNum, and maxNum.

The definition of change is preceded by two utility functions: min() and min3(). They make the subsequent code slightly easier to read.

```
inline int min(int x, int y)      // for readability
{ return (x > y) ? y : x; }


inline int min3(int x, int y, int z)    // for readability
{ return (x > y) ? min(y,z) : min(x,z); }


int* MeasureSystem::change(int a, const int* limit,
                         const int* minNum, const int* maxNum) const
{
   int* retVal = new int[size_];
   for(int i = 0; i < size_; i++)
      retVal[i] = 0;
   // Take care of the minimum number of each measure to be included
   if (minNum) {
      for(i = 0; a > 0 && i < size_; i++) {
         retVal[i] = (values_[i] * minNum[i] <= a) ? minNum[i] : a/values_[i];
         a -= retVal[i] * values_[i];
      }
   }

   for (i = size_ - 1; a > 0 && i >= 0; i--) {
      int v   = a / values_[i];
      int inc = min3(v,
         (maxNum && maxNum[i] >= 0) ? maxNum[i] : v,
         (limit  && limit[i]  >= 0)  ? limit[i]  : v);
```

```
        retVal[i] += inc;
        a -= inc * values_[i];
    }
    return retVal;
}
```

The definitions of the remaining `MeasureSystem` member functions are much simpler than the definition of `change()`.

```
int MeasureSystem :: unitVal(const int list[]) const
{
    int retVal = 0;
    for (int i = 0; i < size_; i++)
        retVal += list[i] * values_[i];
    return retVal;
}

kstring MeasureSystem :: name(int i) const
{
    return names_[i];
}

int MeasureSystem :: value(int i) const
{
    return values_[i];
}

int MeasureSystem :: size() const
{
    return size_;
}
```

The return value for the member function `name()` is of type `kstring`. Returning the name of a measure does not change the measure, so `name()` is a const function. If a const function returns a pointer to some of its data, then that pointer must be a pointer to a const. That shows the convenience of the `kstring` return type.

The `MeasureSystem` class is a substantial part of the solution to the original changemaker problem. Assume `amount` is an `int` with a nonnegative value. The following code illustrates a cash drawer as a kind of `MeasureSystem`.

```
kstring names[] = {"pennies", "nickels", "dimes", "quarters", "ones",
                   "fives", "tens", "twenties"};
int values[] = {1, 5, 10, 25, 100, 500, 1000, 2000};
int moneyInDrawer[] = {50, 5, 1, 0, 0, 10, 3, 9};
// 50 pennies, 5 nickels, 1 dime, 0 quarters, 0 $1s, 10 $5s, 3 10$s, 9 20$s
```

```
MeasureSystem cashDrawer(8, names, values);   // Cash drawer is created
int amount = 89137;                           // amount is $891.37

int* perfectChangeAnswer = cashDrawer.change(amount);
int* imperfectChangeAnswer = cashDrawer.change(amount, moneyInDrawer);
if (cashDrawer.unitVal(imperfectChangeAnswer) != amount)
   // The cash drawer did not have enough of each denomination to make the
   //   requested change
   . . .
```

The following code illustrates how to use a MeasureSystem to solve a "timemaker" problem. Again, assume that amount is a nonnegative int.

```
kstring times[] = {"seconds", "minutes", "hours", "days","weeks"};
int secondMeasure[] = {1,60,3600,86400,604800};

MeasureSystem timeMaker(5, times, secondMeasure);

int* timeDivided = timeMaker.change(amount);
```

Of course, the names and values for the currency and time do not have to be coded into the program. That data could be part of a file on disk. In that case, the input object must be redesigned to be able to read disk data.

The changemaker goes international

We are going to alter the original version of the changemaker problem so that it can make change in different currencies. The new problem statement is as follows.

An international bank must accept checks in various currencies to be converted to cash in other currencies. The bank wants a program to perform the conversions and give out the appropriate change accordingly.

Being able to convert from one currency to another requires knowing the exchange rate for the two currencies. If there are 10 currencies, then there are 45 different exchange rates for the different pairs of currencies. But it is not necessary to know all 45 exchange rates. Suppose instead that you know the exchange rates between one particular currency (for example U.S. currency) and all of the other nine currencies. That is sufficient to determine the remaining 36 exchange rates. For example, if you know the exchange rate between U.S. currency and French currency and the exchange rate between U.S. currency and Italian currency, that is enough information to compute the exchange rate between French and Italian currency.

We will simplify this problem somewhat by making the following assumptions:

- All exchange rates will be in terms of a base currency.

- The exchange rate from any currency to the base currency will always be given in terms of the number of units of the first currency to make up a single unit of the base currency. (This is not how exchange rates are always expressed. Exchange rates for U.S. currency are usually expressed in terms of U.S. dollars rather than U.S. pennies.)

- If no exchange rate is given between the base currency and another, then the exchange rate is assumed to be 1.

A `MeasureSystem` can make change, but it lacks the ability to convert from one currency to another. It cannot convert from U.S. currency to Canadian or French to Italian. However, we will be able to use `MeasureSystem` as a base class to make change in different currencies.

We will derive the `Currency` class from the `MeasureSystem` class. The following is what a `Currency` object will be able to do in addition to its behaviors as a `MeasureSystem`:

1. Tell its own name.

2. Tell the name of the base currency for exchange rates.

3. Set an exchange rate.

4. Convert a number of units of one currency to another.

What about the attributes of a `Currency` object? A `Currency` object must know the exchange rates—a list of exchange rates to be precise—and it must know the base currency. The list and the name of the base currency constitute shared data. Not only that, the three behaviors outlined above are shared behaviors that depend only on the list and base currency.

In Chapter 7 we showed how objects of the same type could share common behaviors and data if the methods were declared as static. Except for the constructor and a method to tell the `Currency` name, all members of the `Currency` class that are not inherited from the base class, `MeasureSystem`, will be static.

This is the `Currency` class definition. Although we do not normally do so, we included the documentation of the protected and private members of the class, in order to show how the exchange rate list is hidden in the protected section of the class.

```
// A currency class for a collection of many currencies.
// The collection has a base currency from which all exchange rates are
//    determined
```

```
class Currency : public MeasureSystem {
public:
    Currency(int i, kstring n[], const int v[], kstring c, double r = 1);
                                    // Creates a Currency of i denominations
                                    //   with names and values n and v. The new
                                    //   Currency name is c; r is the rate of
                                    //   exchange from units of the base
                                    //   currency to units of this currency.
                                    // ASSUME: i > 0; n and v have i elements.
    kstring name( ) const;          // Name of this currency.
    static void setExchange(kstring c, double x);
                                    // Rate of exchange from units of Currency c
                                    //   to units of base Currency is set to x.
    static kstring baseName( );     // Name of the base Currency (on which all
                                    //   exchange rates are based).
    static double exchangeRate(kstring from, kstring to);
                                    //   Exchange rate from Currency with name
                                    //     from to Currency with name to.
                                    //   ASSUME: from and to are Currency names.
    static int convert(kstring d, kstring c, int x);
                                    // Smallest number of units of Currency c
                                    //   with value at least x times the
                                    //   exchange rate from d to c.
                                    //   ASSUME: d and c are Currency names.
protected:
    int index_;                                 // Index of this Currency's
                                                //   name in the list of names

    enum {max_ = 50};                           // Maximum number of currencies
    static kstring currencyNames_[max_];        // List of currency names
    static int currencyCount_;                  // Number of currencies
    static const kstring baseCurrency_;         // Base Currency name
    static double exchangeRates_[max_];         // Exchange rates
    static int findIndex(kstring n);            // Index of name n in the list of
                                                //   Currency names

private:
    Currency(const Currency& c);                // No copying allowed.
    Currency& operator=(const Currency& c);     // No assignment allowed.
};
```

The protected section of the `Currency` class contains a list of currency names. The maximum size of the list is 50. The number of names in the list is `currencyCount_`. The exchange rate is also a list, whose length is the number of names. A `Currency` collection is illustrated in Fig. 10.14. Whenever a new `Currency` is created, it is added to the list that is static data (shared data) of the `Currency` class.

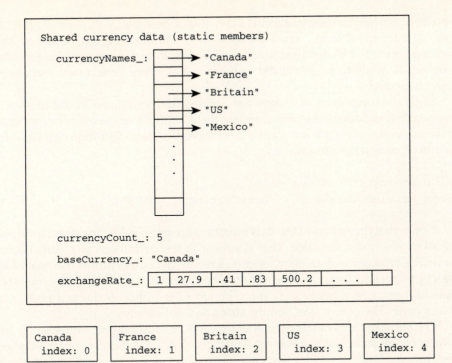

Figure 10.14 A `currency` collection for five nations. The base currency is Canadian.

The `Currency` constructor calls the `MeasureSystem` constructor whenever a new `Currency` is created. It also puts the new `Currency` name into the protected array `currencyNames_` as well as the exchange rate into the protected array `exchangeRates_`. Here is the `Currency` constructor definition:

```
Currency :: Currency(int i, kstring n[], const int v[], kstring c,
                     double r) : MeasureSystem(i,n,v)
{
   if (currencyCount_ < max_) {
      index_ = currencyCount_;
      currencyNames_[currencyCount_] = c;
      exchangeRates_[currencyCount_] = r;
      currencyCount_++;
   }
}
```

The constructor definition brings up a question about static data members. How is `currencyCount_` initialized in the first place? It clearly cannot be set to 1 whenever a new `Currency` object is created. But before any `Currency` object is created, `currencyCount_` must be set to 0 to initialize the list of names and exchange rates. For that matter, initializing `baseCurrency_` amounts to a similar problem. It needs to be initialized only once, not every time a new `Currency` object is created.

Static data members of classes are defined and initialized in the following manner. This code could be placed among the definitions of the member functions of the `Currency` class. Do *not* place the code inside a class definition or inside any member function definitions.

```
int Currency :: currencyCount_ = 0;
const kstring Currency :: baseCurrency_ = "US";
```

Notice that the names of the data members are prefaced by the class name and the scope resolution operator. That is similar to the definitions of member functions. The type of the data member comes before the name, just as the type of an object precedes its name in a definition. The type of the protected class member `baseCurrency_` is `const kstring`. The `kstring` indicates this is a pointer to `const char`. The `const` says that the string will not change.

The initializations of `currencyCount_` and `baseCurrency_` are actually *definitions* of the static data members. The class definition merely contained their declarations. Usually when we see the declaration of a data object, that declaration has also been a definition. That is unlike functions, which may have many declarations.

When a class is defined, its data members as well as its member functions are declared. We have followed the practice of defining the member functions outside the class definition. The data members are not defined in the class definition either. They cannot be initialized in the class definition. Each instance of a class has its own copy of each nonstatic data member of the class. So the data members belonging to a particular instance of a class become defined as soon as an instance of the class is created.

A declaration introduces a name to the compiler. The definition of a class introduces the names of its members by containing their declarations.

We will leave the definitions of the methods `name`, `setExchange`, `convert`, and `baseName` as exercises. Of course, `name` and `baseName` are trivial to define. The methods `setExchange` and `convert` require a design decision on how to find a currency in a list.

Now for some code using the new `Currency` class. Suppose that `aCurrency` and `bCurrency` are two `Currency` objects. Suppose also that `aAmt` represents an amount of units in aCurrency. The following code finds the change that will be given in bCurrency for the equivalent value of aAmt in aCurrency.

```
int aAmt;       // Amount measured in units of aCurrency
int* bChange;   // Amounts of each denomination in bCurrency whose total
                //  values is bAmt;
int bAmt = Currency::convert(aCurrency.name(), bCurrency.name(), aAmt);
int* bChange = bCurrency.change(bAmt);
```

Let's return to the original changemaker problem. Our previous solution from Chapter 7 used a cash drawer. The Currency class can almost serve as a cash drawer. But it is not capable of knowing any limits on the amounts of each denomination of cash on hand. So we will design a new class, CashHolder, to correspond to the cash drawer. The CashHolder will hold various amounts of denominations of a particular Currency in its cash on hand. The currency does not have to be U.S. currency. It can be any currency.

We could design a CashHolder to be a special kind of Currency by deriving it from the Currency class. But that is not quite consistent with a real-world notion of cash drawers. Rather than deriving CashHolder from Currency, we will design CashHolder to have a Currency type member—a CashHolder *has-a* Currency. The CashHolder constructor requires a Currency argument and an optional list of limits on the amounts of each denomination to be placed in its cash on hand. Fig. 10.15 illustrates the relationships among MeasureSystem, Currency, and CashHolder.

The CashHolder class has a reference to a Currency as a private member. The other private member, itemCount_, tells the number of the corresponding denomination of cash on hand. It is used to implement an ordinary CashHolder, which does not have an infinite supply of each denomination.

```
// A cash holder to hold various denominations of a currency
class CashHolder {
public:
    CashHolder(const Currency& c, const int* limit = 0);
                    // Creates a CashHolder for Currency c and limited numbers
```

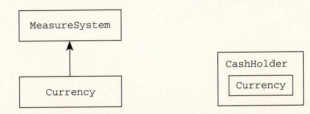

Figure 10.15 A Currency *is-a* MeasureSystem. A CashHolder *has-a* Currency.

```
                // for each denomination. The number of each denomination in
                // cash holder is given by limit; limit[0] is the number
                // number of the smallest valued denomination. If limit is 0,
                // the number of each denomination of cash on hand is
                // unlimited.
    ~CashHolder();                          // Delete cash on hand.
    const Currency& theCurrency( ) const;   // CashHolder's currency.
    const int* cashOnHand( ) const;         // Number of each denomination on
                                            //   hand.
    int* perfectChange(int amt) const;      // Makes change assuming no limit
                                            //   on amounts on hand.
                                            //   ASSUME : amt >= 0
    int* change(int amt);                   // Makes change assuming on the
                                            //   limitations on amounts on hand.
                                            //   ASSUME : amt >= 0
protected:
    const Currency& curr_;
    int* itemCount_;

private:
    CashHolder(const CashHolder &);             // No copying allowed.
    CashHolder& operator=(const CashHolder &);  // No assignment allowed.
};
```

Notice that `curr_` is declared as type `Currency&` rather than type `Currency`. A `CashHolder` does not need to create a new `Currency`. Rather, it can simply refer to an existing `Currency`. When a `CashHolder` object is destroyed, the `Currency` associated with that object will not be destroyed.

The `CashHolder` constructor needs merely to initialize its member data. That can be accomplished through the initialization list.

```
CashHolder :: CashHolder(const Currency& c, const int* limit) : curr_(c)
{
    if (limit != 0) {
        itemCount_ = new int[c.size()];
        for (int i = 0; i < c.size(); i++)
            itemCount_[i] = limit[i];
    }
    else
        itemCount_ = 0;
}
```

The member functions `theCurrency()` and `cashOnHand()` are necessary in order for a user to be able to see what is in the `CashHolder`. They do not allow the `CashHolder` data to be changed.

```
const Currency& CashHolder :: theCurrency() const
{
    return curr_;
}

const int* CashHolder :: cashOnHand() const
{
    return itemCount_;
}
```

The `CashHolder`'s `perfectChange()` and `change()` member functions send messages to its `Currency` to do all of their work. They do not have to repeat the sequence of divisions and assignments. When an object does work by sending a message to another object, the process is called **delegation** or **forwarding**.

```
int* CashHolder :: perfectChange(int amt) const
{
    return curr_.change(amt);        // Example of DELEGATION to curr_ object.
}

int* CashHolder :: change(int amt)
{
    int* chng = curr_.change(amt, itemCount_);   // Delegation to curr_.
    if (curr_.unitVal(chng) != amt){             // Delegation to curr_.
      delete [] chng;                            // Prevent memory leak.
      return 0;                                  // Failure: can't make change.
    }
    for (int i = 0; i < curr_.size(); i++)       // Delegation to curr_.
      itemCount_[i] -= chng[i];                  // Decrease cash on hand.
    return chng;
}
```

These new classes can do a significant amount of work. Together, they have much more functionality than the `CurrencyList` class, which we used in our solution to the changemaker problem in Chapter 7.

Using new classes to solve old problems

The old program from Chapter 7 that solved the changemaker problem can be modified slightly to use our new classes. This new changemaker program solves exactly the same problem as the original version. If you compare the Chapter 7 version with this one, you will realize that the responsibility for determining the denomination names and values belongs to the program, not with the classes.

```
// Name: The changemaker
// Version: 5.0
// Purpose: Determine the count of each denomination from twenty dollar bills
//    down through pennies that constitute a given monetary amount.

#include <iostream.h>
#include "CashHolder.H"

kstring USnames[8] =  {"pennies", "nickels", "dimes", "quarters", "$1 bills",
                       "$5 bills", "$10 bills", "$20 bills"};
const int USvalues[] = {1, 5, 10, 25, 100, 500, 1000, 2000};
const int initialCash[] = {100, 100, 100, 100, 100, 100, 100, 100};

//---------------------------- interfaces --------------------------------
void inputInt(int& aNumber, const char prompt[]);
// arguments:
//    aNumber - out - the integer entered by the user
//    prompt - message displayed to the user
// side effect: reads aNumber from the input stream.  The argument is changed
//    to the number which was read.

void outputChange(const int amts[], const MeasureSystem& aCurrency);
// arguments:
//    amts - list of amounts
//    aCurrency - System with the same number of measures as elements of amts
// side effect: Output each amount and its corresponding measure name on
//    a separate line.

//------------------ teller object implementation -----------------------
void main()
{
    cout << "Change Maker (version 5)\n\n";

    Currency US(8, USnames, USvalues, "US");
    CashHolder cashDrawer(US, initialCash);

    int amountToChange;                      // Amount of money to be changed
    inputInt(amountToChange, "Enter amount to be changed in smallest units: ");
    cout << "Your change:" << endl;
    outputChange(cashDrawer.change(amountToChange),
        cashDrawer.theCurrency());

    cout << "\nRemaining Cash On Hand:" << endl;
    outputChange(cashDrawer.cashOnHand(), cashDrawer.theCurrency());
}
//----------------- end of teller object implementation ---------------------
```

```
//---------------human interface component implementation-------------------
void inputInt(int& aNumber, const char prompt[])
{
    cout << prompt;
    cin >> aNumber;
}

void outputChange(const int amts[], const MeasureSystem& aCurrency)
{
    for (int i = 0; i < aCurrency.size(); i++)
        cout << amts[i] << " " << aCurrency.name(i) << endl;
}
//------------ end of human interface component implementation --------------
```

The new changemaker program uses a cash drawer to make change. The program seeds the cash drawer with 100 pieces of each denomination—100 $20 bills through 100 pennies. We executed the new changemaker program to make ordinary change with an input representing $45.67. The box below shows the output. (The user input is in italics.)

```
Enter amount to be changed in smallest units: 4567
Your change:
2 pennies
1 nickels
1 dimes
2 quarters
0 $1 bills
1 $5 bills
0 $10 bills
2 $20 bills

Remaining Cash On Hand:
98 pennies
99 nickels
99 dimes
98 quarters
100 $1 bills
99 $5 bills
100 $10 bills
98 $20 bills
```

The `CashHolder` class can solve the imperfect change problem in any currency, not just U.S. currency. A program for solving the problem in any currency must do the following:

1. Define an array of names and values of denominations.

2. Define an array of limitations on the amount of each denomination.

3. Define `cashDrawer` with five actual arguments: the number of denominations, the array of names, the array of values, the name of the currency, and the array of amount limitations.

You do not need to define more classes, and you do not need to redefine any methods in the `CashHolder` class. All the `CashHolder` constructor needs is enough information to specify the currency that the object being created represents and to put limitations on the amounts of each denomination available. Once its initial information is specified, the `CashHolder` object is ready to do the rest.

10.7 ▌ Summary

The most important defining feature of C++ is the class construct. C++ programs are built around classes. Class definitions and member function definitions form a substantial part of C++ source code. Inheritance provides the major mechanism to reuse code for different problems and different contexts.

Some of this chapter concentrated on using inheritance to extend existing code. The `BCString` and the `LogFile` are code extensions. Some of the chapter concentrated on using inheritance to build a hierarchy of highly related classes. The `Door` class hierarchy is an example. And of course, C++ has its own rich example in the `ios` class hierarchy.

Class hierarchies provide an organizational framework for programmers who use class libraries as well as for programmers who develop them. By looking at the class hierarchy structure for streams, for example, we can understand how input and output operators on `istrstreams` and `ostrstreams` behave—they behave the same as on `istreams` and `ostreams`. The class hierarchy developer can use that hierarchy to control and clarify the complexity of the design.

Defining a new class from an existing one is a prime example of code reuse. To create a new class with special features from an existing class, we can derive the new class from the original base class, declaring only the new data members and new member functions that make this a special version of the original base. All of the data members and member functions of the base class are automatically part of the derived class. They need not be redeclared or redefined for the derived class. A derived class can hide the methods for the base class, or it can use the base class methods.

The result of creating special classes from existing ones can result in a substantial improvement in the functionality of the old code. Only the new improvement needs to be coded. The original code on which the improvement is based does not need to be rewritten or retested. The code as well as the designs can be enhanced to suit new problems or specialization of old problems.

In subsequent chapters, we will use inheritance as a specialization technique as well as a specification technique. Inheritance is a mechanism to describe interfaces—descriptions of behaviors and attributes—of collections of classes. The code that we developed earlier in this book allowed object-oriented program development, but it did not support object-oriented program development very well. Inheritance and polymorphism are the features of C++ that provide that support.

Glossary

ambiguity In the case of multiple inheritance, the compiler's inability to determine which base class member is being referenced.

base class A class from which other classes are derived.

class hierarchy A collection of classes consisting of a base class and all classes derived either directly or indirectly from it.

delegation One object sending a message to another object in order to complete a task. (Also called *forwarding*.)

derived class A class that is defined as an extension of another class.

forwarding *See* delegation.

hiding Declaring a function in a derived class that has the same name as a base class function. (Hiding does not take place with virtual functions, which are discussed in Chapter 11.)

incremental programming Creating new types by enhancing old ones.

inheritance Creating new classes out of existing ones.

inheritance list In the definition of a derived class, the list of base classes from which the class is derived. The inheritance list includes the name of each base class and the kind of inheritance for each (public, protected, or private).

inheritance of the implementation Private inheritance in which the derived class uses the methods of the base class but does not make them publicly accessible.

inheritance of the interface Public inheritance in which the derived class satisfies all of the specifications of the base class (supports all of the services of a base class).

is-a A relationship between two classes in which one class is publicly derived from another.

multiple inheritance Inheritance in which classes are derived from more than one base class. The inheritance list of such a class contains at least two classes.

private inheritance Inheritance in which public and protected members of a base class are considered private members of the derived class.

protected Access control allowing member access for the declaring (base) class, its friends, and its derived classes and their friends but not outside the class hierarchy otherwise.

protected inheritance Inheritance in which public and protected members of a base class are considered protected members of the derived class.

public inheritance Inheritance in which public members of the base class are public members of the derived class and protected members of the base class are protected members of the derived class.

slicing The compiler's action of disregarding members declared in a derived class when trying to assign or initialize a base class object from a derived class object.

string streams Streams in which input comes from a buffer and output goes to a buffer instead of a file. String stream types are defined in `strstream.h`.

10.8 ▌ Exercises

1. Assume that the following class definitions have been given:

```
class A {
protected:
    int x;
    int y;
public:
    A();
};

class B : public A {
private:
    int z;
};
```

a. How many data members does B have?

b. Which data members of B are public? Which are private? Which are protected?

c. Sketch a diagram of an object of type A and another object of type B. Be sure to show the data members of each object.

2. Assume that the following class definitions have been given:

```
class A {
private:
    int x;
protected:
    int y;
```

```
public:
    int z;
    void f(int k);
};

class B : public A {
private:
    int w;
    int f();
};

class C : private A {
public:
    int w;
    void f(int k);
};

class D : public B {
public:
    void f();
};
```

a. Which of its members can B access?

b. Which of its members can C access?

c. Which of its members can D access?

d. Suppose that the following definitions are in `main()`.

```
A a;            // a is an object of type A
B b;            // b is an object of type B
C c;            // c is an object of type C
D* p = new D;   // p points to an object of type D
```

Which of the following statements are illegal? Explain each illegality.

```
cout << b.f() << endl;
c.f(3);
b.z = p->f();
b.z = 5;
c.z = 7;
p->z = 3;
p->f();
p->f(3);
```

3. Assume that the following class definitions have been given:

```
class A {
protected:
    void f()                {cout << "A::f(void)" << endl;}
public:
    void f(int x)           {cout << "A::f(int)" << endl;}
    void f(double y)        {cout << "A::f(double)" << endl;}
    void f(A a)             {cout << "A::f(A)" << endl;}
};

class B : public A {
public:
    B()                     {cout << "B null constructor" << endl;}
    B(A a)                  {cout << "Constructing B from A" << endl;}
    void f(int x)           {cout << "B::f(int)" << endl;}
    void f(B b)             {cout << "B::f(B)" << endl;}
    void f(int x, int y)    {cout << "B::f(int,int)" << endl; A::f();}
};
```

What output is generated by the following code:

```
A a;
B b;
b.f(3);
b.f(3.14);
b.f(a);
b.f(b);
b.f(1, 2);
```

4. What is printed as a result of executing the following code? (This is an exercise in constructor calls.)

```
class A {
public:
    A()             {cout << "Null constructor for A" << endl; }
};

class B : public A {
public:
    B()             {cout << "Null constructor for B" << endl;}
    B(int x)        {cout << "int constructor for B" << endl;}
};
```

```
class C : public B {
public:
    C()                 {cout << "Null constructor for C" << endl;}
    C(int x) : B(x) {cout << "int constructor for C" << endl;}
};

void main()
{
    A a;
    B b;
    B bAlt(5);
    C c;
    C cAlt(0);
}
```

5. What is printed as a result of executing the following code? (This is an exercise in constructor and destructor calls.)

```
class A {
public:
    A()  {cout << "Null constructor for A" << endl;}
    ~A() {cout << "Destructor for A" << endl;}
};

class B : public A {
public:
    B()  {cout << "Null constructor for B" << endl;}
    ~B() {cout << "Destructor for B" << endl;}
};

class C : public B {
public:
    C()  {cout << "Null constructor for C" << endl;}
    ~C() {cout << "Destructor for C" << endl;}
};

void main()
{
    C c;
}
```

6. Change the definition of the Date class from Chapter 7 so that its private members are protected. Then redefine Calendar (from section 10.3) so that it is derived from Date.

7. Modify the `PasswordDoor` class so that after three consecutive unsuccessful attempts to unlock the door (using an incorrect password), the door is permanently shut. Does your new implementation have any new class members? Rewrite the interface to `PasswordDoor` to reflect its different behavior.

8. All of the following problems concern the `Door` class hierarchy.

   a. Derive a class `TrapDoor` from `LockableDoor`. Trap doors can be unlocked only from the outside. An unlock message to the trap door must include a Boolean value to tell if the message is coming from the outside or the inside. Draw a picture of the `Door` class hierarchy, which includes `TrapDoor`.

   b. Derive a class `DeadBoltDoor` from `LockableDoor`. It is possible to lock the deadbolt when the door is open. If the deadbolt is locked, then it is impossible to open the door if it is closed and it is impossible to close the door if it is open.

   c. Derive a class `SpringLatchDoor` from `LockableDoor`. You can unlock a spring latch only from the inside. A door with a spring latch can be locked and open. It is possible to close such a door.

   d. Discuss the issues of deriving these new `Door` types directly from `Door` instead of from `LockableDoor`. What are the benefits of a short and wide class hierarchy instead of a deep class hierarchy?

9. Derive a new class `FauxUpperString` from the class `BCString`. Alphabetic characters in a `FauxUpperString` "appear" to be uppercase when they are printed or when they are viewed via the subscript operator. The sample code below illustrates `FauxUpperString` behavior.

```
FauxUpperString x("Hello");
cout << x << endl;                    // Output: HELLO
x = "Goodbye";
cout << x[3] << end;                  //   Output: D
x[3] = 'f';
cout << x[3] << end;                  //   Output: F
const FauxUpperString y("Adios");
cout << y.charString() << endl;       // Output: ADIOS
```

Discuss your definition of `FauxUpperString::charString()`. Does the final line of code above cause a memory leak? If so, be sure to document who is responsible for deallocating that memory.

10. Derive a new class `SubBCString` from `BCString` that can return a substring. The new behavior is a member function with two integer arguments, `psn` and `len`. It returns the `SubBCString` representing the

substring of the object according to `psn` (first argument) and `len` (second argument) as follows.

- If `psn` is nonnegative and `len` is positive, the resulting substring begins at the `psn` subscript and contains `len` characters.

- If `psn` is nonnegative and the `len` is negative, the resulting substring ends at the `psn` subscript and contains `len` characters.

- If `psn` is nonnegative and the `len` is zero, the resulting substring begins at the `psn` subscript and continues to the end of the string.

- If either `psn` is negative or `psn` and `len` would specify any invalid subscripts, the resulting substring is null.

Suppose that the `SubBCString` represents the C-string `"abcdef"`. The following table illustrates the values of the substrings returned.

psn	len	*substring*
2	3	`"cde"`
3	0	`"def"`
3	1	`"d"`
-3	1	`""`
5	-2	`"ef"`
3	4	`""`

a. Implement the new behavior as a member function.

b. Implement the new behavior as the overloaded function application operator, `operator()`. This operator must be a class member. There is no restriction on the number of arguments.

11. a. Derive a new class, `TimedDoor`, from `Door`. A `TimedDoor` *has-a* `Clock`. It can be opened only when the time on the `Clock` is between midnight and 6:00 A.M. It shuts itself when the time is after 6:00 A.M. and before midnight. `TimedDoor` should have all of the `Clock` behaviors. (It can implement those behaviors by delegating `Clock` messages to its `Clock` member.)

b. Sketch the new `Door` class hierarchy.

c. Define a `TimedDoor` object named `td`. What message can be sent to `td` to reset its `Clock` to 6:01 A.M.?

d. Redesign the `TimedDoor` so that it *has-a* public `Clock`. Eliminate the `TimedDoor` methods for the `Clock`. Define a `TimedDoor` object named `tDoor`. What message can be sent to `tDoor` to reset its `Clock` to 6:01 A.M.?

What are the drawbacks of implementing a `TimedDoor` in this fashion?

e. Redefine `TimedDoor` so that is derived from both `Door` and `Clock`. (A `TimedDoor` *is-a* `Door` and a `TimedDoor` *is-a* `Clock`.) The behavior of a `TimedDoor` should be identical to the behavior described in part (a). Redraw the new `Door` class hierarchy.

12. a. Redefine the `SimpleList` class from Chapter 7 so that all of its data members are protected. Do not make any other changes.

   b. Redefine the `SimpleListWithIterator` class from Chapter 7 so that it is inherited publicly from `SimpleList`. What new data members are necessary? What new methods are necessary?

   c. Derive the class `SimpleRemove` from `SimpleListWithIterator`. `SimpleRemove` should be able to remove the first occurrence of an item x from its list of items.

   d. Derive the class `SimpleNoDuplicates` from the class `SimpleList-WithIterator`. `SimpleNoDuplicates` should add a new item only if the list does not already contain a copy of the new item.

   e. Derive the class `OrderedSimple` from `SimpleListWithIterator`. `OrderedSimple` keeps its list items in ascending order.

13. Redefine the `BCString` class so that it does not have a `length_` data member.

14. Redefine the `BCString` class so that a `BCString` object *has-a* `String` rather than *is-a* `String`. The new version should have two data members: a `String` and an `int` for the length. What are the advantages of inheriting from the `String` class over including a `String` as a member?

15. Redesign the `CalendarWatch` so that a `CalendarWatch` *is-a* `Clock` and *has-a* `Calendar`. Define a new `CalendarWatch` class as well as all of its member functions.

16. The `istream` class has a member function, `clear()`, which when invoked with no arguments, turns off the three error flags, `fail`, `bad`, and `eof`. When an error has occurred on an attempted read, then at least one of the error flags is turned on. For example, an error occurs when the expression `cin >> x` is evaluated where x is an `int` and the first non-whitespace character in the input stream is `'A'`. Until `cin.clear()` is executed, `cin` will remain in an error state and thus be unable to perform another extraction. See how `clear()` works with `ifstream`s by going through the following exercises.

   a. Create a disk file with the first line

b. Define an `ifstream` object named `in` and open it to that disk file. (See Appendix F for `fstream` syntax.)

c. Define the `int` object named `x` and the `char` object named `ch`.

d. Execute the following statements:

```
in >> x;
if (!in)
    cout << "Read failed" << endl;
else
    cout << "x is " << x << endl;
// What will happen with the next statement?
in >> ch;
cout << "ch is " << ch <<endl;
in.clear();
in >> ch;
in >> x;
cout << "x is " << x << "\nch is " << ch << endl;
```

What can you conclude about the use of `clear()` with input streams?

17. String streams can be used to find the string representation of floating point numbers. Since they are streams, they can be used with manipulators to obtain a string representation from a scientific format or a fixed decimal format.

Suppose that `numString` is of type `char*` and `x` is of type `float`. Write a segment of code that assigns to `numString` the C-string representation of the value of `x` correct to four decimal places.

18. Derive the class `StrCalendar` from `Calendar` so that it has one additional member function, `stringVal()`. The new function has no formal arguments and it returns a C-string that is the `Calendar`'s date in the form `"mm/dd/yy"`. *Hint*: Use the `strstream` class to determine the string representation of an integer, such as the string `"12"` representation of the integer 12.

19. Derive the class `InFileQuery` from `ifstream`. `InFileQuery` has a single constructor, which is null. The constructor repeatedly requests the user to enter the name of the file to be opened and then attempts to open the stream to that disk file until the attempt succeeds. `InFileQuery` has no other additional members from those in `ifstream`. (See Appendix F for determining success of opening.)

20. Constructors and destructors are useful for performing many initialization and termination tasks. The `LogFile` class constructor and destructor provide good examples. Derive a class named `BackupFile` from `ofstream` that makes a backup of an original file before creating a new file of the same name.

```
// class BackupFile
//    Backs up a disk file with the new name extension ".BAK" and creates a
//    new file with the name of the original disk file. All insertions are
//    to the new file.
class BackupFile : public ofstream {
public:
    BackupFile(const char s[] = "");     // Backup the file named s to s.BAK
                                         //    if s exists.

    ~BackupFile();
};
```

21. Write the definitions of the `Currency` class member functions `name()`, `setExchange()`, `convert()`, and `baseName()`.

Programming Projects

22. The `MeasureSystem` class does not have an iterator. But it does implement a list of names and corresponding numbers. Derive a `Measure-SystemWithIterator` class from the `MeasureSystem` class. A `MeasureSystemWithIterator` contains a protected counter and three additional public member functions, `setIterator()`, `next()`, and `more()`.

   The function `next()` must return two values, a name and a number. There are several ways to return two values. One technique is to create a struct type with two members, an `int` and a `const char*` (or a `kstring`). `MeasureSystemWithIterator::next()` can return a constant reference or a constant pointer to that struct. (Make sure the return value from `next()` cannot be used to change any of the class data.)

23. Rewrite the definition for the `CashHolder` so that a customer can request restrictions on the change to be returned. Part of the `change` message to the `CashHolder` are optional lists of the minimum number of each denomination to be returned and the maximum number of each denomination to be returned. A negative maximum number represents the fact that the customer does not care (any negative number will suffice).

24. Write a program that uses the `CashHolder` class to make imperfect change with French currency. Limit the numbers for each denomination to 10.

Chapter 11

Polymorphism and Generic Classes

Chapter Contents

11.1 Ad hoc polymorphism through overloading

11.2 Parameterized polymorphism through templates
Function templates
Using templates to define generic classes
Compile time definitions
Arguments for functions and class templates

11.3 Runtime polymorphism
Virtual functions and runtime binding
Overriding, overloading, and hiding
"Arrays" of heterogeneous elements

11.4 Abstract base classes
Creating a class hierarchy from an abstract base class type
Virtual destructors
Base classes and static members
Warnings on use of abstract base class types
Designing base class types

11.5 Polymorphism and cloning for array-based lists

11.6 The changemaker, revisited again

11.7 Summary
Glossary

11.8 Exercises

T HE hallmarks of object-oriented programming are inheritance and **polymorphism**—a term literally meaning many shapes. In C++, polymorphism means using the same syntax to do or to mean different things depending on the context. This chapter will focus on that meaning.

Polymorphism appears in C++ in three different forms. The first, which is already familiar to you, is function and operator overloading. The second form allows programmers to construct general templates for families of functions or classes. A specific function or class can be created via a template supplying some of the actual types that the class or function uses.

While overloading and templates are very important forms of polymorphism, most C++ programmers think of yet another form when they hear the term polymorphism. That third form involves new concepts called overriding and virtual functions, which have to do with class hierarchies. This form of polymorphism depends on the fact that pointers to base class types can point to objects of derived class types. Those derived types may vary from one execution of the program to the next. So from one execution of a program to the next, the same syntax may be used for invocations of different functions.

The best way to understand polymorphism is to read examples and create your own code. This chapter is full of examples. The final ones show how different forms of polymorphism can be combined to create code reusable in many different contexts. We end the chapter by showing the full implementation of the change-maker solution.

11.1   Ad hoc polymorphism through overloading

We introduced a special kind of polymorphism very early in this book. When you first learned about it, you probably did not give it much thought. In Chapter 2, we mentioned using arithmetic operators such as + with floating point as well as integer operands. Using the addition operator with `doubles` as well as `ints` is an example of special purpose or ad hoc polymorphism. Almost all high-level languages build in this kind of ad hoc polymorphism on numeric types.

Overloading a function means creating a new function with the same name as another function in the same scope so that it can be invoked with different type arguments. An overloaded function can be used in more than one context. The fact that addition is overloaded means it can be used in at least two different contexts, with either `int` or `double` operands (arguments) for example. Calling an overloaded function with two different lists of argument types results in execution of two different methods.

Unlike most other high-level languages, C++ provides facilities to extend this kind of ad hoc polymorphism to user-defined types. Operator overloading is a special feature of C++ that promotes construction of first class types. By treating operators as special kinds of functions, programmers can redefine operator semantics without redefining their syntax. In other words, programmers can redefine the meaning of the operators for different types of operands but not change the form in which the operators must be used.

Operator overloading makes code that uses the operators more general. Without overloading, + is an operation on numeric values. With operator overloading, programs can do generic arithmetic without being concerned about the implementation details of how + is defined or even how numbers are represented. For example, we can write a program to do some arithmetic on integer and floating point data. If we then change that program source code file merely by adding include files and changing numerical declarations to `Rationals`, all the arithmetic will still work. A program that does addition on `ints` or `doubles` could just as easily do that addition on the `Rationals`.[1]

Other functions besides operators can be overloaded. Overloaded functions must differ in their argument lists. (Of course, two functions with different scope can have the same names and the same argument lists. They are not considered to be overloaded.) We have used function overloading most often with constructors. Most of the classes in this text have multiple constructors, including constructors with default arguments.

> Two functions in the same scope with the same name but different signatures are overloaded. A signature of a function includes its name and argument list. Two functions that are members of the same class may have exactly the same name and argument lists if one is a constant member function and the other is not. (The `const` is actually part of the signature, even though it does not appear as part of the formal argument list.)

When an overloaded function or operator is called, the compiler uses the argument lists to determine which function of that name is being invoked. It goes through a complicated set of rules to resolve the ambiguities that may be evident in the call. This resolution occurs at the time of compilation. If the compiler is unable to tell which overloaded function to call, it will generate an error.

It is certainly possible to violate good coding practices by overloading functions that do not serve the same purpose. But overloading functions that do serve the same purpose is a good way to make code correspond to design. The same operation on different types of objects can be given the same name. By referring to code by name, we get a new level of abstraction. We are freed from the implementation details that may differ from one type to the next.

---

[1] The `Rational` class was introduced in Chapter 8.

11.2 Parameterized polymorphism through templates

We will begin our discussion of a new kind of polymorphism by considering an overloaded function named `swap`.

```
void swap(int& x, int& y)          void swap(double& x, double& y)
{                                  {
    int temp = x;                      double temp = x;
    x = y;                             x = y;
    y = temp;                          y = temp;
}                                  }
```

With the exception of the argument and local variable types, these two versions of `swap` are absolutely identical. If we replace `int` or `double` with the identifier `T` (standing for "type"), this is their general form:

```
void swap(T& x, T& y)
{
    T temp = x;
    x = y;
    y = temp;
}
```

A smart compiler ought to be able to generate a function that will swap `int`s, `double`s, `String`s, or whatever type objects simply by filling in the appropriate type for `T`. In the generic swap code, `T` is a formal argument for a type, just as `x` and `y` are formal arguments for objects.

Function templates

Is it possible to write a function that can serve as a generic swap? The answer is yes. If you need two or more functions with identical behavior that differ only in their formal argument type designations, you can write a **function template** to specify what the different versions of the function are to do and how they are to do it. A function template shows the compiler how to generate an actual function by looking at the name of the function and the argument list of an invocation. The compiler uses the template to generate the definitions of the actual functions that will be called.

A function template can be used to create a set of nearly identical functions much the same way a class definition can be used to create a set of nearly identical objects. A class definition tells the compiler the data and methods for an object of that type. The definition of a function template tells the compiler the essential code for the functions. The compiler can substitute actual types later as needed.

A template prototype for a `swap()` function is as follows:

```
template <class T>
void swap(T& x, T& y);
```

Here is an explanation of this two-line prototype, starting from the top.

1. `template` is a keyword. It indicates the definition or declaration that follows is a general form that the compiler will make specific as soon as it sees an invocation to the function named `swap`.

2. `<class T>` is the template parameter list. The list is enclosed in angle brackets, `<` and `>`. This particular list contains only one item, `class T`. The term `class` is a keyword indicating what follows is to be interpreted as a type. (This is one more example of a keyword being used for two completely different purposes. In a template list, the keyword `class` can refer to any type, not just a user-defined class type.) `T` is a generic type name that will be substituted with a specific type when needed.

3. The declaration of `swap()` includes the generic type name `T` instead of specific types such as `int` or `double`. `T` is the formal *type* argument.

4. The scope of the identifier `T` in the prototype extends to the semicolon that terminates the prototype.

The definition of the function template `swap()` also begins with `template<class T>`. `T` represents the type descriptor for both the formal arguments of the function and the local variable. The scope of `T` extends to the entire template definition.

```
template<class T>
void swap(T& x, T& y)
{
    T temp = x;
    x = y;
    y = temp;
}
```

Suppose that `swap()` is defined as a function template. What happens when the following code is compiled?

```
int a,b;
float r,s;
char c,d;
Date e,f;      // Date is a class type defined in Chapter 7

// Code to assign values to the objects goes here.

swap(a,b);     // calls swap(int&, int&)
```

```
swap(r,s);      // calls swap(float&, float&)
swap(c,d);      // calls swap(char&, char&)
swap(e,f);      // calls swap(Date&, Date&);
```

The compiler generates four different **template functions**: void swap(int&, int&), void swap(float&, float&), void swap(char&, char&), and void swap(Date&, Date&). You do not need explicitly to overload swap, making four definitions that are identical except for their types. The compiler does that rote work for you by creating an entire family of functions with argument types and local variable types that depend on the types of the actual arguments of the different invocations. Figure 11.1 shows the definition generated by the compiler when swap() is invoked with int arguments.

> A template function is a function whose declaration and definition are generated by the compiler from a function template. (The programmer writes the function template. The compiler generates the template function.)

Using templates to define generic classes

SimpleList is a simple class that we defined in Chapter 7. It implements a simple list of integers with very limited capabilities. The SimpleList definition shows just how limited those capabilities are.

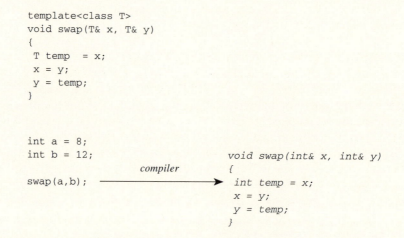

```
template<class T>
void swap(T& x, T& y)
{
  T temp  = x;
  x = y;
  y = temp;
}


int a = 8;
int b = 12;                              void swap(int& x, int& y)
                            compiler     {
swap(a,b);      ─────────────────────▶     int temp = x;
                                           x = y;
                                           y = temp;
                                         }
```

Figure 11.1 An example of how the compiler generates the appropriate template function swap() when it is invoked.

```
class SimpleList {
public:
    SimpleList();                    // Constructs an empty list.
    void clear();                    // Makes the list empty.
    void add(int x);                 // Adds x to the end of the list if there's
                                     //    room.
    bool member(int x) const;        // Is x a list member?
    int maximumCapacity() const;     // Maximum possible list size.
    int currentSize() const;         // Number of items currently in the list.
private:
    enum {maxSize_ = 100};           // Maximum size of the list
    int item_[maxSize_];             // List items
    int size_;                       // Number of items currently in the list
};
```

Implementing a simple list of `doubles` cannot be much different from implementing a simple list of `ints`. How could this definition be modified if we wanted a simple list of `doubles` in addition to a simple list of `ints`? Four changes in the `SimpleList` class would be necessary to define a new simple list of `doubles`.

1. The name of the new class could not be the same as `SimpleList` since it is a different class. We could call it something like `SimpleListOf-Doubles`.

2. The methods `add()` and `member()` would have `double` arguments instead of `int` arguments.

3. The array data member would be an array of `doubles` rather than an array of `ints`.

4. The definitions of `add()` and `member()` would be modified to fit the new `double` element type.

Suppose that we wanted a simple list of `Dates` in addition to the simple lists of `doubles` and the simple list of `ints`? Again, we are forced to make up a new name, change the declarations and definitions of `add()` and `member()`, and change the array element type.

The C++ solution to all of this rewriting is a **class template,** a template that shows the compiler how to generate an actual class definition and the member function definitions when an object of that class template name is defined. Rather than define two new classes, we will define the class template `TSimpleList`.

```
// Template for a simple list class
template<class T>
class TSimpleList {
public:
    TSimpleList();                        // Constructs an empty list.
```

```
    void clear();                  // Makes the list empty.
    void add(const T& x);          // Adds x to the list if there's room.
    bool member(const T& x) const; // Is x a list member?
    int maximumCapacity() const;   // Maximum possible list size.
    int currentSize() const;       // Number of items currently in the list.

private:
    enum {maxSize_ = 100};
    T item_[maxSize_];
    int size_;
};
```

In the class template definition, the arguments to `add()` and `member()` are constant references to the generic type `T`. This is in anticipation of using the template to create a `TSimpleList` with a complicated type that is more difficult for the compiler to duplicate than a type such as `int` or `double`.

The definitions of function members of the class template are function templates. Here are two member function definitions for `TSimpleList`.

```
template<class T>
TSimpleList<T> :: TSimpleList( ) : size_(0)
{ }


template<class T>
bool TSimpleList<T> :: member(const T& x) const
{
    for (int i = 0; i < size_; i++)
        if (item_[i] == x)
            return true;
    return false;
}
```

These definitions have a great deal of new and potentially confusing syntax. We will try to point out some subtleties.

1. Member functions of class templates are considered to be function templates. The definition of a member function must start with the template prefix, `template<class T>`. (Some programmers prefer to put the template prefix on the same line as the function name.)

2. The name of the class template is `TSimpleList<T>`. The `<T>` says that this is not an ordinary class (such as the `Rational` class or `Date` class). Instead, it is a generic class template.

3. The constructor definition does not require the duplication of `<T>` in the name of the constructor. (Likewise, a destructor does not require the extra `<T>` in its name either.)

4. The definition of `member()` is meaningless for a type for which the operator `==` is not defined. If a program tried to use such a type for the actual type corresponding to `T`, the compiler would detect a syntax error.

`TSimpleList` is an example of a **parameterized type**, a definition that allows the compiler to generate an actual type from the name of the parameterized type and an actual type parameter corresponding to the formal parameter `T`.[2] The definition of a `TSimpleList` object requires an actual type to specify the meaning of `T` for that object.

Template syntax may look hopelessly complicated when you first see it. The term

```
template<class T>
```

can be analyzed piece by piece.

1. `template` warns the reader that what is being declared or defined is a template function or template class as opposed to an ordinary function or class. `template` is a keyword.

2. `<` `>` that enclose the formal parameter lists indicate the parameters the template function or class depends upon. They serve the same purpose as `( )` to enclose a formal argument list for a function.

3. `class` tells that the kind of parameter is a type. (The designers of C++ decided against creating a new keyword like "type" to say that the parameter was a type. Instead, they resorted to using a keyword that was already in the language.)

4. `T` is a formal name for the type much the same as formal function argument names are part of the definition of a function. The symbol `T` is not a keyword. (We could have used `template <class Fred>` just as well, replacing `T` by `Fred` everywhere in the template definition.) Most C++ programmers use `T` as a matter of simplicity and style.

Compile time class definitions

Just as a function template is used to create a family of similar functions, a class template is used to create a family of similar class types. Here are three definitions for `TSimpleList` objects. Each one is a different type of `TSimpleList`.

---

[2] The term *parameter* is often interchanged with the term *argument*. They mean precisely the same thing. The term parameterized type is commonly used in the context of template classes.

```
TSimpleList<int> intList;
TSimpleList<double> doubleList;
TSimpleList<String> stringList;
```

The object `intList` is of type `TSimpleList<int>`, the object `doubleList` is of type `TSimpleList<double>`, and the object `stringList` is of type `TSimpleList<String>`.

In these definitions, `TSimpleList` looks almost like a function name and the term `TSimpleList<int>` looks almost like a function call. `TSimpleList` is the name of a parameterized type that requires an actual parameter (argument) in order define an actual type. The actual parameter list, `<int>`, is enclosed in angle braces instead of parentheses. That list informs the compiler which type of `TSimpleList` to define.

When a compiler detects the definition of an object such as `intList` for the first time, it generates the definition for a **template class**, which is an actual class based on the template and the actual parameters. The compiler generates three different class definitions for the three types `TSimpleList<int>`, `TSimpleList<double>`, and `TSimpleList<String>` in order to create `intList`, `doubleList`, and `stringList`.

The compiler can use the newly generated template class definitions for subsequently defined classes. Suppose the following definition followed the ones we just gave.

```
TSimpleList<int> anotherIntList;
```

Then `anotherIntList` is considered to be exactly the same type as `intList`. It is the type `TSimpleList<int>`.

The type `TSimpleList<int>` can be used like an ordinary class type name. As we just illustrated, it can be used as a type for an object definition. It can be used to create a pointer type. `TSimpleList<int>` can be an argument or return type for a function. The following code illustrates using class templates as type names. The code may look strange because the type name has an argument. You will eventually get used to it.

```
TSimpleList<int> list;              // list is an empty list
list.add(27);                       // list contains 27
list.add(51);                       // list contains 27,51

TSimpleList<int>* ptr;              // ptr is a pointer-to-TSimpleList<int>
TSimpleList<int>& ref = list        // ref is an alias for list

// This code uses pointers and references.
ptr = &list;                        // *ptr is an alias for list
ref.add(35);                        // list contains 27,51,35
```

```
ptr->add(10);                    // list contains 27,51,35,10
(*ptr).add(4);                   // list contains 27,51,35,10,4
```

If you have not had much experience with explicit use of pointers and references, those last four statements may be puzzling. Your confusion may have nothing to do with templates, however. Refer to Chapter 9 for a review of pointers, references, and their syntax.

The following function prototypes use the `TSimpleList<int>` type:

```
void one(TSimpleList<int> x);         // The argument is a pass-by-value
                                      // of type SimpleList<int>
void one(TSimpleList<int>);           // Signature form of the prototype.

void two(TSimpleList<int>& x);        // Pass-by-reference argument
void three(const TSimpleList<int>& x); // Const reference argument
void four(TSimpleList<int>* x);       // Array argument
void four(TSimpleList<int> x[]);      // Alternate declaration of four()

TSimpleList<int> five();      // returns a TSimpleList<int> value
TSimpleList<int>* six();      // returns a pointer-to-TSimpleList<int>
TSimpleList<int>& seven();    // returns a TSimpleList<int> object
```

These prototypes show that the syntax for handling arguments and return values that are class template types is no different from handling arguments and return values of ordinary class types. It is merely the use of `<int>` that makes these declarations look strange. Of course you can always make a new notation for `TSimpleList<int>` by writing a typedef.

```
typedef TSimpleList<int> SimpleIntList;
```

This typedef allows the identifier `SimpleIntList` to be used wherever the type `TSimpleList<int>` is appropriate.

Arguments for function and class templates

We have referred to the notation `<class T>` as a formal template argument list enclosed in angle braces and having a single element, `class T`. But there can be formal template argument lists with multiple elements. Different elements in the template argument list are separated by commas.

The elements of a template argument list can be types, which are identified by the keyword `class`. They can also be nontype arguments just like formal function arguments.

The generic type `TIndexedList` is a template class. Its argument list contains two items: a type and an `int`.

```
template<class T, int M>
class TIndexedList {
public:
    TIndexedList();                   // Constructs an empty list capable of
                                      // holding up to M items.
    void clear();                     // Makes the list empty.
    void add(const T& x);             // Adds x to the end of the list.
                                      //  ASSUME: currentSize < M
    bool member(const T& x) const;    // True if x is a list member
    int currentSize() const;          // Number of items currently in the list
    const T& operator[](int i) const; // List item in the position i from
                                      //  the front of the list.
                                      //  ASSUME: 0 <= i < currentSize().
private:
    T item_[M];
    int size_;
};
```

Here are all of the definitions of the TIndexedList class template members. They are simple. Since each member function is a template function, the definitions are preceded by the modifier template <class T, int M>.

```
template<class T, int M>
TIndexedList<T, M> :: TIndexedList () : size_(0)
{ }

template<class T, int M>
void TIndexedList<T, M> :: clear()
{
    size_ = 0;
}

template<class T, int M>
void TIndexedList<T, M> :: add(const T& x)
{
    item_[size_++] = x;
}

template<class T, int M>
bool TIndexedList<T, M> :: member(const T& x) const
{
    for(int i = 0; i < size_; i++)
        if (item_[i] == x)
            return true;
    return false;
}
```

```
template<class T, int M>
int TIndexedList<T, M> :: currentSize() const
{
    return size_ - 1;
}


template<class T, int M>
const T& TIndexedList<T, M> :: operator[](int i) const
{
    return item_[i];
}
```

Of course, to define any `TIndexedLists`, we will need to specify the type of item for the list (the type of array element) as well as the maximum number of items the list can hold (the number of elements in the array). Figure 11.2 shows how the actual type and the actual integer become part of the template class generated by the complier. Here are some examples of `TIndexedLists`:

```
TIndexedList<int,500> integerList; // Indexed list with room for 500 ints
TIndexedList<Rational,30> rList;   // Indexed list with room for 30
                                   //    Rationals
const int max = 40;
TIndexedList<int,max> intList;      // Indexed list with room for 40 ints
TIndexedList<char,max*(max+1)> txt;// Indexed list with room for 1640 chars
```

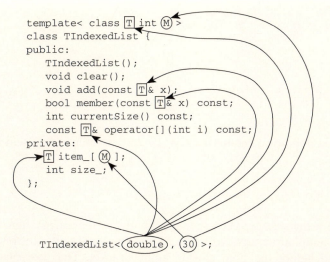

Figure 11.2 The replacement `T` by `double` and `M` by `30` to create the definition of `TIndexedList<double,30>`.

These declarations might tempt you to think that templates allow you to determine array sizes dynamically without using pointers. But that is not the case. The second actual argument in specifying a `TIndexedList` type must be a constant. It cannot be a variable. The following code is not legal:

```
int i = 10;
TIndexedList<int,i> badList;    // illegal. i is not const
```

It is easy to understand why the compiler would reject the definition for `badList`. The compiler itself must generate the definitions for the actual `TIndexedList` types that a program uses. One member of a `TIndexedList` is an array. You learned early in this book that the compiler requires that the number of elements of an array be known when an array is created. But the compiler would have no way of knowing how many array elements were to be allocated for `badList.item_`.

Whenever a template requires a nontype argument, the compiler must be able to determine the value of that argument at the time of compilation. The actual arguments corresponding to template arguments of type `int` or any numeric type must be constant. It does not matter how the value is used in the definition of the actual class template or, in the case of a function template, the actual function template. The actual argument must be a constant value that is known at compile time.

Template types can be used as actual types to instantiate function or class templates. The following definition creates a template for a data type using a struct instead of a class. (Remember that C++ treats structs the same way as classes except that the members of a struct are public unless they are declared to be private or protected.)

```
template <class K, class V>
struct Pair {
    V value;
    K key;
    bool operator==(const Pair<K,V>& p) const {return p.key == key;}
};
```

The next definition creates a `TSimpleList` in which each item has a value `V` and a key `K`.

```
TSimpleList< Pair<int,double> > listOfItems;
```

We are using a `TSimpleList` instead of a `TIndexedList` here to illustrate a subtlety in template syntax. Notice there are extra blanks after the beginning angle bracket and before the final closing angle bracket. That last blank is critical, because it prevents the compiler from incorrectly treating the two closing brackets as the input operator, `>>`.

It is usually easier to compile and test nontemplate classes than class templates. In order to create a class template, first design a nontemplate specific case. After implementing and testing the nontemplate version, use it to design the class template generalization.

11.3 ▌ Runtime polymorphism

Overloading and templates provide a kind of compile time polymorphism. The compiler determines which overloaded function is being invoked by looking at the actual arguments in the call. The function call is "bound" to a particular function body by the compiler. The compiler also determines which template class is being instantiated by looking at the actual arguments of the template class. We call this compile time polymorphism because the decisions about binding and instantiation are made at the time of compilation.

C++ supports another kind of polymorphism called **runtime polymorphism**. Runtime polymorphism is similar to overloading in that it involves the ability to determine what code to execute for a single function call each time that function call is executed. Unlike overloading or templates, that decision is made during the execution of the program rather than by the compiler. It is a decision that can differ each time that particular function call is executed. In object-oriented jargon, runtime polymorphism means determining at runtime which method to execute when a message is sent.

Methods are functions. Messages are sent to objects. So determining at runtime which method to execute when a message is sent must have something to do with waiting until program execution to figure out the type of the object receiving the message. In C++ this can happen only in the context of inheritance and pointers. Before we begin to show you how runtime polymorphism is accomplished, we will remind you how pointers to base class types can be used.

Recall the `Door` class hierarchy from Chapter 10. The base class was `Door`. The class `LockableDoor` was derived from `Door`. The classes `CombinationLockDoor` and `PasswordDoor` were derived from `LockableDoor`. Figure 11.3 illustrates the `Door` class hierarchy.

Suppose the pointer variables p and q are defined as follows:

```
Door* p;            // p is type Door* (pointer-to-Door)
PasswordDoor* q;    // q is type PasswordDoor* (pointer-to-PasswordDoor)
```

We can give p and q legitimate values by creating objects for them to point to.

```
p = new Door;        // *p is a Door
q = new PasswordDoor; // *q is a PasswordDoor
```

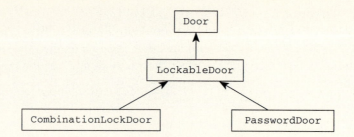

Figure 11.3 The hierarchy of classes derived from `Door`.

A `PasswordDoor` is a `Door`, and C++ builds in a special type compatibility to reflect that *is-a* relationship. The pointer `p` can point to not only a `Door` but also any instance of a class derived from `Door`, including a `PasswordDoor`. The following assignment is quite legal:

```
p = q;        // *p and *q are both names for the same PasswordDoor object
```

After that assignment is made, the type of `*p` is no longer `Door`, it is now `PasswordDoor`. Any variable that is a pointer to a base class type can be assigned the address of an object of a derived class type. In that sense, variables of type pointer-to-base-class are generic pointers within the class hierarchy.

We need to be careful when we talk about the type of `p` or the type of `*p`. The **static type** of `p`, which is the type given in the definition of `p`, is `Door*` (pointer-to-`Door`). However, when the program is executing, the type of `*p`, might not be `Door`. The **dynamic type** of `p` is the type of `p`'s referent—the object that `p` is pointing to. When this assignment is executed

```
p = q;
```

the type of `*p` is `PasswordDoor`. The dynamic type of `p` at this time is `Password-Door*` (pointer-to-`PasswordDoor`). When this assignment is executed

```
p = new LockableDoor;
```

the type of `*p` is `LockableDoor`. The dynamic type of `p` is now `LockableDoor*`.

The static type of a pointer is the type it is defined to be. The dynamic type of a pointer depends on the type of its referent. The dynamic type is pointer-to-referent type.

What does all of this have to do with runtime polymorphism? `Door` has a method named `open`. `LockableDoor` hides `Door::open()` by defining its own version. Keep in mind that at this time `p` has a static type `Door*` and dynamic type `LockableDoor*`. Which `open()` is invoked with execution of this statement?

```
p->open();   // alternate syntax is (*p).open()
```

Which method is bound to the function call? Did the compiler make the decision to call `Door::open()`? After all, `p` was defined as pointer-to-`Door`? Or, since `*p` is at this time a `LockableDoor`, was `LockableDoor::open()` called instead? Did the compiler make the decision about which method to invoke? Or was the decision made at runtime?

When the compiler decides which method to call, the decision is called **early binding** or **compile time binding**. If the decision is made when the program is executing, the decision is called **late binding** or **runtime binding**.

Even though `*p` is a `LockableDoor` object, the expression `p->open()` invokes the function `Door::open()`. The compiler provided the early binding of `p->open()` to `Door::open()` because the static type of `p` is `Door*`. That seems pretty bad, doesn't it? After all, you would think that sending a `LockableDoor` object a message would invoke the `LockableDoor`'s method. But the `Door` class hierarchy is defective in that respect. Fortunately, C++ has a special feature called **virtual functions** to avoid just that problem. Late binding occurs only with member functions declared as virtual in the base class. `Door` has no virtual functions. Runtime polymorphism is not possible in the current `Door` class hierarchy.

Virtual functions and runtime binding

Runtime polymorphism, the ability of an object to respond to the same message in several ways depending on the context, is achieved through inheritance and virtual functions. We will begin our explanation of virtual functions with a simple example, a counting class hierarchy.

`Counter` is the hierarchy's base class. A `Counter` can count. It can tell what its count is, print its count, and increment or decrement its count by 1. `Counter` has three virtual functions in addition to its constructor and two ordinary member functions. You can tell which functions are virtual functions by the keyword `virtual`, which precedes their declarations in the class definition.

```
// A simple counting class
class Counter {
public:
    Counter();                   // Constructs a counter set to 0.
    int value() const;           // Current counter value.
    void nvPrint() const;        // Prints the counter value.

    // virtual member functions
    virtual void print() const;  // Prints the count.
    virtual void increment();    // Increments the counter one unit.
```

```
    virtual void decrement();          // Decrements the counter one unit.
protected:
    int count_;
};
```

We declared the member functions `print()` and `nvPrint()` to illustrate the difference between virtual and nonvirtual functions. These two member functions do exactly the same thing when invoked via a `Counter` type object. They print the value of the data member `count_` to `cout`.

The fact that `print()`, `increment()`, and `decrement()` are declared as virtual does not change how they are defined or how they are used. Here are the definitions for the simple `Counter` methods:

```
Counter :: Counter() : count_(0)
{ }

int Counter :: value() const
{
    return count_;
}

void Counter :: nvPrint() const
{
    cout << "The count is " << count_ << endl;
}

void Counter :: print() const
{
    nvPrint();
}

void Counter :: increment()
{
    count_++;
}

void Counter :: decrement()
{
    count_--;
}
```

We will derive two different kinds of counters from `Counter`. The first derived type is `ModCounter`. It counts modulo a positive integer. For example, if the positive integer is 6, then the modulo counter counts from 0 through 5. If the value of its `count_` is 5 when a `ModCounter` object increments, its `count_` will become 0. If the value of its `count_` is 0 when it decrements, its `count_` will become 5. Here is `ModCounter`'s definition.

```
// A counter which does its counting modulo a positive integer base.
class ModCounter : public Counter {
public:
   ModCounter(int b = 10);  // Constructs a counter set to 0 to count modulo b
                            //   ASSUME: b > 1
   void nvPrint() const;    // Prints the values of the ModCounter.
   void print() const;      // Prints the values of the ModCounter.
   int base() const;        // Base value.
   void increment();        // Increments the count one unit modulo the base.
   void decrement();        // Decrements the count one unit modulo the base.
protected:
   int base_;
};
```

ModCounter has only one new member function, base(), which is not a member function of Counter. ModCounter declares its own versions of nvPrint(), print(), increment(), and decrement(), which are virtual functions in ModCounter even though the keyword virtual does not precede their declarations in the ModCounter definition. Any function that is declared virtual in a base class automatically inherits the virtual designation in any derived class. It is not necessary to declare it virtual once again in the derived class.

ModCounter::nvPrint() hides Counter::nvPrint(). That is no different from what you learned in Chapter 10. Any method declared in a derived class that has the same name as a method in the base class hides the base class member. But the three ModCounter methods print(), increment(), and decrement() override their base class counterparts also. **Overriding** is said to occur when a derived class defines a function declared in the base class and both of these conditions are met.

1. The base method was declared as a virtual function in the base class definition.

2. The derived class method is exactly the "same type function" as the base class method. That means the derived class method has the same return type, the same name, and the same formal argument list, and it is a const member function if and only if the base member function is also const.

Overriding is precisely what is necessary for runtime binding. We'll see what that means with respect to the Counter class hierarchy shortly. But first, let's look at the definitions of the ModCounter methods.

The constructor for a derived class automatically calls the constructor for the base class. No explicit initialization of count_ is necessary in the ModCounter constructor.

```
ModCounter :: ModCounter(int b) : base_(b)
{ }
```

`ModCounter::nvPrint()` and `ModCounter::print()` do exactly the same thing. They print the `count_` and the `base_`. The virtual function `print()` invokes the nonvirtual function `nvPrint()`.

```
void ModCounter :: nvPrint() const
{
   cout << "The count is " << count_ << " modulo " << base_ << endl;
}

void ModCounter :: print() const
{
   nvPrint();        // invokes ModCounter::nvPrint()
}
```

The member function `base()` merely returns the value of the data member `base_`. Both `increment()` and `decrement()` must do their arithmetic modulo the base rather than as ordinary integer arithmetic.

```
int ModCounter :: base() const
{
    return base_;
}

void ModCounter :: increment()
{
    count_ = (count_ + 1) % base_;
}

void ModCounter :: decrement()
{
    count_--;
    if (count_ < 0)
        count_ = base_ - 1;
}
```

Now let's see what virtual functions have done for us. Since virtual functions are used for runtime binding, we will start off with a couple of pointers:

```
Counter* p;                    // p's static type is pointer-to-Counter
ModCounter* q;                 // q's type is pointer-to-ModCounter
p = new Counter;               // *p is a Counter
q = new ModCounter(4);
for (int i = 1; i <= 8; i++)
   p->increment();
q->decrement();
```

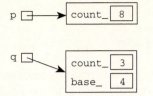

Figure 11.4 Dynamically created `Counter` and `ModCounter` objects.

At this time, `p->count_` is 8, `q->count_` is 3, and `q->base_` is 4. Figure 11.4 illustrates the current values of the objects and pointers.

The message `q->decrement()` invokes `ModCounter::decrement()`. That is no surprise. The output from these messages should not be surprising either.

```
p->print();     // output: The count is 8
q->print();     // output: The count is 3 modulo 4
```

But let's reassign p so that it points to the same object as q. After the assignment, the picture of memory changes to Fig. 11.5. (The old `Counter` object—the old `*p`—becomes lost memory.)

```
p = q;        // p's dynamic type is ModCounter*; static type is Counter*
```

With the assignment, the dynamic type of p becomes `ModCounter*`. Let's see how virtual functions and ordinary member functions are invoked through p.

The function `nvPrint()` is not virtual. When a `nvPrint` message is sent to p, the method invoked is the one corresponding to p's static type. The invocation of a nonvirtual function is bound at the time of compilation to the method of the base class. Nonvirtual functions have early binding.

The function `print()` is virtual. When a `print` message is sent to p, the method invoked is the one corresponding to p's dynamic type. The invocation of a virtual function is bound at the time of execution to the method of the derived class. Virtual functions have late binding.

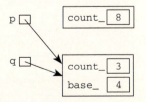

Figure 11.5 Memory after the assignment `p = q`.

```
// p now points to a ModCounter.
p->nvPrint();    // Counter::nvPrint
p->print();      // ModCounter::print
```

The output generated by the two printing messages is quite different. The one bound to the base class function gives just the `count_`. The one bound to the derived class gives the `count_` and the value of the `base_`. The following box shows the output:

```
The count is 3
The count is 3 modulo 4
```

Since `increment()` was declared as a virtual function in the base class, `Counter`, an increment message is bound at runtime to the current type of `*p`. Since `*p` is a `ModCounter` at this time, an increment message via `p` invokes `ModCounter::increment()`.

```
p->increment();    // ModCounter::increment
                   //   p->count_ becomes 0 (3 + 1 modulo 4 = 0)
p->print();        // ModCounter::print
```

The following box shows the output generated by that last `print` message:

```
The count is 0 modulo 4
```

Of course, we can also invoke `ModCounter::increment()` through q. Recall that q and p currently both point to the same object. And since q's static and dynamic type is pointer-to-`ModCounter`, then `print` and `nvPrint` messages via q have the same results. The output from this code is in the box that follows.

```
q->increment();      // q->count_ becomes 1
q->nvPrint();
q->increment();      // q->count_ becomes 2
q->print();
```

```
The count is 1 modulo 4
The count is 2 modulo 4
```

We said that we would derive two classes from `Counter`. So let's turn to the second one, the class `RangeCounter`. A `RangeCounter` can count only in a specific range—for example, from 10 through 100. If its `count_` is at the top of the range when a `RangeCounter` increments, the `count_` remains at the top of the range rather than cycling back to 0 like a `ModCounter`. If its `count_` is at the bottom of the range when a `RangeCounter` decrements, its `count_` remains at the bottom of the range rather than cycling up to the top.

```
// A counter that keeps its count within a fixed range of values.
class RangeCounter : public Counter {
public:
    RangeCounter(int b = 0, int t = 1000);   // Creates a counter set to 0 which
                                 //   counts from a minimum of b to maximum of t.
                                 //   ASSUME: 0 <= b <= t
    void nvPrint() const;        // Prints the values for the RangeCounter.
    void print() const;          // Prints the values for the RangeCounter.
    int top() const;             // Maximum possible counter value.
    int bottom() const;          // Minimum possible counter value.
    void increment();            // Increments the count by 1 up to the maximum.
    void decrement();            // Decrements the count by 1 down to the minimum.
protected:
    int bottomOfRange_;
    int topOfRange_;
};
```

The member function definitions are as follows. Again, remember that the constructor invokes the base class constructor to initialize members declared by the base class (the member `count_`.)

```
RangeCounter :: RangeCounter(int b, int t) : bottomOfRange_(b), topOfRange_(t)
{ }
```

The member functions `top()` and `bottom()` simply report the endpoints of the range.

```
int RangeCounter :: top() const
{
    return topOfRange_;
}

int RangeCounter :: bottom() const
{
    return bottomOfRange_;
}
```

Neither `top()` nor `bottom()` are virtual member functions of `Range-Counter`. They were not declared virtual and the base class does not have `top()`

or `bottom()` methods. Of course, `increment()`, `decrement()`, and `print()` are virtual functions in `RangeCounter` that override the corresponding base class methods.

```
void RangeCounter :: increment()
{
    if (count_ < topOfRange_)
        count_++;
}

void RangeCounter :: decrement()
{
    if (count_ > bottomOfRange_)
        count_--;
}
```

The only methods for `RangeCounter` that require any real design choices are `nvPrint()` and `print()`. This is what we decided:

```
void RangeCounter :: nvPrint() const
{
    cout << "The count is " << count_ << ", top of range: " << topOfRange_
        << ", bottom of range: " << bottomOfRange_ << endl;
}

void RangeCounter :: print() const
{
    nvPrint();
}
```

Before we do any more examples, let's expand the class hierarchy one more time. We'll define a special `RangeCounter` that can detect overflow (the `Range-Counter` receives an `increment` message when its `count_` is the maximum). The expanded class hierarchy is illustrated in Fig. 11.6.

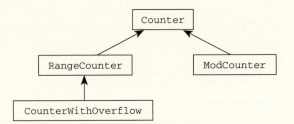

Figure 11.6 The `Counter` class hierarchy.

```
// A counter with a fixed range that can detect when an overflow occurs.
class CounterWithOverflow : public RangeCounter {
public:
    CounterWithOverflow(int b = 0, int t = 1000);
                            // Creates a counter set to 0 which
                            //   counts from a minimum of b to maximum of t.
                            //   ASSUME: 0 <= b <= t
    void increment();       // Increments the count by 1 up to the maximum.
    void print() print;     // Prints the current values.
    bool overflow() const;  // Has overflow occurred?
protected:
    bool overflow_;
};
```

CounterWithOverflow inherits the decrement() method from Range-Counter without overriding it. And it inherits the nvPrint() method from RangeCounter without hiding it. However, CounterWithOverflow does override the increment() and print() methods. Since increment() and print() were declared as virtual functions in Counter, they are automatically virtual in RangeCounter as well as every other class in the Counter hierarchy.

The definitions of the CounterWithOverflow constructor methods are as follows.

```
CounterWithOverflow :: CounterWithOverflow (int b, int t) : RangeCounter(b,t)
{ }

void CounterWithOverflow :: increment()
{
    if (count_ == topOfRange_)
        overflow_ = true;
    else
        count_++;
}
```

CounterWithOverflow::print() overrides RangeCounter::print(), but it can still invoke the RangeCounter method. It is a common C++ programming technique for functions in derived classes to invoke the corresponding base class methods to do some if not all of the work.

```
void CounterWithOverflow :: print() const
{
    cout <<"OVFL: ";
    RangeCounter::print();
}
```

```
bool CounterWithOverflow :: overflow() const
{
    return overflow_;
}
```

Let's see how virtual functions allow runtime binding in the Counter class hierarchy. Suppose that p is a pointer-to-Counter as before. This time, we'll define three objects rather than pointers to objects. The results of evaluating these statements are illustrated in Fig. 11.7.

```
// Counter* p;
RangeCounter rCtr(5,30);
CounterWithOverflow ovfCtr(-10,10);
ModCounter mCtr(8);
p = &ovfCtr;                    // *p and ovfCtr are different names
                                //   for the same CounterWithOverflow
```

We'll go through three segments of code that invoke virtual and nonvirtual printing methods. In the first, p points to a CounterWithOverflow.

```
for (int i = 0; i < 11; i++)
    p->increment();            // CounterWithOverflow::increment
ovfCtr.nvPrint();              // RangeCounter::nvPrint
p->nvPrint();                  // Counter::nvPrint
p->print();                    // CounterWithOverflow::print
```

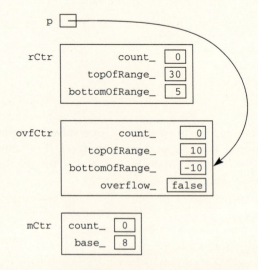

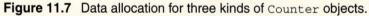

Figure 11.7 Data allocation for three kinds of Counter objects.

The first output that is generated is from the message `ovfCtr.nvPrint()`.
`CounterWithOverflow` inherits `nvPrint()` from `RangeCounter` without hiding.
When an inherited function is not hidden in a derived class, the compiler goes up
the hierarchy tree to find the closest ancestor class that defines the function.

The output from that last segment of code is in the following box.

```
The count is 10, top of range: 10, bottom of range: -10
The count is 10
OVFL: The count is 10, top of range: 10, bottom of range: -10
```

In the next section of code, `p` points to a `ModCounter`. The output that is generated is in the box that follows.

```
p = &mCtr;
for (i = 0; i < 3; i++)
    p->decrement();          // ModCounter::decrement
p->nvPrint();                // Counter::nvPrint
p->print();                  // ModCounter::print
```

```
The count is 5
The count is 5 modulo 8
```

Finally, `p` is assigned the address of a `RangeCounter` object. Again, the output
is in the box following the code.

```
p = &rCtr;
p->print();                  // Counter::print
rCtr.nvPrint();              // RangeCounter::nvPrint
```

```
The count is 0, top of range: 30, bottom of range: 5
The count is 0, top of range: 30, bottom of range: 5
```

Pointers and references are very similar but not quite the same. But polymorphism works with references as well as pointers. References are perhaps most frequently seen in formal argument types. So let's define a function with a `const Counter&` argument.

```
void print(const Counter& c)
{
    c.print();
}
```

Of course, having several functions named `print` does not present a problem. This last function is global. What do you suppose happens when we invoke it with different types of objects? Go back up to `mCtr` (a `ModCounter`) and `rCtr` (a `RangeCounter`) that we just defined.

```
print(mCtr);                    // Actual argument is a ModCounter.
print(rCtr);                    // Actual argument is a RangeCounter.
```

You can guess the output by now. Which `print()` method in the `Counter` hierarchy is invoked depends on the object with which it is invoked. It would be disappointing to find otherwise.

```
The count is 5 modulo 8
The count is 10, top of range: 30, bottom of range 5
```

Objects that are not dynamically created have the same static type as dynamic type. Invocations to member functions through such objects are bound to the methods of that class type at compile time. The message `mCtr.nvPrint()` is an invocation of `ModCounter::nvPrint()`, just as you would expect.

Overriding, overloading, and hiding

Virtual functions give us the versatility of not having to know exactly what type of object may receive a particular message. We know what the message is. But we cannot predict all that the receiving object will do in response to the message. The fact that we know what the message is restricts virtual functions to be part of a class hierarchy. They have no meaning outside of the context of inheritance.

Not just any member function can be virtual. Virtual functions cannot be static class members. Unlike static class member functions, virtual functions must be invoked through a specific class type object. That makes sense, because the object with which the virtual function is invoked determines which function in the class hierarchy is being called.

Virtual functions cannot be global (defined outside the context of any class). Overloaded operators can be virtual functions only if they are class members and not just friends of classes. In the `Counter` class hierarchy, we could not have overloaded the output operator in the ordinary way as a virtual function.

A function that is virtual in the base class is automatically virtual in a derived class. It is not an error if such a function is specifically declared as virtual in the derived class, but it is redundant. Many programmers, however, like that redundancy simply as a reminder to the user that the function is virtual. All virtual functions (except for pure virtual functions, which we discuss in Section 11.4) must be defined. This is true even if the programmer is certain ahead of time that the client code will not invoke the virtual function.

We mentioned before that a function that overrides a base class member must have exactly the same type as the base class method. Its declaration has to look identical—same return type, same name, same formal argument list, and both const or both nonconst. A function declared in the derived class with the same name but a different argument list merely hides the base class method and does not override it. The significance of hiding is that no polymorphism will take place for that method. The method invoked via a pointer will depend on the static type of the pointer, rather than on the type of the object it points to.

Consider the following definitions. One of the derived class members is illegal.

```
class Base {
public:
   virtual void f(int);
   virtual void g(int);
         void h(float);
};


class Derived : public Base {
public:
   void f(int);      // Overrides Base::f(int)
   void f(double);   // Overloads Derived::f(int), does not override Base::f
   char g(int);      // illegal. Return types must match for overriding virtual
                     //  functions.
   char g(char);     // Legal but does not override Base::g(int). Signatures
                     //   are different.
   void h(float);    // No overloading, no overriding. Hides Base::h
   void h(int);      // Legal since Base::h is not virtual. Overloads
                     //   Derived::h(float).
};
```

It is illegal for a function in the derived class to have the same prototype as a virtual function in the base class except for return type.

The terms overriding and overloading mean quite different things. Two functions that are overloaded must have the same scope and the same name but different signatures. Their formal argument lists are different or one of the functions is const and the other is not. A function declared in the base class definition has different scope from a function declared in the derived class.

> Is hiding bad? It can be. It is generally considered to be poor design practice to create a publicly derived class that hides some of the services of the base class.

Let's look more closely at hiding. When a base class method is hidden, that does not mean it cannot be invoked. It does mean that you have to use special syntax to invoke it—namely, the scope resolution syntax. For example, look at those last `Base` and `Derived` class definitions. `Base::h()` is hidden. But it can be invoked this way:

```
Derived d;
Base b;
b.h(3.14);          // Invokes Base::h(float)
d.h(3.14);          // Invokes Derived::h(float)
d.Base::h(3.14);    // Invokes Base::h(float)
```

That last bit of syntax does not look like the normal message-passing syntax. It is awkward for class users and best avoided.

"Arrays" of heterogeneous elements

Our examples so far have not aimed at showing just how useful runtime polymorphism can be. It has always been clear from our code fragments what the dynamic types of the pointer to the base class would be. It is when you cannot determine ahead of time what that type will be that late binding becomes impressive.

We'll continue to use the `Counter` class hierarchy as the basis for our next example. Suppose that you wanted to create a list of `Counter` objects—make that a list of objects of type `Counter` or of a type derived from `Counter`. All of the list items will be related by inheritance. But they will not be the same type. The list will be heterogeneous. It will not be homogeneous like the lists we have discussed in the past.

We have been talking about lists as design objects for a long time. But let's focus on implementation issues rather than design. We know how to use arrays to implement many different lists. In Chapter 6, we implemented a list's attributes with an array and an integer to tell how much of the array was occupied by list items. Since then, we have used those arrays and integer sizes as data members for classes. It does not matter if we think in terms of classes or not; we still need to come to grips with using an array as a buffer to hold the list items.

Suppose that we declare an array in this manner:

```
Counter countItems[300];
```

Then `countItems` is an array of `Counter`s. That is acceptable if all we want in the list are simple `Counter`s. Indeed, the following kind of assignment is even possible.

```
ModCounter hourClock(12);
countItems[0] = hourClock;
```

In making that assignment, some of the data that belong to `hourClock` will not be stored in the first array element. Slicing occurs. There is not enough room for both the `count_` and `base_` members of the `hourClock` in that first element. So `base_`, which is not inherited from `Counter`, is sliced away. Only the hour-Clock's `count_` member is stored in the array element.

Simply defining an array of `Counter`s is inadequate for storing a list of related types. We lose too much information for the different types of counters. The problem cannot be resolved by making the array elements larger either. Consider this array:

```
CounterWithOverflow ovfItems[300];
```

There is enough room in a `CounterWithOverflow` object to hold all of the data members of a simple `Counter` (as well as all other types of `Counter`s we have defined so far). The problem is that the assignment below is not legal.

```
Counter myCount;
ovfItems[0] = myCount;    // illegal
```

C++ does not know how to assign values to members of `ovfItems[0]` that are missing from `myCount`. The type compatibility in a class hierarchy is a one-way compatibility. It is possible to assign a derived class value to a base class object, but it is not possible to assign a base class value to a derived class object.

Arrays of objects simply will not work. But arrays of pointers to objects will. We can define an array of pointers-to-`Counter`. As you become more sophisticated in your knowledge and use of C++, you will appreciate being able to use pointers in many different contexts. And for this problem, pointers are ideal.

Let's define the array as follows:

```
const int max = 300;
Counter* array[max];
```

Each element in the array is of type `Counter*`. Each is capable of pointing to any type of object from the entire `Counter` class hierarchy. We will implement the data for a heterogeneous list by defining a homogeneous array of pointers. (All arrays are homogeneous. An array is a homogeneous aggregate.)

In order to define an array of class type elements, the class must have a null constructor. The null constructor is used to create each of the array elements when the array is defined. In order to define an array whose elements are pointers to a class type, it is not necessary for that class to have a null constructor. Pointers are data objects and not class or struct type objects. C++ provides a default null constructor for data objects.

Consider these assignments for the array pointer elements:

```
array[0] = new Counter;
array[1] = new RangeCounter(-5,10);
array[2] = new ModCounter(12);
array[3] = new CounterWithOverflow;
array[4] = new ModCounter(8);
```

Figure 11.8 illustrates the array and the dynamically allocated objects pointed to by its first five elements.

While it is possible to keep explicit track of the dynamic types of these pointers, there is no reason to do so. The virtual functions provide all the type-specific

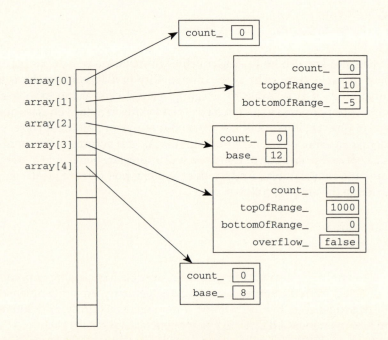

Figure 11.8 A heterogeneous list of counters.

behavior that we need. For example, we could send a decrement message to each of the counters.

```
for (int i = 0; i < 5; i++)
   array[i]->decrement();
```

Similarly, we could send a message for each counter to print itself.

```
for(i = 0; i < 5; i++)
   array[i]->print();
```

Again, given the code fragment that assigned the first five elements of array, the compiler ought to be able to tell the type of each object referenced by the pointer element. But the compiler will not always be able to tell the dynamic type of a pointer. Consider the following function as an illustration.

```
void silly(Counter*& p)
{
   int number;
   cout << "Enter a number ";
   cin >> number;
   if (number > 0)
      p = new RangeCounter(-100, 100);
   else
      p = new ModCounter(23);
}
```

The formal argument type is a pass-by-reference pointer. So even if we could see only the prototype for silly(), we would know that the call silly(array[5]) has the potential of changing the value of array[5]. As far as we can tell, the value can be changed to the address of any object which is in the Counter class hierarchy, or it can be changed to 0 (to stand for no address).

Look again at the function definition. Calling silly() involves creating a new RangeCounter object or a new ModCounter according to the whims of the user. The compiler has absolutely no way to predict the type of object that will be created. It does not matter. Look at these statements:

```
silly(array[5]);          // array[5] will point to a ModCounter or a
                          //    RangeCounter
array[5]->increment();    // Runtime binding to ModCounter::increment or
                          //    RangeCounter::increment
```

The message cannot be bound to a particular increment() method by the compiler because the compiler cannot anticipate the dynamic type of array[5]. For one execution of the program, the dynamic type of array[5] might be Mod-Counter. For a subsequent execution, the dynamic type of array[5] might be

`RangeCounter`. That is why runtime binding is so important. The compiler cannot always anticipate the type of an object even if it maintains fastidious bookkeeping about its pointer types according to the code. The compiler is not able to look into the future any more than the programmer is.

11.4   Abstract base classes

Inheritance can be used for many purposes. In the previous chapter, we used inheritance as an organizational tool and a specialization tool, to create special classes from base classes. The derived classes had additional features that were not present in the base classes—they were special forms of the base classes.

Now we use inheritance as a specification tool. We will show how to create a base class to specify the common interface for its entire class hierarchy—to show the behaviors of the derived classes. The public members of the derived classes will look identical (except for constructors, assignments, and destructors) to the public members of the base class. All of the classes in the hierarchy will appear the same, but they will have their own methods.

Many years ago, libraries loaned only books. Libraries still loan books. But now they loan much more. Many libraries loan journals and magazines, audio-tapes and videotapes, movies, movie and slide projectors, and so on. There is an almost endless variety of different kinds of items a library will loan to its patrons. Not only do libraries loan things besides books, but they do not treat all books the same. Some books, such as encyclopedias, are not available for loan outside the library. Some special libraries have rare books that only certain persons are able to peruse and handle.

We are going to design a class hierarchy of types of items a library loans. The base class, `LibraryItem`, will be a generic class. Since no actual item in a library is generic, it will not be possible to create an object of type `LibraryItem`. Instead `LibraryItem` will serve as a base upon which we can build several related types. These types have a single thread in common. They will all be types of items that a library might loan. The main purpose of `LibraryItem` is to specify the form of all objects that are library items.

`LibraryItem` will be used to derive other classes rather than for creating objects. Such a class is an **abstract base class**. It is impossible to create an instance of an abstract base class.

`LibraryItem` will have nonvirtual members function and member functions that are **pure virtual functions**, virtual functions that are declared with a special syntax but that are not defined. They specify the *what*, not the *how*, of object behavior. Any class containing pure virtual functions is an abstract base class. No objects of that type can be created.

Pure virtual functions are easy to recognize because of their unusual declaration syntax. The definition of `LibraryItem` shows how to incorporate virtual and pure virtual functions in the same class definition. It uses the `Date` type, which was first defined in Chapter 7 and then modified to more of a first class type in the exercises at the end of Chapter 8.

```
// Abstract base class for items in a public library collection
class LibraryItem {
public:
   LibraryItem(int period = 14);          // Initialized as not on loan,
                                          //  with the given loan period
                                          //  in days.
                                          //  ASSUME: period >= 0

   virtual ~LibraryItem();                // Destructor

   bool onLoan() const;                   // Is the item on loan?
   const Date& due() const;               // Date item is due.

   virtual void takeBack() = 0;           // Returns the item to the
                                          //   library.
   virtual void borrow(const Date& d) = 0; // Loans the item starting on
                                          //   date d if it is not already
                                          //   on loan.
   virtual void print(ostream& o) const = 0;  // Prints the loan period to o.

protected:
   Date dueDate_;
   const int loanPeriod_;
   bool onLoan_;
};
```

The `LibraryItem` member functions `borrow()`, `takeBack()`, and `print()` are pure virtual functions. Their declarations begin with the keyword `virtual` and end with the pure-specifier notation, `= 0`. The pure-specifier has nothing to do with assignment or the integer 0. That notation is simply the way of indicating the "pure" part of the pure virtual function.

One reason for declaring pure virtual functions is to spell out the services that every object created from this class hierarchy ought to be able to provide. By making them pure virtual, you defer defining them to the concrete derived classes. Abstract base classes define nonvirtual member functions in order to provide identical, inherited methods for all of the derived classes.

Constructors cannot be virtual for any class, whether the class is an abstract base class or not. Although they are not used to create objects, they are often called to initialize inherited data members of the derived class. Assignment operators cannot be virtual, either. Destructors can be virtual, in spite of the fact that destructors for base classes have different names from destructors for derived classes. In a class hierarchy, destructors usually are declared to be virtual.

Virtual member functions that are not pure virtual functions must be defined. The following definitions suffice for the member functions of `LibraryItem`.

```
LibraryItem :: LibraryItem(int period) : onLoan_(false), loanPeriod_(period)
{ }
```

```
LibraryItem :: ~LibraryItem()
{ }

bool LibraryItem :: onLoan() const
{
    return onLoan_;
}

const Date& LibraryItem :: due() const
{
    return dueDate_;
}
```

The `const Date&` return type specifies that the member function `due()` returns a reference to a constant `Date`. The object that is returned is the `Date` member of the object receiving the `due` message. This return type avoids creating a new `Date` return object as a return value. And it prevents the calling code from being able to modify the protected members of the object receiving the message.

Creating a class hierarchy from an abstract base class type

Until we derive nonabstract classes from `LibraryItem`, all of this talk of what its member functions do is irrelevant. First we will derive an ordinary `Book` class from `LibraryItem`. Then we will derive a `RareBook` class from the `Book` class.

Both the `Book` class and the `RareBook` class use the `String` type from Chapter 9 for their authors and titles. `Book` is a **concrete class** rather than an abstract class—it has no pure virtual functions. A class is concrete if instances of that class can be created. The definition of `Book` is as follows:

```
// A book available for loan from a library.
class Book : public LibraryItem {
public:
    Book(const char a[], const char t[], int p = 14);
                                // Creates a book with the given author a,
                                //    title t, and loan period p.
                                //    ASSUME: a and t are valid C-strings and
                                //       p >= 0.
    ~Book();                    // Deallocates dynamic memory.
    void borrow(const Date& d); // Borrows the book on the given date if
                                //    it's not on loan.
    void takeBack();            // Returns the book to the library.
    void print(ostream& o) const; // Prints the author and title to o.
protected:
    const String author_;
    const String title_;
};
```

Book has three const data members, author_ and title_, which it declares, and loanPeriod_, which it inherits from LibraryItem. The only way to initialize const data members is through an initialization list. It cannot be done through declarations in the body of the constructor. Initialization lists provide more than a mere convenience. The initialization list can initialize most members of derived classes simply by including calls to the constructors of base classes as well as class members.

The Book member functions borrow(), takeBack(), and print() are inherited from LibraryItem. We declared borrow(), takeBack(), and print() because we do not want them to be pure virtual functions in Book. If they were pure virtual functions in Book, then Book would also be abstract and we could not create any Book type objects. The declaration of borrow() in Book keeps it virtual but not pure virtual.

The Book constructor relies on the String and LibraryItem constructors to create a Book object.

```
Book :: Book (const char a[], const char t[], int p) : author_(a),
                                        title_(t), LibraryItem(p)
{ }
```

The Book destructor has an empty body. But that does not mean this code will generate memory leaks. When a Book dies, its destructor is called, the destructors for its individual data members are called, and the LibraryItem destructor is called. In addition, the destructors for its String data members author_ and title_ deallocate their character arrays.

```
Book :: ~Book()
{ }
```

The remaining member functions are fairly straightforward. The definition of borrow() uses the Date::advance() method to figure out the due date.

```
void Book :: print(ostream& o) const
{
    o << "Title: " << title_ << "\nAuthor: " << author_ << endl;
}

void Book :: takeBack()
{
    onLoan_ = false;
}

void Book :: borrow(const Date& d)
{
    if (!onLoan_) {
        dueDate_ = d;
        for (int i = 0; i < loanPeriod_; i++)
```

```
                        dueDate_.advance();
                onLoan_ = true;
            }
        }
```

Rare books are special books in any library. They must be protected against ordinary abuse that comes from everyday handling of books. Books that are very rare are kept in special rooms with carefully controlled temperature and humidity. Not everyone has access to such books. They are often reserved for special scholar patrons.

We will not try to incorporate all of that into our `RareBook` class, but we will prohibit a patron from borrowing a rare book overnight. A rare book must be returned on the day it is borrowed. Many rare books are rare because of their age. So the year of publication will be part of the information that initializes a `RareBook` object.

```
// A rare book in a library. A rare book cannot be loaned overnight.
class RareBook : public Book {
public:
   RareBook(const char a[], const char t[], int y);
                                // Creates a book with author a, title t,
                                //    published in year y.
                                //    ASSUME: a and t are valid C-strings
   ~RareBook();                 // Deallocates dynamic memory.
   void print(ostream& o) const; // Prints the author, title, and year of
                                //    publication to the stream o.
protected:
   const int yearOfPublication_;
};
```

The initialization list of the `RareBook` constructor shows how a rare book must be returned the same day it is borrowed. Look at the call to the `Book` constructor. The last actual argument, which stands for the loan period, is 0.

```
RareBook :: RareBook(const char a[], const char t[], int y):
                                Book(a,t,0), yearOfPublication_(y)
{ }

RareBook :: ~RareBook()
{ }

void RareBook :: print(ostream& o) const
{
   Book::print(o);
   o << "Year of Publication: " << yearOfPublication_ << endl;
}
```

To allow a library to loan more than books, we have derived `Tape` from `LibraryItem`. `Tape` is an abstract base class since it contains a pure virtual function, `print()`, which it inherits from `LibraryItem` but fails to override. From the `Tape` class, we can derive an `AudioTape` class and a `Movie` class.

```
// Generic audio, visual item for library loan.
class Tape : public LibraryItem {
public:
    Tape(int t = 60, int d = 10); // Initializes a tape with playing time t
                                  //   and loan period d.
                                  //   ASSUME: d >= 0
    ~Tape();                      // Deallocates dynamic memory.
    void borrow(const Date& d);   // See LibraryItem::borrow.
    void takeBack();              // See LibraryItem::takeBack.
protected:
    const int playingTime_;
};
```

If we look at the definition for `Tape` without regarding `LibraryItem`, it is not clear that `Tape` is an abstract base class. `Tape::borrow()` and `Tape::take-Back()` override `LibraryItem::borrow()` and `LibraryItem::takeback()`. However, `Tape` also inherits `print()` from `LibraryItem` without overriding it. Since `print()` was a pure virtual member of `LibraryItem`, it is also a pure virtual member of `Tape`.

Every `Tape` has a playing time, which is initialized by its constructor. Here are the constructor definition and the definitions of the member functions that are not pure virtual. Both `onLoan()` and `due()` are nonvirtual functions inherited from `LibraryItem`, and they need not be redeclared or redefined here.

```
Tape :: Tape(int t, int d) : playingTime_(t), LibraryItem(d)
{ }

Tape :: ~Tape()
{ }

void Tape :: takeBack()
{
    onLoan_ = false;
}

void Tape :: borrow(const Date& d)
{
    if (!onLoan_) {
        dueDate_ = d;
        for (int i = 0; i < loanPeriod_; i++)
```

```
                        dueDate_.advance();
                onLoan_ = true;
            }
        }
```

Since `Tape` is an abstract base class, no object of type `Tape` can be created. But the two classes that are derived from `Tape`, `AudioTape` and `Movie`, are not abstract classes. Let's start with the `AudioTape` definition.

```
// Audio tape which can be loaned from a library.
class AudioTape : public Tape {
public:
   AudioTape(const char a[], const char w[], int p = 60, int d = 4);
         // Creates an audio tape with artist a, work w, loan period d,
         //  and playing time p.
         //  ASSUME: a and w are valid C-strings and d >= 0
   ~AudioTape();                  // Deallocates memory.
   void print(ostream& o) const;  // Prints the AudioTape information to o.
protected:
   const String artist_;
   const String work_;
};
```

The `AudioTape` methods are easy to define. Destruction of an `AudioTape` deallocates memory the same way that destruction of a `RareBook` deallocates memory. The `String` destructor for the data members is automatically invoked.

```
AudioTape :: AudioTape(const char a[], const char w[], int p, int d) :
                                        artist_(a), work_(w), Tape(p,d)
{ }

AudioTape :: ~AudioTape()
{ }

void AudioTape :: print(ostream& o) const
{
   o << "Artist: " << artist_ << "\nWork: " << work_ << endl;
}
```

Audiotapes have artists and works, and movies have titles. Furthermore, we might expect a collection of movies for loan in a library would contain many foreign films. So `Movie` declares two data members, `title_` and `countryOf-Production_`.

```
// Movie which can be loaned from a library
class Movie : public Tape {
public:
   Movie(const char t[], const char c[], int p = 120, int d = 2);
               // Creates a movie entitled t, produced in country c, loan
               //  period d, and playing time p
               //  ASSUME: t and c are valid C-strings and d >= 0
   ~Movie();                        // Destructor.
   void print(ostream& o) const;   // Prints the Movie information to o.
protected:
   const String title_;
   const String countryOfProduction_;
};
```

Here are the definitions of the `Movie` member functions. They are similar to their `AudioTape` counterparts.

```
Movie :: Movie(const char t[], const char c[], int p, int d) :
         title_(t), countryOfProduction_(c), Tape(p,d)
{ }

Movie :: ~Movie()
{ }

void Movie :: print(ostream& o) const
{
   o << "Movie title: " << title_ <<
         "\nProduced in: " << countryOfProduction_ << endl;
}
```

Figure 11.9 illustrates the `LibraryItem` class hierarchy that we have just developed. Let's next look at some code that uses that class hierarchy.

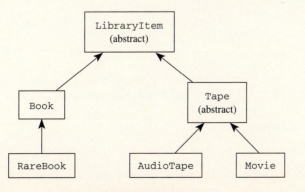

Figure 11.9 The `LibraryItem` class hierarchy.

```
LibraryItem* p;
LibraryItem* q;
RareBook tomSawyer("Mark Twain", "Tom Sawyer", 1876);
p = new Movie("The Graduate", "US");
q = new AudioTape("Bernstein", "Beethoven's 5th Symphony");

// Print all these library items to cout.
tomSawyer.print(cout);
cout << endl;
p->print(cout);
cout << endl;
q->print(cout);
```

The output should be just what you expect. The first output is generated by a message to the RareBook object, tomSawyer. The second output is generated by a message to a Movie. The third is generated by a message to an AudioTape. The box below shows what output is produced.

```
Title: Tom Sawyer
Author: Mark Twain
Year of Publication: 1876

Movie Title: The Graduate
Produced in: US

Artist: Bernstein
Work: Beethoven's 5th Symphony
```

To borrow some of these items, first set up a Date for today. We picked a date from a leap year.

```
Date today(27, 2, 1996);

// Borrow the movie
p->borrow(today);          // *p is a Movie with a loan period of 2 days
Date dueDate = p->due();   // The due date is February 29, 1996

// Now return it to the library
p->takeBack();
```

You can try out some additional code on your own. If you want to see polymorphism at work, you will need pointers or references.

Virtual destructors

Each class in the `LibraryItem` class hierarchy had its own destructor. Furthermore, the destructor for each class was defined with an empty body. So why did we bother to declare destructors in the first place? Why are they virtual? What did we gain through all of this?

Whenever an object is destroyed, either through deleting a pointer to it or when it goes out of scope, a destructor is called. If p is a pointer, then `delete p` invokes a destructor. Destructors supplied by C++ rather than the programmer are not automatically virtual. If p is a pointer-to-base-class type, and the base class does not have a virtual destructor, the base class destructor will be invoked when p is deleted, no matter what the dynamic type of p. The base class destructor may do the necessary cleanup of the data members for the base class, but it cannot do any such cleanup for data members that are not base class members.

When a destructor for a class that has class type members is invoked, the destructors for each of the class members is automatically invoked. This happens regardless of the definition of the destructor. So when `~Movie()` is invoked, the `String` class members of `Movie` are destroyed—the `String` destructor is automatically called for `title_` and `countryOfProduction_`.

Suppose p is of type pointer-to-`LibraryItem`. Consider the following assignment:

```
p = new Movie("Vertigo","US");
```

When a new `Movie` is created, two new strings are also created, `countryOfProduction_` and `title_`. The `String` class contains a single `char*` data member, and creation of a `String` allocates memory for a C-string. Figure 11.10 shows p and its `Movie` type referent.

The data member of `String` is named `info_`. It points to a dynamically allocated string of characters. When a `String` object is destroyed, the `String` destructor deletes `info_`, returning to available memory the array of characters. When a `Movie` is destroyed, its destructor automatically calls the destructor for its `String` members. So when p is deleted, `~Movie()` is invoked, which automatically invokes `~String()` for its two `String` members.

What would happen if `LibraryItem` did not have a virtual destructor? In that case, when p is deleted, the static type of p determines which destructor is invoked. `~LibraryItem()` would be automatically invoked instead `~Movie()`.

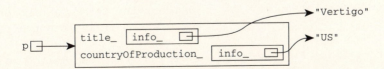

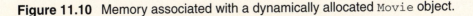

Figure 11.10 Memory associated with a dynamically allocated `Movie` object.

However, since `LibraryItem` does not contain any `String` members, `~String()` would not be invoked for the two members of `Movie` that are not members of `LibraryItem`. The result would be a memory leak. For this example, the arrays `"Vertigo"` and `"US"` constitute that lost memory.

> Always declare virtual destructors for any base class. When a pointer-to-base class is deleted, the destructor that is invoked depends on the dynamic type of the pointer instead of its static type. That ensures that the correct destructor will be invoked for the object that is the pointer's referent.

Base classes and static members

We could have designed the `LibraryItem` base class to include a counter for the number of items in the library. A convenient implementation of that idea is to declare a static `int` member of `LibraryItem` along with a member function that returns its value.

This is the alternate `LibraryItem` definition. The new static data member is private. Derived classes have no access to it. There is a static member access function that returns its value.

```cpp
// Abstract class of library items that maintains a total count of all items.
class LibraryItem {
public:
    LibraryItem(int period = 14);        // Initialized as not on loan,
                                         //   with the given loan period
                                         //   in days.
                                         //   ASSUME: period >= 0
    virtual ~LibraryItem();              // Destructor

    bool onLoan() const;                 // Is the item on loan?
    const Date& due() const;             // Date item is due.

    virtual void takeBack() = 0;         // Returns the item to the
                                         //   library.
    virtual void borrow(const Date& d) = 0;  // Loans the item starting on
                                         //   date d if it is not already
                                         //   on loan.
    virtual void print(ostream& o) const = 0;  // Prints the loan period to o.

    static int numberOfItems();          // Number of items belonging to
                                         //   the library.
```

```
protected:
    Date dueDate_;
    const int loanPeriod_;
    bool onLoan_;
private:
    static int sizeOfCollection_;
};
```

Static class members are not associated with any particular instance of the class. Static data members are shared data and static function members are shared behaviors. While it is impossible to create an instance of an abstract base class, it is possible to invoke static member functions of abstract base classes.

A class definition usually contains data declarations. But those declarations are not definitions. The definition and initialization of a static data member must occur outside the class definition. This is how `sizeOfCollection_` is initialized to 0. (The word `static` is not mentioned in the initialization.)

```
int LibraryItem :: sizeOfCollection_ = 0;
```

The definitions of the member functions and the assignment to static data members are usually placed together into the same source code file. The initialization is executed only once, before any statements in `main()` are executed.

Of course, the static member function from the new version of `LibraryItem` is defined in that source code file also. Even though `numberOfItems()` will not change any data, we did not declare it to be a const member function. C++ does not allow static member functions to be declared as const. (Again, notice that the keyword `static` is not part of the function definition.)

```
int LibraryItem :: numberOfItems()
{
    return sizeOfCollection_;
}
```

The responsibility for maintaining the counter `sizeOfCollection_` lies naturally with the `LibraryItem` base class. That is why `sizeOfCollection_` is private. Derived classes have no reason to change the counter. `LibraryItem` gives read-only access through its member function `numberOfItems()`.

Whenever a new object from the class hierarchy is created, `sizeOfCollection_` should be incremented. Whenever a new object from the class hierarchy is destroyed, `sizeOfCollection_` should be decremented. In light of that, we must redefine the `LibraryItem` constructors and destructor.

```
LibraryItem :: LibraryItem(int period) : onLoan_(false), loanPeriod_(period)
{
    sizeOfCollection_++;
}
```

```
LibraryItem :: ~LibraryItem()
{
    sizeOfCollection_--;
}
```

Even though a `LibraryItem` type object cannot be created, `LibraryItem` constructors and destructor are still called. A `LibraryItem` constructor is called whenever an object from the `LibraryItem` class hierarchy is created, whether it be a `Book`, a `RareBook`, an `AudioTape`, or a `Movie`. The `LibraryItem` destructor is called whenever such an object is destroyed.

> Constructors for derived types automatically invoke constructors for their corresponding base types. Destructors for derived types automatically invoke destructors for their corresponding base types.

Here is a short segment of code to illustrate the new static members of the base class. The output shown in boxes after the corresponding output statements.

```
LibraryItem *pp, *qq;        // pp and qq are pointers to LibraryItems
Book text("ABC's of Programming","Davis");            // Here's item #1.
pp = new Movie("Swamp Thing", "US");                  // Here's item #2.
qq = new AudioTape("Bob Dylan", "Nashville Skyline");  // Here's item #3.

cout << "Current item count: " << LibraryItem::numberOfItems() << endl;
```

```
Current item count: 3
```

```
// Now, we'll get rid of an item
delete pp;                                            // Kill the Movie

cout << "Current item count: " << LibraryItem::numberOfItems() << endl;
```

```
Current item count: 2
```

All of the counting takes place in the `LibraryItem` constructor and destructor. When an object in the hierarchy is created, the `LibraryItem` constructor increments the counter. When it dies, the `LibraryItem` destructor decrements the counter.

Warnings on use of abstract base class types

It is impossible to create an object that is of an abstract base type. Such an object cannot be defined, it cannot be dynamically created, and it cannot be created as a temporary object by the compiler. Abstract base class types cannot be used as pass-by-value formal argument or return types for functions.

Code that explicitly creates abstract base type objects through definitions or the `new` operator is illegal. Code that implicitly involves creating abstract base type objects is illegal. Here are some examples of illegal code. Remember that `LibraryItem` and `Tape` are both abstract base classes.

```
LibraryItem item(5);    // illegal. Cannot define a LibraryItem type object
Tape array[100];        // illegal. Cannot define an array of Tape objects
void f(Tape t);         // illegal. Cannot have a Tape argument
Tape g();               // illegal. Cannot have a Tape return type
```

Although we cannot use objects of abstract base classes, we can use pointers and references to abstract base classes. Unlike the last code, the following code is quite legal and ordinary.

```
Book pearl("Steinbeck", "The Pearl");
LibraryItem* p = &pearl;
Tape* q = new Movie("African Queen","US");
const Tape& f(int);
void g(LibraryItem& lib);
```

As we illustrated earlier, one way to implement a database of library items is with an array of pointers. The pointers can be used to create new library items or to reference library items that already exist.

```
LibraryItem* library[100];
```

The array can be manipulated much the same as the array of pointers to `Counters` from Section 11.3. The main difference is that `Tape` and `LibraryItem` type objects cannot be created.

If we have to be so careful not to attempt to create any abstract base class type objects, why should we even have abstract base classes to begin with? Why not simply avoid pure virtual functions altogether?

There are two good answers to this question. First, it may not make any sense to have an abstract or generic item. And an abstract base class prevents such an object from existing. But perhaps the most important reason for having abstract base classes is to create the same interface for collections of related types. The interface factors out those behaviors that characterize an object as an item for loan at a library.

Designing good base classes

The `Door` class was designed specifically to encapsulate attributes and behaviors common to all doors. It avoided details that are important to some doors but irrelevant to others. Not all doors can be locked. So the `Door` class had no member functions that were concerned with locks, keys, combinations, or passwords. The class `LockableDoor` represented special kinds of doors, doors with locks. Lockable doors have important additional behaviors that doors do not. A `Lockable-Door` is a special type of `Door`. Using inheritance to build special types out of base types is called **inheritance for specialization**.

One of the serious deficiencies of the `Door` class hierarchy was its lack of virtual functions. Polymorphism is simply not possible with that hierarchy. Most programmers would consider that a critical defect that must be remedied before the hierarchy can be of any real use. Of course, in this chapter we have focused a substantial effort on virtual functions and polymorphism.

The design of the `LibraryItem` class was more deliberate than the design of the `Door` class. The `LibraryItem` class was designed to incorporate *all* of the features of items in a library that are important to the library, or at least important to whoever is in charge of loaning out items. If the items had belonged to a bookstore instead, the resulting base class, `BookStoreItem`, would have a different set of member functions from those in `LibraryItem`.

The purpose of defining `LibraryItem` was not to be able to create special types of `LibraryItems` in the future. Instead, it was to provide a description of the behaviors of objects in the library's collection. As far as the library is concerned, every item (object) in its collection can do the following:

- Tell if it is on loan.

- Tell its due date.

- Return to the library.

- Borrow from the library.

- Print its attributes.

As far as the library is concerned, those are the only behaviors that matter. The `LibraryItem` class definition specified those behaviors. It indicated exactly what those behaviors are and the syntax for invoking them. It did not say how those behaviors were to be implemented.

Classes in the `LibraryItem` hierarchy do not have any behaviors beyond those described in the `LibraryItem` class itself. They may have different methods to implement their versions of the behaviors. But they do not have additional behaviors. The base class specified all of the behaviors.

Using a base class such as `LibraryItem` to specify all of the behaviors for classes in its hierarchy is called **inheritance for specification**. Base classes that are used for specification are usually abstract base classes. They are often used as items in lists or collections of different types of objects with the same behaviors.

11.5   Polymorphism and cloning for array-based lists

Most C++ programmers put their arrays within classes when using arrays to implement lists. If an array of pointers is put inside a class, however, we'll need to be especially careful about how we handle assignment, copying, and destruction.

Assignment and copying within a class hierarchy can be tricky. If p and q are pointers to `LibraryItems`, how can we make p point to a copy of q's referent? We do not really have any kind of copy method in the `LibraryItem` class hierarchy. But it is possible to create abstract base classes so that they provide a way of making a copy of an object—a clone of the object.

Rather than trying to modify the `LibraryItem` class, we will show you how to make a clone method in a very simple class hierarchy, the `Gift` class hierarchy. The new hierarchy will contain three classes: an abstract base class, `Gift`, and two concrete classes, `Candy` and `Flower`.

Each `Gift` has a price. Each `Gift` will be able to tell its price, make a clone of itself, and print its data.

```
// Abstract base class for simple gifts.
class Gift {
public:
   Gift(float p = 0);                       // Creates a gift with price p.
   virtual ~Gift();                         // Destructor.
   float price() const;                     // Price of the gift.
   virtual void print(ostream& o) const = 0;  // Prints the gift to o.
   virtual Gift* clone() const = 0;         // Copy of the gift.
protected:
   float price_;
};
```

The definitions of the member functions of `Gift` that are not pure virtual are easy to write. Of course, the method to clone an actual object must be defined in concrete classes derived from `Gift`.

```
Gift :: Gift(float p) : price_(p)
{ }


Gift :: ~Gift()
{ }
```

```
float Gift :: price() const
{
    return price_;
}
```

Here are the definitions of two derived classes, `Candy` and `Flower`.

```
// Gift of candy class
class Candy : public Gift {
public:
    Candy(const char kind[] = "Chocolate", float price = .75);
                                // Creates a Candy with the given name and
                                //    price.
    ~Candy();                   // Destructor.
    void print(ostream& o) const; // (See Gift)
    Gift* clone() const;        // (See Gift)
private:
    String kind_;
};


// Gift of flowers class
class Flower : public Gift {
public:
    Flower(const char name[] = "Rose", float price = 1.0, bool alive = true);
                                // Creates a Flower with the given name,
                                //    price, and live when alive is true.
    ~Flower();                  // Destructor.
    void print(ostream& o) const; // (See Gift)
    Gift* clone() const;        // (See Gift)
private:
    String name_;
    bool live_;
};
```

The definitions of the constructors, destructors, and `print()` methods are similar to those in the `LibraryItem` class hierarchy.

```
Candy :: Candy(const char kind[], float price) : Gift(price), kind_(kind)
{ }


Candy :: ~Candy()
{ }                             // Automatic call to the String destructor for kind_.

void Candy :: print(ostream& o) const
{
```

```
      o << "Candy: " << kind_ << endl;
}


Flower :: Flower(const char name[], float price, bool alive) : Gift(price),
                                            name_(name), live_(alive)
{ }

Flower :: ~Flower()
{ }                     // Automatic call to the String destructor for name_.

void Flower :: print(ostream& o) const
{
    if (live_)
      cout << "Live ";
    else
      o << "Dried ";
    o << "flower: " << name_ << endl;
}
```

The clone() methods are different from what you have seen before. Since
cloning returns a pointer to a Gift, each clone() method defines a Gift* and
dynamically allocates a new duplicate object.

```
Gift* Candy :: clone() const
{
    Gift* p = new Candy(kind_.charString(), price_);
    return p;
}

Gift* Flower :: clone() const
{
    Gift* p = new Flower(name_.charString(), price_, live_);
    return p;
}
```

Why did we bother to go to all of this trouble to create a new class hierarchy
with a cloning method? When can a cloning or duplicating method be useful? We
will answer these questions with an example that uses a special kind of list called
a stack. We will discuss stacks in more detail in the next chapter, but for now here
is a pretty good idea of what a stack is.

A stack is a kind of list in which all items are added to one end, called the top.
Items are also removed from the same end. In computer science lingo, items are
said to be pushed on the stack instead of added to the top of the stack. Items are
said to be popped from the stack rather than removed from the top of the stack.

The class StackOfGifts uses an array of pointers-to-Gifts to keep track of its
Gifts. The array of pointers allows us to have different kinds of Gifts on the stack.

```
class StackOfGifts {
public:
    StackOfGifts ();
    StackOfGifts (const StackOfGifts& s);
    StackOfGifts& operator=(const StackOfGifts& rhs);
    ~StackOfGifts();

    void push(const Gift& g);    // If the stack is not full, pushes g on the
                                 //   stack top. Otherwise, nothing occurs.
    Gift* top() const;           // Item on the top of the stack.
                                 // ASSUME: the stack is not empty.
    void pop();                  // Removes the top stack item.
                                 // ASSUME: the stack is not empty.
    bool isEmpty() const;        // Is the stack empty?
    bool isFull() const;         // Is the stack full?
private:
    enum {maxSize_ = 100};
    Gift* stack_[maxSize_];
    int size_;
};
```

The StackOfGifts null constructor and the destructor do not use the clone() method. The destructor eliminates some of the opportunities for lost memory by deleting all of the pointers in the array which point to stack items.

```
StackOfGifts :: StackOfGifts() : size_(0)
{ }

StackOfGifts :: ~StackOfGifts()
{
    for (int i = 0; i < size_; i++)
        delete stack_[i];
}
```

What would happen if there were no StackOfGifts destructor? Of course, C++ provides one when there is none, so what would the default destructor do? In this case, nothing in terms of the dynamically allocated memory. Although the default destructor calls the destructors for any class type members, there are no class type members of StackOfGifts. There is an array of pointers, but an array of pointers is not a class. It is not even an array of classes.

When a class has an array of pointers, it is a wise programming practice to include a copy constructor, an assignment operator, and a destructor. That is sound advice for any class with simply a pointer member too.

The copy constructor and the assignment operator for StackOfGifts use the clone() method to make copies of the individual Gifts.

```
StackOfGifts :: StackOfGifts(const StackOfGifts& g) : size_(g.size_)
{
   for (int i = 0; i < size_; i++)
      stack_[i] = g.stack_[i]->clone();
}


StackOfGifts& StackOfGifts :: operator=(const StackOfGifts& rhs)
{
   if (this != & rhs) {
      for (int i = 0; i < size_; i++)
         delete stack_[i];
      size_ = rhs.size_;
      for (i = 0; i < size_; i++)
         stack_[i] = rhs.stack_[i]->clone();
   }
   return *this;
}
```

The push() and top() methods use the clone() method. In the push() definition, clone() is invoked by a reference to a Gift. In the top() definition,
clone() is invoked through a pointer to a Gift.

```
void StackOfGifts :: push(const Gift& g)
{
   if (size_ < maxSize_) {
      stack_[size_] = g.clone();
      size_++;
   }
}


Gift* StackOfGifts :: top() const
{
   Gift* p = stack_[size_ - 1]->clone();
   return p;
}


void StackOfGifts :: pop()
{
   delete stack_[size_ - 1];
   size_--;
}
bool StackOfGifts :: isEmpty() const
{
   return size_ == 0;
}
```

```
bool StackOfGifts :: isFull() const
{
    return size_ == maxSize_;
}
```

The `StackOfGifts` class and the `Gift` class hierarchy are ready to use. Let's create a stack and a few gifts.

```
StackOfGifts yourPresents;                  // Empty stack of gifts for you

Candy gumBall("Gum Ball",.05);              // Not-so-extravagant gift
Candy boxOfCandy("Box of chocolates",6);    // Second gift
Flower daisy("Daisy", .5);                  // Simple gift

yourPresents.push(gumBall);                 // You have one gift now.
yourPresents.push(daisy);                   // Now you have two gifts.
yourPresents.push(Flower("Lily",2.3));      // Now you have a lily.
yourPresents.push(boxOfCandy);              // Now you have three gifts.
                                            // A box of chocolates is at
                                            //  the top.
```

Figure 11.11 shows the status of `yourPresents` at this time. There are four `Gift`s in the stack: two `Flower`s and two `Candy`s.

Now we can create more stacks of `Gift`s. The new `StackOfGifts` is named `myPresents`. The assignment that follows its creation will assign it a copy of `yourPresents`. That is the `clone()` method from the overloaded assignment

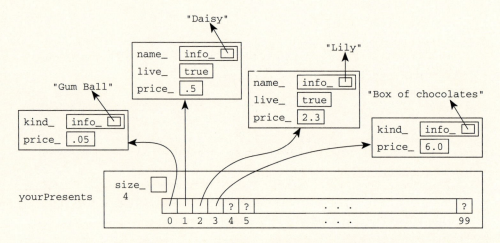

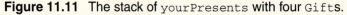

Figure 11.11 The stack of `yourPresents` with four `Gift`s.

operator at work. The two stacks will not share any data; their data will simply look the same.

```
StackOfGifts myPresents;          // Empty stack of gifts for me.
myPresents = yourPresents;        // Now my gifts are just like
                                  //   yours!
myPresents.pop();                 // I just lost a box of
                                  //   chocolates.
myPresents.top()->print(cout);
yourPresents.top()->print(cout);
```

The output from that last segment of code is as follows.

```
Live flower: Lily
Candy: Box of chocolate
```

We can create a `StackOfGifts` through a pointer. The next line of code is a definition and initialization using the `StackOfGifts` copy constructor.

```
StackOfGifts* hers = new StackOfGifts(yourPresents); // She has as many
                                                     //   gifts as you.
Gift* flowers = new Flower("Dozen roses", 45.99);
hers->push(*flowers);                     // Now she has a dozen
                                          //   roses, too.

hers->top()->print(cout);
```

The last line of code is a message to print the top item on "her" stack. And, of course, it is just what you would expect.

```
Live flower: Dozen roses
```

If you do not need all of those stacks, you can always delete `hers`. That does not effect either `yourPresents` or `myPresents`. None of the stacks share data.

```
delete hers;       // Her stack of gifts is gone.
hers = 0;          // Get rid of the wayward pointer value.
```

11.6 The changemaker, revisited again

It is time to reexamine the changemaker once again. That will give us an opportunity to illustrate a very important and powerful use of runtime binding and virtual functions. In particular, we will look at the role of the cash drawer object.

The cash drawer was used to simulate a real-world object that contains items of currency. Another example of such an object is a piggybank. Other examples include vending machines that give change, changemaker machines, and automated teller machines. For all of those objects, cash can be added and removed, change can be made, and there is a total amount on hand.

A different sort of "holder" of monetary value is a bank account with a total amount as the balance, but no specific coins or bills. Your bank account might have a balance of $123.45, but there are no actual bills or coins in the account, just the numerical amount of the balance. A bank account object can perform many of the same operations as a cash drawer. It can add or remove amounts. It can report its total values. In fact, ordinary transactions at a bank or automated teller machine usually involve both sorts of holders. For example, when we withdraw an amount from our savings account, not only does our account balance decrease, but also the teller's cash drawer has coins and bills removed from it.

The class `Repository`, whose definition follows, represents what is common to repositories of bills and coins, such as cash drawers, and to repositories of monetary value, such as checking accounts. It is an abstract class. (You can tell that because of the pure virtual functions.) Therefore it cannot be used to define an object, an instance of a `Repository`. Instead, `Repository` is meant to be a base class from which classes that can have instances are derived.

We designed `Repository` to be a more general kind of holder than indicated so far. A `Repository` may be a repository for any `MeasureSystem`, not just a `Currency`. But that will not concern us here.

```
// An abstract base class to represent a repository of measures.
class Repository {
public:
    Repository(MeasureSystem& m);   // Create a Repository with m for its system
                                    //   of measures.
    virtual ~Repository();          // Destructor.

    void safeDec(int t);            // Decrements the Repository by the amount
                                    //    t if the total Repository value is no
                                    //    smaller than t. Otherwise, the
                                    //    Repository  remains unchanged.
                                    // ASSUME : t >= 0
    void safeDec(const int a[]);    // If the Repository has enough of each
                                    //    measure, the amount of each one is
                                    //    decremented by the corresponding
                                    //    element of a. If not, the Repository
                                    //    is unchanged.
```

```
                                // ASSUME: a has as many elements as
                                // there are measures and each a[i] >= 0
    virtual void inc(int t) = 0;   // Increment the total Repository value by t.
                                // ASSUME: t >= 0
    virtual void inc(const int a[]) = 0;
                                // Increment the total value of the
                                //  Repository by the sum of a[i] times the
                                //  measure's value(i), where the sum runs
                                //  through all valid subscripts of a.
                                // ASSUME: ; a has as many elements as
                                // there are measures and each a[i] >= 0
    virtual bool enough(int t) const = 0;
                                // Is there enough to make up the total
                                //  value t?
                                // ASSUME: t >= 0
    virtual bool enough(const int a[]) const = 0;
                                // Is there enough of each value for the
                                //  corresponding element of a?
                                // ASSUME: a has as many elements as
                                // there are measures and each a[i] >= 0
    const MeasureSystem& getSystem() const;
                                // System of measures for this Repository.
    virtual int getValue() const = 0;
                                // Total value of the repository.
    virtual const int* getAmounts() const = 0;
                                // Amount of each measure.

protected:
    virtual void dec(int t) = 0;           // Like safeDec(int) except there's no
                                           //  check to see if the Repository has
                                           //  enough to do the decrement.
    virtual void dec(const int a[]) = 0;   // Like safeDec(const int[]) except no
                                           //  check to see if the Repository has
                                           //  enough.
    const MeasureSystem& measSystem_;      // System of measures.
};
```

The interesting and important use of runtime binding to be illustrated in this example involves the safeDec() functions, which are *not* virtual. The safeDec() functions are meant to decrement a Repository object (that is, to remove an amount from the Repository) safely. Suppose the Repository is a cash drawer. You cannot pay more out of a cash drawer than the total amount in the cash drawer. You cannot remove more of a particular denomination from a cash drawer than the cash drawer contains. "Safe" increments are not necessary. Our repository always has room for more of each measure. (With a very realistic repository class, there would be limits on the increment amounts also.)

Each `safeDec()` method first checks whether or not it can remove the desired amount. If so, it removes the amount. If not, it removes nothing. The algorithm for safe removal can be stated in terms of checking and removing.

```
void Repository :: safeDec(int t)
{
    if (enough(t))
        dec(t);
}

void Repository :: safeDec(const int a[])
{
    if (enough(a))
        dec(a);
}
```

Since `enough()` and `dec()` are virtual functions, what we have done is to describe a general method that can be polymorphic by sending the same `safeDec` message to objects from different derived classes in which the two virtual functions `enough()` and `dec()` have different definitions. In effect the message identifiers `enough` and `dec` are placeholders for methods that can be specified later—when classes are derived from `Repository`.

An `AmountsRepository` is a class from which we can create objects that simulate holders of coins and bills. The `measSystem_` member, which `AmountsRepository` inherits from `Repository`, describes the kinds of things that the holder contains. An `AmountsRepository` knows not only what kinds of items it holds but also how much of each kind of item it currently has. The `AmountsRepository` is responsible for maintaining those separate amounts. With that design decision, we decided to make the list of amounts a private member of the `AmountsRepository` class. The size of the list of amounts is part of the system of measures on which the `AmountsRepository` is based.

```
// A class to represent a holder of pieces of a measurement system (such as
//    different coins and bills that make up a denomination).
class AmountsRepository : public Repository {
public:
    AmountsRepository(MeasureSystem& m, const int* amounts = 0);
                                    // Create a Repository from m. If amounts
                                    //   is null, all measure amounts are set
                                    //   to 0. If not, measure amounts are set
                                    //   to corresponding elements in amounts.
                                    // ASSUME: amounts is null or has the
                                    //   same number of elements as
                                    //    the number of measures of m
                                    //    and each element is nonnegative.
    ~AmountsRepository();           // Destroy private data.
```

```
    int getValue() const;              // (See Repository)
    const int* getAmounts() const;     // (See Repository)

    void inc(int t);                   // Increment each repository measure by
                                       //   the amount computed by spreading t
                                       //   optimally among the measures.
    void inc(const int a[]);           // (See Repository)
    bool enough(int t) const;          // (See Repository)
    bool enough(const int a[]) const;  // (See Repository)

protected:
    void dec(int t);                   // (See Repository)
    void dec(const int a[]);           // (See Repository)

private:
    int* amts_;                        // Amount of each measure.
};
```

The `AmountsRepository` constructor creates an `AmountsRepository` with an initial amount of 0 for each measure of the associated `MeasureSystem`. The `AmountsRepository` destructor deletes the list of amounts to avoid a potential memory leak.

```
AmountsRepository :: AmountsRepository(MeasureSystem& m, const int* amounts) :
                                                              Repository(m)
{
    amts_ = new int[measSystem_.size()];
        for (int i = 0; i < measSystem_.size(); i++) {
            if (amounts == 0)
                amts_[i] = 0;
            else
                amts_[i] = amounts[i];
    }
}


AmountsRepository :: ~AmountsRepository()
{
    delete [] amts_;
}
```

The `inc()` and `dec()` methods are similar. Here are the definitions for the two `inc()` methods. (We'll leave the definitions of the two `dec()` methods as exercises.) The method `inc(int t)` sends a `change` message to the measure system to determine how to divide the total `t` among the amounts of the individual measures in the repository.

```
void AmountsRepository :: inc(int t)
{
    int* amounts = measSystem_.change(t);   // Increments for each measure.
    inc(amounts);
    delete [] amounts;                       // Avoid memory leaks.
}


void AmountsRepository :: inc(const int a[])
{
    for (int i = 0; i < measSystem_.size(); i++)
        amts_[i] += a[i];
}
```

The definition for enough(const int a[]) is very straightforward. The argument is a list of numbers. If the amount of each measure is at least as great as the corresponding number in the list, then there is enough of each measure in the AmountsRepository to deduct those numbers from the corresponding measure amounts.

```
bool AmountsRepository :: enough(const int a[]) const
{
    for (int i = 0; i < measSystem_.size(); i++)
        if (a[i] > amts_[i])
            return false;
    return true;
}
```

The definition for enough(int t) is subtle. The AmountsRepository must have enough of each measure to remove an amount whose total value is *equal to* t. For example, suppose that the AmountsRepository represents an ordinary cash drawer that is empty except for a two $10 bills. It is impossible to withdraw $2.75 from the cash drawer because the total contents of the cash drawer, $20, cannot be divided appropriately.

The AmountsRepository finds out if its collection of measures is adequate to remove an amount whose total value is t by asking its measure system, meas-System_. The measure system determines the list of amounts of each measure necessary whose total value is as close to t as possible without exceeding it. The calculation is restricted by the maximum amount of each measure currently in the AmountsRepository. After determining the list, the measure system calculates its total value. If the total value is t, then the AmountsRepository has enough to decrement a total of t from its collection of measures.

```
bool AmountsRepository :: enough(int t) const
{
    int* temp = measSystem_.change(t, amts_);
```

```
    int changeVal = measSystem_.unitVal(temp);
    delete [] temp;
    return t == changeVal;
}
```

Before we plunge ahead with another class in the Repository class hierarchy, let's step back and try to figure out exactly how the nonvirtual function safeDec() methods work. Suppose that piggyBank is an object of type AmountsRepository. Look at this message to piggyBank.

```
piggyBank.safeDec(275)
```

The safeDec message is not virtual. There is only one method to be invoked, and it was defined in Repository. Here is the code for that method:

```
if (enough(t))
    dec(t);
```

Both enough and dec *are* virtual. But remember that in order for runtime binding to occur the object receiving the message must be designated by a pointer or a reference. There *seem* to be no pointers involved in the safeDec() definition, which invokes enough() and dec(). So how can there be runtime binding? How can the correct methods be selected? Even though it looks as if no pointers are involved, there are. Remember that within the body of a member function of a class, other members of that class (data or functions) may be referred to simply by name. But that is a shorthand, a convenience. What the compiler understands by the shorthand call enough(t) is really,

```
this->enough(t);
```

There actually is a pointer involved in the invocation of enough. It is the this pointer, which is how any nonstatic member function can refer to the object for which it is invoked. The implicit this pointer refers to an object—the very object that received the safeDec message to begin with. In our situation here, this is a pointer to piggyBank.

Let's look again at the Repository class hierarchy. ValueRepository is another class that we will derive from Repository. ValueRepository represents a kind of holder such as a bank account. A bank account does not keep track of specific items of currency, but it does keep track of a total value (a balance).

```
// A repository to store total amounts without regard to how they might be
//  divided among various denominations.
class ValueRepository : public Repository {
public:
    ValueRepository(MeasureSystem& m, int b = 0);
```

```
                                        // Create a repository from m. The
                                        //   initial Repository value is b.
    ~ValueRepository();                 // Destructor -- does nothing.

    int getValue() const;               // (See Repository)
    const int* getAmounts() const;      // Always returns 0.

    void inc(int t);                    // (See Repository)
    void inc(const int a[]);            // (See Repository)
    bool enough(int t) const;           // (See Repository)
    bool enough(const int a[]) const;   // (See Repository)

protected:
    void dec(int t);                    // (See Repository)
    void dec(const int a[]);            // (See Repository)

private:
    int balance_;                       // Total value of the Repository.
};
```

Most `ValueRepository` member functions have simple definitions. The method `getValue()` returns the `balance_`. The method `getAmounts()` always returns 0. There are no individual measure amounts.

The `ValueRepository` methods with no arguments or with `int` type arguments simply examine or change `balance_` as needed. Those with array type arguments rely on messages to its system of measures to calculate values or lists of numbers.

```
void ValueRepository :: inc(const int a[])
{
    balance_ += measSystem_.unitVal(a);
}

bool ValueRepository :: enough(const int a[]) const
{
    return (measSystem_.unitVal(a) <= balance_);
}
```

It is easy to use the new class `AmountsRepository` as the type of a "cash drawer" variable in the changemaker program. In this version of the changemaker program, we named that variable `moneyBack`.

```
#include <iostream.h>
#include "measure.H"
#include "currency.H"
#include "repository.H"
```

```
//-------------------- Human interface component -------------------------
void inputInt(int& aNumber, const char prompt[]);
void outputResult(const int amts[], const MeasureSystem& curr);


//-------------------- teller object implementation -----------------------
void main()
{
    cout << "Change Maker (version 6)\n\n";
    int amountToChange;                   // Amount of money to be changed
    inputInt(amountToChange, "Amount to be changed in smallest units: ");
    AmountsRepository moneyBack(US);  // US is declared in currency.
    moneyBack.inc(amountToChange);
    outputResult(moneyBack.getAmounts(), moneyBack.getSystem());
}
//----------------- end of teller object implementation -------------------
//----------------human interface component implementation-----------------
void inputInt(int& aNumber, const char prompt[])
{
    cout << prompt;
    cin >> aNumber;
}


void outputResult(const int amts[], const MeasureSystem& curr)
{
    for (int i = 0; i < curr.size(); i++)
      cout << amts[i] << " " << curr.name(i) << endl;
}
//----------- end of human interface component implementation -------------
```

The object `moneyBack` is an `AmountsRepository`. Its associated `Measure-System` is a `Currency`—US currency to be precise—which is a special type of `MeasureSystem`. C++ allows us to use a reference to a derived class when a reference for base class is expected. So the `AmountsRepository` constructor is able to create an object using a `Currency` for the associated `MeasureSystem`.

Our implementation of the `Currency` class introduces a technique useful for creating and making available particular instances of a class as part of the class implementation. We have already experienced this phenomenon (perhaps without recognizing it) with the streams `cout` and `cin`. They are instances of classes `ostream` and `istream` respectively, and are declared in the file `iostream.h`.

Inside the implementation file (`currency.C`), we defined our base `Currency` instance US as follows:

```
static const int usSize = 8;
static kstring usDenoms[usSize] = {"pennies", "nickels", "dimes",
                       "quarters", "ones", "fives", "tens", "twenties"};
```

```
static int usValues[usSize] = {1, 5, 10, 25, 100, 500, 1000, 2000};
extern const Currency US(usSize, usDenoms, usValues, "US");
kstring const Currency :: baseCurrency = "US";
```

Here the role of the keyword static is to make the names it qualifies defined only within the one file (currency.C, for our example). The definition of US is const, meaning that it is not for the user to modify. It is extern, meaning that it is to be made available (by the linker) to any other file.

Our header file, currency.H, contains one additional declaration:

```
extern const Currency US;   // EXTERN gives any client using this header
                            // file access the US currency object
```

This makes the standard definition of US available to all clients. So we omit the definition of US that is present in the version of the changemaker program from Chapter 10.

The program that uses the computing object of the changemaker has not changed much over the course of this book. But how the design and implementation of that computing object have changed! We started out with an object that could compute change. We ended up with a hierarchy of types that could compute change and then some. The MeasureSystem and Repository hierarchies can be used to implement automatic teller machines, international banking systems that can maintain bank accounts and pay out cash in a variety of different currencies, piggybanks, and money belts. They can also be used outside of the context of currencies, translating among various measurement systems when that is desirable.

What we originally organized through a collection of functions with similar comments we have reimplemented as entire class hierarchies. Through inheritance and the polymorphism that inheritance provides, we have revised our solution to have vastly expanded functionality over the original one. The changemaker problem has served to illustrate some of the most important design and implementation principles of object-oriented program development.

11.7 ▮ Summary

Inheritance and polymorphism are the hallmarks of any language that supports object-oriented programming. Polymorphism in C++ comes in three forms: (1) function and operator overloading, (2) templates, and (3) dynamic typing of pointers and references to class type objects.

Templates are generic classes or functions that the compiler can translate into specific classes or functions. They provide for an infinite collection of similar classes or functions for which the programmer needs to write only a single definition. Class templates are parameterized types. Creation of an actual type for a class template by the compiler requires the programmer to fill in the actual parameters on which this version of the template is to be defined.

A more subtle form of polymorphism is runtime binding. This occurs only in the context of inheritance and virtual functions. A pointer to a base class type can point to any type object in the class hierarchy for that base type. When a message corresponding to a virtual function is sent to an object via a pointer or reference to that object, the type of the object (dynamic pointer type) rather than the declared type of the pointer (static pointer type) determines which function in the hierarchy of that name is called. The determination of that function can be made only when the program is executing. It cannot be anticipated by the compiler.

C++ uses static typing (typing determined at compile time) for the most part. But what C++ has over C and most languages is the possibility of dynamic typing in the special case of derived classes. That in turn makes it possible for a function invocation to call different functions for different executions of the program. The execution is tailored to the specific execution conditions.

This final and powerful type of polymorphism is not convenient (and in fact is seldom attempted) in traditional languages such as Pascal, C, and FORTRAN that do not explicitly support object-oriented programming. One of its benefits comes from reuse of code that uses runtime binding. A class hierarchy can be expanded by defining additional derived classes. The code that uses that hierarchy (sending messages via base class pointers) need not be modified in order to use the expanded hierarchy.

Glossary

abstract base class A class with a pure virtual function. No instances of an abstract base class can be created.

class template A template for a class definition. Class templates are preceded by the keyword `template`.

compile time binding A determination made at the time of compilation concerning which function of a given name is invoked. (Also called *early binding*.)

concrete class A class with no pure virtual functions. Instances of concrete classes can be created.

dynamic type (of a pointer) The type of a pointer's referent.

early binding *See* compile time binding.

function template A template for a function definition. Function templates are preceded by the keyword `template`.

inheritance for specialization Using inheritance to create special types from base class types.

inheritance for specification Using a base class to specify the behaviors of all classes in its class hierarchy.

late binding *See* runtime binding.

overriding Definition of a function in a derived class declared as a virtual function in the base class. (The definition of a function in a derived class with the same name as a nonvirtual function in the base class is hiding.)

parameterized type A definition capable of generating different types based on actual parameters.

polymorphism Using the same syntax to do different things depending on the context.

pure virtual function A virtual function in a base class that is not defined. It is declared using the symbol = 0.

runtime binding Deferral of the decision of which function of a given name is invoked until the time of program execution. Runtime binding occurs only with virtual functions and pointers or references. (Also called *late binding*.)

runtime polymorphism The ability of a pointer-to-base class type to cause invocations of different functions depending on the type of its referent.

static type (of a pointer) The declared type of a pointer.

template class An actual class definition generated by the compiler using a class template and a definition of an object of the template class type.

template function An actual function whose definition is generated by the compiler using a function template and an invocation of the function.

virtual function A function in a base class declared with the keyword `virtual`. Virtual functions can be overridden in derived classes.

11.8 ▌ Exercises

1. Consider the following function template.

```
template <class T>
void f(T& t)
{
    T y = t + 3;
    t += y;
}
```

  a. Write the definition of the template function that is automatically generated by the compiler when the following code is compiled:

```
double y = 17;
f(y);
```

  b. What are the restrictions on the actual type corresponding to `T`?

2. Write a function template for a binary search on an array to determine the subscript of an item in the array. If the item searched for is not an array element, the value returned is –1. Use the array element type as the template parameter.

  a. What are the restrictions on the actual array element type?

  b. Test out your definition by doing a binary search on an array of `String`s.

3. a. Write a function template named `maximum` that has two arguments of a comparable type (a type for which the operator < is defined) and that returns the larger of the two.

b. Write a function template named `max` that has two reference arguments of a comparable type and that returns a reference to the larger of the two.

4. Test the definition of the class template `TIndexedList` from Section 11.2 by defining a `TIndexedList` of `Strings` with a maximum capacity of 175 items.

5. Given the definition of the class template `TIndexedList` from Section 11.2, explain why the following code will not compile:

```
int listCapacity;
cout << "Enter list capacity: ";
cin >> listCapacity;
TIndexedList<double, listCapacity> doubleList;
```

6. Assume that the following class definitions have been given, with some of the member functions defined inline.

```
class A {
public:
   A() : aVal_(21)                            { }
   virtual void print(ostream& o) const {o << aVal_ << endl;}
   virtual void increment() = 0;
   void decrement()                           {aVal_--;}
protected:
   int aVal_;
};


class B : public A {
public:
   B() : bVal_(31)                            {aVal_++;}
   void print(ostream& o) const               {o << bVal_ << endl; A :: print(o);}
   void increment()                           {bVal_++;}
protected:
   double bVal_;
};


class C : public B {
public:
   C() : cVal_(41)                            {bVal_++;}
   void print(ostream& o) const               {o << cVal_ << endl; B :: print(o);}
   void increment()                           {cVal_++;}
   void decrement()                           {cVal_--;}
protected:
   double cVal_;
};
```

    a. Why are the following two lines of code illegal?

```
A a;
A* p = new A;
```

    b. The following function definition is illegal. Why?

```
void f(A aObj)
{
    aObj.decrement();
}
```

    c. Which of the following lines of code are illegal? For those that are not legal, explain why not. For those that are legal, explain the effect of executing them.

```
B b;
A& aRef = b;
aRef.decrement();
C c;
c = b;
aRef = c;
```

    d. What output is generated by execution of the following segment of code?

```
A* p = new C;
A* q = new B;
p->increment();
p->print(cout);
q->decrement();
q->print(cout);
```

  7. Suppose the following class definitions are given:

```
class AbstractBase {
public:
    AbstractBase()              { p_ = new int[5];
                                    for (int i = 0; i < 5; i++) p_[i] = i; }
    virtual ~AbstractBase()     { delete [] p_; }
    virtual int f(int) = 0;
    virtual void g(double z)    { p_[3] = int(z); }
    void h(int x)               { p_[x % 5] += x; }
protected:
    int* p_;
};
```

```
class FirstDerived : public AbstractBase{
public:
    FirstDerived() : x_(0)        { }
    ~FirstDerived ()              { }
    int f(int y)                  { p_[1] = y; return y + 1; }
    void g(double z);
    int h(int w);
protected:
    int x_;
};
```

a. Define `FirstDerived::g` so that it invokes `AbstractBase::g` with the argument z.

b. Define `FirstDerived::h` so that it invokes `AbstractBase::g` with the argument w and then returns x_.

c. Trace the following code. After each statement, indicate the values of the int data member and the array elements associated with each object.

```
FirstDerived one;
one.f(3);
one.h(one.f(4));
one.g(27.9);
```

d. Trace the following code. After each statement, indicate the values of the int data member and the array elements associated with each object.

```
FirstDerived* p = new FirstDerived;
p->g(12.3);
```

e. Are there memory leaks in the following code? Are there dangling pointers (pointers to nonexistent objects)?

```
FirstDerived* q = new FirstDerived;
p = q;
q->h(3);
delete q;
```

f. Are there memory leaks in the following code? Are there dangling pointers? Explain your answers.

```
FirstDerived two;
one = two;
```

8. Consider the following class definitions. (`AbstractBase` was defined in exercise 7.)

```
class SecondDerived : public AbstractBase {
public:
    SecondDerived()                          { q_ = new int[10]; }
    ~SecondDerived()                         { delete [] q_;}
    int f(int y)                             { q_[1] = y; return y + 1; }
    void g(double z)                         { p_[3] = int(z) + 1; }
    void h(int w)                            { p_[w % 5] = 0; }
protected:
    int* q_;
};


class ThirdDerived : public SecondDerived {
public:
    ThirdDerived()                           { }
    ~ThirdDerived()                          { }
    int f(int y)                             { q_[1] = y; return y + 1; }
    void h(int w)                            { p_[w % 5] = 3; }
};
```

For each of the following lines of code, tell all of the functions that are invoked when the line is executed.

a. `SecondDerived second;`

b. `ThirdDerived third;`

c. `AbstractBase* ptr = new ThirdDerived(third);`

d. `AbstractBase& ref = second;`

e. `ref.g(35.1);`

f. `ptr->g(35.1);`

g. `delete ptr;`

9. Electric appliances have certain features in common: They can be turned off or on; they have certain power requirements; they can be broken or functional; they have names, such as "refrigerator" or "table saw."

a. Design an abstract class that describes some common features of electric appliances. Put a virtual `print` method in the base class.

b. Build a class hierarchy from the abstract base class. Include in the hierarchy classes to represent kitchen appliances (such as ovens and dishwashers), shop items (such as power drills and saws), and office items (such as copiers and electric pencil sharpeners). How many abstract classes are in your hierarchy?

c. If your abstract base class does not have a `clone()` method, redefine it to include one. Then define `clone()` for each class in the hierarchy that is not an abstract class.

10. A static data member of a base class is shared by all objects from the class hierarchy. The static data member is a single piece of data, rather than one that is duplicated with every instance of the class. Suppose the following class definitions are given.

```
class A {
public:
    A()                           { totalCreated_++; }
    virtual ~A()                  { totalDestroyed_++; }
    static int current()          { return totalCreated_ - totalDestroyed_; }
    static int totalBorn ()       { return totalCreated_; }
    static int totalDied ()       { return totalDestroyed_;}
private:
    static int totalCreated_;
    static int totalDestroyed_;
};

class B : public A {
public:
    B()    { cout << "**** B::B()" << endl; }
    ~B()   { cout << "**** B::~B()" << endl; }
};

class C : public B {
public:
    C() { cout << "**** C::C()" << endl; }
    ~C(){ cout << "**** C::~C()" << endl; }
};

A* f()
{
    return new C;
}

void example()
{
    B bObj;
    C cObj;
    cout << "1. Number of alive objects = " << A::current() << endl;
    A* p;
    A* q;
```

```
    cout << "2. Number of alive objects = " << B::current() << endl;
    p = f();
    cout << "3. Number of alive objects = " << p->current() << endl;
    q = new C;
    q = f();
    delete p;
    cout << "4. Number of alive objects = " << q->current() << endl;
}
```

a. Write the definitions for the static data members of the base class so that they are initialized to 0. Where do those definitions appear?

b. Explain why different calls to base member function current() are legitimate.

c. What is the output of the following program?

```
void main()
{
    example();
    B bObj;
    cout << "main: Number of alive objects after B instance created = "
         << A::current() << endl;
}
```

11. This problem requires that you create a class hierarchy for banking accounts organized as shown by the following diagram.

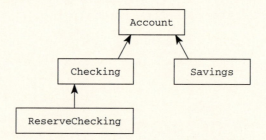

Many of the member functions in the class hierarchy are static. A static function in a class hierarchy can be invoked without an object. (Do not attempt to invoke a static function via a pointer to the base class.) For each part, define the class and methods described.

a. Abstract base class `Account`:

Data:	`balance_`	Account balance.
	`owner_`	Name of owner.
Methods:	`balance()`	Report balance.
	`owner()`	Report owner.
	`withdraw(float)`	Debit specified amount if possible (pure virtual).
	`deposit(float)`	Credit specified amount if possible (pure virtual).
	`addInterest(int)`	Add interest earned for specified days (pure virtual).
	`constructors`	Initialize member data.
	`destructor`	Is it necessary? You decide.

b. Class `Checking`:

Data:	`perCheckCharge_`	Charge per check (static).
	`badCheckCharge_`	Charge per bad check (static).
	`numAccounts_`	Number of checking accounts (static).
Methods:	`withdraw(float)`	Balance should not go negative (except for a bad check charge if required).
	`deposit(float)`	Credit amount to balance.
	`addInterest(int)`	Does nothing.
	`newCCheck(int)`	Set per check charge (static).
	`newBCharge(int)`	Set bad check charge (static).
	`totalAccts()`	Total number of checking accounts (static).
	`constructors`	Initialize member data; increment number of checking accounts.
	`destructor`	Decrement number of checking accounts.

c. Class `Savings`:

Data:	`interestRate_`	Annual interest rate (static).
	`period_`	Compounding period in days (static).

Methods:	withdraw(float)	Debit amount from balance if possible.
	deposit(float)	Credit amount to account.
	addInterest(int)	Add interest earned for specified number of days according to current rate and period.
	newRate(float)	Change interest rate as specified (static).
	interestRate()	Report the interest rate (static).
	setPeriod(int)	Change compounding period as specified (static).
	period()	Report the compounding period (static).
	constructors	Initialize member data.
	destructor	Is it necessary?

d. Class ReserveChecking:

Data:	maxReserve_	Maximum reserve available to cover negative checking balances.
Methods:	withdraw(float)	Debit balance if balance plus available reserve can cover amount. Otherwise, incur a bad check charge.
	deposit(float)	Credit balance with given amount.
	constructors	Initialize member data.
	destructor	Is it necessary?

12. Consider the class StackOfGifts from section 11.5.

    a. Write a class template TStack modeled on StackOfGifts. Make two parameters: the type of item in the stack and the maximum possible stack size.

    b. Write a segment of code to create a TStack of Gifts with a maximum stack size of 100 and a TStack of Appliances (defined in exercise 9) of maximum stack size 200.

13. Modify the Gift class from section 11.5 so that it contains a static private data member numberOfGifts_ and a static public member function numberOfGifts(). The data member tells how many gifts exist. The member function tells what that number is.

14. Lists that are implemented with arrays of pointers do not need explicitly to keep track of the number of elements they contain. In all of our examples so far, lists kept track of their current sizes through an int data member (named size_, of course). All array elements that do not represent items should be null.

    a. Define a new class, PList, which is based on an array of pointers to doubles. A PList can do five things: (1) add a new item; (2) remove the *n*th item (numbering start at 0); (3) tell the *n*th item; (4) tell the current size; and (5) tell the maximum size possible.

    b. Define an assignment operator, a copy constructor, and a destructor. The copy constructor and assignment operator should make deep copies rather than share dynamically allocated memory. The destructor should delete all of the array's elements.

15. a. Design a GiftList list with the same behaviors of the PList of the previous exercise. The items in the list are from the Gift class hierarchy, which was defined in section 11.5. Model the assignment operator, copy constructor, and destructor after the assignment operator, copy constructor, and destructor of the StackOfGifts class.

    b. Design a class template based on the GiftList class. The documentation of the template should include the restrictions on the array element type. (The element type must be a pointer in a class hierarchy with a clone method.)

16. Write the definitions of the members of Repository, AmountsRepository, and ValueRepository. Test your code to discover any mistakes in your implementation.

Programming Projects

17. The initial design of the Repository class declared both SafeDec() and dec() methods to return pointers-to-ints. The pointer returned would tell how the amount decremented was to be distributed over the different measures.

    a. What is the advantage of making that design decision? What is the advantage of declaring all of those functions to be void (as in the final version)?

    b. Change those functions so that they do return pointers-to-ints. Describe the return values for the ValueRepository class decrement methods.

    c. Rewrite the final version of the changemaker program to incorporate this design change. Does your final version have any memory leaks?

18. Solve the following problem:

    Grocery store customers are allowed to pay for their purchases with coupons, checks, cash, or checks for up to $25 over the costs of the grocery orders.

    The grocery store's cash registers are replenished when they run low on denominations. At the end of the day, each register is balanced to determine if the value of its contents match the total purchase value. Design a cash register for this situation.

19. Solve the following problem.

    Design an automated teller machine (ATM) that can dispense bills in either U.S. or Canadian currencies. Limitations on the bills dispensed are as follows:
    Canadian: $2, $5, $10, $20, and $50
    U.S.: $5, $10, and $20
    The ATM accepts deposits in Canadian currency only. Implement your design in C++.

20. Solve the following problem.

    The MidTown bank offers a variety of different accounts including ordinary checking, ordinary savings, checking with interest, checking with automatic reserve, and money market accounts. The bank needs a program to keep track of customer accounts.

    Accounts can be implemented as objects from a hierarchy similar to the Account class hierarchy from exercise 10.

Chapter 12

Container Classes and Linked Lists

A CONTAINER is an object that holds other objects. A typical example of a container is a list. A list of integers contains integer-type objects, and a list of names contains name-type objects. A list that is not empty contains a first item, possibly a second item, and so on. We have been discussing lists and their operations throughout this book.

Some containers are not lists. There may be no item in a container that is distinguished as the first item. Items in a container may not be in any special position. Different types of containers have different behaviors. A substantial body of knowledge in computer science is devoted to the design of different containers and their implementations. Solving a programming problem often involves selecting the appropriate container for the data that a program must deal with.

In this chapter, we will look briefly at several container types and look in depth at a special kind of container called a linked list. We will implement linked lists using C++ pointers, and we will implement other kinds of containers with linked lists.

This chapter introduces the computer science topic called **data structures**, the organization of data and operations that can be performed on that data. The study of data structures is an important topic for anyone learning the basic fundamentals of computer science.

12.1 ▍ Examples of containers

Consider the following scenario. Students who can register to take courses at a community college are required to pay tuition fees. Each student can register for several courses, and many courses have multiple sections.

How can we organize information pertinent to the students, teachers, and administration of the college? That depends to some extent on what is to be done with that information. We could think of several different problems that might need solutions:

- Keep track of which students have not paid tuition.

- Find out the teacher for a particular course section.

- Find out where and when a course section meets.

- Find out the number of sections of a particular course.

- Find out the names of students enrolled in a course section.

All of these problems involve the way information is organized or contained. Some information need not be stored directly, since it can be computed using other information. For example, the names of students in a single section form a **set**, a container in which all items are distinct. The set of names of all the students enrolled at the college can be computed by taking the union of the sets of names in the individual course sections. The registrar merely needs to find the set difference of the students enrolled in the college and the students who have paid tuition to find out the students who have not paid tuition.

A variation on this problem involves a **bag**, a container that may have duplicate items. Figure 12.1 illustrates the difference between sets and bags of numbers. Suppose each student's tuition is based strictly on the number of courses in which that student is enrolled. The registrar can compute the tuition for each student by forming a bag consisting of the names of students in each course section and determining the number of times the student's name appears in the bag.

Consider the problem of determining where and when course sections meet. Each course section is a "key" that is associated with one room and time "value." A **table** is a container used to represent associations between keys and values. Table operations include looking up the value corresponding to a particular key. One solution to the problem of determining where and when course sections meet is to create an appropriate table.

An **association** is a relationship between items in one container and items in another. A table can represent an association—the keys form one container and the values form the other. We can extend associations to more than single keys and values. For example, consider the problem of determining all of the course sections that use a particular room. The room is a single item, but it is associated with many items—all of the course sections meeting in that room. What about associations between students and teachers? A single student can have many teachers and a single teacher can have many students. For each student there is a set or bag of teachers and for each teacher there is a set or bag of students.

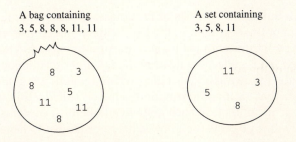

Figure 12.1 Containers: Bags and sets.

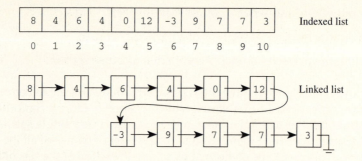

Figure 12.2 Containers: An indexed list and a linked list.

Sets, bags, and tables are containers, and so are lists. Containers can be implemented in many ways. We have already seen two of those ways: arrays (or classes with array members) and streams. In this chapter, we will focus on a popular data structure, the **linked list**. Each element in a linked list is a pair consisting of an item and the location of the next element. Linked lists are important because they are frequently used to implement many different kinds of containers, including sets, bags, tables, and lists.

A linked list is different from an indexed list, in which each item can be accessed through a unique index. An array is a natural implementation tool for an indexed list. Figure 12.2 contrasts linked and indexed lists.

There are almost endless variations on containers. Containers differ according to the types of objects they contain and the things they can do. Each kind of container can be represented in C++ as a class. The class data members represent the items in the container. The class function members represent the operations or behaviors of the container. In this chapter, we will design each of our containers to use a linked list as the underlying data structure to organize the objects in the container.

12.2   Linked lists and traditional linked list algorithms

Every item in a linked list consists of two pieces of information: actual list data and the location of the next item in the list. Items in linked lists are called **nodes**, which are data structures with values and one or more pointers to nodes. The first node in a linked list is called the **head node**. Each node contains information on the location of the following node—either where the following node exists or that it does not exist. That location information, which is called a **link**, is a pointer connecting one node to another. So each node in a linked list contains data and a link to the next node. It is possible for a linked list to be empty, to have no nodes.

The links of a linked list are the glue that hold the list together. A typical linked list convention is to maintain the location of the head node through a data object called the **head pointer**. So the head pointer gives access to the first node in the list, the link of the first node gives access to the second node, and so on. The link of last node in the list is null, indicating that no node follows that last node.

Consider again the items in a linked list. Each item contains the location or address of the next item. In C++, values that are addresses are most frequently represented by pointers. You may now think that linked lists always use pointers. But there are several ways to implement linked lists, and not all of them use pointers. When we discuss algorithms for linked list methods, we will discuss them in terms that can be applied to all implementations of linked lists, not just pointer implementations. We will use the language and terminology of pointers, however.

Linked list algorithms are the techniques that a linked list uses to implement its behaviors. We will describe the algorithms first by words and pictures. The code will come later, after we give definitions for implementing linked lists in C++.

Some of the most common list behaviors are as follows:

- Create an empty list

- Determine if a list is empty

- Find an item in a list

- Add an item to a list

- Remove an item from a list

In our discussion of linked list algorithms, we will use the term pointer to mean the location of a node or to mean a data object whose value is the location of a node. In addition, we will use the following terms for all of our lists and nodes.

- *head* is a pointer to the first item in the list, a pointer to the head node (if one exists).

- *null* is a pointer that does not represent an address. (In C++, null can be implemented by a pointer whose value is 0 or NULL.)

- *info* is a node's data.

- *link* is a node's link member (the location of the next node in the list, or null if there is no next node).

The links hold a linked list together in a single piece. The head pointer is the access to the first node in the list. If the head pointer or one of the links is corrupted, the integrity of the list will be destroyed.

As you write linked list algorithms, be careful when changing the value of a link or changing the value of the head pointer. If you lose one link, you lose the rest of the list, beginning with what that link was the address of. You will be unable to determine the last node in the list.

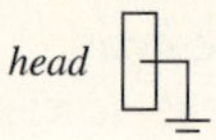

Figure 12.3 An empty list. The *head* pointer is null.

The algorithms for creating an empty list and for determining if a list is empty are easy to describe. An illustration of an empty list is shown in Fig. 12.3. To create an empty list, simply assign *head* the value *null*.

> *head = null*

To determine if a list is empty, check the *head*. If it is *null*, the list is empty.

> *if head is null*
> *   the list is empty*
> *if head is not null*
> *   the list is not empty*

Finding an item in a linked list involves at least a partial traversal of the list. Traversing a list means accessing each item in the list, starting with the first item. The linear search algorithm from Chapter 6 was a list traversal. That search was accomplished by iterating through the subscripts of an array.

A linked list does not have subscripts. But it is possible to go from one item to the next by following the link. Suppose p is a pointer to a node. Then *p->link* is a pointer to the next node if it exists, and *p->link->link* is a pointer to the node after that, if it exists. The last node in the list is indicated by the node whose link is *null*.

This sequence of steps will access each item in a linked list with three items (illustrated in Fig. 12.4). The pointer p is a traveling pointer that accesses each item.

> *p = head*
> *access p->info*
> *p = p->link*   *// equivalently, p = head->link*
> *access p->info*
> *p = p->link*   *// equivalently, p = head->link->link*
> *access p->info*

If access to the last node is followed by

> *p = p->link*   *// equivalently, p = head->link->link->link*

then p will be *null*.

Of course, that sequence of steps to traverse a linked list can be described as a loop. The loop body consists of an access step and the assignment to the traveling pointer, p. Since the last node in the list has a *null* link, the condition that determines loop body execution is: *p is not null*. So the following algorithm traverses a linked list, accessing each list item.

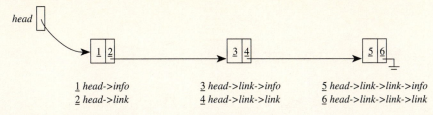

1 *head->info*
2 *head->link*

3 *head->link->info*
4 *head->link->link*

5 *head->link->link->info*
6 *head->link->link->link*

Figure 12.4 Pointers and nodes in a three-item linked list. Node member names are shown according to their corresponding labels.

> *define p as a pointer and initialize it to head*
> *while p is not null*
>   *access p->info*
>   *p = p->link*   // *p points to the next node in the list (or null if there is*
>   // *no next node)*

To find a particular item in a list, do a partial traversal. The loop condition is changed so that the loop is exited if *p* is *null* or if *p->info* is the item we are trying to find. Suppose that *x* is the name of that item. This algorithm will result in *p* being *null* or *p* pointing to the first node whose *info* is *x*. (If *p* becomes *null*, then *x* is not in the list.)

> *define p as a pointer and initialize it to head*
> *while p is not null and p->info is not x*
>   *p = p->link*

The algorithm for finding *x* in a list with four items is illustrated by Fig. 12.5. There are two iterations of the loop body. After the last iteration, *p* points to the node containing *x*.

All of the algorithms that add an item to a linked list require the creation of a new node to insert into the list. In our add algorithms, that new node will be created via the pointer *p*. The *info* for that new node will be *x*.

The algorithm to add an item to the beginning of a linked list is very simple. It requires that a new node be created, with *x* as its *info* and *head* as its *link*. (The old first node will become the second node in the list.) The *head* is then changed to point to the new node. The algorithm, which is illustrated in Fig. 12.6, can be described as follows:

> *define p as a pointer to a new node*
>
> // *Set the data and link members of the new node*
> *p->info = x*
> *p->link = head*   // *the link of the new node points to the old first node*
>
> //*Make head point to the new node*
> *head = p*

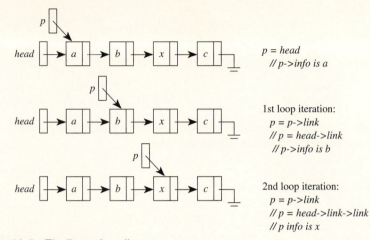

p = head
// p->info is a

1st loop iteration:
p = p->link
// p = head->link
// p->info is b

2nd loop iteration:
p = p->link
// p = head->link->link
// p info is x

Figure 12.5 Finding *x* in a list.

Adding an item to the middle or the end of a list is not as simple as adding one to the front. Often the new node belongs between two nodes that already belong to the list. Sometimes a new node belongs at the end of the list. A standard technique is to use a pair of pointers, *current* and *previous*, to traverse the list until the correct position to insert the new node is discovered. During the traversal, *previous* travels directly behind *current*—the node referenced by *current* appears immediately after the one referenced by *previous*.

Unless it belongs at the beginning of the list, the new node containing the data to be added to the list will eventually go between the nodes referenced by *previous* and *current* or at the end of the list if *current* becomes *null*. To place the new node between *previous* and *current*, follow these two steps.

1. Set the link of the new node to *current*.

2. Change the link of the *previous* node to point to the new node.

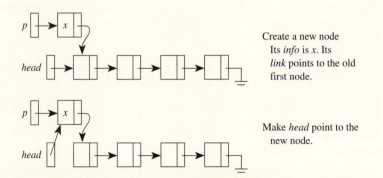

Create a new node
Its *info* is *x*. Its
link points to the old
first node.

Make *head* point to the
new node.

Figure 12.6 Adding an item to the beginning of a list.

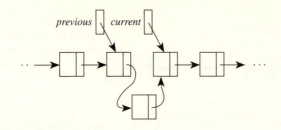

Figure 12.7 Placing a new node between the *previous* and *current* nodes.

Figure 12.7 illustrates the insertion process.

The criteria for selecting the correct position to add the new node depends on the organization of the list. The following algorithm adds an item to a list in which the data are in ascending order.

> *define p as a pointer to a new node*
> *p->info = x*
>
> *// Move current and previous through the list to find the correct position for the*
> *//   new item*
> *current = head*
> *while current is not null and current->info < x*
> *   previous = current*
> *   current = current->link*
>
> *// Insert the new item into the correct position*
> *if current is head*
> *   // The item is to be added to the beginning of the list*
> *   p->link = head*
> *   head = p*
> *else*
> *   // The item is not added to the beginning, insert it before current and after*
> *   //   previous*
> *   previous->link = p*
> *   p->link = current*

Figure 12.8 illustrates adding the number 8 into an ordered linked list consisting of 2, 5, 6, and 9. The new node will be inserted after the node containing 6 and before the node containing 9.

The add algorithm makes a special check to see if the new item belongs at the beginning of the list. It is not necessary to make the corresponding check to see if the new item belongs at the end of the list.

If the new item is to be placed at the end of the list, then the condition that terminates the loop will be: *current is null*. So the new node will have its *link* set to

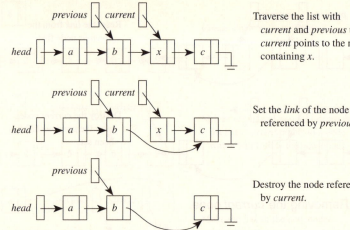

Traverse the list with
current and *previous* until
current points to the node
containing *x*.

Set the *link* of the node
referenced by *previous*.

Destroy the node referenced
by *current*.

Figure 12.10 Removing *x* from a list.

2. Is the algorithm correct if the item is to be added/removed/changed at the beginning of the list?

3. Is the algorithm correct if the item is to be added/removed/changed at the end of the list?

4. Is the algorithm correct if the item is to be added/removed/changed at the middle of the list?

Often the best way to develop a list algorithm is to draw a diagram of the algorithm. Test the algorithm via the diagram before translating it into code.

C++ Pointer Review

Suppose that T is a class type with a null constructor and a constructor with an integer argument. Suppose also that x and n are integers.

T* p	p is a pointer variable whose value can be the address of a T-type object or the address of an array of T-type objects.
p = new T	Creates an object of type T via T's null constructor and assigns its address to p. Memory for the new object is dynamically allocated at runtime rather than specified ahead of time by the compiler.

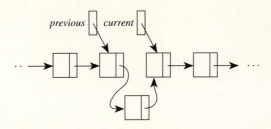

Figure 12.7 Placing a new node between the *previous* and *current* nodes.

Figure 12.7 illustrates the insertion process.

The criteria for selecting the correct position to add the new node depends on the organization of the list. The following algorithm adds an item to a list in which the data are in ascending order.

> *define p as a pointer to a new node*
> *p->info = x*
>
> *// Move current and previous through the list to find the correct position for the*
> *//   new item*
> *current = head*
> *while current is not null and current->info < x*
>   *previous = current*
>   *current = current->link*
>
> *// Insert the new item into the correct position*
> *if current is head*
>   *// The item is to be added to the beginning of the list*
>   *p->link = head*
>   *head = p*
> *else*
>   *// The item is not added to the beginning, insert it before current and after*
>   *//   previous*
>   *previous->link = p*
>   *p->link = current*

Figure 12.8 illustrates adding the number 8 into an ordered linked list consisting of 2, 5, 6, and 9. The new node will be inserted after the node containing 6 and before the node containing 9.

The add algorithm makes a special check to see if the new item belongs at the beginning of the list. It is not necessary to make the corresponding check to see if the new item belongs at the end of the list.

If the new item is to be placed at the end of the list, then the condition that terminates the loop will be: *current is null*. So the new node will have its *link* set to

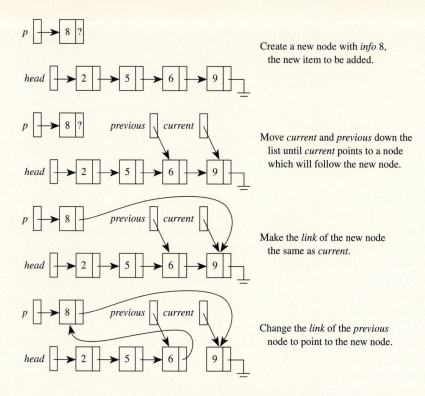

Create a new node with *info* 8, the new item to be added.

Move *current* and *previous* down the list until *current* points to a node which will follow the new node.

Make the *link* of the new node the same as *current*.

Change the *link* of the *previous* node to point to the new node.

Figure 12.8 Adding the item 8 to the ordered list 2, 5, 6, 9.

current, which is *null*. The *link* of the *previous* node, which was the last node in the list, will be set to point to the new node.

The algorithm for removing an item from a list uses a pair of pointers, *previous* and *current*, just as before. The two pointers travel in tandem through the list until *current* points to the node to be removed.

The removal algorithm begins with finding the first occurrence in the list of *x*, the item to be removed. That uses a traversal loop, with the pointers *current* and *previous* moving to the subsequent nodes for every iteration of the loop body. Eventually, *current* will point to a node containing *x*, or there will be no more items in the list left to search (*current* will be *null*).

If *x* is in the list, the node referenced by *current* must be destroyed. However, simply destroying that node at this point would corrupt the list. The remainder of the list that follows the *current* node would be lost. That is where *previous* comes in. Removing the node referenced by *current* is a two-step process, illustrated in Fig. 12.9:

1. Change the link of the *previous* node to point to the node after the *current* node (or *null*, if there is no node after the *current* node).

2. Then, destroy the *current* node.

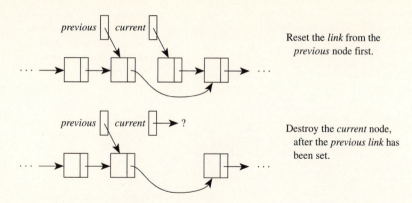

Reset the *link* from the *previous* node first.

Destroy the *current* node, after the *previous link* has been set.

Figure 12.9 Removing the *current* node.

The following algorithm removes the first node in a list whose *info* is *x*. If the list does not contain *x*, it does not change the list. The algorithm works correctly no matter where *x* is in the list.

> // Move current and previous through the list to find x
> current = head
> while current is not null and current->info ≠ x
>   // Move current and previous down the list
>   previous = current
>   current = current->link
>
> // Either current is null (x is not in the list) or current->info is x
> if current is not null
>   if current points to the first node
>   // Make head point to the second node (or null if there is none)
>   head = current->link
>   if current does not point to the first node
>   // Set the link of the previous node to point to the node after current
>   previous->link = current->link
>   destroy the current node

Figure 12.10 illustrates removing *x* from a list for the case in which the node containing *x* is not the first one in the list. When the node to be removed is the first one in the list, the pointer *head* must be changed to point to the second node in the list, or *null* if there is no second node.

It is all too easy to write incorrect algorithms for linked list methods. It is so easy to make a mistake. At a minimum, you should go through this series of checks for your linked list algorithms.

1. Is the algorithm correct if the list is empty?

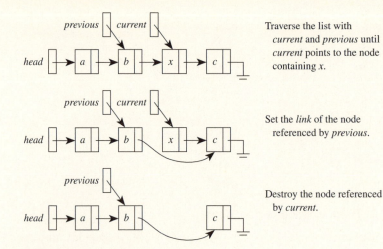

Traverse the list with
current and *previous* until
current points to the node
containing *x*.

Set the *link* of the node
referenced by *previous*.

Destroy the node referenced
by *current*.

Figure 12.10 Removing *x* from a list.

2. Is the algorithm correct if the item is to be added/removed/changed at the beginning of the list?

3. Is the algorithm correct if the item is to be added/removed/changed at the end of the list?

4. Is the algorithm correct if the item is to be added/removed/changed at the middle of the list?

Often the best way to develop a list algorithm is to draw a diagram of the algorithm. Test the algorithm via the diagram before translating it into code.

C++ *Pointer Review*

Suppose that T is a class type with a null constructor and a constructor with an integer argument. Suppose also that x and n are integers.

`T* p`	p is a pointer variable whose value can be the address of a T-type object or the address of an array of T-type objects.
`p = new T`	Creates an object of type T via T's null constructor and assigns its address to p. Memory for the new object is dynamically allocated at runtime rather than specified ahead of time by the compiler.

`*p`	The name of the newly created object. (p's referent.)
`p->funct()`	The notation indicates that `T` is a class or struct type with a member function named `funct()`. `p->funct()` is the alternate, preferred notation for `(*p).funct()`.
`p = new T(x)`	Creates a `T`-type object via the `T` constructor with an integer argument; the address of the object is assigned to `p`.
`delete p`	Calls the destructor for the object `*p` and deallocates the memory allocated to `*p`. (Does nothing if `p` is null.) This is appropriate only if `*p` was created via `new`.
`p = new T[n]`	Creates an array of n `T`-type objects, calling the null constructor for each object; the address of the first element of the array is assigned to `p`.
`delete [] p`	Calls the destructor on each array element and deallocates the memory allocated to the array. This is appropriate only if `*p` was created via `new[]`.
`p = 0`	Assignment to `p` of the null pointer, representing no address. (Equivalent assignment is: `p = NULL`)
`while (p) stmt`	The loop body executes as long as `p` is not null. (Equivalent loop conditions are: `(p != 0)` and `(p != NULL)`)

Errors occur if an attempt is made to dereference `p` when the value of `p` is not the address of an object.

12.3   Implementing a linked list type via `List` and `Node` classes

The items in a linked list are nodes and not simply list data. Our first task will be to define a `Node` class. One of its data members is part of the list data. The other is the address of the next `Node` in the list. In our `Node` class, that address will be a C++ pointer.

What member functions should the `Node` class have? There are many valid answers to this question. Surely there should be a constructor to create a `Node` from list data and the address of the next `Node` in the list (or null, if there is no next `Node`). Our `Node` class will also have a destructor and two access member functions, one which gives the actual list data in the `Node` and the other which gives the address of the following `Node`.

The remaining member functions are special. One adds a new next Node after this Node, thus changing the chain of nodes to which this Node belongs. The other copies the entire chain of Nodes that begins with this one.

```
// Node class: item type for a linked list of integers.
class Node {
public:
    void addAfter(int x);        // Add a new node containing x after this one.
    int info() const;            // List item for this node.
    Node* link() const;          // Address of the next node.
private:
    int info_;                   // List data value.
    Node* link_;                 // Location of next list node.

    Node(int i = 0, Node* p = 0);// Constructor.
    Node* copy() const;          // Pointer to a deep copy of this node.
    ~Node();                     // Destroys the chain of nodes after this one.
friend class List;
};
```

Nodes belong to lists. They are not generally useful in any other context. So the Node class contains a declaration of the List class as a friend. The constructor, the destructor, and copy() are all private members. As a result, no code outside the Node or List classes can create a Node from list data or delete a pointer to one. Nodes are not designed as general-purpose objects to be used by everyone. They are to be used only by Lists.

Private Node member functions: For Lists only

The Node null constructor allows a List (or a Node) to create a Node, initializing its data members with an integer and a pointer. Its definition has an initialization list and an empty function body.

```
Node :: Node(int i, Node* p) : info_(i), link_(p)
{ }
```

The copy() method is unusual. Suppose we call the Node receiving the copy message the target. Then copy() returns a pointer to a deep copy of the target—a pointer to new Node whose info_ is the same as the info_ of the target and whose link_ points to a deep copy of the Node following the target:

```
Node* Node :: copy() const
{
    if (link_ != 0)
        return new Node(info_, link_->copy()); // Send the copy message to the
                                               //   next node.
    return new Node(info_, 0);
}
```

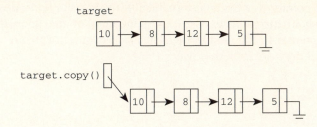

Figure 12.11 The Node named `target` and a deep copy of `target`.

`copy()` is a recursive function, returning a pointer to a dynamically created `Node`. The new `Node` has a pointer to a deep copy of the `Node` following the target. The value of that pointer is determined by sending a `copy` message to the node after the target: `link_->copy()`. That pointer, of course, points to another `Node`, with the same `info_` as the `Node` after the target and a deep copy of the `Node` that follows it. The entire copying process starts with the target, continues to the `Node` after the target, then to the `Node` after the `Node` after the target, and so on. It stops when a `copy` message is sent to a `Node` whose `link_` is null. The result is illustrated by Fig. 12.11.

Think of the original target as being the first `Node` in a chain of `Nodes`. A deep copy of the target duplicates that chain of `Nodes`. After a deep copy of the target is made, there are two disjoint chains of `Nodes` that have exactly the same `info_` values. One chain begins with the original target, the other with the copy of the original target.

A deep copy of a `Node` can be contrasted to a shallow copy. A shallow copy of a `Node` would be an exact duplicate of the `Node`, including the pointer. After making a shallow copy, there are two chains, but they share `Nodes`, as illustrated in Fig. 12.12.

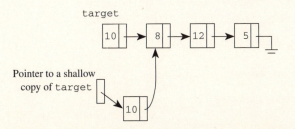

Figure 12.12 The Node named `target` and a shallow copy of `target`.

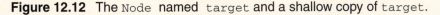

Deleting a pointer to a `Node` automatically invokes the `Node` destructor. The `Node` destructor in turn deletes the `link_` member of the `Node` that is being destroyed—a pointer to the next `Node`.[1] The `Node` destructor is a recursive function, although it does not look that way!

```
Node :: ~Node()
{
    delete link_;
}
```

The deletion of the `link_` member is a very powerful feature of the `Node` destructor. When a `Node` goes out of scope or when a pointer to the `Node` is deleted, the `link_` member of the `Node` is deleted. The result is that the following `Node`, the one pointed to by the `link_` member of the `Node` being destroyed, is also destroyed. And destruction of that following `Node` causes the `Node` after it to be destroyed. This process continues until a `Node` in the chain with a null `link_` member is destroyed. The entire process is illustrated in Fig. 12.13.

When a `Node` is removed from a list, its `link_` member should be made null before it is destroyed. Otherwise, all of the remaining `Nodes` in the list will also be destroyed.

The public member functions of `Node` are easy to define. They could all be declared as inline functions.

```
int Node :: info() const
{
    return info_;
}

Node* Node :: link() const
{
    return link_;
}

void Node :: addAfter(int x)
{
    link_ = new Node(x, link_);
}
```

---

[1] Destructors for node classes with pointer type data members should delete them as well as the links if memory leaks would occur otherwise.

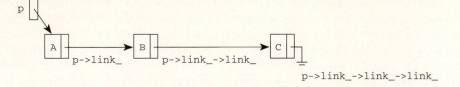

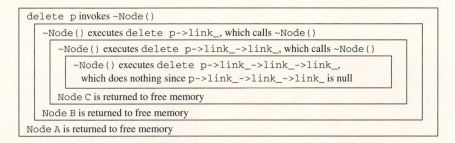

Figure 12.13 Deleting a pointer to a `Node` deletes all the pointers in the `Node` chain.

The declarations of `info()`, `link()`, and `addAfter()` as public makes them usable by any code that has access to a `Node`. You can think of `Node`s as belonging to `List`s. A `List` can prevent access to its `Node`s simply through its interface. A user of a `List` need not even be aware that the `Node` class exists.

Designing a simple `List` class

Design decisions for defining a linked list are the same as those used to define any list. What kind of list is needed? Is the list a simple list, with additions at the front and no removals? Are new items to be added to the end or to the front or somewhere else? Is the list to be ordered according to the values of its items ? Will the list be able to clear out all of its entries at once?

A list can be implemented in C++ with a class. The interface for the list—the information a programmer needs to know in order to create and use a list—is the class definition. The class methods implement the list behaviors. To a considerable extent, the methods determine what kind of list is actually being implemented. For example, if new items are always added to the front of the list, then the nodes in the list are not ordered according to the values of the list data.

We will start our examples of lists by considering lists of integer data. Our list may contain duplicate items. Our list will be able to add a new item to the front and remove the first copy of a particular item. Our list will be able to tell if it is empty and to tell if a particular item is a list member. Our list will contain its own iterator. (In the next section you will see an alternative to incorporating the iterator completely within the list.)

The class `List` implements a linked list consisting of dynamically created `Node`s. It has one data member, a pointer to the `Node` at the head of the list—the `Node` that has the first list item as its `info_` member. When we defined the `Node` class, we intended that it would be used only in a very limited context—only within the context of the `Node` and `List` classes, to be precise. However, anyone will be able to use the `List` class. So we were very deliberate in declaring a `List` copy constructor, a null constructor, an assignment operator, and a destructor.

Any class designed for unrestricted use that has a pointer member should have the following four members at a minimum:

1. A null constructor

2. A copy constructor

3. An overloaded assignment operator

4. A destructor that deletes the pointer member

A `List` will be able to construct itself as empty or as a deep copy of another `List`. Remember that a deep copy of a list is a duplicate of the list. A deep copy (as opposed to a shallow copy) protects against corruption of one list when the other is changed.

The overloaded `List` assignment operator assigns a deep copy of the right-hand operand to the left-hand operand. The `List` destructor deallocates all of the memory allocated to the entire list.

```
// List class: version 1
// List implements a list of integers. New items can be added to the front.
//     Items can be removed according to their values.
class List {
public:
    List();                       // Constructs an empty list.
    List(const List& old);        // Constructs a deep copy of old.
    ~List();                      // Deallocates all list memory.
    List& operator=(const List& rhs);// Assigns a deep copy of rhs.

    void add(int x);              // Adds x to the list.
    void remove(int x);           // Removes the first copy of x from the
                                  //   list, if it exists.
```

```
   bool isEmpty() const;            // Is the list empty?
   bool contains(int x) const;      // Is x a list member?

   // Iterator methods. (The iterator must be set to the first item before it
   //    is used and after the list changes.)
   void setIterator();              // Prepare to iterate from the first item.
   int next();                      // Next list item.
                                    //    ASSUME: There is a next item.
   bool more() const;               // Is there a next list item?

private:
   Node* head_;
   Node* cursor_;
};
```

Some of the methods for the List class will use the algorithms that we just presented in the previous section. We need merely to translate those algorithms into C++ code that is appropriate for the class and the method. Those algorithms used the same naming schemes as the List and Node classes. That is, a Node has two data members, info_ and link_. A List has a pointer called head_, whose value is the address of its first Node. It also has a pointer called cursor_, which the built-in iterator uses to access the list items.

List **constructors, destructor, and assignment operator**

The List null constructor creates an empty list by setting the head pointer to null.

```
List :: List() : head_(0)
{ }
```

The List copy constructor is more complicated than the null constructor. It makes a deep copy of the actual argument. When a List is created from another List, the two will share no Nodes in common. Instead, the newly created List will have newly allocated Nodes to hold its data.

```
List :: List(const List& old) : head_(0)
{
   if (old.head_ != 0)
      head_ = old.head_->copy();
}
```

The List copy constructor relies on the copy() method of the Node class to duplicate the Nodes in the original List. The constructor makes a copy of the first Node of the original List. Since Node::copy() returns a pointer to a deep copy, the entire chain of `Nodes` of the constructor argument, `old`, is copied. The `head_` pointer of the new `List` is assigned the pointer to the new copy.

The destructor for a `List` deletes the `head_` pointer.

```
List :: ~List()
{
    delete head_;
}
```

When a `List` is destroyed, all of its `Nodes` are also destroyed! Why? Go back for a moment to look at the `Node` destructor, which deletes its `link_` member. When a `Node` is destroyed, all of the `Nodes` in the chain following that `Node` are also destroyed. But `head_` is the pointer to the first `Node` of the `List`. And deleting `head_` automatically invokes the destructor for the first `Node` in the `List`. The destruction of that first `Node` results in the destruction of all subsequent `Nodes` in the `List`.

The `List` assignment operator relies on `Node::copy()` similar to the way the `List` copy constructor relies upon it.

```
List& List :: operator=(const List& rhs)
{
    if (this != &rhs) {             // If this List is not assigned to itself:
        delete head_;               //    Destroy all Nodes in this List.
        if (rhs.head_ != 0)         //    If the rhs is not an empty List, make
            head_ = rhs.head_->copy(); //      head_ point to a deep copy of rhs.
        else                        //    If rhs is an empty List
            head_ = 0;              //       make this List empty too.
    }
    return *this;
}
```

The assignment does nothing if the `Lists` on either side of the assignment operator are the same `List`. If they are not the same, the body of the selection statement is executed. The first expression, `delete head_`, destroys all the `Nodes` in the left-hand operand of the assignment. They will not be needed, so their memory is deallocated.

The remaining `if/else` inside the selection statement is almost identical to the definition of the `List` copy constructor. Again, notice how `Node::copy()` does all of the work. At the end of the assignment definition is the standard return of `*this`, the object for which the assignment is invoked.

List operations: `add()`, `remove()`, `isEmpty()`, and `contains()`

The `isEmpty()` method is very easy to code directly from the algorithm presented earlier in this chapter. If the `head_` pointer is null, the `List` is empty. If `head_` is not null, the `List` is not empty. It is that simple.

```
bool List :: isEmpty() const
{
    return (head_ == 0);
}
```

The `contains()` method uses a single pointer that is a local variable to traverse the list. (The pointer `cursor_` is reserved for use only by the iterator methods.) The traversal is written as a `for` loop, which is exited either when the traveling pointer becomes null or when the `info_` member of the `Node` pointed to by the traveling pointer matches the argument.

```
bool List :: contains(int x) const
{
    for (Node* p = head_; p; p = p->link_)   // p travels through the List to
        if (p->info_ == x)                    //   search for x.
            return true;
    return false;
}
```

The `add()` method is very simple. But it does not precisely mimic the algorithm presented earlier for adding an item to the front of a list. (Remember that these `Lists` add new items to the front only.) The `add()` method will take advantage of the `Node` constructor with default arguments. The default arguments allow the `List` to specify not only the `info_` but also the `link_` for a new `Node`. The `add()` method dynamically creates and initializes a new `Node` with the following data:

    `info_`: the actual argument to add to the list
    `link_`: the address of the first node in the `List` (the value of `head_`)

In the definition for `add()`, `head_` is assigned the address of a new `Node` containing the item to be added and the location of the previous first `Node`—the old value of `head_`.

```
void List :: add(int x)
{
    head_ = new Node(x, head_);
}
```

Although the definition for `add()` is simpler than the general linked list add algorithm that we gave earlier in this chapter, the definition for `remove()` looks almost exactly the same as the linked list remove algorithm. It uses two pointers, `previous` and `current`, to find the item to be removed and subsequently to remove it.

```
void List :: remove(int x)
{
    Node * current = head_;   // Eventually points to x, if x is in the list
```

```
   Node* previous;              // Trails current through the list

   while (current && current->info_ != x) {// Find x in the list.
      previous = current;
      current = current->link_;
   }

   if (current != 0) {                  // If x is in the list, remove it:
      if (current == head_)             //    If x is in the first node
         head_ = head_->link_;          //       change the head.
      else                              //    Otherwise set the link of the
         previous->link_ = current->link_; //    node preceding x.
      current->link_ = 0;               //    Destroy the node containing
      delete current;                   //       x but not the ones after it.
   }
}
```

Notice the way the Node whose info_ is x is finally destroyed. current points to it. Before deleting current, the link_ of that Node is set to null. Remember that the expression delete current automatically invokes the destructor for the Node that current points to. Without setting link_ to null, that would destroy all the remaining Nodes in the List.

An iterator implemented by List member functions

Our current version of the List iterator is implemented via three member functions of the List. The function setIterator() sets the list cursor_ to be the same as the head_ pointer. This is analogous to our previous array-based list implementations, where the cursor was positioned to the element with subscript 0.

```
void List :: setIterator()
{
   cursor_ = head_;              // Set the iterator's cursor to the beginning
}

int List :: next()
{
   int x = cursor_->info_;       // Error if the cursor is null!
   cursor_ = cursor_->link_;     // Advance the cursor to the next item
   return x;
}

bool List :: more() const
{
   return (cursor_ != 0);
}
```

The pointer `cursor_` is used exclusively by the iterator methods. This allows mixing iterator messages to a `List` with noniterator messages such as `contains`. But it does not allow having different `List` iterators. There is no way with the current `List` definition to iterate only through the positive data in a `List`, for example. For different iterators, we will need to take the iterator methods out of the `List` class itself and make them part of a separate class, a class that is a friend of the `List`.

Implementation decisions: Dynamic lists vs. arrays

Indexed lists and linked lists are important as both design objects and implementation objects. This chapter uses linked lists rather than arrays for the container class implementations. The choice of which to use is usually based on what performance characteristics are important for the problem being solved. Linked lists are more efficient at adding and removing items. (Not as much data needs to be moved around in memory.) If the list is ordered, arrays are more efficient for searching algorithms.

We have discussed two ways to implement list-type classes: one uses an array of data items, the other requires a linked list of nodes, each of which consists of a data item and a C++ pointer to the following node. Unless the array is created through a pointer, the memory to be allocated to the array is determined at the time of compilation. On the other hand, nodes for a linked list are created dynamically, as the program is executing. Linked lists are sometimes called dynamic lists for that reason.

The obvious question that we might ask is "Which implementation is better, arrays or nodes with pointers?" The answer is not so obvious. Each choice offers different benefits and drawbacks.

In order to create an array, we must anticipate how many items our list might contain in order to give a bound on the number of array elements. (This is true even if the array itself is created dynamically, through a pointer.) Fixed arrays cannot grow in size to accommodate larger lists.[3] They cannot shrink for small lists in order to free memory that could be used for something else. The memory allocated for an array is rigid. That is one of the major problems of using an array in a list implementation. The array does not change in size according to the size of the list.

The memory that is allocated for a linked list with nodes and C++ pointers is almost proportional to the number of data items in the list. A list with twice as many data items as another list requires almost twice as much memory as the other when both are implemented with nodes and pointers. When an item is removed from a list, the memory required to represent that item can be freed for other use. Of course, no computer has an infinite amount of memory. So it is a mistake to think that linked lists with C++ pointers can grow arbitrarily large in size. But the size of a linked list is flexible in terms of the amount of memory that is required to represent the entire list.

---

[3] The exception to this is with dynamically generated expandable arrays (see Chapter 9).

With the flexible size, why would anybody choose an array over a linked list with pointers to implement a list? Think about how a data item is stored in an array as opposed to a node. Each node of a linked list requires two distinct pieces of memory: one for the data item and one for the pointer. With an array, no additional memory is required for a pointer to accompany each data item. Each list item in an array requires less space than the corresponding item in a linked list. Array elements are smaller than nodes.

But the use of memory aside, there is another significant advantage that arrays have over linked lists. Arrays are subscripted, so each item in the list represented by an array is associated with a subscript. In order to examine the five hundredth item in a list implemented by an array named a, we merely need to look at a[499]. It takes the same amount of time to access the five hundredth element of an array as any other element. However, in order to examine the five hundredth item in a linked list, we must go through each item of the list, starting with the first one, counting along until the five hundredth item is reached. The ability to access any item of a list in the same amount of time, independent of where that item is in the list, is called **random access**. Arrays have random access to their list items, linked lists do not.

Random access is particularly nice for lists that are ordered. A binary search algorithm may be used to search for an item in an ordered list that is implemented as an array. A binary search is not possible for a simple linked list. There is no way to find the middle of an ordinary linked list in an efficient manner.

Even though memory may not be an issue for a particular list, you still should not assume that an array is the preferred implementation scheme. Complicated list operations such as adding an item, removing an item, and searching for an item may not be able to take advantage of an array's random access capability. Those operations depend on how the list is organized. If the list is a simple list, for example, all operations can be efficiently coded with either implementation. If the list is ordered by some intrinsic property of the list data, then a linked list implementation may offer a more efficient method for adding an item than an array implementation.

The method for adding a new data item to an ordered linked list is as follows. First, find where the item belongs, then create a new node for the item and place the new node where it belongs. Placing the new node where it belongs amounts to changing the pointer on the previous node and setting the pointer on the new node—two simple assignments. To place a new item in an ordered list implemented as an array, all of the items in the list that would appear after the new item are shifted by one subscript. That could amount to massive shifting of data rather than the creation of a new node and two simple pointer assignments. Removing an item from a list implemented as an array is a similar problem. The items after the one to be removed must be shifted by one subscript, potentially amounting to multiple assignments and moving large amounts of data. If an ordered list is to undergo many additions and removals, then it may be better to implement it as a linked list. If it is to undergo many searches instead, it may be better to implement it as an indexed list via an array.

There are many ways to structure data in order to optimize frequently performed operations. But there is no best way to represent all lists. When doing
a design, you shouldn't be thinking "Do I need an array or a linked list?"
Instead, think "What kind of container class do I want?" When it comes to
implementation, then you can ask the question "Does an array match the
container class better than a linked list?"

12.4   Iterator classes

In all of the list classes we have defined so far, we have implemented the iterator
as part of the class itself. An unfortunate result of this implementation technique is
that it is impossible to iterate over a constant list. Perhaps a more serious result is
that each list has exactly one iterator. There is only one way to go through a list,
starting with the first item and passing through each item as it appears in the list.
But sometimes it is helpful to iterate in different ways. You might need an iterator
that starts with the last item of the list and ends with the first, rather than going
from first to last. You might need an iterator for items that satisfy particular criteria. You might want an iterator that can go back one item in addition to going forward one item.

It is a well-established C++ programming practice to implement list iterators
as friends of classes rather than incorporate them directly into the list classes. That
is what we will present in this section. Our iterators will not change the status of a
list, but they can be used simply to access the list items. This is not a uniform practice, however. Some programmers use iterators to manage a list, including inserting and removing list items.

The original `Node` class needs no change in order to accommodate the new
`Iterator` class. (That is because the `Node` class contains the member functions
`link()` and `info()`, which return the values of the data members of a `Node`.) The
`List` class must change, however. The new version of the `List` class definition is
shorter than the original version. The iterator function declarations are replaced
by an `Iterator` friend declaration. And the iterator pointer, `cursor_`, that was
originally declared as part of the `List` is eliminated as a `List` data member.

We anticipated using `List` as a base class for other kinds of lists. The private
member `head` from the old version is changed to protected in the new version.

The new version of the `List` class can use the same definitions for its member
functions that the original version of the `List` class used. We will not repeat those
definitions here.

```
// List class: version 2
class List {
```

```
public:
    List();                          // Constructs an empty list.
    List(const List& old);           // Constructs a deep copy of old.
    List& operator=(const List& rhs); // Assigns a deep copy of rhs.
    ~List();                         // Deallocates list resources.

    virtual void add(int x);         // Adds x to the list.
    void remove(int x);              // Removes the first copy of x, if it
                                     //   exists.
    bool isEmpty() const;            // Is the list empty?
    bool contains(int x) const;      // Is x a list item?

friend class Iterator;
protected:
    Node* head_;
};
```

Recall that models for object-oriented solutions to programming problems consist of objects and components. A component is a collection of related objects. A list and its associated iterators provide a nice example of a component. The list is one object. Each iterator is another. And, of course, they are intimately related. A list iterator is tied to the list on which it acts.

The Iterator class will provide the same functionality as the iterator behaviors that were part of the original version of the List class—setting the iterator to the beginning of the list, getting the next item, and determining if there is another item. Each Iterator has a protected member, theList_, which is a constant reference to the particular list with which this iterator is associated. That makes an Iterator capable of iterating over a const List.

```
// Iterates over all items in a list of integers. If the list is
//   altered after the iterator is created, the iterator should be reset
//   before using it again.
class Iterator {
public:
    Iterator(const List& aList);  // Constructs an iterator for aList.
                                  //   Prepares the iterator to get the first
                                  //   item (if it exists).
    int next();                   // Next list item.
                                  //   ASSUME: There is a next item.
    bool more() const;            // Is there another item?
    void reset();                 // Reset to the first item (if one exists).
protected:
    const Node* cursor_;
    const List& theList_;
};
```

The single `Iterator` constructor requires the associated `List` for its only argument. It is impossible to create an `Iterator` without a `List`. The constructor initializes `cursor_` to point to the first item in its list. Since `cursor_` is a const pointer, it cannot be used to change the actual `List` argument. Since `theList_` is a const reference, it cannot be used to change the actual `List` argument either.

```
Iterator :: Iterator(const List& aList) : theList_(aList),
                                          cursor_(aList.head_)
{ }
```

Both the constructor and the member function `reset()` position `cursor_` to begin iteration from the beginning of the list. If the list is empty, `cursor_` will be set to null. When the associated list is modified, `cursor_` has the potential to become invalid. The class documentation warns that the iterator should be reset before any further attempt to use it. (Suppose the modification destroyed the node pointed to by `cursor_`. The value of `cursor_` in that case becomes meaningless if not downright harmful.)

```
void Iterator :: reset()
{
    cursor_ = theList_.head_;
}
```

The definitions for `Iterator::next()` and `Iterator::more()` are almost identical to the `List::next()` and `List::more()` definitions from the original version of the `List` class. Since `Iterator` is not a friend of `Node`, the new definitions use the `Node` member functions `info()` and `link()` rather than the private `Node` data members `info_` and `link_`.

```
int Iterator :: next()
{
    int x = cursor_->info();
    cursor_ = cursor_->link();
    return x;
}

bool Iterator :: more() const
{
    return (cursor_ != 0);
}
```

Figure 12.14 shows the relationship between a `List` and a corresponding `Iterator` that could be created through execution of the following code.

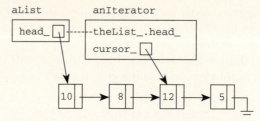

Figure 12.14 `aList` and `anIterator` are aliases for `aList.aList` and `anIt-erator.theList_`. Their `head_` pointers are the same pointer.

```
List aList;                    // aList is empty
Iterator anIterator(aList);   // anIterator is associated with aList

aList.add(5);        // aList is: 5
aList.add(12);       // aList is: 12, 5
aList.add(8);        // aList is: 8, 12, 5
aList.add(10);       // aList is: 10, 8, 12, 5

anIterator.reset(); // (aList has changed -- reset iterator before reusing)
                    //   anIterator.cursor_ now points to 10
anIterator.next();  // value is 10; anIterator.cursor_ now points to 8
anIterator.next();  // value is 8; anIterator.cursor_ now points to 12
```

So far, we have only a single way to iterate over the `List`. But the `Iterator` class serves as a base to derive new kinds of iterators. For example, the class `PositiveIterator` will iterate over the positive integers in the list rather than over all of them.

```
// Iterates over the positive items in a list of integers. If the list is
//   altered after the iterator is created, the iterator should be reset
//   before using it again.
class PositiveIterator : public Iterator {
public:
   PositiveIterator(const List& aList); // Constructs an iterator for the
                                        //   positive items of aList. Prepares
                                        //   the iterator to get the first
                                        //   positive item (if one exists).
   int next();                          // Next positive item.
                                        //   ASSUME: There is a next positive
                                        //           list item.
   bool more() const;                   // Are there more positive items?
   void reset();                        // Reset to the first positive item
                                        //   (if one exists).
```

```
private:
   void setToPositive();
};
```

PositiveIterator inherits the protected member cursor_ from Iterator.
It has a private member function setToPositive(). The purpose of setTo-
Positive() is to make sure cursor_ points to the next positive item or to null if
none exists.

```
void PositiveIterator :: setToPositive()
{
   while (cursor_ != 0 && cursor_->info() <= 0) // Advance cursor_ to the
      cursor_ = cursor_->link();                 //    next positive item
}
```

The PositiveIterator constructor uses the Iterator constructor to initialize cursor_ to the head of the list. And then it invokes setToPositive() to set
cursor_ to point to the first positive list item.

```
PositiveIterator :: PositiveIterator(const List& aList) : Iterator(aList)
{
   setToPositive();
}
```

The definitions of the remaining member functions of PositiveIterator
are straightforward. At the beginning of execution of each one, either cursor_
points to a positive list item or it points to null if there are no more positive items.

```
int PositiveIterator :: next()
{
   int x = Iterator::next(); // Error if cursor_ is null!
   setToPositive();          // Make cursor_ point to the next positive item.
   return x;
}

void PositiveIterator :: reset()
{
   Iterator :: reset();      // Set cursor_ to theList_.head_.
   setToPositive();          // Make cursor_ point to the first positive item.
}

bool PositiveIterator :: more() const
{
   return Iterator::more();
}
```

Because of the way `cursor_` is moved by the other `PositiveIterator` member functions, it is not really necessary to define `PositiveIterator::more()`. But we chose to do so simply to document how it is to be used with respect to the `PositiveIterator` class.

To show how these iterators might be used, we will create a `List`, an `Iterator`, and a `PositiveIterator`. The following code illustrates two styles of loops to iterate over the lists. One style uses a `while` loop and the other uses a `for` loop.

```cpp
List myList;                        // Creates an empty list
myList.add(-9);                     // myList is: -9
myList.add(27);                     // myList is: 27, -9
myList.add(19);                     // myList is: 19, 27, -9
myList.add(-4);                     // myList is: -4, 19, 27, -9
myList.add(6);                      // myList is:  6, -4, 19, 27, -9
myList.add(-5);                     // myList is: -5,  6, -4, 19, 27, -9

cout << "List items are:\n";
for (Iterator iter(myList); iter.more(); )   // iter iterates over all
   cout << iter.next() << endl;              //    items of myList

PositiveIterator pIter(myList);              // pIter iterates over positive
                                             //    items of myList
cout << "\nPositive list items are:\n ";
while (pIter.more())
   cout << pIter.next() << endl;
```

When the loops are executed, `myList` represents the list consisting of the numbers -5, 6, -4, 19, 27, -9. (The order is correct; `myList` adds new items to the front.) The output generated by execution of the code is as follows:

```
List items are:
-5
6
-4
19
27
-9

Positive list items are:
6
19
27
```

`Iterator` is a general iterator class, because an `Iterator` object iterates over all of the items in the list. Since an `Iterator` can access all of the list items, `Iterator` can be used as a base class for every possible iterator on a const `List` type object.

12.5   List variations using inheritance and templates

There are many different kinds of lists. Both versions of the `List` class could be used for an ordinary list in which new items are added at the beginning and from which items can be removed. The second and most recent version of the `List` class provided a base from which different kinds of lists can be derived. We will show how to derive an `OrderedList` class from the `List` class. We will then show how to create lists of different types of items besides integers using a template class.

Our ordered lists will have the same behaviors as an ordinary list. That is, an ordered list will be able to add new items, remove items, tell if it is empty, and tell if a particular item is a list member. The difference between an ordered list and an ordinary list is in how list items are stored. Items in an ordered list are stored according to their values. New items will not generally be placed at the front. An ordered list places a new item into its proper position according to its value.

Deriving ordered lists from lists

The `OrderedList` class inherits much from its base class, `List`. The only member function that the derived class must define is `add()`. This is the only method that distinguishes an `OrderedList` from a `List`. When a new data item is added to an `OrderedList`, it is inserted into its correct position relative to the other items already in the list.

Of course, the constructors, overloaded assignment operator, and destructor must be defined for `OrderedList`. Constructors, assignment operators, and destructors cannot be inherited.

```
// An ordered list of integers type. The list maintains its items in ascending
//  order of their values.
class OrderedList : public List {
public:
   OrderedList();                             // Constructs an empty list.
   OrderedList(const OrderedList& old);       // Constructs a deep copy.
   OrderedList& operator=(const OrderedList& rhs);// Assigns a deep copy.
   ~OrderedList();                            // Deallocates list memory.

   virtual void add(int x);                   // Adds x to the list.
};
```

> Friendship is not inherited. `List` is a friend of `Node`. `OrderedList` is derived from `List`. But `OrderedList` is not a friend of `Node`.

The `OrderedList` destructor does not really need any code. Its only job is to delete the member `head_`, which was inherited from the base class `List`. When a derived class destructor is invoked, the base class destructor is automatically invoked, and the `List` destructor deletes `head_`.

```
OrderedList ::~OrderedList()
{ }
```

The constructors and overloaded assignment operator rely on their `List` counterparts. The arguments to the copy constructor and assignment operator for `OrderedList` are of type `OrderedList`. When reading their definitions, we might ask this question: "Can an `OrderedList` be substituted for a `List`?" The answer is yes. Wherever a `List` can be used, an `OrderedList` can also be used. After all, an `OrderedList` *is-a* `List`.

```
OrderedList :: OrderedList() : List()
{ }
OrderedList :: OrderedList(const OrderedList& old) : List(old)
{ }
```

The overloaded assignment operator uses an explicit call to the `List` overloaded assignment operator. This is standard programming practice—let the base class (`List`) take care of assigning appropriately to the members that belong to it. And since `OrderedList` has no additional data members, its overloaded assignment needs nothing additional except a return statement.

```
OrderedList& OrderedList :: operator=(const OrderedList& rhs)
{
    List :: operator=(rhs);
    return *this;
}
```

The definition for `OrderedList::add()` uses the linked list algorithm from Section 12.2 for adding a node in a particular list position. Since an `OrderedList` is not a friend of `Node`, it cannot access the `link_` and `info_` members of its `Node`s directly. So it uses the public `Node` member functions `info()` and `link()`.

```
void OrderedList :: add(int x)
{
    if (head_ == 0 || head_->info() >= x)      // If x belongs at the front,
        List :: add(x);                         //    use List::add().
    else {                                      // else, find where it belongs
        Node* current = head_;                  //    --before current and after
        Node* previous;                         //       previous:
        while (current && current->info() < x) { //   Move current and previous
            previous = current;                 //       through the list.
            current = current->link();
        }
        previous->addAfter(x);                  // Add x after the Node
                                                //    pointed to by previous.

    }
}
```

The add() method checks to see if the new item belongs at the front of the list. If it does, it can simply invoke List::add() to do the insertion at the front. If not, it must search for the node that will precede the new node to be added. Then it sends a message to that node to add the new node after it.

What about the other member functions, isEmpty(), remove(), and contains(). The List definitions for these three methods are correct for OrderedLists also. There is no need to define them in the derived class. That illustrates some of the beauty of inheritance. An OrderedList can simply rely on the List code to implement most of its operations.

The OrderedList class does not have a built-in iterator, but it does not declare any iterator class as a friend. It does not need to. An ordinary Iterator, which iterates over a List, can be used. That is thanks to C++ inheritance. The Iterator constructor has a const List& argument. But wherever a List is used through a pointer or reference, an OrderedList can be used instead. In particular, an OrderedList can serve as an actual argument of an Iterator constructor.

The following code illustrates how an OrderedList object can be used:

```
OrderedList ord;
ord.add(34);        // ord is: 34
ord.add(70);        // ord is: 34, 70
ord.add(15);        // ord is: 15, 34, 70
ord.add(56);        // ord is: 15, 34, 56, 70

ord.remove(70);     // ord is: 15, 34, 56

Iterator ctr(ord);
for (int count = 0, sum = 0; ctr.more(); count++)
    sum += ctr.next();
// The value of count is 3; the value of sum is 105
```

There are other kinds of lists that can be derived from `List`. In addition to ordinary `List` behaviors, some lists might be able to remove their first or last items. Some might be able to tell how many items they contain, and some might be able to reverse themselves. The varieties are almost endless. The `OrderedList` class provides an example of how to derive one new list type from a `List`.

Node, list, and iterator class templates

Linked lists of integers are not very different from linked lists of other types of items. Integers are not special. In fact, we could readily redefine the `List` type to any type item for which the operators `!=` and `==` are defined. (Tests for equality or inequality are necessary for `contains` and `remove` messages.) Instead of redefining the `List`, `Node`, and `Iterator` classes for each possible item type, many of which we cannot possibly anticipate now, we can use C++ templates.

> Class templates are cookie cutter type templates. Templates are an excellent C++ feature for creating list types that differ only in the types of their items. The main reason templates were made a part of the C++ language was to support container classes.

We will create three class templates: `TNode`, `TList`, and `TIterator`. Those three template classes are interdependent. `TNode` has a friend `TList`. `TList` has a friend `TIterator`. Template classes are different from nontemplate classes. If one template class declares a second template class as a friend, then the second class must be *declared* before the first one is *defined*. So `TList` must be declared before `TNode` is defined and `TIterator` must be declared before `TList` is defined. But `TIterator` uses `TList` and `TNode` in its definition, which means those two classes must be declared before `TIterator` is defined.

It seems that the situation is hopeless. Fortunately, it is possible to declare a class without defining it. Simply leave out the braces and everything that lies between them. Before defining `TNode`, declare `TList`. Before defining `TList`, declare `TIterator`.

```
template <class T> class TList;
template <class T> class TIterator;
```

Now we are ready to define the class template `TNode`. It has the corresponding list item data type as its only parameter. The template definition looks very similar to the nontemplate `Node` class definition.

```
// Template class for a node type.
template <class T> class TNode {
public:
    void addAfter(const T& x);              // Add x after this node.
    const T& info() const;                  // List datum for this node.
    TNode<T>* link() const;                 // Address of the next node.
private:
    T info_;                                // Piece of actual list data.
    TNode<T>* link_;                        // Location of next list node.
    TNode(const T& t, TNode<T>* p = 0);     // Constructs from list data.
    TNode<T>* copy() const;                 // A deep copy of this node.
    ~TNode();                               // Deletes the link.
friend class TList<T>;
};
```

The class template `TNode` is used to create a class that depends on the actual type corresponding to the formal type `T`. The class `TNode<int>` is equivalent to the original `Node` class. The class `TNode<double>` is a class for a node with `double` type data. The class `TNode<String>` is a class for a node with `String` type data.

Many programmers prefer to define node classes so that the `info_` member is a pointer to an item of list data rather than an actual item itself. In the `TNode` template class definition, the `info_` member could be declared as follows:

```
T* info_;
```

The `info()` member function prototype could be changed to this:

```
const T* info() const;
```

If `info_` were a pointer, the `TNode` destructor would be changed to delete the `info_` and the `link_`.

```
template <class T> TNode<T> :: ~TNode()
{
    delete link_;
    delete info_;
}
```

The pointer is a convenience for polymorphism—you might want a list with different types of items from the same class hierarchy. The inconvenience of using a pointer comes from the occasional necessity to dereference it in order to access its referent.

The definitions of the member functions of TNode are as follows. Each member function of a template class is considered to be a template function. So the name of each one is preceded by `template <class T>`. Notice that except for the name of the constructor and the name of the destructor, the TNode is always modified by `<T>`. `TNode<T>` is the name of the type that is being specified by these definitions—a template type.

Here are the public member function definitions for TNode:

```
template <class T> void TNode<T> :: addAfter(const T&  x)
{
    link_ = new TNode<T>(x, link_);
}


template <class T> const T& TNode<T> :: info() const
{
    return info_;
}


template <class T> TNode<T>* TNode<T> :: link() const
{
    return link_;
}
```

Here are the private member function definitions for TNode:

```
template <class T> TNode<T> :: TNode(const T& t, TNode<T>* p) : info_(t),
                                                               link_(p)
{ }

template <class T> TNode<T>* TNode<T>:: copy()
{
    if (link_ != 0)
        return new TNode<T>(info_, link_->copy());
    return new TNode<T>(info_, 0);
}


template <class T> TNode<T> :: ~TNode()
{
    delete link_;
}
```

The TNode class template has no null constructor. There is no way to give a default value for the argument of type `const  T&`. Since a TNode is used only by a list and its iterator, having a null constructor is not necessary. Incidentally, we could have replaced the constructor declaration by this.

```
TNode<T> (T t, TNode<T>* p = 0);
```

Changing the declaration in this manner would have made the first argument a pass-by-value argument. Rather than have complicated types (as opposed to simple types such as `int`, `double`, or pointer types) as pass-by-value formal argument types, it is better that they be passed by constant reference. That prevents construction of a temporary object from the actual argument when the function is invoked.

The definition of the class template `TList` contains a friend declaration for a `TIterator`. The class template definition corresponds to the second version of the `List` class.

```
// Template for a list class. The operators !=  and == must be defined for the
//  parameter T. New items are added to the front.
template <class T>
class TList {
public:
    TList();                                  // Constructs an empty list.
    TList(const TList<T>& old);               // Constructs a deep copy of old.
    TList<T>& operator=(const TList<T>& rhs); // Assigns a deep copy of rhs.
    ~TList();                                 // Deallocates list memory.

    virtual void add(const T& x);             // Adds x to the list.
    void remove(const T& x);                  // Removes the first copy of x
                                              //   from the list, if it exists.
    bool isEmpty() const;                     // Is the list empty?
    bool contains(const T& x) const;          // Is x a list item?

friend class TIterator<T>;
protected:
    TNode<T>* head_;
};
```

The member function definitions for `TList` are the exact counterparts to their nontemplate `List` definitions. Notice how `List` is replaced everywhere by `TList<T>`, except for the constructor and destructor names. Notice also how `Node` is replaced everywhere by `TNode<T>`.

```
template <class T> TList<T> :: TList() : head_(0)
{ }

template <class T> TList<T> :: TList(const TList<T>& old) : head_(0)
{
    if (old.head_)
        head_ = old.head_->copy();
}
```

```cpp
template <class T> TList<T> :: ~TList()
{
    delete head_;
}


template <class T> TList<T>& TList<T> :: operator=(const TList<T>& rhs)
{
    if (this != &rhs) {
        delete head_;
        if (rhs.head_ != 0)
            head_ = rhs.head_->copy();
        else
            head_ = 0;
    }
    return *this;
}


template <class T> bool TList<T> :: isEmpty() const
{
    return (head_ != 0);
}


template <class T> bool TList<T> :: contains(const T& x) const
{
    for (TNode<T>* p = head_; p; p = p->link_)
        if (p->info_ == x)
            return true;
    return false;
}


template <class T> void TList<T> :: add(const T& x)
{
    head_ = new TNode<T>(x, head_);
}



template <class T> void TList<T> :: remove(const T& x)
{
    TNode<T> * current = head_;
    TNode<T>* previous;

    while (current && current->info_ != x) {// Find x in the list
        previous = current;
        current = current->link_;
    }
```

```
    if (current != 0) {
        if (current == head_)
            head_ = head_->link_;
        else
            previous->link_ = current->link_;
        current->link_ = 0;
        delete current;
    }
}
```

As we have recommended in the past, it is prudent programming practice to define an actual class and test the implementation before defining a class template with which the original can be created. You need not worry about template syntax errors when you debug the logic of the original class, and you need not worry about logic errors when you define the template versions.

The definition for TIterator looks a little different from the definition for Iterator. Look at the member function TIterator<T>::next().

```
// Template for a general iterator over a TList.
template <class T> class TIterator {
public:
    TIterator(const TList<T>& aList); // Constructs an iterator for aList.
                                      //    Start iteration from the first item.
    bool more() const;                // Are there more items in the list?
    const T& next();                  // Next item in the list.
                                      //    ASSUME: There is a next item.
    void reset();                     // Resets iteration to the first item.
protected:
    const TList<T>& theList_;
    const TNode<T>* cursor_;
};
```

In the original Iterator class definition, the member function Iterator::next() returned an integer. In the template class version, TIterator<T>::next() returns a constant reference to the parameter type T, which was used to define the actual TList. This is an efficiency issue. By returning a constant reference, TIterator<T>::next() does not create a temporary object of type T. Instead, TIterator<T>::next() simply returns an alias for the next list item. The const modifier to the type T& means that alias cannot be used to alter that item.

The code for TIterator<T>::next() is very similar to code for Iterator::next(). The fact that a reference to type T rather than a value of type T is returned does not alter the logic from the original Iterator definition.

```cpp
template <class T> const T& TIterator<T> :: next()
{
    const T& x = cursor_->info();
    cursor_ = cursor_->link();
    return x;
}
```

The remaining member function definitions are ones that you should have no difficulty in understanding. They are remarkably similar to their Iterator counterparts.

```cpp
template <class T> TIterator<T> :: TIterator(const TList<T>& aList) :
                                    theList_(aList), cursor_(aList.head_)
{ }

template <class T> void TIterator<T> :: reset()
{
    cursor_ = theList_.head_;
}

template <class T> bool TIterator<T> :: more() const
{
    return (cursor_ != 0);
}
```

Now instead of the original List, we use the template class TList<int>. This definition creates a list of integers.

```cpp
TList<int> intList;
```

We can use intList in the ordinary fashion.

```cpp
intList.add(27);        // intList contains: 27
intList.add(520);       // intList contains: 520, 27
intList.add(27);        // intList contains: 27, 520, 27
intList.add(35);        // intList contains: 35, 27, 520, 27
intList.remove(27);     // intList contains: 35, 520, 27
```

To create a list of Dates, this definition is appropriate. (We first defined a Date class in Chapter 7. It is easily modified to a first class type.)

```
TList<Date> dateList;
```

In order for `dateList` to be valid, the `Date` class must have overloaded `!=` and `==` operators. And if the `Date` class is a first class type, it will. To add a new `Date` to `dateList`, we can first create a `Date` object.

```
Date today(1,1,1996);
dateList.add(today);           // dateList contains: Jan 1 1996
today.advance();
dateList.add(today);           // dateList contains: Jan 2 1996, Jan 1 1996
dateList.add(Date(7,5,1997));// dateList contains: May 7 1997, Jan 2 1996,
                               //                   Jan 1 1996
dateList.add(Date());          // dateList contains: Dec 31 2000, May 7 1997,
                               //                   Jan 2 1996, Jan 1 1996
```

The last add messages to `dateList` used the `Date` constructors to add the default `Date` (which happens to be December 31, 2000) and a `Date` representing May 7, 1997 without using an extra, explicitly defined `Date` object.

By defining an iterator over `dateList`, we can see all of its `Dates`. The following code assumes the `Date` has an overloaded output operator.

```
TIterator<Date> day(dateList);  // day iterates over dateList

while (day.more())
   cout << day.next() << endl;
```

The exact form of the output generated by the code depends on the definition of the overloaded `Date` output operator, `<<`. If a `Date` is output in the form `mm/dd/yyyy`, then the output would be as follows:

```
12/31/2000
05/07/1997
01/02/1996
01/01/1996
```

Templates and inheritance

The type `OrderedList` is derived from `List`. It is used to create an ordered list of integers. The type `TList<int>` is used to create a list of integers. Templates and inheritance can be used in conjunction with one another to make an ordered list of any type item for which the operators `<` and `<=` are defined.

`TOrderedList` is a class template derived from `TList`. Notice how the inheritance is specified. The base class is `TList<T>`.

```
// Class template for an ordered list. List items are in ascending order. The
//   operators < and <= must be defined for the type T.
template <class T> class TOrderedList : public TList<T> {
public:
   TOrderedList();                                    // Constructs an empty list.
   TOrderedList(const TOrderedList<T>& old);          // Constructs a deep copy.
   TOrderedList<T>& operator=(const TOrderedList<T>& rhs);
                                                      // Assigns a deep copy.
   ~TOrderedList();                                   // Deallocates list memory.

   virtual void add(const T& x);                      // Adds x to the list.
};
```

The `TOrderedList` member functions definitions are exactly what you should expect. They are almost cut-and-paste copies of their `OrderedList` counterparts.

```
template <class T> TOrderedList<T> :: TOrderedList() : TList<T>()
{ }

template <class T> TOrderedList<T> :: TOrderedList(const TOrderedList<T>& old)
                                                   : TList<T>(old)
{ }

template <class T> TOrderedList<T>& TOrderedList<T> :: operator=
                                      (const TOrderedList<T>& rhs)
{
   TList<T> :: operator=(rhs);
   return *this;
}

template <class T> TOrderedList :: ~TOrderedList()
{
   delete head_;
}

template <class T> void TOrderedList<T> :: add(const T& x)
{
   if (head_ == 0 || x <= head_->info())
      TList<T> :: add(x);
   else {
      TNode<T>* current = head_;
      TNode<T>* previous;
      while (current && current->info() < x) {
         previous = current;
         current = current->link();
      }
```

```
        previous->addAfter(x);
    }
}
```

The following code illustrates how to use the new `TOrderedList` class template together with the `TIterator` class template to define an ordered list of `doubles`.

```
TOrderedList<double> realList;
realList.add(91.4);
realList.add(-64);
realList.add(365);

TIterator<double> it(realList);
while (it.more())
    cout << it.next() << endl;
```

The output generated by this code is shown in the box below.

```
 -64
 91.4
 365
```

12.6 ▮ Stacks and queues

Some containers arrange their items in a particular order. For example, ordered lists arrange their items in ascending order according to the values of the items. There are also containers that arrange their items according to some extrinsic property, such as the times the items are added to the container.

Stacks and **queues** are containers whose items are ordered according to their times of entry into the container. The first item in a stack is the most recently added item and the last item in the stack is the one that was added before all the others. The first item in a queue is the item that was added to the queue before the other items, while the last item is the most recently added item. Figure 12.15 shows a stack of numbers and a queue of numbers.

Stacks and queues are easy to find in everyday life. The previous chapter had one example of a stack. A stack of cafeteria plates is another example. The plate on the top of the stack is the most recently added plate. It will be removed first, before the other plates beneath. That describes the defining characteristic of a stack—the last item added is the first item to be removed. For that reason, stacks are sometimes called "last-in-first-out" lists.

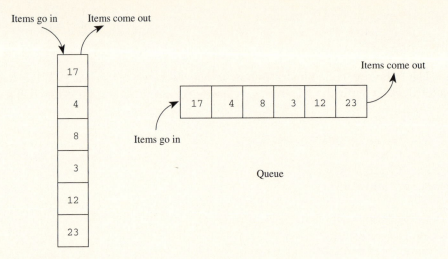

Figure 12.15   A stack and a queue of numbers.

A line of customers in a grocery store is an example of a queue. The first person in the line is the person who has been in line the longest. The last person in the line is the one who entered the line most recently. The first customer in the grocery store line will be the first one out of the line. Queues, which are sometimes called "first-in-first-out" lists, have the property that the first item added is the first item removed.

Stacks and queues are very simple containers. Their simplicity comes from how they behave. Like ordinary lists, stacks and queues can tell when they are empty. But unlike ordinary lists, they add and remove items only at an end, never in the middle. Stacks and queues cannot tell if they contain a particular item, and they do not have iterators.

What do stacks and queues know? What can they do? Let's start with a stack. The front end of a stack is called the **stack top**. Items can be added and removed only at the top. Adding an item to a stack is called a **stack push**. Removing an item from a stack is called a **stack pop**. A stack can tell what its top item is and whether it is empty. That's about it.

Queues are almost as simple as stacks, but not quite. A stack adds and removes items from the same end. A queue adds and removes items from opposite ends. The end from which items are removed is called the **queue front**. The end to which new items are added is called the **queue rear**.

A formal description of the attributes and behaviors of a data structure constitutes an abstract data type or ADT. Computer scientists use mathematical notation to make ADT descriptions precise. The following are formal ADT descriptions of stacks and queues.

```
type Stack<Item>
   NewStack()              →    Stack
   IsEmpty(Stack)          →    Boolean
   Push(Stack,Item)        →    Stack
   Pop(Stack)              →    Stack
   Top(Stack)              →    Item
```

If i is an item and s is a stack:

```
   IsEmpty(NewStack())  ≡   true
   IsEmpty(Push(s,i))   ≡   false
   Top(Push(s,i))       ≡   i
   Pop(Push(s,i))       ≡   s
```

```
type Queue<Item>
   NewQueue()              →    Queue
   IsEmpty(Queue)          →    Boolean
   Add(Queue,Item)         →    Queue
   Remove(Queue)           →    Queue
   Front(Queue)            →    Item
```

If i is an item and q is a queue:

```
   IsEmpty(NewQueue())  ≡   true
   IsEmpty(Add(q,i))    ≡   false
   Front(Add(q,i))      ≡   if IsEmpty(q) then i
                            else Front(q)
   Remove(Add(q,i))     ≡   if IsEmpty(q) then q
                            else Add(Remove(q),i))
```

Defining a stack of Strings

The stack abstract data type translates to a C++ class interface—the public part of
a stack class definition. For our example, we will define a stack of Strings. (The
String class was defined in Chapter 9. An exercise at the end of Chapter 9 indicated how to modify String to make its methods more efficient.)

```
// A class for a stack of Strings.
class StrStack {
public:
   StrStack ();                                 // Creates an empty stack.
   StrStack (const StrStack & s);               // Creates a deep copy of s.
   StrStack&  operator=(const StrStack & rhs);  // Assigns a deep copy of rhs.
```

```
  ~StrStack();                              // Deallocates stack memory.

  void push(const char t[]);                // Adds t to the stack top.
                                            // ASSUME:t is a valid C-string
  bool isEmpty() const;                     // Is the stack empty?
  const String& top() const;                // Top item on the stack.
                                            //  ASSUME: Stack is NOT empty
  void pop();                               // Removes the top stack item.
                                            //  ASSUME: Stack is NOT empty
private:
  StrNode* top_;
};
```

The copy constructor, the overloaded assignment operator, and the destructor do not correspond to any of the operations described in the Stack ADT. Classes do more than simply describe abstract data types. Class definitions usually contain such functions as constructors and destructors to manage allocation and dealloca-tion of resources for an object.

The interface for the StrStack class is the public part of the class definition. However, we can see from this definition that the type StrNode must also be defined. We will not take much time with that. The StrNode class looks like a sim-ple version of the Node class. The big difference is that StrNode has no public member functions. StrNode declares two friends: the StrStack and StrQueue classes.

```
// Node with String data
class StrNode {
private:
  StrNode(const char x[] = "", StrNode* p = 0);   // Data/null constructor.
  StrNode(const String& s, StrNode* p = 0);       // String constructor.
  StrNode* copy() const;                          // Returns a deep copy.
  ~StrNode();                                      // Deallocates the next
                                                   //   node and the String.

  String info_;
  StrNode* link_;

friend class StrStack;
friend class StrQueue;
};
```

Definitions of the StrNode member functions are absolutely identical to the corresponding Node member function definitions, except for the changes in the type names and formal arguments.

```
StrNode :: StrNode(const char x[], StrNode* p): info_(x), link_(p)
{ }
```

```
StrNode :: StrNode(const String& s, StrNode* p) : info_(s), link_(p)
{ }

StrNode* StrNode :: copy() const
{
    if (link_ != 0)
        return new StrNode(info_, link_->copy());
    return new StrNode(info_, 0);
}

StrNode :: ~StrNode()
{
    delete link_;
}
```

A `StrNode` contains two pieces of data: a `String` and a pointer. Figure 12.16 shows some of the data associated with a `StrNode`. The `info_` member is a `String`. A `String` has a pointer to an array of characters (a C-string).

The `StrNode` destructor does not need to do anything with the `String` data member. The `String` destructor is automatically called when a `StrNode` dies.

The `StrStack` member functions are defined the same way as the comparable `List` methods. The `StrStack` constructors, destructor, and overloaded assignment use exactly the same algorithms as those for `List`. `StrStack::push()` is like `List::add()` also.

```
StrStack :: StrStack() : top_(0)
{ }

StrStack :: StrStack(const StrStack& old) : top_(0)
{
    if (old.top_ != 0)
        top_ = old.top_->copy();
}
```

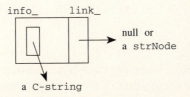

Figure 12.16 A `StrNode`.

```
StrStack& StrStack :: operator=(const StrStack& rhs)
{
   if (this != &rhs) {
      delete top_;
      if (rhs.top_ == 0)
         top_ = 0;
      else
         top_ = rhs.top_->copy();
   }
   return *this;
}


StrStack ::~StrStack()
{
   delete top_;
}


bool StrStack :: isEmpty() const
{
   return (top_ == 0);
}


void StrStack :: push(const char t[])
{
   top_ = new StrNode(t, top_);
}
```

The member functions of StrStack that do not correspond to List behaviors are top() and pop().

```
const String& StrStack :: top() const
{
   return top_->info_;       // ERROR if top_ is null
}
void StrStack :: pop()
{
   StrNode* toDie = top_;    // toDie points to the node to be removed
   top_ = top_->link_;       // ERROR if top_ is null.
   toDie->link_ = 0;         // Don't destroy the rest of the stack!
   delete toDie;
}
```

The StrStack interface warns against trying to pop a stack when the stack is empty. It also warns against looking at the top item when the stack is empty. And of course, it provides the isEmpty() method so the user can guard against such errors.

It is easy to find applications of stacks in the computer world. We will look at a very important one in the next section when we talk about recursion. But our example now is a bit more mundane. We will create a `StrStack` that could represent a student's work and study habits.

```
StrStack toDo;                  // toDo is an empty stack

// Push some activities on the toDo stack
toDo.push("study");
toDo.push("dishes");
toDo.push("eat");
toDo.push("watch movie");
```

Figure 12.17 shows what the `toDo` stack looks like at this point. The item at the top of the `toDo` stack is the `String` representing `"watch movie"`.

The activities can be popped off the `toDo` stack. This loop pops off all of the items except the one on the bottom.

```
while (!toDo.is Empty() && toDo.top () != "study")
    toDo.pop();
```

Defining a queue of `String`s

A queue needs quick access to both of its ends. A typical pointer-based queue implementation uses two pointers: one to access the front of the queue and the other to access the rear. The following `StrQueue` definition implements a queue of `String`s. The `StrQueue` interface warns against sending `remove` or `front` messages to an empty queue.

```
// A class for a queue of Strings.
class StrQueue {
public:
    StrQueue ();                               // Creates an empty queue.
    StrQueue (const StrQueue & q);             // Creates a deep copy of q.
    StrQueue&  operator=(const StrQueue & rhs);// Assigns a deep copy of rhs.
    ~StrQueue();                               // Deallocates queue memory.

    void add(const char t[]);                  // Add t to the rear.
                                               // ASSUME: t is a valid C-string

    bool isEmpty() const;                      // Is the queue empty?
```

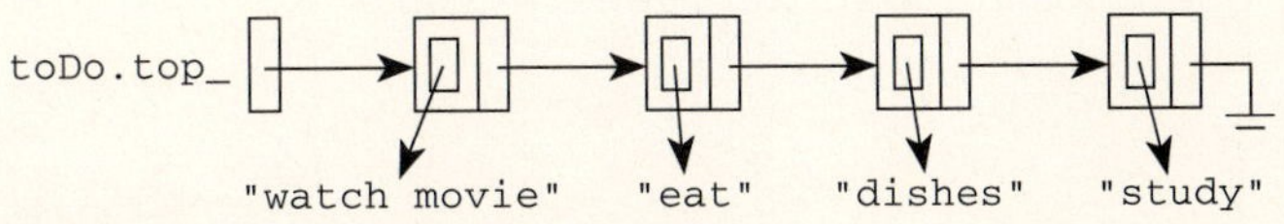

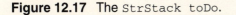

Figure 12.17 The `StrStack toDo`.

```
    const String&  front() const;              // Front item in the queue.
                                                //   ASSUME: queue is NOT empty
    void remove();                              // Remove the front item.
                                                //   ASSUME: queue is NOT empty
private:
    StrNode* front_;
    StrNode* rear_;
};
```

The fact that a StrQueue has two pointers to manage makes its member function code somewhat more tedious than the equivalent StrStack member function code. This is quite evident in the definitions of the overloaded assignment operator and the copy constructor.

```
StrQueue :: StrQueue(): front_(0), rear_(0)
{ }


StrQueue :: StrQueue(const StrQueue& old)
{
    if (old.front_ == 0) {              // Set both front_ and rear_ to null
        front_ = 0;                     //   if the queue is empty.
        rear_ = 0;
    }
    else {                              // Otherwise, make a copy of the old
        front_ = old.front_->copy();    //   queue. Push the rear_ pointer to
        rear_ = front_;                 //   the end of the queue items.
        while (rear_->link_ != 0)
            rear_ = rear_->link_;
    }
}
StrQueue :: ~StrQueue()
{
    delete front_;
}
```

The overloaded assignment operator definition is very similar to the copy constructor definition. In both definitions, the pointers are set to null if the argument is an empty queue. If it is not empty, the rear_ pointer is moved to point to the last item in the queue.

```
StrQueue&  StrQueue :: operator=(const StrQueue & rhs)
{
    if (this != &rhs) {
        delete front_;
        if (rhs.front_ == 0) {
            front_ = 0;
```

```
            rear_ = 0;
        }
        else {
            front_ = rhs.front_->copy();
            rear_ = front_;
            while (rear_->link_ != 0)
                rear_ = rear_->link_;
        }
    }
    return *this;
}
```

The const queue methods do not need to use the `rear_` pointer.

```
bool StrQueue :: isEmpty() const
{
    return front_ == 0;
}
```

```
const String& StrQueue :: front() const
{
    return front_-> info_;      // ERROR if front_ is null (if queue is empty).
}
```

Although new items are added to the rear, the `add()` definition changes the `front_` pointer if the queue is empty when the `add` message is sent.

```
void StrQueue :: add(const char t[])
{
    if (front_ == 0)  {                     // If the queue is empty,
        front_ = new StrNode(t,0);          //    the new item is both the front
        rear_ = front_;                     //    and rear item.
    }
    else {                                  // If the queue is not empty,
        rear_->link_ = new StrNode(t,0);    //    the new item goes to the rear.
        rear_ = rear_->link_;
    }
}
```

The `remove()` definition needs not only to remove the front item but also to reset the `rear_` pointer in case the queue becomes empty as a result of the `remove` message.

```
void StrQueue :: remove()
{
    StrNode* toDie = front_;     // points to the node to be removed
```

```
   front_ = front_->link_;      // ERROR if front_ is null.
   toDie->link_ = 0;
   delete toDie;
   if (front_ == 0)             // Set the rear_ pointer for an empty queue.
      rear_ = 0;
}
```

Queues are as common in the computer world as stacks. Anyone who has used a shared printer realizes that. Print jobs are usually placed in a queue. The job at the front of the queue—the job that has been in the queue for the longest time—is the next one to be printed.

The following code illustrates using a StrQueue. It creates a queue to represent customers in a line at a bank.

```
StrQueue customer;              // customer is an empty queue

// Several people enter the line
customer.add("Charles");
customer.add("Blake");
customer.add("Charlotte");
customer.add("Nick");
```

Figure 12.18 shows what the customer queue looks like at this point. The item at the front of the queue is the String representing "Charles".

In order to see the third person in the customer queue, send it two remove messages.

```
for(int i = 0; !customer.isEmpty() && i < 2; i++) // Remove the first two
   customer.remove();                             //    customers
if (!customer.isEmpty())
   cout << "Next in line: " << customer.front() << endl;
```

The output for the code is as follows:

```
Next in line: Charlotte
```

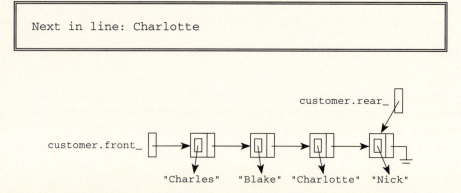

Figure 12.18 The StrQueue customer.

Of course, the front item in the `customer` queue is now the `String` representing `"Charlotte"`. But since `String` is a first class type, that front item can be inserted into `cout` in the usual manner with the expected output.

12.7 ▌ Message passing: Letting the nodes do it recursively

The object-oriented world accomplishes things by sending messages to objects. If you want a list to add an item, send it an `add` message. If you want to see the top item on a stack, send the stack a `top` message.

Class users are not the only ones who can send messages. Lists can send messages to nodes. Delegation is the technique used by objects when they respond to a message by sending that message on to another object. In this section, we will show you how delegation can occur with lists and nodes.

We will implement a list class so that whenever the list is sent a message to do something that involves one or more of its nodes, it will pass the message on and delegate the task its head node. If the head node cannot respond, then the head node passes the same message to the next node—the head node delegates the task to the next node. If the next node cannot respond, then the next node passes the same message to the node that follows it. The message passing travels down the nodes in that fashion until a node that can respond with the appropriate behavior receives the message.

In order for the head node to receive a message from the list, the list must have a head node. That presents a problem with our original concept of a linked list. What if the list is empty and does not have any node? How can the list send a message to a head node that does not even exist?

One solution to the problem is to make sure that *every* list has at least one node, even an empty list. The head node in such a list does not contain a list item. It is a **dummy head node**. The first item in the list will be in the node that follows the head node. All of the list items are in nodes that appear after the dummy head node.

The dummy head node has a pointer to the first node with list data, as illustrated in Fig. 12.19. When the list passes a message to the head node, the message

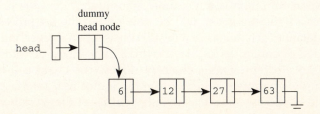

Figure 12.19   A list with a dummy head node. List data are 6, 12, 27, and 63.

should stop at least by the time it reaches the end of the list. That limits the total number of individual messages passed from one node to the next for the length of the list.

Recursive node methods

The nodes in our ordered linked list with a dummy head node do all of the list processing. The essential feature of the processing consists of two distinct parts:

1. *Termination part*: If the node can respond to the message without looking further down the list than its immediate successor, then that node completes the processing.

2. *Recursive part*: If the node cannot respond, it sends the message to the next node to make the response, delegating the task to the next node.

The algorithms that the node methods will use for list-processing tasks such as removing or inserting a new item are recursive algorithms. To say that a node sends the same message to the next node, which in turn may send the same message to the next node and so on, means that the definition of the corresponding member function contains a call to itself via the next node.

The termination part of a recursive algorithm is essential. Without it, the message passing has no way to stop. Every correct recursive list-processing algorithm has a way to terminate the recursion. The Node class copy() method is recursive. It sends the copy message to the next Node to make a copy of the rest of the Nodes in the chain. The next Node makes a copy of itself, then sends a copy message to the Node after itself to copy the remainder of the chain. The recursion terminates when the last Node in the chain of Nodes is copied.

Recursive methods can be applied to many different list variations. We will focus on a single kind of list, an ordered list of integers. We will create an ordered list class RecList which will have behaviors identical to the behaviors of the OrderedList class presented earlier in this chapter. (We used the name RecList to remind you that it illustrates recursive methods. However, the recursion should be transparent to anyone who uses the class.) Templates for lists of other kinds of list items will be easy to construct from our framework.

The name of the new list class is RecList. The name of the corresponding node class is RecNode. The name of the corresponding iterator class is RecIterator. The RecNode definition is much more complicated than the original Node definition. After all, the RecNodes will be doing all of the list-processing work. However, the data for each RecNode will still consist of an integer and a link.

The RecNode definition looks like a hybrid List-Node definition. Keep in mind that a RecNode represents a chain of nodes. The chain is a kind of list. RecList is simply a wrapper designed to make a nice user interface to the list. The user should not be aware of the recursive nature of the work being done. A RecList will pass each list-processing message it receives to its dummy head

node. The dummy head node does not contain actual list items. It looks at its link
or at the next node in the chain, if one exists, to decide whether it can respond to
the message by itself. The work occurs in the chain of nodes that are positioned
after the node receiving the message. In some cases, the link of the node receiving
the message will change. In others, the data in the node after the one receiving the
message are examined.

RecNode is a class with only private members. Only the new RecList class
and its associated iterator class, RecIterator, need access to a RecNode. So
RecList and RecIterator are declared as RecNode friends.

The documentation for RecNode is given for your benefit. Since RecNode has
only private members, its definition could be placed in a .C file rather than a header file. (The same is actually true for the original Node class definition. Node is not
a class for general public use.)

```
// Node type for an ordered linked list of integers with a dummy head node
class RecNode {
private:
    RecNode(int i = 0, RecNode* p = 0);    // Constructor.
    RecNode* copy() const;                  // Returns a deep copy.
    ~RecNode();                             // Deallocates the next node.

    void insertAfter(int x);                // Adds x in the proper position in
                                            //    the chain after this node.
    void removeAfter(int x);                // Removes the first occurrence of
                                            //    x in the chain after this node.
    bool containsAfter(int x) const;        // Does the chain after this node
                                            //    contain x?
    int info_;
    RecNode* link_;

friend class RecList;
friend class RecIterator;
};
```

The definitions for the RecNode constructor, the copy() function, and the
destructor are virtually identical to their definitions in the original Node class.

```
RecNode :: RecNode(int i, RecNode* p) : info_(i), link_(p)
{ }

RecNode* RecNode :: copy() const
{
    if (link_ != 0)
        return new RecNode(info_, link_->copy());
    return new RecNode(info_, 0);
}
```

```
RecNode :: ~RecNode()
{
    delete link_;
}
```

The `RecNode` member functions `insertAfter()`, `removeAfter()`, and `containsAfter()` are different from any `Node` member functions. They are all recursive functions.

A `containsAfter` message returns the answer to the question "Does the chain of `RecNodes` that follows this one contain the value x?" Here is how the `RecNode` receiving the message comes up with the answer:

- If there is no next `RecNode`, it responds `false`.

- If there is a next `RecNode` but it contains a number larger than x, it responds `false` here also. (The data in the chain are ordered, starting with the smallest number in the chain. In this case, the smallest number is larger than x.)

- If there is a next `RecNode` and it contains x, it responds `true`.

- If none of those conditions occur, it sends the message on to the next `RecNode` to come up with the correct answer.

Since the next `RecNode` is accessed by this `RecNode`'s `link_`, sending the message to the next `RecNode` is accomplished by evaluating the expression `link_->containsAfter(x)`.

```
bool RecNode :: containsAfter(int x) const
{
    if (link_ == 0 || x < link_->info_)  // Termination: the chain is empty or x
        return false;                     //   is too small to be in the chain.
    else if (link_->info_ == x)           // Termination: x is in the next node.
        return true;
    else                                  // Recursion: pass the message to the
        return link_->containsAfter(x);   //   next node. (delegation)
}
```

The `insertAfter()` method inserts a new `RecNode` in the ordered chain of nodes that begins immediately after the one receiving the `insertAfter` message. The new `RecNode` may be inserted at the beginning of the chain, in which case there is no additional recursive call. Or it may be inserted somewhere after the next `RecNode` in the chain, for which a recursive call is necessary. A `RecNode` handles an `insertAfter` message in the following way:

- If this is the last `RecNode` in the chain, then it inserts a new `RecNode` containing the new data after it. The new `RecNode` becomes the new last node in the chain.

- If this is not the last `RecNode` in the chain and if the `info_` for the next `RecNode` in the chain is greater than the new data to be inserted, then this `RecNode` inserts a new `RecNode` containing the new data between itself and the next `RecNode`.

- If neither of those two cases occurs, then this `RecNode` passes along the `insertAfter` message to the next `RecNode`.

The `RecNode` that actually inserts the new item does the insertion at the beginning of the chain of nodes following it. Unlike the `OrderedList::add()`, `RecNode::insertAfter()` does not have a pair of pointers to traverse the list looking for the place to insert. This is typical of recursive list processing algorithms. We do not need two pointers when we insert a node at the beginning of a list.

As with most recursive code, the definition for `insertAfter()` begins with a termination check to try to do the work without resorting a recursive call. Look at the `if` condition in the definition of `insertAfter()`. If there is no next `RecNode` (if `link_` is null), then the short-circuit Boolean evaluation prevents the second condition, `x <= link_->info_`, from being evaluated.

If there is a `RecNode` in the chain of `RecNodes` receiving the `insertAfter` message, and if `x` is greater than the `info_` of the next `RecNode` in the chain, the message is delegated to the next `RecNode` to insert `x` somewhere after it: `link_->insertAfter(x)`.

```
void RecNode :: insertAfter(int x)
{
    if (link_ == 0 || x <= link_->info_)   // Termination: insert x here.
        link_ = new RecNode(x, link_);
    else                                    // Recursion: pass the message to the
        link_->insertAfter(x);              //    next node.
}
```

The algorithm for `removeAfter()` has some similarity to the algorithm for `insertAfter()`. The `RecNode` receiving the `removeAfter` message is told to remove the first `RecNode` in the chain beginning after it that contains the value `x`. Here is how it does the job:

- If there are no `RecNodes` after this one, it does nothing because there is nothing to do.

- If the next `RecNode` after this one contains a number larger than `x`, then this chain of `RecNodes` cannot possibly contain `x`. Again, this `RecNode` does nothing.

- If the `info_` of the `RecNode` following this one matches `x`, then it removes that next `RecNode`.

- If none of those cases occur, the `RecNode` sends the next `RecNode` a message to remove `x` from the chain of nodes following it.

A `RecNode` sends the `remove` message to the next one by invoking `link_->removeAfter(x)`.

```
void RecNode :: removeAfter(int x)
{
   if (link_ == 0 || x < link_->info_)    // Termination: x is not in the list.
      return;
   else if (x == link_->info_) {          // Termination: x is in the next node
      RecNode* p = link_;                 //    Remove the node.
      link_ = link_->link_;
      p->link_ = 0;
      delete p;
   }
   else                                   // Recursion: pass the message to the
      link_->removeAfter(x);              //    next node.
}
```

The `RecList` class that uses `RecNode`s has the same functionality as the original `OrderedList` class. Indeed, except for the name of the class, it has the same interface as the `OrderedList` class. The only difference is how the two lists do work.

```
// An ordered list of integers. List data is in ascending order.
class RecList {
public:
   RecList();                                  // Constructs an empty list.
   RecList(const RecList& r);                  // Constructs a deep copy of r.
   RecList& operator=(const RecList& rhs);     // Assigns a deep copy of rhs.
   ~RecList();                                 // Deallocates list resources.

   void add(int x);                           // Adds x into its proper position.
   void remove(int x);                        // Removes the first copy of x,
                                              //    if it exists.
   bool contains(int x) const;                // Is x a list item?
   bool isEmpty() const;                      // Is the list empty?

friend class RecIterator;
protected:
   RecNode* head_;
};
```

The `RecList` null constructor must create the dummy head node. The `info_` for the new head node could be anything. We choose 0, but that choice is arbitrary.

```
RecList :: RecList()
{
   head_ = new RecNode;
}
```

The `RecList` copy constructor relies on `RecNode::copy()` to make its deep copy. Its definition is a one-liner. The overloaded assignment operator relies on `RecNode::copy()` too. Both functions as well as the destructor are exact duplicates of their `List` counterparts, except the identifier `List` is replaced by the identifier `RecList`.

```cpp
RecList :: RecList(const RecList& old)
{
    head_ = old.head_->copy();
}


RecList& RecList::operator=(const RecList& rhs)
{
    if (this != &rhs) {
        delete head_;
        head_ = rhs.head_->copy();
    }
    return *this;
}


RecList :: ~RecList()
{
    delete head_;
}
```

The definition of `isEmpty()` examines the `link_` member of the head node rather than simply the pointer `head_`. Every `RecList`, even an empty one, has at least one node. So the `head_` pointer is never null.

```cpp
bool RecList :: isEmpty() const
{
    return (head_->link_ == 0);
}
```

The methods of the remaining `RecList` members are remarkably simple. All of the work is passed on to the `RecNode` class. Here are their definitions:

```cpp
void RecList :: add(int x)
{
    head_->insertAfter(x);
}


void RecList :: remove(int x)
{
    head_->removeAfter(x);
}
```

```
      bool RecList :: contains(int x) const
      {
          return head_->containsAfter(x);
      }
```

One of the benefits of recursive message passing is the simplicity of the code. Once the `RecNode` class is defined and its methods implemented, the task of defining the `RecList` methods becomes trivial.

The `RecIterator` class is almost identical to the `Iterator` class.

```
// General iterator to access all of the items in a RecList.
// When the RecList is modified, the RecIterator must be reset before
//    subsequent use.
class RecIterator {
public:
    RecIterator(const RecList& aList); // Iterates over aList. Iteration begins
                                       //  with the first list item.
    int next();                        // Next list item.
                                       //    ASSUME: There is a next item.
    bool more() const;                 // Are there more list items?
    void reset();                      // Reset the iterator to begin with the
                                       //    first list item.
protected:
    const RecList& theList_;
    const RecNode* cursor_;
};
```

The `RecIterator` constructor initializes the list reference data member, and it initializes `cursor_` to the address of the node after the head node. That second node is where the first piece of list data resides. The `reset()` definition also makes `cursor_` point to the node following the head node.

```
RecIterator :: RecIterator(const RecList& aList) : theList_(aList),
                                                  cursor_(aList.head_->link_)
{ }

void RecIterator :: reset()
{
    cursor_ = theList_.head_->link_;
}
```

The user of a `RecList` need not know that the underlying linked list has a dummy head node. The `RecIterator` must know about that dummy head node. That is the only way it can tell how to set its `cursor_` to point to the first list item rather than the dummy head node.

The remaining `RecIterator` member function definitions look almost the same as their `Iterator` counterpart definitions.

```
int RecIterator :: next()
{
    int x = cursor_->info_;              // ERROR if cursor_ is null
    cursor_ = cursor_->link_;
    return x;
}

bool RecIterator :: more() const
{
    return (cursor_ != 0);
}
```

Notice how `RecIterator` uses the `RecNode` member data directly. That is possible because `RecIterator` was declared as a friend of the `RecNode` class. (We did not use that technique in the nonrecursive `Iterator` and `Node` classes. As a result, the `Iterator::next()` definition had to use `cursor_->info()` instead of `cursor_->info_`, and `cursor_->link()` instead of `cursor_->link_`.)

Tracing recursive list-processing code

The idea of sending messages to the nodes in order to implement list behavior is naturally implemented by recursive algorithms. The recursive algorithms tend to be simple to code but sometimes not so simple to trace. They all have a similar flavor. In order to demonstrate how to trace recursive algorithms, we will show a very simple model of how recursive functions are executed.

Let's review how `RecList` adds a new item. Two different functions are invoked: `RecList::add()` and `RecNode::insertAfter()`. (Three functions are actually invoked. During one of its invocations, `RecNode::insertAfter()` calls a `RecNode` constructor to create a new node.) Definitions of `RecList::add()` and `RecNode::insertAfter()` are as follows:

```
void RecList :: add(int x)
{
    head_->insertAfter(x);
}

void RecNode :: insertAfter(int x)
{
    if (link_ == 0 || x <= link_->info_)
        link_ = new RecNode(x, link_);
    else
        link_->insertAfter(x);
}
```

We will trace inserting the number 35 into the list consisting of 6, 12, 27, and 63. Our illustration for the list in Fig. 12.20 shows the list with alternate names A, B, C, and D for the list nodes. The name of the list is `myList`, and the insertion is accomplished by sending `myList` the message `myList.insert(35)`.

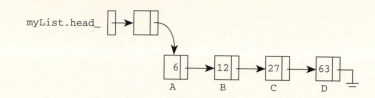

Figure 12.20   An ordered list with a dummy head node. List 6, 12, 27, and 63.

One way to trace the call is to use the function tracing mechanism that we introduced in Chapter 3. But that can become cumbersome for recursive functions whenever the recursion runs too deep—whenever the function invokes itself many times. Instead, we can trace the sequence of function calls generated by the call `myList.add(35)`.

```
myList.add(35)  calls
    myList.head_->insertAfter(35)  which calls
        A.insertAfter(35)  which calls
            B.insertAfter(35)  which calls
                C.insertAfter(35)  which calls
                    RecNode(35,C.link_)
```

If `RecNode` and `RecList` data members were public instead of protected, `myList.head_->link_->link_->link_->insertAfter(35)` could replace `C.insertAfter(35)`.

This trace is easy to understand once you are able to follow the links. But how does the computer keep track of the details? What mechanism does it use to enable the function calls? The answer is best given in terms of a model. We will show a much simplified memory model of how all function invocations work and, in particular, how they work with recursive calls.

A program is allowed a certain amount of memory for its execution: the **runtime stack**, and the **heap** (also called the **free store**). (See Fig. 12.21.) The runtime stack is used for function calls. The heap is the memory from which objects are dynamically allocated. Whenever a new object is created through the new operator, memory for that object is allocated off the heap.

The runtime stack is a stack, just as we described in the previous section. The items in the runtime stack are **activation records**. Each item on the runtime stack corresponds to an activation (or call) of a function. An activation record keeps track of information for this invocation of the function. The information in an activation record includes the following:

1. Pass-by-value arguments

2. Local objects

3. Pointers to reference arguments

4. A return address to tell which code to continue executing when the invocation of the function is completed

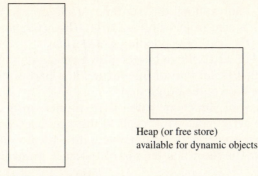

Heap (or free store)
available for dynamic objects

Available for runtime stack

Figure 12.21 Total memory allocated to program execution.

5. Where to initialize a temporary return value if the function return type is not void

When a function is called (activated), an activation record for that invocation is pushed on the top of the runtime stack. When instructions in the body of the function are executed, references to local identifiers in the body of the function are determined by the activation record on the top of the stack.

When the active code calls a function, its execution is suspended but its corresponding activation record remains on the stack. A record for the newly activated function is pushed on top of the stack, with the activation record on the top of the runtime stack corresponding to the active code. Activation records that are on the runtime stack but not on the top correspond to function calls which have been suspended awaiting completion of the calls corresponding to activation records higher in the stack. Since `main()` is either suspended (pending other function calls) or active, its corresponding activation record is always on the bottom of the runtime stack.

At the time a function call takes place, there is two-way communication between the caller and the function. You are aware of the caller sending information to the function to initialize its formal arguments. But a function that is not void also communicates back to the caller by using a special variable that is not explicitly declared—the return value. (That is why the declaration of a function specifies a return type. The caller can tell how much space to set aside for the value returned.) When the function quits execution, it initializes that special variable for the caller much the same way that the caller initializes the formal arguments when the function is called.

Figure 12.22 shows how the runtime stack grows when the message `myList.add(35)` is sent from within `main()`. The activation record on the bottom of the stack is the one corresponding to `main()`.

In Phase 7 of Fig. 12.22, the call `RecNode(35,C.link_)` allocates memory off the heap. While that is not part of the picture, it is part of the memory requirements for the execution of the program.

The sequence of function calls that results from the execution of `myList.add(35)` terminates with a call to the `RecNode` constructor. When the call to the `RecNode` constructor is completed, its activation record is popped off the runtime stack. The record on the top of the stack immediately after that pop

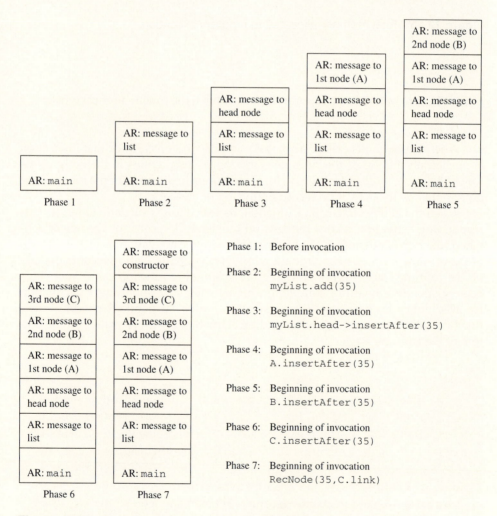

Figure 12.22 Growth of runtime stack resulting from invocation of `myList.add(35)` from `main()`.

corresponds to the `insertAfter` message passed to node C (the node with the data value 27).

The `insertAfter()` code that is executed immediately after the construction of the `RecNode` (the call to the `RecNode` constructor) is the assignment to the `link_` member of node C. When that assignment statement finishes execution, there is no remaining code to execute for that invocation of `insertAfter()`. So the activation record is popped off the stack.

At this point, the activation record on the top of the stack corresponds to the message to node B (the node with the data value 12). In order to do its work, node B merely passed the `insertAfter` message to the node C. There was no remaining work for node B to do in response to the message. So the activation for that message is popped off the stack. The series of pops of the runtime stack described to this point is illustrated in Fig. 12.23.

Keep in mind that we have offered a very simple model of computer memory and activities that occur while a program is executing. This model attempts to make two things clear:

1. There is not an infinite amount of memory in a computer. It is possible to run out of memory so that a function call cannot be executed or so that additional memory cannot be dynamically allocated to new objects.

2. If recursive code is written incorrectly so that the termination of the recursion may not occur under some circumstances, then the growth in the runtime stack may cause the program to crash.

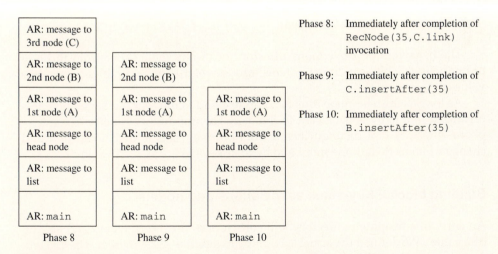

Figure 12.23 The change in the runtime stack resulting from completion of the execution of `RecNode(35,C.link)`, `C.insertAfter(35)`, and `B.insertAfter(35)`.

Modern C++ debugging tools have features that allow the programmer developing code to examine the runtime stack. By examining the stack, the programmer can see the sequence of function calls that have not been completed to this point.

12.8 Tables

A table is a container in which each item consists of two parts: a key and a value. The key for each item in a table is unique. Since no two items in a table have the same key, each table item can be identified through its key. Values are not necessarily unique. It is possible to have two different table items with identical values.

We have already introduced tables, starting in Chapter 6 with the inventory of a hardware store. The key for each item in the store was its bar code. The value was the price of the item. In Chapter 7, we implemented the hardware store inventory through the class `InventoryTable`. That implementation used classes and arrays, but not much more. Now we have more advanced programming tools to implement tables.

We will now focus our attention on a different but familiar table, a telephone directory. Each entry in the telephone directory consists of a name and a telephone number. The names are the keys and the telephone numbers are the values.

A telephone directory is an object that can respond to the following messages.

1. Add a new entry.

2. Remove the entry for a name.

3. Look up a number for a name.

4. Change the number for a name.

The behaviors of a telephone directory or of any table differ from those of ordinary lists. Tables can look up items through their keys, and tables can change values of their items.

As long as the telephone directory can respond to the four messages, how it is organized internally is irrelevant to the user. The important property of the telephone directory that distinguishes it from ordinary lists is that it can find and change its items (telephone numbers) by their keys (names).

Building blocks: Key-value associations and nodes

An entry in a telephone directory will consist of a `String` (the key) and an `int` (the value). We defined the struct `TelEntry` to describe such an item. The `TelEntry` constructor is inline.

```
// TelEntry is an entry in a telephone directory
struct TelEntry {
```

```
        TelEntry(const char s[], int n) : name(s), number(n) { }
                                // ASSUME: s is a valid C-string
        String name;            // Name for this telephone directory entry.
        int number;             // Number for this telephone directory entry.
};
```

The members of a struct are public by default. So a `TelEntry` and its members can be used by any code. That is not true for a `TelNode`, which is the node class for a linked list implementation of a telephone directory. `TelNode` is similar to the `Node` class, which was the type for nodes in a `List`. All the members of a `TelNode` are private except the two which access the `TelNode` member data.

```
// Node for a linked list of telephone directory entries.
class TelNode {
public:
    const TelEntry& data() const;
    const TelNode* link() const;
private:
    TelEntry data_;                         // Name and number for this entry.

    TelNode* link_;                         // Next entry.
    TelNode(const char n[] = "", int x = 0, TelNode* p = 0);
    TelNode* copy() const;                  // Returns a deep copy.
    ~TelNode();                             // Deallocates memory for this node
                                            //   and the following ones.
friend class TelDirectory;
};
```

The member function definitions for `TelNode` are as follows. For the most part, they look like the definitions of the corresponding member functions for `Node`.

```
const TelEntry& TelNode :: data() const
{
    return data_;
}
const TelNode* TelNode :: link() const
{
    return link_;
}

TelNode :: TelNode(const char n[], int x, TelNode* p) : data_(n,x), link_(p)
{ }
TelNode :: ~TelNode()
{
    delete link_;
}
```

```
TelNode* TelNode :: copy() const
{
    if (link_)
        return new TelNode(data_.name.charString(), data_.number,
                                                    link_->copy());
    return new TelNode(data_.name.charString(), data_.number, 0);
}
```

Incorporating an extra data member for efficient methods

The definition of the class `TelDirectory` will serve as our telephone directory design. The `TelDirectory` definition is somewhat similar to the old `List` definition. After all, we are implementing the table as a kind of list.

```
// A table of name-number pairs. Different names for different entries are
//    distinct.
class TelDirectory {
public:
    TelDirectory();                             // Creates an empty directory.
    TelDirectory(const TelDirectory& d);        // Makes a deep copy of d.
    TelDirectory& operator=(const TelDirectory& rhs);
                                                // Assigns a deep copy of rhs.
    ~TelDirectory();                            // Deallocates directory memory.

    void add(const char n[], int x);
            // Adds name n, number x if n is not already in the directory.
            //    Does nothing if n is already in the directory.
            // ASSUME: n is a valid C-string.
    void remove(const char n[]);
            // Removes the entry for name n. Does nothing if n is not in
            //    the directory.
    void change(const char n[], int newNum);
            // Changes the number for name n to newNum if n is in the
            //    directory. Does nothing if n is not in the directory.
            // ASSUME: n is a valid C-string.
    const int* lookUp(const char n[]);
            // Number for name n if n is in the directory, else null.
            // ASSUME: n is a valid C-string.
friend class DirIterator;
protected:
    TelNode* head_;
    TelNode* prevAcc_;
    TelEntry* search(const String& n);
};
```

The TelDirectory is implemented via an ordered linked list with a dummy head node. The ordering is based on the keys. Those implementation decisions are hidden from the public part of the definition. The nonpublic part of the class and the definitions of the class methods determine such issues. They need not concern the user of the class.

The data member head_ points to the dummy head node. The constructors, assignment operator, and destructor definitions are as follows:

```
TelDirectory :: TelDirectory()
{
    head_ = new TelNode;
    prevAcc_ = head_;
}


TelDirectory :: TelDirectory(const TelDirectory& t) : head_(t.head_->copy())
{
    prevAcc_ = head_;
}

TelDirectory& TelDirectory :: operator=(const TelDirectory& rhs)
{
    if (this != &rhs) {
        delete head_;
        head_ = rhs.head_->copy();
        prevAcc_ = head_;
    }
    return *this;
}


TelDirectory :: ~TelDirectory()
{
    delete head_;
}
```

TelDirectory iterators are not incorporated into the TelDirectory class. A single iterator class, DirIterator, is a friend of TelDirectory. When we removed the iterator from the List classes previously, we also removed the traveling pointer from the class definition. So why does TelDirectory have two protected pointers instead of one? What is the purpose of prevAcc_?

The pointer prevAcc_ keeps track of the node in the list that was most recently accessed by a TelDirectory method. It is used to improve the efficiency of execution of two successive TelDirectory methods. For example, a TelDirectory might look up a telephone number and then change it to a new number. The change() method can take advantage of the search done by the lookUp() method if it has access to the TelNode that the lookUp() method found. Figure 12.24 shows prevAcc_ after a node whose key is "John" is accessed.

After each operation, the pointer prevAcc_ points to the node immediately before the node most recently accessed by that operation. Since the underlying list

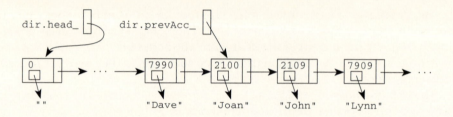

Figure 12.24 The `TelDirectory` dir and its pointer member `dir.prevAcc_` after any of the messages: `dir.lookup("John")`, or `dir.change("John", 2109)`, or `dir.insert("John", 2109)`.

has a dummy head node, `prevAcc_` will never be null. The following rules describe the status of `prevAcc_` immediately after each `add`, `remove`, `lookUp`, and `change` message.

1. `add` message: `prevAcc_` points to the node immediately before the node just inserted. If an attempt was made to add a new entry with the same name as an existing entry (in which case no insertion occurs) `prevAcc_` points to the node before the one with the same name.

2. `remove` message: `prevAcc_` points to the node immediately preceding the node just removed. If no removal occurred (there was no node in the list whose entry name matched the one to be removed), `prevAcc_` points to the node whose key immediately precedes the key of the argument. A `remove` message is illustrated in Fig. 12.25.

3. `lookUp` and `change` messages: `prevAcc_` points to the node immediately preceding the one that was the result of the search (with the name to be looked up or changed). If the search was unsuccessful, `prevAcc_` points to the node whose key immediately precedes the key of the argument.

The private member function `search()` sets the value of `prevAcc_`. The return type of `search()` is pointer-to-`TelEntry`. `search(n)` returns a pointer to

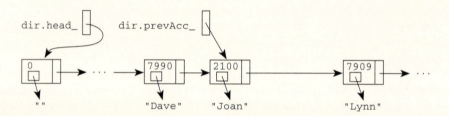

Figure 12.25 The `TelDirectory` dir and its pointer member `dir.prevAcc_` after the message `dir.remove("John")`.

the `data_` member of the `TelNode` that has name `n`. If `n` is not in the directory, `search(n)` returns null.

The other `TelDirectory` operations can invoke `search()` rather than wandering around in the directory on their own. The algorithm for `search()` relies on the fact that the underlying linked list is ordered.

```
TelEntry* TelDirectory :: search(const String& n)
{
    TelNode* current;                   // If n is in the list, current will point
                                        //    to the node containing n.

    if (prevAcc_->data_.name < n)       //    Start current where you left off the
        current = prevAcc_->link_;      //    last time if n isn't too small.
    else {
        current = head_->link_;         //    The last access was too far down the
        prevAcc_ = head_;               //    list. Start current at the beginning.
    }

    while (current && current->data_.name < n) { // Look for n
        prevAcc_ = current;
        current = current->link_;
    };

    if (current && current->data_.name == n) {   // If current points to a node
        return  &(current->data_);               //    with name n, return the
    }                                            //    address of its data.
    return 0;                                    // If not, return null
}
```

When a `change()` operation is performed, the search for the node to be changed might not start at the beginning of the list. If the name for the entry to be changed is greater than the name of the node referenced by `prevAcc_`, then the search begins right after `prevAcc_` instead.

```
void TelDirectory :: change (const char n[], int newNum)
{
    TelEntry* p = search(n);                     // Look for n.
    if (p != 0)                                  // If you find it
        p->number = newNum;                      //    change the number.
}
```

Notice that `prevAcc_` takes the place of the pointer previous in the original algorithms from Section 12.2. The dummy head node is a convenience that guarantees `prevAcc_` will never be null.

The definitions for the `add()` and `remove()` methods are easy to write. They both rely on `prevAcc_` being set to the appropriate position by a call to `search()`.

```
void TelDirectory :: add(const char n[], int x)
{
    if (search(n) == 0)                        // Search for n. If it's not
        prevAcc_->link_ =                      //   in the list, add it in the
            new TelNode(n, x, prevAcc_->link_);  //   correct position.
}

void TelDirectory ::  remove(const char n[])
{
    if (search(n) != 0) {                      // Search for n. If it's in the
        TelNode* toDie = prevAcc_->link_;      //    list, remove it.
        prevAcc_->link_ = toDie->link_;
        toDie->link_ = 0;
        delete toDie;
    }
}
```

The return type for `lookUp()` is `const int*`. A `lookUp` message requires a name for an actual argument. If there is not an entry in the telephone directory with that name, then `lookUp()` returns null. If there is an entry, then `lookUp` returns a const pointer to the item. Const prevents anyone using the pointer from changing the actual item.

```
const int* TelDirectory :: lookUp(const char n[])
{
    TelEntry* p = search(n);                   // Search for n. If it's in the
    if (p != 0)                                //    list, return the address
        return &(p->number);                   //    of its number.
    return 0;
}
```

The telephone directory iterator is designed just like the list iterator.

```
// Iterator for a telephone directory
class DirIterator {
public:
    DirIterator(const TelDirectory& t); // Constructs an iterator for t
                                        //   Iteration starts from the beginning
                                        //   of the directory.
    const TelEntry& next();             // The next directory entry.
                                        //    ASSUME: There is a next entry.
    bool more() const;                  // Are there more entries?
    void reset();                       // Resets to the first entry.
protected:
```

```
      const TelDirectory& theDirectory_;
      const TelNode* cursor_;
};
```

DirIterator is not a friend of TelNode, but it is a friend of TelDirectory. It uses the access TelNode functions link() and data() to return the appropriate information and to move through the list. Remember that the underlying data structure of a TelDirectory is a linked list with a dummy head node. So DirIterator must begin its iteration from the second node rather than from the dummy head node.

```
DirIterator :: DirIterator(const TelDirectory& t) : theDirectory_(t),
                                                   cursor_(t.head_->link())
{ }

const TelEntry& DirIterator :: next()
{
   const TelEntry& t = cursor_->data();// Hold onto the return value.
   cursor_ = cursor_->link();          // Move the cursor for the next access.
   return t;
}

bool  DirIterator :: more() const
{
   return (cursor_ != 0);
}

void  DirIterator :: reset()
{
   cursor_ = theDirectory_.head_->link();
}
```

The following code shows how a TelDirectory and its associated iterator DirIterator can be used. The output generated is in the box that follows.

```
TelDirectory tel;          // tel is now an empty directory.
tel.add("Milly", 3456);    // Milly - 3456 is a new entry.
tel.add("Helen", 7900);    // Helen - 7900 is the second entry.
tel.add("Marion", 4331);   // Marion - 4331 is the third entry.
tel.add("Gordon", 1010);   // Gordon - 1010 is the fourth entry.
tel.add("Milly", 0);       // Milly is already in the directory, so this
                           //    statement does nothing.

const int* p = tel.lookUp("Helen");
if (p != 0)
   cout << "Helen's number is " << *p << ".\n";
```

```
        if (tel.lookUp("Michael") == 0)
            cout << "Michael is not in the directory.\n\n";
```

```
    Helen's number is 7900.
    Michael is not in the directory.
```

The last two `lookUp` messages gave different results. Since `Helen` was a directory name, the first `lookUp` was successful. It returned a pointer to the number associated with `Helen`.

We can create an iterator for `tel`. The output generated from execution of the loop is in the box that follows.

```
DirIterator it(tel);
while (it.more()) {
   const TelEntry& t = it.next();    // t must be const since next() returns
   cout << t.number                  //   a const TelEntry&
        << "   " << t.name << endl;
}
```

```
    1010  Gordon
    7900  Helen
    4331  Marion
    3456  Milly
```

Changing the entries for `Helen` requires a `change` or a `remove` message.

```
tel.remove("Marion");        // tel now contains only 3 entries.
tel.change("Gordon", 2000);  // Gordon's number is now 2000.
tel.change("Alice", 5101);   // Nothing happens. Alice is not in the
                             //   directory.
```

Since the directory changed, the iterator must be reset. Besides, the iterator had already run to the end of the directory. The output from the following code appears after the code.

```
        it.reset();
        while (it.more()) {
            const TelEntry& t = it.next();
            cout << t.number << "   " << t.name << endl;
        }
```

```
2000   Gordon
7900   Helen
3456   Milly
```

Tables as associative arrays: Private inheritance

An **associative array** is a generalized array in which the subscripts are the keys and the elements are the values. Some programmers prefer to organize tables around the concept of an associative array rather than a standard table with its four operations look up, change, add, and remove. Here is what we mean. Suppose that `dir` is an associative array that represents the telephone directory. If `"John"` is in the directory, then the associative array notation `dir["John"]` is a reference to the number associated with the key `"John"`.

We can implement an associative array for a telephone directory by using a table. The interface of an associative array for the telephone directory must have an overloaded subscript operator. The subscript operator will provide the services of the `TelDirectory`'s `lookUp()`, `change()`, and `add()` methods. We named our associative array class `TelArray`. Here is its definition:

```cpp
// An associative array of name-number pairs. Different names for different
//   entries are distinct.
class TelArray : private TelDirectory {
public:
    TelArray();                                 // Creates an empty directory.
    TelArray(const TelArray& t);                // Makes a deep copy of t.
    TelArray& operator=(const TelArray& rhs);   // Assigns a deep copy of rhs.
    ~TelArray();                                // Deallocates array memory.

    int& operator[](const char n[]);            // If n is not in the array, a
                                                //    new element is created with
                                                //    name n and number -1.
                                                // Returns the number for name n.
                                                // ASSUME: n is a valid C-string
    void remove(const char n[]);                // Removes the entry for name n.
                                                //    (Does nothing if n is not a
                                                //    directory name.)
                                                // ASSUME: n is a valid C-string

    friend class ArrIterator;
};
```

There is quite a lot to explain in the `TelArray` definition. The inheritance is private rather than public. (All of our previous examples have been public.) You can tell that the derivation is private from the first line of the class definition:

```
class TelArray : private TelDirectory {
```

Public inheritance is called inheritance of the interface. The public members of a base class are considered to be public members of the derived class. The public members of a class along with the documentation constitute the interface of a class. When a class D is derived publicly from a base class B, we say that an instance of D *is-a* B.

Private inheritance is called inheritance of the implementation. Private inheritance is not inheritance of the interface because all of the members of the base class, including those that are public, are private members of the derived class. No member of the base class is part of the interface of the derived class. If class E is derived privately from a base class B, then an instance of E is not a B. It is illegal to try to substitute an E for a B. What private inheritance buys is the implementation details of the base class.

> Use public derivation when you want the interface of the base class to be part of the interface of the derived class. Use private or protected inheritance when you want to use the base class only as an implementation tool for the derived class.

The TelArray class simply uses a TelDirectory as an implementation detail. You can think of the underlying TelDirectory for the TelArray as being much like the underlying linked list for the TelDirectory. The linked list is an implementation detail for TelDirectory; the TelDirectory is an implementation detail for the TelArray.

Why would one use private inheritance? TelArray provides quite a nice explanation. The operations that one usually associates with an associative array are subscripting and possibly removing (if the associative array is able to purge any of its elements). TelArray has an overloaded subscript operator and a remove that is similar to TelDirectory's remove operation. But the add, lookup, and change operations in the TelDirectory simply are not appropriate for an associative array. And that is quite all right. A user cannot invoke add(), lookUp(), or change() for a TelArray because they are private and not accessible.

The definitions of the TelArray member functions look the same as they might if the inheritance were not private. The constructors, destructor, and overloaded assignment are straightforward.

```
TelArray :: TelArray(const TelArray& t) : TelDirectory(t)
{ }

TelArray:: TelArray() : TelDirectory()
{ }
```

```
TelArray& TelArray :: operator=(const TelArray& rhs)
{
    TelDirectory :: operator=(rhs);
    return *this;
}


TelArray:: ~TelArray()
{ }
```

The initialization lists of the two constructors invoke the corresponding base class constructors. The overloaded assignment invokes the overloaded base class assignment operator. The destructor has an empty body. But that doesn't mean it does nothing. When C++ invokes the destructor for the derived class, it automatically invokes the destructor for the base class, even if the derived class destructor looks like it does nothing.

`TelArray` defines a member function `remove()`. That is one way to make `remove()` a public member of `TelArray`. Its definition invokes the base class `TelDirectory::remove()`.

```
void TelArray :: remove(const char n[])
{
    TelDirectory::remove(n);
}
```

It is easy to see inheritance of implementation in `TelArray::remove()`. The definition of `TelArray::remove()` invokes `TelDirectory::remove()` outright. But the overloaded subscript operator, which does not correspond to any single operation in the base class, is even more impressive. It uses two base class member functions, `add()` and `search()`.

```
int& TelArray :: operator[](const char n[])
{
    String toFind(n);                    // Set up a string to find with name n.
    if (search(toFind) == 0)             // If n is not in the directory
        add(n,-1);                       //   add it, with the default number -1.
    return search(toFind)->number;       // Return the number for n.
}
```

Recall that `add()` is a public member of the base class and `search()` is a protected member. That means both of them are accessible in the derived class. The subscript operator makes one invocation of `add()` and two invocations of `search()`. The first `search()` finds out whether the name is in the directory. If not, then the name is added with a default number -1. The second one simply returns the number corresponding to the name. The code is not quite as inefficient as it looks. Since `search()` caches the last access to the linked list, the second invocation does not require looking through all of the linked list nodes to find the name. That subsequent search begins where the first one stopped, right at the name it is searching for.

The `TelArray` class declares `ArrIterator` as a friend. But think back on the `OrderedList` class, which was derived from `List`. `OrderedList` did not declare any special iterator class as a friend. It did not need to. Instead, an `OrderedList` could use a `List` iterator. So the question remains, "Why is it necessary for `TelArray` to declare its own iterator class as a friend?"

The answer lies in private inheritance. When a class is derived from a private base class, it is not generally possible to substitute an instance of the derived class for a reference to the base class. The `TelIterator` class constructor has a formal argument that is a `const TelDirectory&`. A `TelArray` is not a `TelDirectory`. So an actual argument that is a `TelArray` cannot be used.

The `ArrIterator`, which can iterate over a `TelArray`, looks just like a `DirIterator`, which iterates over a `TelDirectory`. The only difference between the two is that `TelDirectory` becomes `TelArray` and `DirIterator` becomes `ArrIterator` in the new iterator class. Here is the `ArrIterator` definition:

```
class ArrIterator {
public:
    ArrIterator(const TelArray& a);    // Constructs iterator for a, initialized
                                       //    to begin from the start.
    const TelEntry& next();            // Next directory entry.
                                       //    ASSUME: There is a next entry.
    bool more() const;                 // Is there another entry?
    void reset();                      // Reset the iterator to the start.

private:
    const TelArray& arr_;
    const TelNode* cursor_;
};
```

We will leave the implementation of the `ArrIterator` to you. Follow the `DirIterator` member definitions as a model.

Using a `TelArray` is quite different from using a `TelDirectory`. The code that follows is almost parallel to the sample code for the use of a `TelDirectory`.

```
TelArray arr;               // arr is now an empty directory.
arr["Milly"] = 3456;        // Milly - 3456 is a new entry.
arr["Helen"] = 7900;        // Helen - 7900 is the second entry.
arr["Marion"] = 4331;       // Marion - 4331 is the third entry.
arr["Gordon"] = 1010;       // Gordon - 1010 is the fourth entry.
arr["Milly"] = 0;           // Milly is already in the directory. Her number
                            //    is changed to 0.
```

```
if (arr["Helen"] > -1)
    cout << "Helen's number is " << arr["Helen"] << ".\n";
if (arr["Michael"] == -1)
    cout << "Michael is in the directory with a default number, -1.\n\n";
```

```
Helen's number is 7900.
Michael is in the directory with a default number, -1.
```

Any use of the subscript operator has the potential for changing the underlying directory. This time, "Michael" with the default number -1 was added since there was an attempt to use "Michael" as a subscript. A TelArray is a safe array. There is no such thing as a TelArray subscript that is "out of bounds."

How about an iterator for arr. The output generated from execution of the loop below is in the box that follows.

```
ArrIterator iter(arr);
while (iter.more()) {
    const TelEntry& t = iter.next();
    cout << t.number
        << "   " << t.name << endl;
}
```

```
1010  Gordon
7900  Helen
4331  Marion
-1  Michael
0  Milly
```

We can change an entry by using the subscript operator. Removing an entry entirely requires a remove message.

```
arr.remove("Michael");              // arr now contains only 3 entries.
arr["Gordon"] = 2000;               // Gordon's number is now 2000. No new
                                    //   entry is created.
arr["Milly"] = arr["Gordon"] + 1;   // Milly's number is Gordon's plus 1.
```

Let's reset the iterator to see all of the entries. The output from the next segment of code appears below it.

```
    iter.reset();
while (iter.more()) {
    const TelEntry& t = iter.next();
    cout << t.number << "   " << t.name << endl;
}
```

```
    2000   Gordon
    7900   Helen
    4331   Marion
    2001   Milly
```

12.9 ▊ Summary

The discussion of container classes in this chapter was barely an introduction. We first saw container classes with list type classes in Chapter 7, and we saw container objects before that in Chapter 5, when we first mentioned sequences and lists. But this chapter revealed part of a large hierarchy of container classes.

Much of the focus of this chapter was on list type containers, and on linked list containers in particular. Linked lists have been around far longer than C++. Although the linked list algorithms from this chapter were expressed in C++ type syntax, they can be coded in a variety of different languages, including Pascal and FORTRAN. C++ has the advantage over Pascal and FORTRAN of letting us package the list behaviors and attributes into a single object. And C++ lets us create other list types from generic types through inheritance and templates.

Many problem specifications naturally give rise to objects that are containers. Even when the problem does not seem to have a container object involved in the problem, containers are often useful as part of the solution. Problem statements rarely begin with such words as "This is a problem that uses an ordered list." The program designer will figure out what kinds of containers are intrinsic to an object-oriented model of a solution. Is the container an ordered list, a stack, a table? The answers lie in the behaviors of the object. The choice of the container is based on the object's behaviors and the efficiency of the algorithms that implement those behaviors.

Container classes are so important that there are large C++ libraries devoted to them. The most common kinds of classes that are distributed in C++ libraries are either graphical user interface classes or container classes. Knowledge of container class types and their implementation is an extremely important part of the programmer's toolkit.

Glossary

activation record A data structure generated by the compiler for use at runtime during function calls to save argument values or references and return information for use by the body of the called function.

association A relationship between items in one container and items in another.

associative array An array that uses arbitrary strings (keys) as subscripts.

bag A collection of items with no ordering but allowing multiple occurrences of an item.

data structures The organization of data and the operations that can be performed on the data.

dummy head node A node used at the start of a list so that every list, even an empty one, contains at least one node. This is purely an implementation technique to make list processing code simpler.

free store *See* heap.

head node The first node in a linked list.

head pointer The pointer to the first node of a list.

heap The portion of memory used for dynamically allocated data structures. (Also called *free store*.)

link A pointer connecting one node to another.

linked list A list in which each element consists of an actual list item and the location of the next item in the list.

node A data structure with a value and one or more pointers to nodes.

ordered list A collection of items arranged by order of the items.

queue A collection of items arranged by order of entry into collection. The earliest to arrive is the first in collection.

queue front The first item in a queue and the earliest to arrive. Only the front item can be removed.

queue rear The last item in a queue and the most recent to arrive.

random access The property of a collection in which any item can be accessed in the same amount of time as any other item.

runtime stack A stack used at runtime by the operating system for activation records of functions that have been called but have not yet returned.

set An unordered collection containing no duplicates.

stack A collection of items arranged by order of entry into the collection. The latest to arrive is first in collection.

stack pop The removal of the first item (top) from a stack.

stack push The addition of an item to a stack. It becomes the new top item.

stack top The first (most recently added) item in a stack. Only the top item can be removed.

table A data structure that pairs keys with values and allows lookup of a value given its key.

12.10 ▮ Exercises

1. Assume that the following linked list has been given.

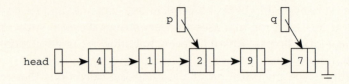

   a. What is the value of `head->info_`?

   b. Write two different statements, each of which changes the `info_` of the third list node to 8.

   c. What is the value of `p->link_->link_->info_`?

   d. What is the value of `p->link_->link_->link_`?

   e. What is the value of `q->link_`?

   f. Suppose the following code is executed.

   ```
   q->link_ = new Node(5,q->link_);
   ```

   What is the value of `p->link_->link_->link_->link_`? Draw a picture of the list.

   g. Given the original picture, write a segment of code that removes the last node from the list.

2. Using the terms *head, null, info,* and *link* described in section 12.2, write linked list pseudo-code algorithms for the following list behaviors.

   a. Determine the length of the list (number of items in the list).

   b. Remove the last item from the list.

   c. Add a new item to the end of the list.

   d. Double the number of list items by duplicating every node in the list. For example, if the original list consists of 2, 5, 8, 4, then the doubled list consists of 2, 2, 5, 5, 8, 8, 4, 4.

   e. Remove every other item from the list, beginning with the first.

   f. Reverse the list so that the first item becomes the last and vice versa. For example, if the original list consists of 2, 5, 8, 4, then the reversed list is a copy consisting of 4, 8, 5, 2.

   g. Reverse the list so that the first item becomes the last and vice versa. Do not make a copy, do not create and new nodes, but instead alter the links.

3. Suppose that one of the methods of the original `List` class from section 12.3 contained the following code:

```
head_ = 0;
for (int i = 1; i < 4; i++)
    head_ = new Node(i, head_);
```

   a. Draw a picture of the list that results from execution of the code.

   b. Is it possible for this code to generate a memory leak? Explain your answer.

4. Jimmy modeled his own `JimsNode` class after the `Node` class of section 12.3, but he made all of the member functions public instead of private. He defined a constructor as follows:

```
JimsNode :: JimsNode(int i, JimsNode* p)
{
    JimsNode* q = new JimsNode;
    q->link_ = p;
    q->info_ = i;
}
```

   Describe exactly what happened when Jimmy tried to execute this code.

```
JimsNode* sample = new JimsNode;
```

5. Use the `Node` class definition from section 12.3, but assume that the `List` class is changed to include some member functions in addition to those in the original version.

   Suppose that the following segments of code appeared in some `List` member function definitions. They are all defective—generating memory leaks, dangling pointers (list pointers that point to nonallocated memory), illegal pointer access, or incorrect results. Describe the nature of each defect, using diagrams when helpful. Describe lists for which the defective code actually performs correctly, if there are any. Correct the errors so that the code is no longer defective.

   a. `// Remove the first node from the list.`
      `head_ = head_->link_;`

   b. `// Change the info_ of the first list node with`
      `// negative info_ to 0.`
      `Node* p = head_;`
      `while (p->info_ >= 0)`
      `    p = p->link_;`
      `p->info_ = 0;`

c. // Remove the first node with negative info_ from
```
   // the list.
   for(Node* p = head_; p && p->info_ >=0;
       p = p->link_);
   delete p;
```
d. // Insert a node with info_ 0 at the end of the list.
```
   Node* p = head_;
   while (p->link_)
       p = p->link_;
   p->info_ = 0;
```
e. // Remove the tenth node from the list.
```
   Node* p = head_;
   for(int i = 0; i < 8; i++);
       p = p->link_;
   delete p->link_;
   p->link_ = 0;
```
f. // Count the number of positive nodes in the list.
```
   int numPos = 0;
   for(Node* p = head_; p && p->info_ > 0; numPos++);
```
g. // (For an ordered list.) Add newItem to the list in
```
   // its proper place.
   Node* p = head_;
   Node* q;
   while (p && p->info_ < newItem) {
       q = p;
       p = p->link_;
   }
   q->link_ = new Node(newItem, p);
```

6. Suppose that the List class from section 12.3 did not define an overloaded assignment operator.

a. Explain what happens as a result of calling f().

```
void f(List& goodList)
{
    List tempList;
    tempList = goodList;
    cout << "Executing f" << endl;
}
```

b. What happens as a result of calling g()?

```
void g(List& goodList)
{
    List tempList = goodList;
    cout << "Executing g" << endl;
}
```

16. Suppose that the `RecNode` class of Section 12.7 contained the following poorly named method.

```
int RecNode :: mystery() const
{
    int adder = 0;
    if (info_ % 2 == 0)
        adder++;
    if (!link_)
        return adder;
    return adder + link_->mystery();
}
```

a. Explain what `RecNode::mystery()` does.

b. Define `RecList::mystery()`, a method that sends the mystery message to its head node.

c. If `myList` is of type `RecList` and `myList` is as illustrated below, what is the value of `myList.mystery()`?

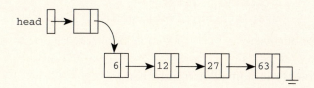

17. The following functions can be used to generate the Fibonacci sequence, which begins with 0, 1, 1, 2, 3, 5, 8, 13, 21,…. Each term except the first two is the sum of the preceding two.

```
int f1(int i)
{
    if (i == 0)
        return 0;
    if (i == 1)
        return 1;
    return f1(i - 1) + f1(i - 2);

}
int f2a(int n, int  a, int b)
{
    if (n == 0)
        return a;
    return f2a(n - 1, b, a + b);
}
```

```
int f2(int n)
{
    return f2a(n, 0, 1);
}
```

a. Trace the execution of `f1(7)`. How many calls to `f1()` were made?

b. Trace the execution of `f2(7)`. How many calls to `f2()` and `f2a()` were made?

18. What output is generated by the call `f("abc",0)`? Explain what `f()` does.

a. Assume `f()` is defined in this manner:

```
void f(char string[], int first)
{
    if (first == strlen(string) - 1)
        cout << string;
    else
        for (int i = first; i < strlen(string); i++) {
            swap(string[first],string[i]);
            f(string,  first + 1);
            swap(string[first],string[i]);
        }
}
```

b. Assume `f()` is defined in this manner:

```
void f(char string[], int first)
{
    if (first == strlen(string) - 1)
        cout << string;
    else
        for (int i = first; i < strlen(string); i++) {
            swap(string[first],string[i]);
            f(string,  first + 1);
        }
}
```

c. Given the definitions that follow, what output is generated by the call `f(sabc,0)`?

```
struct str { char s[10]; };
str sabc = { "abc" };
void f(str string, int first)
{
    if (first == strlen(string.s) - 1)
        cout << string.s;
    else
```

```
        for (int i = first; i < strlen(string.s); i++) {
            swap(string.s[first],string.s[i]);
            f(string,  first + 1);
        }
    }
```

19. The list methods of section 12.7 were implemented via messages to the head node. Suppose that the `Node` definition from that section is amended to include additional member function declarations. Write the definitions for these new member functions.

a. `int length();`   `// Number of nodes in the list after this node`

b. `void removeAll(int x);`   `// Removes all nodes containing x from the`
                              `//    list following this node`

c. `void removeAlternate();` `// Removes every other node in the list after`
                              `//    this node, beginning with the next node`

d. `void doubleEveryNode();` `// Duplicates every node following this node.`

e. `void makeAllPositive();` `// Changes the negative info_ of nodes after`
                              `//    this node to 1.`

f. `void printForward(ostream& o);` `// Prints to o the data in the list`
                              `//     following this node in order of`
                              `//     its appearance in the list`

g. `void printReverse(ostream& o);` `// Prints to o the data in the list`
                              `//     following this node in reverse`
                              `//     order of appearance in the list`

20. The `TelDirectory` has only two constructors: a null constructor and a copy constructor. Use `TelDirectory` as a base for a derived class named `DirFromFile`. `DirFromFile` need not redefine any of the members of `TelDirectory` such as `add()` or `lookUp()`. But since they are not inherited, `DirFromFile` must define its own constructors, overloaded assignment, and destructor.

    Define three constructors for `DirFromFile`: a null constructor, a copy constructor, and a constructor that creates a telephone directory from a text file. The third constructor should have a single C-string argument, which is the name of the actual file on disk. The `DirFromFile` destructor should prompt the user to enter a file name in which the directory information can be written. The format of the input file and the output file should be identical.

21. The `TelDirectory` and its associated classes from section 12.8 create a table type in which each entry consists of a `String` type value and an `int` type key. For this exercise, you will define a collection of class templates capable of creating a table type for generic type values. The keys and values can be any first class types.

a. Define a struct template that has two members, value and key. Base the template on two parameters, one for the value type and the other for the key type. Define a class template for a node with the same parameters. The node template can have a pointer to a struct as its `data_` member.

b. Define a class template for a table class with the same parameters as the struct template of part (a). Model this template class after the `TelDir` class of section 12.8. Define the `change()` method so that the client code can change a value for a particular key but not the key itself.

c. Define a class template for an iterator over the table class for part (b). The `next()` method may return a pointer to a node, a struct, or a pointer to a struct.

d. Compile your collection of templates. (Remember to put the declarations of all of the class templates at the top of your source code file.) Write a small program to test your new code. The driver program should create a table of pairs of items in which each key is a student identification number and each value is a struct consisting of a name (`String`) and an age (`int`).

22. Define an associative array class template based on the templates of the previous exercise. Test your new code by creating an associative array of `String`-`int` pairs, then create an array of `int`-`String` pairs.

23. This project refers to the information retrieval problems at the beginning of section 12.1. For the parts of this exercise, assume that each person (student or teacher) has a unique ID number and that each ID number belongs to exactly one person. Teachers teach one or more course sections, but each course section is taught by only one teacher. Students may be in one or more course sections.

a. Design and implement a one-to-one correspondence of names and ID numbers so that given a name, the corresponding ID number may be looked up, and given an ID number the corresponding name may be looked up. You should consider at least two different designs. First, use two ordinary tables, one with names as keys, the other with IDs as keys. Second, consider deriving from a `Table` class a `TwoWayTable` class that allows either of the items paired to be used as the key. Implement at least one of your designs.

b. Design and implement a one-to-many correspondence of teachers and course sections taught. Your implementation could treat this as a one-to-one correspondence of a teacher and a set of course sections. Make sure your design allows look up in both directions: look up the course sections taught by a given teacher and look up the teacher of a given course section. What are the tradeoffs of using a single list of associations of teachers and sets of course sections versus using two tables?

c. Design and implement a many-to-many correspondence of teachers and students. For a given teacher you should be able to look up the students taught, and for a given student you should be able to look up the teachers who teach that student. You could solve the problem using two one-to-many correspondences of the kind mentioned in part (b). You could also use one *relation*—a list of associations that can have duplicate keys. Relations are the major data structure used in *relational databases*, which are an important technology in many data processing applications. Consider two designs: one using tables and the other using a single relation. Implement the design using a relation.

Programming Projects

24. You may use some of the ideas of the previous exercise to complete this programming project. Suppose the data for the community college is organized into three different files:

    - `id.txt`, containing names and ID numbers of teachers and students. Each line of the file corresponds to one person. The first nine characters in the line are the ID number; the tenth character is a space, and the rest of the line is the name.
    - `staff.txt`, consisting of course sections and teacher ID numbers. Each line corresponds to a single course section formatted as follows:

      XXX NNN ddddddddd

      where XXX is the three-character course abbreviation, NNN is the three-character section number, and ddddddddd is the nine-digit teacher id number.
    - `rolls.txt` containing the class rolls of course sections. Each section roll portion of `rolls.txt` begins with a line in the form:

      XXX NNN

      where XXX is the three-character course abbreviation, and NNN is the three-character section number.

      Each subsequent line of a section roll contains a single nine-digit ID number. The file is terminated by a line consisting of three asterisks.

    Write a program that can process queries about the relationships among students and teachers. In particular, your program should be able to do the following:

    - Find all the teachers for the student John Smith.
    - John Smith is one student that all of his teachers have in common. Find the set of students that all of John Smith's teachers have in common.

25. Electronic mail systems have electronic mailboxes in which users receive incoming mail. Design an electronic mailbox that can do the following things at a minimum:

- Receive a message.
- Delete a message.
- Print a message.
- List all messages.
- List all messages satisfying certain criteria (such as having the same author).

Your mailbox class should have a null constructor, a copy constructor, and a constructor that creates a mailbox from data in a text file. The destructor should deallocate memory and, if the mailbox was originally created from file data, write the current mailbox entries back to that text file.

26. How many words appear in a one-page document more than once?

a. Analyze and design a solution to the problem, making use of a container class.

b. Implement your solution. Test your solution on several text files. Begin your testing with very short text files, then graduate to larger files.

Chapter 13

An Example Reconsidered: Some Issues in Design

THROUGHOUT this book, we have used the changemaker problem to illustrate object-oriented program development and C++ language features. The changemaker problem provided a clear example of how specifications and corresponding solutions can develop over time. The first changemaker solution could solve only the original statement of the problem. The final changemaker solution was much more complex, providing a tremendous amount of functionality beyond the original solution.

In this chapter, we will show you how we designed and implemented the `TypeSetter` library, which was introduced in Chapter 3 to illustrate using class libraries. The `TypeSetter` solves the problem of typesetting a document to conform to specific constraints such as margin size and pagination. We will discuss new design techniques and advanced language features, and we will compare some techniques that you have already learned.

Let's start with the original model from which the final solution eventually evolved. Although some of the implementation of that original model was obvious, there were subtleties that we were quite unaware of when we started. We will show some of the places where we stumbled along the way to the final solution. We will also discuss some of the techniques used to verify that our code was correct as well as some of the programming techniques we used to make the code cleaner and easier to understand (and modify in the future if necessary). We will conclude with a general discussion of organizing all of the code that goes into the solution of a complicated problem.

13.1 ▌ The `TypeSetter` class

The `TypeSetter` class is the earliest example in this book of a nontrivial user-defined class. The class definition was given in Chapter 3 to inform readers how to define and use a class type object. The header file for the `TypeSetter` is as follows:

```
// File = TypeSetter.H
#ifndef _TYPESETTER_H
#define _TYPESETTER_H


#include <iostream.h>

class Worder;
class Liner;
class Pager;

// A TypeSetter object formats text into pages.
//    Each line on the page has a fixed maximum length.
//    Each page has a fixed maximum number of lines.
//    Pages have optional headers at the top and page numbers at the bottom.
//       The header is on the top line of the page followed by a blank line and
//       then the first line of text.  Three lines follow the last line of text—
//       a blank line, a line with the page number, and one more blank line.
//       A form feed character is placed at the end of each page.
//    Characters are divided into "words," where each word is a sequence of
//       non-whitespace characters.  Each word that is too long to fit on the
//       rest of the current line is wrapped to the next line. If a word is
//       longer than an entire line, it is split at the end of the line
//       and continued at the beginning of the next line.
```

```
//    Whitespace characters are translated to blanks or newlines as
//       appropriate. Adjacent whitespace characters are compressed into a
//       single blank (or newline where appropriate).

class TypeSetter {
public:

    enum { minPageNumber = 0, maxPageNumber = 10000, defaultPageNumber = 1,
           minLineLength = 10, maxLineLength = 255, defaultLineLength = 72,
           minLinesPerPage = 5, maxLinesPerPage = 100, defaultLinesPerPage = 55
         };

    TypeSetter(int lineLength = defaultLineLength,
               int linesPerPage = defaultLinesPerPage,
               int pageNumber = defaultPageNumber,
               const char header[] = "", ostream& os = cout);
    // Creates a paged document in the stream os.
    //    lineLength - maximum number of characters per line
    //          (set to be in range minLineLength - maxLineLength)
    //    linesPerPage - maximum number of text lines per page
    //          (set to be in range minLinesPerPage - maxLinesPerPage)
    //    pageNumber - the page number for the first page
    //          (set to be in range minPageNumber - maxPageNumber)
    //    header - is printed at the top of every page
    //          (truncated if necessary to the maximum line length)
    //    os - stream to use for output
    // ASSUME: os is an open, valid output stream.

    ~TypeSetter();              // Ends document, ending current page.

    void endWord();            // Ends current word in the document
                               //    and flushes it to current line.
    void endLine();            // Ends current line and flushes it to os.
    void endParagraph();       // Ends current paragraph and flushes it to os.
    void endPage();            // Ends current page, numbers it, and
                               //    flushes it to os.

    void add(char aChar);           // Adds a character to the document.
    void add(const char aString[]);  // Adds a string to the document.

    // Output operators add characters, strings, ints, and doubles to the
    //    document.
    TypeSetter& operator<< (char aChar);
    TypeSetter& operator<< (const char aString[]);
    TypeSetter& operator<< (int anInt);
    TypeSetter& operator<< (double aDouble);
```

```
private:
    Worder* theWorder_;
    Liner* theLiner_;
    Pager* thePager_;

    enum {theBufSize_ = 25};
    char theBuf_[theBufSize_];
    TypeSetter(const TypeSetter&);                     // no copying
    TypeSetter& operator= (const TypeSetter&); // no assignment
};
#endif
```

Like many .H files, `TypeSetter.H` serves two masters. First, it presents the interface to the `TypeSetter` class so that programmers have what they need to write the client code that uses the class. That interface includes comments and declarations of public members. Second, `TypeSetter.H` provides information needed by the compiler in order to carry out its job of compiling and linking code that is a client of the `TypeSetter` class and the code that implements the `TypeSetter` class. The compiler ignores comments. But it does need to see the public part of the class definition and the private part too—even when compiling client code.

Most of the lines in the file were explained when the `TypeSetter` class definition was introduced in Chapter 3; but a few were not. Consider the first three lines of the file right after the compiler directives:

```
class Worder;
class Liner;
class Pager;
```

These lines are class *declarations*—to be distinguished from the *definition* of the `TypeSetter` class that follows. `Worder`, `Liner` and `Pager` are classes used in the implementation of the `TypeSetter` class. A `TypeSetter` object is composed of three parts that are themselves objects—a `Worder` object, a `Liner` object and a `Pager` object. In other words, a `TypeSetter` object *has-a* `Worder`, a `Liner` and a `Pager`, which are represented by `TypeSetter` data members.

We have encountered the *has-a* relation and its implementation via data members before. What is new here is a simple technique by which the details of the definition of the classes `Worder`, `Liner`, and `Pager` are not needed by the compiler in order for it to understand our definition of `TypeSetter`. The three components are referenced only in the implementation code of the `TypeSetter`. Clients of `TypeSetter` do not need to know the names or types of the members of `Worder`, `Liner`, or `Pager` objects. But client code does need to know how much space is required to store a `TypeSetter` object. By using members that are pointers to a `Worder`, a `Liner`, and a `Pager`, the definition of `TypeSetter` makes it clear how much space is required for those three pointer members. All pointers are the same size, regardless of the nature of what they point to. In fact, the three declarations are needed only to satisfy the compiler's demand that all identifiers be at least declared before used.

Pointers play an important part in achieving information hiding, modularization, and separation of interface from implementation. In particular, the design reflected in `TypeSetter.H` allows arbitrary changes in the definition of any of the component classes—`Worder`, `Liner`, or `Pager`—without recompiling any code that is a client of the `TypeSetter` class (though, of course, the object files would need to be linked anew).

There is one more novelty of `TypeSetter.H` to discuss before considering the implementation of the `TypeSetter` class, the private member function declarations shown here:

```
TypeSetter(const TypeSetter&);                  // no copying
TypeSetter& operator= (const TypeSetter&);  // no assignment
```

The first line declares the copy constructor; the second declares an assignment operator. The purpose of making these functions private is hinted at by the comments that follow them. Because of the specification of the `TypeSetter`, there is no clear and useful meaning for passing a `TypeSetter` argument by value nor is there a use for assigning a `TypeSetter` value to a variable (as opposed to initializing a `TypeSetter` variable with a value). By declaring these functions as private, we make them off-limits to the users of the class. The compiler then becomes our ally and can check client code for improper use of `TypeSetter` variables. If we did not declare the copy constructor or the assignment operator at all, the compiler would cheerfully generate the default versions (member wise copy and assignment) and would not complain at all about code that was improper in this regard. Always accept any help the compiler can offer to proofread your code! You must first announce your intentions in ways the compiler can understand. Prohibiting clients from misusing a class by making certain compiler-supplied member functions private is one way of getting the help you need.

Overall design of the `TypeSetter`

Think of a `TypeSetter` object as supervisor of a small print shop in charge of getting a client's manuscript set into type. Our `TypeSetter` will be provided with a description of the format of the resulting document, maximum number of characters per line, maximum number of lines per page, starting page number, a header string to place at the top of every page, and an output stream on which to publish the typeset document. In addition, the `TypeSetter` will receive the manuscript in the form of a sequence of characters. The sequence of characters might be presented in any of a variety of ways, but our problem takes the characters to be presented in a manner similar to the way characters are inserted into an output stream. In addition, special formatting messages can be sent to indicate the end of a word, of a line, of a paragraph, and of a page. The individual characters to be typeset and the special formatting messages from the client are all received initially by the `TypeSetter`. Ignore for the moment the special formatting messages and concentrate on the incoming characters seen by the `TypeSetter`. The `TypeSetter` employs three specialized assistants: the `Worder`, the `Liner`, and the `Pager`.

The `Worder` is handed individual characters by the `TypeSetter` in the order that they arrive from the client. The `Worder` can recognize the end of a word and can also recognize runs of whitespace characters (which do not go in words). The `Worder` knows the characters that so far are in the current word. The `Worder` can inform the `TypeSetter` when it has accumulated a string of characters that make up a complete word and will hand over the current word when asked to do so. The `Worder` communicates only with its boss, the `TypeSetter`.

When the `TypeSetter` is informed by the `Worder` that a whole word has been accumulated from the client's input, the `TypeSetter` asks for the word. The `TypeSetter` then calls upon its second assistant, the `Liner`, to take the new word and try to fit it on the line currently being set. The `Liner` knows the word it has just been given, the length of the word, the characters making up the current line, the number of characters making up the current line, and the maximum number of characters permitted in a line. Using that information, the `Liner` can decide whether to add the current word to the current line and do so, or it can inform the `TypeSetter` that the current word will not fit on the current line. Depending on what the `Worder` tells it, the `TypeSetter` will either continue as before handing characters one at a time to the `Worder`, or the `TypeSetter` will request the current line from the `Liner`, give the line to the `Pager` to add to the current page, and then give the current word to the `Liner` to use as the first word of a new line. The `Liner` communicates only with its boss, the `TypeSetter`.

The `Pager` knows about the current page; it knows how many lines can fit on a page, the lines on the current page so far, the number of lines on the current page, the heading to use at the top of a page, and the current page number. Our `Pager` is designed to send the lines of a page to an output stream in the proper order, separating one page from the next by an ASCII formfeed character, which is used by many output devices to start a new physical page. When the `Pager` is given the first line on a page, it inserts a header line and some blank lines in the output stream. If the given line fills the page, the `Pager` inserts some footer lines including a page number into the output stream. The `Pager` communicates only with its boss, the `TypeSetter`. Figure 13.1 illustrates the `TypeSetter` design.

Where did this design come from? The short answer is: the design was the result of experience, experimentation (trial and error), creativity, and goals not evident in the problem analysis. The design did not come from a quick look at the original problem statement by means of simple rules of thumb. There is no magic bullet. Straightforward OOA of the problem statement might reveal such real-world objects as words, lines, and pages in addition

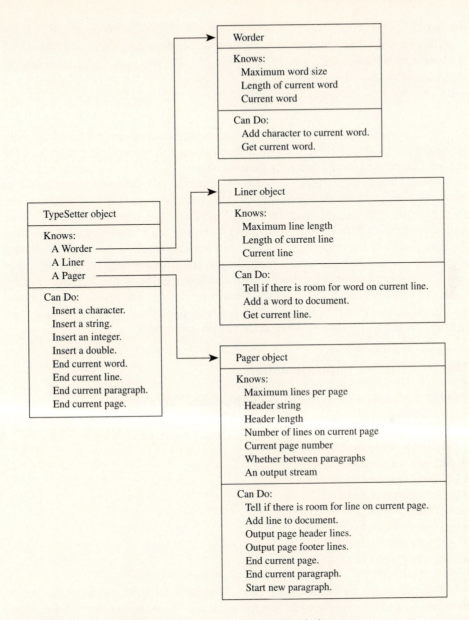

Figure 13.1 Design of the `TypeSetter` and related classes.

> to the `TypeSetter`. Our design incorporates those problem domain abstractions in the form of imaginary print shop workers specializing in words, lines, and pages.

An important goal of a computer-world design is to minimize the complexity of the design by minimizing the interactions among the component objects of the model. Our design model has four distinct objects: `TypeSetter`, `Worder`, `Liner`, and `Pager`. In principle, there could be as many as six different direct paths of two-way communication: `TypeSetter` with `Worder`, `TypeSetter` with `Liner`, `TypeSetter` with `Pager`, `Worder` with `Liner`, `Worder` with `Pager`, and `Liner` with `Pager`. Each path of communication increases the complexity of the design, the complexity of the organization of the implementation code and code files, and especially the job of testing and maintaining the implementation. On the other hand, our design with only three communication paths is much less complex. Consider just the task of testing each of the four classes. The `Worder`, `Liner`, and `Pager` classes may each be tested individually; indeed they may readily be implemented, coded and tested by three different programmers.

The `TypeSetter` Implementation

The file `TypeSetter.C` contains the implementation of the `TypeSetter` class. It begins with several include directives as follows:

```
// File = TypeSetter.C
#include <iostream.h>
#include <strstream.h>
#include <string.h>
#include "TypeSetter.H"
#include "Worder.H"
#include "Liner.H"
#include "Pager.H"
```

A convenience function comes next. It returns its first argument, n, if n is between `lo` and `hi`; otherwise `lo` is returned if n < `lo` or `hi` is returned if n > `hi`. The keyword `static` has the effect of making the definition local to this file and thus avoids conflict with other definitions of the identifier `minMax` in other files.

```
static int minMax(int n, int lo, int hi)
{
    if (n <= lo) return lo;
    else if (n >= hi) return hi;
    else return n;
}
```

The `TypeSetter` constructor recruits a team of experts—`Worder`, `Liner` and `Pager` objects—that the `TypeSetter` object oversees. The `Worder` and `Liner` need only be aware of the maximum line length to do their jobs, but the `Pager` needs to know the number of lines per page, the header string, the number of header characters that can fit on a single line, the starting page number, and the stream to use for output.

```
TypeSetter::TypeSetter(int lineLength, int linesPerPage, int pageNumber,
                       const char header[], ostream& os)
{
    int lineLen = minMax(lineLength, minLineLength, maxLineLength);
    theWorder_ = new Worder(lineLen);
    theLiner_  = new Liner(lineLen);
    thePager_  =
            new Pager(minMax(linesPerPage, minLinesPerPage, maxLinesPerPage),
                      header,
                      minMax(strlen(header), 0, lineLen),
                      minMax(pageNumber, minPageNumber, maxPageNumber),
                      os);
}
```

Since the `Worder`, `Liner`, and `Pager` objects were dynamically allocated by the constructor, the destructor must delete them. The destructor should also ensure that the last page is properly ended and output.

```
TypeSetter::~TypeSetter()
{
    endPage();
    delete theWorder_;
    delete theLiner_;
    delete thePager_;
}
```

The basic way a `TypeSetter` object is used is by sending it a message to add a character to the document being set. The `TypeSetter` delegates the job of adding a character to its `Worder` object team member. The `Worder` replies with information describing the way the characters that have been added form words. Three replies are possible. A reply of `endWordState` signals that a complete word has just been accumulated from the characters added. A reply of `longWordState` signals that the current word has not yet ended, but is already long enough to fill an entire line. A reply of `endParaState` signals that the second of two consecutive newline characters has just been added. When the `Worder` signals that a complete word has been accumulated or that the current word is so long that it requires at least an entire line, the `TypeSetter` performs its `endWord()` behavior. When the `Worder` signals that a paragraph has ended, the `TypeSetter` performs its `endParagraph()` behavior.

```
void TypeSetter::add(char aChar)
{
    int state = theWorder_->add(aChar);
    if (state == Worder::endWordState || state == Worder::longWordState)
        endWord();
    else if (state == Worder::endParaState)
        endParagraph();
}
```

When informed that a complete word has been accumulated, the TypeSetter object gets the word from the Worder object and asks the Liner object if there is room for the word on the current line. If there is room, the Liner is asked to add the word. However, if the Liner replies that there is no room on the current line, the TypeSetter considers the current line to be complete, asks the Liner for the contents of the current line, and tells the Pager to add the line to the current page.

```
void TypeSetter::endWord()
{
    const char* wrd = theWorder_->get();
    if (!theLiner_->isRoom(wrd))  thePager_->add(theLiner_->get());
    theLiner_->add(wrd);
}
```

The end of a line can be signaled to the TypeSetter from "outside" by the client from which the characters to be set into lines and pages originate, or from "inside" when a paragraph is ended. In either case, the TypeSetter performs its endWord() behavior and then requests the current line from the Liner, passing the line on to the Pager.

```
void TypeSetter::endLine()
{
    endWord();
    thePager_->add(theLiner_->get());
}
```

The end of a paragraph can be signaled to the TypeSetter from outside by the client or from inside when a page is ended. In either case, the TypeSetter performs its endLine() behavior and then tells the Pager to perform its endParagraph() behavior.

```
void TypeSetter::endParagraph()
{
    endLine();
    thePager_->endParagraph();
}
```

When the `TypeSetter` receives an `endPage()` message, it performs its end-Paragraph() behavior and then sends the `Pager` an `endPage()` message.

```
void TypeSetter::endPage()
{
    endParagraph();
    thePager_->endPage();
}
```

The following functions are enhancements to the basic interface for the `TypeSetter`. They enable client code to add an entire string of characters by sending a single message to a `TypeSetter` and to use syntax similar to the insertion operator syntax for output streams. However, the similarity to output streams is superficial since the convenient manipulator syntax to control formatting is unavailable.

```
void TypeSetter::add(const char aString[])
{
    for (int i=0; aString[i] != 0; i++)
        add(aString[i]);
}


TypeSetter& TypeSetter::operator<< (char aChar)
{
    add(aChar);
    return *this;
}


TypeSetter& TypeSetter::operator<< (const char aString[])
{
    add(aString);
    return *this;
}


TypeSetter& TypeSetter::operator<< (int anInt)
{
    ostrstream os(theBuf_, theBufSize_);
    os << anInt << ends;
    add(theBuf_);
    return *this;
}


TypeSetter& TypeSetter::operator<< (double aDouble)
{
    ostrstream os(theBuf_, theBufSize_);
    os << aDouble << ends;
```

```
            add(theBuf_);
            return *this;
        }
```

The Worder class

As we saw back in Chapter 5, it is a simple task to chunk together the characters of a word from a stream of characters in which words are separated from each other by whitespace. A slightly more sophisticated version of that job is performed by the Worder, which accumulates the characters of a word until either the end of the word has been reached resulting from a nonword (whitespace) character being sent to the Worder in an add() message, or the word has grown so long that it will fill an entire line. The Worder "compresses whitespace" and recognizes the end of paragraphs as signaled by the use of two or more consecutive newline characters. An enumeration defines a set of values used (1) to report the status of the Worder's analysis of the characters it has been asked to add, and (2) to keep track within the Worder of what the Worder knows about the characters it has seen so far—a straightforward extension of the technique used to recognize words in Chapter 5 in which we keep track of whether we are currently "in a word" or not.

```
class Worder {
public:
    enum { spaceState, wordState, endWordState, longWordState, endParaState };

    Worder(int maxWordLength);
    ~Worder();
    const char* get();       // Null pointer returned instead of empty string.
                             //   String returned is "owned" by the Worder and is
                             //   considered temporary. Client must make a copy
                             //   in most cases. Upon return to client after get
                             //   the Worder considers the current word
                             //   to be empty.

    int add(char c);         // c is added to the current word if it is
                             //   a word character.

private:
    const int theMaxWidth_;
    char* theWord_;
    int theCharCount_;
    int theState_;
    bool isPossibleParagraph_;
    Worder(const Worder&);              // Client can't make a copy, and
    Worder& operator= (const Worder&);  //   client can't assign a Worder object.
};
```

The `Worder` constructor dynamically allocates a buffer through its pointer member, `theWord_`, and the destructor deallocates the buffer. The `Worder` starts out in the whitespace or between-words state, indicated by the value `spaceState` of `theState_`. As a result, the first "word" character encountered will be treated as the first character of a new word. `theCharCount_` keeps track of how many characters have so far been added to `theWord_` and is initially 0.

```
Worder::Worder(int maxWordLength): theMaxWidth_(maxWordLength)
{
    theWord_ = new char[theMaxWidth_+1];
    theState_ = spaceState;
    isPossibleParagraph_ = false;
    theCharCount_ = 0;
}

Worder::~Worder()
{
    delete [] theWord_;
}
```

When a client asks for the characters making up the current word, the `Worder` adds a terminating null character `'\0'` to `theWord_`. For the sake of convenience to the client, a zero-length string is returned as a null pointer rather than as a pointer to a string containing `'\0'` as its first character.

```
const char* Worder::get()
{
    theWord_[theCharCount_] = '\0';
    char* wrd = (theCharCount_ != 0) ? theWord_ : 0;
    theCharCount_ = 0;
    return wrd;
}
```

Two functions, `isWordOrLongWordState()` and `isNewLineChar()`, help the readability of `add()`. Their `inline` declarations have two effects: (1) inform the compiler that it can optimize away the procedure call and put the body "inline," and (2) inform the compiler that the definition is intended for use only within this file.

```
inline bool isWordOrLongWordState(int aState_)
{
    return (aState_ == Worder::wordState || aState_ == Worder::longWordState);
}
```

```
                inline bool isNewLineChar(char c)
                {
                    return (c == '\n');
                }
```

Worder::add() uses isgraph() (which is defined in the standard library ctype.h) to determine its actions. isgraph() returns true if its character argument is a graphical (nonwhitespace) character and false otherwise.

```
int Worder::add(char c)
{
   if (isgraph(c)) {
      // c is a word character, so we are not at the end of a paragraph.
      isPossibleParagraph_ = false;
      // If we are not in wordState, c is the first character in theWord_
      //  Note: we could have been in the spaceState or endParaState,
      //        BUT we could also have been in the longWordState, in which
      //        case we just continued the word on the next line, in effect.
      //        The client is responsible for what happened to the previous
      //        portion of a longWord.
      if (theState_ != wordState) theCharCount_ = 0;
      theWord_[theCharCount_++] = c;
      // If we have just filled theWord_, this is a longWord.
      theState_ = (theMaxWidth_ > theCharCount_) ? wordState : longWordState;
      return theState_;
   }
   else if (isWordOrLongWordState(theState_)) {
      // c is NOT a word character, but we are currently within a word,
      //  so we have just come to the end of the word.
      isPossibleParagraph_ = isNewLineChar(c);
      // In the case that c is a newline,
      // we MAY be at the end of a paragraph too.
      return (theState_ = endWordState);
   }
   else if (isPossibleParagraph_ && isNewLineChar(c)) {
      // c is NOT a word character and we are not within a word.
      // and we have just ended a word with a newline and are now seeing
      // a second consecutive newline - so this is the end of a paragraph.
      isPossibleParagraph_ = false;
      return (theState_ = endParaState);
   }
   else {
      // c is not a word character, and c does not end a word
      // and c does not end a paragraph - so this is MERE whitespace.
      // The client has the responsibility for ignoring this character -
```

```
      // or not.
      isPossibleParagraph_ = false;
      return (theState_ = spaceState);
   }
}
```

`Worder::add()` is, by a substantial margin, the most complex function in the entire `TypeSetter` family. It is not obvious that the algorithm is correct; that is, it is not obvious what exactly the `add()` function behavior is. The comments certainly help—assuming that they are correct. Indeed, one particularly unpleasant error is incorrect comments. The compiler does not ever read the comments, but programmers often do. How could you establish that the comments here are correct? Even if you have assured yourself of the correctness of this code by thorough testing, and even if the code in fact is correct, understanding the code in every detail is important if you ever need to modify the code to change the behavior of the add function. The general problem of establishing code correctness is one of the most important and difficult in **software engineering**, a major branch of computer science concerned with techniques for organizing and managing large software projects. In a later section we will see one technique of determining correctness in connection with the `TypeSetter`.

The `Liner` class

The `Liner` assembles words in a line. It knows the contents of the current line and the maximum line length. It can tell whether or not there is room on the current line for a word, add a word to the current line, and hand over the contents of the current line. Its definition is as follows:

```
class Liner {
public:
   Liner(int maxLineLen);
   ~Liner();
   bool isRoom(const char aWord[]);
   void add(const char aWord[]);
   const char* get();

private:
   const int theMaxWidth_;
   int theCharCount_;
   char* theLine_;
   Liner(const Liner&);
   Liner& operator= (const Liner&);
};
```

The `Liner` creates and manages its own current line buffer, based on the maximum line length. The buffer is deleted by the destructor.

```
Liner::Liner(int maxLineLen): theMaxWidth_(maxLineLen)
{
    theLine_ = new char[theMaxWidth_+1];        // room for \0
    theCharCount_ = 0;
}


Liner::~Liner()
{
    delete [] theLine_;
}
```

The `Liner` inserts spaces between words as they are added to the current line. When there are no characters in the line, the word being added is the first word on the line. When there are already characters on the line, there are already words on the line and a space will be added before the new word is added to separate it from the preceding word. So the number of characters that must be available on the line in order to have space for the word is one more than the number of characters in the word.

```
bool Liner::isRoom(const char aWord[])
{
    if (aWord != 0) {
        int wordLen = strlen(aWord) + ((theCharCount_ != 0)? 1 : 0);
        return (theMaxWidth_ >= (theCharCount_ + wordLen));
    }
    else return true;
}

void Liner::add(const char aWord[])
{
    if (aWord != 0) {
        if (theCharCount_ != 0) theLine_[theCharCount_++] = ' ';
        strcpy(theLine_ + theCharCount_, aWord);
        theCharCount_ += strlen(aWord);
    }
}
```

A null pointer is used to indicate an empty line. The current line is returned as a pointer to a C-string. The client has the responsibility of copying the string to preserve it. This arrangement makes for well-understood ownership of the storage.

```
const char* Liner::get()
{
    theLine_[theCharCount_] = '\0';
    char* line = (theCharCount_ != 0) ? theLine_ : 0;
    theCharCount_ = 0;
    return line;
}
```

The Pager **class**

The Pager is handed lines and places them on the current page. The current page
is part of the output stream specified in the construction of the TypeSetter and
passed on to the Pager constructor. The Pager does not maintain any buffer. Each
line handed to it is almost immediately output to its associated output stream. The
Pager formats the sequence of lines it is handed into pages by inserting additional lines—header lines at the top of each page and footer lines at the bottom. After
output of the last footer line of each page, the Pager outputs the special "formfeed" code, which is ignored by some output devices and used to force a new
physical page by other devices. Thus a physical separation of output lines into
discrete pages occurs for a broad range of output devices. The total number of
lines per page is the body lines specified in the constructor, the header lines (2),
and the footer lines (3).

```
class Pager {
public:
    Pager(int lpp, const char hdr[], int hdrlen, int pgnum, ostream& os);
    bool isRoom();
    void header();
    void footer();
    void startParagraph();
    void endParagraph();
    void endPage();
    void add(const char aLine[]);
private:
    const int theLinesPer_;
    const char* theHeadLine_;
    int theHeadLength_;
    int theLineCount_;
    int thePageNum_;
    bool isBetweenParagraphs_;
    ostream& theOstream_;
};
```

Since the Pager does not buffer the lines, it neither allocates nor deletes any storage. It does keep track of the number of lines output to the current page and the paragraph structure so that it can separate paragraphs by blank lines.

```
Pager::Pager(int lpp, const char hdr[], int hdrlen, int pgnum, ostream& os):
            theLinesPer_(lpp), theHeadLine_(hdr), theHeadLength_(hdrlen),
            thePageNum_(pgnum), theOstream_(os)
{
    theLineCount_ = 0;
    isBetweenParagraphs_ = false;
}
```

The member function isRoom() will not generally be called by a client. The first line of a new paragraph that is not the first paragraph on the current page will require two lines on the page; otherwise only one line is required. The member function header() uses ostream::write(), which has two arguments: the address of a character and an integer to indicate the number of characters to print starting at that address.

```
bool Pager::isRoom()
{
    return theLinesPer_ > (theLineCount_ + (isBetweenParagraphs_ ? 1 : 0));
}

void Pager::header()
{
    theOstream_.write(theHeadLine_, theHeadLength_);
    theOstream_ << endl << endl;
}

void Pager::footer()
{
    const char formfeed = '\f';
    theOstream_ << endl << "Page " << thePageNum_ << endl << endl
                << formfeed << flush;
}
```

The member function endParagraph() will return true only when at least one paragraph ends on the current page.

```
void Pager::endParagraph()
{
    isBetweenParagraphs_ = true;
}
```

Ending an empty page will do nothing. So two successive calls to endPage() will not cause a blank page to be output.

```
void Pager::endPage()
{
    if (theLineCount_ != 0) {
        for (int i=theLineCount_; i<theLinesPer_; i++)
            theOstream_ << endl;
        footer();
        thePageNum_++;
        theLineCount_ = 0;
        isBetweenParagraphs_ = false;
    }
}
```

Starting the first paragraph on a page does not require a preceding blank line.
If there are already lines on the page and there is room, a blank line is added to the
output. If there is not room, the current page is ended.

```
void Pager::startParagraph()
{
    if (theLineCount_ != 0)
        if (isRoom()) {
            theOstream_ << endl;
            theLineCount_++;
        }
        else endPage();

    isBetweenParagraphs_ = false;
}
```

Null lines are ignored. If this is the first line of a page, the header lines are output first. If this line fills the page, the page is ended.

```
void Pager::add(const char aLine[])
{
    if (aLine != 0) {
        if (isBetweenParagraphs_) startParagraph();

        if (theLineCount_ == 0) header();

        theOstream_ << aLine << endl;
        theLineCount_++;

        if (theLineCount_ == theLinesPer_) endPage();
    }
}
```

13.2   *Has-a* vs. *is-a* relationships

The design and implementation of the `TypeSetter` emphasizes an important technique for analyzing and constructing objects—composing an object out of other objects via membership. Each `TypeSetter` class object is composed of `Worder`, `Liner`, and `Pager` objects. The composition is arranged by creating and holding pointers to `Worders`, `Liners`, and `Pagers`. Each `TypeSetter` object *has-a* `Worder` object, `Liner` object, and `Pager` object. On the other hand, the `TypeSetter` does not make use of inheritance nor runtime polymorphism, techniques that are often touted as the hallmarks of object-oriented design and programming. A few observations about these aspects are in order.

During OOA and OOD, objects of many kinds having many kinds of relations to each other can be encountered. For example, one object might be a part of another object; one object might causally interact with another object by banging into it; or one object might be spatially to the northeast of another object. In spite of its flexibility and support of OOP, C++ has very few ways of representing the relationship of one object to another, and even fewer ways of representing the interaction of one object with another. Inheritance is fundamentally a relationship between *classes* (types of objects) rather than between *objects*. We may have a class `Vertebrate` from which is derived a class `Mammal`. Every `Mammal` object is also a `Vertebrate` object. But inheritance does not relate one `Vertebrate` object to another or to a `Mammal` object. We say that a `Mammal` *is-a* `Vertebrate` in this case. *Is-a* is a relation holding between two classes: a subclass and a superclass.

Public inheritance is often called inheritance of interface because each derived class object has the public data and function members inherited from the base class as well as any members unique to the derived class. Inheritance is a tool for organizing, describing, and reusing classes. However, it is a mistake to think of OOD as being solely a matter of developing classes organized into inheritance hierarchies. The world of real and computer objects is very rich, and a large part of many OOD and OOP tasks will involve describing and representing the relationships among objects. *Has-a* relationships are common. There are several kinds of *has-a* relationships, among them whole-part relationships, owner-possession relationships, client-provider relationships, and supervisor-staff relationships. Our analysis of the `TypeSetter` problem involved a version of supervisor-staff relationship between a `TypeSetter` object and its `Worder`, `Liner`, and `Pager` collaborators. A slightly different model could lead to a whole-part relationship. The important point here is that we do not consider a `TypeSetter` to *be* a `Worder` or vice versa; rather we consider a `TypeSetter` to *have* a `Worder`, to *make use of* a `Worder`, or to *be composed of* a `Worder` together with other parts.

Is-a relationships are usually implemented by inheritance and *has-a* relationships are usually implemented by including in one object a data member representing another object. These are only implementation techniques. *Is-a* and *has-a* relationships can be implemented in other ways too. Consider the base class `B`, derived class `D`, and the class `C` defined as follows:

```
class B {
public:
   int f(int);
private:
   int i;
};

class D : public B {
public:
   int g(int);     // g doesn't reference members of B
private:
   int j;
};

class C {
public:
   int g(int);    // same definition as for D::g()
   int f(int n) { return pb->f(n); }
private:
   int j;
   B* pb;
};
```

We could use an object c of type C in essentially the same way we use an object d of type D. Indeed, as we have seen with the TypeSetter members such as theWorder_, the constructor for C could also dynamically create a B object and store a pointer to it in c.pb. Then each C object would have its own, unnamed B object. The B members would be accessed through a pointer rather than grafted on the C object, which is what happens in inheritance.

We have not here spelled out an entirely general method for replacing inheritance by use of a pointer to an object of the pseudo "base" class type, nor do we suggest that both implementations of *is-a* relationships are equally good in all cases and in all respects. Public inheritance clearly is a superior technique when the base class has many public member functions. In that case the compiler automatically makes all the base class public members available as public members of the derived class. The alternative technique requires the programmer specifically to include *all* the public members as part of the class definition. Compare the example classes D and C above. In the case of the LogFile class (see section 10.5) inheritance saves us much effort. We inherit a very large set of public members from the hierarchy of stream classes by deriving LogFile from ofstream. There are few reasons for using inheritance instead of member objects, but private inheritance can be used to implement some cases of *has-a* relationships.

There are some reasons to prefer member objects over inheritance as an implementation technique whether *is-a* or *has-a* relationships are being implemented. One of the reasons concerns separating implementation details from interface information. The other concerns multiple inheritance. C++ language features for multiple inheritance are significantly more complex to understand and use than are the language features for single inheritance. So in cases where other issues such as the size of the interface to be "inherited" do not override the benefits of avoiding multiple inheritance, implementing with multiple member objects can be simpler and more reliable.

13.3   Memory leaks: A common flaw

Whenever storage is dynamically allocated, there is the possibility of a memory leak. Under the assumption that unlimited storage is available, a memory leak is not a bug—it will not adversely affect a program. However, storage is never unlimited and is often in short supply. A memory leak is a kind of performance flaw, as is using an algorithm that is correct but takes 100 years to produce the correct result.

Memory leaks are hard to diagnose because the undesirable result—running out of storage—is built up gradually and the code executing at the time the program fails is only randomly related to the code that is in error. Testing does not easily reveal memory leaks because developers often have powerful computers and use small quantities of test data compared to the eventual consumers of the program. In the case of libraries and other components for reuse, the diagnosis of memory leaks is even more difficult. For these reasons it is important to be vigilant concerning memory allocation and deallocation throughout the development of code. The `TypeSetter` serves as a case study in memory leaks; we inadvertently had a memory leak in early versions of the code.

Memory leaks arise when storage is dynamically allocated and not deallocated. In the `TypeSetter` storage is dynamically allocated in the constructor, creating `Worder`, `Liner`, and `Pager` objects. The `TypeSetter` destructor deletes each of the those objects. The `Worder` and `Liner` constructors allocate character buffers, which are deleted in their destructors. So, it seems, there are five `new`s and five matching `delete`s and no memory leaks. But life and programming are not so simple. Memory leaks generally arise out of two types of circumstances: (1) when a dynamically created object outlives the lifetime of the function execution in which it is allocated and there are no clear guidelines determining which procedure should delete the object, and (2) when the allocation is disguised and can easily be overlooked.

One benefit of using classes in a disciplined way is that many opportunities for memory leaks (and other common errors) are avoided. Constructors that allocate storage via `new` should always be paired with destructors that deallocate that storage via `delete`. The `TypeSetter` follows this pattern. Three objects are allocated by the constructor and deallocated by the destructor. However, there are other opportunities for memory leaks to arise. An early version of `TypeSetter::operator<<(int)` looked like this:

```
TypeSetter& TypeSetter::operator<<(int anInt)     // Version with memory leak
{
    ostrstream os;
    os << anInt << ends;
    add(os.str());                                // This leaks!
    return *this;
}
```

The expression `os.str()` returns a `char*` that contains all the characters inserted so far into `os`. The string of characters is created dynamically. Responsibility for deallocating the storage for the string belongs to whatever function calls `ostrstream::str()`. If no other compensating changes are made to the `TypeSetter`, there is a memory leak—after return from `add(char*)`, the pointer returned by the call `os.str()` is forgotten and the storage becomes a lost block, never to be referenced or reclaimed. Since `TypeSetter::operator<<(int)` always creates a new string about which it does not care after the call to `add(char*)`, there are two possibilities for assigning responsibility for deallocation. Responsibility for deallocation could be turned over to `add(char*)` or it could remain with `TypeSetter::operator<<(int)`. Since `add(char*)` will be called from `TypeSetter::operator<<(double)`, which also creates a string that should be deleted, it may seem like a good idea to give `add(char*)` the responsibility for deallocation of its `char*` argument. But that decision would make the call on `add(char*)` within `TypeSetter::operator<<(const char[])` dangerous. A later version of `TypeSetter::operator<<(int)` looked like this:

```
TypeSetter& TypeSetter::operator<<(int anInt)     // No memory leak
{
    ostrstream os;
    os << anInt << ends;
    char* temp = os.str();                        // Inefficient
    add(temp);
    delete[]temp;                                 // No need for new buffer
    return *this;
}
```

This version solved the memory leak problem, but it was inefficient because it repeatedly allocated and deallocated storage. Since there is a maximum size to an integer value, there is a maximum length to the string representation of an `int`; likewise for a `double` value. So a single buffer could be used for all the temporaries needed by `add(int)` and `add(double)`. Fortunately, the `ostrstream` has a constructor that supplies a buffer to use for the stream. Our final version avoids the memory leak and the needless overhead of allocating and deallocating each successive string of characters.

> If you are tempted to ignore memory leaks early on with the intention of dealing with them only if they cause problems later on, don't do that! If there is even a slight possibility that memory leaks will turn out to be a problem, you should design with that in mind from the start.

Some memory leaks will not be problems. In the `TypeSetter`, for example, the allocation of a `Worder`, `Liner`, and `Pager` is not likely to cause a problem even if the destructor does not deallocate them. This is a case of fixed storage overhead, three objects lasting during the entire program. On the other hand, the memory leak in the earlier version of `TypeSetter::operator<<(int)` is potentially a serious problem. It is an unbounded memory leak. The more calls made on `TypeSetter::operator<<(int)` the more memory is lost. With enough input and a small enough supply of memory, the leak could cause the program to terminate when it runs out of memory.

13.4 ATNs for specification and implementation correctness

The augmented transition network (ATN) is an important element of the computer scientist's toolkit for character-processing algorithms. ATNs can be found in three different forms: (1) machines for processing streams of characters; (2) diagrams representing character-processing algorithms; and (3) mathematical structures. The fundamental idea in all three forms of ATNs is that character-processing algorithms can be thought of in terms of a set of states, a set of transitions between states, and the actions that take place during each transition.

It is not common for published source code to contain known errors. Even less commonly published are the series of designs and implementations that make up the versions leading to debugged and published source code. As a result, there are few concrete examples of what is involved in "getting it right." Our earlier remark that `Worder::add()` is the most complex function in the `TypeSetter` package is based on experience as well as analysis of the code. `Worder::add()` went through three versions previous to the published code. The earlier versions contained bugs of varying degrees of subtlety. Here is pseudo-code for an intermediate version of `Worder::add()`.

```
int Worder::add(char c)
// Does NOT check for overflow of buffer. Just signals endWord state.
// Client has responsibility to call get() after add() signals endWord
// before calling add() again. get() resets charsPresent to 0.
{
    if (wordChar(c)) {
        // a word char, add to current word
```

```
        theWord[charsPresent++] = c;
        possPara = false;
        if (charsPresent == Max) return (state = endWord);
        else                     return (state = word);
    }
    else if (possPara && (c == newLine)) {
        // second consecutive newLine after word end
        possPara = false;
        return (state = endPara);
    }
    else if (state == word) {
        // whitespace ending a word
        possPara = (c == newLine);
        return (state = endWord);
    }
    else {
        // whitespace that doesn't end a word or mark paragraph end
        possPara = false;
        return (state = space);
    }
}
```

What is the bug? Take a few minutes and see if you can detect the problem. Comparison with the final version of the code in section 13.1 will provide a hint.

The bug reveals itself when a word of exactly the maximum line length is immediately followed by two newline characters. In that case, instead of signaling the end of a word and then the end of a paragraph, the end of paragraph signal is erroneously omitted. When the last character in the word is seen, `charsPresent == Max`, and `endWord` is signaled. So when the first newline is seen, `state == endWord`, and the newline is treated as "whitespace that doesn't end a word." The second newline is then treated as "whitespace that doesn't end a word or mark paragraph end." In the version of `Worder::add()` in section 13.1, this bug is absent. The design presented there introduces an additional state, `longWord`, which is used to signal that a word filling an entire line has been accumulated so far. The additional signal is useful because the correct action to take for such a case is neither the action for an `endWord` signal, nor the action for a `word` signal.

Two separate but related problems involve correctness of `Worder::add()`: (1) to specify correctly the desired behavior; and (2) to code the behavior correctly. Some techniques for establishing correctness concentrate on the match between the specified behavior and the behavior of the implementation. These techniques are highly mathematical and difficult to apply beyond elementary cases. Regardless of their merits in an ideal world, they are not yet in the everyday toolkit of most programmers. Another approach to correctness involves concentrating on specification using notation that makes implementation a routine task, one that could even be automated. For all but the simplest specifications, English may not be the best choice of notation. Indeed much of the general problem of creating correct software can be reduced to the choice (or creation) of a suitable language in which to express the specification of the software. An ideal very high-level language would be powerful and natural enough to make possible English-like specifications that are intuitively correct and precise enough to make possible compilation directly into executable form.

Such a language has yet to be discovered. But reasonable facsimiles exist for specialized kinds of programming problems. We are fortunate that the task assigned to the `Worder` object in the `TypeSetter` problem can be solved by an "executable specification." The `Worder` performs the job of **lexical analysis** (or lexing) of the input sequence of characters, which means chunking them together into units called **tokens**. The `Worder` recognizes three classifications of characters: word characters, newlines, and all other characters (whitespace). Our job is to specify precisely the signaling behavior (output) of the `Worder` given its current state and its current input character classification. We will create an ATN for that task.

A `Worder` **ATN**

We start with a simple example: the job of chunking the input sequence of characters into words with no length limit to a word (and no special paragraph ending characters). We need to decide character classifications, states, and transitions from one state to another. We chose three character classifications, W (word character), N (newline character), and S (whitespace). We chose two states: the state SPACE, representing the condition that the most recent character added is whitespace, and the state WORD, representing the condition that the most recent character added belongs to the current word. Figure 13.2 is the **state-transition diagram** corresponding to our notation. The states are represented by labeled circles and the transitions between states are represented by arrows labeled by character classifications.

We start processing input in the SPACE state as indicated in the diagram by the bold circle. The arrows leading from WORD to SPACE are transitions that signal the end of a word. The arrow leading from SPACE to WORD is the transition that signals the start of a new word.

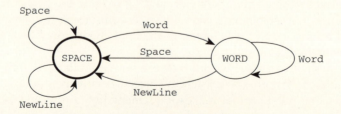

Figure 13.2 SPACE and WORD state transition diagram.

A sample use for this diagram is a word counter. Transitions signaling anything other than the end of the word are ignored, while those signaling the end of a word are counted.

How can we reduce the specification of behavior described by the state-transition diagram of Fig. 13.2 to executable code? The first step is to re-describe the state-transition diagram as a **state-transition table**, displayed in Fig. 13.3. Each line of the table represents a transition. The signals determined by the transitions are in the rightmost column of the table.

The following pseudo-code implements the behavior described in the state-transition table.

```
signalType stateTransitionMachine(char c)
{
    signalType signal;
    static stateType state = SPACE;
    switch (state) {
    case SPACE:
        switch (wordClass(c)) {
        case Word: state = WORD; signal = beginWordSignal; break;
        case NewLine:
        case Space  :   state = SPACE; signal = spaceSignal; break;
        }
    case WORD:
        switch (wordClass(c)) {
        case Word: state = WORD; signal = withinWordSignal; break;
        case NewLine:
        case Space  :   state = SPACE; signal = endWordSignal; break;
        }
    }
    return signal;
}
```

Current State	Character	New State	Signal
SPACE	Word	WORD	BeginWord
	NewLine	SPACE	WithinSpace
	Space	SPACE	WithinSpace
WORD	Word	WORD	WithinWord
	NewLine	SPACE	EndWord
	Space	SPACE	EndWord

Figure 13.3 State transition table corresponding to Fig. 13.2.

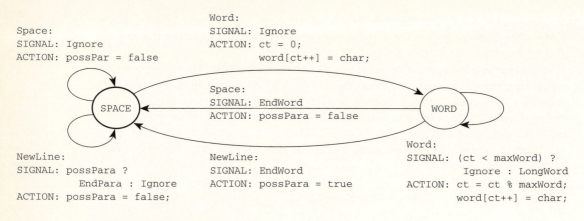

Space:
SIGNAL: Ignore
ACTION: possPar = false

Word:
SIGNAL: Ignore
ACTION: ct = 0;
        word[ct++] = char;

Space:
SIGNAL: EndWord
ACTION: possPara = false

NewLine:
SIGNAL: possPara ?
        EndPara : Ignore
ACTION: possPara = false;

NewLine:
SIGNAL: EndWord
ACTION: possPara = true

Word:
SIGNAL: (ct < maxWord) ?
        Ignore : LongWord
ACTION: ct = ct % maxWord;
        word[ct++] = char;

Figure 13.4 An ATN for `Worder::add()`.

There is a well-developed mathematical theory and computer-based technology for creating state-transition machines, describing them in the form of state-transition tables, and automatically translating the table description into a function definition. In simple cases such as the `Worder`, intuitive design methods and hand translation into code serve admirably. Figure 13.4 is a slightly more complex ATN diagram for the full `Worder::add()` behavior. The actions taken after a transition are more complex than merely signaling information about the current word, and so pseudo-code statements are used to describe the transition actions and signals. In the previous state transition diagram, the signals simply described the transitions. In the new diagram, the signals are the replies that the ATN makes to the client code in response to processing the characters.

Figure 13.5 is the `Worder::add()` ATN diagram expressed as a state-transition table. For brevity the transition actions are described in English. The precise and full description is given by the pseudo-code labeling the arrows in Fig. 13.4.

Facility in reading and in creating ATN diagrams or tables comes with practice motivated by a desire to succeed. Nonetheless, expressing a desired behavior as an ATN is usually at least as easy as expressing the specification in informal

Current State	Character	New State	Action	Signal
SPACE	Word	WORD	add character to word	Ignore
	NewLine	SPACE	check for paragraph	EndPara or Ignore
	Space	SPACE		Ignore
WORD	Word	WORD	add character to word, check for long word	WithinWord or Ignore
	NewLine	SPACE	possible paragraph	EndWord
	Space	SPACE		EndWord

Figure 13.5 State transition table for `Worder::add()`.

English prose. A specification in the form of an ATN diagram or table is straight-forward to code in a way that is easy to verify as meeting the specification. Fur-thermore, it is a simple task to come up with correct code given a modified ATN diagram or table and the code implementing the original ATN.

We have reimplemented the `Worder` using the design expressed in Fig. 13.4 and 13.5. Though not strictly necessary, we have also made minor changes to the `TypeSetter` itself, the better to reap the benefits of the ATN specification of `Worder::add()`.

Other than the trivial renaming of files reflected in comments and include directives, the only changes are better names for the signals returned by `Worder::add()`.

```
void TypeSetter::add(char aChar)
{
   Worder::signal sig = theWorder_->add(aChar);
   if (sig == Worder::signalEndWord || sig == Worder::signalLongWord)
      endWord();
   else if (sig == Worder::signalEndParagraph)
      endParagraph();
}
```

`ATNWorder` design and implementation

The most important change in `Worder` design is the hiding of implementation details in the new class `WorderStateInfo`. That class is declared in the header file for `ATNWorder` and referred to via a pointer to an instance that is created by the `ATNWorder` constructor. `ATNWorder` defines an enumeration type, `signal`, for values used by `add()` to return information about the lexing of the input sequence.

```
class WorderStateInfo;

class Worder {
public:
   enum signal{ signalEndWord, signalLongWord, signalEndParagraph,
                signalIgnore };

   Worder(int maxWordLength);
   ~Worder();

   const char* get();
   signal add(char c);

private:
   const int theMaxWidth_;                    // max word size
```

```
    char* theWord_;                        // current word buffer
    int theCharCount_;                     // chars in current word
    WorderStateInfo* theStateInfo_;        // implementation details

    Worder(const Worder&);                 // prevent client copying
    Worder& operator= (const Worder&);     // prevent client assignment
};
```

Most of the novelty in the implementation of the ATNWorder resides in the language features and syntax of C++. When we have explained the manner of describing the ATN algorithm, you will see that the code is a straightforward implementation of the state-transition table in Fig. 13.5. Indeed the implementation presented here is even more closely related to the corresponding state-transition table than was the case in the sample code for Fig. 13.3. Here we will create an array data object that represents the table. So the table presented in Fig. 13.5 will have a concrete representation as a data object, rather than being scattered throughout the cases of a switch statement.

The class WorderStateInfo is strictly a detail of this implementation of the class Worder; it is declared a friend of Worder and has only private members. The Worder has access to all the members of its friend, WorderStateInfo. But by being private, the members of WorderStateInfo are inaccessible to any other code. This is just one of a variety of techniques available in C++ for information hiding, a version that makes the fewest assumptions about what features of C++ your compiler can deal with.

```
class WorderStateInfo {
friend class Worder;
private:
    // Identifiers naming the ATN states and character classes.
    enum state { stateSpace, stateWord };
    enum {theStateCount = 2};
    enum token { tokenWord, tokenNewLine, tokenSpace };
    enum {theTokenCount = 3};

    // Variables used to implement the ATN transition pseudo-code
    state theState;
    bool isPossibleParagraph;

    const int& theMaxWidth;    // References to members of Worder
    int& theCharCount;         //  initialized by WorderStateInfo constructor;
    char* theWord;             // simplifies communication.

    WorderStateInfo(const int& mw, int& cc, char w[]) :
        theState(stateSpace), isPossibleParagraph(false),
        theMaxWidth(mw), theCharCount(cc), theWord(w)
    { }
```

```
// Classifies characters as W, N or S.
static token theTokenType(char);


// The transition actions — behavior of arrows in Fig. 13.5.
// The "transAction"s take an explicit char argument and implicitly use
// the value of theState as an argument. The explicit result is the value
// of type signal returned and implicit results are updated values for
// theState and isPossibleParagraph.
Worder::signal transActionSpaceW(char);   // Curr State = Space, char is W.
Worder::signal transActionSpaceN(char);   // Curr State = Space, char is N.
Worder::signal transActionSpaceS(char);   // Curr State = Space, char is S.
Worder::signal transActionWordW(char);    // Curr State = Word, char is W.
Worder::signal transActionWordN(char);    // Curr State = Word, char is N.
Worder::signal transActionWordS(char);    // Curr State = Word, char is S.


// To be explained below
typedef Worder::signal (WorderStateInfo::*TRANSACT)(char);
static const TRANSACT transAction [theStateCount] [theTokenCount];
};
```

The members `theMaxWidth` and `theCharCount` are declared in
`WorderStateInfo` so the `Worder` will not have to pass them as function arguments. All members of `WorderStateInfo` are initialized via the constructor initialization list.

The transition actions are stored in a table so that one can be selected using
a state and `char` as subscripts of an array. The selected function is then called in
order to perform the correct action and return the correct signal. The idea is
simple: we want to declare and initialize a two-dimensional array with state
and `char` subscripts, the elements of which contain the corresponding transition action functions. Conceptually, the array (named `transAction`) looks like
Fig. 13.6.

It is easy to declare an array like this for ordinary elements, such as integers.
The problem for us is that the elements we want are functions that we can call.

	State	Character		Array Element
transAction[	SPACE	][Word	]	transActionSpaceW
transAction[	SPACE	][NewLine	]	transActionSpaceN
transAction[	SPACE	][Space	]	transActionSpaceS
transAction[	WORD	][Word	]	transActionWordW
transAction[	WORD	][NewLine	]	transActionWordN
transAction[	WORD	][Space	]	transActionWordS

Figure 13.6 Table of transactions actions bases on state and character
classifications.

Fortunately C++ allows us to declare and store **pointers to functions** and to use a pointer to a function to call that function, pass arguments, and return a value. A pointer to a function is the address of the entry point (first instruction) to the function.

Functions, represented by pointer values, can be treated as data and assigned to variables. How? First we must define the type that describes the function pointers. We want a pointer to a function that takes a character argument and returns a signal value. A typedef notation lets us define an identifier with just that meaning, which can then be used to declare the element type of the desired array. Taking for granted, for the moment, that TRANSACT is a typedef name for "pointer to a function that takes a character argument and returns a signal value," we can declare our array this way:

```
TRANSACT A [theStateCount] [theTokenCount];
```

If we make the array elements constant by prefixing const, then we can make a single array of constant elements belong to the class as a whole by prefixing static. All that remains is the definition of the type TRANSACT.

A typedef definition introduces a new name for a type. In general, prefixing typedef to a declaration of an identifier has the effect of defining that identifier to be the name of the type described in the declaration. Examples of this are as follows:

```
char A[15];              // Declare array of 15 chars named A
typedef char aType[15];  // Define name of type of array of 15 chars
aType AA;                // Use aType to declare array of 15 chars

char* s;                 // Declare pointer to char named s
typedef char* sType;     // Define name of type of pointer to char
sType ss;                // Use sType to declare variable pointing to char
```

The first of each triple is an ordinary declaration, the second is a definition of a type name, and the third is a use of the type name to declare a variable. Similar syntax can be used to declare functions, pointers to functions, and corresponding type names.

```
int f(char);                   // Declare function from char to int
int (*fp)(char);               // Declare pointer to function from char to int
typedef int (*fpType)(char);   // Define name of type of pointer to function
                               //  from char to int
fpType ffp = &f;               // Use fpType to declare a pointer to a function
                               //  and initialize pointer to point to function f
```

A pointer to a function can be used to call the function by dereferencing the pointer with operator*. For example, (*ffp) ('X'), will call the function pointed to by ffp—f() in this case—with the argument 'X'. C++ compilers automatically dereference a pointer used in the position of a function name in a function call. So, `ffp('X')` also calls the function pointed to by `ffp` with the argument `'X'`.

Additional syntax is required to create pointers to member functions of some class type object. The crux of the matter is to use the class name and scope resolution operator along with the familiar pointer notation. Consider the following definitions:

```
class C {          // sample class
public:
    int f(char);   // member function f
};

int C::f(char x) { return x; } // sample definition of C::f

C c;                    // declaration of object of class C
```

The need for special syntax with pointers to class members results from the fact that they are not actual addresses but offsets relative to the start of a class object. Each member of a class object is located at a fixed position for all the objects of that class. Because pointers to members are offsets, dereference of a pointer to member requires different action than dereference of an ordinary pointer.

The symbol `::*` is used to declare a pointer to member—`C::*m` declares m to be a pointer to member of class C. For example,

```
class C {
public:
    int i;
    int j;
    float f;
};
int C::* m;
```

declares m to be a pointer to an `int` member of class C. So m can be assigned a value, an actual pointer to member.

```
C c;
m = &c.i;       // m points to c.i
m = &c.j;       // m points to c.j
m = &c.f;       // ILLEGAL, a type error. c.f is a float.
                //    m must point to an int.
```

A pointer to member is dereferenced using `operator.*`, as the following example shows:

```
int n = c.*m;
```

It is even possible to combine a pointer to an object and a pointer to a member using the operator `->*`, as the following example shows:

```
C* cp = &c;
int n = cp->*m;        // equivalent to (*cp).*m
```

Here are further examples of declaring and using pointers to members for function members:

```
int (C::* fp)(char);   // Pointer to member-of-C function with 1 char arg
                       //   and returning an int value
fp = & C::f;           // Assign pointer to C::f as value of fp.

int j = (c.*fp)('X'); // Call member function of c pointed to by fp.
                       // Note: first set of parens are required,
                       //        c.*fp('X') does not parse correctly.

typedef int (C::* fpType)(char);   // Definition of type name, fpType,
                                   // for pointer to-member-of-C function
                                   // with 1 char arg and int return value

fpType ffp = & C::f;               // Definition of fpType pointer
                                   // initialized to point to C::f
                                   // similar to definition of fp above,
                                   // but uses type name and initializer.
int i;
i = (c.*ffp)('X');     // Call member function of c pointed to by ffp.

C* cp = & c;           // cp is pointer to object c.
i = (cp->*ffp)('X');   // Call member function pointed to by ffp
                       //    of object pointed to by cp.
```

Now we are ready to explain the new syntax used to declare the data representation for a state-transition table. Let's review the typedef and the two-dimensional array declarations:

```
typedef Worder::signal (WorderStateInfo::*TRANSACT)(char);
static const TRANSACT transAction [theStateCount] [theTokenCount];
```

The identifier being defined in the typedef is TRANSACT—it is the only symbol in the typedef that is not yet declared. TRANSACT is defined to be a pointer to a member function of WorderStateInfo, with one char argument and returning a value of type Worder::signal. Finally, we understand the definition of transAction: it is a two-dimensional array of elements of type const TRANSACT. In addition, it is a static member of class WorderStateInfo, a single object shared by all instances of WorderStateInfo.

Now we are ready to write the implementation of `Worder` and `Worder-StateInfo`.

```
// Implementation of Worder and WorderStateInfo
typedef WorderStateInfo WSI;      // Abbreviation for convenience.

Worder::Worder(int maxWordLength) : theMaxWidth_(maxWordLength)
{
    theWord_ = new char[theMaxWidth_+1];
    theCharCount_ = 0;
    theStateInfo_ =
        new WorderStateInfo(theMaxWidth_, theCharCount_, theWord_);
}


Worder::~Worder()
{
    delete [] theWord_;
    delete theStateInfo_;
}

const char* Worder::get()
{
    theWord_[theCharCount_] = '\0';
    char* wrd = (theCharCount_ != 0) ? theWord_ : 0;
    theCharCount_ = 0;
    return wrd;
}
```

`Worder::add()` now just looks up the appropriate transition action, which is determined by the current state and the kind of character to be added. `tfp` is the pointer to member of class `WSI` that represents the state-transition behavior as a function. `theStateInfo_` points to the object of type `WSI` containing the values used to implement the `Worder` object that is receiving the `add()` message. So `(theStateInfo_->*tfp)(c)` calls the `transAction` function with the character to be added as its argument.

```
Worder::signal Worder::add(char c)
{
    WSI::TRANSACT tfp =
        WSI::transAction [theStateInfo_->theState] [WSI::theTokenType(c)];
    return (theStateInfo_->*tfp)(c);
}
```

Since `WSI::TRANSACT` is static data, it can only be *declared* in the class definition. Fortunately, it can be *defined* outside the class by repeating the declaration and following the declaration with an initializer specifying the pointers to member functions associated with each of the pairs of subscripts—the state and token type for the `transAction`.

```
const WSI::TRANSACT
      WSI::transAction [WSI::theStateCount] [WSI::theTokenCount] =
      { { &WSI::transActionSpaceW, &WSI::transActionSpaceN,
          &WSI::transActionSpaceS },
        { &WSI::transActionWordW,  &WSI::transActionWordN,
          &WSI::transActionWordS  } };
```

The classification of a character can be determined with the help of the standard library function `isgraph()`.

```
WorderStateInfo::token WorderStateInfo::theTokenType(char c)
{
    if (isgraph(c)) return tokenWord;
    else if (c == '\n') return tokenNewLine;
    else return tokenSpace;
}
```

The next six functions implement the state-transition behaviors. They determine the new value of `theState`, add a character to `theWord` if that is called for, and return a `signal`.

```
Worder::signal WorderStateInfo::transActionSpaceW(char c)
{
    theState = stateWord;
    theCharCount = 0;
    theWord[theCharCount++] = c;
    return Worder::signalIgnore;
}
```

```
Worder::signal WorderStateInfo::transActionSpaceN(char)
{
    Worder::signal retSignal =
       (isPossibleParagraph) ?
          Worder::signalEndParagraph : Worder::signalIgnore;
    isPossibleParagraph = false;
    return retSignal;
}
```

```
Worder::signal WorderStateInfo::transActionSpaceS(char)
{
    isPossibleParagraph = false;
    return Worder::signalIgnore;
}
```

```
Worder::signal WorderStateInfo::transActionWordW(char c)
{
    if (theMaxWidth == theCharCount) theCharCount = 0;
    theWord[theCharCount++] = c;
    return (theCharCount < theMaxWidth) ?
        Worder::signalIgnore : Worder::signalLongWord;
}


Worder::signal WorderStateInfo::transActionWordN(char)
{
    theState = stateSpace;
    isPossibleParagraph = true;
    return Worder::signalEndWord;
}


Worder::signal WorderStateInfo::transActionWordS(char)
{
    theState = stateSpace;
    isPossibleParagraph = false;
    return Worder::signalEndWord;
}
```

The implementation of Worder is now longer than in the original. However, it is now easier to verify that the implementation is correct with respect to the design, and it is also much easier to alter the design and determine exactly what portions of the implementation will require alterations. Much of the design and code is readily reusable for other lexing behavior.

13.5 Separating public interface from implementation details

One aspect of program design and implementation we have not so far emphasized concerns how the source code for a complete program is organized into files. This may seem to be a minor detail, far removed from the important tasks of analysis, design, and implementation, but that appearance is misleading. An important part of understanding C++ and how to use it effectively is understanding the impact of how code is organized into files and the language features and design techniques that provide control over the file organization of the code.

In principle, all the source code for a complete program could be in a single file compiled to produce a single object file. However, there are many reasons against a single-file organization of source code. Some of the reasons are purely practical, such as limits on the size of files that may be conveniently edited and compiled, and the undesirability of printing out a 100-page listing when only a single short procedure has been changed. But some of the reasons against single-file organization of code have to do with what is needed to achieve such vital goals as reuse of code and ease of debugging and maintenance as well as the realities of a commercial software marketplace.

The `TypeSetter` is a cooperating set of classes that are meant to be used as part of a complete program. If it is useful, it will be used in more than one program, possibly in many programs. The include directive of C++ is helpful in cases in which source code is part of more than one program. For example, whenever a change in the `TypeSetter` source code is needed—either to add a feature or remove a bug—the person in charge of the `TypeSetter` need only edit the master copy of the source code and notify all clients of the change. Include directives are but one of the means for organizing code into files. Users of the `TypeSetter` will need a main program source file and any other files into which their source code has been partitioned. They will also need access to `TypeSetter.H` in order to compile their code, and access to `TypeSetter.o`, `Worder.o`, `Liner.o`, and `Pager.o`, in order to link it.

Notice that the source code in `TypeSetter.H` reveals almost nothing about the source code for the `Worder`, `Liner`, and `Pager`. `TypeSetter.H` contains no include directives for the files `Worder.H`, `Liner.H`, and `Pager.H`. The result is that code using the `TypeSetter` is almost totally independent of the design and implementation of the `Worder`, `Liner`, and `Pager` classes. No matter what changes are made to `Worder`, `Liner`, or `Pager`, users of the `TypeSetter` would only be required to relink their object files to updated versions of `TypeSetter.o`, `Worder.o`, `Liner.o`, and `Pager.o`. They would not be required to edit their source code or to recompile it. This degree of independence between the users' code and the `TypeSetter` code is desirable, but it does not come about without care and effort.

Has-a relationships such as those that exist between the `TypeSetter` and `Worder`, `Liner`, and `Pager` can be implemented with class members, pointer (to class object) members, or reference (to class object) members. If a `Worder` class object was a member of `TypeSetter` rather than a pointer to a `Worder` class object being a member of `TypeSetter`, then `TypeSetter.H` would need to include the file `Worder.H`. In that case every client of `TypeSetter` would be dependent on the definition of the `Worder`, even if the `Worder` member is private. Any change to the `Worder` involving a change in the class definition (`Worder.H`) will require that all clients recompile their code. On the other hand, the version presented here, using a pointer to a `Worder` object, requires only linking the existing client object code to the updated object files `TypeSetter.o`, `Worder.o`, `Liner.o`, and `Pager.o`.

Even more complete independence of client from class implementation is illustrated by the files `TypeSetter.C`, `Worder.H`, and `Worder.C`. The `TypeSetter` implementation in `TypeSetter.C` is a client of the `Worder` as represented by the interface in `Worder.H`. In the first version (section 1), `Worder.H` contains details that reveal aspects of the implementation and make `TypeSetter.C` depend upon `Worder.H` and `Worder.C`. A substantive change of implementation, reflected in a change in the private part of the interface of `Worder`, will require client code such as `TypeSetter.C` to be recompiled. But in the `ATNWorder`, the independence of a client of the `Worder` and the implementation of the `Worder` is much increased. `ATNWorder.H` contains a pointer to a class that hides many of the details of the implementation. Since that class is represented by a pointer, changes to its composition—including changes in the number, names, and types of members—will not require recompilation of clients that include `Worder.H`.

Is-a relationships, using inheritance in a class definition, make for dependence between the derived class and all it base classes. So inheritance can cause dependency problems unless the client of a class and the class are maintained by a small cooperative group of programmers, or the interface of the class is "etched in stone."

13.6   Summary

It is difficult to look at a solution to a complicated problem and understand the process by which the solution was developed. This chapter was a case study of such a process: a case study plus more.

From the discussion of the original model of a print shop complete with supervisor and workers to the final discussion of using an array of pointers to functions, this case study runs the gamut of problem solving. Well, sort of. The end is never really in sight as problems evolve over time.

As you continue to develop your programming skills, you will find new design techniques to help you with hard problems. (Easy problems do not need sophisticated techniques—that is why they are easy.) You will exploit old features of the language in new ways as well as learn new features to solve new and difficult problems. The road ahead is interesting. We have all just begun.

Glossary

Augmented Transition Network   A mathematical system for specifying an algorithm in terms of input symbols, states, transitions, and actions. Transitions take a system from one state to another determined by the current input symbol. Actions are performed during each transition.

lexical analysis   The classification of characters and chunking of characters into tokens. Details depend on notation or language being lexed.

pointer to function   The address of first instruction (entry) of a function. It can be stored as value of a variable and used to call the function it points to.

software engineering   A major branch of computer science concerned with techniques for organizing and managing large software projects. The aim is to produce software that works, is cost effective, and meets production schedules.

state-transition diagram   A representation of an ATN using circles for states and labeled arcs connecting circles for transitions. Transition labels specify actions in pseudo-code.

state-transition table   A representation of an ATN using a table with columns for current state, next state, input symbol, and action. Each row shows what next state and action occur when the input symbol and current state are as specified on that row.

tokens   The symbols or words of a language.

13.7 ▌ Exercises

The following exercises are all projects in themselves. Some of them are major projects.

1. Extend the `TypeSetter` so that whenever a paragraph is started, the first line is indented by `parIndent` spaces. `parIndent` should be an argument for the constructor.

2. Extend the `TypeSetter` so that the sequence of characters (two characters) `'%'` followed by `' '` will always put a space into the output—unless it would overflow the current line. `'%'` followed by `'n'` should start a new line but not a new paragraph. `'%'` followed by any other character should insert that character into the output.

3. Extend the `TypeSetter` so that tab characters are interpreted.

   a. Tab stops occur at every `tabInterval` position. For example, if `tabInterval` is 4, tab stops occur at positions 1 5 9 13 17 21 25 29, etc.

   b. Tab stops can be at any position—for example, at positions 1 4 10 25 30 35 on a line. The settings are fixed *once* for all lines of the typeset document. Interpret `\t` characters in the input so that enough blanks are placed in the output that the next character is at the next tab stop.

   c. Tab stops can be at any position and can be reset at any time, taking effect on the next line.

   d. Tab stops can be (i) left aligned (normal tabs), (ii) center aligned, (iii) right aligned, or (iv) decimal point aligned.

4. Extend the `TypeSetter` so that lines can be justified—left, center, right. Use an escape sequence such as `'%'` followed by `'L'` or `'C'` or `'R'` to indicate that the next line should be suitably aligned.

5. Extend the `TypeSetter` so that the page left and right margins can be moved inward and remain at whatever position they are set until explicitly altered.

6. Extend the `TypeSetter` so that output can be set into two (or more) columns from the next line until the number of columns is changed.

   a. Allow side-by-side columns. Use `'%'` followed by `'1'` or `'2'` to set the output from that point on into the appropriate column.

b. Allow "newspaper" columns in which output snakes from the bottom of the left column to the top of the right column.

7. Extend the `TypeSetter` so that it hyphenates words where possible rather than moving the whole word to the next line.

   a. Base the hyphenations entirely on a "dictionary" listing words and legal points of hyphenation for the words.

   b. Base the hyphenation on an optional hyphen occurring in the input. Use `'~'` as the optional hyphen character. For example, the input `"regi~ment~al"` would appear in the output as `"regimental"` if the word would fit on one line. Otherwise, it could be hyphenated as indicated by the `'~'`.

   c. Remember the hyphenation for a word so that, for example, subsequent input of `"regimental"` would be treated as if the optional hyphen information were present.

   d. Use a set of rules to hyphenate input words that are not in a hyphenation dictionary or explicitly hyphenated with `'~'` in the input.

8. Design and implement typesetting of variable width fonts. Assume access to data giving the width of each character of the font in terms of some basic unit of measure.

9. Create a class (or set of cooperating classes) to use wherever an ATN is desired. In other words, generalize the ATN mechanism of the `ATNWorder`. Emphasize ease of use, generality, and efficiency—in that order of priority.

10. Design and implement an interactive version of the `TypeSetter`. Start with the job of handling deletion of characters. Add as many of the features in exercises 1-7 as you care to. Emphasize object-oriented design. Try to design in stages and aim to reuse as much as possible as you move from one stage to the next. Start your project with simple word wrapping and no pagination. This is very open-ended.

ASCII Character Codes and Escape Sequences

The non-whitespace printable characters have ASCII codes greater than 32.

Code	Char	Code	Char	Code	Char	Code	Char
0	NUL	32	blank	64	@	96	`
1	SOH	33	!	65	A	97	a
2	STX	34	"	66	B	98	b
3	ETX	35	#	67	C	99	c
4	EOT	36	$	68	D	100	d
5	ENQ	37	%	69	E	101	e
6	ACK	38	&	70	F	102	f
7	BEL	39	'	71	G	103	g
8	BS	40	(	72	H	104	h
9	TAB	41	)	73	I	105	i
10	LF	42	*	74	J	106	j
11	VT	43	+	75	K	107	k
12	FF	44	,	76	L	108	l
13	CR	45	-	77	M	109	m
14	SO	46	.	78	N	110	n
15	SI	47	/	79	O	111	o
16	DLE	48	0	80	P	112	p
17	DC1	49	1	81	Q	113	q
18	DC2	50	2	82	R	114	r
19	DC3	51	3	83	S	115	s
20	DC4	52	4	84	T	116	t
21	NAK	53	5	85	U	117	u
22	SYN	54	6	86	V	118	v
23	ETB	55	7	87	W	119	w
24	CAN	56	8	88	X	120	x
25	EM	57	9	89	Y	121	y
26	SUB	58	:	90	Z	122	z
27	ESC	59	;	91	[	123	{

(Continued on next page.)

Code	Char	Code	Char	Code	Char	Code	Char
28	FS	60	<	92	\	124	|
29	GS	61	=	93	]	125	}
30	RS	62	>	94	^	126	~
31	US	63	?	95	_	127	DEL

C++ uses escape sequences for characters that are difficult to express. The effect of output of some of the characters varies among computing systems.

\a	alert	Depends on the system and the terminal. For some, alert sounds a bell; on some the terminal may blink; on others, no noticeable output.
\\	backslash	Distinguishes the backslash character in a string or in a literal character from the beginning of an escape sequence.
\b	backspace	Behavior varies according to the system.
\r	carriage return	System dependent. Some systems will back the cursor to the beginning of the current line.
\"	double quote	Distinguishes a double quote as a character in a string literal from a string delimiter.
\f	formfeed	For printing text files, sends a formfeed character. Many printers respond by ejecting the current page and starting a new one.
\t	horizontal tab	
\n	newline	Used to mark the end of a line of text. (Different systems have different ways of terminating lines of text.) For terminal output, a newline moves the cursor to the far left of the next line.
\0	null character	Distinguishes the string terminating character from the digit character '0'.
\?	question mark	Used for extended character sets, especially helpful for some non-English languages.
\'	single quote	Distinguishes a single quote from the literal character delimiter.
\v	vertical tab	

Appendix B

C++ Keywords

There are 48 C++ keywords.

asm	float	signed
auto	for	sizeof
break	friend	static
case	goto	struct
catch	if	switch
char	inline	template
class	int	this
const	long	throw
continue	new	try
default	operator	typedef
delete	private	union
do	protected	unsigned
double	public	virtual
else	register	void
enum	return	volatile
extern	short	while

Appendix C

Operator Precedence

The following chart shows the precedence of operators that are used in this text. The operators are organized into numbered groups. The lower the number on the group, the higher the precedence of the operators within that group. All operators in the same group have the same precedence.

Number	Operator	Meaning	Example Code
1	`::`	Scope resolution	`void List::add(int x);`
2	`.`	Member selection	`l.add(25)`
	`->`	Member selection	`p->add(30)`
	`[]`	Subscripting	`array[2]`
	`()`	Function call	`swap(x,y)`
	`()`	Grouping	`3.1 * (2 + 17)`
	`sizeof`	Size of object or type	`sizeof(x)    sizeof(int)`
3	`++`	Pre and post increment	`x++    ++x`
	`--`	Pre and post decrement	`x--    --x`
	`!`	Not	`!x && y`
	`-`	Unary minus	`-27`
	`+`	Unary plus	`+27`
	`&`	Address of	`&a`
	`*`	Dereference	`*p`
	`new`	Allocate	`new char`
	`new[]`	Allocate array	`new char[20]`
	`delete`	Deallocate	`delete p`
	`delete[]`	Deallocate array	`delete [] p`
	`()`	Type conversion (cast)	`int (3.1 + a[7])`
4	`*`	Multiply	`3 * 12`
	`/`	Divide	`4 / 5 4.3 / 5.2`
	`%`	Modulo	`37 % 28`
5	`+`	Addition	`1 + 2`
	`-`	Subtraction	`1 - 2`

Number	Operator	Meaning	Example Code
6	<<	Shift left (and insertion)	`cout << x`
	>>	Shift right (and extraction)	`cin >> x`
7	<	Less than	`x < 27`
	<=	Less than or equal to	`x <= 25`
	>	Greater than	`x > 30`
	>=	Greater than or equal to	`x >= 40`
8	==	Equal	`x == 0`
	!=	Not equal	`y != 1`
9	&&	Logical and	`x < 5 && y > 7`
10	||	Logical or	`x < 5 || y > 7`
11	=	Simple assignment	`y = 27`
	*=	Multiply and assign	`y *= 4`
	/=	Divide and assign	`y /= 2`
	%=	Modulo and assign	`x %= 25`
	+=	Add and assign	`x += 3`
	-=	Subtract and assign	`x -= 4`
12	,	Comma (sequencing)	`x = 4, y = 7`

Appendix D

Stream Input

All of the examples in this appendix use the input stream `cin`, which is defined in the input output stream library. Most of the techniques for using `cin` can be identically applied to other input streams. The include directives necessary for the code in this appendix are as follows:

```
#include <iostream.h>
#include <iomanip.h>
```

Input streams use a temporary storage area in memory called a buffer to keep the next stream characters to be processed. Many operating systems line buffer input by default. That means the operating system does not put any of the characters that you type into the input stream until you press `<return>`. When the line is entered, newline character, `'\n'`, is placed into the input stream.

There are two ways to process input stream characters, thus removing them from the stream. One is to use the input operator,`>>`, to extract information from the stream and store it into an object—to read data into the object. The other is to use a stream member function to read data.

Each input stream has a state. The state of a stream determines how subsequent input is processed. The state of a stream can be changed by stream manipulators, some stream member functions, and some input operations. This appendix shows ways to change the state of the stream as well as ways to read different types of data.

Numeric input

Input streams can translate appropriate character sequences into numeric values. Assume that `x` is a floating point variable. Execution of the statement

```
cin >> x;
```

proceeds as follows. `cin` skips leading whitespace characters. If the first non-whitespace character begins a sequence of characters representing a number, `cin` translates that numeric sequence into a floating point value and stores that value in `x`. The leading whitespace and the characters in the numeric sequence are removed from the stream.

Integer input is similar to floating point input. The numeric input is translated as a decimal number unless the sequence of digits begins with `0`, `0x`, or `0X`. If the

sequence begins with 0x or 0X, then by default the input is translated as a hexa-decimal number, with valid digits '0' though '9', 'a' though 'f', and 'A' through 'F'. If the digits start with 0 but not 0x or 0X, by default the input is translated as an octal number with digits '0' though '7'.

The input manipulators dec, oct, and hex change the state of the input stream to force integer input to be interpreted as decimal, octal, or hexadecimal numbers respectively, regardless of the leading character. Manipulators are not extracted from the stream in the same sense that data are extracted, but the syntax for manipulators uses the operator >>.

The following code shows some results from using manipulators for integer input. Here, assume n is an int variable and cin is initially in the default state for reading integers.

```
cin >> n;                // Input 010 gives n the value 8
cin >> n;                // Input 0x10 gives n the value 16
cin >> dec >> n;         // Input 010 gives n the value 10
cin >> oct >> n;         // Input 10 gives n the value 8
cin >> hex >> n;         // Input 10 gives n the value 16
cin >> n;                // Input 20 gives n the value 32
```

Single character input

By default, cin skips whitespace when it reads any variable. Suppose ch is a char variable. Execution of the statement

```
cin >> ch;
```

skips over leading blanks, tabs, and newlines. The value stored in ch is the first non-whitespace character in the stream. Any leading whitespace and the first non-whitespace character are removed from the stream.

When cin is in the default skip-whitespace mode, you cannot execute cin >> ch to find out when the user has entered <return> or a blank. So how is it possible to read a whitespace character? The member function cin.get() provides an answer. To store the next input stream character into ch, regardless of whether or not that next character is a whitespace character, execute the following:

```
cin.get(ch);       // Removes the next character from cin, storing it in ch.
```

Use cin.get() whenever the whitespace characters are important. The function skipToNextLine() defined as follows uses cin.get() to remove all of the characters from the input stream up to and including the first occurrence of a new-line.

```
void skipToNextLine()
{
    char ch;             // Next character to be read
    do
        cin.get(ch);
    while (ch != '\n');
}
```

Occasionally it is useful to "look ahead" at the next character without removing it from the input stream. There are two ways to accomplish this: (1) peek at the character and (2) get the character and then put it back. Suppose that ch is a char variable. The following statement peeks at the next input character, storing it in ch but not removing it from the stream.

```
ch = cin.peek();
```

Alternatively, use cin.get() to remove the character and look at its value. Then use cin.putback() to return the character to the beginning of the stream.

```
cin.get(ch);        // Removes the next character from the stream.
// ...
cin.putback(ch);    // Puts the value of ch at the beginning of the stream.
```

cin.putback() is designed to do a single character putback before performing a subsequent read operation. It is unwise to try to put back two or more characters in a row.

Input streams have a flag named ios::skipws that is on by default. That flag is part of the state of the stream. Turning off that flag forces the stream not to skip whitespace when the operator >> is used to read character, string, or numeric data. There are two different ways to turn off ios::skipws. One way uses a manipulator and the other way calls a stream member function. The results are identical in either case.

Member function style	Manipulator style
`cin.unsetf(ios::skipws);`	`cin >> resetiosflags(ios::skipws);`

Turning off ios::skipws forces cin >> ch to behave the same way as cin.get(ch). However, turning off ios::skipws may not be a smart thing to do when reading numeric data. Leading whitespace is not ignored. Attempts to read a number when the leading character in the input stream is a newline or a blank result in a read failure. To turn ios::skipws on again, use either of these statements:

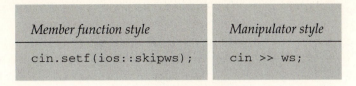

Member function style	*Manipulator style*
`cin.setf(ios::skipws);`	`cin >> ws;`

String processing

The default skip-whitespace behavior of input streams can be a problem for C-string processing. Suppose that your program contains the following code:

```
char name[50];
cin >> name;
```

If the input stream contains no characters when the user enters *John Doe*, `cin` will store the string `"John"` in `name`. It skips whitespace before the *J*, and it terminates those characters in `name` with the null character, `'\0'`. But `cin` stops reading into `name` as soon as it encounters the blank after *John*.

That behavior may not be what you had intended. The stream member function `getline()` provides different behavior for string input. `getline()` allows an input stream to read blanks and tabs as part of the string. To store the entire `"John Doe"` in `name`, use the following statement:

```
cin.getline(name,50);       // Alternatively: cin.getline(name, 50, '\n');
```

The expression `cin.getline(name,50)` does the following things:

1. Removes at most 49 characters from the input stream up to and including the first occurrence of a newline but not beyond.

2. Stores all of the characters removed from the stream except the newline in `name`.

3. Places a null character, `'\0'`, at the end of the characters stored in `name`.

One difficulty with `getline()` requires some defensive programming. Assume that n is an integer variable in the following sequence of statements.

```
cout << "Enter number --> ";
cin >> n;
cout << "Enter name -->";
cin.getline(name,50);
```

Suppose that output and input appearing on the terminal is as shown below where user input is in italics—the user enters 26<return>Jim Doe<return>.

```
Enter number --> 26
Enter name --> Jim Doe
```

The results are unfortunate. The integer input is fine, but `cin` stops reading into the numeric variable n as soon as it encounters the newline after the 26. When `cin.getline(name,50)` is executed, it removes the characters up through the first newline from the stream, storing all of them but the newline in `name`. But there were no characters in the stream before that *first* newline. Therefore no stream characters are put into `name`, `cin` does put '\0' into name as a terminator, and the result is that `name` becomes the null string. The process is illustrated in the figure below. The arrow shows where the reading of n stops and where the reading of `name` subsequently begins.

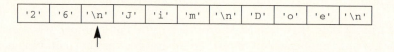

Immediately after `cin >> n` is executed, the newline after the '6' in 26 is a pending, unwanted newline, still remaining in the input stream. Execution of `cin.getline(name,50)` removes the newline but stops there. When the reading of name ends, the next character remaining in the input buffer is 'J'.

You can get around this problem by reading n, ignoring all of the rest of the characters already in the stream up to the first newline, and then reading `name`. The stream member function `ignore()` is useful here. Execution of the statement

```
cin.ignore(80,'\n');
```

removes at most 80 characters up through and including the first newline from the stream. Assuming that the user does not insist on entering extraordinarily long lines (more than 79 characters), the next character to be processed by `cin` (with `cin.get()`, `cin.getline()`, or with the input operator) will be the first character that follows the newline. The input-output code fragment for reading a number then a string can be replaced by the following code:

```
cout << "Enter number --> ";
cin >> n;
cin.ignore(80,'\n');
```

```
cout << "Enter name --> ";
cin.getline(name,50);
```

The effect is that the value of n is 26, the value of name is "Jim Doe", and all of the characters up through the newline following the 'e' are removed from the input buffer.

When newlines in the input buffer affect the way information is read, it is good programming practice to leave the input stream in a clean state after using >>. This is particularly important when character, string, and numeric input are intermixed.

Error states: What happens when an input operation fails?

Input streams do not have any "look ahead" to figure out if the next input operation will succeed. If all previous input operations have been good, you cannot tell whether or not the next one will fail until you try it. Fortunately, having an error on input does not crash the program, but it does put the stream in an error state. You still have to deal with the errors in some fashion.

An input operation can fail for three different reasons:

1. The input data are not in an appropriate form. For example, when evaluation of cin >> n is attempted on the integer variable n and the next character in the input buffer is 'Z', an error occurs.

2. The system encounters the end of the file when the input operation is attempted.

3. There is a catastrophic failure such as a hardware input device failure. With catastrophic failures, it is unlikely that any additional input operations can occur on the stream.

Some errors are not really errors at all but conditions that the programmer expects to occur. For example, the anticipated input could be a sequence of numbers terminated by the letter Q (or any non-whitespace character that is not part of a number). The following loop will find the sum of that sequence. Assume sum and num are numeric variables.

```
sum = 0;
while (cin >> num)
   sum = sum + num;
```

Evaluation of the expression (cin >> num) reads a numeric input value into num and controls execution of the loop. The reading part is easy to understand. The loop control is subtle. The *value* of the expression cin >> num is cin. The value of the expression cin.get(ch) is cin. When cin is used as the value of a Boolean expression to control the execution of a loop or a selection statement, then it is considered to be true if the stream is in a good state and false if it is in an error state.

You can process all of the characters in an input stream by using a model similar to the one for numeric input. To process all of the characters in the input stream one at a time, use the following looping structure:

```
while (cin.get(ch)) {
// loop body to process ch goes here
}
```

Go back to the loop for finding the sum of a sequence of numbers terminated by Q. When an attempt is made to read the sentinel character Q into num, the character Q is not removed from the input stream. The following three things occur:

1. An error flag is turned on and cin goes out of its good state into an error state.

2. The value of num is not changed.

3. The body of the loop is skipped and loop execution terminates.

At this point, if you want to read more input from the stream, you cannot. It is not a mistake. It just does not work. The variable num, the state of the stream, and the characters in the stream do not change.

When the stream state is not good, it is impossible to continue reading from the stream. In order to continue to read from the stream, you must change the stream state to good. The stream member function clear() does just that.

```
cin.clear();     // Makes it possible to attempt more input operations
```

How does the stream know when it is good? Input streams have three different error flags to indicate their error status. When no error flags are on, the stream is in a good state and input operations are possible. The purpose of clear() is to turn off all of the error flags.

It is possible to find out not just whether an error has occurred but also what type of error occurred. Streams have four member functions to indicate their error status: good(), eof(), fail(), and bad(). Each member function returns true or false, according to the following chart.

Function	Return value
good()	All error flags are off.
eof()	End-of-file has been detected in attempting the last input operation.
fail()	An error occurred on the last attempted input operation.
bad()	A catastrophic error has been detected.

The four stream state functions are not independent. If `cin.good()` returns true, then the other three functions return false. If `cin.eof()` returns true, then so does `cin.fail()`. If `cin.bad()` returns true because of an attempted input, then so does `cin.fail()`. So `fail()` covers all failures at attempted input, while `eof()` and `bad()` cover more specific problems.

Stream Output

All of the examples in this appendix use the predefined output stream cout. C++ has two other predefined output streams, cerr, which is commonly used for reporting errors, and clog, which is commonly used to log some program activity. All three of them are defined in the input output library. Most of the techniques for using cout can be identically applied to cerr, clog, and all other output streams.

The state of an output stream determines how it formats the output. Streams use data members to keep track of their states. Some of those data members are flags that belong to the base class ios from which the streams are derived. Those flag names are qualified, beginning with the symbol ios:: and followed by the specific flag name.

A stream can change state if it receives an appropriate message (a call to a member function) or in response to a special object called a manipulator. The member functions of the stream class and the comparable manipulators used for formatting are as follows:

Member function	Manipulator	Meaning
width()	setw;()	Set the field width for next output.
fill()	setfill()	Set the fill character for any necessary field padding.
precision()	setprecision()	Set floating point output precision.
setf()	setiosflags()	Turn on a format flag.
unsetf()	resetiosflags()	Turn off a format flag.

Manipulators are defined in the manipulator library. The include directives for the iostream library and the manipulator library are as follows:

```
#include <iostream.h>
#include <iomanip.h>
```

Field width

You can position the output of a number or a string by specifying the width of the field in which the output is to appear. Force the field width for the next item output by inserting the manipulator `setw()` into the stream directly. Alternatively, call the stream member function `width()`.

Member function style	*Manipulator style*
`cout.width(8);` `cout << 3 << "Hello";`	`cout << setw(8) << 3 << "Hello";`

In both the manipulator and member function styles, the output generated is as follows. The 3 is right-justified. It is preceded by seven blanks (or a specified fill character). `Hello` appears immediately thereafter.

```
3Hello
```

Setting the field width is not persistent—it does not carry over from one value output to the next. If you need the same fixed field width for a sequence of values, you must set the field width for each value. That is why the `Hello` in the output above is not preceded by any blanks. Specifying too small a field width has no effect. The default value for field width is 0.

Justification

When you specify a field width for the subsequent output, the output will appear right justified by default. You can force left justification by turning on `ios::left`, the flag for left justification.

Member function style	*Manipulator style*

`cout.setf(ios::left);`
`cout.width(8);`
`cout << 3;`
`cout.width(8);`
`cout << "Hello";`
	`cout << setiosflags(ios::left)`
	`        << setw(8) << 3 << setw(8) << "Hello";`

The left-justified output produced by both sets of code consists of 3 followed by seven blanks and then `Hello` followed by three blanks.

```
3      Hello
```

There are actually three justification flags, `ios::left`, `ios::internal`, and `ios::right`. Even though the default justification is right, all of those flags, including `ios::right`, are initialized to off.

When more than one justification flag is on at the same time, the format of the output is unpredictable. You can ensure that only the left flag is on by using the following statement:

```
cout.setf(ios::left, ios::adjustfield);
```

The two actual arguments for that last call to `cout.setf()` are as follows:

- `ios::left`   Turn on the left-adjust flag.
- `ios::adjustfield`   Turn off the other adjust flags.

Unlike the field width, the justification flags are persistent. They remain in effect until they are reset. To turn off the left-adjust flag, use the stream member function `unset()` or the manipulator `resetiosflags()`.

Member function style	Manipulator style
`cout.unsetf(ios::left);`	`cout << resetiosflags(ios::left);`

Padding

When the field width is set, output is padded by characters if necessary to fill in the remainder of the field. The default for the fill character is blank. You can change the fill character to another value by using the stream member function `fill()` or by using the `setfill()` manipulator. Both use a single character argument, which becomes the next fill character.

The following two sequences of statements are equivalent:

Member function style	*Manipulator style*

```cout.fill('*');```
```cout.setf(ios::left);```
```cout.width(8);```
```cout << 3;```
```cout.width(8);```
```cout << "Hello";```
	```cout << setfill('*') << setiosflags(ios::left)```
	``` << setw(8) << 3 << setw(8) << "Hello";```

Assuming the justification flags are off immediately before execution, the output generated by both sets of code is as follows:

```
3*******Hello***
```

Floating point output

There are three format choices for floating point output: (1) fixed decimal, (2) scientific, and (3) the default. The number 13.5213 in fixed decimal form with two digits to the right of the decimal is 13.52. In scientific form with two digits to the right of the decimal, 13.5213 is 1.35e+01. The default for floating point output is neither fixed decimal nor scientific, and default behavior varies among compilers.

Two "floatfield" flags, `ios::fixed` and `ios::scientific`, force floating point output format to be fixed decimal and scientific format respectively. Both of the floatfield flags are initialized to off. You can turn on a flag through the `setiosflags()` manipulator or by calling the output stream member function `setf()`. Both styles are shown below. You can set precision, which is the number of digits to the right of the decimal, by a manipulator, `setprecision()`, or via the stream member function `precision()`.

Member function style	*Manipulator style*

```cout.setf(ios::fixed);```
```cout.precision(3);```
```cout << 21.5163;```
	```cout << setiosflags(ios::fixed)```
	``` << setprecision(3) << 21.5163;```

Assuming that the only floatfield flag turned on is `ios::fixed`, the output generated is the same for both styles.

```
21.516
```

If both floatfield flags are on at the same time, output is unpredictable. To avoid that problem using the member function style, replace the statement

```
cout.setf(ios::fixed);
```

with the statement

```
cout.setf(ios::fixed, ios::floatfield);
```

The meanings of the two floatfield arguments to `setf()` are similar to the adjustfield arguments.

- `ios::fixed`   Turn on the fixed flag.
- `ios::floatfield`   Turn off the remaining floatfield flags.

Floatfield flags and the precision are persistent. They remain the same until they are changed. Floatfield flags can be turned off with the `resetiosflags()` manipulator or with the `unsetf()` stream member function.

Member function style	Manipulator style
`cout.unsetf(ios::fixed);`	`cout << resetiosflags(ios::fixed);`

To set floating point output in scientific notation, use `ios::scientific`. If the fixed flag is off, these two sequences of statements will print 21.5163 in scientific format.

Member function style	Manipulator style

`cout.setf(ios::scientific);`
`cout.precision(3);`
`cout << 21.5163;`
	`cout << setiosflags(ios::scientific)`
	`        << setprecision(3) << 21.5163;`

The output generated is as follows:

```
2.152e+01
```

Turning off the scientific flag is similar to turning off the fixed flag. You can use the `resetiosflags()` manipulator or invoke `unsetf()`.

Member function style	*Manipulator style*
`cout.unsetf(ios::scientific);`	`cout << resetiosflags(ios::scientific);`

Decimal points that have only zeros to the right are not printed, independent of how the precision is set. To force them to be printed, turn on the flag `ios::showpoint`.

Member function style	*Manipulator style*
`cout.setf(ios::showpoint);`	`cout << setiosflags(ios::showpoint);`

Turning off the showpoint flag has a familiar look.

Member function style	*Manipulator style*
`cout.unsetf(ios::showpoint);`	`cout << resetiosflags(ios::showpoint);`

The floatfield and showpoint flags are persistent. When they are turned on, they remain on until they are explicitly turned off.

Integer output

By default, integers are output in decimal (base 10) form. Output can be forced to be octal (base 8) or hexadecimal (base 16) instead. Manipulators provide an easy way to switch bases.

```
cout << hex;    // sets integer output to hexadecimal
cout << oct;    // sets integer output to octal
cout << dec;    // sets integer output to decimal
```

The settings are persistent. They remain in effect until explicitly changed. Assume that `n` is an `int`. The output generated by

```
n = 11;
cout << n << ' ' << hex << n << ' ' << oct << n << ' ' << dec << n;
```

is as follows:

```
11 b 13 11
```

Use the `ios::showbase` flag with `setiosflags()` or `setf()` to show the hexadecimal or octal base. Turn the `ios::showbase` flag off with `resetios-flags()` or `unsetf()`. The output generated by this set of statements is shown in the box below.

```
n = 11;
cout << setiosflags(ios::showbase) << n << ' '
    << hex << n << ' ' << oct << n << ' ' << dec << n <<  endl;
n = 5;
cout << n << ' ' << hex << n << ' ' << oct << n << ' ' << dec << n;
```

```
11 0xb 013 11
5 0x5 05 5
```

Uppercase or lowercase letters in numeric output

The `x` in hexadecimal output will be printed as an uppercase `X` when the `ios::uppercase` flag its turned on. Turning it on also forces the `e` in floating point output to appear as an uppercase `E`.

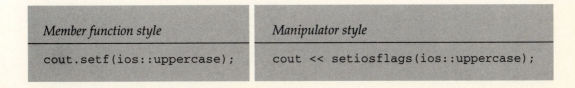

Member function style	*Manipulator style*
`cout.setf(ios::uppercase);`	`cout << setiosflags(ios::uppercase);`

The output generated by this segment of code appears in the box below.

```
cout << setiosflags(ios::showbase) << setiosflags(ios::uppercase)
        << hex << 35 << '\n';
cout.setf(ios::scientific,ios::floatfield);
cout << setprecision(4) << 213.12345;
```

```
0X23
2.1312E+02
```

Turning off the uppercase flag is just like turning off all the other flags.

Member function style	Manipulator style
`cout.unsetf(ios::uppercase);`	`cout << resetiosflags(ios::uppercase);`

Appendix F

File Streams

File streams are C++ class objects associated with disk files. They can be used for input (reading) or output (writing). Input file streams are of type `ifstream`; output file streams are of type `ofstream`; file streams that can be used for both input and output are of type `fstream`. The C++ file stream library, which defines these three stream types, is accessed through the following include directive:

```
#include <fstream.h>
```

One word of warning about this appendix is in order. Different operating systems have different ways of handling files. Do not be surprised if files created in one environment are not yet portable to other environments.

Defining and opening `ifstream` objects

A file stream must be attached to a particular disk file in order to be usable. Attaching a file to a stream is known as opening the file. An `ifstream` object can be defined without opening a file. Alternatively, the definition of an `ifstream` can include the actual file opening. The following code shows the two different styles of definitions:

```
ifstream inA;              // inA is not yet usable.
ifstream inB("text.in");   // Opens text.in and attaches it to inB.

char filename[80];         // Disk file name entered by the user.

cout << "Enter name of input file. -> ";
cin >> filename;

ifstream inC(filename);    // Opens the disk file named by the user and
                           //    attaches it to inC.
```

The definition of `inA` creates an input stream object that is not usable until a file is opened for it. The definitions of `inB` and `inC` create input stream object and open files at the same time. Both `inB` and `inC` are ready to use unless an error occurs in opening the files. (Errors will occur if no disk file of that name exists or if the user does not have read access to the disk file.) The streams of characters associated with `inB` and `inC` come from their associated files.

The file stream member function `open()` is used to open a disk file. It should be used only when the stream is not already attached to an open file. The following code opens the file whose name is the string `filename`, attaching it to the input stream `inA`.

```
inA.open(filename);    // File named filename is opened and attached to inA.
```

If `filename` represents the name of an accessible file, then the opening is successful and `inA` becomes a usable stream. You can tell if there was success by using `inA` as a Boolean expression to control a selection statement or a loop.

```
if (inA)
    // Opening was successful.
else
    // Opening was not successful.
```

Once an `ifstream` object is successfully attached to an open file, either through a definition or a subsequent call to `open()`, it is ready to be used. The `ifstream` object can be used in the same way with *exactly* the same syntax as `cin`. All of the input operations, manipulators, member functions, and error functions behave the same for the `ifstream` object as for `cin`. That is part of the beauty of inheritance and the stream class hierarchy. Once you learn how to use `cin`, you know how to use any input stream.

Processing to end of file

The C++ paradigm for processing data all the way to the end of the file uses the stream as a Boolean condition indicating when no more data remain unprocessed. Typically, evaluation of the Boolean condition involving the stream has the side effect of reading data. When the attempt to read data fails, the value of the stream is interpreted as "false."

Suppose that `in` is an input stream attached to an open file and `character` is a `char` variable. The following loop will process all of the remaining characters in the file:

```
while (in.get(character))
    // process character
```

Similarly, suppose that `in` is an input stream attached to an open file whose lines are 80 characters or less. If `string` is a C-string variable (with room for 80 characters), the following loop will process each line in the file.

```
while(in.getline(string, 80, '\n'));
    // process string
```

Finally, suppose that `in` is an input stream attached to an open file representing a list of integers. If `number` is an `int` variable, the following loop will process all of the numbers in the file.

```
while (in >> number)
    // process number
```

All three Boolean expressions, `in.get(character)`, `in.getline(string, 80, '\n')`, and `in >> number` evaluate to `in`. If the result of the attempted input leaves `in` in a good state, the expression is considered to be true. If the result of the attempted input places `in` in a fail state, the expression is considered to be false. Any expression evaluating to `in` will have the same control effect. Remember if `in` is good, it does not change to a fail state before an attempt to read fails—there is no "look-ahead" to see that all of the file data have been read.

Defining and opening `ofstream` objects

The following code shows two ways to define `ofstream` objects. The first definition creates an output stream object but does not open any file. The last two definitions create output stream objects and open the associated disk files as well (assuming no file access errors occur):

```
ofstream outA;               // Output file stream is not yet usable.
ofstream outB("text.out");   // Opens text.out and attaches it to outB.

char filename[80];
cout << "Enter name of output file. —> ";
cin >> filename;

ofstream outC(filename);     // Opens the disk file named by the user and
                             //    attaches it to outC.
```

If the file openings for `outB` and `outC` are successful, two new files will be created: `text.out` and a file with the name entered by the user. If a file named `text.out` already exists when `out` is defined, the old file is destroyed and a new one will take its place. The same is true for the file named by the user.

The output file stream member function `open()` can open a disk file for an output stream. Assuming no errors, this code makes `outA` usable for output.

```
outA.open(filename); // File named filename is opened and attached to outA.
```

If the opening of the disk file is successful, outA can be used exactly the same as cout. Output stream objects are to cout as input stream objects are to cin. The output operator, <<, writes data to actual files just as the input operator, >>, reads data from actual files. Output manipulators such as setprecision() and member functions such as unsetf() work with output stream objects the same as with cout.

It is possible to open a file to an output stream, specifying "at-end" opening mode, ios::ate. If the file already exists, then output to the stream is placed at the end of the file rather than overwriting the contents of the file. The following code illustrates opening files in at-end mode:

```
ofstream outD("D.dat", ios::ate);  // Output to outD will be written to the
                                    //   end of the file D.dat.
ofstream outE;                      // outE is not attached to an open file.
outE.open(filename, ios::ate);      // Output to outE will be written to the
                                    //   end of the file named by filename.
```

Defining and opening `fstream` objects

An fstream is a file stream that can be used for both input and output. C++ streams provide modes to determine how the file is to be opened. The modes include the following:

Mode	Meaning
ios::in	Open the file for input.
ios::out	Open the file for output.
ios::ate	Attach the new output at the end of the file.

The following code illustrates several ways of defining fstreams and opening attached files:

```
fstream fin("myIn", ios::in);            // Open the file myIn for input.
fstream fout;
fout.open(filename, ios::out);           // Open the file named by filename
                                         //   for output.
fstream dir;
dir.open("telDir", ios::in | ios::out);  // Open the file telDir for input
                                         //   and output.
```

The operator | is the bitwise inclusive-or operation that can combine modes.

The last statement allows the stream `dir` to be used for reading from as well as writing to its associated file, `telDir`.

Closing files

Once a disk file is opened and attached to a stream, it need not be attached to the stream for the entire duration of program execution. The stream can be associated with several files, but never with more than one file at a single time.

In order to attach a new file to a stream, you must first detach the old file from the stream. Use the stream member function `close()`. Input and output files can be closed as follows:

```
inA.close();          // Detaches inA from its associated disk file.
outA.close();         // Detaches outA from its associated disk file.
```

Closing files makes the streams to which they are attached unusable for input or output until they are attached again via `open()`. Closing is not necessary if the stream is to be attached to only one file during program execution. C++ automatically closes a stream at the end its lifetime.

Stream arguments

While `cin` and the file stream `inA` (defined earlier in this appendix) are different types of input streams, both of them can be used as actual arguments to functions with `istream` type formal arguments. (Input stream classes are derived from the base class `istream`.) Similarly, `cout` and the file stream `outA` can be used as actual arguments to functions with `ostream` type formal arguments. The following functions have formal input and output stream arguments:

```
void getInteger(istream& in, int& x)
{
    in >> x;
}

void putInteger(ostream& out, int x)
{
    out << x;
}
```

Assume that `x` is an `int` variable and `inA` and `outA` are input and output file streams attached to open files. The following are valid calls to `getInteger()` and `putInteger()`.

```
getInteger(inA, x);
getInteger(cin, x);
putInteger(outA, 3 + x);
putInteger(cout, x);
```

Functions with formal stream type arguments almost always change the corresponding actual stream. The formal `istream` and `ostream` stream arguments should be reference arguments.

If `dir` is an `fstream` attached to a file opened for output, the following invocation of `putInteger()` is also valid.

```
putInteger(dir, 59);
```

If `dir` is attached to a file opened for input as well as output, `dir` can be used as a first actual argument for `getInteger()`.

Random access to files

Files are sequences of bytes. The bytes of a file are implicitly indexed: the index of the first byte is 0, the index of the second byte is 1, and so on. Input streams have a "seek for getting" member function, `seekg()`, to position files for input beginning at a particular byte index. Assume that `in` is an input stream attached to an open file. If `N` is a nonnegative integer, the statement

```
in.seekg(N);
```

positions the file for input of the bytes starting at `N` bytes from the start of the file. Therefore `in.seekg(14)` will cause the next input operation to start at byte with index 14. It is possible to cause end of file to be set by trying to seek past the end of the file.

Output streams can "seek for putting" through the member function `seekp()`. Assume `out` is an output stream attached to an open file. If `N` is a nonnegative integer, the statement

```
out.seekp(N);
```

positions the file for output at the position starting at `N` bytes from the start of the file. Therefore `out.seekp(25)` will cause the next output operation to start at the byte with index 25.

If `f` is an `fstream` attached to an open file for both input and output, `f` can use both `seekg()` and `seekp()`. The following statement positions `f` for input at byte 14:

```
f.seekg(14);
```

The next statement positions f for output at byte 25:

```
f.seekp(25);
```

Seeking can be done relative to three file positions: `ios::beg` (the beginning), `ios::end` (the end), and `ios::cur` (the current position). Both `seekg()` and `seekp()` have optional position arguments, with default value `ios::begin`. The following statement is appropriate for seeking to put at the end of the file.

```
f.seekp(0, ios::end);
```

The input stream member function `tellg()` returns the index of the current input position. The output stream member function `tellp()` returns the index of the current output position. The index of the current position for `in` is `in.tellg()`; the index of the current position for `out` is `out.tellp()`. If f is an `fstream` attached to a file open for input and output, then `f.tellg()` is the input index position and `f.tellp()` is the output index position.

Binary files

Binary files, as opposed to text files, consist of bytes that are usually interpreted to be some type besides `char`. File streams can be associated with binary files as well as text files.

Streams were originally designed for text files. Operating systems treat text in different ways. The most clear-cut evidence comes in how they mark the ends of lines. Unix uses `char(10)` to mark the end of a line, Macintosh uses `char(13)`, and DOS and OS2 use `char(13)` followed by `char(10)`. Because of this treatment of ends of lines, the bytes stored in a file may not be identical to the bytes that were inserted into the stream. Binary files require exact identity between the bytes inserted and the bytes stored. To adapt input and output streams so they are suitable for binary files, the draft of the ANSI C++ standard introduces the file opening mode `ios::binary`. Some current implementations conform to the standard; others do not. For the implementations that do not have a binary stream mode, programmers can make calls to the C standard input and output routines that are universally included in C++ implementations.

In a system supporting binary mode, the following statements create an `fstream` named `dat` and open it for reading and writing in binary mode.

```
fstream dat;
dat.open("mydata", ios::in | ios::out | ios::binary);
```

Binary data cannot be read directly with the input operator, >>, because of the automatic translation provided by >> from characters to other types. To support reading of binary data, the class istream has a member function read() with two formal arguments, an array of characters, and an integer indicating a number of bytes. A prototype for read() is as follows:

```
istream& read(char array[], int number);
```

The purpose of read() is to extract number of bytes from the stream starting with the current input position of the stream and store them in array, with one character per byte. The bytes in the file are stored directly in the array without further translation.

Although the first actual argument for read() is an array of chars, read() can be used to read in any type of data, not just char data. The trick is to typecast the address of the object to be read to a char*. (Typecasting is a tool that should rarely be used, but it is critical in this situation.) The following code illustrates using read() to read a float from a binary file. It uses a file stream numF, which is attached to a binary file opened for reading and writing.

```
fstream numF("numbers.data", ios::in | ios::out | ios::binary);
float x;
numF.read((char*) &x, sizeof(x));
```

Binary data cannot be written directly with the output operator, <<, which translates the inserted information into a character sequence. The class ostream has a member function write() with two formal arguments, a const array of characters and an integer indicating a number of bytes. A prototype for write() is as follows:

```
ostream& write(const char array[], int number);
```

The purpose of write() is to write number of bytes of the array to the fstream starting at the current output position. Writing to a binary file is almost a mirror image of reading. The following statement writes x to numF.

```
numF.write((char*) &x, sizeof(x));
```

Typecasting is not limited to floats or other built-in types. Assume aType is the name of a type and that y is an object of type aType. The following code writes the byte representation of y to the fstream named dat, which was defined at the beginning of this section.

```
dat.write((char*) &y, sizeof(aType));
```

Using file names from the command line in Unix systems

All of the programs in this book so far use a `main()` function with the first line like this:

```
void main()
```

A more elaborate first line is as follows:

```
int main(int argc, char* argv[])
```

In the Unix environment a program, represented by its `main()` function, is simply another function that is called by the operating system in response to a command entered by a user. With this first line, `main()` is considered to be a function returning an integer and with two arguments: an integer and an array of strings. The user supplies string arguments and the function `main()` returns an integer "status code" value.

By convention, Unix takes a return status code of 0 to indicate that everything was OK. Nonzero status codes are interpreted as error codes, and each program can choose to signal as many different kinds of errors using whatever arbitrary nonzero values the program designer chooses.

There are really two sets of arguments to `main()`: those supplied as part of the command line by the user and the actual arguments supplied in a call to `main()` created by the operating system in response to the user's command. Unix makes two ordinary function arguments available to `main()`: an integer count (`argc`) and an array of C-strings (`argv`). The count indicates how many strings are in the array. It is the job of the program to interpret the strings as needed. Unix always places the program name (the first item of the command line) at index 0 of the array `argv`.

The following program illustrates using `main()` to copy one file into another, translating all of the alphabetic characters into uppercase. It uses the function `toupper()` from the built-in character handling library to get the uppercase equivalent of characters.

```
#include <fstream.h>
#include <ctype.h>
int main(int argc, char* argv[])
{
    if (argc != 3) {
        cerr << "ERROR: Must specify input and output files.\n";
        return 1;
    }
    ifstream in(argv[1]);
ofstream out(argv[2]);

if (!in || !out) {
    cerr << "ERROR: Cannot open " << argv[1] << " or " << argv[2] << ".\n";
    return 2;

char ch;
while (in.get(ch)) {
    ch = toupper(ch);
    out << ch;
}
    return 0;
}
```

Assume that the name of the executable file created by compiling this program is `copyUp` and that the name of a text file available to the user is `text.in`. The following Unix command creates a new file named `text.out` from the file `text.in`.

```
copyUp text.in text.out
```

If the user fails to supply exactly two file names, `main()` returns an error code of 1 and the message `ERROR: Must specify input and output files.` appears on the terminal. If the user supplies inappropriate file names so that the streams `in` or `out` cannot open, `main()` returns an error code of 2 and a message of the form "`ERROR: Cannot open <argv[1]> or <argv[2]>.` appears on the terminal.

Bibliography

C++ Language References

Ellis, M. and B. Stroustrup. 1992. *Annotated C++ Reference Manual*. Reading, Mass.: Addison-Wesley.

Plaugher, P. J. 1993. *The Draft C++ Library*. Englewood Cliffs, N.J.: Prentice-Hall.

Stroustrup, B. 1991. *The C++ Programming Language,* 2nd ed. Reading, Mass.: Addison-Wesley.

————. 1994. *The Design and Evolution of C++*. Reading, Mass.: Addison-Wesley.

Teale, S. 1993. *C++ IOStreams Handbook*. Reading, Mass.: Addison-Wesley.

Intermediate C++ Use

Bergin, Joseph. 1994. *Data Abstraction: The Object-Oriented Approach Using C++*. New York: McGraw-Hill.

Budd, Timothy. 1994. *Classic Data Structures in C++*. Reading, Mass.: Addison-Wesley.

Cargill, T. 1992. *C++ Programming Style*. Reading, Mass.: Addison-Wesley.

Cline, M. P., and G. A. Lomow. 1995. *C++ FAQs*. Reading, Mass.: Addison-Wesley.

Gorlen, K. E., S. M. Orlow, and P. S. Plexico. 1990. *Data Abstraction and Object-Oriented Programming in C++*. New York: Wiley.

Graham, N. 1992. *Learning C++*. New York: McGraw-Hill.

Meyers, S. 1992. *Effective C++*. Reading, Mass.: Addison-Wesley.

Murray, Robert B. 1992. *C++ Strategies and Tactics*. Reading, Mass.: Addison-Wesley.

Sessions, R. 1992. *Class construction in C and C++*. Englewood Cliffs, N.J.: Prentice-Hall.

Wang, Paul S. 1994. *C++ with Object-Oriented Programming*. Boston, Mass.: PWS Publishing.

Advanced C++ Use

Coplien, J. W. 1992. *Advanced C++ Programming Styles and Idioms*. Reading, Mass.: Addison-Wesley.

Gamma, E., R. Helm, R. Johnson, and J. Vlissides. 1994. *Design Patterns: Elements of Reusable Object-Oriented Software*. Reading, Mass.: Addison-Wesley.

Soukup, Jiri. 1994. *Taming C++: Pattern Classes and Persistence for Large Projects.* Reading, Mass.: Addison-Wesley.

Young, D. 1992. *Object-Oriented Programming C++ and OSF/Motif.* Englewood Cliffs, N.J.: Prentice-Hall.

Object-Oriented Analysis, Design, and Implementation Techniques

Booch, G. 1994. *Object-Oriented Analysis and Design with Applications*, 2nd ed. Redwood City, Calif.: Benjamin Cummings.

Coad, P., and J. Nicola. 1993. *Object-Oriented Programming.* Englewood Cliffs, N.J.: Prentice-Hall.

Cox, Brad. 1992. *Object-Oriented Programming: An Evolutionary Aproach*, 2nd ed. Reading, Mass.: Addison-Wesley.

Graham, I. 1994. *Object-Oriented Methods*, 2nd ed. Reading, Mass.: Addison-Wesley.

Love, Tom. 1993. *Object Lessons.* New York, N.Y.: SIGS Books.

Meyer, Bertrand. 1988. *Object-Oriented Software Construction.* Englewood Cliffs, N.J.: Prentice-Hall.

Pree, W. 1995. *Design Patterns for Object-Oriented Software.* Reading, Mass.: ACM Press, Addison-Wesley.

Rumbaugh, J. M. et al. 1991, *Object-Oriented Modeling and Design.* Englewood Cliffs, N.J.: Prentice-Hall.

Other Object-Oriented Languages

Budd, T. 1987. *A Little Smalltalk.* Reading, Mass.: Addison-Wesley.

Lalonde, W., and J. Pugh. 1990. *Inside Smalltalk Volume 1.* Englewood Cliffs, N.J.: Prentice-Hall.

———. 1991. *Inside Smalltalk Volume 2.* Englewood Cliffs, N.J.: Prentice-Hall.

Meyer, B. 1992. *Eiffel: The Language.* Englewood Cliffs, N.J.: Prentice-Hall.

Paepke, A. 1993. *Object-Oriented Programming: The CLOS Perspective.* Cambridge: MIT Press.

Reiser, M. 1992. *The Oberon System.* Reading, Mass.: Addison-Wesley.

Reiser, M., and N. Wirth. 1992. *Programming in Oberon.* Reading, Mass.: Addison-Wesley.

Network Information Sources

Usenet news `comp.lang` groups: especially `comp.lang.c++`, and `comp.std.c++`

WEB object-oriented information sites, `http://cuiwww.unige.ch/OSG/OOinfo` and `http://www.yahoo.com`

Index